THE
DUCK
THEORY

by
Lawrence J Rupp

ISBN: 1495427307

ISBN 13: 9781495427305

Library of Congress Control Number: 2014902649

CreateSpace Independent Publishing Platform

North Charleston, South Carolina

I dedicate this book to the following individuals that I have had the pleasure of working with, as they affected my life dramatically, and yet departed so quickly in the rush of my career:

George Barthel
Walt Pickering
Gary Saunders
George Arthur
Jack Williams
Larrell Smith
Lou Wallace
Brian Wines
Stanley Pate
Tommy Ellis
Charles Ley
Roy Chester
John Russell
Raul Adauto
Mike Ismerio
Lawrence Lavieri
Charles Anderson
Nelson Yamamoto
Jimmy Hollingsworth

Each one of these men has a story. Although painful feelings exist through this writing, a footprint of their warmth, character and integrity will live on.

PREFACE

This is an autobiography of a man in his earlier years characterized as stubborn, creative and vivacious. He was born and raised in the southern California area, in the city of Long Beach. His childhood immersed within a family of five siblings with modest living accommodations. Larry blended into the middle child of this group and indeed the most troublesome.

Both his mom and dad were set in their ways of raising five children in a disciplined environment, and if compromised, it was followed up with immediate corporal punishment. His parents possessed a strong Catholic religious protocol, where church attendance and prayer was a daily, mandatory occurrence. His father was an immigrant from Russia, and his mother was born in New York City.

Larry's life was indeed full of excitement. He seemed to be heading in the wrong direction from all avenues of life, experiences and parental direction. Although channeled by strict discipline he was abundantly full of mischievous notions and childish pranks. Those pranks seemed to guide his adventurous ambitions and behavior into laughter and countless paths of intrigue.

Any threats or demands directed towards him simply caused him to ignore those challenges. It ushered him closer to seek a larger thrill from an impending life of excitement and enthusiasm. He studied police science in college while seeking out a career in law enforcement. Those classes stimulated his interest and easily focused him toward an exciting job of combat and action.

One evening while Larry was at work; his brother Vince, who was already a Compton police officer, made a traffic stop, and was jumped by four suspects who were in the car. Although Vince was beaten with his own nightstick and nearly killed with his own pistol, he survived and informed Larry of the incident, and described it in detail. That event incensed Larry's motivation and perseverance and literally pushed him aggressively into a law enforcement career and a deep desire to come to his brother's aid.

This new career placed Larry into an era where racial strife was in full battle amongst arrogant militant black gangs and the existing governmental establishment. The City of Compton just several years beforehand was essentially a small quiet bedroom community full of hard working everyday folks. However, over a period of several years the whole area transformed into a haven for criminal activity and chaos.

The City of Compton had only seventy-five officers and inundated with all sorts of crime and not nearly, enough police personnel to handle the criminal onslaught. The officers were caught up in the surge of radical racial hate groups coming into the city as well. Those same hate groups took advantage of the insufficient and diminutive number of its police officers.

From the start, while still in the academy, Larry was put to the test by a city that carried the highest crime rate per capita in the United States. There were murders galore, shootings, stabbings, bomb threats, robberies, burglaries, rapes, and mounds of dope dealing and usage. That basic, raw experience in a law enforcement career could not be matched in a better place than Compton.

As a Compton cop, you were virtually pushed to "man-up" from the onset; because most of the units were one-man patrol units and many times with no backup. A legacy of violent crime and hate was amidst a majority of good, decent black folks, most of which were in fact afraid of its militant radical parasites.

That is when a Compton cop had to decipher each eventuality of the persons involved, and determine if they were good or bad folks, or just plain wicked, imported radical racists. Those radical, political agendas sported social unrest that up-heaved the standard of living and imposed a levy of threats and violence upon every decent citizen's way of life.

Larry's career started in December 27, 1967. This was just before Martin Luther King's murder April 4, 1968. That unfortunate murder fueled the racial militants of a current event that flamed their ilk of hate and outright defiance of law. In fact, Larry graduated from the L.A. Sheriff's Academy in April as well, and stepped right into the cop-hating morass of evil street thugs stirred up by socialistic militant schemes. Whenever there was a police car, militants would rush to the scene in their cars. They would tout, torment and provoke the surrounding crowd with radical, racial hating epithets. All the while attempting to aggravate and provoke the situation by yelling hateful and threatening slogans towards the officers, like "Kill the red-neck, cracker, mother fucking pig!"

Regardless, this was the hand Larry was dealt; he was naïve to the racial turmoil and brushed all of their antics, challenges and claims of racial prejudice aside. He did not pay attention to their constant jeering and babbling. He knew he was being watched by all, whether or not visually present, but seen by many from secreted vantage points. Those venom-spewing radicals were very cautious not to be identified, or expose their evil sleight-of-hand invoking racial hatred. Although the loud, brash, racial comments stated in various degrading tones, cops had to negotiate through the morass of sneers and outright callous behavior.

Through the next thirty years of law enforcement, a full series of these stories or vignettes came to fruition and Larry was in front of it all. Some of the stories are funny, some are sad; some are still full of feelings and sentiments that are heartfelt and virtually molded Larry's career and his vision of right from wrong; and good from bad. Pure luck seemed to enhance Larry's observations for finding trouble. If it was there, he frequently stumbled right into it. Many times, when provoked by a combative suspect, his own fellow officers aided him. They had a major influence in helping temper Larry's aggressiveness.

He was a father of three boys from two marriages and really was not a hugsy, kissy kind of guy; or the exemplary model for a perfect husband. His attention was directed mostly toward his law enforcement career and how to handle any criminal situation or calamity. Larry arrested as many thugs as he could; and that was his forte. He put *countless hours into the preparation of urban criminal arrests and combat techniques that would aid him in their capture.*

The Los Angeles County Sheriff's Department was his life and commitment. Several executives of the department were once Larry's lieutenants or sergeants at the infamous Firestone Park Station.

Those same Firestone Park lieutenants and sergeants always seemed to support his endeavors and officer survival skills and training. They also seemed to embrace his enthusiasm and trusted him to a point where Larry never suffered any disciplinary repercussions and allowed him to stay and endure the ghetto atmosphere of his own choosing.

At home was another story, trouble found him there as well. Stories of his criminal contact stemmed from sporadic encounters in his daily home activities and in his own neighborhood. Many neighbors appreciated Larry's zeal, alertness, enthusiasm and capturing techniques as they witnessed the local police interaction with him, and the stories of adventure that followed.

His wife Gloria was instrumental in Larry's fight for preventing criminal activity from entering their neighborhood, and of course his own family's protection. Gloria herself was involved in several of the exciting situations and provided a good and healthful conduit and psychological tolerance to backup a man who was a self proclaimed male chauvinistic shield of machismo, touting he needed no help at all. Larry stood for the good of the neighborhood and let it be known that his family was not to be touched, tormented or molested.

This book entitled "The Duck Theory" is primarily derived from the common sense term still widely used in today's acknowledgement of human behavior. "If it looks, walks, talks and acts like a duck; then it's a damn duck." Most folks understand this basic principle of recognizing any situation or individual who acts strange or out of the ordinary.

Just because a street thug is "be-bopping" down the street; wearing gangster clothes, wrap around shades, and sporting slick back hair, with death defying tattoos licking up the side of his neck and "fuck off" tattooed on the back of his neck in fine, scrolled in cursive writing, seems a tad suspicious. The thug may accentuate his mannerisms by swaggering and bouncing his head in total defiance of anyone who may even look at his antics as threatening; well, those thoughts are "just plain accurate as hell."

This is what Larry was faced with on the streets and on many situations. He knew very well he would need to let all of those obvious signs of political sensitivity and correctness to a more sanitary proclamation and a cleaned up version. Suspicious movements coupled with other mitigating factors would certainly satisfy a judge and jury's thirst, differentiating from just another plain "Joe Blow" on the street.

Larry's philosophy and observations as a "duck theorist" on the go was relatively easy. He could spot suspicious behavior on the run, or their slithering around and carefully peeking from behind some distant edge of a building or obstacle. In Larry's view, it got to a point that someone with dope, a gun or a knife acts almost the same way in all eventualities.

Luck seemed to follow and shadowed Larry from harm's way when several situations went awry. He was shot at many times and he attributes those close calls as pure luck and nothing to do with strategically sound maneuvers. Most of the officers killed in the line of duty were clumped up in the high crime areas or the ghettos of South Los Angeles. Unfortunately, those officers killed did not have the same luck as Larry.

Larry knew those killing fields very well, because he went through many of the actual reports in officer survival classes that he taught, and felt a deep sense of grief in each one. Larry's intentions of these heartfelt stories are to share some of the depth of personal visions and feelings he encountered and how he viewed them as they occurred.

He retired in July of 1998 from several injuries sustained while on duty, which retired him early in a disabled status. He spent two years going from doctor to doctor to remedy his pain management and carefully regained almost all of his restricted movements.

Larry then became a private investigator and worked for the conflict panel in Riverside County. There were about 12 attorneys that he performed investigative defense work. Those attorneys worked for defendants involved in violent crimes as well, but this time Larry and his partner were doing investigations for the other side of the counsels table.

In 2002, he began to perform bodyguard work in the Los Angeles area for entertainment celebrities. In 2003, he and two other bodyguards went on a "road tour" for four months. It was with a female country-singing trio, completing sixty-five shows throughout the United States and eight shows throughout Canada.

When Larry returned that same year he was hired as a bodyguard and security specialist for a well-known entertainer in the Hollywood area and remained with him and his family until May 2008. Larry then became a bodyguard for the entertainer's children sporadically over the years when the entertainer's family was in town.

As of this writing, Larry is working for a large ranch in the San Diego area and is part of a security team for the ranch. He is working alongside a friend, Ray G. a former police officer and big city motor cop, from the Los Angeles Police Department. Both Ray and Larry continue to work as partners together. They are the ranch's security and are to appear ominous. They are paired together to back each other up for trespassers, illegal hunters and wayward environmentalists' who frequent the vast borders of the ranch.

The setting is quite beautiful for its innate beauty and rolling hillsides. High flowing wind swept grasses conceal coyotes, rattlesnakes, wild turkeys and quail. The ranch borders are on five individual Indian tribal territories.

This ranch setting is a stark difference from the radical rabble they were accustomed to in Los Angeles and the surrounding communities. There are many deer and of course, mountain lions, mostly lingering in the shadows of thousands of shady oak trees and vastly peppered volumes of poison oak. The ranch is surrounded in several deep valleys and plateaus by mountains reaching up to the four thousand foot level. The raging waters many times wash out the roads that race down the steep slopes during the winter season. Although paid for their protective services, both Ray and Larry certainly appreciate the beauty of the ranch and the peace and quiet of its surroundings.

I hope that these short stories will invite you, the reader, to view a cop's feelings of excitement, torment, compassion and zeal. Larry seldom had a boring shift without some stimulating raucous popping off right in front of him. He lived and loved his job with a great amount of enthusiasm and passion.

Today, no one will seem to have the same thrill and enthusiasm Larry enjoyed. Yet he can easily wallow through each of these events without wavering and still enjoy telling the captivating stories.

CHAPTER INDEX

CHAPTER 1

"ROUGH HOUSE": THE RUPP HOUSE

I was born at Seaside Hospital, Long Beach, California, in 1944. I was classified a baby boomer, because my mom and dad were entwined in a momentous moment of marital bless one night around December 1943.

We lived in Belmont Shore, Long Beach, a short while, but we moved inland because I had asthma, and the doctors suggested getting away from the beach area. So we relocated to a small three-bedroom home with one bathroom on the corner of Fifty-Fifth Street and Dairy Avenue in the North Long Beach area.

World War II was in full force, and my dad worked for the Union Pacific Railroad as a machinist, while Mom worked off and on in downtown Long Beach as a secretary for either Buick or Ford car dealerships. These dealerships were right along Long Beach Boulevard, back when and where the red trolley cars used to run.

There were five of us. Diana and Vince were a little older than me, and Mary Catherine and Hank were the youngest by about ten years. I, of course, was in the middle of this group of puppies and of course the least smart and suave. I was the one in the most trouble. I received the worst grades, and I was always on someone's list for least likely to assimilate and advance. I admit that I was a tad odd and very creative with anything thrown at me and never gave it much thought.

Our mom and dad were basic blue-collar workers and made homelife relatively comfortable and well disciplined. They kept us in clean clothes and instructed us well how to sew, iron our own clothes, and mend them as well. We were all well fed and made to eat lots of vegetables and fruit. Our mom baked quite a bit and kept us in homemade cakes, cookies, and pies.

Mom was also an expert cook and made many delicious, unique specialty dishes from scratch that came from recipes of Irish, German, Russian, English, and Mexican cuisines.

Many times I was sent to the local bakery to pick up two loaves of freshly baked bread. The problem was that by the time I got home, a lot of the bread was consumed. The smell was absolutely compelling, and the taste was irresistible, so I convincingly massaged my brain to justify why I ate nearly half a loaf.

I'll always remember Mom's famous New York family endearment. If I was hurt or crying about something, she would always express her motherly love by saying, "Ah, shut up!" instead of the basic hug, close to the mother's bosom, and giving warm and cuddly words of affection. She was Germanic as well; love in this home was within reach of the disciplined hand.

We all pitched in to clean the house—dusting, washing the floors, doing dishes—and keep up with the wash. The weekly cleaning of course began every Saturday. The siblings were always involved, with Mom and Dad doing the majority of cleaning. We had no doubts about what to do on Saturdays—clean and straighten up the house and yards. During the week our rooms were expected to be clean. We made our beds daily and placed dirty laundry in the hamper.

On the weekdays, Dad liked to leave long lists of things to do, and he expected to have the entire list completed before he got home. Dad always took the electrical connector to the television set to ensure that time wouldn't be wasted frivolously watching TV.

Unbeknownst to Dad, Vince had purchased an identical electrical connector at the old Dooley's Hardware store on Long Beach Boulevard near Del Amo. If we watched TV we had to make sure that we unplugged it at least two hours before Dad came home, so the TV had time to cool down. When Dad came home, he would always feel the sides and back of the TV set to see if it was warm. I think Dad was on to us, but never really said anything.

The dinner table was set daily around four thirty, and everything was primed and ready to go as soon as he pulled up in his blue 1953 Chevrolet.

Food was always a family cooperative affair. We prepared some of the food, and when our parents came home they cooked the meat and completed the dinner's preparation.

We never went hungry, and many times I was stuck at the table because I didn't want to eat the heaping pile of squash or eggplant stacked on my plate, I hated the food and refused to eat it. But I'll tell you this; I still had to eat it all, and remained seated at the table, often hours after dinner was over, usually until around ten o'clock at night.

Mom always insisted on following the bible of table manners, *Emily Post's Etiquette*. Oh yeah, that huge book was always close by for our perusal. The knives, forks, and spoons were to be in their proper placement next to the traditional blue, Chinese motif dinner plates, accompanied by the napkins and glasses.

The glasses filled with milk and were placed in the center of the table, away from the intended individual. These glasses of milk were strategically positioned by our dad, who insisted that we shouldn't swallow our food with milk. They remained in the center of the table until we had consumed our dinner.

Another table-setting rule Dad had was that he positioned his butter knife, placed always upside down, on the right side beside his plate. If any of us—except Mom, of course—dared to reach beyond the edge of our plate closest to the center of the table without first asking for permission, we would get rapped across the knuckles with the handle of the butter knife. We all caught onto this one real fast, but we would occasionally forget.

Our dad was the dictator in our family, and there was no questioning his authority. We all knew that, and Mom did, too. Dad was a cool six feet tall, about two hundred pounds, and Mom was five foot three and weighed around 170. Dad's philosophy was very simple: obey or get punished.

The one thing about Dad you could count on was that he never threatened us, and if punishment was to be doled out, it was immediate. That philosophy worked, and we stayed within his strict guidelines and never strayed too far.

He told us that he would pick our friends, and if he didn't like them, he'd tell us. That meant if he saw us with that person again, later on, he would kick our butts and our friend's butt as well. He also advised us if the friend's dad came over to complain about his son getting his butt kicked, he would kick that dad's butt as well. We didn't need to be told what would happen if the police captured us doing some nefarious deed. We would rather stay with the police than be handed over to Dad.

We all went to bed early, around eight o'clock, and Mom let us listen to many radio suspense and detective stories, as they were the best and most comforting and relaxing. Kate Smith songs were played in the evening hours, I believe to calm us down and fade our minds into sleep much quicker. To this day I still remember those radio shows and how they tapped our imagination.

Television came into our home around 1956. There were only a few shows that were broadcast, including *Harry Owens and His Royal Hawaiians,* with Hilo Hattie, country musician Spade Cooley, the *Who Do You Trust?* game show with Johnny Carson, *You Bet Your Life* with Groucho Marx, *The Ed Sullivan Show,* and finally, the always-funny *The Soupy Sales Show.* All of these shows were very entertaining for a long time, especially Johnny Carson and Ed McMahon. No current entertainer comes close to them at all.

At Christmas time, Vince and I were locked in our room, which at that time was a called a solarium, separated by large glass doors and locked from the inside to keep us from getting up too early. All of our yelling and screaming while opening the pretty wrapped packages irritated Mom and Dad immensely.

Around nine o'clock in the morning on Christmas Day, Dad would unlock our interior glass door and allow us to rush to the tree and unwrap our present.

We anxiously tore the wrappings off and ripped the boxes apart. We were just tickled pink with joy that all three of us would get brand-new flannel bathrobes. We could barely hold back the excitement, and pure jealously set in when Vinnie got the blue-plaid robe and mine was the red one. Funny thing, though, we never fought over our bathrobes.

I don't know why, but that still seems funny today. I still can see the expression on Vince's face as we looked at each other on those mornings. Diana was, of course, still in bed, sleeping like a log. She stubbornly refused to get up early to see her new flannel bathrobe.

My dad was born in 1910 in a city called Balzer, Russia. My grandfather on my father's side was a soldier in the Russian army, although in the Russian army he was attached to a German regiment, mainly German-speaking soldiers. (These Germanic groups were also known as Volga-Germans.) Come to think of it, maybe that's why we ate pork chops in a steaming bed of sauerkraut and backed up with borscht soup. Hmm, mighty suspicious.

An eight-inch framed picture of a uniformed Russian soldier, sitting in a chair, legs crossed, clearly displaying his high top shiny boots, honors my front room. If you look closely, my grandfather's hands were huge and strong looking, like mine when I became an adult.

When my dad immigrated to the United States in 1913, he and his whole family were processed as immigrants through the infamous Ellis Island, New Jersey. Dad's family then traveled to Grand Island, Nebraska, and remained. Dad read, spoke, and wrote German but never taught any of us that language because, he said, it was not a very popular language at the time—1944. Duh!

After immigrating to the United States, my grandpa was also a machinist for the Union Pacific Railroad.

My mom was born in the borough of Queens, New York. Her whole family was involved heavily in the US Navy. Her father was a chief petty officer in both World War I and World War II. He was short, stocky, and immensely crabby. He had more uniform patches and medals than one could imagine, but because of his brutal personality, no one cared what he had achieved.

My mom informed me that Grandpa was a bare-fist boxer in the US Navy, hence his tightly clustered cauliflower ears. He had the curious habit of constantly ducking his neck slightly and dodging his head from side to side, and an extremely gruff personality. I don't think I ever got a hug from grandpa either.

Mom also informed us that our dad was not welcome in her parents' San Pedro home near the top of Santa Cruz Street. One day, my dad and my grandpa got into a fight, and my dad got his butt kicked. So every time we went to San Pedro, my dad was dropped off at the small liquor store on Gaffey Street, while we visited grandpa in his old home near the top of the hill.

Whenever we visited any of our relatives, the order was that we sit on the sofa, with our legs together and mouths shut. No interruptions, small talk, or whining. Mom's old theory, that "children are to be seen and not heard" was in full order.

Three of my mom's brothers were chief petty officers in the navy during World War II. She also had another brother, who was the black sheep in the family. He was in and out of prison for bank robbery, heroin addiction, and murder, among other things. The person my uncle killed was his best friend in the Lake Isabella, California, area. Other than that, he seemed like a pretty nice guy. He drove by our house one night and tossed a brick through our front-room window. I think he and Dad didn't like each other very much.

My dad was a Lutheran who had converted to Catholicism, and our family was very much Catholic. Prayers were always offered before dinner and mildly enforced when going to bed at night. We all went to Saint Athanasius grammar school, which was approximately a mile and a half away from our three-bedroom home in North Long Beach. When I was preparing for school, washing my face, brushing my teeth, and combing my hair, there was an entourage of my friends and fellow classmates who waited outside my bathroom window. They would wait until I was ready, and then all of us, anywhere from six to eight kids, would walk to school together. I enjoyed this experience daily, because of their company. We all told stories about what had occurred the previous night.

I really didn't do too well in school and brought home report cards that would cause most parents to think that I had a brain disorder. I failed third grade by getting twenty-three Fs. I was not the best student nor the worst, and I was extremely active in the classroom. In class, I was purposely placed directly in front of the Sister's desk. This was to help curb my marginal deportment and help me focus on good behavior and pay full attention. However, during class when the nuns spotted my desk empty, they knew I was up to no good. I personally think they were onto something.

Every time the sister turned her back to the class, I took the opportunity to drop to the floor and crawl to the rear of the classroom just to get a laugh from most of my fellow students, who roared with laughter when I got caught. I was the class clown.

I was punished each time, either by detention or a swat by the Sister Superior with her one-by-four-inch-by-two-foot paddle—the same kind often used by college fraternities to paddle new applicants.

Any fights on the school grounds resulted in a meeting with the Sister in charge of discipline, who slapped a three-foot birch pointer across the knuckles of all combatants. This happened to me maybe five or six times while I was in grammar school.

One day in fourth grade, all students in the school were assembled in line formations to sing national songs and pay respect and homage to the American flag, as we did every day. I was the second-tallest student in my class and close to the front of the line; that left the smallest student at the rear. I had turned my head slightly and was talking surreptitiously to the student right in front of me, probably about some unique scientific fuel formula for space flight.

The Sister Superior was vigilantly perched at an open casement window on a wooden box located right at the base of the wall, just below the window on the second story of the brick school, from which she was able to look out over the entire lineup of classes, first through eighth grades. She apparently spotted my deplorable antics, talking in formation, and called out to me in a loud voice, "Mr. Rupp, go home!" She bellowed my name in a heavy Hungarian accent. She stuck her arm and hand out of the casement window. Her long-sleeved, brown-and-black robe draped from her right arm and wrist, looking kind of like the oversized robes of Merlin the Magician.

She apparently was aware of my poor deportment and shameful school antics—like lifting up all of the girls' dresses and peeking at their underwear while they were playing on the monkey bars—and a whole catalogue of incorrigible activities.

I left immediately, without even going back into the classroom, and walked home alone. I loafed and malingered around the house until my mom and dad came home, around four or five o'clock. I wasn't too alarmed for what I was caught doing; it was only talking in formation. It seemed trivial compared to other things I've been caught doing.

Usually, the Sisters would call my the parents and advise them of what I had done, but on this occasion they hadn't. This was out of the norm, and something seemed askew. I didn't say much about what had happened at school, because I knew the Sister would call real soon and update my father about my deportment and what was going to happen to my scholastic career.

Around seven that evening I heard the phone ring. My dad answered it, and there was no doubt who it was. The Sister informed my dad that she was at the end of her patience with my disturbances and class disruptions.

They talked for almost an hour. I couldn't believe the length of time they spent talking about me. I was listening through the heat grate in the floor. There, I would lie on my stomach, at the edge of the heater, which was partially on the floor and on a wall that divided the hallway to our bedroom, the front room, and the door area. A small clothes closet acted as a telephone booth, with a small end table snuggled in the tight opening. The walls were covered with many telephone numbers scrawled on them.

The Sister and my father conversed for almost an hour, and I felt as if maybe they were comparing me with my brother and sister. They were in a couple of classes ahead of me and apparently doing very well in all areas of study and deportment.

I could hear the good-byes from my dad's side of the conversation, so I jumped up and ran into my bedroom, climbed to my top bunk, and waited.

Dad obviously was swayed by the nun's evaluation of my poor performance, grabbed the two-foot black neoprene hose that was nestled atop the secretarial cabinet in the front room. He made this robust implement to dole out punishment to us whenever we got out of line. (Personally I believe he made this hose from some special German technical torture manual from World War II.)

He came in, and I don't really remember if Vince was in the room or not, but Dad laid into me as he had never done before.

That hose had "cattails" slit into one end. each tail was six or seven inches long. There were about five of those cattails on one end of the hose. When Dad was laying into me, he was yelling at me about what I had done and called me a bastard and a son of a bitch. He slung that hose into my bunk bed—a wooden two-tiered bunk bed—and made contact with every blow. This was the first time he whaled on my face and arms dramatically. Each contact actually made five or six welts, so you do the math.

I cried and yelled for him to stop, but he continued for at least five full minutes. When he finally stopped, he informed me that I was to report to school the next day and retrieve my books. I was suspended from school for two weeks. (Several people have declared that this was the reason I got into law enforcement. Hmmm, I wonder. Could that be?)

I couldn't really understand why my dad talked so much with the Sister. It seemed like maybe I was caught trying to kill the pope. He was definitely pissed, and he left welts on my face, neck, arms, chest, stomach, and legs to point out how upset he was. I sobbed for a short while and then fell asleep, obviously exhausted.

The next morning I rose early to have our luscious, lumpy cream of wheat or oatmeal breakfast and was reinformed of what I was to do and warned not to make any mistakes, or I knew what would happen.

I rushed through breakfast, dressed in my school attire that I ironed, and quickly walked to school. I immediately went to church, which was expected, received communion, because I confessed all of my sins in a timely fashion to remain constantly pure in mind and thought. This spiritual endeavor was an everyday ritual, where we all assembled prior to the morning report in line formation.

When we left the church, a lot of my classmates came over to me to get a closer view and feel all of the obvious long bumps and welts. Some of the welts had opened small abrasions on my face and arms. There were quite a few bumps and bruises, and many of my classmates began to cry, as did our Sister/ teacher.

I overheard one of the Sisters say that she would never again call my dad to report my deportment. A psychiatrist would definitely analyze this as the reason why I became a cop. So much for the accuracy of Aldous *Huxley's Brave New World, which portrays how to manipulate a child from a young age and develop a focused hunger or appitite for specific areas of development.*

Other classmates started to come over but were shepherded quickly away by other vigilant nuns, who observed what was happening and wanted to prevent their charges from seeing any of my injuries.

I was alone just outside my class and allowed inside briefly to get my books. Then I scurried out of the class and walked home. Many of my friends looked at me with great sorrow and empathy, nodding slightly as I left the room.

I guess it worked pretty well—you know the adage "spare the rod, spoil the child"—I stayed out of trouble pretty much for the remainder of the year and made a complete turnaround.

I realized that if someone sees a little harshness, with an occasional hose beating, somehow things happen and poor behavior is modified. Maybe this should be studied in a college setting.

Dad didn't discriminate, either; he whipped Diana's butt as well, whenever she sassed him. I still remember when he was slapping her around with the hose, and she slammed into the bedroom closet doors, which made a tumultuous noise. Her room was right next to the kitchen, where we were, and was only separated by a wall. God, she was screaming loud and really interrupting our morning lumpy cereal breakfast of Wheat Hearts.

One day my brother Vince was on the rear playground at Saint Athanasius and the "big cheese," the school bully, had Vince snugly in a headlock. Quite a few other wannabe thugs were watching my brother getting the snot knocked out of him, and of course no one was willing to help him. The bully was punching Vince in the face quite dramatically, and Vince couldn't break free.

The reason for the fight was very simple; Mom and Dad had bought both of us a couple of silly-looking woolen plaid caps, like they wear in Grand Island, Nebraska, during the cold winter months.

You know the type of cap—a heavy woolen material, with long flaps that draped over the ears to protect them from the cold. But if Mom or Dad bought them for us, we wore them or faced the disciplinary music. I'll let you guess what we did.

Anyway, when I saw my brother getting his ass kicked by some school bully, I knew it was time for me to step in. Scared? It didn't even cross my mind. I just leaped onto the thug with great exuberance, because it was my brother, and in my mind nobody kicks my brother's ass except me. You know, it's a family thing! I grabbed the bully's right leg with both of my hands, pulled it backward, and chomped down on the back of his right calf. I bit as hard as I could and tore flesh from his leg, which sent him, wailing, away from my brother.

I slowly wiped the bully's blood from my mouth and checked if Vinnie was okay. He had a bloody nose and mouth, but he was pretty much all right. A little while later, the school bully was taken to the hospital and received seven stitches for that wound. From there on, no one ever attacked my brother again as long as he was in grammar school.

Another time, my brother and I were walking home and passing by a small malt shop that was just two houses away from our elementary school. The malt shop was *the* place to stop and get a "suicide soda," which was a cherry and a cola mixed. God those drinks tasted great; I can remember the taste even today.

Anyway, we were walking home together, and another school bully drove right up the rear seat of my pants and buttocks with his front bicycle tire. As I turned around, he challenged me by saying in a rather cocky tone, "You want to do something about it? Let's fight!" He was nodding his head up and down as if prompting me to take him on.

I looked at my brother and said, "Phh, Why not? But let's get away from here." My interest was that the school's nuns wouldn't see the altercation. His reply was a quick, "Okay!"

Another bit of info I failed to mention was that our mom and dad bought each of us two pairs of brilliant solid-colored pants, one red and other green. I figured Dad found them on a broken freight box in the Union Pacific Railroad train yards.

Those goofy-looking slacks had to be worn every day and got us in many fights, because they were so gaudy. Both of us were challenged and made fun of, every turn we made, but mostly by public-school kids. We never balked at following up on the confrontations. We never would allow the philosophy, "Turn the other cheek," to invade our understanding of acceptance. During this time Vince and I fought with each other quite regularly, so to fight and get a bloody nose, split lip, or one of many black swollen eyes was nothing but kids' play, a display of brotherly love.

We walked about three blocks away, with about twenty other students following us, to a vacant dirt lot, shed our shirts, and squared off. The young hooligan swung at me five or six times with his clenched fists; I easily ducked each blow. I reacted by whisking him slightly past me on his final swing and judo chopping him in the back of his neck as hard as I could five or six times.

He remained stooped over slightly and then stood up—quite slowly, I might add. When he stood erect, it was the first time I noticed he was bawling. Tears were pouring down his face like a little girl. He grabbed his shirt from one of his buddies and briskly walked away. The majority of the twenty classmates there cheered me to no end. I apparently had just kicked the shit out of the guy who had been bullying most of them for their lunch money and property. He apparently was hated by most everyone, and they celebrated my knocking the snot out of him. They knew very well I was one of them, not at all a belligerent punk making life miserable for everyone.

Many came up to me, patted me on the back, and expressed their happiness. My brother and I continued on our way home.

The next day as I came onto the playground bench seats, where most of the school assembled prior to reporting to morning lineup, I was met with cheers and applause. I felt like a hero coming home from a war. As I drew closer I could see the ex-ruffian seated toward the rear, away from the majority of students. I noticed he was looking at me, and when our eyes made contact he lowered his head. I was very proud of the applause and all of the notoriety.

But as I came closer to the ex-ruffian, I nodded to him, acknowledging the fact that he'd been humiliated and was no longer a threat to anyone. Basically the animosity between us was now vacated. He noticed my friendly response, and we became friendly after that, because there was no need to express being tough anymore.

———

My dad didn't like blacks or Mexicans and made no bones about it. The problem was that our best friend and neighbor, Phil, was Mexican, and his dad hired Vince and me to help rip out linoleum and tiled floors and paid us a pretty good day's wage, about ten dollars a day.

Mr. T. was a floor contractor, and the whole family was as friendly as anyone could be. Dad always confronted us and wanted to know why Vince and I hung around "greaseballs" and "beaners." We always had to defend the whole Mexican family when Dad went into his tirade about his deep-seated feelings.

We spent an exorbitant amount of time at Phil's house, because he had many more unique things than we did, including a powder-blue 1957 Chevrolet Nomad, a station wagon. I'll let you guess how we got around. Phil was a great friend, and we learned to play poker at his house with his mom for money. We enjoyed their company and laughed quite a bit. The whole family was very opinionated about our father's strict disciplinary habits. They, of course, noticed the welts and bruises from our bouts with the disciplinary hose. To make matters worse, Phil's family never made any negative remarks about our dad or mom and remained neutral.

So the Mexicans we knew weren't prejudiced at all, and they made quite an impression on us by how well they treated us throughout the years. We obviously didn't pay any attention to Dad's prejudices and just brushed it off as basic racism. Dad never went further than to issue us his philosophy about blacks and Mexicans, so we chose our own direction when the time came to have personal opinions.

Many times Vince, Phil, and I went to the area over by a miniature golf putting course called Shady Acres. Besides miniature golf, this place had quite a few pinball machines and small bowling games. It was the place to hang out and dawdle and have fun. We spent an ample amount of time there. Right next to Shady Acres was the unpaved Los Angeles riverbed. We were in that place as often as we could manage. There were large bushes and weeds surrounding the area, and it was loaded with frogs and tadpoles congregated in the small streams that washed through the wide bed. The riverbed was our own watery hangout, like the Mississippi River in *Huckleberry Finn*.

Right next to the large bridge that spanned the entire riverbed was a small short dirt trail surrounded by large bushes. That trail snaked along the northeast side of the bridge, where there was a small horse-rental spot. You could rent horses for traipsing the narrow dirt pathways into and alongside the meandering riverbed. This alone added to the anxious ambitions and imaginations of all of us, trotting together and thinking of the Wild West and imagining being a part of it.

We did all sorts of things there, like playing hide and seek, war, army maneuvers, and of course cowboys and Indians. Yeah, we made our own rifles and pistols out of wood and conjured up lots of childhood imagination.

We were accosted several times, together and sometimes alone, by the itinerant bums, hobos, and drunks who sometimes frequented the protection of the bridge and camped there. They weren't too aggressive, and we generally ran away from them easily and climbed back to the top of the bridge to avoid any dangerous encounters.

When they finally paved the riverbed, it rained for several days, very heavily at times, right after its completion. One or two days later, the riverbed was almost twenty feet from the top road. Those rains made the riverbed at least thirty to forty feet deep.

This was very unique and the fullest it had ever been. So I ran home, grabbed my surfboard, and ran back to the riverbed. I took off all of my clothes and sported only my trunks. I stacked my clothes under the Long Beach Boulevard Bridge and carried my board to the water's edge.

I looked at the amount of water going past me and wondered if it was safe. It looked okay, but Jesus, there was a whole lot of water, with lots of debris. It seemed more pleasant and appealing than dangerous. I noted how it ran against the large cement pilings supporting the bridge. The speed of the water caused the rapid level flow to rise about a foot and a half, not a lot, but still a little concerning. I figured it looked relatively safe, so I went for it and jumped in with my knees atop my board.

Unbeknown to me, the speed was about 30 mph. When I landed on my board, the speed of the water threw me and the board in the air, and I landed near the top of the road, twenty feet away. It was like someone had thrown me a good distance. I believe I had a divine intervention that stated, "Hey, stupid, don't try that again or you'll die."

The sheer power of being tossed aside with such force spooked me, and that didn't happen very often. I picked up my clothes and quickly left, and passed on the story of near peril to my brother, friends, and Mom and Dad. Dad just shook his head slowly, as if to say I was an idiot. Hmm! They all laughed and remarked just how dangerous a situation I had missed. I know now that if that vast volume of water hadn't grabbed me right out of the water, once in the riverbed I would've immediately been taken downriver with no obstructions. In fact, it would have killed me for sure just because of the speed; draw and drag would have pulled me to the bottom quickly. That meant that I would have been washed into the ocean within a half hour. I realized I was taking things to the limit and had better change my brazen exploratory ways or face death again and not be so lucky next time.

Months later, about six of us found huge completed cement chambers of flood control drains that connected with the vast flood control system. These chambers were at least eight feet in diameter and had a shallow one-foot-wide flow of water, one inch deep, which caused the water to ultimately empty into the riverbed. The edges of the slow-moving water were green with algae.

These had just been completed, so we all ventured into these cement tubes and walked inside for miles, going into the northern cities of Compton, Lynwood, and Southgate. We went into the chamber so far, we came upon a giant manifold where four of the giant chambers came together. We had a lot of fun screaming and yelling in those chambers and couldn't imagine how water could fill these giant tubes.

Could you ever envision what would have occurred if there was a large release of water while we were in those tubes? Yeah, we would have all probably died.

This is also about the time my sister Diana was around sixteen years old and a cheerleader at Saint Anthony's Girls High School. She came home from school often, and we sat up eating crackers and avocados, which were sprinkled with garlic salt and pepper and tasted delicious. We talked about school and the boys and girls who had contact with her that day. She was really a preppy and belonged to all sorts of school organizations and functions and didn't know squat about how young men functioned. In the kitchen in the evenings, she questioned me many times about all sorts of cuss words she had heard; she wanted to know what they meant. This was a lot of fun, because she had no clue what was being said about her or her friends, or what they were implying. Many times we sat up together at the kitchen table and laughed a lot about the meanings of the words she threw at me. When she asked me what "cunt" meant, I about fell backward. So I told her the story about coming home one afternoon and spotting Dad working on the stairway leading up to the studio apartment above the garage.

He was painting the stairs battleship gray and was about midpoint, near the banister. I asked him if he knew what the word "cunt" meant.

Dad stopped, holding the four-inch paintbrush in his hand, and asked, "Did someone call you that?"

I said, "Yeah, Steve M. just called me that and I didn't know what that meant." Dad courageously stood up and stated, "You don't let anyone call you that. That's a woman's wee-wee."

Well, that didn't help much at that age, because I didn't know what a woman's wee-wee was. I scrunched up my face and paid little attention to my father's description, because it meant nothing to me other than a "hairy nothing."

Diana laughed and snorted at my ignorant explanation, but we still had fun talking to each other.

One day I had to go to the bathroom and do the big "choo-choo" (aka defecate). Our small home only had one bathroom, and Diana was inside taking one of her never-ending beauty baths.

I pounded on the door, and she yelled out, "It's busy, please go away." I had to go real bad, so I grabbed three small washcloths from the cabinet, "jimmied" the bathroom door with a bobby pin, and walked right in.

There she was naked and sloshing around, screaming like a banshee for me to get out. But I didn't pay any attention to her and dropped my pants and drawers, sat on the toilet, and began to unload.

I tossed her the three washcloths as I sat down and told her to calm down and cover up her stuff so I couldn't see. I did remark, "Gee, Di, your boobs are getting kind of big, huh?"

She was initially very mad but cooled down eventually. I was only in there for a few minutes and left. She did in fact use the washrags to cover up and thanked me for being so thoughtful. We still discuss that event even today, because she was so traumatized.

Just before the summer of 1957, my brother Vince had a really serious operation performed on his chest. He was stuck at home after the operation for two weeks straight, with a stainless steel bar poking out one side of his chest.

The rest was implanted inside his chest cavity. Mom and Dad were very worried about him, and so was I.

His rib tips were all clawing into his lungs, a childhood condition, and the tips had to be removed and replaced with nylon. This was quite concerning to all of us. He was in serious shape, but in time he was going to be much healthier.

Well, he recovered within a couple of weeks and to our surprise Mom and Dad sent both Vince and me to a small cabin in the nearby San Bernardino Mountains, just above Lake Gregory. We cooked our own food in our little cabin. It must have been five or six hundred square feet, with a small loft.

We were alone, without any parental supervision for a full two weeks. I'll always remember that adventure, because we were left alone to our own devices with no orders or demands. We were well behaved and had a friend over as well.

The area was absolutely beautiful, and there were lots of little things to do. We got to walk to the lake daily and swim most of the day. One night we walked to the small town and saw the 1957 Walt Disney movie, *Old Yeller*, which had just come out.

One evening we walked all the way to Lake Arrowhead and slept overnight in our sleeping bags on a remote finger outlet right next to the shoreline.

At night the carp would swim with their heads slightly out of the water. The carp would make strange noises in the early morning hours so we decided to throw some dirt clods at the carp to tease them. We laughed a lot and had a fun time. In the morning we found out the dirt clods we were throwing were in fact "road apples" (horse dung).

Our parents were very kind to allow us out on that adventure. Our deportment was quite tempered from then on, and I believe Mom and Dad stopped beating us with the hose.

I continued on with my classes until I was out of grammar school and went on to Saint Anthony's Boy's High School in downtown, Long Beach, at Seventh Street and Olive Avenue.

At Saint Anthony's, I regressed to my nonscholarly ways and received detentions routinely. There were so many rules and regulations, and this school strictly adhered to those laws of discipline and deportment.

Let me explain the detention disciplinary method. If you talked in class, chewed gum, or misbehaved in any manner, you would be notified that you had a detention by either the teachers or the Catholic brotherly order that administered the rules and regulations and ran the school.

At the conclusion of school regular hours you would report to the basement detention room. There the heavyset proctor Brother, an avid boxer and one big dude, would duly note your attendance. You would take a seat among maybe fifty to a hundred classmates on a half table desk.

You would sit at attention with your legs together, shoulders rolled backward, and your hands lying next to each other on the top of the desk. You knew you were supposed to sit still and not talk or slump down; your feet were together, and your eyes looked straight ahead.

The proctor, every once in a while, would come around near your seat. If he saw you talking, fidgeting, or surreptitiously chewing gum or candy, he would suddenly, with an open half-curled knuckle and slam that puppy right alongside your head, just above the ear line. He would inform you of another detention the following day. That contact hit would really snap instantaneous pain to the side of your head. And you didn't dare snivel or yell out, because the proctor/disciplinarian was usually an obdurate man with a face like the sole of your shoe. As a matter of fact, one of them was as excessively brutal, Brother Mel, and we all kidded about his foul-smelling butt odor that reeked as he passed by our desks.

If you were caught moving, you would be ordered to raise your arms and hands above your head for the remainder of the detention. If you moved too much again, then you would be ordered to kneel at your desk with your arms and hands elevated above your head, in addition to being cracked on the side of the head. If you were seen moving—or any other infraction they could conjure up—the proctor would order you to the front of the room beside his desk, easily within the proctor's reach. He would toss a half-inch-by-three-foot birch dowel at you, and you would kneel on that dowel with your arms and hands up straight. Now you were facing the entire detention group, and some of the classmates started to quietly snicker. They would make facial gestures at your dilemma.

Of course the proctor would whip out that half knuckle of his and throw it right to the side of your head. Let me tell you, that always hurt. If the Brother hit you of course, that automatically meant another detention the following day.

Midway in my junior year, I was expelled from Saint Anthony's for having too many detentions—twenty-one, to be exact—and failing religion and Spanish classes. I'll admit I wasn't too displeased, because I had to pay my own tuition from my part-time jobs. This was also a requirement by our parents to help lighten the family's economic load.

I left Saint Anthony's Boy's High School in the middle of the 1961 school year and arrived at Long Beach's Polytechnic High School. As I casually walked in through the portals and along a large sidewalk, a lone female yelled at me from atop one of the walkway ramps, "Hey, hold it right there!" She came running down the stairs and right up to me and asked, "Boy, you're good-looking. Can I have a kiss?"

I was shocked and excited that such a floozy, harlot, jezebel, slutty-type female would accost me, as I was trying desperately to assimilate into a new coed academic environment. I thought for a moment, *Was this Eve, likened to the apple she gave Adam?* I wondered, *Do I look cheap and easy, or am I just another male thrown into the mix of coed education?*

In order to just get along, I replied, "Yes, you may, but I must warn you that I'm from Saint Anthony's Boy's High School and haven't had much contact with women." We locked lips, and I was in heaven. I thought, *Classes with women are a gift from the gods.*

I walked into my English class and was assigned a desk where there was a woman seated on my side. I leaned over and asked her if she was good-looking, because I didn't know who was good-looking or not. She giggled and said she didn't know! Let me tell you, she wasn't that hot, but I was happy she was there anyway. Just knowing she was nearby made me feel good.

I had a wood shop class one semester and was caught cutting out a wooden gun while working on a band saw. When the teacher spotted me he confiscated the gun and brought it to the attention of the entire class, who laughed. The following day, the instructor cut out a large wooden star for me to wear around the shop and informed everyone that I was now the sheriff of the woodshop. That got a lot of chuckles for a couple of days.

This is also where I met my first wife. She was introduced to me by my brother Vince's girlfriend. We met each other off and on at the weekend meeting place for all students called the Hutch.

At that time, the black students went to another weekend assembly called Teen Tavern. Most black students went to the Teen Tavern, and no white students went there. But at the Hutch several blacks came there often, and we had no racial problems.

Go figure. I felt the blacks just didn't want to be around white folks, for some reason. All you would have to do was ask one of the black students, they'd surely give you a reason.

When I first arrived at Long Beach Polytechnic High, I bought food at the school food shops and took it over to a shady area where there were unoccupied wooden benches. I sat down and began to eat my lunch. A couple of guys approached me and asked me why I was sitting in their quad area. I told them I was hungry and eating my lunch. They became agitated as if they were going to throw me out, but I stood my ground and continued eating.

I came to the same spot for a couple of days, and those same two, and others, moved closer to me as if to intimidate me. My response was to get up and move closer to them.

They seemed puzzled. I know someone told them I was a transfer from Saint Anthony's, and they could've challenged me again, but they didn't.

One day as I was eating, they were planning something, but I don't know what it was. They were talking quietly when my girlfriend came by with her girlfriend and a guy named Steve, the girlfriend's boyfriend. He was a big guy like me, and we shook hands and greeted each other. The fraternity boys seemed to become really concerned when we shook hands. I spoke to the guy I had just met as if they were included in the conversation and informed him of their antics.

He turned his head and addressed all of them, about fifteen of them, and asked, "You guys got a problem with this guy eating here? Do ya?"

They all collectively answered, "No, it's okay with us!"

I was shocked at their comments and couldn't figure out why they answered the way they did. I shrugged it off until a little while later when I found out the guy I met was the toughest fighter in the school and had everyone eating out of his hand. We got along great and from there on, no one challenged me at all. That was awfully nice of them.

A few other guys like me who were kicked out of Saint Anthony's went to Long Beach Poly as well. We hung around each other and carried on as if we were longtime buddies. Several of them were very active like me and enjoyed life as it was, going to the movies and cruising around in cars to drive-in restaurants like Grisinger's and movies at the Town and Crest theaters in the Bixby Knolls area of Long Beach.

Oddly enough, most of us who went to Long Beach Poly from Saint Anthony's were surfers. We went surfing many times in the early morning hours, around four o'clock, during the school week. We'd surf before sunup and still be able to get to class on time. Now, we may have not been the sharpest minds in the room, but nevertheless, we were very healthy and energetic.

I distinctly remember the 1962 movie *Mondo Cane* was playing at the Circle drive-in theater, which was right at the infamous traffic circle where most of us met up and hung out. Of course the drive-ins were a great place to make out, and gab about all of our problems and enjoy one another's company.

In 1959 Vince, Phil, and I decided to catch the Catalina Cruiser and go to Catalina Island over the Labor Day weekend. We were going to camp out in the hills above the golf course, and during the daytime hang out at the fountain in Avalon and watched all the college guys sign the bodies of the hot babes and write letters in ballpoint pen across their bodies. We were also going to rent an electric car and go driving around, squirting women in the belly button with squirt guns. That sounded like a pretty good plan at the time, huh?

Well, it didn't turn out that way. First, we went to the shore and walked through Avalon, looking at all the girls. God, there were a lot of people. We enjoyed our short day but needed to scout out our sleeping area, just off the nearby golf course.

It was getting dark, so we drifted onto the golf course and ran across a whole bunch of college kids trying to go to sleep on one of the putting greens.

They were all spread out, covering the whole green, and were actually quite a bit rowdy, so we walked right past them and up into the small hills just above them. We nestled among the tall shrubs and bushes in a small clearing, maybe fifty yards away from the college students.

Around three in the morning we heard noises coming toward us, and we couldn't figure out who in the hell would be coming by us. It turned out it was a whole bunch of those same college kids, running from the deputy sheriffs chasing them up the hill. Needless to say they stumbled right onto us. This just so happened to be the first year (1959) that the LA County Sheriff's Department (LASD) took over Catalina Island's law enforcement.

Our camping adventure ended quickly when the deputies literally ran right on top of us. We were ordered to wrap up our sleeping bags, collect our personal gear, and walk down the hill to the golfing runway and green.

At the bottom of the hill, right next to the golfing green, was a nice big sheriff's paddy wagon. It was full of drunken college kids yelling and singing rowdy songs. Once we were loaded up, they drove us to the center of town and unloaded us in the courthouse, where they were conducting hearings for all the various violations. Our charge was vagrancy.

Vince was the only adult, and he was jailed until noon and charged a twenty-dollar fine. He was also given explicit instructions to come pick up Phil and me, pay the ten-dollar fine for each of us, and then personally escort us off the island on the next Catalina boat leaving the island.

That meant both Phil and I were in jail for at least twelve hours. Vince showed up at about three thirty in the afternoon and paid our fines. We went directly to the dock and caught the next boat out of there. Wow, what a time.

When we got home and told our dad, he laughed and said he was never contacted at all about our arrests. Later on, we found out there was no evidence of an arrest on any of our records, and therefore it didn't happen.

In my freshman year in college, my brother and I continued with surfing, which was the answer to all of our problems. We surfed as often as possible. A lot of times we went surfing at Ray Bay, by the smokestacks at Seal Beach, because the curl of the wave was a good shape. That was the first place I was able to hang ten—that's ten toes—over the nose of my nine-foot-two-inch, candy-apple red Allen surfboard.

There, the warm waters coming from the power plant caused a number of stingrays and small sharks to gather and loll around. Unfortunately one day, wading chest high with my surfboard, I stepped on a stingray. It was like someone stabbed me with an ice pick. I jumped onto my board and noticed the quarter-inch puncture wound on top of my right foot. Apparently when I inadvertently stepped on the sting ray, its tail curved upward and jabbed the top of my foot. It bled pretty well for about ten minutes and then stopped.

I was more concerned about the small sharks in the area that might want to chew away on the bleeding wound.

Surfing was nearly an everyday lifestyle for all of us, but others thought we were all nuts because we were surfers. My entourage wore garb similar to high-class beach bums. A white Penney's T-shirt, blue Levi's pants with the belt loops carefully cut off. Also we removed the W in orange stitching from the rear pockets, and folded over the cuff seams of our pants twice, real close to where there was about a half inch of light cuff exposed.

That was the most important thing—to have your Levi's right. Then came the Jack Purcell's low-cut black tennis shoes with the white rubber toes and sides. Across the toes was a well defined blue quarter-inch stripe, approximately two and a half inches long. This outfit was topped off of course with a green US Army military jacket, Vietnam era, with lots of pockets. This was everyday wear and handsomely worn by all of us. That was the cool way to dress, if you surfed. To top off all of that necessary regalia, I went a step further and peroxided my short hair to an orange color.

We hung out at the Long Beach Pike. One of the guys I knew and hung around with was Tom Nevin. His mom owned Nevin's Locker Room. It was right on the pike. All of the sailors from the Port of Long Beach came to stow their personal gear while they were on shore leave; they'd hit the beach over by Rainbow Pier. Not too faraway was a place on the bay called Woody's Goodies, where most of the high-school and college kids hung out.

Most of us were very naïve and lay around, gabbed, and drank beer moderately. We were all concerned about the draft coming up when we turned eighteen, so a lot of talk was about joining the navy or the marines as soon as possible to avoid the draft and joining the masses in the army.

A lot of us went on the weekends to the Rendezvous Ballroom, located in Newport Beach. Everyone wore the same Levi's and T-shirt, but instead of Jack Purcell tennis shoes, we wore huaraches. These were brown, strapped, leather sandals with car-tire bottoms attached to the leather base.

Everyone loved the live and loud music of Dick Dale and the Deltons. Oh, there always a few hoods looking for fights, and we never shied away, fighting with fists and feet, nothing really serious.

The only ones who smoked marijuana were the hoods, who sported slicked-back hair and wore khaki pants, buttoned up Pendleton wool shirts, and shined-up, pointed-toe leather shoes. Those were the ones who were always getting arrested and jacked up by the police.

A short time later I finally made the grade and graduated from high school. We were the first class to graduate from the Long Beach Sports Arena in 1963 with a class of eight hundred seniors.

I enrolled at Long Beach City College and took general education classes along with my girlfriend, Rosie. Quite a few things were going on, but it felt like a going to school was an educational rut and just killing time.

I distinctly remember on November 22, 1963, I was playing handball across the street from the quad at Long Beach City College. When we finished, we showered and got dressed and came back to the quad, right around noon. To our surprise, quite a few students were crying about the killing of President John F. Kennedy in Dallas, Texas, earlier that morning. We were all stunned by this announcement. We were already on pins and needles because of the Cuban missile crisis, and the Vietnam War was intensifying. Boy, everyone was glued to the TV, awaiting the next calamity. It seemed like a nuclear war was about to occur.

That's what we were planning for throughout my elementary and high school years. You know, all of the "duck, roll, and cover" practice. We practiced that maneuver many times each month, and it never really meant too much. We were in rooms with entire walls of windows. What do you suppose would have occurred if a blast occurred near all of those windows?

My girlfriend, Rosie, and I were seeing each other quite regularly, and I desperately needed to get a job. Vietnam was getting real hot, and the draft was calling. I got a job at Lucky's Supermarket as a box boy in Lakewood, a city just east of Long Beach.

This job was near the college and my girlfriend's home in Long Beach, near All Souls Cemetery on Cherry Avenue and Tehachapi Road. While I was working at Lucky's, I hung around the meat shop during break time and talked a lot to the meatcutters. I became interested in cutting meat.

Then a test came up at the unemployment office in downtown Long Beach. I was encouraged to take the test, which turned out to be a dexterity test that was fairly simple. I passed it with flying colors and landed a job with Safeway Stores. I was sent to a training store over on Manchester and La Cienega, in Los Angeles. I hustled and went as fast as I could, and the meat managers loved it.

Soon the Selective Service notified me to take a physical exam, and of course I passed with flying colors. They were about to pick my number, so I filed for a deferment, because I was a meatcutter in training. That deferment allowed me to complete my apprenticeship training first, and then I was susceptible to the draft.

That training was two to three years long, and I was in no hurry. I had to go to Gardena Adult High School once a week for meat-cutter training, and I became a member of the local meatcutters union on 111th Street, Los Angeles. The majority of my apprenticeship training was at Safeway at Vermont and Gage Avenue.

This also was the hot spot where the Los Angeles riots kicked off in 1965. At lunchtime I walked outside to the front parking lot, and there were fires all around me, as if we were at war. I don't think being scared ever entered my mind. I had my Forschner German-made knives in a metal leg scabbard. They were all keenly sharp, and I knew how to use them very well.

The streets were cluttered with military personnel and equipment, and I was battle ready, with my white Safeway meatcutter's smock and my paper hat with a red trim line running along its edges. I really never saw too much of the LAPD, but who needed them, when I was at work? Good thinking, huh?

I was stopped a couple of times while driving to work in my '63 off-white Volkswagen by the LAPD with five officers in the patrol cars. They all had shotguns and questioned why I was on the freeway all by myself.

The word was out that there were snipers shooting at cars and trucks on the freeway. No one else was traveling on the freeway except me and the LAPD, and that alone was amazing.

I explained to the officers that I was an apprentice meatcutter and had my knives ready for any problems I might encounter. They all smiled and wished me luck. For nearly a week I cut my travel time to work in half because of the vacant freeways.

I finally got married in 1965 and became a proud pop in 1967 when my first son, Brian, was born. That same day I drove to the local Selective Service Office with my son's birth certificate. I was then classified 3A, with a dependent, now actually one of the last to be selected.

One month later I became a journeyman meatcutter. I was "suit-cased," meaning I was sent to a whole variety of Safeway stores for the next five months.

That's about the time when I decided to apply to several law enforcement agencies, like LAPD, Long Beach PD, El Monte PD, LA Sheriff, Compton PD, and quite a few others. I was attending Compton College and taking law enforcement classes and ready to get into the career and become a cop. I was being primed by my brother Vince, who was already a cop with Compton PD and pretty well informed how to answer most of the questions for my oral interview.

I took all of the written tests and was about to go to the oral interviews. My meat-cutting union was now in a major strike and all of the money I saved for the cost of uniforms and equipment was exhausted for my family's survival.

Several of the agencies had given me quite a few hypothetical situations that I did not answer too well, so they asked me to try again in six months.

Then came the Compton interview. The main question they asked me was, "If all of the agencies that you applied for called at the same time, who would you want to work for the most?"

My response was, "The first one to call!" They loved that answer, and I passed and went on to the physical and psychological testing.

The meat-cutters strike went right into deep December of 1967, and I was running out of money. Fortunately, Compton PD called, and I was hired effective December 27, 1967. I was elated and anxious to quit meatcutting and start my new career as a police officer.

To top it off, I could keep an eye out for my brother, so he wouldn't get his ass kicked anymore, because his little brother was coming. Actually both Vinnie and I were very anxious for me to start the academy and get into the field as soon as possible.

The academy was going to start on January 8, 1968 and was a cool sixteen weeks long. It was going to come quickly. I had to get new uniforms—khaki utility uniforms that were going to be used extensively for the academy—and of course my class A uniforms, which were dark blue and expensive.

All of my equipment needed to be purchased as well; i.e., Sam Brown belt, handcuffs, nightstick, sap, whistle, gun, and ammo. There was a lot to prepare for. Plus, being ready with an intricate knowledge of the city was imperative. Radio codes were a must, and we needed to be ready for intense questions from the academy staff; and of course, we needed this knowledge for our own survival.

To start with, there were five of us coming from Compton, three white guys and two black guys. We immediately got along with one another and made a pact that all of us were going to make it and help one another.

Race never was an issue, because we were all thrown into the mix. This was the easy part. The academy was the way to our success, and we were about to land right in a race that made us stick together like glue.

CHAPTER 2

A COP IN TRAINING: APPRENTICE MEATCUTTER

My brother Vince was already a clerk with supermarket called Safeway in Compton. He was making a decent wage, so I tracked along his career path. He also was waiting to quit his clerk job and become a policeman for the City of Compton. Oddly enough the store where he was working was just across the street from the old Compton city hall that housed the police station, which was another entity within city hall.

I attended meatcutting school once a week at Gardena Adult High school, as well as working roughly a forty hour work week. The pay at the time was about $109 per week.

My car was a 1954 Ford, dull green with primer black, and the engine would overheat by the time I made it to work. By the end of my working shift, I would fill it with fresh water, but by the time I made it back home, it was again overheating. Several weeks later I purchased a used 1963 Volkswagen Beetle. With all the money I was making, I felt as if I was on top of the world.

About this same time I finished several months of training as a meatcutter and was shipped off to Vermont and Gage to a much more demanding store where they sold twenty-nine cents a pound, frying chickens; pig snoots, ears, tails, and a whole bunch of animal offal. This store was in the heart of a real rough and crime-ridden area, just south of a large Sears store, smack dab in the city of Los Angeles.

I worked hard and hustled around a crew of about eight meatcutters and enjoyed their company and listened to their stories.

My meat manager was a gentle man who always called on me to hustle and stay up with the second man, who was manning the saw and rapidly cutting all sorts of meat like beef, pork, chickens, lamb, and several times a year, sloppy buffalo. (The buffalo was sloppy because it wasn't aged like beef for twenty-one days, which caused the meat to be flaccid. It damn near draped over your forearm like a heavy overcoat.)

These same meatcutters encouraged me to get out of the meat-cutting business, because it was a dying trade. The whole trade, they said, was going to be centralized meat processing from one giant meat plant. This encouraged me to continue with my college education part time.

The second man was actually the second man in charge and worked very fast, telling the other meatcutters what meat product was needed. He also had to keep me, the apprentice, busy cutting and packaging the retail cuts and not let me catch up with him. Actually, we all hustled and processed a lot of cuts of meat daily and had an excellent rapport with each other.

When a meat load of approximately thirty thousand pounds came in on the delivery trucks, I promised the manager it would only take me thirty minutes to unload the delivery and put all the bulk meat away. I would casually leave the processing room, as the second man was intently cutting the various cuts of meat as fast as he could in order to get way ahead of me. His purpose was to bombard me with a whole bunch of cuts that needed trimming, brushing, and packaging.

I didn't show any anxiety or pressure as I left the room and casually walked into the cooler. Once in the cooler, the heavy refrigerator door slammed behind me, and I rushed out to the delivery truck and began to unload the truck by hand. (Palletized trucks were just coming into the picture but rarely used; access doors were still narrow and wouldn't allow anything palletized past its portals.)

My meat load was unloaded by hand, at least three times per week, and that meant unloading the thirty thousand pounds of beef, pork, buffalo, lamb, boxes of delicatessen meat items, and at least forty-five wooden crates of chickens, surrounded with crushed ice.

The chicken crates were the sloppiest to handle because all of the melting ice saturated with chicken odor would spill out of the crate and onto my clothing, and the foul odor would remain throughout the day.

Each crate contained thirty-five chickens and approximately twenty pounds of ice in a light, wired wooden crate, a combined weight of approximately 125 pounds each.

All of this heavy meat load had to be moved fast and along the snake-shaped long meat rails, on their way from the meat cooler onto the loading dock and nearby the delivery truck. When hanging the large quarters of beef like chucks, rounds, loins, and buffalo, it was imperative to hang these large bulky pieces by hanging them onto tree hooks. Each had about ten large hooks.

These heavy pieces weighed between 130 and 150 pounds apiece. If these quarters of beef were hung in the wrong spot, it could very well damage the various cuts of meat to the point where they wouldn't sell, mainly because the hook would cause a dark spot to show up and look like spoiled meat.

In order to hustle, I hired a young black kid named Lonnie R. who was about eight years old, to watch over the meat load on the dock as I was going in and out of the cooler putting items away. I paid him three bucks, and he helped me tremendously and was fun to talk to while I was working.

Several times local thieves would linger, awaiting an opportunity to move in and grab a piece or a box of the idle shipment and run down the alley, which was an easy avenue of escape.

Lonnie would sit atop the delicatessen cases and talk with me as I went in and out of the cooler. This worked great, and I was pleased to give him money for keeping a watchful eye. With his help watching the load, I was able to quickly unload all items without interruption in less than thirty minutes. The meat manager was extremely pleased when I returned to my abundantly loaded workbench and continued to hustle and catch up with the processed cuts of meat.

This occurred quite frequently throughout each day. As soon as I came close to catching up with the processed cuts of meat, the second man would invariably assign me to work in another area, fill the case with wrapped meat or bag frying chickens.

Our store sold approximately four thousand frying chickens a week. It was time-consuming to bag each chicken from the 135-pound wet wooden crates. I was pretty fast bagging each chicken, filling an entire block bench three feet high with all the bagged chickens.

Next came pushing the two chicken drumsticks protruding from the bag, twisting the bag closed, and wrapping a wire-tie around the end. The problem was that a lot of the legs were broken and when you pushed the legs with the palm of your hand the broken splintered bones would jam into your hand approximately a quarter inch. It hurt like hell. These wounds would inevitably become infected and slowed my performance down considerably.

During the week, the time would come to cut beef liver. These large livers needed to be skinned first of an opaque, thin membrane that encased the organ. Then we'd cut the large oversized arteries that were embedded on one side and clean up any oddities that made the liver appear unappealing or distasteful.

Occasionally while slicing each cut, if you were lucky, a light-greenish color might appear on one of the cuts.

This of course was an obvious hint of a boil or pus-filled abscess. You would cut the entire abscess from the dark-colored liver and continue cutting up the whole liver. If you weren't so lucky, you would cut into the boil directly and the pus would spew onto your hands, apron, and many times into your face. The odor was foul. You learned quickly to close your mouth when this occurred, because the outcome wasn't pleasant. When I finished cutting and packaging the liver in small one-pound plastic tubs, they were processed by the meat wrapper, who labeled them with what type of liver they were and the cost. The whole process took probably two hours.

If the meat buzzer sounded off, your job was to drop what you were doing and immediately respond to the front and see what the customer wanted. Many times I answered with my whole white apron, sleeves, and surrounding smock covered with blood, saturated to the point where I could feel the wetness seeping through my white shirt and T-shirt. As I greeted the customer I could see how my blood-soaked clothing shocked them. Their eyes opened wide, and they jerked their heads backward.

When my day finished, I would go home and take a shower to try to rid myself of the powerful odor of liver that permeated my skin and nostrils. Unfortunately the stench of liver would remain for several days, but that was part of the job.

Several times a year, fresh hog heads would be ordered. As they would arrive they would come in large boxes, three to a case. I, of course, would be assigned to process them. I would grab a four-wheel dolly and load up two cases at a time. Anything more and the partially damp cases would start to collapse and fall over. The heavy hog heads sometimes moved around and easily slipped out.

I positioned the cart nearby the band saw, which was right next to large windows, affording an opportunity to watch what was being processed. I carefully opened the large box, and immediately three large hog heads were revealed, eyes wide open and peering in my direction. I would carefully lift the thirty- to forty-pound head out of the box and place it onto the band saw table, with a noticeably loud bang. I would then open the throat of the saw blade guide and lock it into place. I carefully directed the head, nose first, right down the middle of the head slowly. As the blade cut into the jawbone, it made a higher whining noise and began to drag as it cut into the teeth and jawbone. Then white-colored dust kicked into the air and caused a small amount of the dust to remain round the head until passed the teeth area. Several customers would congregate around the window and watch as I processed the heads. I found it rather comical; it seemed to broaden the customers' interest in the grisly task.

There was an older meatcutter named Stan who was always kidding around. He was in his sixties and was not too faraway from retirement.

Sometimes Stan would pull himself on the rail guide where the heavy pieces of meat would roll out near the large band saw. Stan would then literally hang from that rail by his shod feet, which was about seven and one half feet in the air.

When I answered the buzzer, I would open the swinging door and immediately greet the customer. As I conversed with the customer, they would catch the sight of Stan hanging upside down with his arms and hands dangling. The bottom part of Stan's apron would dangle as well, leaving a smeared blotch of blood on his white smock with the green trim to signify authentic meat removal. A lot of customers would smile, realizing the joke as Stan would come down from the rail right after the swinging door closed.

We all had a special rapport with the customers and being very friendly was essential and encouraged by the infamous Safeway motto, "The customer is always right."

CHAPTER 3

RIOTS COME TO TOWN

It was right around August 1965 while I was at work when suddenly the Watts riots broke out. All sorts of law enforcement and the National Guard were running here and there with red lights and sirens. Fire trucks and emergency vehicles were traveling up and down Vermont Avenue. I went outside into the front parking lot and took a quick look around. I saw many fires and smoke surrounding the neighborhood.

A large Sears store was a couple of blocks north of my store. It was ablaze, with the pungent smoke billowing upward, hugging an area about fifty to sixty feet from the ground. It seemed as if we were at war because of all the fires, military personnel in jeeps with mounted machine guns, and police cars loaded with cops armed with shotguns noticeably sticking out their windows. However, all fires were still three or four blocks away from the store.

The constant chatter from the media was that the LAPD incited and provoked this riot because of all the degradation and abuse they foisted on the black community, which had reached its limit. The media consistently painted an extremely ugly picture of the police and starkly pointed out this riot was inevitable.

Presumably, as illustrated by the media, this was all brought to a head when a car was signaled by a police unit to pull over for speeding. The driver was refusing to pull over, although the police car had its red lights and siren on. The driver's noncompliance to yield to the police car now developed into a pursuit, with the suspect driver waving a white handkerchief out the window, allegedly because there was an emergency medical situation inside the car.

Once he stopped, the officers were upset because the suspect would not yield. As the officer approached with his gun drawn, the car lunged forward which caused the officer's gun to discharge. The bullet struck the driver in the head.

This situation was sensationalized by the media because it sold newspapers, and the television media loved it. The media's antics did fan the hatred of the local black community, as if they were all waiting for a cause to rebel. These carefully contrived news releases spread twisted views of police brutality that was not at all evident.

I worked in the ghetto area, and whenever I saw the police they were always professional and relatively friendly, even when they stopped me.

This area where I worked was loaded with criminals and all kinds of terrorist activity occurred daily. I can't remember how many times our store was robbed, but at least three or four times a year.

If you were in the parking lot of our store, you might have been subjected to auto theft or armed robbery. It happened all the time. We all knew very well what was happening by all the petty thefts that were occurring in our own store.

It wasn't just the blacks who were preying on everyone. Our store was inundated weekly by various bands of gypsies. Whole families of gypsies would come into our store and wreak havoc.

As many as ten or fifteen gypsies would enter the store, and they would create a diversion or grab large amounts of food like canned hams, luncheon meat, or whole trays of steaks, and make a mad rush for the door. This was unbelievable to watch, and there wasn't a thing you could do about the thefts. It was tantamount to a wholesale "grab and run." Managers of the store were getting ulcers from all of the trials and tribulations that confronted them on a daily basis, but there was little that could be done to remedy the many problems.

During my tenure at the store I chased down many a shoplifter outside and ordered the culprits to return the stolen meat packages. In fact, several times I chased robbery suspects down the alleys in an attempt to retrieve the cash stolen from our store.

Even though I was good with my knives many of the meat-cutting crew warned me that guns were superior.

My brother Vince who was in his first year as a Compton police officer, told me of being shot at all the time as the riots were beginning. Vince also told me of an incident when he was at Rosecrans Boulevard and Central Avenue. Several shots rang out when he was out of his patrol car. He said that when the shots were whizzing by, he dove right into a Salvation Army recycling bin and was able to avoid all of the randomly fired bullets.

CHAPTER 4

REVENGE: WHO BEAT MY BROTHER?

I was already enrolled in Compton City College, taking police science courses, and preparing myself for a law enforcement career. My brother, Vince, was already a cop and constantly discussed his daily adventures with me. I was admittedly very jealous. I knew very well that if I quit my meat-cutting job and became a cop, it would satisfy my thirst for a more exciting and active job.

In May 1966, my brother was making a car stop with four black male adult occupants. As he approached the left side of the car, the driver suddenly sped forward. My brother rushed back to his radio car and gave chase.

The suspect car zigzagged through traffic and sped away through the narrow streets, but Vince was slowly catching up with them. The suspect car traveled at a high rate of speed northbound through the city streets of Compton, and then went into the southern county area of Willowbrook, just south of the Watts area of Los Angeles.

The short pursuit ended in a residential driveway on an unknown street. My brother gave the general location over the police radio, but he did not know the name of the street. All of the occupants quickly exited the suspect car as my brother stopped and jumped out of his patrol car.

Three of the young adults stopped on my brother's command, but one of them continued to run away. Vince thought the one who got away was going to hide, so he focused on confronting the three remaining suspects. He held his police baton at port arms in an attempt to dissuade them from running.

As he stood there waiting, fellow units were coming to his aid, but they were unable to locate him, so they were slow to arrive

Suddenly, as Vince was waiting for help, the other suspect who had run away returned to Vince's rear and jumped on him from behind, driving him to the ground. The three other suspects joined in and pried the baton from my brother's hands. They began beating him and kicking him on the head and back. Vince, fortunately, had his helmet on, and it took the brunt of the beating he was receiving. He was struck fifteen or twenty times with his own baton.

One of the suspects grabbed his .357 magnum revolver from its holster as he was attempting to crawl away between two large street-sweeper brushes and ordered him to stop what he was doing. Vince was then told at gunpoint to stand up. He was struck again by the suspect who had his baton. Vince blocked the strike and was able to grab his baton, wrench it from the suspect, and clobber the suspect in the face.

They told him to move his patrol car from the driveway, so the suspects could leave quickly in their own car. The gun was pointing in his face as he got into the unit and sat down. Vince carefully and surreptitiously grabbed the microphone and placed it in his lap and repeated "Officer needs assistance, code three, I'm being held at gunpoint." Vince heard the radio operator ask him to repeat his last transmission, but at this point he couldn't.

Finally the first of the assisting units located him. The blasting siren and screeching of tires and brakes came upon all of them quickly. All of the suspects ran together, and they were captured shortly thereafter without any further trouble or aggravation.

My brother went to the hospital and was treated for injuries sustained from the beating. Fortunately he only suffered multiple bruises and bumps to his back, arms, and legs.

Vinnie lived several blocks from me, and the next day, when I heard that four guys jumped him and kicked his ass, I went over to his house immediately. The next day an article was in the newspaper about his assault. He showed me the article. It infuriated me that four punks jumped my brother and beat him like a dog. Retaliation was the only thing that came to my mind, but all suspects were in custody.

Vince then showed me his wounds, all along his back, eight or nine nightstick marks darkened by the bruising and reddening. Then he displayed his arms and legs with multiple defensive bruises. In my mind, that did it. I had to become a cop now to protect my brother from scum like the ones who beat him. And to make matters worse, they took his gun, but by the grace of God he didn't get shot.

A year later, two of the four suspects, who were brothers, were arrested, charged, and found guilty of seven local gas station robberies and murders, all within the Compton area. In their robberies, they kidnapped the lone attendants and forced them into the gas station bathrooms, where they shot and killed them.

CHAPTER 5

THE ACADEMY: LA COUNTY SHERIFF'S ACADEMY CLASS 122

During the first week, it was exciting from the get-go. I came to the Compton Police Station at 100 W. Almond Street. This was a station that was just a little over a year old and crispy clean. The training lieutenant introduced himself and several of the seasoned training officers.

We assembled in the briefing room, and all of the new recruits were introduced to each other, John G., Barry C., Ed H., Tom M., and of course me. John was the eldest by at least ten years, and the rest of us were close to twenty-four years old.

From all outward appearances, John was going to have a little trouble because of his age difference. He had a slight paunchy gut. The rest of us seemed strong and ready for whatever they threw at us.

We were all very attentive and somber as the day went on. The lieutenant would handle the majority of our training and lecturing time. He was very nice, informative, and sincere about our chosen profession. He focused mostly on what gear we needed immediately, and all necessary equipment for the classes, which were to start in thirteen days.

Our days initially were to expose us to the city, its government and size, and the police department—how many personnel, special problems, and areas. It was all very interesting and we, the recruits, had an insatiable appetite for information as we prepared for the sixteen-week course.

Compton had just recently contracted with the LA County Sheriff's Academy in lieu of Compton's own academy, which was a basic eight-week police officers standards of training approved course. Two other Compton officers had just graduated from the last sheriff's academy, and that was the actual first class since the changeover.

The lieutenant gave us a lot of information that we would need through our course of training. He emphasized what would happen and how to prepare and study for the quasi-military training. Several of the training officers took us outside and taught us how to march, make facing movements, and more important, how to succeed when questioned by the heavy-handed drill instructors. This instruction occurred every day until we got it right.

It all was new and very informative, without a minute to spare.

Everyone was warning us of the impending stress of training and that several of us might very well fail. Those warnings instilled a certain amount of pride in all of us and we, the recruits, made a pact with one another that we would help one another without any unnecessary prompting. The pact we made was the best thing we could have done to make it through the training and in our future in law enforcement.

We learned how to shine our shoes, prepare our everyday khaki uniforms that were cotton wash-and-wear. All uniforms were neatly ironed with three perfect creases on our shirts and centered creases on the legs of our pants, clean and crisp. No strings, Irish pennants, holes, smudges, or any stains whatsoever would be tolerated.

All buttons were buttoned, snaps were snapped, and zippers zipped, no argument. Belts were shined, and all police belt equipment was in its proper place, even down to an extra flashlight bulb and a dime in the bottom of the handcuff case. The dime was to be used when circumstances allowed the use of a pay phone for emergencies.

Within the thirteen days we all parroted the radio codes feverishly among ourselves; knowing full well the drill instructors would attack our knowledge and skills on the use of the "lifeline," our police car radio.

The importance of minuscule details was brought to our attention. The drill instructors, DIs, would not give in on anything that could possibly save our lives or cause injury to other officers. That meant knowledge of the city and all of its unique characteristics. This was essentially going to be a sixteen-week course of intense cramming.

When the training started, we decided to carpool each day, and of course it was in my '63 Volkswagen.

The first day, January 8, 1968, we were all dressed in suits and assured that there wasn't going to be any running. Well, guess what. Those DIs apparently didn't think that way. They met us as we were parking our cars.

From that point on, as soon as we stepped from the car, we were screamed at. "Hustle and run like you've never run before!" As we ran we could hear maybe four or five drill instructors screaming and yelling commands with no letup.

We scurried and were driven like cattle into our classroom with a total of approximately one hundred cadets. The instructor was microjamming us with anything that law enforcement does or could ever do. The unrelenting yelling didn't stop unless an instructor was coming to the podium.

As the instructor would step away from the front of the class, all hell would break loose. The key to success was the ability to detach yourself from all outside influences; focus on what is at hand; do what you're told; and don't get scared. That alone would provide enough impetus to make it through the class. The drill instructors would watch very carefully, and try to make you flub up, and watch your reaction microscopically. And your reactions had better be proper and look professional.

John G., our fellow Compton cadet, was jumped on from the get-go and the DIs made him do fifty sit-ups at each break. He was well liked and encouraged by all of us, but he still had to complete his sit-ups before the end of each ten-minute break. This was to remedy his paunch and an attempt to see if he could withstand the DIs' physical appearance readjustment program plagued with pain. Within three weeks a noticeable flattening of his stomach was visible, and he continued without complaint. We were very proud of our small group and assisted one another in every way possible.

We were in competition with all our fellow cadets, and especially the sheriff's cadets, who was about 75 percent of the class.

We, the Compton cadets, bragged about our city's crime rate and the on-the-scene combat training that occurred every time we were on patrol. The other cadets couldn't match the life-threatening adventures we faced even on our normal and routine calls for service. We rode on patrol as much as we could each weekend, and it became more exhilarating as time passed. Every week was a new adventure. Our training lieutenant at Compton had said that Compton had the highest crime rate per capita in the United States. We didn't yet realize how deadly and dangerous it really was.

CHAPTER 6

THE COMMENDATION

About the fifth or sixth week we were sitting in class, and my drill instructor went to the podium in front of the class. He began reading a commendation for someone in class. The event that he was reading about seemed familiar. Then he read my name aloud. I was amazed. What he was reading was actually relating to an arrest my training officer at Compton PD, Stan P., and I had made over the past weekend.

The drill instructor read the accolade aloud and with great enthusiasm. The entire class was noticeably attentive when he stopped for a few seconds and ordered me to stand up near my desk. He continued with the description of my adventurous arrest and capped the whole thing off with emphasis on my valor and courage.

As he read the proclamation, I felt a strong sense of pride and accomplishment. Here, where I was alien to all and only a cadet, my peers praised me as the report outlined the arrest in minute detail. I was very proud that my training officer took the time and effort to write such a commendation; he had never led me to believe that he would write such praise.

Stan and I were working a two-man evening car in the northern part of Compton. It was relatively quiet at around eleven o'clock, and we were driving along the curb line with our headlights off. An in-dashboard toggle switch was hooked up to cut out the patrol car's brake lighting so people would think we were continuing forward, as opposed to braking. Also hooked to the lighting system was another toggle switch to shut off all headlights and rear lights, which helped immensely.

We were traveling at approximately 3 mph, sometimes even slower, and looking for anything that could possibly jump out in front of us. This was the Compton casual patrol way to rout out suspects. We and the patrol cars had to be as quiet as possible. Usually in this mode our guns were out of the holster and lying across our laps. Because of the narrow streets and alleyways, suspects could suddenly appear at your door, and you had better be ready. If you weren't ready, you might very well be involved in a fight for your life just outside your always-open patrol car window!

Stan was giving me instructions on a variety of hypothetical situations that might occur and what I should do. Stan was very cool and informative on every topic and prepped me for many situations.

My brother Vince and several other officers had previously informed me that Stan P. was one of the best officers in Compton. He had been involved in several hair-raising shootings. He was described as an extremely hard worker, dedicated, and attuned to the law enforcement ethic.

We were working the shift from 7:00 p.m. to 3:00 a.m. This shift was very active, and arrests were frequent. The police radio started to chatter, and we received a call for a situation that was very close to us. Stan said that I should look out for two auto thieves who were running nearby, away from the scene of a car crash.

The dispatcher reported that the stolen car had just crashed into the front room of a home, narrowly missing the occupants. The suspects had abandoned the car, its rear end resting on the front porch. The front and middle parts of the car were deeply embedded in the house.

Stan repeatedly instructed me to keep looking out my window and let him know if I saw anything move. We drew closer to the incident, but at the same slow speed.

Suddenly I spotted two silhouetted figures skirting across the bright moon backdrop. They were running parallel to us but approximately a block away. I told Stan what I saw, and he increased the speed, careful not to give away our position.

We made a right turn at the next corner and drove northbound quickly, drawing closer to the corner where we would most likely intersect the thieves. About a hundred feet from the corner, we noticed the thieves crossing in front of us, looking in our direction. The suspects immediately changed direction and jumped over the six-foot wooden fence on a slight incline.

Stan yelled, "Go get 'em, Larry!" My door was already prepped, partially ajar. I bolted from the car and vaulted the six-foot fence quite easily.

I landed in a backyard and spotted one of the thieves partially hidden in the shrubbery that encircled the yard. I went over to the suspect and grabbed him with my left hand. My pistol was in my other hand. Actually it wasn't necessary. There wasn't enough time to point the gun at him because I came upon him so quickly.

He began screaming for me not to hurt him, when suddenly the other suspect appeared running toward the back of the home.

He looked at me. I shouted, "Hold it right there, or I'll drop ya!" Although I was struggling with the first suspect and pointing my gun at the other about eight feet away, they both surrendered and lay face down on the grass. This all occurred within about thirty seconds.

I cuffed one of the suspects and stood him up in a headlock using only my left arm. I holstered my gun, grabbed the other suspect by the back of his shirt collar, and began dragging him behind me.

I brought both suspects toward the front of the house. The one suspect I was dragging was cuffed up behind his back, and I was very concerned about what he might try to do. I thought he might try to escape from my grasp, because the opportunity was evident.

When I reached the front yard, I saw my training officer standing beside the open driver's door of the patrol car and talking over the police radio. The spiraled wire of the Motorola microphone was stretched to its limit. I overheard him stating our position. He said we'd been separated briefly, and he was waiting for me to reappear. I was only gone from his view for about a minute or two.

When he spotted me, he smiled and asked, "Are you okay?" I nodded that I was okay, despite the anxiety about what had just occurred. He continued to smile as he dropped the mic and walked toward me. I still had both suspects in tow, and we came upon each other in the street. Stan seemed to be belly chuckling at my appearance with both suspects.

Both suspects commented that they were glad that I didn't hurt or shoot them, and they were very sorry for stealing the car and crashing it into the house.

Several fellow Compton units arrived as I was getting personal information from the suspects and jotting down the address and the intersection we were near.

Most of the officers who arrived talked briefly with Stan, who was giving them the details. They all began to smile and came over to me and complimented my capture, patted my back, and shook my hand. I was elated.

Both suspects were placed in the car, and we drove to the scene of the crash. As we arrived at the scene, Stan commented, "Holy shit!"

The stolen car was deeply embedded into the house. The occupants clustered in the front yard with several other policemen and firemen.

Another unit was assigned the crash site. Stan and I were en route to the station to book and charge both suspects and write the reports.

Later on, when we'd finished the reports, Stan again congratulated me on the tactics and rapid capture. I thanked him. I appreciated the acknowledgment, however short-lived.

Time in the academy dragged on. At times the work was very strenuous and time-consuming. We all stuck together very close and continually had the attention of the whole class because of the array of felony arrests we made each weekend.

I received several other commendations, but none as dramatic and complimentary as the one Stan P. gave me. To my amazement, few if any commendations were given to any other cadet. I really felt gifted. My commendations were from some of the better and more generous training officers.

We were coming up on the eleventh week, and I had just received another low grade in my weekly tests. I was concerned. I approached my drill instructor and brought my concerns and my grade point average to his attention. He quickly advised me, while looking through my folder, that there was no cause for alarm and that everything else was really good. He assuaged my concern, saying that I was okay and there was nothing to worry about. I felt relieved and reassured, so I returned to my seat in class.

The very next day, in morning formation, I was called out to the front of the entire class. While standing front and center, in a position of attention, my drill instructor and the staff sergeant boldly announced that I was now the new class sergeant. In this position I was placed in the spotlight and given a whole host of rules and instructions to operate and control the class. If anything occurred, it would rest on my shoulders. Basically it was my turn in the bucket, and I had to perform flawlessly or get washed out.

With that in mind, nothing could be further from my mind than to do an excellent job and withstand whatever the academy staff threw at me.

The class sergeant's position was stressful, but to be honest, the whole class helped by just doing what they were told to do. No matter what happened, I would endure. I had the routine down and performed fairly well, and nothing much diverted my focus.

—————

By the way, an important detail that I omitted occurred on April 4, 1968. I was in my apartment, prepping my Compton class "A" uniform and getting gear ready for the upcoming graduation in several days. My clean and perfectly pressed blue uniform hung on the cabinet handle above the bedroom closet, and my spit-shined uniform shoes lay beneath the closet doors, carefully placed together and handsomely displayed. I was going over my blue steel revolver, serial number 74100, a six-inch Colt Python .357 magnum. It was very important that everything was perfect, so I focused on the details of what the inspection would entail.

I carefully loaded the magnum shells into the cylinder and wiped off any semblance of dust or fingerprints with a lightly oiled cloth. I extended my arm slowly pointing at one of the specks on the ceiling, visualizing my training. I pulled the hammer back.

I had done this hundreds of times at the range, and I was very careful not to pull the trigger. I knew very well that when the hammer was pulled back, the trigger-pull poundage was cut virtually in half, and it was highly likely to discharge with the slightest light pull.

With that in mind, my finger gently touched the trigger, and it fired. *Holy shit,* I thought as the dust and smoke was clearing. I nervously spotted a small hole in the spackled foam ceiling, just one foot away from the small closet doors above the two wide closet doors.

I knew the round had entered the ceiling and the attic and exited the roof as well, but I had no idea where the round went after that.

I looked at my impeccable dark-blue police uniform and realized it was covered with ceiling spackle as if it was coated with powdered sugar. It scared the bejesus out of me, and I realized what could occur from that errant bullet. I sat back on my bed and thought that if anyone found out about this, I'd be crucified.

I thought about reporting my incident to the authorities but carefully drew the conclusion that that wouldn't be very wise, considering the drastic consequences it may create. So I kept this incident to myself, and it has indelibly etched my brain about such a foolish situation that could have been avoided.

The remainder of the sixteen weeks went fast, and we were all grateful we succeeded. Upon graduation, the police cadets went to our patrol assignments and unfortunately the sheriff cadets, except for the number one cadet, went to their jail assignments. If that sheriff cadet was nominated number one, the sheriff's staff would ensure he would be assigned one of three stations of his personal selection.

Women were in our classes, but not viewed in contention with the men, because most would be assigned a jail division assignment. I actually didn't remember that any women were in my class until I viewed the class photo after we graduated.

My focus during the academy class was committed, determined, and fixed to the point where gender never entered my mind. I viewed everyone as an equal unless it was brought to my attention, and it never was. No female was ever class sergeant.

———

Several years later Stan P., the training officer whom I rode with and admired, left Compton PD and went to a neighboring police department in the city of El Segundo. Stan worked with El Segundo for several years. One day he went to a hospital in the Long Beach area to have a tumor removed from his forearm.

That surgery was classified as a "therapeutic misadventure," and Stan died on the table. The anesthetist screwed up, to put it bluntly.

May God bless Stan P. for his integrity, dedication, and enthusiasm, and the direction and training he gave me that I have used throughout my career, and damn his early demise. He was an excellent role model for anyone in uniform and truly dedicated to the law enforcement profession.

CHAPTER 7

A COLORFUL PICTURE: COMPTON, THE MODEL CITY

The city of Compton is roughly eight and one half square miles. It is located just southeast of the Los Angeles. The actual borders are Long Beach, Los Angeles, Lynwood, Paramount, and Gardena.

Several years before I hired on as a policeman, Compton was known as a quiet, beautiful suburban city occupied mostly by white, middle-class people mixed with a robust variety of Hispanic and blacks. It was relatively calm and serene. Crime was minimal and unremarkable.

Unfortunately, a dark cloud of anguish and despair enveloped this suburban city. A vast array of criminals permeated the area and swallowed what good was left. They brought the city into the position that it still exemplifies today.

When I hired on in Compton in December 27, 1967, it had the highest crime rate per capita in the United States. Now, this may sound rather vague to some; but to those who know what that means, is profound. In other words, Compton had more crimes committed per person than anywhere else in the entire country.

During the initial days of indoctrination, my attention was directed to the northern border limits of Compton, specifically on Carlin Avenue at Bullis Road. The southern side of the street was within the Compton city limits, and the northern side was in the city of Lynwood.

I was told that all of the homes on the north side were up for sale. I didn't really comprehend what was going on, but I was told it was called blockbusting and white flight. Over the next several months, those terms were mentioned many times as the former residents fled the area, and its new occupants arrived.

Local residents were in fear that blacks were coming into their neighborhoods and coming quick. The flight was to avoid the gloom and doom about to take over the entire area. They were told to move out quickly—cut their economic losses and run.

Compton was virtually a quagmire and haven for thieves, gangs, drug dealers, shooters, murderers, rapists, pipe-bomb makers, and a plethora of other criminals. Biker gang wars were also prevalent and added to the mix of the highly dangerous criminal element.

The Black Panther Party, the militant Malcolm X faction, and police-hating "community alert patrols" were in full operation. They all followed and shadowed police officers as they were rushing or responding to their calls for service and hung around, voicing their angry opinions and epithets. (In today's setting, circa 2013, does this sound a tad familiar?) Those community misfits were very active and organized and well entrenched in all that happened in the city. They did not hold back with their hateful antics and tormented the law-abiding community as well, as the officers went on to their calls for service. Many times those same arrogant misfits came into the lobby of the Compton police station demanding radical entitlements. Or they were very upset if one of them was captured while involved in a crime.

The radical militants would demand their comrade's release solely because he was arrested because he was black, and not because he was the main suspect involved in a crime.

The radicals confronted the police many times, taunting and provoking them. The whole atmosphere seemed like a stage for a much bigger operation and radicals were in fact testing our integrity and stamina, probably because we were a small police department, and we didn't have the resources that other nearby departments employed.

The US Organization, headed by the Marxist leader Ron Karenga, was at odds with the Panthers in Oakland and Los Angeles. A shoot-out in the Oakland area had occurred at this time, and that incident stirred up that same racial hatred here locally as well, at the UCLA campus.

I certainly wouldn't want to overlook that infamous bow-tie-wearing, bean-pie salesman and "pitchman" Louis Farrakhan. He's in a league of his own. His plan was to scare "whitey," and send all of his little pull-toy thugs out to act as "snide white haters." We never crossed paths, and I think we never will. Farrakhan is no different from any other nose-picking, booger-eating, trailer-trash Klansman who hates blacks. Personally I feel he'll get what he deserves sooner or later, and I'm sure that's with the devil, his twin conjoined at the hip, as he designs and cultivates a new brand of hatred for whites.

These incendiary conflicts were in the news and televised daily. All of this nonsense was a heavy cocktail of dangerous intrigue and diatribe that added to the scheming and plotting of the criminal element. This demonstration of anger, pomp, and parade was only stifling the black community and no one else.

"Nihilist" would be a good word to apply to these hate-mongering tactics, and law enforcement was the ideal commodity for both the radicals and the media to exploit. Yes the media is part of those ideas because it is profitable—even with a little bit of twisting of facts about what actually occurred in order to establish a spectacular made-up story and promote controversy.

Another major event was the murder of civil rights leader Martin Luther King. This occurred just as I was starting my career. It was brought up continuously by the media who were placating the blacks.

The Black Panther gang arrogance was amplified by Cassius Clay, now Muhammad Ali, who was rambling on about his allegiance to the Black Muslim movement. He was a boxer, and a good one, too, but his outspoken anger for the establishment was reported daily as a constant reminder of his defiance and despair. The media loved him for his brash, snide poetic comments and the support of his sports-reporting lackey, Howard Cosell. Cassius Clay's behavior was mimicked by a lot of young blacks when they were questioned by the police and added more curt rude behavior to stimulate law enforcement overreaction.

Stokely Carmichael, the honorary leader of the Black Panther movement, was vocal as well. He and his local thugs all sang out of the same twisted radical racist cookbook. He was always in the mix because of his use of large hand-painted signs advocating black power when the media showed up. The Panther gang used their incendiary slogans for basic media sensationalism.

But who am I to say such things? I was there with my fellow officers, and the radicals knew it. If they would misbehave in the slightest way or break the law, the radicals knew who would put up with their antics by sizing up each officer.

We all knew some of us had the appearance of command presence to control them. So the Panthers chose to sneak around the outer periphery just out of our reach and egg on the onlookers to defy the cops and to do something.

Occasionally these cop-hating Panthers would fire a few rounds at us, or toss glass bottles and rocks toward our positions. They were really scared of what we could do to them, so they would stay far enough away that they couldn't get a good line of fire on us, and many objects fell short, but very close by.

Each officer had to be aware of his surroundings all of the time because it meant survival. To put it bluntly, Compton was not the place for the weak or indecisive, and our guys stood their ground at unbelievable risk.

The big shoot-out at Forty-First Street and Central Avenue in Los Angeles between the Symbionese Liberation Army and the LAPD occurred around this same time. This was sensationalized even more by a local female reporter, who went to the doorway to get the scoop from the kidnapper, murderer, and bank robber.

Even Patty Hearst was in the mix with the Symbionese Liberation Army to pick up any slack that might have been missed. She fell conveniently into the psychological profile of the Stockholm syndrome. This was, in my opinion, another political twist conjured up by the media, where a kidnap victim becomes entwined with her captors and becomes part of the gangster crew. She was wanted now for bank robbery and a whole slew of other criminal antics, and wanted posters were being distributed throughout the Los Angeles area for her arrest as well as the rest of the gang.

No one had the guts to say what was happening, because it was highly racially sensitive and had to be politically correct at all angles. That caused more fear and grief, and the media worked those radical elements to the maximum. What it was, in fact, was a strong affront and major push for anarchy. Oddly enough, the media never covered the Watts Summer Festival except to report positive reviews for the celebration. Boy, was that a freak show and a political joke. We'll discuss that event later.

The fire department had to be escorted by the police many times to fight fires in the more densely populated areas. While fighting those fires, the fireman were attacked and assaulted with rocks and bottles and shot at frequently by militant blacks in order to obtain more entitlements. Our job was to protect those firemen, let them fight the fire, and discourage civilians, led by the thugs, from shooting at them. Was the press there on those occasions? Hell no. Somehow the media would miss these events and pop up at all others that weren't as dangerous. Again, it all seemed very much contrived.

Most of us couldn't understand the obvious manipulation of the criminal and political aspects. Why? It was absolutely not safe for them, and it was much easier to cover police malpractice if there was a claim of racism. Racism is a wild card and always used when entitlements will further the radical agenda. The radicals knew very well if they incited the local community by screaming and yelling and starting the fires and destroying property, they would obtain more and more entitlements. To me it seemed just like it was a free ride for the radical thugs and gangs, but their efforts were scaring everyone, but it was working, and they knew it. To top it all off, all of these provocateurs continued with their gangland antics throughout the day and evening hours.

Compton criminal behavior was strangely enough absent from any publicity by the local media. In my young mind it was obviously concealed as if to disguise the behavior of this racial group as law-abiding and pro-American.

Black gangs were just starting to form and grew incrementally, like rabbits, from the late sixties until the late nineties. Their death toll was astounding, but who's counting? Everything had gone to hell, and hope for their ending was severely diminished. It seemed like the more radical they became, declaring racial strife and touting the reasons why they were committing all of the crimes, the more they demanded entitlements. These claims can be verified by reviewing the local papers of the time. It was always about terrible police behavior, overreaction, and brutality against the poor black community.

Oh, sure there were some police officers who did some of what they were accused of. And the media played up those few, but 98 percent of the officers did not participate and did a splendid and outstanding job.

To this day I embrace those officers who performed well, stayed away from the media and racially prompted views, and held their course of action and never compromised their ethical standards.

I believe the media absolutely abuses their self-imposed journalistic protocol and most likely helped create "gang behavior." One can see evidence of their insensitive behavior whenever you see a pursuit by police on television. Although asked not to broadcast by most agencies, because it brings civilians into the mix of the ever-present danger, in fact it provides a way for the suspect to call his or her fellow gangsters or "homies" to create diversions or pick up any items of evidence they might have tossed while fleeing.

When asked to stop, the media rationalizes their position by saying that it's news. You have seen this behavior when O. J. Simpson was being chased shortly after the murders of Nicole Simpson and Ronald Goldman. When suspects rob a bank and are being pursued by the police, and the suspects start tossing money out of their car windows, it creates mass confusion as civilians come onto the scene to gather up the loot. I'm sure you've seen this as well.

These pursuits have been addressed many times to the media over many years. They have been asked to delay their "live" broadcasts because someone might be severely injured or killed. In my opinion, we need a law to stop the media's live-pursuit broadcasts. They should be fined heavily in order to stop these "blaze" moments of indiscriminate televised information. Of course the First Amendment will be drawn out and used to support freedom of speech ahead of personal safety.

Watch what the courts will do when one of these media-caused injuries or deaths are attributed to their negligence.

CHAPTER 8

HISPANICS/LATINOS/MEXICANS

The Hispanic/Latino groups in Compton were located on the east side near Atlantic Avenue and on Wilmington Avenue. These two areas were heavily infested with two different gangs. Again, I will not mention their names because it gives credence to the thug mentality. In my short year and a half stint with Compton, one of the gangs was nearly wiped out by all of the shootings. These two gangs were the most active at the time.

I'll admit my view point toward Hispanics, Latinos, and Mexicans is biased because my wife and her entire family. My wife says that she's not Hispanic or Latina, but she is 100 percent Mexican.

What I can say is that because of familiarity with individuals and their cultural traits, I do not see notable differences between races.

CHAPTER 9
SKEWED REPORTS

Statistics can be verified through the Federal Bureau of Investigation's yearly statistical guide and are provided in book form. However, that book, although loaded with statistics, pie charts, and graphs illustrating various major crimes in all the cities and jurisdictions in the United States, is not accurate, and in fact is very misleading. For instance, if a jurisdiction wants to lower a specific crime, all it has to do is twist or change the name of that crime to another classification, as they do in several cities in the Southern California area.

I know this because I ran a suspicious vehicle's license plate one night to see if it was a possible stolen auto. The car came back as "missing." I asked what the hell a missing auto was, and our communications center replied they didn't know either. I returned to the station and made an inquiry into the matter. To my surprise the city representing the missing auto, instead of taking a stolen auto report, is now reporting stolen autos as missing autos. This is done primarily because the city, in an attempt to improve its image, is very much aware that most stolen cars are recovered within two weeks. So their reasoning was why not reclassify a stolen car as a missing car for a two-week period. If the car is still not located within that time frame, then it can be changed to an auto theft or another lesser criminal classification favored by the city administrators and welcomed by the media.

That way, when the yearly jurisdictional report from the cities are submitted to the FBI, the city involved in the manipulation will report a drastic drop in their auto theft cases. The cities involved in these misrepresentations can then boast of their lower national car theft ratings than most other cities in the United States.

With that in mind, think of the consequences those skewed statistics could have on insurance companies. Those cities with the lower crime ratings will certainly draw more folks to their low-crime neighborhoods.

There was a major change about to be sprung on the city of Compton in 1968. A briefing was called to order at the police station, and a new city manager came to our briefing and made a declaration to all officers in attendance. He stated that Compton was now in the "model cities program," and we were ordered "to cater to the needs of the black community."

I was brand-new, a rookie, and I was perplexed. The attitude of most of the officers was that everything had changed. No more going to the troubled areas where most of the crime was being committed. The hot spots were no more. We, the officers, were now ordered to stay away, and leave alone whatever went on in those areas. Unless directed otherwise.

The racial makeup of the Compton officers was mostly white, fifteen Hispanics, a couple of Asians, and maybe ten or fifteen blacks. The total department was approximately seventy-five male personnel and maybe five females.

Under the new "model cities program," race was not to be an issue and therefore not to be used in any statistical data. If the murder rate was high, those statistics were to be skewed by all involved. They were adjusted to guide the city into a new pleasant atmosphere and portray the city as an aspiring and law-abiding community.

This was an implied edict by the new black city manager, and never expressed aloud other than at the first briefing, but well understood by all of us. The grumbling increased, and most of the officers were displeased. They determined there was no alternative but to look for another job elsewhere.

Shortly after that meeting, around two weeks later, arrangements were made for twenty-three Compton officers, to take the LA County Sheriff's Department written test at the city of Industry sheriff's station. We initially thought this exam was arranged for Compton officers only, but when we arrived we saw the exam room was full of approximately another one hundred applicants.

I distinctly remember it was raining like crazy, and I saw water shooting about one foot high out of the heavy lid in the middle of the street.

Why do I remember that event so distinctly? I believe I was confused about the whole ordeal, and perplexed. I felt I was easily swayed by the older and seasoned officers to take the test and get the hell out of Compton. This was because of all the obviously imported racial strife that was in place and a future with the department seemed unstable and very bleak.

An example of the new order was our simple police patch. The older one depicted a barrel with spokes radiating from the center indicating the "Hub City." That was the one I wore while I was employed by the city. Shortly after I left they changed that patch to a new upbeat patch depicting a beautiful sailing ship.

Later on, that sailing ship was referred as the "Compton Yacht Club." This was funny to most of the officers, who knew about the city's extraordinary crime rate, but not funny at all to the residents. It was later learned that the sailing ship depicted was a figure that celebrated the slain civil rights leader Martin Luther King.and celebrated annually on the third Monday in January to honor him as the chief spokesman for non-violent activism in the civil rights movement which successfully protested racial discrimination.

Around that same time I was visiting a zoo in the Southern California area with my family. Someone broke into my locked van by prying the wing window open. They stole several pieces of my wife's jewelry, a camera, and about ten dollars in change. Officers responded, took a report, and gave me a report slip indicating the crime and the file number. Several days passed, and I called the police department to get any details from their investigator. The detective wasn't available, and a secretary was connected with me to answer any questions.

In our conversation I was informed by the secretary that the classification was changed from auto burglary to malicious mischief and miscellaneous car prowl. I asked why, and she replied that that was the way they did things in their department. Why in the hell would anyone do that? The secretary was just as baffled as I was, but in reality, it all made perfect sense. All jurisdictions could very well redirect and skew their crime statistics like any other topic, adjust it accordingly for whoever was the concerned entity, which might or might not have a negative impact on their city. If a sizable state or federal grant or loan was available, all they would have to do is convert or skew the present statistics toward that specific grant or loans to fit the loan parameters. The concerned entity could use whatever brush the jurisdiction wanted to paint their area as a beautiful thriving metropolis, boasting of their low crime status, clean streets, and nice people.

If you search deeply, you will find that this has been going on for a long time and is accepted by all government resources as truthful and responsible. But if you have anyone who is in law enforcement, ask about their statistics and see for yourself. If they are forthright, you will be startled to see that statistics can fool anyone.

City managers and administrators are the ones who pressure law enforcement to improve their specific crime problems no matter what, including deception. By the way, city administrators would be the first to describe these revelations as hyperbole or just plain nonsense.

Remember the movie *Jaws?* In that movie, the city of Amity, a beach community, the mayor used very harsh language toward the concerned police chief, Brody. The chief knew very well that there was a killer shark in the waters and wanted to close off the beaches in order to save lives. In the movie, Chief Brody was slapped in the face by a mother who had lost a son in a shark attack and found out the chief knew there was a previous shark attack a week earlier. The mayor's comment to the chief right after he was slapped was, "She's wrong!"

However, the mayor and city council believed it would ruin their city's reputation and appeal to tourists and beach goers. They believed the crowds would stay away, and the city's economic status would be trashed. This comparison is almost a perfect analogy to the city of Compton's skewed reasoning and heavy-handed police control. Because the city of Compton has a mayor and a city council, it is well known that the city manager directs the police department, not the police chief.

This comparison is right on track with Compton's crime rate. In my own mind to this day all city and county governments manipulate their classifications in a similar fashion and simply skew negatives into positives, or eliminate the name altogether. That way, they have no data to criticize.

In today's environment, each department now usually employs a statistician. These individuals are specifically hired to prove or disprove behaviors, crimes, and descriptions of suspects and gangs for the area's own economic and social agendas.

They can tone down the stats of gang activity and violence by making minor adjustments and altering the boundaries of any reporting districts. They merge it into a different area by nudging the designating lines on maps and switch zip code borders or area code designations, which are rather broad.

This was demonstrated by the city of Los Angeles. Several years ago, the city administrators said that "South Central LA" was not to be used anymore because the very name tainted the already muddy crime-infested waters. So now all you hear is South Los Angeles, and negative connotations have simply disappeared. Given these new demographics, this minor adjustment spreads the actual crime rate to a much larger area and covers up the specifics of the actual area, which wreaks havoc with all major crime statistics. And guess what—the media goes along with the adjustments and name changing without a hitch or a comment about what the city is doing. The crimes the police were targeting have almost disappeared. This crime cleanup is simply done with ghost teams of officers, justifying their work as the team responsible for the crime eradication.

I guess you could draw a parallel to redlining. The insurance industry did this to certain areas that have high insurance risks. When the insurance companies were redlining, they were charging additional costs for policies in designated high-crime areas, or where a high number of traffic accidents occurred. Local governments expressed their dissatisfaction with the redlining and wanted it stopped.

Has redlining stopped? I'm sure the term redlining has stopped, but rest assured something else under a different name and classification has taken its place. This practice will always remain, but under different names.

It's pretty much like profiling, which is not liked by the courts, attorneys, and the ACLU. Much of the criminal element dislikes it as well, because it supports the adage, "If it looks like a duck, walks like a duck, and talks like a duck, it's probably a duck." What they want is something described as "warm and fuzzy!" So whom do you trust?

CHAPTER 10

"KILL THE PIG"

Before the Martin Luther King Hospital was even built, Compton was stuck with the infamous Las Campanas Hospital, Dominguez Valley Hospital in the local area, or the older and much larger Los Angeles County General Hospital, located way north just above the I-10 freeway at Soto Street.

Las Campanas was constantly being picketed by Compton citizens, who called it a "killer hospital." Their claims included a dismal hospital care facility with a constant crowd of sick, injured, and dead. I was there nightly because the emergency aid plan (also called EAP) we (the Compton PD) used required us to respond to all individuals who called with a variety of ills and have them transported to a nearby emergency medical facility. Las Campanas was the preferred hospital.

I certainly didn't see any abnormalities, but I knew a lot of people were kept there for quite a period of time before they were shipped off to the county hospital, primarily, for further medical treatment.

The Compton police were targeted for their bungling of all enforcement amenities, charges, and entitlements. I believe these Compton cops were the first in line to be criticized for anything not going on well within the city.

Police could be charged loosely with racial bias, backed by the media, because the police were the specific ones catching the brunt of the immense criminal element and physically touching individuals to process their legal consequences and enforce the law. In other words the police were easily identified by their uniforms and marked patrol units, which created a distinct opportunity for the community and media to falsely accuse them of wrongdoing, because they were doing their jobs in front of an extremely critical society upset with its government.

Essentially, and with an extreme prejudice; the city of Compton, the new politicians, and the community, coupled with the ambitious orchestration by the media had successfully caused a significant twist to Compton's local government and law enforcement. Their intentions were to criticize and confront the entire decision-making process and the enforcement arm of the law by arbitrarily wreaking havoc on common police protocol.

Groups of fifty to a hundred could be summoned quickly in the close-knit or racially divided neighborhoods to promote many attempts to either rescue or lynch suspects in police custody, regardless of what crime had occurred.

The radicals threw racial comments such as "Kill the pig!" frequently at the police to provoke an overreaction. If that was the case, the officer would be overwhelmed with the sheer numbers of adverse complaints for being racially prejudiced and overreactive. The media would advance those racial claims and cash in on how the community would support them, as long as it agreed with their racial overtones and claims of police malpractice and brutality.

Meanwhile, among all of this present and mounting racial strife and government displeasure, another problem surfaced intermittently—the biker wars. It seemed that Compton was a haven for motorcycle gangs from all over. A lot of the bikers were from the Dominguez Hills area just west of Alameda Boulevard.

———

Most intelligent persons know full well that gangs are developed by individuals with limited intelligence, and nearly all suffer from some sort of psychological disorders. That's why attorneys can defend criminals so easily in court, because a plethora of prison studies account for the makeup of inmate profiles, stemming from another batch of skewed (or twisted) concoctions of parental abuse, social injustices, and police abuse.

Dominguez Hills was a quiet area near the Dominguez Catholic Seminary, just south of the 91 freeway in what was called the presidential housing tract. The name came from the streets of that area, which were named after many former presidents of the United States.

Bikers coming through Compton were being shot and killed on their bikes or in their cars. Riders and their bikes sailed through storefront bay windows and venetian blinds and obviously had an impact on the business community.

Because dope was so prevalent in Compton and large amounts of narcotics were being scored locally, it added to the crime quagmire. It made me think that this city was an outpost of hell, and my job was to move around, be seen, and try to contain these problems within the city. To me, Compton was an unofficial but very well-defined magnet city for crime.

CHAPTER 11

FIRST HOMICIDE

I received a call about a suspicious man seated in a truck on Glencoe Street in the Richland Farms district. I received the call around sunup, at about six o'clock in the early morning.

When I arrived as a one-man unit, I saw a fifties pickup truck parked across the narrow street facing westbound.

I went directly to the driver's side of the truck and saw an elderly white male, clad in everyday street clothing, with his chin resting on his chest, seated in an upright position, on the right side of the front bench seat. The windows were rolled up, so I drew closer and tapped on the window with my knuckle to get the person's attention. He remained motionless. He appeared to be in a deep sleep or passed out. I looked down at the street at the side of the driver's door and noticed a large amount of blood leading away from the truck, diagonally across the street.

Each step seemed to have more blood, suggesting that someone was traveling southbound, then onto the front walkway of a home, and then to the front door of that same home.

The informant didn't want to be contacted. This was a common practice, because most folks in Compton didn't want to be seen informing on anything, let alone talking to the police, because of their constant fear of retaliation.

Large globs of blood stained the front door and the adjoining stucco wall. The blood splotching was about shoulder height and tapered down the stucco wall, indicating that whoever was hurt had curled up momentarily, leaning forward slightly. The blood trail then returned down to the cement pathway into the street and toward the tailgate of the truck. The tailgate of the truck revealed more bloody splotches across the tailgate section, rounding the right side of the truck up to the right front door and handle.

I knocked on the passenger-side window harder to let the man know and see that I was a policeman and wanted to talk to him. He remained motionless, so after several seconds, I reached for the handle and opened the door. The man didn't move. I tapped on his shoulder and shook him slightly. I called to him, "Hey, are you all right?" He didn't answer. I then put my fingers on the left side of his neck to check his carotid artery for any pulse.

He was cold to the touch and lacked any sign of a pulse. I looked down his chest, which was partially concealed from view from the outside, because his shirt was loose and draped over his lap, concealing the gravity of his obvious wounds. I noticed a heavy coagulation of blood on the front of his shirt. I also noticed the blood was all along his right shoulder. I checked to see if he was breathing, and noted the lack of a heartbeat and the massive blood loss, which convinced me that he was dead.

I called the station over the radio and requested detectives and a crime-scene officer at my location. I was careful not to mention a death, for it would surely alert the media to my location. The media constantly monitors all police radio frequencies in a quest for any potential hot news item. I went back to the truck and noticed a two-inch hole in the middle of the front windshield, toward the bottom edge. There were several rags stuffed into the hole from the inside.

My job at that point was not to touch anything and attempt to ascertain what had happened based on my basic observations. I would reduce those observations to writing and submit the report in a timely fashion.

Backtracking to when I first came upon the scene, I didn't recall seeing a single soul on the street the whole time.

This was an obvious indication that the neighborhood knew very well what had happened. This included the entire time I was there on the scene, until I was relieved by the crime-scene officer about an hour later.

It was revealed several days later that this poor soul was apparently the victim of kidnapping and carjacking from the city of Bellflower. He was forced by gunpoint to Glencoe Street and shot once while he was in the driver's seat.

As the suspect left he turned and fired one more time through the front windshield and struck the victim in the chest. The suspect left the location around two o'clock in the morning. No witnesses were found.

Based on the blood evidence and shoe prints, it was determined that shortly after the suspect left, the victim got out of the car by way of the driver's door. Information later obtained from unidentified sources indicated that the victim called out for help quite a few times, but no one helped or even called.

The victim, severely wounded, staggered to the front door of the home across the street, where he called for help. He pounded on the door for a couple of minutes and then returned to his truck. He managed to open the passenger's door and then sat in the truck to rest.

That night was chilly, and the victim fought off the chill by stuffing several small rags into the hole in the window caused by the parting gunshot. There he passed away while seated in his truck, and no one even called to alert the police or fire department.

The victim was about seventy-two years old and weighed approximately 150 pounds max. He didn't seem too intimidating to most, but apparently his death was necessary in order for the suspect to get away with all the loot and not be identified. Oh, how much loot did he get away with, do you ask? About thirty bucks! What a cheap price for life.

This was my first homicide, and it made a deep negative impression in my chosen career path of law enforcement. It has remained in my mind throughout my thirty-one years of experience just how cold, calculating, and sordid this job was about to be. I also thought that if that victim was my dad, I would never waste time capturing the suspect. I thought it over many times. Would I even the score?

Put yourself in those same shoes and think seriously about what you would do. The answer should be relatively easy.

CHAPTER 12

OVERSTRETCHED AND LIMITED

It took a little while, maybe a couple of months, to realize this city was absolutely crammed full of crud, crime, and corruption. I knew I had a big job to do.

During the day, there were as many as five units on the streets, and in the evening hours only two. Between all of the calls and reports, units were easily tied up with investigative duties as well as clerical duties. The only car left in the field had to move around and not get involved in anything that would tie the car up. If you were that car, you knew you could be overwhelmed quickly, and no help would be coming.

Most of the Compton units were one-man units, and there were no females in patrol at all. During the evening hours there would be one two-man unit working from seven to three in the morning.

Strangely enough, other surrounding city police and sheriff units were seldom seen. At that time I couldn't understand why we wouldn't bump into each other more often. I thought maybe they were just as busy as we were, and their force was stretched as much as ours was but the real reason was that Compton was alone and inundated with crime.

Compton was both isolated and insulated from all. Speaking from my vantage point as a new officer, what I knew and observed was rather limited. The field personnel anxiously awaited every shift and felt that we were always up to the task of law enforcement but apparently very much alone.

Although we were impeded by an obvious absence of information and hobbled by new rules pertaining to handling a specific race, we, the officers, felt obligated to follow the edicts of our employer, the city of Compton.

In my opinion, the new and refined rules of engagement, coupled with any adverse suggestion indicating that a certain race was getting out of hand, was similar to Chinese foot-binding. The Chinese for many years believed that foot binding was sensual and compelled all wives to bind their feet. This custom was very painful and resulted in small but mutilated feet, which of course assured the women of their beauty. Much later it was revealed that the true intention of foot binding was not to ensure beauty, but to keep the wife or woman at home and not allow her to travel around, because walking would cause intense pain and prevent promiscuity. I'm sure the media in those years supported that restrictive policy as it remained a tradition for a long period of time.

Since the proclamation by the new city manager in 1968 that Compton was now a model city we, the field officers, had no idea of what that really meant. Oh, but over the next thirty years, the grooming and coddling by the entire governmental bureaucracy molded the city into what it is today.

A new two-story police station had been recently completed (1967) and located directly across the street from the old city hall and police station. Most of the officers were characters, some gruff, some humorous, some very somber. To me, they were the makeup of a good line of defense and purpose. It was imperative for all of us to work together and confront any and all criminal activities that threatened the community.

In roughly a year and a half, my brother and I both left the Compton Police Department and transferred to the Los Angeles County Sheriff's Department. After a brief stint at the transportation bureau, we transferred and were reassigned to Firestone Park located just north of Compton. When my brother and I arrived at the station, we both were summoned to the captain's office of the Firestone Park sheriff's station.

The captain greeted us with pleasantries and asked us both to be seated. I thought maybe he was going to formally greet us for a short discussion, and we would be on our way to receive our field assignments.

There was a brief diversion after the greeting. The captain was very polite and went right into the reasons why Los Angeles sheriff units never came to Compton PD's emergency requests for help. Specifically identified were the calls from the area at 150th and Central, near the Jack in the Box drive-through. Of course both my brother and I were very much aware of what went on at that location but never really thought much of it or realized something was going on behind all of the chaos.

That location was inundated with an extremely large crowd of blacks, approximately three or four hundred of them, stopping cars on the street, pulling the occupants out, and beating them up. The crowd would then turn the cars over, torch them, and leave the beaten occupants on the roadway.

Nothing could get through. Emergency crews, like the fire department and ambulance attendants, were too frightened to even approach, because they feared being pulled out and beaten up as well.

Several times I was summoned to the location, usually Friday and Saturday nights around nine o'clock through midnight. I would usually position myself about three blocks away and watch the crowd terrorizing whoever came across the crowd's path. There was no way a single one man unit could go to that call because that unit would be attacked immediately and have to use deadly force to survive. Those decisions were not even discussed because deadly force would be viewed as an overreaction and brutal.

Although the citizens, mostly whites, were being dragged from their cars and beaten, they were simply chalked up as collateral damage, because our requests for backup and assistance fell on deaf ears.

This went on for quite some time and the captain at Firestone Park Station stated that the events at 150th and Central were routine situations. The city of Compton knew it existed and didn't do anything about it. The police department didn't cancel all days off and vacations nor logistically plan for this serious recurring event. The city of Compton relied on the routine request for assistance from LA to respond to and help break up the situation. This cost the sheriff's department resources for events that were foreseeable by the city of Compton.

Furthermore, when the Sheriff's deputies arrived in significant numbers and resolved the criminal antics by arresting and dispersing the crowd, complaints from the Compton community would pour in heavily to the sheriff's department, and no complaints were generated to the Compton PD.

This information the captain gave us was important to him, because the weight of not sending units to our location was causing significant consternation about him and his command. However, to be honest, none of us were really aware that this situation and its problems or ever considered the event uncontrollable by surrounding law enforcement personnel. In this case, ignorance was bliss, and my brother and I informed the captain that we had never considered the reason other law enforcement agencies never helped us.

We brushed the situation off by reflecting that Compton was overwhelmed with crime. We thought the cities that bordered Compton were in the same overstretched conditions. But that was not the case. Compton was indeed a special place where criminal activities were hidden by government entities, such as the police and city administrators, municipal courts, local, state, and federal law enforcement, and the media, all of whom deliberately clouded crimes and racial identifiers to minimize the true scope of the racial makeup and the magnitude.

Wouldn't this be an interesting study at a university level? It would compare early 1960 crime reports (not statistics) to present-day calls for service, which have changed dramatically? That study would create volumes of books about how not to govern.

The study would be called "The City of Compton," and it would reveal what really took place with city government, the attempts to hide what was actually going on and who was profiting from this deliberate cover-up, and why?

CHAPTER 13

BOMBS GALORE

Many other departments minimized the Compton Police Department's experiences, but only from a safe distance. No one was close to our dangerous and deadly list of serious situations.

On top of the Marxist black brigades stating their aims to shoot it out with the police, the media catered to the wishes of the militants. The media was not giving objective information about what the police were combating and produced skewed evidence of assaults by the police on a daily basis.

During the year 1968, when all of the radical racists were preparing their caches of weapons for the big onslaught against police, huge caches of weapons were being found in Compton. Areas known as "fruit town," north of Rosecrans Avenue, and "corner pocket," Aranbe and Stockwell Streets were areas where these anarchists loitered, resided, and did their business of torment and racial hatred and planning.

Just as I left the Compton Police Department in March 1969, the infamous Compton bomber was walking alongside the new police station. He had his two-and-a-half-inch galvanized pipe bomb in his hands. Apparently he was tightening the end cap before he set it down on the police department's front porch. Fortunately, that tightening caused the bomb to explode. Flesh and blood flew upward and stuck to the second-story windows of the detective bureau. One of terrorist's arms flew across the railroad tracks and landed on the northbound lanes of Willowbrook Avenue. Thank God, he was the only one who died, and remarkably, no one was injured. The frequent use of bombs to make a point is no different from today's ideological fundamentalists' beliefs, those people willing to kill anyone to aid their extremist views.

The Black Panthers were in the north end of Compton and had two houses where they proudly boasted of their hatred of "Whitey" but couldn't handle aggressive police scrutiny and screamed help from the community and the media. The Black Panthers would pass out free food to the black community and coloring books to entertain the little ones. Those coloring books were rife with graphic illustrations of pigs in police uniforms, beating and eating small black kids. Only in America could some radical gang come up with free food that was given to them by Americans and claim it came from their extremist group. Only in America could a radical group print up coloring books, supported by donated American money, defaming law enforcement.

In my opinion, it's no different than today's presidential friends Bill Ayers, Jeremiah Wright, and Louis Farrakhan, who spew the same radical views of the police and government from forty years ago.

There are many followers of these types of extremists who hate this country, but refuse to leave. Except Eldridge Cleaver, another radical Marxist who fled this country to Liberia to avoid criminal trials, and just recently returned pleading for forgiveness.

To me they are nothing to but two-bit shoe clerks, snake -oil salesmen and pitchmen.

CHAPTER 14

EDITOR OF CHINESE NEWSPAPER KILLED

Her car was stopped along the side of the 710 freeway in the Compton city limits at around eleven at night. She was apparently lost. She was at a yellow emergency call box and asking for directions to North Long Beach.

As she was speaking to someone on the emergency phone, probably a CHP operator, a car pulled up with two male adults and parked right behind her car. One of the men got out and approached her and asked if she needed help. Meanwhile, the other man got into the driver's seat of her car and started the engine.

She was talking with the man who walked up to her initially, and she was still on the phone. She was able to see the second man get in her car. She dropped the phone, ran over to her car as it was pulling away, and grabbed the door post of the driver's door in an attempt to stop the auto thief from stealing her car.

The man who was talking with her by the emergency phone ran to his car and drove away, southbound on the freeway. Her car had been stolen right from her grasp, and now she was alone, on foot, on the freeway in Compton, feebly attempting to stop the thief.

Approximately an hour later, (Possibly delayed because the initial call was about being lost and needed directions) several calls came in to the local California Highway Patrol emergency desk, describing what appeared to be a large animal in the southbound lanes of I-710 being struck repeatedly by cars and trucks, nearly causing several traffic accidents.

When the CHP arrived on scene they discovered that the large animal the callers were describing was the woman who'd attempted to stop the thieves from stealing her car a little over an hour earlier.

She was later identified as a well-known editor of a Chinese newspaper located in the city of Montebello. She was well liked and respected throughout the Chinese community and the Montebello area.

Her abandoned car was located a couple of days later near the intersection of Santa Fe Avenue and Pine Street, Compton.

The moral of this event was that it took another valuable and praised life. So if your car breaks down or you're lost, do not stop in or near the city of Compton, because you too will be a mere statistic, neither more nor less.

This murder (Because the death was caused during a felony, robbery or grand theft, and the seriousness of injury or death was foreseeable) could have been any one of our family members just trying to get home. Think about this incident the next time your daughter or wife goes somewhere alone in the evening hours.

CHAPTER 15

A SUBURBAN SANCTUARY

To put this opinion into the proper perspective, when I was working with the sheriff's department in the areas near and around Compton, we were ordered to stay out of the city. Arrested criminals were informing all of us that the police department was taking down sheriff's department license plate numbers and turning them into the chief of police of Compton. The chief of police constantly reported that when the sheriff's units came into their city, they would wreak havoc and then leave, so he ordered the city police units to seek out any sheriff's units within the city limits.

Furthermore, the criminal element said that the police chief of Compton also informed gangsters from Compton that he wouldn't bother them as long as long as they didn't commit their crimes in the city, giving them an umbrella of protection and leniency. This involved all major racial gangs on both ends.

Keeping the sheriff's units out of their city was the primary focus. Wow, it's just plain amazing that something like this could happen, but it did. I was there and saw it happening, all under immunity, with no documentation whatsoever.

The sheriff's units that patrolled the nearby areas viewed Compton as a "cherry patch" full of criminals who were wanted for a wide range of crimes. We were viewed as troublemakers, because our units would quickly duck into Compton, snag several of their criminals afoot, arrest them, and take them to our station in Lynwood.

At times, some of the deputies were charged with lying on their reports and in court, because they simply changed the arresting location to an area within the sheriff's jurisdiction a few blocks away.

Let's say you saw someone suspicious, justifiably stopped him, and found him to be a major gang member armed with a gun. What would you do? Would you arrest him and take him to your jail and book him? Or would you call the local police, who would be upset that you were in their city "jacking up" their citizens when you should not have even been there in the first place? The arguments were endless, but it happened, and the local law enforcement wouldn't do anything. I might add that the deputies who changed the locations when making arrests in Compton were ultimately charged with perjury and falsification of reports.

The sheriff's department travels throughout all of Los Angeles County going to their respective patrol areas, passing through all cities within the county. The only city that insists that the sheriff stays out is none other than Compton.

To more firmly illustrate what was going on, let's put a different perspective into play. Going back forty years ago when the City of Compton was introduced as the "model city" anyone coming into the city was at extreme risk. Ask most folks from that area at that time and listen to what they say was happening in the city and why it was happening.

It was specifically a racial injection of tolerance that the entire area was accepted by the local government, Compton, and the follow-up proof was carefully skewed by the media to prevent any mentioning of criminal behavior. If you question my opinions and experiences, go to the public library, or just Google the local news about what was going on in Compton at that time. Keep in mind that media coverage of Compton was biased, and accurate information has to be researched in order to reveal the causes of this errant conduct. Note: little or nothing was said about the crime that was actually going on in the city, but there's a nice coating of good over bad. If an opportunity arose where anything positive could be introduced, it was embellished and amplified.

Ask anyone who was in the area if they avoided the city at all costs, and their answer will undoubtedly be a resounding yes. Most of the residents were well aware of the dangers. But the truth wasn't stated in the media. Why not?

Just calling the police was viewed by the controlling gangsters as snitching. If the rat was identified, he might be hunted down and killed. Today it is no different; informants may suffer severe consequences, although the police department has been replaced by the sheriff's department.

Ask anyone in their right mind if they'd go to or pass through the Compton today. The answer would be a resounding no. Oh yes, they may be on the freeway, passing by Compton, but they won't stop for gas or a quick bite to eat. That would be just plain nuts.

And if your car breaks down near the Compton's city limits, call for help quickly and leave. You've been warned!

CHAPTER 16

COMPTON POLICE DEPARTMENT TRAINEE

Well, I made it through the academy, and now I was in training with my newly assigned training officer. He was a little shorter than me and had a face that looked like a scrunched-up toy lion. He was a little gruff and rough, and definitely not the same caliber as Stan P.

He guided me through the briefing that started off all patrol shifts and helped ready my paperwork and supplies for a busy night. He wasn't harsh, by any means, but he was very firm on his personal beliefs about how things were to be done. He explained in detail the infamous written-paper protocol and assured me that I would eventually get it right because of the vast number that I would be doing daily.

We finished briefing, went into the rear parking lot, and went over several hypothetical situations as we were preparing our car, shotgun, and equipment for a night's busy onslaught. We slowly exited the police parking lot. I was filling in the blank spaces in the police patrol log, jotting down the required date, time, mileage, etc. as my training officer drove carefully from the lot.

He was giving me all of the specific details of what I should do in the event of a gunfight and any other conceivable emergency setting. He also advised me that all I had learned in the academy would not apply itself in real-life police scenarios. I thought that bit of info was a little strange. I felt that this guy was going to do things I was not familiar with at all. I figured this was going to be much more adventurous than I could have imagined.

We drove casually northbound for about a mile to a small L-shaped shopping center and parked our patrol car just outside a Laundromat.

We got out of the car and went into the small Laundromat. My training officer looked around the vacant shop for any human activity or signs of wrongdoing. I followed his lead and remained quiet, looking for anything that looked suspicious or out of the ordinary. The place was quite small, and I didn't catch on to what we were looking for. I tried to avoid looking puzzled. My TO went around looking carefully at each machine and the attached coin mechanisms.

He announced suddenly, "All right, let's go!" He walked out the front door, passing by several washing machines and carefully examining their outward appearances. We returned to our patrol car, and drove across the narrow street, and parked in the driveway of a closed drive-through dairy. He turned off the engine and said, "Keep your eye on that Laundromat, especially people who go in and those who leave."

I assumed that something serious must have happened here recently, and my training officer was going to catch whoever was doing it. He slumped slightly in the driver's seat, all the while keeping an eye on the place. We sat there for approximately thirty minutes, listening to the Compton radio putting out calls and responding to requests from other units. I just couldn't figure out why we were so close to the Laundromat, facing it, easily seen by all in our marked patrol car.

Every once in a while we would hear from units S1 or S2, who were chattering back and forth to each other and their dispatch. The radio frequency Compton used was shared by the Signal Hill Police Department, and S1 and S2 were their assigned units in the field. (Signal Hill is a small city surrounded by the City of Long Beach.) Oddly enough, this was just a minor disruption. They were very professional and courteous when communicating with one another.

Several cars raced through the nearby intersection, and we would go after them and issue citations for various infractions. I was carefully jotting down the info for the citation as my TO looked around and occasionally checked on my citations for accuracy and progress. When each citation was completed, we would return to the dairy and again watch the Laundromat.

After several hours of this routine, my TO finally broke loose and informed me that he had just purchased the Laundromat and was watching for people who were bringing in their wet laundry and using the dryers to dry their wet clothing. Those individuals were obviously using my TO's newly acquired Laundromat utilities for a free dry.

I'll admit I was caught by surprise; I would have never guessed that this was all part of my training package and apparently the department wasn't aware of my training officer's ulterior motives either. But who am I to complain? All we were doing was watching his Laundromat and enforcing local traffic laws and killing time. What a dud.

CHAPTER 17

FIRST ARREST: AN EVOLVED PASSION

Suddenly the radio announced our call sign and gave us a call of a drunk in the street. He was trying to stop cars on Compton Boulevard, just east of Willowbrook Avenue. It was already dark out, so we drove toward the location at a normal speed.

We approached from the east, and my training officer advised me that I was going to handle this one by myself. He told me to just relax and not get too excited. I assured him I was all right and ready for the call.

As we drew near where the drunk might be, we spotted him in the number two lane—second lane from the center—waving at us to stop. We did and exited our unit and approached the drunk, a white man approximately twenty-eight to thirty years of age.

I calmly asked the man to step over to the sidewalk so we could talk. He complied and stood right in front of us, listing from side to side and making back and forth motions, swaying uncontrollably in an awkward circular motion.

He was obviously very drunk and unable to care for himself. The stench of booze permeated his soiled clothing. I drew closer as my training officer stood slightly to my rear and off to my right side. I stated to the man that he was "highly inebriated and causing a lot of problems with the traffic."

He replied, "What the fuck did you say?" Feeling that my vocabulary was too confusing to him, I repeated myself in a manner more attuned to his level of street talk.

I repeated myself in a slightly different way and stated; "You're very drunk and apparently causing a lot of problems with the cars in the street!" He was grimacing and cantankerous. He pulled back, frowning, and in a confused manner said loudly, "Well, fuck you!"

He took several more steps back, away from me. He made a quick sidestep to his left and drew closer to my training officer. The suspect raised his right arm, made a fist, and punched my TO right in the nose. This of course knocked my training officer down to the pavement. I quickly grabbed the suspect with both of my hands. He passed out almost immediately, going limp in my grasp.

My TO jumped up, pulled out his sap (a leather-bound hand weapon used for close order battles), and began to clobber the passed-out suspect several times. He apparently did not realize the drunkened suspect had passed out while in my grasp. My TO was cussing and was actually striking me like crazy as he attempted to hit the suspect.

I released the suspect, and he fell to the ground still unconscious, but slowly starting to recover. My TO then took out his tear-gas spray canister and generously sprayed the suspect. The suspect was screaming from the pain and finally submitted to our demands to place his hands behind his back.

He wrestled from our grip as we were placing him into the backseat of our patrol car. We both were also feeling the effects of the tear gas, and it was hard to manage driving the car. Fortunately we were only a block or two from the station and drove slowly.

I didn't want to smile or laugh, but the suspect really caught my TO off guard and decked him rather easily. I remained quiet and cautiously waited for my TO to say something critical, but he was silent other than a few choice cuss words for the surprise knockdown.

He wasn't hurt very much, just a slightly bloody nose, and I'm sure he mentally rehashed the episode many times and tried to figure out why in the hell the suspect stepped away from me and pounced on him. My guess was that he had a kinder face and outwardly appeared warm and cuddly.

I continued for several more weeks as a trainee with hardly any significant events, considering the determination of my training officer. His special interests outside his duties have been discussed before and are certainly not worth repeating.

CHAPTER 18

KICKED LOOSE

Tom M. and I, both trainees, were seated in the briefing room one evening, about to start our usual shift 6:30 p.m. to 3:00 a.m. In the room were our TOs and maybe eight other officers. The sergeant was a small, thin, gruff, and firm figure with a stern voice. He was going through the briefing board, reading through significant arrests, crimes, and notable situations that had occurred within a twenty-four-hour span.

The sergeant began handing out radio car keys from a small steel index-card box and calling out who was assigned to specific patrol areas. He then tossed the keys across the room to where officers were seated.

We trainees were in the rear of the room, patiently waiting for our names to be called along with our training officers. Trainees were generally assigned areas that favored the east side of the city, where the heavy stuff hadn't started yet. That meant that the felony pervasive crime was lower near the riverbed bordering the city of Paramount but still raising its ugly head occasionally.

The sergeant continued calling the names and then said, "Well, it's about time." He called out Tom's name and tossed him a set of keys, and then casually picked up another set and threw them toward me as he called my name out as well.

A set of keys came flying toward me as the sergeant said, "You guys are about ready, aren't you?" Both Tom and I looked at each other and grinned, realizing what the sergeant had just done. At that moment, with no warning, we were in our own patrol cars, assigned the east side of Compton. I gulped and felt tension within.

Both Tom and I knew if we displayed any apprehension on this gift to be off training, it would mark us as choking and buckling under minimal pressure. It would mark us as weak. We kept our mouths shut, went to our assigned cars, and prepped them.

We quietly made commitments to each other to keep a sharp eye out for each other's safety and pay close attention to each other's calls for service. We shook hands, got into our units, and left the lot.

I drove my car eastbound Compton Boulevard, carefully keeping a suspicious eye on everyone. I drove carefully toward my patrol area close to Compton Park, where heavy drug trafficking took place. It was a bit precarious being alone without anyone to shepherd me through tough problems as I drew closer to known hostile locations.

This was mid-1968, when black radical groups were rife in the city and had their own patrols that raided police calls for service. Usually two to three of these guys appeared out of nowhere on my calls and criticized anything and everything I did. They would announce who they were and make snide comments just loud enough so I would hear them, in an attempt to draw me to their preplanned verbal confrontations. It seems a little funny they always made racially challenging remarks to me without any provocation, counting on the system not to do anything to them.

Before I was in law enforcement, I would have popped them on the head with bottom of my fist and easily knocked them out. But here in Compton, the system seemed to embolden this behavior. The media sensationalized the reactions of the police when their tolerance and patience wavered and broke down.

Martin Luther King had been killed earlier that year, on April 4, 1968, in Memphis, Tennessee. In my opinion, that incident propelled the radical ambitions and fervor of the Black Panthers—Huey Newton, Angela Davis, Bobby Seale, Stokeley Carmichael, Ron Karenga, and others—to go in and out of Compton. They were spewing their revolutionary thoughts up and down the California coastline and occasionally in New York City. Most of their shootouts, however, were with each other and intended primarily as internal power plays.

You might remember when the Black Panthers went into the California General Assembly with loaded weapons to demonstrate their anger at the changing of gun-carrying laws. That incident pretty much set the tone of the hatred and antiwhite sentiment of the radical racial groups. The media still painted the radicals as a nonviolent and sensationalized police misconduct.

The media and several self-righteous groups clamored for police reform, recruiting all communities to stop the alleged "terrible police behavior." These antics will be addressed later on.

It was easy to avoid these political gangs and their comments by just not paying attention to their rhetoric and focusing on the mission at hand. They were probably armed the Compton way, but there was nothing I alone could do about shaking them down.

I completed my service calls as if they were not present, yet I cautiously watched them at a safe distance. The Compton way of being armed is that although you don't have a gun or knife on you, there are weapons easily within reach. I'll go into the specifics of that technique when I discuss Compton Park.

CHAPTER 19

DOUBLE WHAMMY

I received a call on a suspicious person wandering the street just west of Atlantic Avenue near Cookacre Street. The radio gave a brief description of what the suspect was wearing and the direction he was traveling. I maneuvered my car to where I thought I might intercept the suspect, and bingo, there he was, right in front of me, staggering away. He was Hispanic, about six feet in height and maybe two hundred pounds. I pulled up nearby and noticed he was looking toward me. Suddenly he turned around and walked much faster.

I called to him to stop and said that I wanted to talk to him. He said, "No thanks, I'm going home." I moved away from my car and closed our distance, and I asked the suspect to turn around. He stopped and turned slowly, swaying all over the place. He reeked of alcohol. I noticed he had urinated in his pants and appeared to nearly fall over several times. I grabbed him and brought him over to my car with little resistance.

I took out my handcuffs and cuffed him and advised him he was under arrest for being drunk in public. I placed him into the right front seat and buckled him in with no problems. I announced my return to the station for a booking over the radio and arrived at the station about five minutes later. This was actually my first solo arrest, and I felt pretty sure I'd done everything in a procedural manner.

At the station I brought the suspect inside the jail area and prepared to book him. Procedure required me to uncuff the suspect, empty his pockets of all property, and search him thoroughly.

I was just outside the booking cage, near a painted concrete-block wall, and the suspect was standing with his back to the wall. I was facing him as I went into his pockets and placed everything into a plastic bag. The suspect became belligerent as I was talking with him. He slowly clenched his right fist and swung at my face. I dodged backward, and he narrowly missed me.

I pushed myself against him, forcing him into the wall, and told him to cool it. His reaction to my comment was to swing again toward my face, only this time I struck him in the mouth and nose, sending him into the wall, which was a few inches away from his head. The wall, I believe, did the trick, because he hit it pretty hard, slamming his head against it. He passed out almost immediately, slithering down the wall, leaving a two-inch blood swath trailing behind his head as it slid. I backed away from him and heard the jailer, a policeman assigned as jailer that night. "Are you okay?" He obviously overheard the ruckus and was concerned with what had just happened.

The jailer came over to where I was and commented, "What the shit did you do, kill him?" I was concerned, because this was the first time I really ever struck anyone as a policeman, and I felt a little bit insecure because of what I allowed the suspect to do. I think he was actually kidding me about what I had done and wanted to see if I would reply as if I had done something wrong.

First off, we needed an ambulance to take him to the hospital as soon as possible, and I had to quickly go into the sergeant's office to inform him of the use of force and what had happened. The sergeant came in to see the condition of the suspect as he lay still on the concrete floor, with a sizable amount of blood surrounding his head. He started to laugh, because I'd hit him so hard, he actually was hit twice in quick succession, because of the block wall's proximity and hard surface.

An ambulance arrived, and a two-man unit assisted with the transportation to the hospital and the medical aid.

This was my first solo arrest, my first use of force against a combative suspect, and my first written police report.

It weighed heavily on my abilities to perform and required close careful scrutiny to make sure I made no errors—or grammatical mistakes—in my report. I finished my work and went over the paperwork several times to make sure everything was perfect. I brought the completed work to the sergeant for his approval and waited for him read it carefully and ask any questions about anything I might have overlooked. With very few corrections, he gave it his stamp of approval, smiled, and stated, "Good work, Rupp."

That was it, completed work in every detail, from start to finish. I felt good that I understood the job. All of my training proved very valuable, and I was ready to launch my career as a cop.

The job was indeed self-motivating. I established early on in my own mind I was going to arrive at least an hour before my shift started. This would enable me to read the multitude of completed reports on several ring boards leaning against the base of the chalkboard trays. These report boards were distinguished by the areas where the crimes occurred. Reading these reports gave me many ideas about how to lay out the narratives and improve my writing skills. On top of that, I would learn about all of the crimes, both big and small, within the city.

CHAPTER 20
KEEN OBSERVATION

I was on patrol going around looking for something to happen. I was making myself visible in the late evening hours. Around ten, I received a call about a burglary in progress at Naples Winery on North Willowbrook Avenue.

When I came upon the scene, three other units were already there, and I asked if they needed help. The officers there were all seasoned officers. They guided me around to the rear of the building, and we met up with at least three other officers standing near a small fence. The small fence surrounded one of those old Coca-Cola coolers with a lift-up top.

From our position we could see at least two other officers atop the one story roof of the winery apparently looking at an entry hole cut through the roof. One of the officers asked me to stay where I was. They were going inside to look for suspects. I watched several of the officers silhouetted on the rooftop, moving around, and another standing directly by the rear door. Apparently the front was covered as well.

The officers on the roof moved down, and I assumed they were lowering themselves into the store. I was far enough away that I was going to miss the excitement and felt a bit jealous that I couldn't be up close.

I could hear the officers calling to each other and using the car radios to communicate what they were doing. (Handheld radios hadn't come into our department yet.) I stood at my post and kept my head moving around to spot anything that moved or appeared suspicious. More important, I kept a close eye on where my fellow officers were located, ready to move quickly if I heard gunshots, or the suspect was escaping.

I heard someone say, faintly, "Officer!" I winced and frowned turning my head slightly, listening carefully and trying to figure where the voice came from.

Again I heard a faint voice calling, "Officer!" This time it came from behind where I was standing, right next to the old Coca-Cola machine. I turned around slowly and scanned the lid of the machine, glistening in the moonlit night, and the small fence directly behind it.

My gun was already in my right hand, and my large flashlight was in my other hand, and off. I couldn't see anything, but the voice came from very close by. I didn't want to shine my flashlight, for it might backlight the officers as they were searching.

Then again I heard it, but the voice this time came from a small foot-and-a-half crevice, darkened by the Coca-Cola machine and the wooden fence. It said a little more loudly and coherently, "Officer, please don't shoot me!"

I focused all of my attention on the crevice and detected a person curled up into the darkened area. I pointed my gun directly into the space and ordered, "Get up real slow, or I'll shoot!"

The scrunched-up man slowly uncoiled himself and stood erect right in front of me. He repeated that he was sorry for trying to break into the store. I announced loudly and proudly, "I got one back here!" Several officers came from inside the store and over to my position. I had the suspect already hand-cuffed. "Good job, Rupp. Where did you find him?"

I pointed directly where the suspect stood up, and the officers said, "Are you kidding?" I replied, "No. He was all wadded up between the Coke machine and the fence and very hard to see without any light." I pointed out that they didn't have any flashlights on, because they were afraid to give away their positions or backlight one another.

The officers apparently felt satisfied with my explanation. They all seemed pleased with my catch and added that I had done a good job watching their backs and preventing the suspect's escape.

Now, did I find him, or did he expose himself thinking I might very well blow his head off? He could have easily jumped me or cracked me over the head with something hard, but he didn't. Due to the suspect's lack of aggressiveness and being forthright, I treated him with respect and a tinge of kindness and compassion.

I thought about this incident frequently over my career, because many things could have occurred but didn't. Maybe it was just pure luck, or possibly it was a divine intervention.

CHAPTER 21

A MOTHER'S BROKEN HEART

I began working in the afternoon hours around three o'clock. I was assigned a traffic accident on Compton Boulevard near Wilmington Avenue. The assignment was a code three run—red lights and siren—because the accident involved a six-year-old child. I got there rather quickly and noticed a small crowd of people surrounding several parked cars and a Ford Mustang two-door convertible, double-parked, facing eastbound.

A tall, black man was standing near the Mustang, visibly depressed and very somber. Another black man came to me and stated that a small child had been struck by the Mustang and killed. He added that the child was lying under a white van parked by the south curbline.

I walked directly over to the white van and saw a light-colored tarp covering what appeared to be a small body. I dropped to my knees and stretched under the van and lifted the tarp and noticed the partial head and face of a small black child approximately six years old. The entire top three inches of the child's head was missing and empty of any brain matter. This was quite an awful sight. It is terrible for anyone to see such a death blow—very sobering.

The male who approached me initially told me he'd asked someone for the tarp and placed it over the obviously deceased child to prevent anyone else from seeing him. He added that the man by the Ford Mustang was the driver of the car that struck the child.

I looked to my left and saw what appeared to be human tissue splattered across the number two eastbound lane. I surmised that it was the remnants of the deceased child's brain, skull, and skin tissue, spread for approximately fifteen feet from where I was standing. I went over to my car and advised that a coroner was needed. I said that the driver was with me and cooperative.

I walked over to the driver and asked for his driver's license and registration. He already had his license and registration in hand and gave them to me. He was distraught. I asked him to tell me what had happened.

He stated he was traveling eastbound on Compton Boulevard at approximately 45 mph, when suddenly a small child came running out into the street from between two parked cars.

He added the height of the parked cars concealed the child's presence until he was almost right in front of him. He couldn't do anything because it happened so quickly. He struck the child with his right front head-lamp assembly and slammed on his brakes.

At this point, the driver was so upset, he broke down and cried. He was really hurting, so I went up to him and consoled him. I talked to several pedestrian witnesses who repeated the same series of events that the driver had already stated. I was really attempting to persuade the driver that he had done nothing wrong; the accident was unavoidable.

The driver admitted he was in fact going slightly over the speed limit, 45 mph in a 40 mph zone. He thought maybe he could have avoided the accident. My theory was that the accident would have had the same effect at 25 mph, and his speed had nothing to do with the child running directly into the street.

As we were talking, and unbeknown to both of us, a woman was wandering around the sidewalk looking for her missing six-year-old child. One of the onlookers told the woman there was a small child who had just been struck by a car and the child's body was under the white van, under the tarp.

The woman went directly over to the van and dropped to her knees. She raised the tarp and recognized her son. She screamed loudly and wept.

This was one of the worst scenes any mother could have ever imagined. We all stood witnessing the tremendous grief and turmoil and knew that our pain didn't compare. Upon hearing the mother's anguish, the driver buried his head into his hands and bawled. I was absolutely floored by the outward display of passion and pity. It was as if a bomb had gone off and killed everyone but me.

I ran over to the woman and attempted to console her. I questioned her about the boy's identity and hers as well. Once those details were established, and that it was in fact her son, I told her to go home. I advised her I would be by in several hours to get more specific information. I told her that the coroner was in en route, and they would need to know to which mortuary she wanted to have her son assigned. Fortunately, a friend of hers came by and assisted her home.

Due to of the gravity of the situation and the emotional breakdown of the driver, I asked him to accompany me to the police station to confirm his identity and let him calm down. Often, church ministers are attached to police departments, and they help in many situations where compassion and relief could ease the heavy load of sorrow, guilt, and grief.

At the station the driver finally regained his composure after I assured him it wasn't his fault. I then went to the mother's home, finished the details of this very sensitive report, and gave her my sincere condolences for her loss.

This event was one of the most sensitive and awkward situations that I was involved in. It has remained with me for decades and probably will remain until I die. I didn't know the child, but I felt the overwhelming grief and torment, very touching from all parties. It was quite a learning experience.

Oh yeah, there were a few times during this turmoil I felt myself breaking down, but it was my job to keep calm and steady, so I could finish the reports and attempt to ease the pain of the grieving mother and the shaken driver as well.

May God continue to bless the mom and her little boy who was swept away at such an early age.

CHAPTER 22

SEE SHELLS

It was around nine in the evening when I received a call of a burglary alarm at the Sears Roebuck Store on Long Beach Boulevard and Pine Street, right next to the city line of Lynwood.

I arrived pretty fast and circled the huge building with my car lights off. I spotted a smashed display window on the north side, which was partially hidden from the main boulevard, yet very close. Obviously someone had smashed the window. Either they had run away, or they might be inside the huge store.

I quietly made my announcements over the radio and was informed that all other units were tied up and unable to assist. That meant that I was all alone. The pedestrian traffic was minimal, as I expected, because it was night and the street was not well lighted.

I advised the desk of my observations over the car radio and my intentions of going inside the store. My thinking was to see if I could spot any evidence that someone might have entered and constantly reassess the situation in my mind as I progressed slowly. I began walking across the shards of glass that were strewn all over the display case floor. As I drew inward past the display case and away from the noisy broken pieces of glass that I was stepping on, I briefly stopped and carefully listened.

It was very quiet, and I could still hear the car traffic passing by on Long Beach Boulevard. I took several more steps with my pistol at the ready, constantly looking from side to side and intermittently shining my flashlight briskly toward the dark areas.

About every ten steps I would draw near some object, whether for cover or concealment, it wasn't all that critical; I stopped just to listen to whatever I could hear. Everything remained quiet. I was already deep inside the store, approximately twenty-five to thirty-five yards, hunkered down, and slightly bent over, so my tall torso would hardly be seen. I stayed close to the hanging clothes racks, which provided good concealment and softened any noise that I made while I was moving around.

I was drawing close to the center of the store and still saw nothing. (Please keep in mind that handheld radios were not available yet, and I was all alone with no backup.) I moved very slowly and quietly in order to notice any movement or noise caused by other human activity.

Several times I backed up, slightly leaning over and against many large support pillars. I stood still for several seconds, cautiously hoping to draw activity from the possible suspect or suspects. I was using noise and light discipline to my advantage, which meant using the flashlight sparingly, aware of all of the noises cops make when moving around surreptitiously.

I could faintly see objects twenty feet away. If someone was moving around and standing above the clothing and shelving racks, I'd be able to see that, but below those same obstacles, my view was extremely limited and nearly impossible alone. If someone else was there, they could easily remove their shoes and move around me with little trouble. I was considering just going back and waiting for the manager to respond so we could turn on the lights. I also realized that my fellow officers were very quick to spot a lack of brevity and easily branded a boot officer as spooked at the slightest provocation.

As I came from behind one of the pillars and onto the main floor aisle, my shoe kicked something small on the floor. I looked down quickly and saw a red live shotgun shell spinning erratically across the floor. I hid underneath one of the clothing racks full of clothes. I thought, *Holy shit!* I saw maybe five or six other red live shotgun shells lying in plain sight on the tiled floor.

Obviously someone was in the store, armed with a shotgun and most likely watching me. This also meant I was also outgunned. Accuracy wasn't an issue for whoever had the shotgun. Now I was alarmed and focused on any slight movement from any of the many clothing displays that easily could conceal the shiny dark barrel of a shotgun following my position.

I quickly and carefully retreated the same way I came in. I was cautiously alert to any surprises that might jump out suddenly; knowing full well a shoot-out was imminent. As I withdrew, I stalled my movements purposefully to confuse anyone who might be following my departure.

Once outside, with my pistol still in hand, a breath of relief was definitely in order. Brevity wasn't an issue at this point, and I called for several units for backup and the field sergeant to assist.

The sergeant and other units arrived quite quickly as I announced to everyone what I observed. I even displayed one of the shells in my hand.

The sergeant smiled and reminded me to be careful at burglaries like this, where stores are likely to have guns and ammo. No further explanation was necessary, and his warning was well received.

Later when I turned in the burglary report indicating no one was captured, the desk sergeant asked me if I knew how many officers it would take to search that same building. I knew it would take quite a few, but he informed me it would take at least forty officers to completely search the basement and the third story.

(This was also in an era where canine units were not around. They were seen by many law enforcement agencies and politicians as a terrible tool for the black community to cope with. In their minds, police dogs were used in the South for suppressing the blacks. So the political reasoning was that no dogs would be used, as their use would imply police brutality and racism.)

CHAPTER 23
DRAINAGE PROBLEMS

One Sunday I was working a day-shift car. It was relatively quiet for the first hour. I was meandering close to the southern border of Compton. Occasionally I would go toward the south end because it was right next to vast open fields, about a half mile deep, of tall grass and shrubs. Those fields paralleled the city limits between Greenleaf Avenue and Artesia Boulevard. I liked to drive along that route, especially on Sundays, because it appeared so serene and appealing for such a fast and troubled city.

Just as I was moving along Greenleaf Avenue, an announcement came over the radio that a unit was in pursuit on various streets near the south end of Compton. The unit claimed the car he was after might be a stolen auto right off the hot sheet.

The unit advised that there were two occupants. I heard the speed and a description of the car, its plate numbers, and the street they were traveling on. I was near Wilmington Avenue, so I turned my unit around and sped in the direction of the pursuit.

Another broadcast indicated the car was now racing off the paved road and in the open field I had just passed not two minutes earlier. The suspects were driving wildly across the tall grass and closing in near an eight-foot storm drain. (That drain dumped flooding rain into the vast green fields. A larger culvert carried the water toward the local riverbed.)

The suspects were now out of the stolen car and running toward the storm drain. That storm drain had a large heavy steel grate partially covering the drain. Before the pursuing officer went after the suspects, who had abandoned the stolen car, he broadcast his position and the arrival of another assisting officer. Both were now in foot pursuit and going into the storm drain together.

I arrived right behind the first unit and two one-man units and reported my observations over the car radio. I saw the officers squeezing through a narrow opening in the grate and entering with their guns out and ready to go. I met up with them about twenty feet inside the drain, and we discussed our strategies.

We could hear the suspects running, because their steps were amplified by the splashing shallow water, sloshing with each step. We surmised the drain was large and long with many turns and twists, connected to many smaller drains.

The shallow, meandering water that covered a two-foot lower span of the drain was laden with green and brown algae. It reeked of dampness and mold.

One of the officers went outside and communicated our dilemma to the station. He was advised that a sergeant was en route. Several minutes passed by and to our surprise, the chief of police arrived on the scene, alone. He told one of the more seasoned officers to go and get the station's three-wheel motorcycle.

Several officers remained inside the drain as the rest stood outside with the chief awaiting the three-wheeler's arrival, discussing how big the drain was, and just how far it might go.

Once the three-wheeled motorcycle arrived, we assembled outside the drain, and together we managed to lift the heavy steel grate to about four feet. We wedged the grate open with some abandoned pieces of lumber.

At the chief's recommendation, five of us entered the drain and began walking slowly. The three-wheeler was right behind us. We were essentially acclimating ourselves to the dimly lit, moist environment. Another officer remained inside the drain and another stood outside, manning the car radio.

The suspects were inside and couldn't get out, because the manhole covers weighed a little over a hundred pounds and were hard to open from the inside. (If the manhole covers were rusty they would require nearly double the effort to dislodge them. A special tool, an eight-foot, solid steel octagonal pole is required. To remove the cover from the manhole, it must be done from the top, street side. You must wedge the eight-foot tool in a one-inch hole and rock it back and forth to break the rusted coating from the edges. Then it will slowly dislodge the cover.)

By the time we started to move, at least twenty or thirty minutes had passed. We all mounted the three-wheeler, a Harley Davidson motorcycle used primarily for issuing citations and traffic enforcement. The motorcycle had a three-foot box situated just behind the broad leather seat and right above the rear axle. The box carried boxes of flares, wheel markers, yellow tire crayons for marking tires, and several other traffic sundries.)

Three officers were riding on the small rear bumper and another was atop the heavy lid. We started out going about 5 mph with the high-beam lights glaring. As the motorcycle traveled inside the large, nearly empty drain, the motor made tremendous noise that reverberated throughout the drain, and actually prevented hearing noises or voices.

We decided to holler out to the suspects to surrender, knowing full well they could definitely hear us coming toward them. We decided to increase the speed to approximately 8 mph, which seemed a better speed to close in and capture the elusive suspects.

We were now nearly a mile into the drain and came by several foot-and-a-half-wide tributaries feeding into the larger drain.

The tunnels were dark and narrow. The depth of water was about half an inch, with a minimal amount of current coming into our larger tunnel. The base of the moisture was at least three to four inches wide These smaller tributaries were spaced about two or three hundred feet apart. As we came upon them, we paused momentarily and investigated any telltale signs of movement..

As we directed our bright flashlights into the smaller tunnels, we couldn't detect any disturbed moisture that would indicate evidence of any movement. Had any one of the suspects diverted into this avenue, they would have caused the shallow water to spread higher than the bordering green-and-brown algae. This also would have created a virtual dead end for anyone to enter.

We then noted splashes of water above the green and brown algae that provided evidence they were still running blindly in the dark and attempting each laddered manhole to escape. They were persistent and desperate not to be caught. We tracked onward. Several times we stopped and shut down the motor and lights to enable us to hear any movement. This also proved fruitless, but still we pressed on.

As we were nearing the second mile, the older officer driving the motorcycle, decided to turn on the red lamps as well as the bright head lamps.

He also began to sporadically activate the siren, hoping the noise and lights might induce the suspects to surrender. The wail of the siren was unbearable and deafening. but seemed effective as we continued onward still noting the splashed remnants and possibly partial footprints.

The suspects were, in fact, running above the low-water line, occasionally crossing the shallow water and splashing water along the sides. The suspects were attempting to hide their trail, knowing full well we were tracking their moistened footprints.

We had come into what appeared to be a manifold of sorts at about the fourth mile, where five large drains converged into ours. We stopped and shut down everything. The suspects might have split up or continued on together, but the convergence was perplexing. The suspects were now careful not to step into the water and there was no evidence of which way they chose to travel.

It was about an hour now since the foot pursuit started, and time was on the suspects' side. This meant we must reexamine our priorities. This incident was an auto theft, and the stolen car was damaged but recovered. There were five officers tied up on a low-grade felony, and because we had no idea how long the tunnels were, the decision was relatively easy.

At about the five-mile mark into the drain, in the absence of any footprints, we all concluded it was time to turn around and get back into service. It still took us another thirty minutes to go back to the opening, but it was quite an adventure in the tunnel. I'm sure the suspects were highly relieved, and our persistence probably forced them into leading exemplary lives after hearing all the noise we made, including the deafening siren.

CHAPTER 24

THE MAGGOT

Close to the station, just off Compton Boulevard, was a small mortuary with a prominent name. They had called the station because of a break-in by some unknown person. The person jimmied the window and crawled into the clean, quiet, and quaint mortuary late in the evening hours and rummaged through many of the loose items lying around near one of the desks. The person then apparently came into the parlor area, where there was a closed metal casket sitting alone atop a polished high-set dolly.

The intruder opened the casket. It contained the made-up and decorated body of an eighty-year-old woman, lying in her beautiful laced gown. She had been prepped the night before because she was going to have a viewing early the following morning.

What the suspect did next was unthinkable. He lifted the elderly lady from the casket and draped her body over the opening, face first, head inside the casket. He lifted her gown and raped and sodomized the deceased woman. It is not known how long the necrophiliac was in the funeral parlor, but he had left his bodily fluids and fingerprints everywhere.

The fingerprints were lifted and researched immediately, because solving the crime as soon as possible was paramount and rushed through with unbelievable speed. The culprit was identified by his fingerprints as a Compton resident who had done this act before. The rush was not only because it was a terrible crime, deplorable conduct that greatly upsets the entire community. It was also because the elderly lady was the mother of a California Highway Patrolman. He was livid and made no bones about it. He would do just about anything to physically get to the suspect.

The suspect was a diminutive white man around thirty years of age. He had a meek and tender-looking face like a typical mama's boy; and in fact he still lived with his mother in Compton. His had semilong hair and a well-manicured moustache and goatee. He remained very quiet and wouldn't look at anyone. I guess he knew very well that he was an outcast to all, and his despicable act was about as low as one could imagine, displaying a total lack of human decency.

I'm sorry I couldn't let the CHP officer near the suspect because we all know what would have happened, and I'm not so sure that would have been wrong.

But let's wait a minute, although he was found guilty and sentenced to prison, he's probably out by now, fully recovered from his twisted and sick behavior.

Now, if this victim was your mother, would you feel a sense of relief? Was justice truly done?

CHAPTER 25

ROUND ONE

It was another busy night, and the calls had us running all over the city. All Compton city units were trying to chase after mostly the priority calls. Some were bogged down handling reports, and several traffic accidents occupied the rest of the evening crews' time. We had no other units available, and everyone was hoping nothing major would develop.

One unit contained a fellow cadet and a newly off-training officer named Barry C. He was traveling around freely after completing several minor reports.

He was a lone officer, excited about his recent off-training status, and he was looking for significant issues to pop up in front of him. We all knew that in Compton, significant crimes were only a breath away, if you keep your eyes open. Unbeknown to Barry as he pulled into a small alleyway on Long Beach Boulevard near Temple Street, something was about to raise his stature, level of performance, and pucker factor.

This alley looped around the back end of a McDonald's, busy with the early evening crowd. Just a few minutes prior, a lone male suspect had stuck a gun into the clerk's face at McDonald's and demanded the money from the cash register. The clerk complied, and quickly handed over all of the cash from his drawer.

Once the thief had taken the money, he stuffed it into his pocket and slowly walked toward the side door. He then casually walked out of the restaurant westbound across the rear parking lot.

At the same time, Barry was coming into the alleyway from the north, casually driving in his police car, nearing the back end of the very same restaurant. Neither Barry nor the suspect had any idea that they were within fifty yards of each other as they continued to close the gap.

The suspect was alert and focused on getting away from McDonald's as fast as possible, but with care not to reveal what he had just done. Barry, on the other hand, was relaxed and relatively blasé, but he was still looking ardently for a good contact to improve his newly acquired officer status.

He watched several individuals casually walking around, but nothing suspicious was occurring, so he slowly came upon the rear of McDonalds, still looking around.

As the robbery suspect drew nearer the alley, his view of traffic coming from the north was concealed by a six-foot block-wall area. (That walled-in area and gate concealed a wheeled trash Dumpster commonly used by restaurants.)

The suspect had a pistol in his waistband. He constantly looked around for any signs of persons coming after him. When he turned his head slightly toward the north, he spotted the police car Barry was in.

At that same time, Barry spotted the suspicious way the suspect had looked at him and noted the suspect reaching into his waist area as if he was going to draw a gun. Barry slammed on his brakes, stopping the patrol car, and began to get out of the car. The suspect already had his gun in his right hand, and he raised it toward Barry.

Barry quickly armed himself as he was getting outside the patrol car, and managed to squeeze off one round at the suspect. The suspect was now at least fifteen feet from Barry.

He sensed the suspect was about to fire at him and backed quickly around toward the rear of the patrol car for cover. To Barry's amazement, the suspect never fired, and more puzzling, Barry couldn't see him at all.

Barry thought maybe the suspect had run away and never was able to fire off any rounds because Barry was much quicker. (Keep in mind Barry didn't know anything about the robbery.)

As Barry inched slowly around the rear of the patrol car and started carefully up the right side of the patrol car, he spotted the suspect lying on the asphalt, face down and facing away from his position.

Barry thought, *Maybe I hit him.* He yelled to the suspect several times, but the suspect never answered and never moved. Barry kept the suspect in view and reached into his patrol car and grabbed the microphone. He alerted everyone to what had just occurred and said that he was standing by, awaiting backup to assist in checking on the suspect.

Several minutes went by, and then units arrived en masse and assisted checking on the suspect. The suspect's gun was lying several feet away to the south of his body and couldn't be seen from Barry's position, close by his radio car.

As it turned out, the suspect was dead on the spot. The one shot fired from Barry's revolver, dropped him like a rock. The round struck the suspect in the right shoulder, went directly across the suspect's chest, and lodged in his other arm.

That shot was an absolutely great shot, done while Barry was on the move, coming out of his car and then backing quickly toward the rear of his car. The suspect couldn't even fire off one round because of Barry's quick reaction and one-round accuracy.

Furthermore, as it turned out, Barry's fired round that had killed the suspect was a single wad-cutter round. That bullet type is a blunt-ended target round, used primarily for target practice. Barry had fired a few rounds for practice just before briefing in the small pistol range, located in the basement at the police station. When Barry finished practicing, he didn't have enough full-size field rounds to fill his cylinder, so he supplemented one empty chamber with a wad-cutter. That wad-cutter was the round that struck the suspect.

(Wad-cutter rounds usually do not possess enough penetrating velocity or the proper shape to be used as combat rounds and are discouraged from use in the field.)

Although this situation turned out well for Barry, dire consequences were averted because Barry was alert, well trained, and conditioned to combat readiness. Fate had brought them together and the bullet used coincidently was fired by a person who was now destined for a law enforcement career.

CHAPTER 26

FATEFUL TRIP

I was working a busy day-shift car and went on duty at around eight in the morning. I had already stopped for coffee. I drove around for an hour, answered several calls, and stopped a few cars. Nothing out of the ordinary was occurring until several Compton units received an emergent call to respond to a helicopter crash, occurring at Pop Leuder's Park, at Rosecrans Avenue and Bullis Road.

I was a lone car and responded code three, red lights and siren, with a two-minute arrival time. As I drew near the park, I saw the fire department already on the scene, dousing the remnants of flames with their fine spray of water.

As I first came onto the scene, my attention was drawn to a black silhouetted figure, appearing frozen in time, atop the charred crash site. One arm was outstretched slightly, and the other arm was cocked slightly backward. The ghostly figure appeared to be looking toward my position. The mouth was slightly open as if calling out for help or gasping for air.

The pungent odor of fuel and the burning of human flesh permeated the air. The heavily charred pile of wreckage was twelve to fifteen feet in height, fifty to sixty feet in length, and approximately thirty to forty feet wide. The craft had missed the trees and buildings and settled on a mat of flat green grass.

Initially a crowd of maybe one hundred onlookers was standing close by the yellow caution tape, approximately fifty feet away, carefully watching the outcome of the crash and fire and the various tasks firemen were performing.

Several individuals came forward to me and stated they heard and saw the helicopter when the engines stopped. The witnesses graphically described the crash as coming down fast and hard. When it did hit, it partially crumpled, and quite a few people were still alive inside.

They were screaming and attempting to grasp anything along the edges of the aircraft; frantically seeking help and escape from impending death. The witnesses added that the craft actually bounced at least three times before it settled down on the open grassed area.

Then a small amount of flames appeared and suddenly the entire craft erupted into a heap of fire. They added that they still could see people inside as the flames were consuming them, screaming with anguish and obviously suffering from a great deal of excruciating pain.

As I took the witnesses' information about themselves and what they had seen, they were crying because there was absolutely nothing they could have done. Still, they looked on, because they were captivated by the calamity.

Based on the witnesses' ghastly observations and the description of the horrid event, I had no doubt this tragic memory would also be permanently etched in their minds for the rest of their lives.

The LA County coroner and the Federal Aviation Administration were en route to the site. Copious amounts of yellow barricade tape were strewn all around the crash site, keeping all onlookers back at least a hundred feet from the wreckage area.

Our police procedures demand that nothing is touched in these situations and the entire area must be cordoned off. The whole investigation was to be completed by the Federal Aviation Administration, the county coroner's office and the LA County Sheriff's Department. Our primary job was to protect the security of the crash site and preserve everything until relieved.

We stood by for a short while until the investigative crews arrived approximately an hour later. Pictures were being taken of the whole site, and measurements were charted by the investigators.

I was assigned to a spot just inside an eight-foot chain-link fenced-in area that was a new car holding lot, containing an abundance of cars for "Bill Barnett Chevrolet," a local dealership in the city.

Several deputy coroners were in the process of attempting to remove the charred remains of the pilot from the cockpit. The pilot was wrapped and entwined in a collage of melted plastic, wire, and metal shards. To further complicate matters, the pilot's body parts would detach quickly when grasped, and this caused each one of the deputy coroners to fall backward onto the burned rubble, with the pilot's appendage still in their grip, but detached. When the coroners would fall backward from their pulling efforts to remove body parts, the majority of the crowd would moan aloud, "Ohhhh!"

Dramatic and more troublesome were the numerous bundles and batches of thin- and thick-gauge electrical wires. As the pilot was being pulled from the cockpit, these wires scraped skin and flesh from the bones in a gruesome display.

My position was only five feet away from the actual cockpit area, in a fixed security spot. I was near a crowded and confined area. Although I was surrounded by an eight-foot fence and near the last two cars. I was able to squeeze near the corner end of the fence, where several small globules of brain matter were splattered on the side windows and painted surfaces of the cars. These globules might have come from the charred pilot, who was entangled not five feet from the fence. I advised the investigators of the brain matter and said that I wouldn't mind helping them pick the matter up. I explained that I was a recently a retired journeyman meatcutter and had a much stronger stomach for foul odors and chores. A deputy coroner asked if I would be kind enough to use several thin sheets of paper to capture the matter and pass it through the fence to them. I collected the apparent brain matter carefully, maybe ten pieces in all.

The entire crash site investigation and security lasted for a full two days. At times there were as many as three to five hundred onlookers at the scene. They were cooperative and solemn as each passenger was removed. The handling of all of these charred bodies by the investigators was quick and reverent, as expected.

Watching this entire ordeal had a major effect on my career and psychological behavior. The most moving was the sight of stuffed children's toys that I saw near the aircraft's empennage, the tail section. A lot of luggage was crushed in this area and not burned at all. Each piece was open at the corner seams, yet their shiny latches were still secured. To me this indicated the ferocity of the impact. Seeing those toys made me feel very sorry for the kids who died in the crash, because the evidence indicated that the crash alone had to have been a terrible ordeal, prior to their demise in a horrible fire.

Later on, research of this crash revealed it actually occurred on August 14, 1968, at 10: 35a.m. The flight was en route to Disneyland Heliport in Anaheim from Los Angeles International Airport, resulting in the loss of twenty-one lives.

Oddly enough, three months prior, on May 22, 1968, another similar crash occurred in the city of Paramount, resulting in the loss of twenty-three lives. This helicopter was the same type and was en route to Los Angeles International Airport from the Disneyland Heliport in Anaheim.

CHAPTER 27

"EXCUSE ME, SIR; WHAT ARE YOU DOING?"

Part of the patrol route in Compton was its alleys. The alleys are narrow and have many places to hide. If you're lucky enough to be in a two-man unit, it's much better than a one-man unit, because you're definitely going to run into some rough stuff, especially at night when your lights are out, and you're moving slowly, with very little noise.

A former mayor of Los Angeles announced that he was a former LAPD officer. He claimed that in his twenty years with the LAPD, he never drew his weapon. That statement seemed to me to be perplexing and ridiculous. Where the hell did he work?

When I started as a Compton officer, I found it very difficult not to pull my gun out quite a few times per shift. In fact, when I patrolled the alleys in Compton, I had my gun lying in my lap, because several times in the alleys I came upon suspects who were armed and very close to my car door.

In some of the alleys, it was sometimes difficult to fully open the car door. I found it necessary to keep the driver's window down, in case I had to poke my gun through the window to convince a suspect not to move.

No doubt the crooks had the lookout situation down pat. When a patrol car came down the street, it was easily spotted because of its shape, and whole groups acted in concert by whistling or yelling out certain words to let everyone know the police were coming. From little kids to big kids, they announced that police were coming, to help out the criminal element or to gain their favor. It was a kind of neighborhood sycophant choir toying with dangerous gang liaisons.

In the alleys, crooks were less likely to be vigilant. Hanging out in the alley didn't generate much notoriety or glamour and limited their visibility. So that's where I loved to go. I'd suddenly pop in on some streets from the alley access.

One night I was working with a partner, silently patrolling up and down alleys and streets for the first hour. We decided to stop briefly for a cup of coffee. We chatted for a short time, sipping our coffee, while listening to the police radio put out one or two calls that were routine for two o'clock in the morning.

Very little traffic was on the streets, and the coffee shop attendant was busily making dough for morning business; everything else was quiet and calm. After the brief break and stretching of our legs, we got back into our patrol car and headed toward the west end of the city. We were westbound in an alley that paralleled Compton Boulevard on the north side, about four blocks from Wilmington Avenue. Our headlights were out, and we were creeping slowly westbound, traveling at about a mile or two an hour. Nothing out of the ordinary was happening. The radios were down very low as we passed various small businesses to our left and fenced residential yards to our right. As we continued our slow-moving patrol, some dogs, awakened and alerted to the noise from our car engine and tires, would bark occasionally.

We ventured onward, still peering into the alcoves behind the businesses. There were Dumpsters, cardboard boxes, and scantly spread sundries of trash.

Cats would scatter and scurry around as we came by, disturbing their early morning meals. There were those good-size roof rats meandering through the trash for food as well, avoiding the stealthy cats.

If it moved, we spotted it pretty quick. We had just crossed one of the streets and were coming upon midblock, and we heard some very loud noises a short distance away.

We slowed even more to focus on where the noise was coming from. Suddenly we were at the rear of a liquor store. It was very dark, and we could barely make out a human figure, but the noise coming from him was loud, as if he was hammering on something. He was about fifteen feet away from our car and apparently not aware of our presence.

We carefully opened our doors. Together we illuminated the figure with our flashlights, as he was striking the back-door area with a full-length axe. He turned his head around and then his whole body. He was clutching the handle in his right hand and the sharpened edge was slightly dragging on the asphalt.

I asked him in loud voice, "Excuse me, sir, what are you doing?" His clothing was drenched in perspiration, and he was slightly out of breath.

He didn't say anything initially because he was shocked by our presence. Both of our guns were pointing at him and we were grinning and chuckling slightly, knowing full well what he was up to.

Our chuckling irritated him significantly, and he started to pick up the axe, but we warned him that getting caught red-handed was no reason to die. He released the handle, and the axe lazily fell to the side.

We order him to turn around and walk back toward our voices, because he probably couldn't see us from our blinding flashlights.

We handcuffed him without incident, and we were still chuckling about how brazen he was, focused as he was chopping on the back door and not noticing us right behind him. We asked him how long he had been chopping the door, and he responded, "About a half hour!"

Once he was arrested and in the back seat of our car, I went over to the back door and noted that he had really damaged it extensively, but still the door was intact. Our desk personnel notified the owner. He arrived about a half hour later and led us inside the liquor store and to the rear door.

As I looked at the back door, I was amazed at the various locks, triple two-by-four boards of lumber used as bracing for the top, middle, and bottom portions, and steel brackets that locked the bracing lumber in place. The owner stated that he had been burglarized so many times that he and a friend had developed the armored door.

We felt very good about our catch and capture; it resonates even today in my mind as good basic police work by patrolling our area, both in a car and afoot.

That's what folks expect. So we bragged about our catch to our fellow officers, knowing full well they would try our tactics out and look for a better catch.

CHAPTER 28

MY BROTHER'S KEEPER

I was in the Compton PD's jail, booking a male suspect and filling out the booking paperwork when an announcement came over the station's public address system stating that a unit needed help. It was reported that a Compton unit was involved in a fight with a man on Keene Street, just west of Wilmington Avenue. I recognized the unit number as my brother Vince's unit, and no one was able to assist.

I quickly shoved the suspect I had just searched into the booking cage, removed my gun from the gun locker, and ran out the back door. It was a very foggy night, around three in the morning and there was very little traffic.

I announced over the radio that I was en route, with an ETA of at least five minutes, considering the heavy fog. As I darted from the parking lot I found that the fog was so dense, I could hardly see past the hood of my radio car.

I was nervous as hell because of the delay of the heavy fog, I had to open my car door to aid in locating the painted stripes on the road. It didn't help much, as I blindly traveled at approximately 10 mph. I was busily trying to adapt my vision from the dense fog, to the poorly visible street signs.

I was desperately trying to orient myself to what streets I was passing. I was in a state of anguish and hoping I wouldn't cross paths with another car going in either direction. My speed was marginally safe, but my door was ajar, and I was leaning outward slightly. I knew it was dangerous, but it was my brother in trouble, and no one else was coming to his aid. If I got into a crash, it might very well cause serious injury or death to some innocent persons, and it would surely be perceived as my fault. On the other hand, I knew my brother; Vince was fighting with someone, and I anxiously hoped he would hang on until I got there.

I informed my desk that I was going to be a few minutes longer because of the dense fog. It actually took me about eight minutes.

Finally I arrived on the scene and noticed a black female adult standing at the foot of a stairway, pointing upward toward the second floor. There was also an open door, and the bright interior lights were diffuse, because the dense fog shrouded the two-story building as well.

I was up the stairs in a flash. I ran into the front room and heard the commotion in the adjoining bedroom. I crossed a narrow hallway, and I saw my brother holding the wrists of an equally large black man who was holding a giant bag of bright red capsules, commonly called "red devils," a controlled substance that was predominantly used in the area. They were wrestling with each other, and both seemed very tired.

I casually leaned against the right side of the doorway and jokingly chided my brother, "Jesus, Vince, I rushed over here in this damn fog to help you and nearly got killed. Now I come to find out you're just dancing with this guy, in bed!"

Vince angrily yelled at me, "What the shit? Help me with this guy!" Fortunately, when I stepped over to the bed and grabbed the male suspect by his hair and trousers, pulled him upward, and threw him into the wall, he meekly surrendered and easily submitted to arrest.

We quickly handcuffed the suspect and called the station to let them know that everything was okay and that both of us were en route to the station. I admit that I was very concerned for my brother's well-being and the time to get there was very troublesome.

I joked with Vince later on and reminded him that the only person who got to beat him up, was me, and me alone.

I guess because of our positions in law enforcement I would indeed be my brother's keeper, and with no regrets.

CHAPTER 29

CHEF OF THE DAY

I came in early to read the briefing boards and prep myself for the day shift. When I was in the locker room preparing my uniform and gear for the day's activities, I was called over the public address system to report to the sergeant's office. I ran up to the sergeant's office, and he stated that I was going to be the jailer for the shift.

I informed him I had no jailer experience and had never worked that position, even as a trainee. His response: "Well, that's too bad You're it!" I said, "Yes, sir!" and went to the jail immediately. I was about thirty minutes early, but that was not at issue. I just needed whatever help I could get, and real quick.

I located the jailer and begged for instruction, and he laughed. He said, "I'll show where everything is and give you a rundown on what to do, but I am out of here in about twenty minutes." I thought, Well, what else can I do?

The jailer guided me through all of the things I was supposed to do, including feeding breakfast to the twenty inmates, eighteen males and two females. The law stated that all of the inmates needed to be checked on every half hour. They were also required to be fed prior to court lineup at 8:30 a.m.

The jailer, also a Compton policeman, pointed out red two-inch buttons situated outside each cell and all along a block wall about four feet above the ground—panic buttons in case I got into a fight or had to wrestle an epileptic inmate. When activated, an alarm rang in the jail, and a buzzer sounded at the front desk and in the sergeant's office in case a fight broke out, or I spotted someone trying to commit suicide, or there was any other conceivable emergency.

I was also guided to a separate cell that was much smaller and only had a toilet opening in it and an iron-frame bunk along the wall. This was the isolation cell for those who were belligerent or sloppy drunk on drugs or alcohol.

The jailer pointed out jail rosters and follow-up bed checks that were to be made out every half hour. Bail books and procedural notifications of next of kin were filled out in case of emergencies. If these forms were not filled out by the officers during booking, then it was up to the jailer to persuade the inmate to complete the forms. With the inmate's permission, the jailer would make the contact.

There were many peripheral tasks to complete, and so I began completing the first half hour bed checks as the early morning jailer left and went off duty.

Prior to leaving, he showed me what to feed the inmates and briefly stated frozen pancakes and sausage, with instant coffee. The problem was getting the meals and coffee ready for the inmates at the 8:30 a.m. deadline.

It was actually the first time I ever used a microwave to prepare these meals, and when I was finished some were hardly cooked through, but the importance was getting it to the inmates on time, so I did. The biggest complaint was the instant coffee. It tasted terrible to me, and the inmates complained as well, but not too rudely.

About twenty minutes later I came around to collect the paper plates and cups from each cell. Prior to entering the women's block of cells the jailer was required to announce his entrance, so if any females were using the toilet facilities they would have enough time to finish their personal hygiene matters.

I paused for at least one minute and entered to collect the plates and cups. As I walked in I heard some laughter from one of the females and didn't think much of it. I stopped by the first cell and collected her paper plate and cup. Then I heard a female voice laughing and commenting "Look at me, honey!" She sounded like the Wicked Witch of the East in *The Wizard of Oz*. I turned my head toward the voice. I saw the other female, who was totally naked, with her legs spread atop the walled bunk. Her bed mattress was torn across one end and lay partially on the cement floor. She was pulling the stuffing from the mattress and cramming it into her vagina. She raised her voice. "Do you like this?" She grabbed another wad of bedding material and stuffed it into herself.

I was caught off guard by her brazen demonstration and left the cellblock immediately. I went to the jailer quarters and called the desk sergeant and stated what I had observed and questioned her sanity. The sergeant came in right away and both of us went into the block and announced our entrance.

She was in the same position, naked, and she repeated her graphic behavior. Because of her offensive conduct, we came to the same conclusion—that she was was emotionally unstable and needed to be clinically examined for her well-being.

In this case, a unit was ordered to come pick her up and take her to a Norwalk facility for a seventy-two-hour psychiatric evaluation by a professional. This was the standard policy of the department for inmates who were unable to care for themselves or their own personal safety. Those persons would then be evaluated and perhaps committed, or they would sign themselves into a special psychological program to remedy the problem.

CHAPTER 30
ROOKIE PURSUIT

Pursuits were a common daily event and consequence of all police activity. Foot pursuits of fleeing suspects—chasing them down and then arresting them—were challenging, to say the least. But auto thefts were absolutely out of control in Compton. There were days when vehicle pursuits would occur several times per shift. Bets were on that two pursuits might occur at the same time, which would tax the entire shift of patrol cars and would cause Compton to ask for help from other agencies.

Computers weren't even in the stations yet, let alone in the police cars. Our department operated off a sheet of paper handed out at each briefing that contained approximately a hundred license plate numbers in columns across the entire sheet. These numbers reflected local stolen cars that were put into the law enforcement teletype system for display to aid in the capture of suspects and the recovery of the stolen cars. This was commonly was called the "hot sheet."

When a license plate was broadcast over the radio, the police station desk personnel would run that number over the teletype system and the information would return within five minutes or longer. By using the hot sheet, you would know right away if it was a stolen car and announce your intentions over the radio.

The desk personnel or dispatcher would simply parrot your words and announce them to other units. There were usually two band frequencies on most police radios. One was used from the desk broadcasting to all units and the other frequency was used for car-to-car communications.

We both had several court cases that were going to be heard, so we were sitting around on several benches just outside the courtrooms.

Tom and I were in our relatively new dark-blue uniforms, highly polished brass and spit-shined shoes. We were absolutely bored to death. We had never practiced this waiting routine in the sheriff's academy nor while in training. It was tedious and time-consuming to wait for the call of the deputy DA. Although we were being paid to wait, the mere thought of the astronomical costs attributed to one arrest several weeks prior seemed mind-boggling. However, one could argue that the costs were a cheap price for freedom. This time was spent waiting for our cases to be called and could conceivably take the entire day.

Because we were bored with all of the idleness, Tom and I were discussing the idea that working in the field and not receiving routine calls for service would be much more advantageous for the city. Because we were recently off training and on our own, maybe we could get permission from the desk sergeant to take out a unit and work the field together.

This would be in lieu of sitting around and doing nothing but waiting to testify. We advised the deputy DA of our thoughts—if he needed us all he would have to do is call over to the station, and we would respond within minutes.

The deputy DA agreed to our terms, and we immediately walked back to the station and sought out the desk sergeant. He sarcastically called out that we should be in court.

We asked if we could talk for a short bit and make some minor adjustments to the routine of just sitting around court and waiting all day. The sergeant also reminded us that the waiting was also for the district attorney to arrange for all the victims, witnesses, and informants to testify in court as well, and for us to have the evidence ready to be presented.

We agreed with the sergeant about his concerns and the importance of being ready to testify. We pointed out that although we are paid for our court time, we could make an offer he couldn't refuse. He laughed and allowed us to make the offer. He listened carefully and gladly agreed with the reasoning. He allowed us to take out a unit and patrol the streets while on call at the court. The one thing he wanted us to assure him was that whatever we were doing in the field, it must be dropped immediately if we were called to testify.

We agreed with his requests, and the feeling of elation set in. We quickly retrieved our field gear and checked out a patrol car. We imagined making a spectacular catch to really drive home our energy of enthusiasm and persistence.

We advised the desk of what we were about to do and said we could actually back up units in the field if necessary. This meant we wouldn't receive any calls for service and drive around and look for trouble. This might prove to be beneficial to the department, because we were actually an extra two-man unit in the field, fully able to free up other units.

Tom and I got to our car, prepped it quickly, and left the parking lot. Tom was driving, and I was the bookman, which meant I took care of most of the paperwork, like filling out the log, writing reports, and handling radio communications.

We headed north of the station toward Rosecrans Avenue. We were driving slowly, carefully looking for suspicious behavior. It was already around eleven. The residential streets were pretty much empty, and foot traffic was minimal. It was pretty free of any perceivable crime, so we decided to go back near the courthouse, where there was a treasure trove of criminals.

We knew full well that the courthouse was a great place to look for crooks, because that's where they go during the day. The crooks are being dropped off by other criminals to show up for court for their pending criminal cases. Those criminals would oftentimes commit more crimes while waiting for their cases to be called. It was a kind of criminal alternative to what we were doing. Or simply invoking commonsense reasoning, because most people worked during the day, as opposed to the criminals, who would be showing up for court from nine to five, while their crime partners whom they came to court with, would sneak around the local neighborhood and marauding the close-by homes. I wonder—if court was held from nine in the evening to six in the morning, would it drastically impact daytime crime like burglaries, robberies, and auto theft? What do you think?

We were southbound on Acacia Street and drawing close to the courthouse, not a half block from Compton Boulevard when we spotted a brand new red and white two-door Plymouth right in front of us, with two men inside. There weren't any license plates, probably because it was so new. Their car was stopped almost right in front of the courthouse steps, and they were talking with another man standing in the street by the driver's door.

As we came right behind the Plymouth, the man in the street looked toward us and said something to the two occupants. They turned around inside the Plymouth, apparently realizing we were about to confront them.

Suddenly their rear tires started to smoke heavily and screech as they took off on us, racing southbound on Acacia Street with their rear end beginning to swerve dramatically from side to side. Tom and I were talking while I was attempting to contact our desk over the radio, announcing our pursuit.

The desk repeated our directions and the description of the Plymouth to all other units as it fled from us. The Plymouth was traveling so fast it couldn't manage the narrow street and slammed into two parked cars. The impact caused both cars to fly upward and land on their sides, narrowly missing pedestrians on the sidewalk.

We continued southbound on Acacia Street as the Plymouth picked up speed again and continued slamming into parked cars, large and small, knocking several more cars on their sides and some in midair, their rear ends landing solidly on the hoods of the neighboring parked cars. Smoke and debris covered our car as we enthusiastically chased them. We didn't notice anyone being struck by the car or any pieces flying off the car from the collisions.

The Plymouth made a left turn onto Indigo Street, coming up to and passing a grammar school that was in session. That didn't seem to bother the two crooks very much, because they slammed into at least five to six more parked cars on either side of Indigo Street, and those cars as well were knocked up and onto the sidewalk area. Two were on their sides. One of the collisions in front of the school caused the driver's door of the Plymouth to rip off and fall into the street. It was sparking and spinning on its outer side and jetted across the street right in front of us. At least two cars directly in front of the school were tossed up on their sides as well.

The Plymouth's top speed was about 60–70 mph. It was now coming onto busy Alameda Street nonstop and made another left hand turn, cutting clear across Alameda Street into oncoming traffic. Fortunately, the two idiots didn't hit any moving autos as they sped northbound in the now-ruined brand-new Plymouth.

It veered sharply right and slammed into the curb and stopped. The driver jumped out, and my partner Tom grabbed him just as the passenger attempted to run across the double railroad tracks, but I was on top of his movements in about thirty steps. Both suspects turned out to be juveniles who lived locally, and both had extensive prior arrests and criminal records.

About five of our Compton fellow units showed up at the end of the pursuit and assisted us by going back to see if anyone was injured. We retraced our pursuit, and as it turned out, there were nine cars knocked onto their sides, and three or four others tossed on top of other parked cars. Fortunately, no one was injured.

A couple of collisions caused several other cars to slam on top of one another over on Acacia Street. Those cars were a little more complicated to pull apart and needed extra effort and care to disengage. The fire department had several of their trucks nearby because of the leaking gasoline and in case of any problems when the towing companies righted all twelve cars.

The patrol sergeant, lieutenant and chief of police all came over to where we apprehended the suspects and congratulated us on the outcome of the pursuit and the two arrests. The sergeant was pleased that this had a good outcome, since it could have easily had disastrous results. He was also pleased this occurred when we were on call from Compton court. He congratulated us for our perseverance and for welcoming difficult tasks faced by law enforcement.

As we tracked backward and viewed the disarray and damage to the cars involved, a thin haze of smoke hung in the air. Drawn outside by the noise, there were multitudes of people out on the street and the sidewalk. It was apparent that we handled this event as best as we could, and that a power much greater than the justice system was watching over us. We were very pleased and thankful when we realized that many others could have been seriously injured or easily killed.

The Plymouth was so smashed up it was evaluated as total loss and as it turned out, it was stolen, taken several hours prior to the pursuit.

Both suspects were booked on auto theft charges. The passenger suffered a broken ankle. No other injuries were sustained in the entire episode.

In the my next thirty years of law enforcement, no one even came close to such a vibrant pursuit, so full of crash-and-bang conduct and diversity of damage with no injuries.

We were two rookies on court standby, freelancing against Compton's plague of crime. On top of it all, we did not damage our patrol car and didn't get hurt. It was a prelude to a career destined for adventure. I can distinctly recall thinking, *Oh, the glory of it all, this is going to be an exciting career.*

CHAPTER 31
DEAD END

I was out in the field patrolling my area and had already taken several reports. I found a spot to conceal myself safely to complete my reports. Sometimes as much as two or three hours of writing is needed to complete the reports, so anytime an officer gets a chance, he will find a spot to perform his writing tasks.

As I was writing, my brother Vince called on the radio and wanted to meet with me. He came to my location and wanted to tell me about a call he had just handled. He stated he was on the south side of the city handling a suspicious circumstances call. He contacted the informant who was complaining about a terrible smell coming from their next door neighbor's home. Vince said he could smell the odor himself, and it was extremely foul.

He left the informant's home and went next door. He encountered a thirteen-year-old black girl at the front door. Vince asked for her parents, and she said that her mom was the only person living with them, but she wasn't home right now. Vince observed several kids running around and asked how many kids live here and the thirteen-year-old said there were ten. "Ten," he repeated. She stated "Yes, sir!"

Vince then stated that the reason he was there was because the neighbors were complaining about the smell coming from their home. At that point the thirteen-year-old led Vince inside the squalid home and to the bathroom.

She opened the door to the bathroom, and Vince almost vomited at first sight. The toilet and bathtub were both full of human feces and smeared all over the walls and floor. Apparently everyone there was still using the toilet and bathtub for their personal business, and because there was no toilet paper, they were wiping the excreta from their hands onto the walls and floor. The young girl stated that the water hadn't worked for a long time.

The girl then led Vince through the kitchen and near a bedroom. The door was shut, and there was the odor of rotting flesh very nearby. The young girl said it was coming from the bedroom, but the door wouldn't open anymore.

Puzzled because of the terrible living conditions and feeling something might be dead on the other side of the door, Vince decided to kick the door open, and when he did he was aghast at what he saw. Lying on its side was a full-sized dead horse, tawny colored, extremely bloated, lying right next to an unkempt bed.

Dried horse excreta covered an area of five to six feet on the rug and wooden floor, near the rear end of the horse. The bloating caused the swelling of the horse to expand from its normal size to about four feet in height, sideways. The horse's rear end had the wooden handle of a corn broom shoved into its anal orifice, where only the corn bristles were exposed.

The girl explained that they were trying to stop all of the excreta from escaping from the rear end of the horse about a week ago, so they took the corn broom and pushed the long wooden handle into the horse in order to stop the stuff from coming out.

The girl was a little unsure of herself and a little scared because of all the attention Vince was giving her. She added that the horse had been dead for about a week and a half.

Vince requested the Department of Child Protective Services to respond and remove all the children from the home. He found out that their mom was a local prostitute. She had an extensive criminal record for prostitution and drug-related charges. She was away at the time, apparently taking care of her business, and left all of the ten children in the care of her thirteen-year-old daughter.

All of the children would be given proper care and facilities, fresh clothing, food, and drink. Of course all of the kids would be examined by medical personnel and relocated to foster homes until their cases were adjudicated.

Because of the large number of kids, it would be very difficult to keep them together as a whole family.

———

Approximately seven years later, when I was with the Los Angeles County Sheriff's Department and on assignment at the Wayside Honor Rancho, near Magic Mountain in Valencia, I was involved with training approximately 150 law enforcement cadets at the training facility. We had finished our weapons training on the range and were en route to lunch at the huge mess hall located in the central area of the large detention facility.

The training was a week long and came at the end of the twenty-four weeks in the sheriff's academy. Staff and cadets were quartered there for the extensive final week of training.

I was walking by a very large pigpen where inmates were working. This area was a farm atmosphere, where the inmates raised several hundred pigs for their self-sufficient food supply. They were carefully watched by deputy personnel.

The vast pen that had just been hosed down and cleaned. The odor of pig excreta was repugnant and nearly overpowering. Most of the waste was running down the cement grade into a giant concrete-block pit where it went into a renovating process. Every once in a while the large grate became plugged and prevented any filtering whatsoever. So when the grate was plugged, it was necessary for someone to get into the pit and clean the grate and unplug any pieces of large debris.

One trusty was in the pit as we were passing by and I easily recognized the individual as a young man named Spencer. I knew him very well from Compton and had many contacts with him and his mother. Spencer was one of the ten kids who had been taken into custody by Child Protective Services when they were called by my brother Vince to remove them from that home.

I called to him, "Hi, Spencer, How's it going?" He smiled, apparently recognized me, and stated, "Pretty good!" He was covered with the pig matter. He was shirtless and had Levis on, with tall rubber boots.

I felt a deep sense of sorrow and empathy for Spencer. I knew full well that whatever he was in custody for was brought upon him from his upbringing. Now seven years later, he was still deep in the squalid conditions he was raised in.

This was another event that formed my opinion about the causes of criminal behavior. It will also remain with me forever.

CHAPTER 32

JUST CAUSE FOR A WOMAN BEATER?

The call came as a code-three run to a home on the west side of the city as an assault. A man was beating a woman. We arrived shortly and a black woman came out to talk to us. She informed us that her husband was just picked up by the ambulance and transported to the emergency hospital.

We asked what happened, and she anxiously told us of her plight. I might add that she had a swollen and bruised eye and cheek, contusions all over her arms and legs, with small lacerations oozing a small amount of blood from her eyebrows and nose.

She said that her husband of five years had been punching her and kicking her repeatedly throughout the entire marriage. The reasons for the beatings ranged from burning his food and not cleaning the house to not providing enough sex for his satisfaction. She added that the day before, she'd found out her husband was having an affair with someone in her family. She'd confronted him with the accusations of infidelity and began yelling at him. He became enraged at her anger and took off his inch-and-a-half-wide leather belt, folded it neatly in half, and came into the living room. He beat her with the belt quite a few times until he lost his grip, and it fell to the floor. He began to punch her all over her body and then slapped her in the face. As the woman blocked many of his slaps and punches with her arms and hands, he began to kick her repeatedly in the stomach and back. She was begging him to stop and crying for help, but no one came to her aid.

After several minutes of beating her, he became tired and ordered her to hurry up and finish cooking dinner for him. He allowed her to stand up and hobble off into the kitchen. As she was going into the kitchen her husband went to the front-room couch and calmly lay down, placed his tired hands behind his head on the armrest, and fell asleep.

Meanwhile she was busily finishing their dinner preparation. She carefully brought a large pot of thick, split-pea soup to a boil and double-checked on her husband, making sure he was asleep.

He was sound asleep and not moving, with his hands still directly behind his head. She grabbed several kitchen towels in one hand and a hot mitt in the other and cautiously picked up the heavy pot. She crept quietly to his resting area and stood near the armrest of the couch.

She then dumped the entire pot of boiling split pea soup onto her husbands face, neck, chest, and arms. He woke up screaming like a banshee. The thick soup stuck to his skin and severely burned all of his exposed skin.

She then ran out of the house as her husband was running around inside their house bumping into everything, because his eyes were affected as well. She went to a neighbor's home and called for an ambulance and the police and informed them of what she had done.

I explained to her that she might very well be arrested because of the injuries that happened to her husband, but that she'd have to seek her own medical attention for her injuries from the beatings. I made substantial notes of her injuries and encouraged her to have the medical staff do as well as they identified and described her wounds and bruises.

———

Several years later I ran into the same woman in the central part of Compton, walking along Compton Boulevard accompanied by a man who was lingering ten feet behind. I asked how she was doing and whatever happened to her husband. She remarked that the man behind her was the same man, and his injuries had been substantial.

He looked like a spotted giraffe with real light one-inch skin channels separating darker splotches on his face, nose, neck, scalp, arms, and hands. His vision was slightly impaired with stretches of pink skin webbing from his eyebrows and upper cheeks. His ears were stubs of twisted gristle and very grotesque.

She advised me that she was still married and they are in still in love, only this time without any more turmoil. She added she was given only probation for the soup attack, because it was viewed as a defensive reaction to her husband's initial attack. Her husband was given probation as well and didn't serve any time in jail.

I smiled at both of them and wished them the best of luck. I said I hoped their physical injuries would improve as well as the psychological injuries.

I'm sure their physical and psychological injuries will improve with time. This is an excellent example of human turmoil that resulted in severe injuries. However, the outcome was more emotionally draining and consigned the couple to a life of perpetuity, or a lasting love forever.

CHAPTER 33

THE ANGRY TRUCKER

A radio call directed us over to Wilmington Avenue on the western side of Compton. We were assigned to keep the peace between a husband and wife. We arrived and a woman met us outside the house with her mother.

Both of them were crying. They demanded that we stop her husband of ten years from ruining their house. I asked for her the reasons why he would be doing such a thing, and she stated, "He just flipped!" I asked her and her mom to stay outside while we went inside to talk with her husband.

We went up to the porch and knocked on the door. The husband came to the door and invited us into the home. He was about six foot five in height, 280 pounds. He was wearing a dark baseball cap and wiping his eyes with a handkerchief. He wept as he began to tell us what had really happened.

He stated he was a truck driver and had been out on the road for the last three days. He came home at least a day early and walked into his home. He went looking for his wife and opened the bedroom door and saw his wife in bed with another man, having sex. The man jumped up and ran out of the bedroom, completely naked, into the backyard. He left his clothes and shoes in the bedroom, and the wife remained in bed covering herself up with a bed sheet.

The husband became irate and started to yell at his wife as she dressed and went into the front yard. The husband began to smash his fists through the drywall and was mumbling something about her and her boyfriend. The wife went next door and summoned the police to stop him from damaging his home.

I went back outside while my partner stayed inside with the husband. I related what the husband had told me, and she confirmed his observations and statements.

I informed her if they had been married for ten years, the home belongs to both of them. I went on to state that if he wanted to destroy the house, he certainly could do it, as long as it didn't threaten the safety of the neighbors.

She said that that was not right to destroy the whole house because she had been caught having sex with another man. I advised her there didn't have to be a reason. Either one of them could destroy the home as they saw fit. Again, however, if they decided to destroy the home, it could not jeopardize the safety of the neighborhood.

I left her and her mom on the sidewalk and returned to the inside of the home. I explained the situation to the husband, and he asked me outright,

"So I can destroy the home as I see fit?" I responded, "Yes, as long as you don't jeopardize the safety of the neighborhood!"

The husband agreed and commenced to destroy his home, ranting about his wife's lack of loyalty to him. He added that if he couldn't keep the home, then there wouldn't be much of a home left after he got through with his demolition.

I informed him of my concerns about the safety, specifically the gas and electrical connections that must be guarded against any damage that might cause sparks and or an explosion.

We walked around the home as the husband was destroying everything in sight, throwing articles from drawers and closets.

He came into the kitchen and tossed all of the kitchen utensils, plates, glasses, and pots and pans everywhere. He grabbed the refrigerator and pulled it from the top and sent it downward, gashing the double-door kitchen stove. All canned goods and boxed foods were ripped open and tossed throughout the home. He came down his hallway and stopped at the full-length wall furnace and began punching the ribbed steel vents that distributed the heat. About the fifth punch his hand began to bleed quite a bit from the sharp steel vents, so I grabbed several kitchen towels and handed them to him so he wouldn't damage his hands anymore. He then resumed punching the vents until it was all caved inward. He punched through walls as he walked throughout the home. He was of course weeping and venting all of his frustrations as much as he could.

I kept quiet most of the time, empathizing with his trauma, but I gave him guidance about what not to damage for fear of fire or electrical shortage. He cried nearly the whole time and was very responsive to me and the other officer.

Near the end, he picked up a metal folding ironing board and tossed it three times at the center of the large front living-room window. Finally the window broke, and he announced that he was finished.

The husband rinsed off his bloody hands in the kitchen sink and carefully covered them with fresh kitchen towels. We walked him outside and over to his truck as he got in and closed the door, still crying.

He drove off, and we discussed the situation with the wife and her mother, who were now coming into the home. The wife was crying, and the mother was consoling her. There wasn't much more that we could help her with, nor was there any need for any more talking. Enough was said in word and deed.

CHAPTER 34

HOLY CAPTAIN

It was a busy night, and everyone was rushing all over the place. The desk was busy shoving out calls, and the night seemed like it was going nuts with all sorts of activity. Several units were inside booking five or six suspects, a couple of other units were at Los Campanas Hospital getting suspects treated, released, and approved prior to booking. I had just dropped off several completed reports and was going back into the field. As I left the parking lot, another patrol car was coming in with another suspect in custody.

One of the older officers was showing the watch sergeant in his office several confiscated weapons he found in a suspect's car. Several other officers were carrying out various tasks and procedures.

One of the rifles being examined in the watch sergeant's office appeared to have a hidden serial number inside the stock assembly. He was in the process of removing the stock, holding the rifle away from himself and slightly above his head, while he was seated at his desk.

Suddenly a loud report of a gun blast came from the rifle as it discharged a round directly across the sergeant's desk. It narrowly missed the officer standing in front of the desk and went through the opened doorway, across the hall, and into the glass that surrounded the captain's office. It passed through the window on the door, and into three neatly pressed police uniforms that were hanging on hangers, on a hall tree, with the dry cleaner's thin plastic shrouds covering them.

The sergeant was embarrassed and very concerned about where the bullet had ended up, hoping no one was injured or killed. After a diligent search they found the round. It was lodged in one of the wall units that encased the office.

Twenty-four holes were punched into those uniforms, because they were so neatly and tightly packed. That meant eight holes for each set of uniforms.

By the time all of us on the shift found out about the accidental discharge, the shift had ended. But the lesson of the damage something like that could do was well demonstrated by the sergeant. Furthermore it was much better for the accident to occur when the sergeant had the weapon, rather than one of us.

It was a good lesson on weapon safety.

CHAPTER 35

UBIQUITOUS DOPE

Narcotics were absolutely everywhere. There was so much dope, it was unbelievable. Almost every arrest involved at least one of the major drugs: reds, rainbows, yellow jackets, black mollies, bennies, heroin, LSD, and marijuana. (Not so much cocaine or methamphetamine, because the other drugs were abundant; cocaine and methamphetamine really didn't really become common until the eighties.)

Seeing individuals standing in the middle of the street or on the sidewalk, totally naked men and women, stoned completely out of their minds was a common occurrence. Capsules would be in their hands or stuck to their naked bodies. Bubbling and gurgling sputum dripping out of their mouths was a common sight.

A lot of the juveniles were intoxicated on a whole variety of toxins like airplane glue, spray paint, and gasoline. I went into many areas where young juveniles had a gasoline saturated rag lying atop their faces, inhaling its deadly contents. Most juveniles were literally "stuck" on inhaling airplane glue. All of the doctors who examined these kids said that if they kept using either of these two toxins, gas and toluene, they would inevitably perish as a consequence within a year's time depending on their usage.

Toluene was the toxic ingredient and went several years without any intervention by any state laws prohibiting its usage. Many young teenage children permanently lost their minds or perished because of using it. It was in airplane glue, found in most retail store and paint suppliers.

The brain would actually shrink because of its poisonous elements and effects. When their parents were told what they were doing, they were also told that an end was near if they continued. I'll bet that today you won't find too many of those individuals alive. But if you do, they won't be the sharpest knives in the drawer, and they might still be in isolation because of their antics years ago, awaiting the end.

I was following a suspicious auto and was about ready to stop the car when suddenly a motorcycle, a "hog," sped past my unit in the opposite direction. I dropped my attention to the car I was about to stop, went after the motorcycle, and attempted to stop it near Compton High School.

The driver was a heavily bearded bare-chested adult. He was wearing his colors and biker Levi's pants, chains and heavy black motorcycle boots. I don't believe he even thought of pulling over; he decided to give me a run for my driving skills; meanwhile I was radioing my course and speed and a description of the biker.

The pursuit lasted for about three minutes and finally came to an end when he was southbound on Acacia Street from Compton Boulevard. He spilled his bike, slipped off the spinning wreckage, and began to run up a driveway. His hog was now spinning slowly in the street just a few feet in front of me.

I jumped out, running full bore after him, and caught up with him just as he was going around a small business and relatively dark, narrow walkway. As I grabbed him, he tossed two huge bags of "bennies" off to the side and began to turn around.

I dropped him to the ground quickly and cuffed him. I think the chase had tired him out. That, coupled with the fact that I was bigger than him, may have had an influence on his decision to fight.

I could hear other units converging to my location, and by the time I came from behind the small business, three units had just arrived. Several of the officers assisted me in placing the hairy thug into the backseat of my unit, and then I went to retrieve the two large bags I saw him toss.

As I came out I was more able to view the contraband and realized I had two one-thousand-tablet bags of "bennies." This amount not uncommon in the area. It was transported by many different methods throughout the city. I was elated by the excitement of the chase, the ease of the arrest and the amount of dope I recovered.

This type of pursuit occurred nearly every day and night. The thought of abandoning my police unit with the keys still inside was tempting, but to leave the keys with the engine running was simply out of the question. Radio cars and were stolen just as easily as civilian cars. I made it a practice that when I left my unit, the shotgun was locked, and the keys were removed every time, no excuses. Also, every time I chased someone I would avoid the same route the suspects took, because it would be easy for the suspects to hide and await you coming right behind them. So if the suspects fled and rounded a corner, I avoided the temptation to round the same corner where they might easily be lying in wait.

Most of these chases and apprehensions were so frequent that it forced one how to track the crooks when the situation arose and became an instinct.

You must remember that to survive, every event must be evaluated. You must sharpen your skills of detection, pursuit, and capture every time or you will become a statistic.

CHAPTER 36

MURDER OF AN IN-LAW

Around the latter part of November 1968, a young, white male, nineteen years old, was on his way to work at the McDonald's located on Long Beach Boulevard and Temple Street. He was trying to get to work by 6:00 p.m. He was going to be a little early.

The young man was driving his hopped-up, clean, two-door Volkswagen southbound on Bullis Road, approaching the red signal light at Rosecrans Avenue. As he stopped his car for the red light, two black men approached on both sides. His windows were already down, and one of them stuck a gun in his face and demanded entry into his car. There wasn't much he could do when both of the thugs entered his car; one sat in the rear, the other sat in the right front seat. They ordered him to drive on, so he continued southbound on Bullis Road and made a right turn onto Elm Street and stopped at Long Beach Boulevard.

There something occurred, and one of the suspects shot the young man in the head. He died seated in his car. Both suspects fled the scene and no description of either suspect was given. The suspects took no money and left the Volkswagen in the street. It was a scenario that was occurring frequently in the city of Compton. There were no workable leads. However, this case was going to be quite a bit different, and handled with great care and fervor.

First off, that young man was the brother-in-law of Tom M., my fellow cadet, friend, and fellow officer. Second, that young man's dad was an officer with the Los Angeles Police Department, presently at the rank of captain of the LAPD Narcotics Bureau. This meant that this was going to be handled quickly, efficiently, and with extensive and amplified zeal.

The very next day around three o'clock, fifty LAPD detectives came to the Compton Police Department to assist on that specific case. Before the end of the shift was over, they would round up well over two hundred suspects to be interviewed at the station. Later the same day, it was learned that one of the suspects had lost a shoe. That shoe was found under a mobile home in a small trailer park on the southwest corner of Bullis Road and Rosecrans Avenue, right across the street from where the carjacking took place. Within a week, the killers were arrested and charged, and later they were convicted of the murder.

That episode of police assistance impressed many of us. The number of officers available for a thorough investigation was astounding. They weren't impeded like us, by the rising of political and racial obstacles being erected to paint a picture of a model city.

If we were to be killed in the line of duty, we wondered, who would help our investigators? Would the city of Compton even want to acquire additional investigators? Most likely not. Compton was so caught up with catering to the slightest suggestion of police abuse or impropriety toward the black community, they would stop at nothing to improve the overall picture of the city. They might toss any one of us onto the pyre. This situation caused many of the officers to reevaluate their employment in the department. It was an incessant reminder that reverse racial prejudice would raise its ugly head many times over the next year.

CHAPTER 37

THE CODE THREE RUN

One of the more seasoned and well-liked officers was working one rainy evening. Nothing much was happening, and he was going from call to call. He was doing his best to stay as dry as possible like the rest of us, although he made several suspicious car stops. He received an assistance call from another Compton unit who needed backup. So he responded with the shortest ETA over the radio to the dispatch center and therefore was assigned the assist.

He was traveling southbound on Wilmington Boulevard, focusing on getting to the assistance call as soon as possible. The wet road was inhibiting his quick response, creating problems like visibility, road, and traffic conditions. In addition, the performance of the patrol car's acceleration and brakes was compromised. He was traveling southbound at around 65 mph into an intersection that appeared to be clear of vehicles. His red lights and siren were on.

As he entered the intersection, another car appeared going westbound on Alondra Boulevard at approximately 35 mph, perpendicular to the officer's direction. They both collided in a T-bone configuration and crushed both cars massively.

That crash killed a mother and two of her small children instantly and severely injured the father. The officer was himself severely injured with major back injuries. The officer was able to come back to work, but with restrictions.

This collision was terrible and caused great deal of pain for all of us, because it was determined that it was the officer's fault for not driving with due regard to the safety of others. To a police officer, the term prima facie speed actually means traveling at a speed with due regard to safety of others and the conditions of the road. In this case, the officer was determined to have been driving at an excessive speed and not considering the rainy conditions that inhibited his control of the car and his visibility. It was determined as well that the officer also lacked the consideration of the opposing traffic and unfortunately caused the deaths of three individuals, and significantly injured the only survivor, the father.

This decision also had a great effect on my future and added a sense of decency and common sense to my career. An officer must be considerate of others. Although consideration is many times visually absent when completing police functions or tasks, it must remain one of the critical traits. Merely being tough, rough, and indifferent to all cannot prevail. A policeman must be cautious in all endevors or serious consequenses will occur.

CHAPTER 38

HORSE SENSE

No doubt the Sheriff's Academy taught many things to survive the atmosphere of law enforcement. Many special situations were addressed and thought over carefully, in order to avoid confusion and give guidance to all involved on how to handle nearly everything. However, there are many things that arise that were never discussed at all, and unfortunately, those would be handled by "the seat of the pants," also known as "flying blind."

It was a slow night, and I was working the early morning shift from 11:00 p.m. to 7:00 a.m. For some reason it was very slow and cold; nothing was happening. Even the radio was silent. I was working with a partner, and we were gabbing back and forth about how to correct all the ills of society and make the world a better place to live in.

It was around three, and we decided to go and grab a cup of coffee over on the east side of town. over by Compton Airport. The radio then gave us a call of loose horses on Greenleaf Avenue in the Richland Farms area.

We kind of chuckled at the call because of what we could do. We were in uniform, and we were going into a farm environment to chase down a few horses. But we acknowledged the call and gave an ETA of a few minutes. As we came onto Greenleaf Avenue, we noticed the street lighting was minimal. As we drew close to where the horses were seen last, we parked our car, turned off our head lamps, shut the engine off, turned down the radio, and got out. We were trying to see if we could hear the horses or see them with the aid of our flashlights.

We saw nothing. It was very quiet and very, very dark. We assumed the animals probably strayed across Greenleaf Avenue southbound into the huge vacant dirt and grassy area just north of Artesia Boulevard.

We were about thirty feet apart, walking around casually. We intermittently shone our flashlights and talked back and forth to each other as we looked for the horses. With no lights on, it was pitch black and a bit unnerving. We descended into the vacant lot approximately a hundred feet. I then detected a strange noise coming from my right side. My partner was to my left thirty to forty feet away from me, so it couldn't be him. I turned my flashlight and saw something moving. I was hoping it was several of the horses just aimlessly walking about or grazing on the tall clumpy grass that flourished closer to the creek bed several hundred feet farther south.

I informed my partner that something was over toward my side and moving around, and we drew closer to the muffled sounds. I intentionally kept my flashlight off and so did my partner, so we wouldn't upset the usually quiet atmosphere the horses were enjoying.

Without any doubt I heard many thumps coming straight toward me, so I turned my flashlight on and saw four horse faces coming directly at me about twenty feet away. I yelled to my partner, "Holy shit, they're here!" I ran about twenty feet over to where I'd just seen a large tree off to my left. I hid behind the tree, just as five or six of the full-size horses passed my position.

I yelled for my partner, who was out in the dark somewhere. He replied as he came upon my position and stated he was okay. We both laughed at the situation, because it scared the hell out of both of us and considered the outcome lucky. No one would have believed it if I'd been trampled to death by a small herd of horses, which meant I should have known better.

My uniform was an absolute mess, covered with the lightly powdered soil and damp clumps of grass across my shoes and pants cuffs.

We discussed how close the horses had come to me and visualized the possible outcome. I learned from the episode what not to do the next time a similar call came through.

Again, this surprising event taught me that noise and light discipline weren't the only important survival tools that I possessed; common sense guided me to the tree and to safety. Fortunately the running horses returned to their corral not a half block away and were secured without our intervention.

CHAPTER 39

LANDMARK DECISION

I was working the day shift when, close to noon, I received a call to a robbery that just occurred at the Compton Feed and Grain store, located on the northeast corner of Wilmington and Greenleaf Avenues. That day was a little different, because my brother Vince was riding along with me. He was wearing a suit for his court appearance and decided to ride along with me for a little while as he waited for court. (Personally, I think he was trying to learn a few good patrol procedures from me so he would look better for the brass.)

When we arrived, I walked through the front door of the store and called out to whoever was there. No one answered, so I crossed the front sales area, which was rather small. Vince shadowed my approach as we came in the front door, and we met near the cash register. We looked around, waiting for someone to respond to my notice.

I advised Vince that no one was answering my calls. We both felt rather suspicious and pointed our revolvers in front of us as we moved inward. We cautiously walked past the front counter area and cash register and into the rear of the store.

The storeroom was slightly darker, with old bare wood that covered the ceiling, open rafters, walls, and floor area. It also had a bland animal smell of "feed and seed" with a mix of the urea, from urine, that rats and mice leave behind when scurrying around open feed and seed storage.

We passed neatly stacked large bags of animal feed in low rows, about five to six bags in each stack, and saw a pair of legs in dark pants and brown street shoes sticking out near one stack of feed bags. The legs were motionless.

We looked around carefully for any movement and listened for any sounds. As we drew closer to the legs, we observed an older white male, around seventy-three years old, lying in a supine position, his eyes were closed.

I saw a four-inch blotch of dark-red blood, on the front of his plaid flannel shirt and a small hole like a gunshot wound near his heart area. I felt his carotid artery on the left side of his neck and couldn't sense any pulse. Vince watched my actions and the area behind my position.

I determined that the man was dead. Then I noticed a slightly heavyset woman lying face down on the cement floor near the rear loading dock.

There was a wide receiving door that was open wide, allowing an ample amount of sunlight inside the darkened loading area.

I moved closer to the motionless white woman, who was about sixty-five years old. She was clad in a light cotton dress and a white apron. I saw one small hole in her back surrounded by a small three-inch blotch of dark-red blood. I felt the left side of her carotid artery and couldn't detect a pulse in her neck, either.

I motioned to Vince that she was dead as well, and we moved around the storeroom and thoroughly checked for any other victims or suspects. I walked carefully into a small room just off the storeroom and looked inside the room. It was a small kitchen with a round table and a couple of chairs away from the table's edge, as if someone just stood up from them and walked away.

On the table were two small bowls of partially consumed spaghetti with the forks sitting inside the bowls. It appeared that the owners were interrupted while eating, and they got up together and were confronted in the rear storeroom.

Both the man and the woman were shot in the storeroom area. I believe if, instead of shooting him, a hundred-pound feed sack was placed on the elderly man, it would have prevented him from getting up.)

After we concluded that the place was empty and safe, we walked to the radio car and radioed for detectives were needed. We had to go next door and call the report in via the telephone. Procedures required that homicide detectives be summoned over the hard-line telephone, because the media monitors all police radio frequencies. Any mentioning of a homicide over the car radio would alert the media and they would respond immediately to the crime scene and cause unnecessary interruptions while the crime scene is being handled.

Not that human life has a value, but in these two senseless murders, the crooks got away with, was a mere thirty dollars.

The investigation led detectives to a seventeen-year-old black kid named Buzzy, and his friend. This thug used his father's unique pistol and bullets. The bullets were a rare find, because they had distinctive red-colored wadding that was from England.

What took place next was baffling. When the detectives were questioning the juvenile who shot the couple, he asked to speak to his mother and father. The detectives refused and stated that he could only talk to an attorney. The California Supreme Court reversed the conviction and ruled that when a juvenile defendant asks to speak to his parents, it's the same as requesting an attorney. Buzzy was asking for help from his parents, and for that reason alone, he escaped the conviction and was freed because his right to communicate with his parents was abridged.

I've heard this case many times and was in fact extremely sensitive to the outcome of that trial. I have nothing nice to say about that situation or the court's decision to let a double murderer loose to kill again.

But I'll leave anyone to look up that case decision and review the outcome. Don't forget to take the time to run the juvenile and see what happened to him. Is he dead now, in prison, or raising a family and paying his taxes like a good American? You be the judge!

Oh, don't even ask about the dead man and his wife. I'm sure they weren't read their rights to remain alive or even to finish that damn spaghetti.

What if that was your mom or dad? What would you think?

CHAPTER 40

LOS ANGELES SHERIFF'S DEPARTMENT, FIRESTONE PARK STATION: THE ARRIVAL

My brother and I had just arrived on May 20, 1969. We scurried into a meeting with the captain, who welcomed us to the station and explained the turmoil in Compton. We didn't have a clue what the meeting was all about and felt a bit uneasy. The introduction was very cordial and he asked Vince and me to sit in two chairs positioned in the front of the captain's desk. He introduced himself as Melvin W. and right away directed our attention to the turmoil at the Jack in the Box located at 150th and Wilmington, in the city of Compton.

The captain advised us that the reason that the LA County sheriffs didn't come to Compton's numerous requests for backup or emergency assistance was that Compton failed to apply themselves directly into the mix. He went on to say that Compton knew very well that that particular spot had been a hotbed of assaults and racial tension for months on end.

He advised us that although the police department knew very well what was going on, they never cancelled days off, vacations, or reserves to that area because Compton always relied on the sheriff's department to come and save the day.

To me, his explanation seemed way above our pay grade, but we understood why the captain found it necessary to explain in detail. Please keep in mind that my brother's time at Compton Police Department was roughly three and a half years, and I had a year and a half of service.

When the Compton officers were overwhelmed with a large violent crowd, the sheriff's department came in and kicked some serious ass in order to help the Compton officers. The cops were very thankful, but the city blamed all of the unnecessary use of force on the sheriff's department, and the sheriff's department was offended at the numerous accusations of brutality went without the city taking part in the justification for the use of force.

Vince and I were both assigned training officers who seemed rather strange, but for indoctrination and learning the sheriff's way it was understandable. Vince's training officer had less time in law enforcement than he had. He was very amiable and simply glad they both paired up. He had a great personality, he was a hard charger, and he was just as big as my brother, who was six two and about two hundred pounds.

My training officer was a little strange. He was small in stature, and had a cocky and arrogant personality and a mean streak that was easily visible. I was six three and 215 pounds. He treated me rudely and as if I had no idea what I was doing, but that was okay; I had been there before, and I knew the routine.

We were assigned to work the shift from 5:00 p.m. until 1:00 a.m. Our area of assignment for the most part a Willowbrook car called 15B. The area was really busy—and hot with all sorts of crime. It was the area just north of the city of Compton, the same area where my brother, Vince, was beaten like a dog and had his gun taken away about two years before.

Willowbrook is a rough and tough area, and it had a lot of nice folks living in the plagued community. However, the community as a whole could be described as a sponge that absorbed all crime and criminals from the surrounding areas of Watts, Compton, Athens, and Firestone. On the eastern side of these communities was the Los Angeles riverbed that paralleled the 710 freeway. Oddly, the infusion of crime stopped at the riverbed.

Gangs were forming in the early seventies and would grow significantly over the next thirty years. The gangs' strength came from families that literally gave up on their children and couldn't handle the constant onslaught of assaults, murders, and the crude, blatant disregard for life and property. Most of the communities could be racially categorized as black, with a few groups of Hispanics sporadically intermingled. Samoans were mostly around 215th and Avalon Boulevard.

The idea at Firestone Park Station was to make arrests quickly and avoid being given calls for service. Routinely we went to our area and within minutes we had already made our first hook. We hunted for the most deadly and dangerous felons and, of course, dope dealers.

When returning to the station you would announce your car and that you were coming in with two or three arrests. This would alert the desk that you could not handle any calls for service until you finished your booking and processing, which usually took up to an hour. Once finished, you needed to check the desk for any calls or assignments in your area and get into the field as soon as possible. The reports would be completed in the field as you were driving around and adapting to all of the bumps, turns, stops, and accelerations. Of course, while completing the reports in the field, you and your training officer would answer any calls for service and make car and pedestrian stops frequently.

Arrests were so plentiful that the feeling of accomplishment when hunting for crooks was diluted. We were selecting the more important or higher categories of felons. It seemed that there were so many felons in the area, I couldn't imagine anyone on the street not being a felon.

You might not agree with me and feel I was just a felon zealot, but we filled the entire backseat of our car many times. Each arrest could represent an individual crime or a group arrest for robberies or assaults with deadly weapons.

Robberies, assaults, and burglaries were rampant, and coming in with three felonies was not a stretch. Foot pursuits went on every hour, and it was important to respond quickly to calls for assistance without dispute or delay.

Food flew every time you chose a slow moment to take a lunch break. The food wouldn't be any good anyway, and you could always order another later on.

We were always ready for vehicle pursuit; the number of stolen cars in the area seemed infinite. Radio communication was kept at a minimum, but we had a communication system to call for help for any fellow car.

Firestone Park Station's area started at Fifty-Ninth Street to the north to just south of Sepulveda Boulevard in the city of Carson. The western border was Central Avenue, the eastern boundary on the eastern city limits of Cudahy; farther south, the Los Angeles riverbed arched around Compton and the northern city limits of Long Beach.

Gunplay happened every night, whether you pointed your gun at nearly every stop, held your own firearm along your leg, or just rested your gun on your lap. A gun was just as important as the pencil to write your reports. Even as a trainee, I relished the idea of walking into building and being confronted by an armed assailant. I was good with my weapon and carried a boot knife for backup.

Several of the other deputies carried two guns, just in case they lost their primary weapon in a fight or brawl. My feelings were mixed. I felt very comfortable with my single sidearm and my boot knife. Of course my thinking was that I was a retired journeyman meatcutter and could handle a knife better than most other officers. I carried the knife just in case something occurred and I couldn't get to my gun in time. I knew exactly where to put the blade.

Most of the deputies were enthusiastic, sharp, and very funny. They goofed off around about me and where I came from and really had a good time screwing around with anything I was near. This meant they tried many times to provoke crooks into setting me up. I took anything and everything with a grain of salt in order to avoid being classified as a "fish," or newcomer, oblivious to what was really going on in the streets. Other trainees weren't so lucky. They confided in me, because they knew where I came from and that I knew the ropes pretty well from my Compton experience.

Several of the trainees were really scared about what was happening to them with their training officers and asked many questions, which I was glad to answer. I was very attentive to my own training officer and watched him closely. Something just didn't gel and seemed out of place, but I carried on with full enthusiasm and attention to details.

During the first several weeks of training we rushed around and were involved in many arrests and many calls. My training officer put us in the forefront on everything possible and then some.

Shootings and knifings were rampant every night, and a variety of tasks were thrown at me to see if I could handle the pressure and still maintain the focus for report writing and deputy protocol.

CHAPTER 41

THE MIRACLE MARKET

My training officer and I were just clearing the station from booking two suspects at around 9:30 p.m. We were eastbound on Firestone Boulevard and a call for assistance came from our sister unit at 130th street and Willowbrook Avenue. That request was for a burglary now call, and the suspects were in the location.

My training officer hit the accelerator and we sped to Alameda Boulevard and southbound at approximately 100 mph. We were dodging cars in and out of the southbound lanes with our red lights on and siren blaring.

Normal traffic was traveling around 35–40 mph, and my training officer wanted to get there fast, so he sped up and swerved many times, negotiating around a moderate amount of southbound civilian traffic.

We were coming to a very busy intersection at Imperial Highway and saw many cars crossing perpendicular to us, east- and westbound, at approximately 40–45 mph. My training officer was almost at the intersection when a car in front of us turned into our southbound lane and direction of travel.

My training officer tapped the brakes slightly, which caused the patrol car to spin to the right. We spun around full circle, at least two times, and actually came into the intersection backward in a straight trajectory at approximately 90 mph.

The traffic on Imperial Highway continued to cross directly in front of and behind us, so close it was as if we had a protective shroud or cloaking device around our car as we sped out of control, backward, for at least two full city blocks. Our car traveled diagonally across Alameda Boulevard and the rear wheels slowed enough to where they gently bumped the eastern curb and stopped.

We looked at each other and caught our breath, and leaned our heads backward and breathed a sigh of relief. We both knew full well that we just kissed death on the lips, and somehow we didn't get killed or kill someone else.

My training officer the slammed down the accelerator and sped out in a fishtail, smoking the tires and continuing our course to 130th and Willowbrook Boulevard. A follow-up call coming from the same sister unit, stated they were holding their positions for our announced estimated time of arrival (ETA).

As we came upon the location, called the Miracle Market, we saw at least six to eight units there already, reacting to the initial assistance call. Several units were on the north side of the small market, and several more were on the south side of 130th street.

When we stopped, I ran across another deputy as I was scaling a ten-foot wooden and corrugated-steel fence swathed with barbed wire along the top. He cautioned me that several other deputies were already in the back of the market. I looked down the tall fence, and saw deputies grabbing a suspect as he ran by them trying to get away. They threw him down in the center of the yard, which was covered with dirt and rocks.

The deputies and the suspect were yelling, and I figured no one had checked the back door yet, so I jockeyed myself to the back door, just as the deputies were cuffing the suspect they had captured.

I quietly turned the handle, located on the left side of the door, and pushed in lightly. I felt something stopping the door from opening any farther than a foot and a half. I shone my flashlight onto the lower level and saw the bottoms of a pair of black high-top tennis shoes against the door.

I shut off my flashlight and leaned my shoulder against the door. I pushed harder and carefully peered around the door and over the black high top tennis shoes and spotted a black man lying motionless, face down and away from the door. I shone my light on him. His eyes were closed and blood was coming from his mouth. I spotted brain matter splattered from the top of his head onto the cement flooring and other miscellaneous items nearby.

Oddly enough, no one had mentioned that shots were fired, and fortunately, I came across the dead body first so I could announce to all that a dead body was partially blocking the rear door. I stepped farther into the store, and other deputies came in behind me. We quickly cleared the market of any other suspects.

Then the handling unit deputy pulled opened a corner of the solid sheet of plywood that was blocking the entire front window. That same window was apparently smashed a week earlier during another burglary. The deputies crawled into the market and met up with us inside and stood near the dead body.

My training officer then came into the market and asked the handling deputy why he didn't let everyone know that he had fired off rounds. He said it happened just as everyone was arriving, when the second suspect was coming out the back door. The handling deputy stated he was pulling the sheet of plywood away from the window with one of his hands and had his gun in his other hand. He started to come into the market by stepping over the window ledge. Suddenly the suspect appeared at the back door with a rifle in his hand, and he was pointing the rifle in the deputy's direction.

The deputy immediately fired one round from his revolver as he backed up and dove outside the market through the boarded-up window. He and his partner stayed in their outside positions until help arrived, and he didn't know if he had hit anything.

We all looked around and found the rifle the dead suspect had in his hands. It was resting on top of a nearby refrigerator not three feet away from the deceased suspect. The only problem was that the rifle was in fact a pellet gun instead of a real rifle. Why in the hell would a suspect point a pellet gun at a deputy armed with a real gun? Was he trying to scare the deputy or make the deputy back up and out of the market? Who knows?

The deputy went on about his business and was awaiting the homicide unit. The owner arrived about thirty minutes later. He came into the market and stood about thirty feet away looking at the body that was on the floor. When the owner was asked about any weapons in the market, the owner said the only weapon he owned was the pellet rifle on top of the refrigerator.

So based on that new information, it was agreed that the deceased suspect took the pellet rifle from atop the refrigerator when the deputies were coming in through the window. He then pointed it at the deputy and may very well have tried to shoot it. When he was shot, the rifle was tossed or thrown right back on top of the refrigerator exactly where the owner kept it.

Whoa! You've got to be kidding me. That story was a bit unpalatable, but I was a trainee. What the hell did I know? I'm sure there would be many that will come to that same conclusion.

We were then ordered by radio to return to the station and contact the watch commander. We came into the station and contacted the watch commander. He wanted us to transport the sole captured suspect from the Miracle Market, attempt to find out his identity, and try to find out who the deceased suspect was. Unfortunately when we spoke to the suspect, it turned out the he was in a complete state of oblivion. He'd had the living snot knocked out of him when he was captured and was not responding to any questions whatsoever. It was as if he was drunk and out of his mind as we placed him into our car and headed back down to the Willowbrook area.

We drove around with the suspect and had him peer out the window and attempt to identify his or the deceased suspect's home. That detail took us at least two hours of traveling around slowly until he was finally able to identify his home. We went up to the door to confirm his identity. His mom answered the door, and my training officer took her name, her son's name, and the name of the deceased suspect, without letting the mom know that her son's best friend was dead.

We advised her that because he was eighteen years old, he was going to be taken to the jail ward of USC Medical Center and treated for his injuries. He was going to be charged with burglary. It was left up to the detectives if an additional charge of homicide would be added.

CHAPTER 42

CAUGHT BETWEEN A ROCK AND A HARD SPOT

Later on, several other situations developed where I was placed in a position where my integrity was tested and strained. I viewed it as a very compromising position to be placed in, and I felt my career was turning into a series of illegal acts for which I could very well go to jail. I was quite puzzled how my training officer was doing things that seemed illegal, but I didn't stop or question his tenacious abilities.

We continued on for another month and a half, but the position I was in was becoming very strained and unstable, pushing me to make a decision that scared the living hell out of me. I was thinking that jail was imminent if I continued. I knew I couldn't say anything to anyone, because common wisdom said that "snitching off" on your training officer would mean you're through with law enforcement, and there was the possibility of physical retaliation, too.

I talked it over with my brother, who was concerned on several occasions when he saw and noted things that were not right where I was in on part of the operation, but as a trainee, an unwilling participant.

Several weeks went by and I was conversing with another trainee who was scared to death of what his training officer was doing and couldn't stop worrying. He was shaking like crazy. He said he was scared of the overall attitude his training officer had against him, and that it involved some very serious crimes he might be linked to if his training officer was ever confronted. All I did was to listen to him vent, but it made me think twice about my own position, which seemed even more challenging and risky. After just about four months of training it was enough for me. I was forced to do something I dreaded, but it had to be done, or I was going to face going to prison for something I could have stopped.

I walked into Firestone Park Station and went directly into the sergeant's office at around 5:30 p.m. I asked the desk sergeant if I could talk to the on-duty lieutenant. The desk sergeant asked me why a trainee needed to speak to a lieutenant about anything. His tone indicated I was much too dumb to talk to anyone above the rank of sergeant. I advised him that I wanted to quit the department and go back to the Compton Police Department. He nearly fell out of his chair. His cocky, arrogant attitude changed immediately. I was serious, and he knew it, and he asked me to follow him to the watch commander's office.

I followed him, still wearing my street clothes, and met with the lieutenant. The lieutenant, who was pretty easygoing, asked me why I wanted to leave the department and seemed politely concerned. I replied that I just wanted to return to Compton and get out of the whole training program and the Los Angeles Sheriff's Department. I indicated that I was very comfortable with Compton PD. I said that I missed the personnel there and liked the whole Compton operation much more than the sheriff's department.

The situation was obvious, and the lieutenant knew I wanted out, and now. He stated that he wanted me to go home and talk it over with my wife. I needed to realize what was about to occur. He added that tomorrow I could return and give him an answer, but with a much clearer mind.

I knew it was a delay tactic, but the lieutenant was kind and decent with his offer, and it seemed more beneficial to discuss the situation with my wife, as well as give myself a little time to reconsider what I was about to do.

The problem was that my wife had no idea what I was doing at work, nor was she aware of what was going on with my training officer. I kept all serious issues to myself and shared some of the concerns with my brother and him only.

I left the station and traveled slowly south to Compton Police Department and talked with the administrative captain. I informed him that I was considering coming back to work with the department, because I missed the atmosphere and personnel.

He was extremely encouraging and quickly hustled me back into the department in a matter of thirty minutes. I knew he had an ulterior motive other than seriously caring about my return; but my return would dampen the terrible attitude among fellow Compton officers about the changing city. We shook hands, and he repeated that he was highly appreciative of my return. He expected me to come back the next day for finalization.

I'll admit he made me feel very good about coming back. But I was then rehashing the negative thoughts about the changing city and the reason why twenty-three of the city's police officers, including my brother and me, fought to abandon the police department in the first place. Boy, I felt rather numb and dumb about everything, but I knew if I returned to Compton, I wouldn't worry about winding up in jail. These thoughts were going through my mind as I was leaving the administrative captain's office and coming down the central staircase.

Lo and behold, as I was coming down the stairs I ran into my fellow Compton PD officer and friend, Tom M., and he was with none other than another Firestone Park training officer named Bob S.

Just seeing these two together startled me enough, but what was even more ironic was that Bob S. was the other source of field strife for the trainee who had the shakes and was emotionally near his breaking point.

Tom on the other hand, had quit Compton Police Department about a month ahead of me, and went to the Los Angeles Police Department and was very happy with his choice. I had completely forgotten that Tom had mentioned before that he had been good friends with Bob S. for quite a while, so our chance meeting was very unique and timely. They both greeted me with a handshake and casually asked why I was there. Knowing Tom very well and trusting his judgment encouraged my candid answer. I admitted my deepest concerns to Tom and Bob, even though Bob was a training officer and apparently friends with my training officer; I felt a strong sense of trust and sincerity with them together. So I laid out my training officer's method of harsh training and rudeness as the primary concern; but never mentioned the real acts of concern that were ultimately going to land me in prison.

Bob S. was very warm and casual and remarked that my training officer was a major prick, and everyone else at the station thought of him in the same way. He added that he was kicked out of West Hollywood and Antelope Valley stations because of his rude and crude behavior and that all personnel at those stations thought he was an arrogant prick with a capital P.

Now I was really confused. Why had Firestone Park Station taken him and made him a training officer in the first place? If they knew about his behavior and past problems, then why in hell did they even consider him as training officer material? Did the term "vicarious liability" seem to fit this situation? Like a glove!

Bob assured me several times that my training officer wasn't shit, and that I was about to get kicked loose off training anyway, so I wouldn't have to put up with him at all. He assured me as well as Tom that coming back to Compton Police Department was not a good idea because the immense internal turmoil was about to explode.

We spent about thirty minutes in the stairwell discussing the ordeal, and it helped me reconsider my options. I realized I must make a choice overnight. Jesus, I felt as if I was between a rock and a hard spot and really couldn't confer with anyone but myself about my choices, because future conflict with my training officer at Firestone Park Station was inevitable.

We finally parted, and I left to go home after discussing some of the anxieties I was confronting. When I got home, I sat down with my wife and told her that basically I was a deputy sheriff and a policeman at the same time. She didn't question me very much but started to cry about my indecisiveness. She sensed something else was bothering me, but I couldn't tell her. I didn't want her input into something that it was so obvious I had to do, I didn't want her to encourage me to go to the captain at Firestone Park Station and let it all out.

I was up and down all night long, dismayed and perplexed. I finally came to a mature conclusion later the next morning. I informed my wife of what I was about to do, and she wished me good luck as I left for Firestone Park Station.

I arrived early in the afternoon hour and came in with my chest high, poised and ready to talk with the watch sergeant about changing my mind and remaining at the station. The sergeant immediately picked up the phone, called the lieutenant, and told him I was in his office. The sergeant hung up the phone and said the lieutenant wanted to talk with me in his office.

He led me down the hallway, past the briefing room and the small kitchen to the lieutenant's office. The door was closed. I was a little nervous as the sergeant told me to wait outside; he'd be right back. Seconds later the door opened. The sergeant held it open and motioned me inside. As I walked inside I saw two lieutenants and three sergeants, all in uniform. They greeted me and told me to come in and sit down.

I could only guess why so many supervisors were there. All appeared very concerned about what I was about to say. Nervous wouldn't even come close, but my pride and intuition kicked in about my formative decisions and explanations. One of the lieutenants was the first to ask what was going on for me to decide to quit the department after four months as a trainee.

I responded that I simply missed the camaraderie at Compton Police Department and yearned to be back where I knew I was welcome and needed.

The lieutenant asked, "Is it the training?" I answered, "Well, kind of, but not everything!" Another lieutenant spoke up. "It's the training, are you sure?" I repeated, "I'm tired, and have been on training for four months with no end in sight."

Oddly enough, they seemed genuine about their concerns, but something was troubling them about my answers.

A sergeant asked, "Can you handle yourself in the field alone?" I answered, "I was a one-man officer at Compton, and on my own with no problems."

Another sergeant asked, "There must be something else bothering you; what is it?" I said that nothing else was a problem. We went back and forth, and the questions were mostly aimed at finding out just exactly what was the main reason for quitting.

After twenty minutes, one of the lieutenants said, "All right, effective in two days, you're off training! How, do you feel about that?"

I answered, "Great, I'm really pleased."

The same lieutenant then stated, "Your training officer indicated that you are extremely good and hardworking. He said that you would like to stay together. Would you like that?" I hemmed and hawed for about ten seconds and never actually said anything. Finally another lieutenant said, "Okay, if that's it, you're by yourself. What you think about that?"

I said, "Absolutely fine!"

I had been in the watch commanders office for thirty or forty minutes. The lieutenant asked if I had any questions. I said no. "Anything else," said the sergeant? I said no again.

With that, the meeting concluded and all three sergeants and the two lieutenants shook my hand as I stood up. I felt a lot of relief because the strain of the subject matter was effectively avoided.

I opened the door and stepped out, and to my amazement my training officer was three feet away from the door. He said, "What the fuck are you doing in there? I told you that if you want to talk with anyone you must see me first, you dumb fuck!"

At that point, I'd about had it with this guy, and I leaned over to talk to him. I responded sarcastically, "Listen up, I've got two more days with you and then I'm off training. If you talk to me that way in two days, I'm going to kick your ass! I'm going to go get the toys— I'll meet you in the car." That meant I was going to get all the gear ready for patrol and meet him in our assigned unit.

He looked at me with his little squinty eyes and said nothing more as I walked away. He had to retract his comments now and knew full well I didn't give a damn anymore for his training antics and was not in the least bit intimidated.

I took a few minutes to call Compton Police Department. I spoke with the administrative captain and informed him of my change of mind. I said I was sorry for causing such a fuss. He stated that he understood and still left the door open for any other future changes of mind.

A little while later, my training officer came out and got into the car. We rarely talked the whole night. You could cut the anger and hatred with a knife. We didn't stop any cars or anyone on foot. He met with quite a few other deputies and sergeants surreptitiously in the field, and I remained in the car. I knew he was deathly afraid of what I might have told the lieutenants and sergeants, and he didn't have a clue what I had said. At several field meetings with other cars, I caught him pointing his finger at me, obviously critical of what had happened.

I was alone and ready to prove myself as a formidable individual rather than a feebleminded, sycophantic trainee.

The next day, Friday, was no different. We did absolutely nothing. At the end of the shift we parted ways with nothing said. Fortunately, no issues arose.

The next day was Saturday. I was off training and assigned to another older deputy. We worked the north end in the Firestone Park, Florence, and Walnut Park areas and the contract city of Cudahy.

What a great time that was—no drama and a nice, kind, and friendly partner. We worked very well together and made several hooks each evening. After two or three days I was assigned a day car in the east Compton area alone and felt as if I was back in the Compton PD.

One month later another group of trainees hit the station. I was surprised that my training officer was assigned another trainee. That trainee was a light-skinned black deputy who seemed pretty nice and smiled a lot. We made eye contact many times at the station and nodded, but we never talked very much.

I knew very well my training officer was bad-mouthing me to his new trainee, but I watched him for a reaction like I had, and I knew it was coming. I felt a strong sense of empathy for the trainee, and I didn't think he was going to survive as well as I did. I'm sure his training officer focused on not talking to anyone other than him first and used me as an example. He probably said that I was going to get hammered by everyone in retribution somehow.

Within a month, both my former training officer and the trainee were administratively removed from the field. My former training officer was given thirty days off and terminated. The new trainee was given fifteen days off and transferred to Lennox Station. I really felt sorry for the trainee, because he had no clue about what was going on. He was suddenly and totally immersed with his training officer on issues that should have been known by the administration. Or was the trainee an Internal Affairs plant? I'll never know.

Several days later a huge black narcotics deputy, nicknamed T-Bird, bumped into me at the municipal court. He informed me that all of our arrests were being personally reviewed by the captain, and multiple charges against my former training officer were being processed. The charges against him were: planting narcotics on arrested persons, multiple charges of assault with a deadly weapon, using challenging language and berating a local municipal judge, and kidnapping and false imprisonment of a local snitch who was being used by our department's narcotics and detective bureaus.

The last individual was beaten up in the backseat of a patrol car for three hours and then dumped and wheeled out of the back door in the auto salvage yards where Century Station and Detention Facility stands today at Imperial Highway and Alameda Boulevard. I might add that all of the sergeants and lieutenants who were in the office when I came back to the department ended up being chiefs and assistant sheriffs twenty years later. They were very good at the station and well liked by most deputy personnel.

Enough has been spent on the likes of my training officer and good riddance. The punishment was always the same. In order for the department to keep in the favorable eye of the public, nearly all officers who go sour are given an opportunity to resign in lieu of prosecution. The thinking was just to get rid of them at all costs. So that's what happened, and I never saw him again.

CHAPTER 43
DEPUTY ARRESTED

Several months passed. I was driving home on the Long Beach freeway, coming from LA Superior Court around two in the afternoon. The news channel I was listening to broadcast that a deputy sheriff from the Los Angeles County Sheriff's Department named Bob S. had been arrested for murder. Few details were given, but I knew him very well. He was the guy who'd encouraged me to stay on the sheriff's department when I was thinking of quitting. The person who put him away was his trainee, whom I talked with many times, who was always on the brink of an emotional breakdown.

I learned it all was a series of poor judgments, possession of illegal rounds of ammunition, possession of a firearm without a serial number. The most incriminating factors were the notching of his gun for the past five shootings he was involved in, and the keeping of a "gore book" that depicted all of the gruesome incidents that were prevalent at most shootings and knifings.

His latest episode was at a small liquor store in the north end of the Firestone Park area by Ninety-Second Street and Beach Boulevard. There he came across a sixteen-year-old juvenile who was in a hidden room, hiding behind a four-by-eight-foot piece of wall paneling.

The questioning was focused on whether Bob first asked, "How old are you, asshole?" and then shot and killed him, or whether he shot the juvenile first and then asked him, "How old are you, asshole?"

That shooting, coupled with the gore book, notching the handle of his firearm to indicate how many people he had shot, and the special rounds he was using, which happened to be handcrafted exploding rounds, did the trick. The jury found him guilty, and he was sentenced for three years in prison.

I later found out that Bob's trainee, who gave him up as well, suffered a major psychological breakdown and was hospitalized for an extended period of time. He retired from the department. Other deputies who knew and worked around Bob were put into precarious positions and were humiliated and angered by sitting in the superior court hallways waiting to be deposed by the district attorney. That testimony they were about to give was a strain on each deputy because it was part of an undiscussed "silence" they had with one another and it was now going to be forced into the open and used against Bob for his prosecution.

The dilemmas for the deputies were the calls where Bob's use of force was viewed as overly aggressive behavior, and they were there, as indicated in the reports and radio transmissions. Bob's behavior was determined to be way over the legal parameters of justifiable force and in fact viewed as assaultive.

From then on, Firestone Park Station was under suspicion for many things and the internal affairs unit was at the station for a long time.

Quite a few other deputies were arrested and terminated for a variety of charges including theft, planting narcotics, perjury, assault, pimping, possession of stolen merchandise, and the use of throwaway guns and knives.

Aside from the shenanigans that were being revealed, there were a whole lot of good things going on as well. The pride and humor in being a Firestone Park Station deputy was beyond comparison.

It is still said today, "If you never worked Firestone Park Station, you were never a deputy!" Many deputies on the sheriff's department got quite irritated and scoffed at that assumption, but deep inside they knew very well that Firestone Park Station was a very dangerous and deadly place to work. The aggressive behavior, social skills, and teamwork ethic were superb and trusted to be above reproach.

Serious situations that occurred every day at Firestone Park Station were never seen by many other stations. In fact it was literally viewed as a frontline combat zone.

Anyone from Firestone Park Station who is alive today displays a high sense of pride, more than any other unit, that the experience was career molding and helped them form the ability to handle virtually anything pertaining to law enforcement.

CHAPTER 44

RED PANTS

There was the noisy hustle and bustle going on in the locker room as we were all changing our clothes, opening and closing lockers, cleaning our brass, shining our boots and shoes. This of course was all necessary prepping for a possible snap inspection of our uniforms.

We were getting ready for the afternoon briefing, around four o'clock. Two of the funniest deputies, who were partners for quite some time, had lockers in proximity to each other. The two were Paul F. and Walt P. These two guys could keep most of us laughing until our stomachs hurt.

There were about twenty guys prepping themselves in the locker room and talking loudly, laughing, and discussing their sexual exploits. They were just rowdy, short conversations bouncing all over the room's poor acoustics. There was a short lull in the talk, and Paul and Walt yelled out, "What the hell happened to your shorts? That question, coming from Paul and Walt, alerted all of us that something was about to make us all laugh, and we all needed to take a look at what they were talking about. Most of us were in various stages of dress, and drifted over to where Paul and Walt had their lockers.

They were querying another deputy whose locker was next to theirs. That deputy was trying to get his green uniform trousers on as fast as possible, because these two guys would just hammer you with jokes that would embarrass any living soul. Walt echoed Paul. "What the hell is wrong with your shorts?"

They were referring to the deputy's white underwear shorts, which were covered with dried blood, as if he'd cut off his private parts. That deputy's name was Stephen R. He was a very thin male, semibald, and rather unkempt for the most part. Stephen's remark to their question was, "Well, my wife sometimes borrows my shorts when she's on her period, and she forgot to wash them!"

You couldn't imagine the roar of laughter, moaning, and groaning from everyone. They all just ridiculed the hell out of the guy. Stephen really didn't seem to understand why we were shaking our heads and nodding in contempt.

Stephen pulled his pants on over the dried bloody mess and finished dressing rather quickly.

Most of us knew him as out of touch, but not to this extreme, and we just let it go. Nothing else was said other than the usual raised eyebrow when his name was mentioned.

Stephen R. will be mentioned several more times, and each time it becomes more extreme. Obviously "out of touch" is putting it lightly.

CHAPTER 45

A WOMAN SCORNED

I was working the north end with a partner and responding to a fight call at a small bar on Compton Avenue, just north of Firestone Park Station. The male victim was reportedly inside and seated at the bar.

As we walked, our presence created a slight commotion. Everyone in the bar was black, and a few were muttering inaudibly as we moved through various small groups. We were working our way toward the main bar and watching a lot of hands and the reactions of many faces in the dimly lit room. Several of the customers were nodding and motioning us through the crowd toward the bar, indicating the location of the person who called us.

When we reached the bar, a large man came over to us and stated that he was the one who called. He was about six three in height, 240 pounds, casual in his conversation, and a little inebriated. He began to fill in the details of what had occurred.

Earlier that evening, he was at home with his wife, who confronted him about his having an affair with another woman. The conversation between the two deteriorated rapidly and became a screaming argument. He said he had had enough and walked down the street to the bar.

He was determined to get a drink in order to cope with the frustrations and attempt to calm down. He wanted to meet with some of his friends. While he was seated with his friends, his wife came into the bar looking for him, and he didn't know it. Apparently she spotted him seated at the bar and came up behind him. With her right hand, she slammed the rounded face of a medium-sized ball peen hammer into the back of his head. He fell slightly forward and braced himself against the bar. He shook his head slightly, turned around, and saw his wife standing near him with the hammer still in her hand.

She was yelling at him about his affair and how disgusted she was with his lack of loyalty. He punched her in the face and knocked her to the ground. She recovered from the blow, dropped the hammer, and ran out of the bar, furious.

As the male victim stood in front of me, he was very calm and direct about what happened. I noticed he was occasionally feeling the back of his head with his right hand and fingers. As he was feeling the back of his head, he squinted and winced as he touched a certain area. It seemed rather obvious his injury was painful, but he was attempting to minimize his wife's attack because of his breech of sexual loyalty.

I asked him if I could see the injury on his head. He turned his head to display the injury. I looked at the wound and was shocked when I saw a one-inch hole in his skull and a bulging one-inch piece of torn brain matter protruding from it. The brain matter was covered in a light film of blood that shimmered in the poorly lit room, and it seemed as if it was pulsating.

I said, "Jesus Christ, man, that's got to hurt." He responded, "No, I'm okay, it'll stop bleeding pretty soon!" I surmised he was definitely in shock and possibly intoxicated enough to minimize the pain.

I told him that we were getting an ambulance here right now, and he must get medical care immediately. He didn't argue much and followed us out of the bar and on the sidewalk. Once outside and awaiting the ambulance, we obtained the necessary information for our report.

His wife all of a sudden appeared ranting and raving about his infidelity. We immediately informed her that she was under arrest for assault with a deadly weapon, handcuffed her, and placed her, still ranting of course, into the backseat of our patrol car.

I never followed up on this event, but I can only imagine the violence in the entire community was nothing short of an epic human struggle.

CHAPTER 46
TRIBUTE TO A DEPUTY

Walt was assigned alone to work the east Compton area and received a call around 10:30 a.m. to assist an apartment manager on Rosecrans Avenue near Gibson Avenue. When he arrived, the manager informed him that he hadn't heard or seen one of the occupants for at least two weeks. The manager seemed concerned, because no one had seen the forty-year-old lady go in or out of her apartment, and other residents had expressed their concerns as well. (Walt P. is the same deputy who was one of the funniest deputies at Firestone Park Station along with his close friend Paul F.)

Walt assured the manager that together they would first knock on her front door and ask to speak with her to check on her safety. They went to the second floor of the west-facing apartment on the north side of Rosecrans Avenue. It was a little warm and relatively quiet, with very little foot or vehicular traffic.

Walt knocked loudly three times and announced who he was and that the manager was with him. No one answered. He asked the manager to unlock the front door with his passkey. He complied, and Walt knocked on the door again and then opened the door fully and announced, "Sheriff's department, is anyone home?" Still, no one answered.

Walt walked in slowly, thinking that perhaps the woman might have passed away. He was preparing himself for something of that nature. Walt had both hands free as the manager stood by the front door. Walt walked slowly into the living room and then toward the narrow hallway leading to a bedroom.

Every two or three steps he took, Walt announced who he was, to alert the woman that he was a deputy sheriff, accompanied by the apartment manager, to check on her health and make sure everything was okay. Everything remained quiet as Walt went down the hallway. He saw the bedroom door slightly open, four to six inches, from the left side.

As he reached the doorway to the bedroom, he pushed the door open slightly and saw the woman standing not three feet in front of him. She had a crazy look on her face. Her eyes were wide open, and she was pointing a .32 caliber pistol directly at Walt's chest. She fired. Walt was struck in the chest. He grabbed the door as he fell backward, and the door closed behind him.

He fell to the carpeted floor and crawled backward quickly to a nearby closet and scooted himself inside. Walt yelled for the manager to get help quickly, that the tenant had just shot him, and closed the closet door quietly.

Walt said it was quiet for a short bit of time while he was seated on the floor of the closet. He felt cold blood coming down his stomach and pooling in his lap. He thought, *Holy shit, I'm going to die in Compton. This ain't right!* Just then he heard the bedroom door creak slightly as it opened slowly.

(This shooting occurred in the early seventies and bulletproof vests were not yet available.)

Walt was poised inside the closet, his pistol already drawn and pointed, at the ready if she opened the closet door. He heard her walk past the closet door, down the hallway, and into the front room. Walt remained quiet, because his life depended on it.

He listened carefully and thought about what could happen in the next few seconds. He knew full well she was in the front room. He needed to get out of the closet as quietly as possible and see where she was—take the attack to her. Walt knew he was still bleeding. He needed to move cautiously, so he wouldn't bleed out too fast.

He slipped quietly from the closet and focused on anything that he could direct his fire toward. He came to the front-room doorway and saw the woman standing in the open door.

Walt saw bright rays radiating from the female tenant, who was dressed in a light flowered bathrobe, while she stood in the doorway.

The tenant was partially leaning outward and looking slightly to the left as Walt crept up behind her and realized she was looking at the manager, who was downstairs, standing by Walt's patrol car, attempting to use his car radio.

Walt carefully pointed his pistol directly between her shoulder blades and lower back area and did not know if she had abandoned the pistol or not, and felt she was possibly going after the manager to stop him from getting help. Walt then shot her five times in the back. Arresting her was not an option, because Walt felt he was about to lose conciousness and needed to end the threat immediately. She fell forward and out of the doorway— lifeless, facedown—onto the narrow pathway in front of the apartment. She died on the spot.

Walt stepped outside, straddling her corpulent body, which was slowly oozing blood onto the light-colored walkway. He looked toward the manager and yelled to get some help real quick. Walt scanned her body several times and confirmed, based on her not moving or breathing, that she was dead.

Walt saw the manager was having great difficulty attempting to transmit over the microphone he had pulled outside the car. So Walt walked slowly across the narrow pathway, leaving the dead tenant lying on the pathway, and made his way to the stairs. When he reached the stairs, he realized that he was going to have to walk slowly and get to the radio car in order to get help. The manager was still fumbling with the microphone on the open driver's door but was unable to make it work.

Walt was really concerned about his chest injury. He might very well pass out from the blood loss. His tan uniform shirt and green pants were saturated with blood. The manager handed the microphone to Walt, and Walt transmitted his request for emergency assistance for a shooting with a now-deceased suspect and added that he might be gravely injured with a bleeding chest wound. (Walt had the presence of mind to speak slowly and distinctly when he gave his location and condition. In serious situations, deputy radio transmissions may be garbled because of the urgency and cause what is called "rushing the mike.")

A Lakewood Station unit acknowledged the call for help and had the closest ETA. He was assigned the task of a code-three run to get to Walt fast. Fortunately that unit was a former Firestone Park deputy who had transferred to Lakewood Station just two weeks earlier. The responding deputy was about three minutes away.

Many cars driving by the patrol car where Walt was standing in the street slammed on their brakes and careened out of the way when they saw Walt bleeding all over his uniform. Several of them called minutes later about the bloody deputy on Rosecrans Avenue who needed help.

Walt waited patiently for several minutes until the assisting car arrived. The deputy started to get out of the car when Walt opened the rear door of his unit, and asked the deputy to just get him to the hospital quickly. Walt lay halfway down and was coming close to losing his consciousness, as he was telling the deputy what had happened.

Something strange happened when the deputy asked Walt which hospital he wanted to go to. Walt stated, "Saint Francis, of course!" The deputy sped westbound on Rosecrans Avenue and passed Atlantic Boulevard. Walt was puzzled why the deputy passed Atlantic Boulevard, which is a better street to travel, and was continuing westbound on Rosecrans Avenue. The transporting deputy seemed a little baffled and stunned at what Walt was asking him when he should've known the route and the routine. He then admitted to Walt that he didn't know which way to go.

Walt grew very impatient with the deputy and expressed his thoughts about how he might very well cause Walt's death because he was lost. Walt said to the deputy, "What the hell is wrong with you, man? You just left (Firestone) two weeks ago, and you worked there (Firestone) for three years!"

The deputy became more rattled, so Walt sat upright and started telling him the directions on the code-three run. The deputy did admit later that he was absolutely shocked when he first saw Walt covered in blood, and he felt he was put in a rougher situation when he was asked to get him to the hospital.

A department psychologist later on informed Walt that sight of the bloody uniform alone caused the deputy to become disoriented. He couldn't think very well, because he was in shock. That explained the loss of his memory while en route to Saint Francis Medical Center. The doctor further explained that many individuals go through this syndrome when exposed to violent situations like the one he had gone through.

Walt told me that the roughest part of the whole shooting ordeal was when the doctors had to cut Walt almost in half to gain access to the bullet lying near the inside of his spine.

This shooting is one of many that deputies will risk when checking on the welfare of the people they are protecting. In today's world, deputies wear their bulletproof vests religiously. Those vests protect the trunk of the body, although in the same circumstances as Walt's assignment, deputies could still very well get shot in the face or exposed limbs just as easily.

Walt survived this shooting and acted in true Firestone Park fashion. He worked many more years on the department and retired around 1990 because of the physical impairments of the shooting.

CHAPTER 47

GRENADE

It was a little after midnight on a relatively quiet Wednesday night at Firestone Park Station. Most units had already come in and gone home. A few cars occasionally would come in and out of the parking lot to drop off completed reports or make a head call. Occasionally a detective or a uniformed officer or two would be in the rear parking lot completing fastidious chores, emptying their cars, and getting ready to go home.

As you came through the swinging double back doors of the station, you would immediately see the sergeant's twelve-by-twelve office right in front of you, only thirty feet away. It had glass windows surrounding the office so the sergeant could easily see the front desk, secretariat, booking cage, jailer's gate, book area, and counter for suspect processing.

Usually crime tapered off near midnight. The early morning crews already hit the streets and were shaking the remaining crooks trying to pull off one more theft before they turned in. There were sporadic burglar alarms going off, most likely on doors or windows jiggled by burglars to see if the alarm was working and to wear down the deputies responding to false alarms.

Suddenly there was a very loud explosion just thirty feet outside the rear doors. Nearly everyone ran outside to see what caused the explosion. Five radio cars were on fire and in shambles. The fire department was called to put the fires out. Pieces of shrapnel had struck the solid concrete wall and trusties' quarter's glass blocks approximately thirty feet from the explosion.

Fortunately no one was injured, but we lost five patrol cars. There was minimal damage to the building. The investigation revealed that a single military grenade was lobbed over the rear wall on the alley side.

Two outposts were erected on the interior wall of the parking lot, with direct phone lines to our front desk. Each outpost was approximately a four-foot-high platform, four feet wide and six feet long, with a chair.

These outposts were designated "10p1," the southern corner on the Compton Avenue side and "10p2," the alley corner just south of Nadeau Street. Initially these posts were manned by one two-man unit pulled from the field for three-hour shifts. These posts were mainly used for observation points and as deterrents for future grenade attacks or criminal threats to law enforcement.

From the outset, 10p1 and 10p2 were in place for additional security for the station, but frequent arrests came from those posts as well.

The announcement over the station's public address system was "10p1 is 1015 with one or two," which is the radio code for suspect in custody.

When you worked that post, you would drop off your prisoner, book him/her, and get back out to the post as fast as you could. While on post you would write your arrest report and complete it quickly. Boy, what a station!

I wonder why Bill Ayers of the Weather Underground never came to our station to blow it up. Maybe he was tired from making so many bombs and blowing up New York Police Department stations. Or maybe he realized he would be a university professor and could have much more to talk about when he was with his friends, students, or other bomb-making friends. Or, maybe he was just too _____! You be the judge.

CHAPTER 48

WATTS SUMMER FESTIVAL

Preparation for this event started at least four months prior. Fast mass-booking-arrest forms were in citation packets. Crown Buses to cart off at least fifty inmates each were lined up. Box lunches from the jail, nylon ties, cameras, additional personnel from surrounding stations, crowd and riot gear, public address systems, tear gas, smoke grenades, plastic booking bags, indelible marking pens, first-aid gear, and written material for practicing crowd and riot formations, and emergency contingency plans were all at the ready. Extra units from other stations and personnel from the jail to help in the mass bookings, extra probation and parole personnel, and preparation for use of outside police agencies were added into the mix.

No doubt this yearly event cost a lot of money, and the primary purpose was to let the folks have fun at this event and immediately stop any criminal activity that may raise its ugly head.

The Special Enforcement Bureau (SEB) was poised to transport all arrested suspects from the park and deliver them to Firestone Park Station for the booking teams to process.

In Will Rogers Park there were ten two-man foot-patrol teams assigned to walk throughout the park and be visible in order to prevent crime.

When making arrests you would broadcast over your radio that you had someone in custody and walk directly toward the curbs surrounding the park. The SEB unit would then come to your spot, take your prisoner, and take a picture of you and the suspect, so you would remember who you arrested. That picture would also have a large file number across the suspect's chest to connect the suspect with the report and the file number. This process worked great, and very few problems occurred while the operation was in existence.

The Watts Summer Festival lasted a week, generally from noon until midnight. When it started, we had a small command post in the center of the park to assist with drawing file numbers and identification of suspects with deputies, and assisting with radio communications. From the onset the park was absolutely packed like sardines, with almost no space for folks to turn around. Most attendants were black and very cordial. People brought their kids during the day. The usual windy politicians spoke, with equal rights as the main topic.

Several black guests of honor spoke of the joyous event and freedom from the tyranny of police brutality. Our two-man teams were casually walking through the huge crowd, looking for the obvious crooks selling dope, stealing, or carrying guns and knives. There were occasional rapes and every crime that could be imagined as it grew darker.

Many times I went into the men's restroom, which was packed, and saw four persons around the sink, peeing into the sink that was already full to the brim. As I came into the bathroom wearing my sheriff's uniform, shiny Corefam boots, and beige-and-green helmet, I would greet the packed bathroom with "Hey you guys, how are you doing?" Usually everyone responded politely as possible as I walked around the small three-toilet facility.

We were usually paired up with like-size partners. We needed to be cool and chill for the most part. I was lucky because my size was at least six five with helmet and boots, and I weighed 215 pounds; with a partner my size, we set the tone for obedience. Generally command presence and a tapered and tempered attitude prevailed.

During the course of the twelve-hour shift, most of us on foot patrol were making at least twenty-five or thirty arrests each day. A lot of the arrests were for being drunk on drugs or booze. Everything was pretty cool, although it had the potential to explode into a riot, but it never did.

I believe it was successful because of our training and supervision by the sheriff's department, which was firmly aware of the surroundings and cultural differences. We all knew something simple could set the whole thing off, but we were constantly reminded to empathize with the folks and that our sheriff was an elected position. Our lieutenants and sergeants from Firestone Station were probably the best in the department and really attuned to major conflicts. Several of our lieutenants were majors in the active and reserve military organizations and applied their knowledge to our conditions. When they gave directions, you knew they were good. Later on in my career, supervisors like the Firestone Park type ended up in the top administration levels because of their glowing attributes.

The same applies today with the Firestone Park experience; you'll know immediately who they are by their command presence and postures.

CHAPTER 49

RUDE PHONE ANTICS/DEAD TRAINEE

About twice a year at Firestone Park Station, each deputy would be assigned the front desk. I hated it, as did most deputies. The field, with all the excitement, was the place I wanted to be. On the other hand, working the desk you answered telephones and handled front desk reports and miscellaneous activities like helping the jailer. It was a good way to learn all aspects of station activities.

At that time when deputies finished calls for service, details, and other assignments, they needed to call the station and clear each and every call. This meant filling out the small call sheet, listing the details of the call, and receiving a tag number for your car log indicating everything you did that night. When a deputy called in, there was a set method to clear the sheet so the clearance would get done quickly. Generally everyone got it right, but some didn't.

One night I was talking with a trainee who seemed unsure of himself.He was giving me the wrong information and in the wrong sequence. I became upset at the delay and screamed at the trainee, "Goddamn it, if you don't have it right, don't call!" I slammed the phone down and called him several impolite names. I knew his training officer and informed him later on about his trainee screwing up and what I had done. He acknowledged my information and most likely addressed my complaint to the trainee.

Later on I felt bad about yelling at him so harshly, because he was one of the calmer trainees, and his training officer was one of the better deputies at the station. I figured if I saw the trainee, I would explain to him the reasons I was so upset, and apologize for jumping in his face so hard.

The next night it was pretty busy and things were popping off all over. Those of us on the desk had to pay particular attention to what was being stated over the radio so we could assist the dispatcher without him asking for help.

There was a shooting over near the Florence community and one of the units was in foot pursuit of several gang members involved in the shooting. The unit was the training officer I spoke with the night before criticizing his trainee. Both the training officer, Harvey H., and his trainee, Gary S., were in foot pursuit of two separate suspects. The suspects had separated and the training officer and trainee split up.

This area is well known for its gangs and violence, and splitting up is discouraged but still allowed. The trainee was coming upon the suspect he was running after when the suspect ran up to a large front porch and began to pound on the door, demanding someone to open the door quickly. The trainee grabbed the left shoulder of the suspect, who twisted the opposite way from the grab, spun around, and punched the trainee off the large three-step porch. The trainee fell backward and landed on the lawn. His pistol fell out of his holster. The suspect quickly jumped from the porch and retrieved the pistol. He hovered over the trainee, who realized the suspect had his gun. The trainee begged for his life with his hands held outright.

Although the trainee's palms were facing outward and he was begging the suspect not to shoot him, the suspect fired three times. The bullets hit the trainee's chest. One passed through the trainee's extended opened palm and landed in his chest, killing him instantly.

The suspect quickly fled farther down the street and was captured alive by several California Highway Patrolmen a short time later, hiding in a garage, behind a water heater. The trainee had only two months at Firestone Park Station and was the same guy I hung up on the night before. He was married and had one child. Boy, what a fool I thought I was for slamming the phone down on him; he lost his life the very next day. I would never do that again; it set the tone of consideration for anyone on training.

The suspect survived several more years and killed yet another undercover officer in the city of Huntington Park. Now, I believe, the suspect resides in the city of Carson. This form of justice—allowing a killer to go free—isn't justice at all. Now picture this type of exposure. You know full well what will happen if you or your partner is killed. The killer will most likely get away with an extremely light sentence. What would you do?

If your answer is arrest the individual, because it's the right thing to do, knowing he may not have had a chance because he was involved in a "youth group" (street gang). The name "youth group" is now what gang members are referred to rather than "gang member" because it has a better connotation. That youth group philosophy conveniently pays more attention to him—because his mom and dad disowned him, because of his incorrigible behavior, or perhaps maybe he wasn't breastfed by his mother. Or the poorly treated youth may have been sexually abused by his father, or maybe his father painted his hobbyhorse pink, and all these things individually or in combination made him angry at authority figures. His psyche was twisted to just be mean and kill.

Don't laugh. All of these things are constantly brought up by attorneys as a justification for homicide, and the killers are coddled by the court system.

CHAPTER 50

A DUMB MOVE

An assistance call came out of an assault with a deadly weapon just north of Firestone Boulevard on Fig Street. My partner and I arrived within three minutes and saw the handling unit there already with two other units. We surrounded the location and waited for the handling unit to knock on the front door.

I moved around to the rear of the home and discovered there was neither cover nor concealment nearby. I noticed there was an easy access to the roof area, and climbed onto the roof. I figured if I could hover above the small rear porch I would be able to order him to stop in midair.

Several seconds went by while the deputies were waiting at the front door for someone to answer. Suddenly a lone man came running out the rear door. I decided to jump on him as he was passing by directly underneath me. I figured that if I landed on his shoulders, boots first, I could easily stop him from running away. So I jumped, leading him slightly and allowing for the nine foot fall.

I landed right on top of his shoulders which caused the suspect to fall forward, head first, onto the narrow sidewalk. This forward motion caused me to fall backward between the suspect's ankles, striking the back of my helmet on the sidewalk. I nearly knocked myself out from the impact.

The suspect was out cold from the impact and was readily captured and handcuffed. Several seconds later, the suspect regained consciousness. He was taken to the hospital and examined by the emergency staff, and then he was released to be booked.

In retrospect, this was one of the dumbest moves I could have come up with, and I readily passed this information along to as many officers as I could over the next twenty-nine years.

CHAPTER 51
THE GRASSY KNOLL

I was working a one-man unit in the city of Carson on Sepulveda and Avalon Boulevards, near the south end. There were a lot of burglaries and lots of dope in the area.

The early morning shift was generally from 11:00 p.m. until 7:00 a.m. It is a little more quiet, with fewer report calls and not as many people and cars. Usually activity spikes close to when the bars close; the drunk drivers hit the road. Inebriated individuals show up at the hamburger and taco stands and create commotions.

As a one-man unit you are expected to drive around and be seen to alleviate problems that typically show up but dissipate when you're seen. This is also the time when everything in the entire area closes, and the only thing remaining open are the donut shops. Around two-thirty in the morning, I had just purchased a cup of coffee and was slowly driving southbound on Avalon Boulevard at 2–3 mph. I made a right turn onto Fries Street and was coming near the end of the street. Then I saw something move off to my left. I had my rear stop lights switch engaged, which prevented my brake lights from illuminating. I stopped briefly and listened for any noise out of the ordinary. My window was open most of the time, like any good attentive officer's would be, and I was ready to dump everything, if necessary.

I paused for thirty seconds and continued onward very slowly thinking I was going to see something or someone pop out quickly in my rearview mirror. It was just a hunch, but I spotted the top of a head poking up from the hood of a car parked almost adjacent to my patrol car. It seemed as if he was concealing himself, waiting for me to pass by. Or was he was going to ambush me as I drove past?

I stepped out quickly and told the figure to stand up so I could see his hands. I dumped my coffee onto the street and began to go around the rear of the car where he was hiding behind. He took off running lickety-split.

I returned to my car and put out my location and announced that I was in foot pursuit of a possible auto thief.

I threw the mike onto the bench seat and ran after the suspect as fast as I could. He ran into an unpaved alley that was full of grass and assorted trash. I could still see the suspect, who'd apparently tripped on some of the larger pieces of rubbish and fallen into the high grass and debris. I was closing in on top of him, but he continued down the alley, high-stepping to miss all the bumps, small knolls, and holes that cluttered the path.

The suspect then turned left into a dilapidated wooden fence that was almost falling over and leaped it without missing a step. I was gaining on him, only five feet away at times, and I was about to grab him when he dove to the ground under an old abandoned car that was sitting atop four cement blocks.

I was able to grab one of the cuffs of his pants with my left hand as I was reaching for my pistol. My holster was empty!

I thought, *Holy shit, I'm unarmed; I sure hope this guy is unarmed as well!* He was holding tightly onto something under the car. I put both of my hands, arms, and legs into motion and yanked real hard. He might have hit his head on something when I dragged him out.

He screamed as he was extricated from under the car, and I plowed my knee into his back and neck and placed his hands behind his back as instructed. Once he was hooked up, I was extremely relieved. I needed to search for my pistol.

We were backtracking on the foot pursuit's course of travel as I was desperately looking for my gun, holding the suspect with one hand and my flashlight in the other. I could hear sirens coming to my aid, but I was still a block away in the raunchy alley.

When we were halfway back to my car I finally spotted my blue Colt Python, 6-inch bbl, .357 magnum revolver lying on the opposite side of a small grassy knoll in the center of the alley.

Boy, was I relieved, and the suspect never knew about my temporary loss. Apparently while I was stepping through the high grass somehow my Buckheimer swivel holster unsnapped, and the pistol fell out.

This event has stayed with me throughout my career. I changed the type of holster to one that rode much higher, and whatever I was doing, I would always arm-check my pistol with my right arm; tapping on the gun grips frequently to make sure the gun was always in its place.

I arrested the suspect for possession of burglary tools and stopped his thieving antics for a short while, but more important, I spread the importance of checking your gun at all times.

CHAPTER 52

A FOGGY NIGHT

They had been working together for several weeks and were assigned to work the east side of Compton. Lou was driving, and Al was booking. Both of them had several years on and were comfortable with each other and pretty good friends as well.

They had a pullover routine method down to shake as many people as possible in the shortest amount of time. They would bring the suspect(s) out of the car, and Al would shake them down, unless something seemed to be wrong or suspicions were elevated, then both would remain as the suspect(s) would be searched. Lou would search the suspect car for any contraband while Al would watch the suspect at a safe distance. After the car was searched, Lou would return to Al's position and let him know what he found, combining their information and observations for report writing purposes.

This night was no different. They were over by Jerry's Drive-In on Long Beach Boulevard at Cypress Street. They spotted a character acting funny as he was driving; it seemed rather suspicious. When they decided to pull him over, they were just past the milk stand right across the street from Jerry's.

Lou approached the driver's door as Al lay back and watched from the right rear, slightly out of view of the driver. There was a short conversation between Lou and the sole occupant, the driver.

Lou asked the male driver to step out and guided him over toward the curbside where the radio car was parked offset and about three feet from the curb. Al was watching and slowly tracking the movements of both Lou and the male driver as they approached the right front fender of the patrol car.

The driver was cooperative and did nothing suspicious to alert either Lou or Al. Lou mimed to Al that he was going to search the car. Al would pat down the driver, following the routine they did every night.

Lou was in the driver's car, and Al had the driver's hands on the hood of the patrol unit and one leg between the driver's legs. As Al placed both of his thumbs into the front waistband, the driver stood up and started to turn around and face Al. Al tried but couldn't stop his rapid movements. As the driver turned, Al felt the man's right hand move into his waistband. Al could feel something hard, like a pistol, so he grabbed the driver's right wrist. They wrestled each other to gain control of the shooting end of the pistol. Al was trying desperately to force the barrel away from him. Al's hands were firmly locked on the driver's wrists. Al yelled out to Lou for help. Lou heard him and came out of the driver's door fast.

Lou saw Al wrestling with the driver and drew closer to aid his partner, coming between the driver's car and the patrol unit which was about ten feet apart. Al yelled, "Gun!" to Lou.

Lou was about eight feet away from Al and the driver as Al was pushing the gun hand above the driver's shoulder and away from them. This caused the barrel to point directly toward Lou as he was approaching them.

Then it happened. The driver pulled the trigger while the gun was above him and literally upside down. The gun discharged, and the bullet slammed into Lou's chest and dropped him like a rock onto the asphalt, near the curb. He was out for the count and no help to Al now.

Al and the driver continued to fight when the gun fired again. This time it hit Al's right knee, causing him to buckle slightly. Al, admitted later on, he knew this might very well be the end of his life. He tried to fight off the pain of the gunshot and felt himself losing the strength to continue. Then the gun discharged again.

This time the bullet struck his middle finger. Al fell to the ground and felt he was going to pass out. The suspect saw Al drop to the sidewalk and turned away from Al, going southbound, and started to walk away from both officers lying in their own blood.

As the suspect walked away, Lou regained consciousness, drew his pistol, elevated his arm on the curb, and fired five rounds into the driver's back. Fortunately all five rounds from Lou's gun found their mark and the driver fell forward onto the sidewalk, dead.

Unfortunately, Lou passed out again, pistol in hand. Al regained his composure enough to crawl to the partially open passenger door and grabbed the microphone. Al was able to announce that he, his partner, and the suspect were shot and needed immediate assistance. The RTO (Radio/telephone operator) repeated his exact words and units started to race toward their position.

My brother Vince and his partner were in the Willowbrook area and were the closest, so they were given the authority to respond code three, red lights and siren. Unfortunately, it was extremely foggy and their response was at least eight minutes in the dense fog. When they arrived on the scene, Al informed them he was wounded, but Lou really needed attention quick.

Vince and his partner picked Lou up and placed him into their car as other units began to arrive to help Al.

Vince and his partner then took an aggravating "Code 3" slow run in the heavily blanketed fog. By the time they arrived at Saint Francis Hospital and brought Lou into the emergency room, he was pronounced DOA (dead on arrival). Al made it to the hospital and was treated for his wounds and survived physically, but emotionally he was really shaken up, and rightfully so.

The suspect was pronounced dead at the scene. Lou and Al's method of stopping cars and suspects was seen as unsafe and will never to be repeated.

This event was recreated many times for training purposes by the academy staff. Training officers were cautioned to avoid any similar incidents.

Al retired early from his injuries and opened a bar in Huntington Beach, California, called the Wounded Knee. Later he became an attorney for several years until he passed away in the early nineties.

I always considered Al a very sharp, friendly, and easygoing officer, and I was very proud to have known him for many years.

May God bless both Lou and Al for their service and their tenacious abilities to spot crooks and take them to jail. I'm sure their names will never be used in vain; they will be used as a primary tool for officer survival classes.

CHAPTER 53

ANOTHER DUMB MOVE

I was working a one-man unit and received a burglary alarm at a two-story business on Avalon Boulevard, just south of Main Street in Carson. It was very foggy again and difficult to see addresses of the businesses, but I knew I was close. When I arrived, several other units were already there and checking the perimeter. I was usually the one to go to the roof, because I was pretty good at climbing and anxious to catch a roof burglar and show off to deputies that my efforts paid off.

Typically roof burglars are more experienced and very quiet. Often they avoided alarm detection, because they probably worked for an alarm company or were very familiar with their wiring systems. Of course they would need a rope to lower themselves into the business, several cutting tools, and wiring pliers.

The old theory that a roof burglar only needed a garden hose—which is widely overlooked by officers—is true, and in fact it is a much better climbing tool than a rope. The hose is usually rubber and pretty strong, and generally it comes in lengths of fifty, seventy-five, and one hundred feet. If you've ever tried to climb a rope and experienced a little difficulty, it's probably because your hands slipped down the rope pretty easily. Now try it with a hose. Your climbing and lowering techniques will be greatly enhanced.

When someone is walking down the street with a hose under his arm, it seems very innocent behavior; it's never looked at as a burglar tool.

I began climbing the two-story structure alone and was nearly at the top. I could easily see other deputies below who had already searched the perimeter for obvious signs of entry and found nothing.

The deputies were assembled on all four sides, waiting for me to finish searching the roof for any signs of tampering with the ventilation units and air conditioning duct systems and grids. It took me about five minutes. When I finished, I informed everyone that everything was cleared. Several deputies stated they would stick around until I came down.

I told them to go ahead and leave, because it would take fifteen to twenty minutes to crawl down. To make matters worse, it was real damp, and everything had quite a bit of moisture on its surface.

They all took off, and I remained for several minutes relaxing on the roof. I was sitting on top of the small wall on the perimeter and looking through the thick fog, as it covered nearly everything. In fact, noise was muffled, and a surreal atmosphere set in and felt very peaceful, tranquil, and dreamlike.

I saw two tall utility poles bordering the front of the building and they had several pieces of wood connecting the two poles and two large electrical canisters containing PCBs (A hazardous chemical used to assist in conducting electricity). These poles were about eight feet taller than the roof, and both had half-inch guywires strapped to each pole. They angled down to the ground and were anchored in the earth to secure the poles in their upright positions. The guywires were only about eight feet from the roof's edge and reachable with a slight leap.

I thought, *Why go back the same way and get all dirty crawling over the many wet obstacles on my way down when I can easily jump to the guy wire and slide down the wire to the ground in maybe ten seconds?*

The wire seemed a little steep at about a forty-five-degree angle, and it was probably moist from the fog as well, but it seemed plausible, if a little risky. But what the hell, no one was around to see me screw up, and it shouldn't be that bad.

I stepped back about ten feet from the roof and ran to the edge. I placed my foot on top of the small wall, leaped out, and grabbed the guy wire. I had my leather gloves on, and down I went. The one thing I really didn't realize was that the speed coming down the wire would be very fast, but I held on. I believe the proper word to describe the movement would be "zing." What if one of the wires was frayed, you might ask. Another oversight was the twelve-foot heavy plastic shroud that prevents rats and mice from climbing the guy wire, usually at the base by the half-inch eyebolt that secures the guywires to the anchor rod.

When my hands hit that shroud I went flying and cartwheeled at least five times into the muddy English ivy that surrounded the poles and guywires. I landed on my back and literally knocked the crap out of myself. I struggled to catch my breath and hoped I wasn't hurt too badly.

I got up and looked around to see if anyone saw my brilliant move. Fortunately, the heavy fog provided the best cover for my performance. I was covered with mud and water. It was so bad I had to make a trip back to Firestone Park Station and change my uniform and shoes.

I told that same story many times to many persons, as well as other cops. The reason was to let them know how dumb some ideas are. I hoped no one else would attempt such a brilliant move.

CHAPTER 54

ELA RIOT

When this riot broke out, East Los Angeles Station was overwhelmed by a local mass insurrection. Many deputies were injured. They were confronted by large groups of rioters and had to abandon areas to the looting and burning buildings.

The entire Special Enforcement Bureau, which was located right behind ELA station at the time, was activated to assist the ELA Station with out-of-control riots, looting, and burning.

The ongoing melee cornered the entire group of responding deputies; both ELA and the SEB units were overwhelmed as well. Many deputies were beaten, driven into submission and retreated by the crowd of organized rioters, who included local Hispanic gangs.

That's when Firestone Park Station was summoned and put on emergency status for mobilization to the East Los Angeles area. Many of us were mobilized from our homes to report to Firestone Park Station immediately. No questions were asked, other than what was going on and where we were going. Everyone responded quickly, and three entire platoons were assembled for the roll to East Los Angeles.

Fortunately, several of our lieutenants were active in the US military reserves, seasoned and trained in crowd and riot control. They had prepped us many times for any civil disruptions that might occur in the Watts area, when any of the Watts Summer Festivals were about to happen.

These lieutenants were demanding and adept at their jobs, probably the best on the department. They were also admired for their forceful demeanor and command presence. Most of us knew very well these lieutenants knew their business, and they had the supervisory charisma to direct us in any event or emergency. Several years later these same lieutenants became upper administrative personnel, undersheriffs and assistant sheriffs who directed our department on an unmatched grand scale.

Let there be no doubt that our preparation for crowd and riot control, convoy tactics, command post operations, tear gas training, and deployment was drilled into all of us to the point we felt confident that we could control the most unruly mobs. I might add a majority of our personnel were six foot and above. Our uniform appearance was exceptionally good with spit-shined Cochran boots, highly shined black leather gear, buffed and shining helmets, and polished brass. Our equipment was always clean and ready for deployment. A mere order from one of our sergeants would trigger our preconditioned command responses, and we knew exactly what to do.

The order was no more than two hits per mobster, or we'd tire quickly, so pick and hit our marks well with the nightstick. Our backup, directly behind the line, was several shooters with twelve-gauge, Ithaca-pump shotguns in case someone wanted to shoot at us. On our flanks were protected with predetermined counter snipers and spotters.

Mass bookings and transportation were set up at the Sybil Brand Institute for Women at the top of the hill, just above the sheriff's academy.

We formed a large convoy of patrol cars and came to the area on the 710 freeway to Floral Avenue. We traveled eastbound to the Floral Drive-In Theater, located on Floral Avenue and Arizona Boulevard.

We assembled there, about two hundred units standing by, briefed on what had occurred, and tactically prepped to swarm into the onslaught of the crowd to control the riotous mobs.

Other station personnel from Norwalk and Lakewood were mixed in with us. Their lieutenants and sergeants were captivated by our Firestone Park staff and fell in on all ordered formations.

When the time came, off we went down Arizona Boulevard to Whittier and Olympic Boulevards in a convoy, five deputies in each car. When we arrived, the crowd was about thirty yards in front of us, acting out as rampaging thugs and thieves. We jumped out of our cars and formed the skirmish line and on command started our forward movement. The rioters scurried several times for a short run and then resumed their pillaging.

This formation lasted for several hours. We persisted in our skirmishes and diagonal lines, with strict discipline not to overreact. We completed our tasks at hand, dealt two blows per contact, and moved on. Our formations were impeccable, and our sergeants let us know how we were doing as we went along. That small exchange of accolades made us feel good and we were determined to do a good job. We were all proud of our accomplishments.

We still came toward them. One idiot in the crowd fired a couple of rounds toward us. Our rear men with shotguns took them out, and they dropped onto the street. Several rioters came to their aid but ran from us as we drew close.

Our paramedics assigned to the platoon formations handled the wounded quickly but needed to catch up with our formation as soon as possible. One rioter was dead, lying on Whittier Boulevard near Kern Avenue. We had them on the run. The rioters were allowed to run and escape through our predetermined routes and avenues of escape.

In a matter of hours, we cleaned up the mobs and restored order. Fire teams were assigned fixed posts until adequate replacements came onto the scene. (This is when my brother Vinnie and I were accidentally assigned together on Ford Avenue and Whittier Boulevard. Usually family members are not assigned with each other for fear of the possibility of losing multiple personnel from the same family.)

Once the main riot was over, static posts were put into place primarily to stop independent looters from returning. The looters would most likely come back to reap the economic booty. It was an easy harvest because of all of the smashed windows and doors.

This entire operation lasted several days, and when peace was restored, we returned to our regular stations of assignments.

CHAPTER 55
COMMAND

It should be noted that there were several riots in the ELA area, and I was assigned to all of them. I had a certain respect for all ranks and supervisors. Some of them came from areas where the criminal activity was minimal, and they had limited experience and rather dull routines, such as paper shuffling and processing. Those individual supervisors were very noticeable. Their lack of command and direction was obvious.

Experience showed up quickly in high crime areas. Our ghetto sergeants and lieutenants took command and were in charge, no questions asked.

You needed to know your job very well. Directing and command had to come from an authoritative voice with command presence and posture. Certain weak supervisors hid among the stronger ones and rode completely on their coattails. The riots really exposed them for what they were, as they kept their mouths shut and hid within the ranks of the larger-size deputies. This always occurred and most likely continues even in today's command.

The latest McArthur Park riotous melee with the LAPD a couple of years ago, was nothing more than line supervisors not doing their job controlling their personnel. In that event, several of the media were treated as part of the melee.

That never happened with the sheriff's department. Why? There's no comparison. The sheriff has a media liaison specifically for the interaction. Funny thing, it works and is always promoted in the policies and procedures manual.

Of course the sheriff is an elected official, and that is the great strength. All chiefs of police are selected and appointed by the mayor or city council government and controlled by the city manager.

This is way too much interference and politicking, referred today as political correctness. It's a no-brainer. Just watch the next faux pas in any law enforcement situation. The sheriff is least likely to err, because he generally has the community's ear.

The chief of police is more inclined to err because of all the mixed signals coming from the city administration and political cronies, and he or she will capitulate under pressure in order to keep the position. Sounds familiar, doesn't it? A good word to classify these cornballs is "Sycophant!"

Weak command will always happen when weak supervisors are put in a position they can't handle. The term "vicarious liability" should be understood in supervisory school that is taught to all new sergeants on the sheriff's department.

When broken down, it is easy to see where the liability lies for a supervisor. They all had better take heed of all important elements of vicarious liability. It has legal consequences that will be enforced and the department's personnel will suffer if it's not addressed.

Personally, I have always looked at the shape of a person's head. I believe that's called phrenology. The next time you see someone out of kilter, just not in step with "normal" behavior, look at the shape of their head—it may be conical or bumpy, or their face will not be symmetrical.(Ha Ha)

This is especially apparent to those with a lot of education, the ones placed into professorship or a political position. (Another term, of course not politically correct, is your basic "kiss-ass" or toady sycophant.)

CHAPTER 56

DEEP GASH, NO BLOOD

I was working a two-man unit in Carson on the night shift. My partner's name was Louie H. We were just given an assault with a deadly weapon call on Sepulveda Boulevard near Main Street. It was about eight as we pulled in front of the address and noticed a small crowd about fifty feet north of us.

They were in a semicircular configuration and moving away from two adult men who appeared to be fighting each other. One of them had a six-inch knife in his right hand. Just as we were stepping out of the patrol car, the knife was thrust forward into the other man's open right hand as he attempted to fend off the attack. The crowd yelled something undistinguishable as the knife was withdrawn. Blood appeared quickly, and the victim grabbed his hand in pain and looked at his wound, wincing in agony. The suspect with the knife noticed our presence and ran away from us, northbound around an apartment complex with my partner, Louie, in foot pursuit.

I went to the street side of the complex, and waited to see if the suspect would circle around the rear of the apartments and come running toward my position. I was standing near the center of the two-story buildings, anxiously awaiting the suspect and my partner to come running toward me. Suddenly the suspect rounded the apartment building just to my left, and our eyes met. The suspect went wide into the street to avoid my approach and capture and ran past me as I drew closer.

I was suspicious that my partner wasn't close behind. I was thinking that he might have been attacked as well and was possibly lying behind the apartments, bleeding to death.

The suspect was about ten feet in front of me running full bore. He turned left toward a home on the north side of the street. I was closing in but realized he might very well live at this home he's running toward, and if he got inside, it would further compromise my safety.

I had my nightstick in my right hand. I threw it hard and saw it strike the suspect in his back, knocking him to the sidewalk near the front porch steps. I still didn't see or hear my partner, Louie, and I was thinking he might be seriously hurt, and this better end quickly.

The suspect entered the large front door and latched it just as I hit the door on a forward thrust of my right leg and foot. I hit the mark just near the handle and slammed the door open as it swung widely.

In amazement I saw the suspect about four feet in the air horizontally going away from me. He dropped to the floor near the opposite wall of the front room. He was completely knocked out. I hovered above his face.

There was a gash in his face below his left eye, and all the way down to his bottom lip. This gash was at least a quarter to half inch deep with no blood whatsoever coming from the wound. This wound was apparently caused by the front door's leading edge that struck the suspect directly in the face as I kicked it open. Unfortunately, the suspect must have held the handle by the latching mechanism, and it struck him full blast.

My partner, Louie, came up behind me and was about to clobber the suspect, but I extended my arm and informed Louie that the suspect was out cold. We picked the suspect up and carried him across the room near the front door and laid him out in a reclining, overstuffed chair. As the suspect was lying in the chair the gash was even more apparent, but still no blood was seen coming from the serious wound.

Louie mentioned he had slipped and fallen on the sidewalk behind the apartments and put two holes in his pant legs, which caused several small abrasions to his knees, explaining his slight delay.

The suspect lay motionless for several minutes. All of a sudden, the wound started to bleed slightly. Then blood spilled heavily onto the suspect's face and down his clothing. He awakened and started to kick and flail his arms and legs as if his was in a fight by himself. Blood was flying everywhere.

We handcuffed him with little effort, and carried him to our patrol car, and placed him in the backseat for a short ride to Harbor General Hospital, which was fortunately close by. When we arrived at the hospital, we carried the suspect into the emergency room, which was packed with people and patients waiting. We separated ourselves from the mass of people and patients so they wouldn't hear our suspect, who was screaming, still kicking and flailing his arms and legs.

We were supplied a hospital gurney. We picked the suspect up and placed him on his back on the gurney and handcuffed him to the rails. We held his feet and legs still at the gurney base. He was apparently on some type of drug and booze, acting bizarrely, screaming obscenities that could be heard all over the emergency rooms and hallways.

The attending physician came in to quiet the suspect but was not successful. The doctor was very patient and a bit under strain as the suspect was nonstop with his spewing of vulgarities.

We remained for at least two hours. Forty stitches later, we were allowed to take the suspect to Los Angeles General Hospital, jail ward on the thirteenth floor, for booking.

CHAPTER 57

NEW NEIGHBORHOOD

Both my brother and I had just moved to the new community in Orange County called Mission Viejo. He was about three blocks from my house, just off Geronimo Boulevard and south of Alicia Parkway. Several other friends of ours also moved into the neighborhood, mostly from Firestone Park Station. We were all excited to come to this new community and hunker down in an area that had minor criminal problems. We became used to the new riches of a planned community and boasted about it. This area was cluttered with small hills, which made it much more inviting than the typical LA flatland.

Everyone seemed so busy landscaping and adding all sorts of small improvements to the new development. The neighborhood hardware store was bustling with many of its new customers. Fences, pots, plants, ladders, nails, saws, and wood were needed by even the least ambitious of families.

The drive back and forth to work was at least an hour without traffic, but worth every bit of the comfort of living in the new community. Everyone seemed very happy and pleased with the surroundings. Laughter was no stranger to this area, and it seemed appropriate considering all of the activities and the neighborhood's indulgence in helping one another.

My next-door neighbor owned a small record shop nearby and was a very friendly sort of guy. He was about as "hippie" as one could get. He had long hair down to the middle of his back and wore the paisley loose garb seen commonly in and around the San Francisco area.

His wife was a young good-looking brunette, rather shapely and pleasant to look at.

We were into our second or third month of living at the top of a small hill with view lots facing an unobstructed view of Saddleback Mountain approximately five miles to the east.

One of my new neighbors was a Huntington Beach fire captain, and we hit it off very well and became good friends. We would help each other with small projects and encouraged each other in all ventures.

One morning I got up at my usual time, to see the sunrise and enjoy a cup of coffee in the backyard, and take in the beautiful view. I stood by one of the tall wooden posts holding up my large patio cover, about five feet from my three-foot fence. That fence had an unobstructed panoramic view of the mountains that enhanced my simple morning pleasures immeasurably.

It was around six, the birds were chirping as I sipped my special blend of morning coffee, the kids and wife were asleep, and it couldn't have been any more peaceful.

Unbelievably, small groups of hummingbirds came by and sucked from the splashy crimson bougainvilleas that surrounded my low fence on both sides. The neighbors to the rear were approximately fifty to sixty feet below my view.

I heard the next-door neighbor's door open, and his wife stepped outside in a paisley silk bathrobe. I was admiring her appearance as she stepped into the backyard and up to a two foot, split-rail fence that bordered their rear yard.

A six-foot block wall bordered our properties and tapered down to a three foot wall as it drew toward the rear wooden fences. This was erected by design to allow for a more broad opening of the grand view of the surrounding hills, homes, trees, and of course Saddleback Mountain.

I continued to sip my coffee and could easily see her as she came right up to the fence and laid out a beach towel on the green grass. She then straddled the beach towel while she was standing. She was midyard, and apparently the small trees between our property lines concealed my position, maybe twenty feet away.

As she faced the mountain, the oncoming sunrise struck her well-defined body and face; she was aglow. God, she looked good. But maybe it was my highly caffeinated coffee consuming my brain and overwhelming all the other beauty of the morning and the view.

I didn't want to keep looking, but she untied the bathrobe's silk belt and opened her robe, exposing her totally nude body. She let her silken robe fall to her feet, and sat on the towel cross-legged, displaying her gazelle features and human flexibility. Her hands opened up with the palms facing upward atop her knees, which allowed the sun's rays to outline her nude shape. She said nothing and remained there for about a half hour, not moving at all.

Although I ran out of coffee, I was not about to leave these pleasant surroundings and just remained still, praying to the gods not to disrupt this moment with screaming kids or barking dogs. This was the start of a ritual that occurred at least three to four times a week, and I enjoyed it immensely.

My problem was that I informed the fireman neighbor, Bob L., who for some reason wanted to come over every morning and enjoy a delicious cup of coffee. He was ever so anxious to see the beautiful sight and lusted for her like a dog in heat. Of course not me, because I was a cop, and all cops control their emotions with elegant restraint.

Bob kept asking if she had ever turned around while I was there, and caught me looking. I told him no, but to be that unaware of the surrounding neighbors was near impossible. So we surmised that she was aware but didn't object as long as we kept quiet.

We remained friends but never really got together much because her husband was a full-blown dope smoker and toked up frequently in his backyard.

As a matter of fact, several times he grew marijuana plants in large pots in his backyard. I made several runs into his yard late at night and salted the plants with a small saltshaker. He never caught on to my midnight raid antics and just stopped putting the plants out, because they turned brown quickly, possibly due to the ocean air not ten miles away.

He knew I was a cop, but I guess he didn't put two and two together. I did it because of the principle of the matter and let it slide because he was really a nice neighbor.

Unfortunately, they moved away after five years of the same old nudity, which became…well, we'll let that remain unsaid. I'll let you figure that one out!

CHAPTER 58

SIX SEEDS

I was working a day-shift car in Carson on a weekday, and it was a little slow and quiet. So I started to pay attention to the abandoned cars that sometimes litter the streets. The community wanted them off the streets as soon as possible.

This task would entail writing out a red tag, marking the tires with yellow chalk, and filling out forms that would entail rechecking the auto in seventy-two hours or a period of three days.

I was in the area of Lincoln and Fries Streets, just south of Sepulveda Boulevard, when I noticed an apparent abandoned early-fifties black panel truck that had many cobwebs attached to the lower frame and a lot of old debris settled near the tires. The panel truck was obviously abandoned and within the guidelines for an immediate tow.

I sat in my car for several minutes with my engine running, comfortably and casually filling out the form to have the panel truck towed from the location. I filled out as much as I could and finally got out of my car to open the door of the panel truck in order to mark down its mileage, which was a requirement for the infamous CHP 180 forms. My patrol car was parked a little offset from the curb and facing the front of the panel truck. No one was on the street, and it was fairly quiet as I walked up to the driver's door.

I'll admit I was relaxed, and actually didn't expect complaints, because most neighbors are grateful the trashy cars are removed from their neighborhoods. I reached for the handle and opened the door, and a strong waft of marijuana smoke poured out of the opening. I stepped back and looked toward the rear interior of the truck. There was a dark paisley-print fabric sagging from wall to wall, covering whole width of the truck. This prevented anyone from peering inside beyond the front seats.

I surmised one or two individuals were beyond the paisley barrier and were smoking dope the whole time I was in my car filling out the necessary forms for the tow. I left the truck went to my car to request a unit backup for a narcotics follow-up investigation.

The panel truck was moving slightly, and I imagined that whoever was inside was consuming all the marijuana one could eat for at least five minutes.

Another unit arrived. We talked over what to do and decided we would stand by one side and another directly behind the rear door of the panel truck and order the occupants to step outside the truck. I ordered all in the truck to step out from the rear door and could hear and see a lot of movement inside.

About one minute passed. The back door started open, and the first male juvenile stepped out. He didn't say anything. I asked him to open his mouth and it was cluttered with marijuana debris. Several seconds passed and another male juvenile came out. This time the male was chewing on something. I stopped him and asked him to open his mouth as well. His mouth was also cluttered with marijuana debris. I didn't ask either of them to spit it out and let them finish up swallowing the debris. Several seconds later the third, fourth, fifth and sixth male juveniles came out, all chewing frantically. I stopped them all and inspected their mouths as well. They all had marijuana clutter and debris in their mouths, on their tongues, teeth, and cheeks.

After they were finished with their marijuana chew fest, I asked them all to take a seat on the curb and confirmed they were all juveniles.

The law at that time was that a juvenile who was in possession of any of the narcotics controlled substances list was arrestable for a felony.

I went into the truck to see what was left and after fingering my way through the entire rug I came up with six seeds. Yep, that was it. A total of six seeds caused these juveniles to go to jail, because their parents were all away for the day, and I couldn't drop them off to anyone else.

So with aid of my assisting officer all six were arrested and transported to Firestone Park Station, and the abandoned panel truck was taken away by the local tow yard.

Today, marijuana is nearly legal. I firmly believe law enforcement will probably require each officer to toke up during briefing so they can go out and display compassionate feelings for the liberals.

If that's representative of the present-day American political ethic, that's fine with me, but let me give you a final analysis. Many officers were killed because of this drug and many others as well. Several were my friends and still are today, although they're dead. You can rationalize that smoking dope is harmless, but you are factually wrong in my eyes.

Dope is dope. Research it all you want. What has happened is marijuana has gained favor as of this writing by those who broke the law in the past and they will continue to beg its helpful benefits with easing the pain of cancer.

If you are dying of anything, including cancer, Alzheimer's, heart ailments, blood diseases etc., you should be able to ingest dog crap, if you choose. Now that's a fair thought, right?

Most all of my captured narcotics suspects indicated that they all began their dope habits with marijuana. I can hear those snickers and groans coming from all of those who doubt me, so go ahead with your condescending notions, but I'll stick by that same philosophy.

It is well known that today's cop doesn't possess the same standards as we had in our day (1967), and today it is much more difficult to find someone who hasn't tried dope in many other forms, so what do you expect?

So the bar has been lowered to allow more candidates into the law enforcement profession. How do you feel about that? Recent presidents have admitted to using it, as well as cocaine, so why not a cop?

If you are looking for a more compassionate, touchy-feely kind of cop, good luck. My feelings are etched in stone, and I don't sway away from the fact my friends were killed because of dope.

If you smoke dope, or use dope in any way unless prescribed, I don't care for you or your friends, period.

CHAPTER 59

KIDNAPPED

It was early morning in the City of Cudahy, and as usual, the activity was a little slow. Working in this city was quite a bit different from the other Firestone Park communities. The first hour or two was spent writing at least a whole book of parking citations—twenty-five in each book. There was no overnight parking, and the citations caused the folks to pay attention to the crowded parking conditions. This was created by the vast array of apartment complexes that were built without adequate parking facilities. So much for the Cudahy city planning that allowed this problem to increase incrementally over the years with no remedies other than overnight parking restrictions.

My partner was Stephen R., whom I've worked with before. Remember the guy with bloody shorts? We polished off the remnants of the parking citations by both writing tickets and zigzagging back and forth on each street quickly before we got any calls or details. We were on the west side of Atlantic Avenue just off of Live Oak Street, gabbing about everything and anything. We decided to go get a hot cup of coffee. I turned northbound on Atlantic Avenue, which was practically free of any moving vehicular traffic. I was traveling slowly, looking around for anything out of the ordinary, listening for any unusual noises. A good patrolman always keeps his options fully open by keeping the front windows down. How else would he be able to hear a woman crying for help or any burglar-type noises that would not be discerned through a closed car window?

We were lazily traveling toward Florence Boulevard when I spotted six male pedestrians walking southbound on the western sidewalk of Atlantic Avenue. Actually, they were the only persons visible on the street. I guided my patrol car diagonally across the opposing traffic lanes, noting there was no other traffic. I mentioned to Stephen, "Let's check these guys out and see what they're up to!" I pulled up slowly and was able to see everyone's hands because they were spaced three to four feet apart.

I asked in a loud voice, "Where are you guys going?" One of the guys did the talking. "Long Beach. Our car broke down!"

Now that same man was walking toward my car, and I asked him to step aside and not block my view of the other pedestrians. My door was already partially ajar, and I was stepping out of my car. As the person drew closer to me, I noticed one of the others near a large display window, slightly waving at me for some reason. I thought maybe to get our attention. He then mouthed that the guy in front of me had a gun.

The warning was unmistakable, so I quickly raised my gun, which was already in my hand, pointed it at the man approaching me, and told him to stop moving and turn around. I quickly got away from my car and ordered all of them to lean against the large bay window.

As I approached, all six had their hands braced on the window, I turned slightly to notice my partner's position. Steve was atop the patrol car in front of the light bar. Yes, on top of the patrol car, not the hood. Steve's gun was at the ready and he had it pointed it toward all six pedestrians.

I started searching the first male, who was about twenty-one years old. He was shaking and whispered to me that the guy in the middle had a gun in his waistband. He said that he and the rest of the guys were being kidnapped. This guy was very nervous. His legs were trembling as if something very serious was going on, and his story was believable.

I went to the next guy, about twenty-three years old and spoke softly to him while searching him and asked him to tell me what was happening. His response was the same as the first person's, and this one also indicated the guy in the middle had a gun in his right waistband. This man was also extremely scared. He was trembling and in tears.

This drama was now going to ripen quickly. I backed up and told Steve, my partner, that the guy in the middle apparently has a gun.

Steve focused more on the adult in the center. I went to the next guy, who also was about twenty-one, and he parroted the same story about being kidnapped as his companions. He too was trembling and very thankful for us stopping them because he said the guy was going to kill them.

As I searched each male adult, I cautioned them not to move or talk. They all complied. I then moved toward the next man, who was approximately twenty-five years old. He said they were just walking through the streets going to Long Beach, because their car broke down on the on-ramp to the Long Beach freeway, and they were coming from the 10 freeway interchange.

I positioned myself behind the suspected gun-carrying male and told him if he moved, he could get shot real easy. Of course he knew full well Steve was somewhere directly behind me. He said he understood. I ran my hands around his waistband and located the handle of a large pistol stuck inside his right front waistband.

As I grabbed the gun, I withdrew it and backed away immediately so my partner could have an easy shot.

The gun was a .357 magnum, Smith & Wesson revolver, loaded with five live rounds and one spent round. I conveyed my findings to Steve, who was still focused intently on the suspect. His firearm was pointed directly at the suspect's back. I returned to the now-unarmed suspect and ordered him to place his hands behind his back. I handcuffed him for the weapon violation. I completed searching the suspect and went around our car and placed him into the rear seat.

I went back to the fourth man, who was approximately twenty-one years of age, and began searching him. Not surprisingly, he repeated the same story as the others. He was greatly relieved when I had arrested the man as well. The fifth pedestrian was about twenty years old, and his story was convincingly the same as the other four.

Once I finished with the searching, Steve came down from the roof of the car and stood by the seated suspect. I took each guy aside and asked what had happened. Their stories were similar and very compelling.

Their remarkable story began as all five were coming from Hollywood. They picked up the suspect, who was hitchhiking on Sunset Strip Boulevard. They traveled to the 10 freeway and were headed eastbound when the suspect, who was later identified as Ralph N., pulled out a gun and stuck it in their faces and said, "This car better not fuck up, or I'm going to kill all of you!"

Suddenly, and without any reason, the engine stopped working. They had to pull the car to the shoulder on the eastbound transition ramp, to the southbound Long Beach Freeway.

All of them began to beg for their lives when "Ralph" came out of the car with his gun in hand;, very angry, and insisting that he was going to kill them all.

Ralph, during his tirade then fired one round into the right rear tire and said, "You see, this fucking thing works!" They all witnessed the tire deflate and they began walking with him from the freeway until we stopped them. (Note: that would account for the empty casing in the gun when I retrieved it from Ralph.)

They also stated another police car had stopped and talked to them, just north of Cudahy, and asked them where they were going. Ralph responded, "To Long Beach!" The police said, "Good, keep moving and don't stop!" They said that the police didn't even get out of their car, just brushed them off. They didn't know what else to do.

All five were very elated, shook our hands, and hugged us several times. They were jubilant because we arrested the suspect, and they were extremely relieved to be out of a situation that seemed very grim and could have had much more serious consequences for them.

The lesson of this event is that you shouldn't pick up a hitchhiker, even though it might seem the friendly thing to do, and even if he appears to be a good guy.

"Ralph" was transported to Firestone Park Station and booked on five counts of kidnapping, five counts of assault with a deadly weapon, and one count of possession of a stolen firearm.

An added feature to the arrest was that the gun "Ralph" had in his possession was stolen from Binghamton, New York, in a burglary. Also it was learned that suspect Ralph was also recently from New York City as well.

The victims were all given a ride to their car which had already been stored at a local towing yard. They were then transported home by another unit.

I need to mention something about Stephen R., who was my partner in this and several other situations I was involved with. He is presently on death row in the California prison system, and as of 2012, he just lost his appeal.

Stephen turned to a life of crime in the mideighties and was sentenced to eighteen years in prison for a whole slew of armed robberies in the Southern California area. He served ten of those years in prison, and within one year of his early release in 1994, he robbed and murdered a supermarket manager in the Yorba Linda area. Part of his defense for his abhorrent criminal behavior was that he had witnessed many ghastly crimes and emergencies while working out of the Firestone Park station for several years.

He also worked out of the sheriff's West Hollywood station, where he witnessed a man trapped inside a burning car after a traffic collision. That man burned to death and was trying desperately to get out of the car. Stephen witnessed this entire ordeal and did his best to save the trapped man, but to no avail.

Stephen's lawyer tried desperately to locate someone to help persuade the appellate court to rescind Stephen's death penalty judgment because of his exposure to real life events that afflicted his mind and caused him to change to the life of crime, claiming a kind of post-traumatic stress disorder.

He lost his appeal and remains on death row in California.

CHAPTER 60

THE DEATH QUAGMIRE

The Willowbrook area was a hotbed of violent crimes that were always racially stirred up and active. Willowbrook is nestled just south and adjacent to the Watts community within the City of Los Angeles. Willowbrook is separated mostly by Imperial Highway to the north and Alameda Boulevard to the east. Central Avenue is on the west side and its southern border is the city of Compton.

There was so much dope available, people were literally standing on corners swaying from side to side, absolutely bombed out of their minds on narcotics. To fill a unit with drunks on drugs would have been an easy task, but it would have taken all working units out of the field. Clogging the jail with drunks only and leaving the area open to the ever-present, entrepreneurial, slick, jive-ass, ready and willing, enthusiastic criminals was frowned on.

One place in particular that was rife with narcotics was called Lyon's Lounge. It was on the west side of Willowbrook Avenue just north of El Segundo Boulevard.

It was next to an open dirt lot slightly covered with weeds and lots of small pieces of trash. This was the place where drugs and guns were being sold twenty-four hours a day. Countless arrests came from the perimeter surrounding the sleazy bar, with no letup in sight. I was there nearly a hundred times and made at least thirty or forty arrests during my first year working out of Firestone Park Station. On top of it all, it was smack dab in the middle of our patrol area.

One night my partner and I were slowly passing by the location and spotted several black men who noticed us coming toward them, quickly lowered their hands, and turned away from our approach.

I got out of the car first, because my partner was driving. I walked toward the group and watched who was watching my movements on the approach.

It was dark and eerie with small pockets of fragmented street lighting scattered throughout that helped conceal minor hand movements. The area had a strong stench of human urine that only added to the fragrance and tang of crime, emphasizing that serious shit was about to happen.

One guy gave me a real snide look, maybe because I was eyeballing all of them. I was careful to discern who was acting out a diversion, and who most likely had contraband. It was obvious someone in this group did and all I needed was for one of them to make a foolish hand gesture or movement. My partner, Paul, was behind me, off to the side and few feet away, watching my backside.

I was now coming upon the small group, and the one with the snide looks turned away and moved both of his arms from my view. He was obviously doing something near his front belt area, and my focus was more on him. I thought perhaps he was putting away a gun or dope to avoid my detection. I had my pistol out now, resting along my leg, ready if something deadly popped out.

The others in the group moved away from this guy. That alerted me even more as I came upon him about three feet away. I ordered him to stop and not to turn around, or I was going to do something he wouldn't like.

Oddly enough, he complied and remained motionless. At this point I had my gun almost to his back. I told him to put his hands behind his back.

He still hadn't turned around, but his hands moved behind him. I quietly put my gun in its holster, took out my handcuffs, and cuffed the man up. Then I brought him backward toward my partner.

My partner watched the remainder of the group as I was focusing on the one at hand. I reached into his waistband and found a Smith & Wesson 9 mm automatic pistol, fully loaded with one in the magazine.

In his front pants pockets were some rather bulky items that seemed like large bags of pills. I pulled the bags out of each pocket and saw that they were heavy-gauge, sealed plastic bags of "red devils," or sodium secobarbital. The bags had a small white pieces of paper displaying the name of the drug and the number of pills, five hundred in each bag. The packets were similar and apparently right from a hospital pharmaceutical supply. This was a substantial find, and along with the gun, it meant that he was obviously selling the drugs and carrying the gun so he wouldn't get ripped off himself. Oh, the glory of it all, a true crook.

His name was Thomas R. We took him to jail and booked him for possession of a controlled substance for sale and possession of a loaded gun as well. This was in fact a pretty good observation and arrest and we felt pretty good about our luck at that location. We opted to stay away for the next few days so we wouldn't burn the location out. Everyone would obviously stay away because of our vigilance.

Approximately two weeks later, we received a call to the Lyon's Lounge. An assault with a deadly weapon had occurred there, and we were the handling unit's backup. As we pulled up to assist the handling unit, we could see two men lying face down near the front steps of the bar, and another just around the corner lying on his back. They all appeared to be dead; large amounts of blood had already poured onto the sidewalk, dirt, and rubbish.

The handling crew had already determined that they were indeed dead and were placing the call to have detectives roll out to this one, because of the grave consequences.

I walked over to the one male clad in a plaid shirt lying on top of the dirt, small rocks, and rubbish. I recognized him as Thomas R. from two weeks earlier and nearly in the same exact spot. Only this time he was dead.

It seemed the obvious took place here. Three were dead, and there were many more to come, given the criminal atmosphere and activity that blanketed the Lyons Lounge area. It would be interesting to get the unskewed statistics for that area, within fifty feet in either direction of Lyon's Lounge, and see exactly how many people have died there in the past forty years. What do you think? Would you like to know? Can anything be done to change that data?

CHAPTER 61

WHUPPED

We were over on Mona Boulevard, just above Imperial Highway near 111th and Grape Streets, right on the edge of the Nickerson housing projects. Special attention was given to that area because of the random shots fired at law enforcement.

My trainee and I were shaking down quite a few gangbangers who were caught bunched up and all pretty much startled when we slipped up on them around nine o'clock in the evening. There were about fifteen to twenty of these hoods, dressed to the max like street gangsters, so we had our hands full keeping an eye on all of them. They were all leaning, both hands against one home's stucco wall and a fence, grumbling about the harassment we were initiating. That was our job.

If you really want to place blame on who enables gangs to organize, then think about all of these gangsters' parents. At this time of the night, where were the parents, and why were these thugs out at all?

As we were shaking them down, a certain hood across the street was shooting his mouth off. "Fuck these pigs, jump 'em!" He was a little smaller than the ones we were dealing with, but he had the same gang mentality and aggressiveness. He repeated himself many times, as we were pretty much tied up for at least a half hour.

As we neared the last several of the unsearched hoods, another unit came by and backed us up. I had made mention to the assisting unit that I needed to talk with the mouthy one as soon as we were done, and they assured me they would grab him for us as they pretended to leave.

A short time later we concluded with our pack of hoods, and we were returning their various assortments of ID. The backup crew feigned going to their car, circled the one loudmouth, and nabbed him without further ado.

The crew promptly brought the mouthy thug over to our car and turned him over to us as we placed him against the same wall where the others were before. While we searched this mouthy, cantankerous one, he kept up his tirade as if he wanted to be seen and heard by all to amplify his visibility and rating in the community. He had an especially thick and heavy overcoat on, which could easily conceal all sorts of guns or weapons. I asked him to take it off so I could search him more thoroughly.

Once his overcoat came off, it revealed a kind of skinny thug with small muscular development. Without his coat, he was pretty much stripped of any threat and was just left with his foul mouth. As we were discussing his antics, a black male, approximately forty years of age, came up to us and asked us if his son had done something wrong. I stepped back and discussed the situation with the man, and informed him of what his son was saying and that he was apparently trying to gain favor with the group of thugs we were searching.

The man was very displeased with what we told him about his son's challenging behavior and asked if he could take him home now. He would take care of his behavior immediately.

I informed him that we weren't really done yet. It seemed his son really wanted to go to jail, so he would be like one of the "boyz in the hood."

His dad said he would take his son home and take good care of him. I asked the father if he could handle the gangster, and he assured me he could, and if I wanted to come over to the house, he'd show me as well.

I agreed with his remedy, and we walked several homes up the street and went to a dimly lit home with the man.

His son followed us with his head down and went right into the home. His father and I stayed in the living room. The father yelled to his son to take off his jacket and return quickly. He grabbed a high-backed wooden chair and placed it in the middle of the room.

When his son returned, he ordered his son to drop his pants and lean over the chair. Now that same tough guy started to whimper and cry without any punishment whatsoever, but not to his father's satisfaction. His dad again repeated his order for him to lean over the back of the chair, and the son reluctantly complied.

His dad then drew his black leather belt from his waist and folded it in half. He began to slap the gangster's rump quite professionally, at least ten times. Each lashing pulled a yell from the thug as the pain was delivered home.

When he was finished, the father stated, "You yell like that again at the officers, and you'll get double the whuppin' you got here today." With that final warning, the hoodlum ran immediately to his room crying.

I thanked the father for his support, understanding of the local gang problem, and his immediate remedy. I praised him and said that if the same situation occurred again, I would certainly report his son's behavior to him rather than haul the sissy gangster off to jail.

This was one of many instances where mothers and fathers approached me and begged for their children back instead of going to jail. Their awareness and alertness to these community problems were helpful and persuasive enough to cause the problems to go away. They were in contact with law enforcement when the situation arose and quickly approached the officers in a way that was friendly and intuitive. I wish more parents would be involved in these kinds of efforts, but unfortunately, not enough are.

If these so called gangsters suffered the same consequences as this wannabe thug, think of what the gangster would say to them when his dad or mom
spanked his rump. He wouldn't say anything. But had we hauled him off to jail,
he would have brandished that as a trophy and gained sympathy from all the
hoods for being picked on by the police.

CHAPTER 62

CHILDHOOD DISCIPLINE?

We arrived on Gibson Avenue in East Compton after receiving the call that there was a family disturbance. The location was a nice, small one-story home. Several kids were running around in the front room when their father walked in and asked us to sit down.

The four kids ranged from eight to eighteen years of age. Everyone seemed very somber. The father was a big man, about six three, 240 pounds, well groomed, and very upset about what had happened approximately forty-five minutes earlier. He said that the whole family was seated for dinner around five. The mother said that their eighteen-year-old son had gotten into some trouble earlier in the day. It was learned the son was hanging around gang members from Compton Park.

When the mother finished, the eighteen-year-old spoke up and argued that he wasn't hanging around the gangsters; the people who told the mother that he was, were lying.

The father became irritated and ordered the son to keep silent about what his mother was saying. The son was noticeably upset that his father cut him off, and he began mumbling incoherently about the incident. A short time passed, and the father could hear his son still mumbling over the incident. He told the eighteen-year-old to stop mumbling and that he, Dad, would look into the matter after dinner and get to the bottom of it by speaking to several neighbors.

This irritated the son, who slid his chair back and pounded the table, vocalizing his displeasure that everyone was talking about him.

The father said he saw his son remove something from the table, possibly a napkin. Then he stood up rapidly and walked away from the kitchen table, passing behind his dad, who was still seated at the table and comfortably eating his dinner. Dad heard a growl from his son, and he was struck in the back with something very sharp, which drove Dad's face nearly into his dinner plate.

Dad stood up quickly, and grabbed his son by his shirt, and began to punch him all over his face and body until the son fell to the floor crying. Unbeknown to the dad, he had a three-inch meat fork firmly stuck in his back. This was the kind with the small levering piece of metal that teeters halfway, close to the handle, in order to separate meat.

When he finished disciplining his son, the father strained with his right hand and arm reaching behind his back and withdrew the two-pronged meat fork from the middle of his back. There wasn't very much blood and his wounds on the upper right side of his back had somehow missed his vital organs.

The dad was adamant that his son needed to go to jail and that he would go to the hospital immediately to have his wounds evaluated and attended to.

We went to the eighteen-year-old son's bedroom and talked to his son, who was seated on his bed, sobbing. We explained that he would have to be arrested and held accountable for what he had done to his dad. We arrested him without incident for assault with a deadly weapon and booked him at Firestone Park Station.

Now, although the son was arrested and jailed for assault on his father, I'll bet that boy suffered more than anyone else about his gang affiliation. I would also be willing to guess that the son didn't get into a gang and is probably more appreciative of his parents for their concern than others in similar situations.

CHAPTER 63

DRIPPING OIL LINES

I was working the north end in the Firestone Park community with my partner and was driving in the alley just south of Firestone Boulevard, just off Compton Avenue. It was about three in the morning, and we were slowly traveling westbound with our patrol head lamps off. Not much was going on, but we were coming onto a fairly new car parked near a garage, but slightly off-angle. It was a nearly completely stripped-out Plymouth, four door, blue in color, no doors, bald tires, no seats, no hood or trunk lid. The license plates were missing as well.

We quietly walked around the car and noticed its engine was missing. The only things left were the dangling hoses, wires, and thin tubes. It seemed that the stripped car had just been dropped off because the metal framework was still a little warm and dry to the touch.

I noticed the oil lines dangling and still oozing a small amount of oil. I looked to the rear of the car and could see the dripped oil path that followed the stripped-out car. I could follow the drip path in reverse and plainly see the oil path trailing from where the car had been pushed. I asked my partner to follow me with the patrol car as I tracked the oily path.

The path went two and one half blocks, crossing two streets and back into the alley to a white framed garage and detached home. I couldn't believe the dripping lines led directly into the garage, as if they completely forgot to tie up the lines so they wouldn't give away their original position in the garage.

I reached for the handle of the garage door and pulled it up. Lo and behold it was unlocked, and there were all of the parts of the stripped-out car neatly stacked along the sides of the garage walls. Even the engine was still hanging from the engine hoist which was in the rear portion of the garage. They must have finished about an hour earlier and were probably all tuckered out from stripping the car down to nothing. Then, because they were so tired, they forgot to tie up the oil and fuel lines to keep the fluids from dripping onto the road.

We requested two units to back us up as we went up to the house, which was dark inside, indicating the occupants were possibly asleep. I moved around to the backyard and near a roughed-in room addition next to a patio area. There against the studs were two of the car's fenders near the back door. No dogs were around, and it was quiet until I heard something fall inside the home by the back door.

At this point I felt we were being watched, and our safety was being compromised without an announcement that law enforcement was in their back and front yards. I went to the back door and knocked loudly as the lights on the three patrol cars went on.

A black man approximately thirty-five years of age came to the door in his shorts and asked what was happening. I asked if he was the owner of the home, and he said he was.

I asked if anyone else was in the home, and the man said his brother, who was asleep, and a male friend were there. They had just gone to bed about an hour earlier, because they were playing cards and drinking most of the night.

I asked if I could come inside to talk with the man about certain things had occurred, and it involved everyone in the home. He seemed concerned about exactly what was happening, but I withheld that info until he was able to get his brother and friend up. They came outside for an interview with other officers.

Once everyone was purportedly out of the home I asked the owner if it was okay for me to search the home for anyone else and evidence of his utility bills. Those utility bills would establish and confirm ownership of the home if his name and address were on the invoices. My partner and I then went into the home, while the other deputies watched the three occupants, who were seated in three separate patrol cars incommunicado.

We were looking primarily for any other persons who might be hiding in the home, so we began carefully examining anywhere someone could hide. I was near completion and noted an oily handprint on an attic hatch in the small narrow hallway. I decided to just poke my head into the small hallway attic access hatch to satisfy my curiosity. I grabbed a strong kitchen chair and placed the chair beneath the access door. I grabbed the edge of the supporting rafters and pulled myself upward until I was just able to peer into the small attic with the aid of my flashlight. I saw an unusual firearm near the attic hatch ledge opening.

I lowered myself back onto the kitchen chair and reached into the attic where I felt the gun and picked it up by the stock. As I withdrew the gun and brought it down I noted it was a machine gun with a fourteen-inch magazine attached. It was an Apache .45 caliber submachine gun, fully loaded with one in the chamber. The magazine held twenty-five or thirty rounds.

Possession of this firearm was a felony. It also indicated to me that the owner could have fired upon us in the backyard and wiped out several of us quite easily. Thank God he wasn't that bad or felt he couldn't get away with that type of resolution!

All three male adults were arrested for grand theft auto and possession of stolen auto parts, and the owner was also charged with possession of a machine gun.

CHAPTER 64

CITY OF CUDAHY

The city of Cudahy is a small city that was originally a contract city assigned to Firestone Park Station. This is the city where I had made an arrest for kidnapping and false imprisonment involving five victims. The city was no stranger to crime, but did not have as many rich targets.

Many situations occurred there, because it was a working-class city, loaded with apartments and several trailer parks. We did a lot of work there and controlled the crime pretty well. Just before I left Firestone Park Station the staff detailed me to a ceremony of transferring the "law enforcement baton" to the city of Bell, which was located immediately north of Cudahy. It was a sort of sad ceremony, even though I was honored to pass the wooden baton to the Bell police sergeant. I liked working in the city, because I knew it well and liked the folks who lived there.

Cudahy was disenchanted with the operational costs the sheriff's department charged them for law enforcement services. They also wanted a more compassionate police force and specifically an agency that would take on more of the minor tasks police departments do to assist the city government, like cater to the city staff and city council. Apparently the city of Bell insisted it could do the job cheaper and more graciously, so Cudahy cancelled the sheriff's contract and went with city of Bell.

Cudahy was out of the picture from Firestone Park's perspective, and shortly thereafter, 1973, I transferred to the sheriff's academy as a drill instructor for the cadet classes.

As fate would have it, one of my cadet classes had a certain special cadet within the ranks of one class. I was told he was the mayor of Cudahy. That didn't bother me much, except he was so special, he needed help in all endeavors of instruction. So that cadet was given an exemplary cadet to be his mentor, to make sure he didn't fail. This job was tough, very time-consuming, and really unfair to the cadets trudging through on their own merits. But that's politics, and that's the way the sheriff wanted it.

Years later, when I was assigned as a sergeant to the East Los Angeles station (1993), I was called in to the captain's office. He was a good man and treated me very well. He had a special task for me—to go to Cudahy and in a ceremony to receive the law enforcement baton from the Bell Police Department. This gesture was to signify that Cudahy was now back as a contract city, and I was designated as the person to receive the baton.

The city's only request was that they did not want any connection with the Firestone Park Station or its personnel. East Los Angeles was now to be the contracted station.

I begged the captain's pardon to exclude me, because I was in fact a former Firestone Park deputy and the very one who passed the law enforcement baton to the city of Bell nearly twenty years earlier. The East Los Angeles captain was adamant that I accept the baton and not to say anything about my past assignment to Firestone Park Station. Well, now I was part of the political mix, ordered to keep my mouth shut, and I did.

There was no serious breach, but still deception was part of the mix. I really felt humiliated and embarrassed to be the recipient, but everything went down without a hitch, and I managed to survive.

CHAPTER 65

FIRESTONE PARK'S TRIANGLE

As a deputy working out of Firestone Park Station, the day would start by coming into the station from the rear parking lot and through the double doors.

Once inside and clear of the swinging doors, you would be about twenty feet from the watch sergeant's office door, which was wedged open most of the time. It was easy for the desk sergeant to see what was going on, and we could overhear his warm verbal appraisals. Many times comments poured out of that office about arrests, suspects in custody, deputies' uniforms, combative suspects and overstimulated reactions to what was going on in the booking cage.

Firestone's booking cage was a constant den of activity. The cage was approximately twelve by fifteen feet, with a short solid wall and two-inch heavy-gauge screen from three and a half feet up to the ceiling on two sides. Two stainless steel counters bordered the screens, which allowed deputies and other personnel to fill out booking slips and all other types of book work. The gate was a heavy framed two-foot wire door with a heavy-duty electric locking mechanism.

These three areas—back swinging doors, watch sergeant's office, and booking cage were configured in a relatively tight pattern, forming a triangle. Within this triangle something was always about to happen. Ongoing activity could develop in to a fight between combative inmates, deputies against inmates, or deputies coming in with a combative suspect fighting the officers as they were walking him or her through the doors.

Blood was no stranger to this area, and generally wiped up immediately by the station's own trusties, who were housed there for a variety of menial tasks.

The watch sergeant was always the one to set the tone of attention, making sure the booking cage, front desk, and his office were orderly and within the guidelines of the department's policies and procedures. Some sergeants were excellent, some not so excellent. Actually, several of the sergeants were toadies, who were about as inept as hell, but they kept real close to some of the stronger lieutenants, like silly lapdogs begging for a bone.

Hearing a commotion was generally the clue that a fight was in progress in or near the triangular area. "Hit the gate!" will always resonate in a Firestone deputy's mind. No other station would experience such a hotbed of activity.

I can't remember how many times I escorted someone in custody, coming through the back swinging doors and falling on the light-tan tile floor and fighting all the way, nearly into the watch sergeant's office. Then we would swing left near the booking gate, and desk personnel would come running up to assist me in securing the suspect. The jailor would many times have to stand back and watch other unrelated inmates inside the booking cage to make sure they didn't get involved in the ruckus. Several times when a fight broke out, the lieutenant would come by to watch the battle and offer guidance and directions. Once while I was rolling around on the floor attempting to control a violent suspect who was punching me, someone suggested, "Hit the son of a bitch harder!" That person was the night lieutenant, his spit-shined shoes near my face as he yelled for me to fight harder while staying out of the physical confrontation.

Later that same lieutenant became one of the most valued officers in our department and was looked up to by most hardworking deputies who were proud of our department. Unfortunately, that same lieutenant was retired from the department rather early, because of his excessive care, concern for details, and ability to run the department in a positive role. He was an excellent assistant sheriff. (May the gods bless him, his steadfast determination, and his excellent work ethic.)

It also seems rather peculiar that most of the sergeants and lieutenants who had worked at Firestone Park Station became major administrative icons for our department. Those selected individuals spoke reams about what was going on within the department, and those individuals' exposure had immersed them in an unbelievable amount of experience.

Yearly statistical books taken within the department would clarify any offered outside embellishments that seem to minimize how much action and just how busy the activities were at Firestone Park Station.

CHAPTER 66

COMPARATIVE DUCK THEORIES

The activities of my time as a deputy cannot be compared to today's activities because back then, prior to the nineties, car and pedestrian stops were encouraged. Reasonable cause and observation arrests were made night and day without much prompting from our supervisors.

If it looked like a duck and quacked like a duck and acted like a duck, then it was a duck. So if you spotted a strange person acting suspiciously, you would stop and talk with him or her without question. Today's officers are discouraged from profiling—or operating under the duck theory—and they only make arrests when necessary and legally compelled to do so.

Our proactive supervisors condoned arresting as many as you could handle, which meant to pack as many crooks in the car as possible and haul them off to the station for whatever the charge was. That meant sometimes a hardened thug could be brought to jail for spitting on the sidewalk. That arrest could very well violate his or her parole or probation. Guess what? It worked. There was an endless supply of hardened thugs in our area, and we took advantage of it. We skipped compassion toward crooks.

If you paid attention to your work—being seen and moving around your area of patrol—you could easily bring in three to five arrests per night and keep yourself busy. There wouldn't be any time to do anything else except drink coffee and have a donut.

Today, unfortunately, units don't rush to calls; they take their time, because getting to the call quickly might generate a complaint for the handling deputy. Arrests would take place if you got there too soon, so by delaying response, what do you think? Minimal complaints!

Because arrests are discouraged, deputies are now are inclined to drive around and not shake down or search many individuals, because it would generate complaints for violating their civil rights. Remember, reasonable or probable cause is always necessary. If a deputy has too many complaints today, let's say five to be a medium standard, the deputy couldn't transfer anywhere until the complaints were cleared up. Does this method bother you? It should.

Presently, law enforcement is under pressure to try to make themselves appear more effective based on the generated personnel complaint system. To check on this theory, the next time you call for service from your agency on anything, see how long it takes for a unit to get there.

In my day, a code-three response was three minutes away, maximum. If you didn't get there in three minutes then you weren't in your designated area. Today, I'm sure they have an excuse for the delayed response, but that won't hold up against any timeline study. Calls will be held up and given out to allow the heat of the battle to settle down. Once it's over, then a car is assigned.

I feel that the deputies are not to blame. The system has changed to pacify the public and neutralize law enforcement to the point where they are ineffective.

Actually the duck theory is now known as profiling. I believe the Feds made the term up and caused its meaning to appear to be picking on minorities. Gee, I can't imagine why! (Check the unskewed stats.)

It was common sense and nothing more. Entire communities, including attorneys, judges, businessmen, councilmen, and children, know full well what a gangster looks like, what is guilty behavior, and what is innocent behavior.

Police aggression now appears to be identified as moving toward the front doors of the police station. Oh yes, it has gone that far. Technology will reveal incoming 911 calls as disputed sources of information in court. These beliefs are pursued by attorneys and will probably initiate future proceedings to stop police aggression as soon as cops start getting into their uniforms. You may laugh and think that's absurd, but time will tell where this is headed.

Folks in my neighborhood complain all the time that it is no use to call, because the deputies don't show up for hours at a time. That's essentially the way the LAPD turned around since the appointed chief, Bratton, was brought in from the New York Police Commission. Under the Christopher Commission, federal agencies concluded that law enforcement here was way too aggressive, and their behavior was focused primarily on minorities.

Gee, I wonder where the feds got their information. Not from the ACLU. Hopefully not from the deplorable "Perez gangsters" who were allowed to work out of the Hollenbeck Station. Not to digress, but where were Perez's supervisors? Boy, was that situation overblown. Ask any ex-LAPD officer who worked there when it was going on. It is no different from any other police station. There are always two or three idiot cops who do stupid things and get everyone else in trouble—kind of like your kids, huh? The mere fact that Mayor Hahn pulled an appointed commissioner from the New York Police Department says a lot.

Chief Bratton had virtually no police experience at all and was brought into an agency that had tons of experience and good qualified members. All Bratton had to do was everything the city council and mayor directed him to do, and he'd have the best smarmy position available. On the sheriff's department, it's a little different; the best position available for an elected official is the sheriff. He or she is the chief law enforcement officer in the county. So if any riots occur, he can elect to stop them at his will and settle any delays of local law enforcement agencies that actually fuel a riot. If the sheriff decides to move in, the riot will be stopped and dealt with accordingly.

For the sheriff to cater to any individual city's government would inhibit his influence, response, and judgment. He must be held accountable for any wrongdoing within local police departments and stay above any fraternization claims by miscreants. That means whoever is elected sheriff had better know law enforcement very well. It doesn't mean putting a federal agent in that top position or pulling in someone else's political appointee or sycophant to a commissioner's position.

You need to know what each position does and why commissions are put into place. If commissions were put into place to oversee police activities, then why create them? To appease the wronged public, and more specifically, for their political influence. If they are a political buffer to intervene in investigative matters, then who put them into the commission? There is always taint, and it is difficult to unveil it when the commission is every part of the problem.

If there are good, strong supervisors in the field, then little can go wrong. If the supervision is weak, at any level, then anything could go wrong.

Observation arrests are critical. Receiving a complaint over the phone and dispatching a car quickly is critical. The quick arrival of the dispatched car is a necessity, not an option. Combine all three, and your service is unmatched.

The complaint system in place is terrible, and law enforcement cannot do its job. If the powers at hand criticize any of the above criteria or delay the response in any way, then they are not acting with due diligence, and they're slowing down basic apprehension techniques.

If there is an area of heavy crime or high murder rate a footbeat is needed. Whenever crime is so prolific, it needs to be addressed with a two-man footbeat until it is resolved. The footbeat meets all citizens and crooks and knows exactly where they're located. They cannot be replaced with bicycle patrols or car patrols, because those entities are much too removed. Footbeats allow officers to meet everyone, so if the problem area is several blocks, let's say eight blocks, then two officers having a four-block area is not asking too much.

Every four-block area should have two officers, and in an eight-block area, four officers who have a random patrolling unit ready to pick up any arrests if made. This always leaves the four footbeat officers on the beat and ready to react to any calamity. Any area will greatly improve, and moreover, the community will meet the officers protecting them and mend any differences. This would be an ideal training environment for trainees and their training officers.

The problem is that in today's society, the requirements had to be lowered to become a peace officer. Too many new applicants have used dope at one time or another, and there are not enough applicants to pass the high bar developed in years past. The facts are that there is a tolerable amount of past drug usage for the selection of the new order of becoming a police officer. I wonder if they still take random yearly urine tests from all of its personnel, including everyone from deputy to sheriff, policeman to chief and commissioners.)

If you really want to know why more cops are off the street now then ever before, just ask the sheriff or chief of police how many personnel, lieutenants, sergeants and deputy investigators, work in the internal affairs unit? Once you find out that specific number, you will find out that's enough to man an entire station and more. That number of personnel requires how much money to operate? So what you have is cops investigating cops.

You might compare that number of personnel to any other large company. How many employees are at each store, and how many internal security personnel are assigned to the store as well? In my opinion, it's outrageous and a waste of money and resources.

CHAPTER 67

NEW YEAR'S EVE

The evening shift runs past midnight on New Year's Eve. Everyone is always ready and on the same page for the onslaught of the New Year's activities.

Generally, you patrol in the marked unit and let your presence be known. There are going to be a whole lot of calls for service come midnight, and the plan is to quit moving around maybe an hour to an hour and a half before the clock strikes midnight. This is probably the most dangerous night of the entire year. The entire area is about to be rained on with bullets, more than you could ever imagine. As the time gets closer to midnight, you and your partner will be looking for a place to hide, preferably with a hard cover to keep the lead from hitting you.

The deputies, desk personnel, and supervisors are aware that patrol cars will be shot at, and the persons shooting may very well get away with it because of the celebration. Of course their legal defense will be an overzealous patriotic nationalism and excessive public drunkenness. The shootings usually start at a little after ten thirty. At that time you will be well hidden from everyone. Several more rounds be discharged around eleven. Various calibers can be distinguished as heavy caliber and the rapid firing of machine gun rounds.

At about eleven forty-five, you had better be hunkered down because here it comes, and what a downpour. The entire area is riddled with gunfire, and if you or your partners come out for anything, more than likely you will catch a round or two, hopefully not in your body.

A whole slew of calls will report a man with a gun. No one will respond for at least an hour. The desk will let all callers know that there is an abundance of emergent calls, so the deputies will be late to most calls. Yeah, you'll hear some of the units running from call to call and getting shot at, but that's what happens if you don't hunker down.

No matter where you are, bullets will be falling on top of everything—a virtual "hail of bullets!" There are so many people involved in this gunfire, it is impossible to enforce any laws without casualties on both sides.

You can only imagine this type of turmoil, but next New Year's Eve, go to the corner of, say, Seventieth Street and Compton Avenue, and see if you can count the independent rounds. I'll bet you can't!

Since those hair-raising years, laws have been crafted to make it a felony, because of the deaths that had occurred. Those laws help, but shots continue to endanger anyone nearby.

Wait a minute, isn't it a felony to shoot someone? Does that still go on? Ever wonder why?

CHAPTER 68

TRAINEE FROM HELL

I knew he was coming, and I was not going to screw this up. The trainee would be here in a couple of days, and I was preparing myself for his arrival. I gathered all the pertinent paperwork and familiarized myself with the trainee exposure list.

My experiences as a trainee would never include the same type of instruction that I was exposed to. I was ready to set this one straight, and when I finished, I hoped he'd be a good deputy with a strong sense of integrity.

It meant long and tedious hours of instruction and report writing and the neverending process of paperwork.

The day he arrived he was very pleasant and attentive, and we hit it off right away. He knew very well I was willing to go the whole nine yards with him and broadly illustrate for him all avenues of success. I was very methodical and threw everything on the training list, which was rather exhaustive. We started off slowly and were very busy with many calls, details, and arrest reports. About two weeks went by, and things were becoming a little queer.

As we stopped suspicious cars I would ask Dave, my trainee, to do certain things, like watch the persons we stopped as I would turn away. A short time later, I would see Dave smoking a cigarette and casually talking with whomever we had stopped. I brought it to his attention every time, but somehow he would talk with almost everyone. It seemed he didn't understand the position I was attempting to mold him into. I stopped more and more individuals and brought his easygoing attitude to the surface. I took him to task and said that if he wasn't careful, he was going to get into trouble real quick.

We focused on the error each time, but he still didn't seem to understand. He was polite and attentive to a certain limit, but then just let go all of the survival points that he had learned in the past.

On several occasions, he was watching a suspect carefully, but then all of a sudden I would look toward him, and he wasn't watching the suspect at all. His attention span was rather limited and short-sighted. It became apparent he couldn't stop his behavior. He lowered his officer survival skills and techniques to a point where he was going to lose the suspect, who would run away, or one of us was going to get hurt, wounded, or killed.

His report-writing skills also suffered. He would start to write and he would forget what was needed in the same empty spaces that he had done quite a few times before.

Something was wrong, and I just couldn't my finger on it, but I was determined to find out. Unfortunately the same ailment spread to almost everything, and I came to realize he was unable to focus for more than the first several moments on anything he was doing. It could be report writing, stopping suspicious persons, or on calls, details, or assists; he was fatally flawed. As I brought each matter to his attention, he would earnestly try to correct his problems, but to no avail. I think he may have been suffering from ADD or ADHD or some other D ailment. I don't know, but something had to give.

One evening we pulled over a suspicious car with three male adults. I believe it was on Fir Street just above Firestone Boulevard.

It was about seven thirty, and I had just asked the three males to step out of their car and back to the patrol car, where we patted them down. Once they were checked and okay, I left Dave to watch the three as I searched their car for contraband. I got the acknowledgment from Dave that he understood what was to be expected, and I went to the driver's side door and opened it.

I was searching around inside the car under the front seat, and I heard and felt something pop, like the rear trunk.

It seemed rather puzzling, so I looked up and looked through the slit opening of the trunk lid, which was wide open, and saw Dave leaning forward into the trunk.

I leaned back to catch a quick view of the three males and noted they were behind my trainee, watching him!

I quickly came out of the car and back to the trunk and looked at Dave leaning fully into the trunk, almost off his feet, and then back toward the three males. Fortunately, they were pretty cooperative. They remained in their same positions and did not take advantage of my trainee's failure to provide a proper or reasonable level of care.

I scolded Dave as he was leaning into the trunk rummaging through various items. As he stood up, he seemed puzzled about why I was yelling at him. I didn't want to demean him in front of the three male adults, but I did anyway. He accepted my ranting about officer safety and lowered his head in shame. After a serious "butt chew," he came to realize what he had done wrong. This was one of the more serious absentminded situations I had ever seen, and I told Dave if he did it again, I was going to send him back for remediation of basic skills.

We were nearing four months and should have been near completion of his training, but I refused to sign off on many of his coverage forms that stated he had been exposed to and fully understood each area of instruction and protocol. He was floundering and couldn't redeem himself for his mistakes, and he knew failure was near.

My training sergeant was adamant that Dave had been on training long enough and wanted him kicked loose. I had told the sergeant many times that he was near failure. But despite my evaluation, the sergeant blindly compelled me to sign off his training sheets. I refused. Let's face it, my sergeant was not the sharpest knife in the drawer and he pushed for me to let Dave off training, and now! I argued that he was too much of kick-back kind of guy and probably not suited for law enforcement at all. The sergeant said, "Bullshit, he's been on long enough! I'm taking him off training today and effective today he is your partner."

My argument that he was unsafe and could very well get someone hurt or killed was not enough. The sergeant released him without my approval. Dave was now released and fully off training. I told the sergeant that in the past four months, he had never driven. I was going to let him drive and stop cars that he wanted to shake down.

The sergeant agreed and away we went as Dave drove his first night off-training. I told him I was ordered to let him off, although I thought he was not ready at all. We were working the earlymorning shift, twelve to eight a.m., in the north end and made an abandoned vehicle stop on the southbound side of Beach Boulevard just north of Ninety-Second Street. The car smelled like there was a dead body in the trunk of the car, but we were not sure; it could be just rancid meat. So we examined it, and put a tag on it for a second review in seventy-two hours, and left the location.

We continued southbound on Beach Boulevard, made a right turn onto Ninety-Second Street and one block westbound to Graham Avenue and then northbound Graham Avenue at approximately 30 mph.

I was writing Ninety-Second Street and Beach Avenue into my car log and felt my side of the car coming slightly upward. I looked up and saw a cement light pole coming at me.

I believe I was knocked out for at least ten to twenty seconds and awoke to Dave yelling at me from outside the car. He was screaming at me to get out of the car, because it was on fire! The radio car was awkwardly balanced, riding upwards along the pole, approximately eight feet in the air.

I could see Dave's head positioned on the bottom rear of the front seat, his hands cupped over his mouth as he attempted to get my attention.

I noticed the front windshield was smashed as if my head had slammed into it, but I didn't go through, as evidenced by the circular spider web of shattered glass radiating outward for approximately ten inches.

I tried to exit my side door, but it was jammed shut from the impact, so I dove out the opened right front passenger window. Unfortunately my Buckheimer swivel holster and grips of my pistol were stuck on the door jamb, and I found myself hanging upside down just outside the window.

My top lip was bleeding and felt like some one had just smacked me right in the nose. My upper lip was bulging, and blood was pouring from the abrasions on my upper lip and nose. I noticed my blood was dropping from my nose and lip and down on top of the dusty barron dirt beneath me.

After I realized I was stuck, I pulled myself backward and was able to release my gun grips and holster, and fell to the dirt about six to eight feet below. I distinctly remember the dust billowing upward and outward as I dropped to the ground.

I'll admit I was a bit delirious when I hit the ground. I crawled southbound for about thirty feet. I overheard Dave, my new partner, making an emergent request for three units to assist at Eighty-Seventh Street and Graham Avenue, regarding a car crash and fire, and a partner in need of emergent care.

That request was way too overreactive, so I stood up with blood dripping down my uniform and yelled at Dave to change that request to one car only, and to get me to the goddamn hospital.

Dave made the correction and just as he finished transmitting the request, a unit was seen racing around the corner and arrived within seconds.

The deputies came out of their car and assisted me into the backseat of their car. We were about to take off when Dave came running up to me and asked, "Larry, what should I tell the sergeant?"

I responded, "Tell him the damn truth! Oh, by the way what did happen?" Dave looked at me then lowered his head and said, "I fell asleep!" My response was, "Holy shit, Dave, we just checked that damn car on Beach Avenue!"

I was indicating to Dave that we were both wide awake no more than one or two minutes ago. With that in mind, the assisting unit sped me to Saint Francis Hospital in Lynwood, where I was treated for a minor concussion and released.

When I returned to Firestone Park Station, I walked by the sergeant who had demanded that Dave come off training. I just nodded my head as if he was overwhelmed with ignorance and complicity and left it at that.

I knew that he, his peers, and his superiors knew very well that he, the sergeant, was way out of line when he called the trainee ready to be released, and he may have very well caused me to be injured because of his blundering foolishness with an obvious ulterior motive.

Believe it or not, that same sergeant made it to captain level several years later. We never crossed paths again, I believe by design, because everyone knew I would not put up with his foolishness again and could make a spectacle of him quite easily.

To make matters worse, I learned the following day that Dave had hurt his back severely in that same crash and was retiring from the department. The steering wheel was bent and crushed from the impact against Dave's chest, and he was never able to return to work.

Later rumors were that Dave had become a wonderful and thriving professional bartender somewhere on the Colorado River and enjoyed by many folks.

CHAPTER 69

SPOOKED

I was working alone in the Willowbrook area just south of Imperial Highway when a call came over the sheriff's radio as a "see the woman" call regarding some strange article that was in her home. It was a rather routine lazy radio call on the day shift among the many report calls that occupied the day shift.

For the most part there were so many burglaries and thefts it seemed a lost cause for anyone to possess anything at all. Empathy is a key ingredient in all calls and reports, and there was a high sense of trying to help the people in this area. Gangs ran the whole area and stole nearly everything available to their little sticky thieving hands.

As I pulled up to a driveway in a small group of bungalow style homes, a black woman came up to me all excited and screaming something indistinguishable. She had a gray pallor as if someone had scared the living hell out of her, and she was in shock. She screamed and pulled on me to hurry into her small home and see what she was afraid of. I kept asking what the matter was, but she was out of breath.

Still not able to understand what I was getting into, I pulled my gun just as several other female neighbors came to the woman's aid and tried to calm her. They were also trying to find out what the problem was, but they couldn't understand her. She was just too hysterical and vapor locked, unable to say what had happened.

I walked to the front porch and opened the wooden screen door. It had the common squeak like a weak spring being stretched. I crept inward slowly and walked around the small front room and couldn't see anything out of order. I drifted into the small, apartment-type kitchen and snooped around as well. Still nothing. The owner came near the open front door and yelled out through the screen door, "It's in the bedroom! Go look in the bedroom!"

My gun was at the ready as I walked into the small bedroom and looked around the made-up bed and still couldn't see anything out of order. After about a minute the owner said, "Look inside the dresser drawers, it's in there!" I thought maybe someone put a snake inside the drawer, and it spooked her. That's what I had on my mind as I opened the top drawer, but again I saw nothing.

The second drawer was void any strange items as well, so I went to the third drawer and opened it slowly. I saw the bloody severed head of a German shepherd dog looking right at me with its tongue partially hanging from its mouth. It kind of spooked me as I stood there with my gun in hand, and I damn near had a bowel movement. I guess it caught me off guard as well.

I left the small home and came outside to talk to the woman, who was finally recovering and regaining her composure. She told me she had just taken a shower and went into the bedroom as she was drying off with a towel and opened the drawer to get some underwear. When she saw the grisly sight, she screamed and slammed the drawer and ran outside, screaming and crying. Another neighbor friend had called, but was unable to understand her problem.

My understanding was that quite a few of the kids in the area frequently performed operations on many of the local junkyard dogs in the neighborhood. I guess they were just trying to pull a prank on the woman to see what she would do.

I picked the severed head up from the drawer and placed it into several plastic bags that were lying around. I took the head with me when I left the location.

The first chance I got, I tossed the bags into an alley trash can. A basic malicious mischief report was taken to cover the incident.

CHAPTER 70

COMPTON PARK

This was a rather unique park in the city of Compton. It wasn't real big, about a city block long and maybe a half a city block wide. More dope and guns were sold there than anywhere else in the area. It was open and visible to everyone who came by and open for whoever was in the park to see what was coming.

This alone aided anyone selling dope, guns, and anything else because of the unobscured view from anywhere in the park. Law enforcement was impeded, because it was nearly impossible to approach from any angle.

It also provided ample time for escape. Criminal lookouts were posted and apparently paid well, because if any patrol car would come near, the lookout would give out a distinctive whistle or yell out "one time," "five-o"(a term from *Hawaii Five-0* that meant police), or some other prearranged word.

The scenes of attention were in and around the children's play area, sand-boxes, bushes, small trees, and expansive lawns. Guns would be secreted in the sandbox, wrapped in a blanket or towel four to six inches below the surface. The sand would be leveled out so it blended in with the surrounding sand, so it wouldn't appear disturbed by anything other than children's foot traffic.

The spot of concern would be marked with an empty white foam cup, partially filled with sand and slightly submerged. If the cops or rival gangs came by, you wouldn't have the guns on your person but very close. You had the ability to rapidly arm yourself by jamming your open hand into the sand, near the cup marker, and grabbing the blanket or towel, pulling all the guns up in one move, ready to go.

If the guns were found, trying to connect the guns to any one person would be too invasive and involve too much guesswork to make an arrest, especially if the guns were wiped down with an oily rag. (Most of the guns were stolen and the importance of their maintenance was far from care and concern.) The best cops could do was to confiscate the guns and get them off the street for a short time, pending if any were stolen, and of course they would be returned to the rightful owners as soon as they were found out.

Drugs could be secreted as well, usually marked by an empty soda can, and the plastic bags that contained the dope were free of fingerprints. Another way to secret handguns and dope was to cut the turf or lawn down two or three inches on three sides. Remove the excess soil on the underside, place the guns or dope in plastic bags, and close the grassy flap on top of the cutout. If the grass had a dandelion embedded in the sod, it might serve as a natural marker for the spot for instant recovery, but it was easily overlooked by law enforcement.

There were other ways to hide shotguns and rifles from cops and rival gangsters or dope dealers. In Compton Park, they would place the barrel downward in a large bush. It would easily blend into the array of radiating half-inch limbs at the base of the bush, and the stocks would be covered by the green foliage. Because of the vast number of bushes in the park, it was extremely hard to find any weapon contraband. Trees also served as places to hide shotguns and rifles. The cops would arrive, and the guns were there but undetected in the overhead branches.

Many shootings occurred in the park, often by the local gang shooting at a rival gang who thought no one had any firearms. To their dismay, the guns were there morning, noon, and night, and ready for any eventuality.

One night I was walking through the park, trying to remain hidden. I was fortunate the lookouts weren't posted. My partner was tracking me silently about a block away in the patrol car. The park was quiet, and there was not much foot traffic at all, so I was overlooked in my uniform.

I spotted two black men riding together on a single beach-cruiser bicycle, coming my way as I stood hidden by a small tree.

One of the men was on the handlebars, and the other was pedaling the bicycle lazily down the path. As they came near, I stood right in front of them and ordered them to stop. They complied and stepped from the bike.

I warned them that my gun was not in my holster. I suggested that they not to try to figure out where it was as long as they cooperated. It was actually in my right hand and easily brought up.

They turned their backs to me and placed their hands behind their heads as I shook them down. Both had loaded pistols in their waistbands, and they were set to fight off any attacker. I handcuffed each of them, held them at the elbows, and walked them to the curb near Atlantic and Compton Boulevard to meet up with my partner, who was watching from a distance.

This would be another perfect spot to get murder rate statistics—within a two-block radius of the park. It should be quite high, but it was skewed to deflect criticism of the park, because the city and county would do anything to keep murders from being connected to the park at all.

That was the hidden method for officials to claim the parks were safe when they really weren't. Oh, but the statistics said they were safe. Those claims would be dismissed by all of those who lived near the park and of course the local patrolling officers, but don't go any higher than that to get at the truth.

CHAPTER 71

SHERIFF'S ACADEMY: THE DRILL INSTRUCTOR

The purpose of going to the academy was to improve my personal skills and get as much training as possible.

Once you've mastered the fundamentals of law enforcement you go into instruction. After instruction, promotion will come when the higher-ups are satisfied with the level of competence you've generated. There are several basic philosophies and rules most deputies and cops agree they must follow:

1. Don't lose sight of why you became a cop.

2. Arrest as many crooks as you can before you retire, so you can help God sort them out.

3. Those who can, do; those who can't, teach!

4. Murphy's Law is true. What can go wrong, will go wrong!

5. The Peter Principle is top heavy. People are promoted to the level of their incompetence!

6. Enjoy your work or go back to selling shoes!

When I arrived, the other instructors felt we were all in the same mix. They were very methodical in everything and intended to drill everything in the cadet training manual as much as possible. The importance could not be over-emphasized. It cost lives if errors were made; some of them would die or get injured in the course of their duties. Their training would be subject to criticism and review throughout their careers. Some would be arrested and imprisoned for violating the most treasured resource: trust and decency.

What I was exposed to on Compton PD as well as at Firestone Park Station was a mix no one else had, and my exposure brought my skill and diligence to this position as an instructor, and it would not falter.

I was adamant that I would only let the best through and fight off any signs of favoritism and compromises of law enforcement's work ethic. This didn't mean the smartest or the highest IQ, it meant those who tried earnestly—with a good wholesome character, a healthy and robust personality, and good leadership qualities—would pass through.

I arrived in August 1972. I was quickly taught that marching was a major tool for all training. I needed to learn how to deliver every move for about four weeks. I was given many opportunities to march with the class and improve my command voice and cadence delivery.

My first cadet class was class #150.There were about 140 cadets in the class and we met them as they arrived in the parking lot on their first day. I'm sure most were stressed initially, but it would shock most people.

Most of the stress training was being replaced with a more fathomable, moderate discipline that wasn't as blindly obedient as before. The administration wanted more of a thinking deputy, one who would reveal himself or herself as kinder and more empathic.

The staff was good and wholesome and selected on their merits of good character and willingness to teach others their attributes and pass them on.

Most of us were braggarts—arrogant, self-righteous, pompous, and narcissistic. Outside of these few colorful descriptions, we were just willing to go forth and train as many as the department threw at us. This included regular deputy cadets, outside police department cadets, state agencies, Los Angeles city school officers, US military personnel with ambitions to become deputy sheriffs when separated from their tour of service.

Many agencies preferred the sheriff's academy because the structured curriculum and standards implemented were excellent.

The timeline for cadet classes was extended from sixteen to twenty-six weeks. To me, that was entirely too long. There was a whole bunch of downtime without any agenda. There were replacements for instructors who just didn't show up. Sixteen weeks was more than sufficient, as long as the cadets were linked to patrol operations every weekend. But that's my opinion.

Most classes had their own characters and tried their best. If I saw an honest endeavor in each one, I would make adjustments accordingly. If any deviation was spotted, it was immediately stopped and corrected. If a cadet was doing poorly on his or her exams, I would help so they would pass. If any deficiencies surfaced, I would do my best to direct them to a staff member who would remedy the problem and push the cadet to pass and go on to the next obstacle.

There were some who could not perform and were helped to a certain point, and then either they were terminated or recycled, or they resigned.

Several had severe problems handling role-playing scenarios and basic command presence, which alone are enough to control many situations.

CHAPTER 72

ARE YOU NERVOUS?

All would be told initially that to make it through the academy, they would need support from their families and loved ones. This was emphasized at family orientation, and most abided by the warning. If they didn't have that support or help, it would have a drastic effect on their performance and most likely they would fail.

Let me give you an example: In one particular class there was an individual waiting for the staff to come to their platoon, and check their uniforms and ask pertinent questions relating to what they were taught at least a week prior. As I drew closer, one female felt excruciating pains in her stomach. She would snap to attention, march off to the rosebushes, and throw up green stomach bile. She said it couldn't be helped; she was nervous on my approach. It became necessary to have her reexamined medically to see if she had a preexisting condition that might be detrimental to her career in law enforcement. The examination revealed she had a duodenal ulcer. She would not be coming back to the academy, because the stress aggravated her condition.

Her dad was a captain and her uncle was a lieutenant, both in our department, and they claimed I had scared her so much I gave that condition to her. That meant the dad and the uncle were focusing on me as the villain and needed me to lighten up on their loved one. After a brief interview with her, I learned that her dad and uncle had placed tremendous pressure on her to make it through the academy in order to be like them. She admitted that she didn't want to be in law enforcement at all but was forced to continue under the intense pressure from home. That pressure, in conjunction with the stress of the academy made her body react to anguish her mind couldn't handle. She was pleased the pressure had been revealed so she could go on with her life in a career of her choice.

As it turned out, similar situations would surface with each class as two to five male and female cadets would simply pass out from the apprehension of my coming near them. This was discussed in each class and helped many other cadets cope with external pressures.

CHAPTER 73

TOO FOCUSED!

Another example was a male cadet, who had his master's degree in chemistry. He was assigned to work at the Lennox sheriff's station for his weekend riding assignment. His awareness and attention to detail was great. He would write good reports and complete excellent car logs. His personal skills were a bit inhibited, but he was improving.

On this ride though, something appeared to be out of sync, and his training officer found out the hard way. They were on a call and both were out of the car and keeping the peace. They were winding down and returning to their car and a heated argument started to escalate again. The training officer told the cadet to continue writing his clearances and log entries, and he would step out for just a moment and reaffirm his prior admonishments.

The training officer apparently thought it was going to be minor, and he didn't need the cadet to stop his written tasks. The cadet said he understood his instructions and would continue on with his work.

It was a warm summer night, and the cadet rolled his window up to get the benefit of the car's air conditioner. The driver's window remained open, but the cadet was comfortable. The training officer was about twenty feet away from the cadet's right-side view. As the cadet was writing, unbeknown to him his training officer became involved in a fight for his life with the informant's adult children. He was being clobbered by both of them. The duo tag-teamed the training officer about five feet from the right front door of the patrol car.

The fight went on for several minutes and the training officer was calling for help from the cadet, but he, the cadet, was busy writing his car log and was so focused on the log, he never heard or saw the affray.

The problem is that whatever you are involved in, you must be able to adjust your priorities and adapt to whatever emergency is at hand. If not, then you shouldn't work in the field, because it will happen all the time.

The cadet understood he was no help to his training officer when he was being beaten. Only when someone called the station and told them an officer was being beaten up by two guys, and the assisting units arrived, did the cadet realize he failed to back up his training officer, and the consequences could have been fatal.

That cadet realized his error and decided to resign the following training day, because he couldn't bear the peer pressure from other deputies and his fellow cadets at Lennox Station.

Cadets would start off their day standing in formation and waiting for the staff to approach at seven o'clock exactly every morning. This would cause many to stiffen up and nearly faint from the apprehension of approaching staff. After a week or two, most would adapt. The day of instruction would start with the morning report of those who called in sick, absent, or just didn't show up.

Our pressure was consistent and routine and needed to be closely monitored at all times. In several weeks, these men and women would be issued guns and have the ability to shoot shortly thereafter. Their characters would blossom when the power of arrest was given to them.

Some in the class would be administrators, getting out of patrol as fast as possible, because if they're not productive, and easily spooked, they could get into trouble. To work in the field of law enforcement as a patrolman was an easy task or hard work. They could be slugs with a diminished level of energy, or hard chargers, active and driving around handling calls, details, and assignments, all the while looking for crooks. Some were absolute embarrassments to the career. They had never had been in a fight, their command posture was that of a wet noodle; they had voices like mice and the strength of anorexics.

These were individuals who somehow had got this far and should have been eliminated much earlier.

CHAPTER 74
THE MORGUE

I was introduced to the morgue while I was on the Compton PD. I went to the coroner's office just to see what it was like, accompanying bodies from Compton, mostly natural-cause deaths.

The corridors were loaded with dead bodies sitting along the walls; there must have been at least fifteen to twenty of them. They were laid out on hospital gurneys in supine positions and randomly placed head to foot, foot to foot, and head to head. I might add there was no refrigeration or any cooling system in that area. It was dark and dingy and poorly lit with flickering fluorescent lighting.

I walked down the ramp into the lower level and was allowed in because I was with the body. I was to surrender my charge, a deceased person from Compton, to one of the ghoulish deputy coroners in one of the autopsy rooms.

He signed the acceptance form, and I asked if I could look around and in on some of the autopsies. He smiled and said, "Sure, go right ahead, there's one going one in that room."

I walked into the room and saw a deputy coroner working on a man; his scalp was already cut open from the nape of the neck, but still within one inch of the hairline. The separated scalp was lying inside out, flapped and still attached to a five-inch front of his skull, also just about an inch behind the hairline, covering his forehead, eyes, nose, and mouth.

It actually appeared as if a small glob of thinly pressed hamburger covered the entire facial area. The top of the skull was sawed off and set off to the side.

The coroner lifted the brain from the rear lobe and severed the stem at the base of the brain so it could be removed and weighed. He then set into a stainless steel pan. When the brain was removed, you could plainly see the filmy tissue that separated the eyeballs from the brain cavity. The open skull with no brain revealed where the brain stem was severed, but it now was a void that exposed a hole large enough to drop a quarter into.

He then made the V cut from the bottom of the clavicles to the center of the sternum and then straight down to the abdomen and out to the top of the inner thighs. He took a pair of long-handled pruning loppers and cut both sides of the ribs along the sides, in a whole piece containing the sternum. He placed that large piece aside and went into the body cavity and removed the heart and lungs and weighed them. He examined them very closely, and if something seemed suspicious, he would cut into the heart with fine, evenly spaced slices and examine those pieces as well.

He reached into the cavity and removed the kidneys and liver, carefully examining each organ. When through, he set them into a stainless steel pan and removed the stomach, intestines, and bladder. He was very methodical and a wealth of information.

Although this sounds gruesome to most, remember I was a journeyman meatcutter in my previous career, and it was very interesting to watch the deputy go through the procedures of the entire autopsy.

He was very friendly. He was smoking a cigarette and flicking the ashes on the cement floor. I guessed this was to mask the stench of aging bodies and expelled body gases.

He asked me if I was getting sick and was surprised when I told him it didn't bother me at all. I told him I was really interested and let him know of my meatcutting background.

Reacting to my interest he led me over to a thirty-five-year-old woman whose autopsy was already partially completed. Her skin splayed outward on both sides, revealing the open cavity in her body, filled with approximately two inches of the liquid preservative formaldehyde. With her chest split open, I could easily see the eight-inch flank muscles behind each breast. The muscle structure was similar to what I'd seen in animals.

I was grateful for the demonstration and his willingness to give me his time. I didn't realize it until a few years later, but that same deputy coroner came over to the sheriff's department and was a deputy sheriff for many years. I ran into him several times, and he was surprised I still remembered him; however, he still looked ghoulish because of his eyes and unmoving, stoic expressions.

His instruction was so well received it caused me to introduce autopsy indoctrination to the Sheriff's Academy cadet classes when I was a ramrod and drill instructor for at least ten cadet classes. As we walked into the autopsy room with a group of cadets, there were as many as eight stainless steel tables lined abreast and all the coroners' staff was as busy as bees, cutting the bodies open in various stages of examination. Some cadets immediately got sick and needed to leave the room to toss up their stomach contents. As a class, we stood by and watched the deputy coroners work on the bodies and explain the important procedures. The cadets found it very interesting, along with a tour of the facility, now located over by Los Angeles County Medical Center.

This place was much more modern and well kept, with large refrigeration units. Inside these units there were three bodies stacked together on each large metal tray. All bodies were well mixed: Negro, Caucasian, Hispanic, Asian, Native American, and so on. There were the rich, poor, homeless, good-looking, ugly, homely, thieves, murderers, dope dealers, politicians, priests, rabbis, imams, child molesters, and whatever else you could mix into the batch. It was a thorough mix of the humanity.

Two things they all had in common was that they were part of the entire human race, and all had a single toe tag. The toe tag was a stiff piece of paper, two by five inches, with a piece of string running through a reinforcement washer seal that reinforced the hole in the tag, which was affixed to their toe on either foot. That toe tag identified the deceased and the lengthy county file number that was given to each body, regardless of what city the deceased was from.

In order for someone to arrive at the morgue, the death had to be suspicious or unexplained. Trauma from a murder, shooting accident, collision, home accident, and a plethora of other classifications would cause the body to be legally examined.

The most moving was the exhumation room. It was loaded with a vast number of fans to deal with the foul-smelling bodies that were exhumed and cleaned off for autopsy. The smell will never leave your thoughts, because it is just like any other type of rotting flesh—foul.

Another shocking room was the room where they autopsied small children. That was painful and very hard to see. I don't care how tough you think you are; you'll cringe.

We were also shown a cage made out of rigid chain-link fencing and welded angle iron. The cage had a keyed lock on the gate and was a special area fencing off would-be intruders from making contact with a well-known celebrity, politician, or important figure. Anyone of fame or prominence, would be segregated and placed into this caged area where only certain assigned persons had access. I can only imagine what caused this isolation cage to be erected. It was inside one of the main refrigerators where many other bodies awaiting autopsies were kept.

Meanwhile, on one of the tables in the autopsy room was a male about thirty-five years of age, being autopsied and evaluated.

The coroner took the heart out and examined it. Then he carefully sliced quarter-inch slices through the majority of the heart. He searched through the pieces, extracted one piece, and looked closer, turned around to us standing behind him, and stated, "Here it is; his artery is closed!" I looked closer and saw a small artery; it was about the size of ballpoint pen filler. The entire opening was blocked by what the doctor explained was cholesterol actually closing off the entire small artery. The man appeared to be in good physical condition. He was muscular and didn't appear to have any fat at all. He looked rather like a sports enthusiast. It was a true eye-opener that we must watch the food we ingest, no matter how we look.

In yet another room, we saw a stainless-steel table covered with what appeared to be Caucasian skin with a pair of feet and ankles attached. The feet, toes, and ankles were pointing downward and hanging from skin that was about a half inch thick coming from the calves and all attached to the large, nearly whole body of human skin and skin alone. It was covered with small rocks and twigs, grass, pine needles and other minute natural debris found typically in the mountainous terrain.

The deputy coroner let us surround the remnants of a human body that somehow died a terrible death, literally skinned from the entire torso and was only attached to its feet. We couldn't tell if it was male or female, but it was an adult. The deputy advised us that this was the body of a male pilot of a small plane that slammed into a mountainous rocky outcropping. They had been looking for him for several hours because the (ELT) emergency locator transmitter was signaling his whereabouts. That transmitter is typically secured in the internal tail components of the aircraft.

When the wreckage was finally located, the tail empennage was nearly flush with the outcropping of rocks. A sheriff's department Choctaw helicopter was summoned, and ropes were attached to the empennage and assembled with various winches to pull it from the rugged outcropping. Unfortunately, when the plane was released, the remains of the pilot, the sole occupant, dropped free from the wreckage and fell approximately two hundred feet. It made contact with the mountainous terrain and rolled a significant distance as well, picking up all the small debris that attached to the moist remains quite easily.

Later in my career I learned that in a typical small-plane crash, based on its angle and trajectory, the portion that strikes the impact point first, literally compresses the soft body tissue and pushes all of the tissue away from the bones.

Basically the impact "bones you out" because the much harder metal, springs, screws, glass, and plastic are sent flying, crushing you on impact alone.

To put it simpler terms, you can say the propeller, if directly in front of you when you crash, will probably go through you. I'm sure you get the point. And to top it off there is probably not much pain, and it's a quick death.

Another example was a naked woman lying on her side. On her inner thigh was a vibrator with the cord still attached and plugged into a wall outlet. The skin beneath the vibrator was blackened and covered a six-inch area circling the whole vibrator. At first observation, it appeared to be an electrocution because of the blackened skin tissue. However, the actual cause was listed as a heart attack, and the lady actually died from that, not an electrocution. The vibrator was apparently on when she died. She was not able to shut it off, and it ran for hours, the motor in the vibrator ultimately burning out on her skin.

The morgue was a good tour and a show of frequent and unique situations causing death. Electrocutions, shootings, heart attacks, poisonings, strange medical malfunctions were covered and how they appeared when first arriving on the scene. The cadets also learned much about scene preservation and how to not handle evidence.

CHAPTER 75

THE BEE CAPER

This case is about a cadet from a city south of central Los Angeles. He was extremely out of step and did little to surface or project himself for the staff to see his attributes. He was the weakest cadet in the class. He had very thick glasses, because he had problems seeing clearly. I couldn't understand why the police agency that hired him had bypassed the standard 20/20 vision requirements.

However, if they wanted him they must have been a sensible reason, so I would let it go unless it resurfaced as a problem.

One Friday near noon, we had just finished a formal inspection with the cadets wearing their class A uniforms, which are the working uniform the cadets would actually use in the field. This inspection was a special one because the cadets were to display their uniforms without any errors.

I marched and drilled the cadets in their formations, and they chanted "Jody-calls," which made them feel very good and proud of their accomplishments. After thirty minutes of marching, I wanted to see who would like to go home, and who wanted to stay and march for an extended period of time. Of course, the ones who fell for the gimmick remained, as the rest of the class was discharged to go home early. About thirty remained, and oddly enough, they were the weaker ones of the class.

We continued to march for approximately fifteen minutes when a bee landed on the helmet of the cadet with the thick glasses. The helmet was white with a black band around the bottom. I announced to the cadets that an intruder had landed in our group and must be a spy trying to get secret information from its law enforcement host.

I explained that the bee must know our cadence. The cadets would have to shout out this cadence as loud as possible to make the bee go away. Several minutes passed and the bee took off as if in cadence with the entire group. They were pleased at the bee's departure and were released shortly thereafter.

The following Monday, a sergeant from the city southeast of Los Angeles came into the training office with a misdemeanor report in his hands, written by the cadet and listing me as the suspect in a malicious mischief. The report went on to say that during marching the Friday before, I had noticed a bee on the cadet's helmet, and to belittle him I took a wooden ruler and tapped his helmet fifteen or twenty times, causing chips of white paint to flake off and damaging his helmet. No other explanations were given, and it was signed by the cadet.

I was summoned into the cadet training office and into the lieutenant's office where the accusing sergeant was seated. My lieutenant had the report in his hands, handed it to me, and asked if I could explain what had happened.

After reading the report, I was infuriated and stated exactly what had happened. I suggested that the cadet was making a false charge, because he knew he was very weak and near faltering. The sergeant stood by the cadet and accused me of lying.

That did it. I asked that he give both of us a polygraph exam, and the results would point to the one who was lying. That person must resign from law enforcement. The sergeant refused, and I called him a blind sycophant and nothing but an errand boy for the city.

I had just learned that the city had a vested interest in this cadet because his father was the attorney for the city he worked for. Talk about a conflict of interest! And on top of it all, the report listed me as a suspect. Does libel or slander count? How about conspiracy? Fortunately, my lieutenant, John K., saw through this scheme and advised the sergeant to destroy the report and dismiss any charges against me. The whole issue was dropped immediately.

The point I was trying to make was that some of cadets were special and had special and conflicting interests were always present and ominous and could stifle the academy's integrity.

To squeeze those special persons into a standard cadet class was extremely unfair and morally wrong. I could easily spot those individuals and I asked the administration to form a special class for them, because they couldn't and wouldn't pass muster or critical evaluations. However, the administration was ambivalent to our strict selections and acquiesced to the anointed ones, because many came from the upper echelon of the sheriff's department as well as contract police departments.

CHAPTER 76

BALLS OF FIRE

Day in and day out regardless, formation was at 0700 hours and the academy staff stepped out and marched to greet the enlisted swine and pounce on them if they didn't know their stuff. The inspections started at 0700 hours and not a minute later, and you'd better be ready. If you're a running a little late, you'd better hide and not let us see you, or you'll feel the pressure all day.

If their uniforms were out of whack, research papers were given for each violation. Perfectly straight gig lines, snaps snapped, buttons buttoned, zippers zipped, and no Irish pennants. They were all important, and they had better be done correctly.

If they didn't know their radio codes or the exact penal code definition of a crime, they would be expected to drop immediately and crank out ten pushups and one for the sheriff. Then they would be expected remain in the front-leaning rest position until recognized.

If you felt sick from all of the induced pressure and wanted to throw up, make sure you snap to properly and remove yourself quickly. Go over to the rose garden and toss up your stuff, and then get back into formation. Oh, you had better ask permission to return to your position, or you will be charged with being late.

Right after each morning inspection, the class was given instructions to get into the classrooms without delay and be ready for the first instructor. Once inside and classes began, it was hands off the cadets unless they stepped away from the training atmosphere, like going to the bathroom, or getting a drink of water.

Just after lunch the class would dress in running shorts, shirt, and tennis shoes, and get ready for a three to five mile run. I had been running with nearly every class and enjoyed the weaponless defense classes as well.

A lot of times I was sweaty most of the day and remained in my physical training gear. Not the big baggy type, but the shorter ones that showed your upper thighs.

Most of the baggy stuff was used by the gangsters who had legs so skinny you would think they must have been teased a lot, because they looked so skinny and sickly, that's why they turned to guns and dope.

Constant visual inspection of all the cadets was a necessity, and it was important to watch them closely.

They knew the twenty-six weeks of academy classes was to determine if they were capable to handle themselves in any endeavor as deputies or peace officers in the field.

I went home several nights and realized I had a rash developing on my inner thighs. I started to put powder on the area to stop the rash, because it was starting to itch more and more each day. I was running every day, and the itching became more prevalent and irritating. One evening I was at the store and noticed an item on the display area advertising different remedies for athlete's foot and other muscle strain ointments.

My curiosity led me to a small package called NP-27. This was a small bottle and seemed rather innocuous, and I thought a small amount might very well cure the rash. The ointment was actually for athlete's foot, which is a fungus between the toes. Well, that's all the rash I had between my thighs was—a rash from probably the very same thing, a fungus. Or so I thought!

I purchased the item and went home and took a long, warm shower and cleaned the area well, so the chemicals in the ointment would have a good chance to penetrate my skin deeply.

After the shower I dried myself well and squirted the ointment into the palm of my hand. I sloshed the ointment into both hands and applied it liberally to my entire scrotum and crotch area including my private parts. I had the feeling it was surely was going to penetrate easily. I sensed the itching would stop and could feel the slight heat coming from the ointment.

It was beginning to work and I began to go into my bedroom to put on my underwear. Seconds passed, and the ointment began to heat up more and more until it began to hurt and finally started to burn my skin.

I ran down the hall naked and past my wife, who happened to be sitting in the living room. I envisioned smoke billowing from my groin as the pain intensified. I yelled to her to get some baking soda and vinegar and meet me in the shower real quick. I jumped into the shower with cold water only and waited for my wife to come to me with the items. Then I thoroughly doused my entire groin with vinegar first and then baking soda.

Nothing was helping except the cold water that ran for at least fifteen minutes. I was moaning, groaning, and pitching my voice with all sorts of high tones from the pain and misery.

I finally left the shower, with humility in pursuit and close behind. I gently dabbed my groin with a dry towel and noticed skin was in fact peeling off of my testicles, penis, and inner thighs.

I ended up in bed on my knees and blowing on myself to cool down the burning sensation, obviously not a very pretty picture. Jesus, it hurt. And I felt like I did a really dumb thing. Duh.

During the night the area finally cooled down, and the burning sensation subsided.

The next morning I had to get up real early and when I went into the bathroom I noticed my entire groin was covered with a large scab formations and it was cracking all over the bends and folds in my skin. A clear liquid was seeping out, and it was painful each time it moved.

I arrived at the academy and was in the locker room with a lot of the other staff members. I told them about my experience. I showed them my groin, and they all yelled, "Holy shit, man; you're fucked!"

There was no doubt about it; the area looked revolting, as if I had a serious sexually transmitted disease. One of the more scientific staff members was talking while I was relieving myself at the urinal and stated that one of his friends had something just like what I had. He said that when he went to pee, his penis broke off and fell into the toilet.

That did it, I informed everyone that I was going to the hospital. I'd let a doctor tell me about the cure, if there was one. Oh, did some laugh, you dare ask?

I believe there wasn't a dry eye in the locker room. They were all roaring with laughter at my plight.

It took about twenty minutes to get to the hospital, and I had to wait another twenty minutes to get to an examination room. The doctor examined me as I was telling him what I had done and he was reading the ingredients on the NP27 label, shifting his eyes from the label to my scabbed groin. Suddenly the doctor started laughing. He was bending over from laughing so much and holding his stomach. As he laughed he was making all sorts of apologies for laughing so much. He wiped the tears from his eyes. He saw that I wasn't in the mood to laugh. I was concerned about the peril of my genitalia.

He straightened up and came over to my side of the room and, still smiling and laughing softly, pointed out a long scientific word on the ingredients label. "Do you see this long word? This is wart remover!"

He was laughing so hard he was leaning against another gurney to support himself. "Do you see this word here?" The word was at least fifteen letters long and not at all easy to pronounce. He said, "This one would burn the brass balls off of a monkey!"

He laughed again and was repeating that he was really sorry, but this was an obvious error by the company who provided this ointment. He advised me that I had good cause for a lawsuit for the injury and pain I had gone through.

I informed him that I really wasn't interested in suing anyone; all I wanted was to get rid of the embarrassing injury.

He stated that the itch was "jock itch," as I had originally diagnosed, a fungus just like athlete's foot. However, the chemicals in the remedy are quite different. The chemicals used for athlete's foot are much stronger because of the toughness of the skin around the foot. Now for the genitalia, it requires a much weaker solution because the groin is so soft and sensitive.

He told me to get out of my wet jockstrap as soon as possible during the day, and when I go home to change my briefs to boxers so the genitalia would be able to breathe.

He then added that the chemicals in the ointment caused second-degree burns. For the next two weeks I had to put a creamy salve all over the burned area every four hours, in order to repair the damaged skin, and soften the scabs. I guess it was kind of like caring for a pet snake with acne.

He then asked me if he could take the small bottle of NP27 and write a report on the incident for the medical field and the company to inform them of the injury I sustained. I replied, "Sure, go ahead."

He apologized again for his laughter, and said I was going to see results from the prescription cream within two days and complete cure within a week and a half. I was relieved and thanked the doctor.

I guess the doctors lounge was nearby. When I started to leave, I overheard the doctor and several others laughing their butts off. I could hear his loud voice, and his quips were easily distinguished, and I heard a snort or two.

CHAPTER 77

A TWIST OF FATE

Cadet G. was from an outside police agency and had several obstacles to overcome as he went through the academy. He was polite, patient, and did well on his exams every week. He studied hard and tried very hard to please us and that allowed him to pass through the academy. His biggest fault was his weight. He was fifty to seventy-five pounds overweight and struggled through all physical training, including running. His body shape was that of an avocado. His rump was very big, and he suffered many cruel remarks from cadets as well as staff for his poor appearance.

I took him under my wing and focused on getting him through, no matter what. His appearance changed for the better, and he never fell out of a run. I assigned several mentors from his class and they assisted him with all of his shortcomings.

His stamina and endurance were exemplary, and he had the grades to match. I could see very good qualities in his outgoing personality. He was very likable and clean-cut. I was very proud of his role-playing abilities, which were sound and on track with a professional image. I watched him carefully, and he was least likely to err in all endeavors of academy instruction.

Amazingly, he made it through, and I was very proud of him. He knew I wanted him to do well and become a thriving, hardworking, diligent officer. I congratulated him on his accomplishments and wished him luck in all endeavors.

Several months later he was working at a school when he spotted a trespasser on school grounds. It was a sixteen-year-old boy who had a cocky and surly attitude. Officer G. arrested the trespasser, handcuffed him, brought him to the security office, and sat him in a chair. The boy wouldn't stop gabbing about what he was doing on school grounds, which didn't make sense to Officer G.

He asked him several times why he was on school grounds and the sixteen-year-old was very evasive. Officer G. was irritated. He took out his service revolver, cocked it, and stuck it in the sixteen-year-old's mouth to scare him into submission and talk about why he was on school property.

Suddenly the officer's weapon discharged and the bullet went right through the kid's mouth and out the back of his head. The handcuffed juvenile was dead on the spot.

Officer G. was interviewed by detectives, and by the time his interview was over he was arrested and booked for manslaughter. Within a year Officer G. was tried and convicted and sentenced to prison.

Conveying this situation to other cadets was crucial. No matter how hard you try in the field, you must abide by the rules and regulations, or you might never survive the consequences of your poor decisions, especially when one of your daily tools is a deadly weapon. This was a classic warning to all and served well as an instruction tool for many classes.

CHAPTER 78

DIRTY LAUNDRY

In a small and quaint yet tattered and grungy theater in Los Angeles, a team of LAPD vice officers were trying to apprehend a man who was having oral sex while a throbbing movie was fluttering its erotic images on the screen.

When the vice unit interrupted the two engaged in the throes of love, the man took off running and left the vice officers in the dust. They commented he was so quick they could hardly believe his speed.

Meanwhile, back at our academy, we were busily tending to our cadets and running their rear ends off and exercising two to three hours a day. Sometimes four to five hours were spent on exercising, baton tactics, and weaponless defense. The physical training staff sergeant was focused on all elements of exercise that help develop many skills in combat training.

There were as many as four cadet classes on the hill at any one time. The maximum in any one class was class #165, which had 180 cadets. Many of the cadets had never been involved in any hand-to-hand combat training, some cadets were proficient in a variety of martial arts combat, some were senseis in their martial arts specialties. We used the sensei to help instruct, as well as individuals who were just recently released from the military service.

Our physical training sergeant was in top condition and an awe-inspiring individual on his way up the promotional scale of the department. He had a great personality and had a lot of talent forming combat-ready men and women for our department. He was single and a powerful, handsome image in uniform for our department. He enjoyed many women chasing him all of the time. He drove a black Corvette and always had a different woman hanging on his arm every time I saw him. He was also very humble and very easy to talk to.

Everyone admired him and trusted his judgment and leadership qualities. All seemed well. No one could imagine what was to follow.

One day we were summoned to the cadet training office and informed by our lieutenants that our physical training sergeant had been just arrested by an LAPD vice detail for indecent exposure and having sex in a porn theater.

The sergeant's explanation was that he was inside the theater watching from the vestibule when his gold bracelet mysteriously fell off his left wrist and fell below the legs of a man sitting next to him. As he bent over to pick up the bracelet, he had no idea the man next to him was exposing his love muscle and masturbating. When he bent over, he accidentally fell onto the man's love muscle with his mouth. That's when the LAPD vice unit arrested him. The

LAPD added that the sergeant was the same one who had run from them several months prior but got away from them due to his superior athletic ability.

The sergeant, like anyone else in our department who is involved in any scandalous situation, or even criminal conduct, was offered the opportunity to resign in lieu of termination or prosecution.

CHAPTER 79

AN EXAMPLE OF A GOOD MAN

The academy's instruction was very good, and time spent on each cadet was well worth it. One of the previous classes from an outside agency to the north of Los Angeles was recuperating from the loss of one of its officers, who had recently graduated.

After a robbery, two suspects were being pursued by an officer on foot. One of the robbery suspects stopped, turned around, and shot the officer in the face, which caused him drop to the ground.

Both suspects continued to run; however, the officer regained his strength and momentum, suppressing his injuries, and continued to pursue both suspects on foot. There was a violent shootout, and the officer ended up shooting both suspects and killing them.

The officer's injuries to his face were substantial, and he was unfortunately retired from his department because of that shooting.

Several months after the shooting, the officer came to the academy and was directed to the cadet training lieutenant. He asked to speak with me; however, I was on vacation and unavailable.

He told the lieutenant about what had happened during the robbery. When he was shot he could hear me yelling at him, "Don't you dare die, just because some idiot surprised you! You hunt him down, and at least take him with you! Never ever give up. Take the pain and go after him, no matter what!"

He said he wanted to thank me for the inspiration and stamina I drilled into him that made him successful and a survivor. That compliment made me feel very proud and speechless. I don't think there is a better accolade. It made me tear up.

This incident, too, remained in my series of instruction over the next twenty years and hopefully benefited many officers in their careers. I certainly hope the officer lives for a long time and is not in much pain from his brief chosen career.

CHAPTER 80
A CLASS FROM HELL

I was very fortunate making "ramrod" of several classes and had a good crew of deputies working with me. We all were very comfortable with each other and helped one another in all aspects of training. We became very adept at selecting good qualified cadets and did not vacillate or shy away from paperwork to justify any terminations, resignations, or recycles. We were well set up and in a team network; we were given most of the recycles, also termed retreads, from other classes. These were individuals who had already been in the training program for weeks or months at a time but needed to remediate to comply with the state mandated training, called Peace Officers Standards of Training, frequently referred to as POST. Their training was stopped because of minor injuries, failing too many exams, or not adapting to the quasimilitary discipline that was possibly not understood, or failing to qualify for the shooting requirements.

We were preparing to receive a new class and were warned this was the bottom of the recruiting barrel, or the end part of an old recruitment batch. On top of this revelation, we were told that a bunch of county employees who were being cut from their assignments with other departments, like social services, hospital employees, janitors and clerical staffs, were offered a job with the sheriff's department as long as they made it through the academy. This meant that these individuals didn't even think about being a cop on their own merit. Many hadn't passed a drug test or the background tests necessary for law enforcement, which caused much consternation about their abilities and qualities coming into the academy. We were also warned that we would not know who those individuals were, so we wouldn't pick on them too much.

Of course those individuals would not be probationary cadets, because they were already permanent employees with a track record of poor acknowledgment and acceptance for quasimilitary discipline. Okay, we were ready, and here they came, 180 of them. This meant that on class runs, two columns of ninety would be rather loud and a bit cumbersome; but we could handle them carefully and cautiously.

This batch would take up the entire classroom, butting against the staff's desks. When they arrived, we met them with great gusto. The selection process started immediately when we started shouting out commands to move and in what direction. Just sitting in the class took stamina.

To sit at attention, your hands are on your lap, shoulders rolled back and erect, head looking straight ahead, and of course, feet together. If you were not used to someone yelling at you, you would shrink your shoulders, tuck your head downward, and squint in defiance.

We began losing cadets daily. They would come to their staff member and offer their resignation. Weekly we would reassign and readjust their seating positions. If the class uniformly performed poorly, they would be placed into their original seating positions. This left gaping holes in the seating arrangements and specifically pointed out how many cadets have left the class.

If a cadet wanted to speak to a staff member, the protocol was strict for many reasons. The cadets needed to formulate what they were about to say with precise words to make sense as if they were confronted by the media on a crime scene. If something personal occurred and needed attention quickly, formalities were dispensed with, depending on the gravity of the issue at hand.

If a cadet ran into trouble or had an issue with his ride along at his or her station weekend assignments, they were to let us know as soon as possible so we would be aware of their indiscretions or poor judgment situations.

I came in from the morning inspection, grabbed a cup of coffee, and came into the class. The cadets' first class was already underway, and I spotted a cadet seated at attention in the chair next to my desk awaiting my arrival.

His name was cadet T.M. I knew just to sit in that chair was chilling and apprehensive. I was firm and unwavering about any violations of protocol and discipline. Yet this cadet was seated with a firm intent to talk with me and stood his ground. I sat my coffee on my desk, arrange a few papers, and set them aside. The cadet knew full well that he would not speak unless spoken to first.

He was trembling and near tears. He raised his head, took a deep breath, and unloaded the following story:

"Sir, I was assigned to Temple Station last weekend and rode with a deputy named Tom V. He seemed pretty good but was very demeaning. I knew I could handle anything he could throw at me because I used to be a reserve deputy prior to coming on as a regular deputy. He asked what week I was in, and I responded the twelfth week and who my staff officer was.

"He was elated that I was a reserve for several years and started to relax. We drove around for a couple of hours not doing much. Then we went to a private parking area near a supermarket. Deputy Tom met a young lady and had her sit in the rear seat of our patrol car.

"We drove to a small liquor store. Deputy Tom got out alone, went inside the liquor store, and came out shortly with a bag containing vodka, orange juice, some small plastic cups, and a bag of ice. Deputy Tom came to the driver's window and told me to drive, and he got into the rear seat with his lady friend.

"I didn't mind driving, but I was concerned what he was going to do next. Deputy Tom poured drinks for him and the lady and drank several cups. He told me to drive around, deflect the rearview mirror, and not to look back.

"I followed his instructions and became very worried about how drunk they would become and about whatever he had planned next. Deputy Tom told me to go over to a riverbed area by a bridge, and meet up with several other units. When we got there, I was told to stay in the car and not to turn around, and listen to the sheriff's radio.

"Deputy Tom and his friend got out of the backseat and went to the rear of the car and met up with about six to eight other deputies. They were all consuming the mixed drinks Deputy Tom was making and were having a good time, laughing and talking loudly. Deputy Tom came over to the driver's side and told me to turn the radio up, deflect the side mirrors, and close all the windows. Deputy Tom reminded me not to turn around at all, no matter what happened. I acknowledged his orders and remained in the car listening to the blaring sheriff's radio.

"Then I felt the rear trunk area dip as if someone was sitting on top of the trunk lid. The entire patrol car began rocking up and down and side to side. To me it seemed they were all having sex with Deputy Tom's girlfriend. After approximately twenty minutes, Deputy Tom came over to my window and ordered me to leave with the patrol car and do some patrolling around the city.

"I seemed a little puzzled, but followed his directions immediately and left the sister units as well as Deputy Tom and his girlfriend. I drove around for a little over an hour, made several car stops, and searched several people. Then a lieutenant from Temple Station called me on the radio and wanted to meet up with me. I acknowledged him, and we met about five minutes later. As I got out of the car, the lieutenant asked where Deputy Tom was, and I told him he was with about eight other deputies by the riverbed bridge.

"The lieutenant seemed a little surprised I was alone. He informed me that I received three complaints from three independent parties about the way I treated them like common criminals. I responded that I was sorry for the complaints and didn't mean to cause trouble. The lieutenant then ordered me to return to the station immediately and go home. I was very concerned about what was going to happen and whether I was in any trouble for following orders."

When the cadet finished his story, I calmly thanked him for the heads-up information and said I would personally look into the matter. I also promised him that he would not suffer any repercussions for the information he provided.

When he left I went directly into the cadet training office and informed my sergeant and lieutenant of the situation and said they should expect an onslaught of critical insinuations. They agreed, and we were poised for follow-up investigations. Two weeks went by and nothing much was passed on to us. I had just finished physical training with the class when several cadets came to me and informed me that Cadet T.M. was being roughed up inside the locker room. They were afraid something serious was about to happen if they didn't inform the staff. I thanked them and when Cadet T.M. came into the classroom in his uniform, I pulled him aside to find out why he was being roughed up and by whom.

He indicated he didn't want to talk about the matter. Something was wrong, so I took him to the cadet training office, summoned the sergeant, and informed him of the incident. We went into a private office and sat the cadet down. He broke down emotionally and said that two cadets from the class were acting on behalf of the accused deputy from Temple Station. They told T.M. that he had better withdraw his observations and admit it was all made up, because the deputy was about to be fired.

When I found out who the cadets were, I wasn't surprised. One of them was a follower, the other was in trouble every week to a point where he should have been fired long before this incident occurred. However, he was also the president of a local labor union, and that union supported the election of the sheriff.

Need I say more? Was there a conflict of interest? You bet! The second week of tenure, this cadet, who also happened to be named Tom, was pushing for his own termination because of his numbskull antics.

Let me identify one of those antics that, if done by any other cadet, would have resulted in immediate termination.

This incident was done right at the time the gasoline crisis was in full swing. I received information from a gas station attendant that the line waiting for gas was about three blocks long. It took quite some time to get to the pumps, sometimes close to an hour, before you could pump gas.

An individual in a black Porsche, Cadet Tom, came directly to the gas station business desk, flashed his deputy sheriff's badge, and demanded to be placed ahead of everyone else because he was going to a police emergency.

He added that Cadet Tom was very gruff and would not put up with any delays. The attendant/owner felt suspicious about the demand and called the local authorities. They directed him to the sheriff's department personnel bureau, who in turn found out he was my cadet.

They gave the gas station attendant the academy phone number, and he pursued an explanation for Cadet Tom's antics. When he called, and I talked with the man, I apologized for the cadet's behavior and that if he experienced any further antics, not to hesitate to call.

I pulled Cadet Tom from the class and questioned his deportment, he admitted to the incident because he was running late to the academy and needed gas immediately.

I couldn't fathom anyone doing such a blatant thing for any reason other than a major emergency, let alone a probationary cadet who was unarguably on a quest to display poor behavior in all human traits. The cadet's judgment was seriously flawed, and we were only in our second week, with only twenty-four more weeks to go.

Regardless of why I wanted this guy terminated, my requests were squashed every week. He was a major headache, and the academy knew full well he should have been terminated, but instead denied all of my requests for termination. My question was why he was in a class at all, and I suggested he should be pushed out and sent directly to the unit of his choice immediately. This was a mockery of our academy's integrity, and I was livid.

Because of this cadet's special position, I classed myself as hypocritical, with a loss of self-pride and integrity. However, I was determined to proceed with my own expectations and duly noted each week's reports of the free-ride cadet.

The class proceeded with its instruction and training. The incident at Temple Station resulted in several resignations and was over. Cadets were falling out of the physical training classes, failing tests beyond any saving remedies, getting into trouble right and left in situations occurring outside the academy, resigning, and just plainly giving up on their chosen career. Most admitted the discipline for a deputy was too much for them, viewing themselves as failing basic working skills that were necessary when working in the patrol environment.

Many resigned and some were terminated, and the numbers grew so high our results were monitored closely as if we, the staff, were too harsh. As time pressed on we still reseated the remainder of the class weekly, and until the twenty-third week, we set them in the original seating positions.

Toward the end of class #165's training, the seating had a major effect on their pride and revealed an attrition rate of nearly 64 percent. This was a milestone; no other class had lost such a great number. We, the staff were proud of the remainder of the class. Their accomplishments were superior, and we expected them to be an example of good training.

Today, the academy is run like a college. Very little stress. Quasimilitary instruction has been put aside. It is not part of any selection process, because the training costs are too high, and the department would rather allow all to remain and confront anxiety through catharsis.

The system now brags of losing no one. Everyone who goes into the academy comes out, unless some extraordinary situation develops or occurs. The academy now feels the type of training in the past produced an aggressive, hardworking deputy who is looked down upon today as too mean, indifferent, and racist.

I wonder who would mostly benefit from such an adverse philosophy. Would it be skewed statistics, certain racial groups that are mostly involved in criminal activity, or lawyer groups like the ACLU, who condemn law enforcement as a whole?

Today's academy is much more passive and apathetic, and leans mostly on nonaggressive deputies who are deeply immersed in cultural diversity and how to improve an image that only time pushes in an opposite direction.

We've discussed this before and the results will surely show that law enforcement is not interested in arresting people now, because the jails are too full, and processing inmates is too costly. So what do you think they do now if a whole gang of thieves enters their area?

Go after them? Are you nuts? That will generate a whole series of complaints from the ones they stop and talk to. Everyone knows to complain against every officer who stops them. That alone will curb the appetite for doing police work and stopping the obvious. Remember the duck theory?

There will be more officers killed and injured than in the past, because the cops are so restrained and hobbled now from doing what they should be doing. You can judge the next several decades by comparing killed or injured statistics with those of the past. See the results. You shouldn't be surprised.

CHAPTER 81

UNDER THE GUN

Running the classes was an honorable job, and I was left to follow strict guidelines of protocol in instructing each cadet. Our method was usually creative, as long as we compared it to viable field activities that deputies use frequently.

Fortunately, the 1964 movie *Zulu*, with Stanley Baker, Jack Hawkins, and Michael Caine was an excellent movie, and I mimicked the Zulu war chant when we were running through the hills of East Los Angeles. This chant was repetitious yet excitable, and it drew energetic responses from the class and the staff, instead of the boring counting and left-right-left mantra. Oh, the sounds we made were spectacular and reverberated all over the ELA alps, the class was in step and pumping blood through their bulging carotids as we tromped on command. My orders were for the men to yell until their testicles rose from their jockstraps and the women until their breasts separated from their bras. (Today you couldn't even mention jockstraps or bras, or you would be ostracized.)

The class was also primed in case someone came by and shot at our group. There were approximately eight armed cadets, with guns hidden in towels sporadically sprinkled throughout the running formation, and ready on command to drop to one knee and open fire if anyone attempted to shoot at us. The entire class practiced dropping down to the ground and lying flat as possible, not standing up unless ordered.

We were on a run, and it was raining pretty hard, so I had the cadets put on their raincoats. (Gun bearers, of course, had their guns in plastic wrap.) In order to comply with the rules, I had promised the captain that I wouldn't do anything to the cadets that I wouldn't do myself. As we ran, we counted out cadence and sang "Jodi" calls with clear tone and robust volume. Because it was raining, the sound was magnified, and everyone could hear us a half mile away.

We were about two miles out on the run, and though it was raining, we definitely stayed dry from the rain. What I didn't count on was the humidity generated by the body heat inside the raincoats. It was hotter than hell, so I decided to make it a short run of only a three and a half miles.

Every one made it without any complications, but as soon as I came in, the academy captain wanted to see me. I ran to the captain's office and was escorted in front of him directly. He wanted to know why in the hell we were running in the rain—and in raincoats, which seemed a bit risky. I admitted it was my idea and that all the staff, including me, wore the same gear. I told him it was for just a quick jaunt, and the cadets as well as the staff thoroughly enjoyed it.

The captain's eyebrow went up as he seemed to question my zealous behavior, but he smiled and nodded. I assumed that my idea was okay, but it suggested that he was watching me and the class closely.

I knew the biggest problem was that other classes saw the extra considerations my class got for doing well; they were viewed as privileges. Every class was complaining, asking why their class couldn't do the same things as our class. So their staff sergeants would criticize my every move to the captain.

What pleased me is that the cadets loved all the stuff I threw at them. It was beneficial and made street sense. I could always connect whatever they did to field maneuvers.

For a run several days later, I went to the Emergency Operations Bureau and picked up ninety M-17 tear-gas masks. They were distributed to each cadet, and they were given instruction on how to use the mask in emergency operations. They were also shown how to apply the mask in combat, and in routine crowd and riot formations.

When we were through, the cadets were all pumped up and excited, because this was not a normal run-of-the-mill approved class. We all stepped out onto the parade grounds with the other classes, including the senior class, for their daily run.

When our class stepped out with the M-17 gas masks on their waists the senior class didn't know what to make of it, but they viewed it as something special.

As we took off, I reminded the class several times what the commands were, and I went over them as we marched off going down the hill. The commands were very basic: Take the masks out, don the masks, take them off, and put them away. These were all done in cadence time, as we all were walking and occasionally running, but never more than a block at a time.

We were gone for probably two hours, and we went through the whole process as many as fifty times. The cadets did great. They loved it, and their pride was finalized as we came in past the senior class, counting cadence with the masks on.

I was summoned to the captain's office as soon as I came in. Again I was escorted to the captain's office, and he again questioned the exercise. I explained the practice and said that the reaction of the class was very good.

The captain was concerned the exercise was never given to other classes and I explained it was not part of the academy curriculum but a part of classes that I taught to regular deputies for in-service training. Again he smiled and allowed me to return to my class, but I knew he was watching me like a hawk.

Several senior class staff members came to me and stated that the senior class was miffed, because my class was given more privileges than they were getting, and they wanted to do the same.

I said that my class was better than theirs, and they needed to get lots of extra training for a better performance. All in all, these exercises developed a healthy competitive spirit—for the classes and the staff.

CHAPTER 82

SUIT AND TIE

My classes were competitive and performed well compared to all other classes. They were bursting with class pride. Once in the latter weeks of training, I was sure they were ready for patrol, and they knew they were well prepared. The constant pressure and instruction paid off with their ability to perform all tasks with a reasonable pass rate.

I was comfortable as the ramrod of the classes and let it be known that cadet training was enhanced with a first-class act and could not be duplicated.

Well, my arrogant comments apparently got to the captain, who had always had his eyes on me and challenged my methods of training. He ordered me to come to an interview to see if I was able to qualify for the academy's administrative staff and write scenarios for each class. I informed the captain that I wasn't interested, because the administrative staff were nothing but effeminate lackeys. They had no training or experience in the eyes of real law enforcement.

The captain apparently didn't like my answer and ordered me to take an oral exam in three days anyway. He reminded me to be sure to wear a suit and tie and be ready for an extensive interview. I couldn't believe the captain was that serious and adamant that I go through the administration selection process.

Although I wanted nothing to do with the group, I figured it was a power play on the captain's part to prove who was in charge of the whole facility and to repay me for my scoffing remarks about the administrative body. The next couple of days I was humiliated by all of the admin staff about my oral interview and that I was being forced into the position of possibly working with them. I went along with the ribbing as a front for the captain in his attempt to redeem the wholesale clutch of nerds and obsequious toadies who worked directly under him.

The captain was a well-known prankster, but with a double-edged sharp sword, if you didn't go along with the joke but offered resistance. I knew him well, and he knew me well, and we were about to bump heads where he *must* win. I figured out that I must follow his orders in detail and show up at ten o'clock the next morning without any further provocation.

Everyone knew that something would give, because the captain was going to test my commitment to his command, and if I didn't comply he would send me packing and boot me off the hill. I arrived early to prepare myself and freshen up. I walked to the administration building, fully ready for whatever they would throw at me and braced myself for the topic of complete ridicule.

As I was led into the captain's office, at least ten of the nerdy staff were seated in their suits and ties and dresses. The captain was in his chair at the head of the table. They all had pens and tablets of paper to jot down whatever nerds jot down.

They all looked in my direction and broke out laughing, hissing, and snorting because of my suit and tie, I think! The captain himself was laughing but then voiced his displeasure. "I told you to wear a suit and tie. Where is it?"

I had to point out that I had a blue swim trunks on, and a very narrow tie, which was popular maybe ten to fifteen years ago, and a yellow patrol raincoat, which met his exact order. The captain was saying other things, but the laughter was too boisterous to hear him.

I also was carrying a brown briefcase, which I laid on the interview table. In my left hand were three large garden snails. As I began to open my briefcase I noticed the captain pointing toward it. Later on it was revealed that he was ordering me not to open the briefcase, but unfortunately I couldn't hear him because of all the exuberant laughter.

Inside the briefcase, I had twenty-eight two-by-two-inch pieces of torn yellow tablet paper with the number twenty-three written on each piece. Their significance: absolutely nothing. Of course those pieces of paper went along with two hard-boiled eggs soaking in about three ounces of mustard locked in a plastic sandwich bag.

Everyone finally sat down, and the captain declared that I had better be in a suit and tie in fifteen minutes, or I was going to suffer his wrath. When I followed the captain's directions and started to leave, I surreptitiously dropped the three garden snails into a large ashtray that was near the center of the conference table. Later I learned the three snails surfaced without anyone seeing me place them into the ashtray.

The picture I was given, was that they suddenly came alive and crawled to the top of the ashtray edges and spread their foamy residue, gyrating their silly squiggly eyeballs noting the nerdy staff as well.

Fortunately, I did bring a real suit and tie and met once again with the whole administrative staff. I came in this time with a suit and tie, well groomed, and silent, and sat at the opposite end of the table facing the captain.

The show then started. Each administrative staff member at the table asked me why they should let me come to their unit. They smirked their way through their independent questions, knowing full well I wouldn't stand for their contrived insolence. Each one of the questions was met with a contrarian viewpoint. I reminded each of them of something they had mentioned to me that they did not want to come to the attention of the others. I also mentioned that they condemned the administrative sergeants and lieutenants, and of course having to be around the captain all of the time.

This interview went on for at least a half hour. Then the captain ordered me to step out of the room and wait in the lobby for the results of the interview.

About ten minutes went by and the lieutenant, John M., came out to the lobby and informed me that I failed the interview. I was to remain in the cadet training office.

Boy, was I relieved. I scurried down the hill to the cadet training office to let everyone know I was remaining. I had avoided the administrative plague of the "people of a feather..."

CHAPTER 83
FINAL FINALE

I had now been at the academy for about three and one half years. I had instructed at least ten classes since I came, and with class #165, I had the infamous accomplishment of having the highest attrition rate the department ever had.

I was proud of most of the cadets who had graduated, but there were a few specials who could not be tossed. To me it was a black spot on my integrity for not getting rid of them, but higher influences prevented me from doing so.

Everything seemed fine until when one day around one o'clock in the afternoon when I was summoned to the cadet training office by my sergeant, who said I was in trouble with the lieutenant for saying something about a cadet who was stuck atop a block wall. Apparently that cadet was on top of the six-foot climbing wall. He couldn't get down and was literally stuck.

I told the sergeant I hadn't said anything about anyone, and that I hadn't been out to the obstacle course for at least three days.

The sergeant led me into the lieutenant's office. As I came into the office, the lieutenant, John K., had a pale face and the look of shock and dismay. It seemed as if he was going to be a harbinger of ill will. I couldn't imagine what the problem could be, and the situation the sergeant had mentioned was not on the radar at all. The lieutenant, whom I respected very much, was in fact one of the most knowledgeable law enforcement supervisors on the department. He stated that he just got off the phone with the captain, who ordered me to transfer out of the academy within an hour. I asked, "What the hell did I do?

The lieutenant then repeated the same accusation and added that a cadet with a very large bottom was stuck on top of the block wall over by the obstacle course.

Someone overheard me make a comment that the cadet's large buttocks were nothing compared to a chief's son, who just happened to have a similar affliction, but much worse, and he was not as agile as this one.

I asked, "Who the hell said I was the one who said such a thing?"

The lieutenant said it was someone from the sheriff's information bureau. I told the lieutenant that I hadn't said anything of that sort; the accusations were totally wrong.

The lieutenant told the captain that I was denying the whole episode. The captain said he didn't care; he knew it had to be me, and that I must leave.

So the lieutenant said you've got to leave. The captain wouldn't vacillate. I shrugged and nodded and complied with the orders. I packed all my gear in haste and called Carson Station, who was pleased to take me on such short notice.

As I started to load my car and leave, the lieutenant called me and said that the captain wanted to see me again, immediately. I went directly to the captain's office. He began to say that he was sorry for what had happened. He had researched the accusation and found out it was not me at all. He rescinded the transfer order. I could stay on the hill, in cadet training.

I informed the captain that I had never been treated so badly in my entire career, and the way this whole affair went down was in fact a revelation that he, the captain, didn't trust me, and our integrity was too damaged to recover.

I said that I felt it best to leave honorably, with my head held high for a good performance while on the hill. He shook my hand and stated he understood and wished me good luck in my career.

I received word that cadet class #171, which I was in charge of when I left, had a going away present for me. The lieutenant asked me to return to the classroom and accept the class's going-away presentation.

As I came into the room, the class sergeant approached me and handed me a box. The class was cheering as I tore the paper from the box, revealing a Smith & Wesson .357, stainless steel, four-and-a-half-inch revolver. It was beautiful, and a wonderful gift from cadets to whom I'd been rather harsh and demanding for nearly twenty-three weeks.

As I accepted the gift, the academy captain came into the rear of the room, probably to see if I would say anything damning about him or the training. Of course I didn't, and at that time I felt it was about time to move on. I thanked the class for their attention and wished them good luck in all their endeavors and reminded them that some day we would possibly be assigned together. They applauded me as I left the room.

I packed up my gear and equipment for Carson Station. A sense of despair was lingering in my mind, but I knew I would get over it. Carson Station was ready and willing to accept me, and I always bounced back from any adversity. I knew many of the brass at Carson Station and several of the older deputies, so it was encouraging to look forward to arriving there. I knew I would make the best of my recent transfer and enjoy getting back to arresting crooks.

Note: That very gun the cadet class gave me, and maybe ten of those cadets in class #171, later were involved with me at the Special Enforcement Bureau/Special Weapons and Tactics team when our sergeant was killed.

That gun was the instrument that was used in a shooting that will never be forgotten. Two people were killed and irreparable psychological damage was on every part of the menu. This shooting will be discussed in detail in a later chapter.

CHAPTER 84

SPECIAL ENFORCEMENT BUREAU:
A CULTURE OF MEN

Several former Firestone Park deputies were now working at the new Carson station. Working there was pleasing and relaxing and just getting back to working the streets and taking thugs to jail was an inspiration. I was offered the position as jailer or training officer, but I refused and had to surrender my two stripes, as a deputy IV rank, to a slick sleeve, and lose the additional bonus pay for that rank. I was actually still in the doldrums from my abrupt academy transfer, but comfortable the way Carson Station treated me, and it was nice and refreshing getting back to the patrol environment.

After working patrol for a short stint of eight months at Carson Station, I was called and asked if I would like to body swap with a deputy who was leaving the Special Enforcement Bureau. My response was an unequivocal "Hell, yeah!" The voice on the other end stated that in two days I would be transferred to SEB. I was elated, because I was twenty-third on their waiting list to transfer to that unit, and at that numerical position, it would take at least one to two years.

In addition, to be selected to go to SEB, each applicant could not be blackballed by anyone of excellent reputation, which meant the background of any applicant must pass the work ethic of wherever they came from. Most of the hardworking deputies in the stations where you were working or had worked, were queried about the applicant's work achievements. One complaint could stop the applicant from transferring. Approval had to come from other deputies and limited information from station supervisors.

I was honored to be selected and anxious to leave Carson Station for a new and invigorating assignment. I knew very well that going to SEB was going to be a challenge, because a lot of the guys there were former combat-trained military veterans from the Vietnam War.

The armament used in SEB were Ar-15s, M-16s, and Remington bolt action .308 sniper rifles. I needed to get to those weapons and study them well.

The day came when I arrived, and I immediately went to the training office and acquired the AR-15. I took it to the basement and briefing room area every chance I could get. I spent hours reading and practicing with the weapon, taking it apart and putting it back together until I could do it blindfolded.

I did the same in the dark until I knew I was very fast and well informed about the AR-15's nomenclature. Then I did the same to the M-16s, with slight modifications and adjustments.

During this time, I also practiced everything I was taught, so I would excel in all endeavors relating to Special Weapons and Tactics. This unit was probably the best unit to work patrol and make arrests at every station. We were allowed to work out for three hours a day, mainly to stay slim and trim for all the rigors the Special Weapons and Tactics team were confronted with.

My interests in sports included handball and volleyball, and I was pretty good at both. In fact, my volleyball serve was well known and the very fast ball knocked many to the ground in an attempt to rebound. Several of the sergeants and lieutenants were handball enthusiasts and asked me to play against them. That pretty much set the tone, because several of the supervisors were injured and nearly beaten like dogs when I finished the games. We played mostly at East Los Angeles City College, where I was attending classes.

Most of the personnel assigned at SEB were well known and very cordial with introductions. I knew quite a few of them, and they assisted me in everything I needed to know. The sergeants were mostly very sharp, except for a couple of them who must have come from the administrative trail rather than on their own merit. At first glance, it was relatively easy to spot some of the weak ones, because their physical stature and command presence were rather weak.

The difference between the Special Enforcement Bureau and other units like detective bureaus, training units, and patrol stations was that this unique unit was a group of men; no women could pass the existing physical tests.

These men were excellent patrol deputies and generated many quality arrests on their own enthusiasm, and wrote equally important arrest reports. The SEB personnel all had a command presence that was excellent, and just by standing in a room demanded obedience. Any orders, within the policy and procedures, were followed up immediately, and no questions were asked.

After workout, most of us suited up in our class A uniforms, with spit-shined boots, polished leather gear, and brilliant brass badges, name tags, and helmets. The uniform was representative of the inspection gear at the academy and hopefully an inspiration to all stations where we worked.

Once dressed, we went to our briefing in the assembly room and found out what station we were going to work with. We were often assigned to ghetto areas, where we could put a dent into the criminal activities. It was great to work all around the county. Some stations were inundated with gang activity, and the reports would point out the locations where the gangs would hang out. There we would go, and if the crooks didn't know we were coming, they would suffer a multitude of arrests. This pleased the local community for a while, so after one or two shifts we would leave the area until the problem emerged again.

Getting to know the guys was relatively easy. You couldn't come to this unit with any poor comments from anyone in the department, and that meant we would get along with everyone. Everyone was politically correct until someone pissed down their leg, and then all hell would break loose. This was great because everyone pretty much knew who you were prior to ever coming to the bureau.

Sure, there were always the ones who tried to act tough, but they knew sooner or later you would find out about them. In the training mode it was very difficult to hide ineptitude in physical coordination and patrol skills. I felt very comfortable because most of the personnel were good, hardworking cops from the streets. They came here to work and improve their own patrol techniques.

I was going to work with another ex-Firestone deputy named Bobby P. Bobby and I had some history from Firestone Park. Digressing to this history is very important and causes me reflect about my time at Firestone Park Station. When I was assigned there, Bobby had stolen his training officer's radio car to answer an "officer needs assistance" call. This type of call indicates help was needed immediately and essentially allowed immediate code-three response.

Bobby, being a former US Marine, had no reservations about coming to the aid of a fellow officer who needed help, and I was that fellow officer. I was thoroughly involved in a fight, attempting to handcuff a large man under the influence of phencyclidine, commonly called PCP, and "whacked out of his gourd." What I mostly recall was that I was throwing the individual around, unable to handcuff him, although I had a firm grip on his testicles and pants. I was in fact right outside the station, right next to the health department parking lot, street side, very close to the station's 10p1 position—the corner outpost I mentioned earlier, at the southeast corner. When I saw and heard a radio car coming toward me warp eight, out of the station lot, tires screeching, I sensed relief and help was upon me.

That's when Bobby jumped out of the car alone and rushed toward me. Together we were able to handcuff the "studly muffin" quite easily. One of the nice things I remember was that this trainee had a slight smirk on his face, which alone assured me he knew what to do. (Those damn Marines—always first in, and no questions asked.) Normally there was never much contact with another's trainee, but I was grateful for Bobby's assistance, because he was alert and paying attention to the radio at the time of my request.

When I came into the station with the suspect and began to book him, I sought out his training officer and commended Bobby's diligence and spirit for coming to my aid. His training officer was upset that his trainee took his car and left him without wheels to come as well. But my thoughts were that Bobby was way ahead of his training officer, just by paying attention to the radio when

I first called. He also knew that I was close by and never wavered knowing someone needed help.

It wasn't long after I had transferred to the sheriff's academy when Bobby came as well. We had already developed an excellent rapport with one another, and now he seemed to be tracking my enthusiastic career path.

To add to our personal interaction, there were about six or seven of us deputies, all from Firestone Park Station, who had moved into the brand-new Orange County housing community of Mission Viejo. So my bond with Bobby was relatively close, and working with him at SEB was not an unplanned rendezvous at all.

Another deputy came to me and asked if I would mind being his partner. He explained he was in somewhat a predicament and needed a partner quickly. He seemed pretty nice and friendly, and I agreed to work with him, noting that Bobby P. and I had previous plans. With that in mind, a change wouldn't be that troublesome and would enhance my standing, because I was flexible enough for an interim change in partners.

His name was Doug D. and he was the scout on the blue team. Being his partner put me in a very good position on the team as backup for the scout, and second man in, on all SWAT operations. Quite a few of the older guys on other teams hadn't ever been on entry team positions, and they had been at the unit for years already. Those guys came up to me and wanted to know if I was trained in a specialized unit or in some US military group to justify being pushed ahead of everyone else to be part of the entry team. My response was that I had no specialized training and was just lucky when selected for the vacated position.

My job in that position was to back the scout up on all special weapons operations and maneuvers. Basically, I tracked the team scout wherever he went. I was armed with a sawed-off shotgun with a sling and my sidearm, and I brought up the rear and flanks as he moved along.

Training was a key point to all SWAT operations and the training staff was quite innovative. VIP protection was a must and practiced often. Finding and locating booby traps was always practiced, some very uniquely positioned and armed. Day- and night-movement operations were practiced at the Los Alamitos Naval Reserve Base in Orange County and the Los Angeles County's Pomona Fairgrounds.

A lot of team movement problems were "capture the flag" and the "Stokes litter recovery" at the Pomona Fairgrounds. We would have to locate a Stokes body litter hidden somewhere on the fairgrounds property in an unknown quadrant. The team set out to find the location of that litter and carry that litter with a 180-pound dummy tied to it. When you located it, you and your team had to carry it to the opposite corner of the fairgrounds.

The opposition in turn, were all mobile in the police units, roving around attempting to find the other team members. If you were spotted, they would light you and your cronies up with the bright spot lamps and honk the horn. Inside the patrol car were movement monitors who regulated each team's behavior. Each team must abide by the set rules and finish within three hours.

In the capture the flag problem, teams would compete with one another in capturing a positioned flag. This type of tactical problem incorporated extremely stealthy movements and actually made the opposing team converge upon the other opposition force and totally surprise them.

We engaged in competitive movement problems with the US Marine Corps and the LAPD quite often and performed excellent tactics against them. Each time, we won. Well, I'm going to tell all who engaged against my team: you really won, because I cheated. I have really felt bad since then. You knew deep down something was amiss, and you were correct.

———

We often worked the day shift, because the criminal element was working heavily during the early day hours. Most of the time we were paired up and worked the busy stations like Firestone Park, Lennox, East Los Angeles, where we arrested many thugs. These assignments gave us the opportunity to swoop into the tough areas and relieve the regular patrols to answer their calls unabated and with ample backup from our units.

I think my partner and I usually hooked up crooks faster than anyone else on our team or on other teams assigned to the same station. Our arrests were mostly felonies and occasional misdemeanors. Guns were very important and felonies in progress were more important.

We made countless "reasonable cause" arrests which meant lots of dope, and a plethora of robberies, burglaries and sales of dope. A few of those arrests made landmark decisions by the court system and encouraged us to make many more.

Working the field as a supplemental support to patrol allowed us to mingle with other deputies and establish good relationships. If there was an officer-involved shooting or an officer was wounded we would fill that space quickly, as the station personnel helped their fellow officers.

On days when a station lost one of their personnel, our units would work the field and fill in for the allotted time for the funeral. No questions needed to be asked, because we all were very familiar with the desk, dispatch, jail, and patrol systems. As soon as the funeral was over the station deputies would return and take their places without any interruptions.

One year I kept stats on my inner locker door, just to know how many felons and misdemeanors I hooked during that time frame. The number revealed 250 felony and 93 misdemeanor arrests. I felt proud as peaches and also noted we were only in the field for a little over 193 days out of 365.

What that proved is that we generated a lot of arrests and focused on a booking and writing system that made our time spent inside the station minimal. We were fast and had all of the details down so we would eliminate any impediments.

We knew our job was to be seen in the field as much as possible in order to generate accolades from station supervisors. Guess what, it worked and was duly noted. Our sergeants loved our work, and we generated few complaints.

When training came, I was lucky when I accelerated and thoroughly enjoyed rappelling from the Crocker Bank in downtown Los Angeles, in the empty bowels of elevator shafts, from whole variety of tall buildings and of course the Choctaw helicopters.

This entire rappelling experience was mostly generated by one of the most efficient and effective lieutenants I've ever worked for. He was a master in all officer survival situations and an excellent specialist. What this training did was create a confidence and effectively reduce fear of heights. His name was John K., and no one could be compared to him. He was very well vested in all tactical training matters and had worked SEB in the startup years. John K. was also my lieutenant in the academy when I was drill instructor. His best asset was his training in damn near everything, not to mention his leadership skills, which were threatening to many of the established administrators of the department.

John K. also taught us rappelling while a drill instructor in the sheriff's academy. This flash of genius was never forgotten, because I did another dumb move by rappelling from the LA County fire tower in my nylon shorts and shoes. Everything went well until I unhooked my carabiner, aka snap ring. When unhooked from the "eight ring," the carabiner dropped and fell right next to my groin, protected only by thin layer of nylon shorts and a jockstrap, and once again I burned the hell out of my private parts with that hot piece of metal. I'll admit I never did that again.

John K. was dedicated to all sincere training and officer survival classes. No one came close to his conviction, excluding one person—one of John K.'s closest friends, named Carroll H.

Carroll H. was one of the finest sergeants one could meet and knowledgeable as hell. He wrote a column for the sheriff' department's *Star News* called "Keys to Survival," pumping out this monthly article with little effort.

Some narrow-minded individuals have forgotten who wrote those articles and have given accolades to another individual who was not the writer. The information was incorrect, but it was to be expected from the many sycophants who loitered about the administration level.

I knew Carroll H.'s work and read all of his important writings. I have nothing but pride and respect for these two, John K. and Carroll H. Between them, I think they've covered all deployment angles and strategies. Both of them were workaholics and seldom relented.

My experience was enhanced by their ideas and thoughts on almost all officer safety matters, and I embraced their teachings and instructions. No one could match their tenacity and exuberance of leadership. I learned a lot from them and will always remember them and their characters as true law enforcement professionals.

At the time we practiced, practiced, and then practiced more. In between all of that practice, I practiced even more, drawing my weapon for speed and using blank ammo to blank fire and reload. I did this nearly every day and several times in isolated areas.

When I walked into the briefing room just before evening briefings, I would throw out the challenge to all in the room, it didn't matter how many were present, to empty all guns and load up with blank ammo. There were at least twenty in the room.

Once all loaded up, the practice was to draw your weapon on a given signal, point, and shoot all blank rounds. Then dump that brass and load up with new ammo and be ready as fast as possible. This was done with and without lights. I won nearly every time, primarily because I practiced so much. But also when I walked in and challenged them, I had already psyched most of them out with my pompous, boastful, narcissistic attitude. This was done competitively, and the object was to be able to be ready for any eventuality. The practice was done repetitively, and it kept us all on an even keel as long as we practiced.

All teams practiced extensively with the department's arson/explosives detail, where we made explosive entries and used a variety of small explosives to gain advantage and entries. We used diversionary tactics that were unlimited and left to the imagination as long as they conformed to a certain level of deployment and decency.

Our companionship was essential and everlasting, although several of the bureau's men fell into wrong choices and were ordered out of the bureau. However, most were very team-oriented and extremely good comrades in arms.

As time went on, a lot of the bureau members left because they were promoted, and they were sorely missed. We had developed a bond that no other unit in the department could enjoy as total backup when emergencies arose. We actually developed relationships as if we were one big family.

Our uniform appearance was maintained as drill-instructor quality, and we wore our highly polished helmets with chin straps attached when in the field to help differentiate us from other station deputies.

Our class A uniforms had to be in excellent condition, well cleaned, neatly pressed with the proper number of creases. Our name tags and shooting badges were kept exceptionally clean and well maintained. We collectively approached other deputies in the field and at the station to help in all activities and always asked them if our help was needed.

In fact we practiced, while en route to different stations, changing out of our "class A" uniforms into our SWAT gear. This was done while on the roll and in midrange change positions with the driver to allow him to change as well. Our units did not have cages in them, and this allowed us to crawl into the backseat and change pretty damn fast.

There were several adverse comments by some jealous deputies and supervisors who disliked our unit because they perceived us as troublemakers. Those individuals were few at most, but apparently they'd had poor contact with one of our crews.

It was the first citizen's complaint I had ever had, and it came from a gay man I stopped in West Hollywood. He complained that I treated him like a common criminal when we had first stopped him and started to pat him down.

As I was searching him for weapons he wiggled and squirmed around as if I were groping him romantically. Boy, what a complaint that one turned out to be. The investigating sergeant spoke with the complainant's high-pitched voice and effeminate delivery. The entire complaint was that I treated him like a common criminal. Fortunately the complaint was identified as unfounded, with no evidence of misconduct whatsoever.

I know of one black lieutenant who referred to our bureau, SEB, as the most racist, and said we only arrested black people. Gee, what a profound statement. I would express this as basic black rancor in an attempt to fortify racial hatred.I think he may have been recruited from the Social Services Division as an undercover socialist.

Now think about those accusations coming from ghetto stations like Lennox and Firestone Park stations. All I could say is that those stations were in a predominantly black area. During one shift at any of those stations there could conceivably twenty to thirty persons shaken down for a variety of reasons, so most of those shaken were black.

We had several black deputies assigned to our unit, and some were our sergeants and one captain. Their race was never at issue, and they were the best picks of our department. Many of our SWAT coppers were Mexican, not Latinos or Hispanics, but Mexican. We were all very comfortable with one another and never thought much about anything except team tactics, interaction, and camaraderie.

———

Yearly we were honored to be the primary security team for the Academy Awards. We would suit up in tuxedos and personally guard the ceremonies.

In fact, when the naked mustachioed man ran across the stage as Elizabeth Taylor was receiving an award in 1973, our guys were the ones who captured the culprit. This was an event where nothing happened except that one incident, which was unavoidable. The Academy Awards were definitely fun, and we were directed to only scare the less than law-abiding so they would scurry away, rather than make an issue out of their poor behavior or choices.

At break time at one of the ceremonies, I walked into the men's bathroom and there were maybe fifteen or twenty band members inside, lounging around leisurely chatting with one another and smoking pot. I walked into the bathroom in my tux and used the urinal. Then I washed my hands for several seconds, and turned around as I was drying my hands with a paper towel, identified myself, and addressed the small crowd of dope smokers.

When I announced to the musicians, who also happened to be dressed in tuxedos, that it was time to put their dope aside and get back to playing their fiddles, horns, and drums, now, they all scooted out the doors quickly and scurried back to the orchestra pit.

Outside of being alongside the movie stars, we all were very focused on our jobs to make sure no one disrupted the festivities. Instead of being starstruck, we were vigilant and cautiously focused on admirers and stagehands.

The biggest problem for most was the special closeness that developed when we worked as a team. The sergeant was every part of our efforts and although he was our supervisor, the separation from us was flawed. We all became too close to one another. The sergeant to appear too close to the enlisted swine, who would defend his life; yet he would be condemned for not keeping a supervisory distance in the eyes of the lieutenants. This occurred with every team. We all became too close, because we depended so much on each other, and keeping our distance was nearly impossible. Excluding a few, most of the lieutenants were nearly the same mix. They too would be too close to the teams for the same reason.

The Special Enforcement Bureau was unique and our companionship was not matched anywhere else on the department. Many of the sergeants and lieutenants who became executives in our department had been assigned to the unit as well.

On the other hand, a few weasels sneaked through from the administrative level and were immediately seen as politicians rather than cops. This rare breed of lieutenants—and one captain—was immediately identified and the top executives of the department somehow were given their profiles and picayunish command decisions, which caused their early departure.

———

Rappelling took us into a whole different perspective when we rappelled off tall buildings in downtown LA or down bridges that overhung a river or creek a couple hundred feet feet below. This fabulous training instilled confidence in all when exposed to varying heights.

I must admit the elevator shaft in the Crocker bank was awe-inspiring, a sixty-story darkened shaft. We would know the floor location of our role-playing terrorists, take the floors below and above their level, and work from there.

We practiced very hard and varied the scenarios and the number of terrorists on each problem. When we finished each time there was a debriefing, and criticism was abundant. In fact each member had something to say, so we could evaluate each other on strategic points of movement.

Lieutenant John K., whom I've mentioned earlier, would certainly have a scenario that would be well thought out and lucid, and you could count on his criticism and support just by the way he conducted himself.

Our snipers and spotters practiced all the time, and several were champions in the US rifle matches. These rifle matches included all US military units and private organizations. Their targets, at one hundred yards, would have a grouping within the size of a postage stamp. That's ten shots.

So if a shot was necessary, on command and cue, they would take a shot, and rest assured all they would need to hit the target would be a half inch inch exposed. Think about it the next time you grab someone in jest and expose yourself from behind, pretending to be a terrorist, just peeking from behind your captive's head. Your head would pop like a cantaloupe, splattering on a sidewalk from a ten-story building, and drop you right in your tracks. Many times there were as many as three snipers and spotters to obtain better angles for the kill.

The outside perimeter would have team members ready with a canine and ready to pursue or physically take down any individuals. Gas members were at the ready with a plethora of tear gas to obtain the best possible results. These individuals would be armed with a variety of weapons that might be necessary to deploy against whatever obstacles they might encounter.

The inside team scout, backup, and third man were separated, to eliminate one shot hitting two, and followed up by third man to cover the scout and backup. If the third man entered the home, a fourth man would stand just outside the door and watch where the interior team was going.

If the fourth man went in to maintain a good picture of the entry team, another man would stand by the door. That person by the door would always be replaced by another until informed to stop. The man by the door was also the one to bring in the extra ammo can if necessary, which would be by the door at all times, just in case a high volume of rounds were expended.

If each team practiced each position and cross-trained with all firearms, there would be no room for mistakes. It was instinctive, and each operation was different. We also practiced various martial arts and went through the motions when role playing.

My specialty was weapon retention and takeaway. I guess my size, coupled with my large hands, enabled me to manipulate most into submission quite easily. I was very proud that in every encounter with a suspect I had to hit them only once and knocked many of them completely out. Of course, I was under pressure from other team members, who would criticize me if I spent too much time on each combative suspect I encountered. They would rib me about hitting like Shirley Temple and almost getting beat up by some "pansy-ass" doper.

Well, that never happened. I would grab most and throw them into walls, corners, furniture or counter tops, or simply throw them out the window, depending on how many stories were in the building.

Going through the home, no matter how big, had to be quick and careful, like clockwork. Being ready for any eventuality made the team and inflated our boasting talents, although we all knew there was a match out there somewhere. We knew that most individuals in their own home would have the upper hand, because they knew their homes in complete darkness. If anyone bumped into something in the dark, the mere sound of that object, would lead them to know exactly where that object was located, and your position would be given away. Try it in your own home. Have someone sneak in during the darkness and see if, by noise alone, you know where that person is positioned. It works all the time, even if something is thrown to divert your attention.

We also practiced crowd and riot control extensively. This was imperative, because we were the first to respond to all civil disturbances and were a necessary force to quell most unruly mob behavior.

Our unit was expected to be up-to-date on all formations, the use of tear gas, and the strict use of physical and deadly force when justified. Aggressive and passive situations were practiced many times with the use of our own video cameraman and canine services. We all became skilled in this area, because we also taught the department and stations on many occasions.

We practiced immediate setup and implementation of primary and secondary command posts to handle calls for equipment and extra personnel. We had covered this topic so many times, it seemed quite natural for implementation of services performed in all major emergencies. This also incorporated the coordination of helicopters, buses, motorcycle units, horse details, and specialty items of generators, foul weather gear, utilities, tables and chairs, charts, display maps, mass booking equipment, flex cuffs, bedding, tent procurements, and toilet facilities. These procurements were swiftly achieved, because an emergency check list was used so nothing was overlooked.

That list had to be amended after each event in order to cover areas that may have been overlooked or could be better resourced on the next situation. In all emergencies, it was necessary to have ample fire department equipment close by, and depending on the situation, a number of ambulances needed to be strategically positioned so they could respond in a timely manner and safely direct their ingress and egress.

Another matter that differentiated our unit from all others and most other departments was the use of our patrol cars in convoy tactics. This was critical when quickly driving from the ELA area to the outer areas where our units were needed. Driving on the streets anywhere in Los Angeles County can be unnerving and unsafe unless the mobilization is coordinated and extremely flexible.

We practiced this maneuvering many times code-three, red lights and sirens, and became extremely aware of impediments that popped up quickly and created a major mess and traffic accidents. We didn't want to contribute to any injuries or deaths while responding to emergencies. Most other departmental units didn't have the time or the resources to practice this maneuvering and were hobbled by the intense traffic conditions at all hours of the day.

Mobil tactics was another matter when we were asked to respond to other stations for help. Those station commanders would view us as a necessary and viable resource, but also perceived us as "goons with guns," way too brutal and regimented to peacefully resolve their quiet neighborhood disturbances.

So what they usually did was hide us nearby, hidden from direct and aerial view. This happened quite a few times when sporadic, sizable demonstrations developed. When the anti-Shah of Iran demonstrations popped up in 1977 in Beverly Hills, our units were close when the demonstrators were blocking the entire street to the Shah's home.

A female sheriff's deputy put out a call for help when she was being beaten up by the demonstrators. Our units heard the cries for assistance. She needed help without delays. The lead SEB unit was being driven by one of our lieutenant's named Chuck W.

The crowd was not letting anyone through, so the lieutenant hit the gas and slammed into the crowd with his car and two were hit on the roll. One of the male demonstrators was thrown into a gutter and curb. A female demonstrator was struck, and both of her legs were broken by the car bumper. An infamous photo of her rolling over the radio car hood and hitting and breaking the windshield of the unit was publicized. The unit was followed by at least five other units that raced to assist the female deputy, who was not too seriously injured.

The tactic we practiced is using the radio cars to race toward the crowd at about 50 mph. As we approach we tap the brake slightly. The ass end of the unit comes around and may clip nearby demonstrators for a dramatic effect. They retreat because of the effects of the screeching brakes and tires. We practiced this often and with proper spacing the effect is very successful.

Another time we used mobile tactics, but this time it was at the federal building on Wilshire Boulevard near the 405 freeway. It was another Iranian demonstration, except this time it was planned.

The commander of West Hollywood Station was very concerned about our presence and personally let us know his feelings. He conversed with our sergeants and made it clear that he didn't want us seen by anyone, so he had us hidden from view and hunkered down in a large parking complex a couple of blocks away. We were directed not to be seen by anyone, including the snoopy media, which always was around in all demonstrations.

This commander even met with us in the parking garage to make sure we wouldn't be seen. He was primarily concerned about what we would do if the demonstrators got out of hand. He knew our tactics were swift and firm, and that there would be a quick reaction when we were deployed, should any riot situation raise its ugly head.

In addition to our hidden presence, there was an LAPD mounted detail of about twenty-five horses lined up and facing the crowd of approximately five hundred demonstrators.

These mounted officers were in full uniform and firmly seated on big steeds. They had no trouble directing large groups in certain planned directions. Just the presence of the mounted detail alone seemed ominous enough to cause the demonstrators to temper their aspirations. They were lined up along Veterans Avenue on the east side of the federal building on the lawn area. Everything seemed okay initially, but then the demonstrators started to become unruly, throwing things and breaking car windows in the rear parking lot.

Then the call came to us that a news media truck, with several media personnel inside, was being knocked around, and the crowd was trying to tip the van over. We received the signal to activate from the command post, and I was the lead patrol car coming out of the multistory parking lot within two minutes of the call. There were four in our car, including myself, the driver, another deputy in the back seat, and the new sergeant, Mike K., who was seated in the right front seat.

Mike had just come to the bureau and wasn't really familiar with mobile tactics. But it was a little late now, since we were in the midst of deploying the tactic as soon as we came out of the garage. There were about ten units behind me, all with four in each car. The rear and front doors were slightly ajar and my speed was getting up to approximately 50 mph. I was headed just to the left side of the crowd, where the media van was located. As I accelerated toward the crowd, I glanced slightly at my sergeant, Mike K., who appeared somewhat edgy.

As I drew closer, Mike asked me, "Larry, you're not going to hit them, are you?" When he asked me he placed his hand on my right leg as if to grab it. I smiled and said, "I sure hope I don't."

I started to tap the brake and let the rear end swing around from the right. The patrol car just cleared the group as they ran from my car. The tires were squealing and smoking. We all jumped out of our cars and quickly formed a skirmish line. We stood erect and slowly marched toward the crowd. This maneuver motivated the crowd to run into the large central area of grass just as the mounted posse was converging on their right flank.

Another mounted sheriff's posse was now deployed on the northern perimeter of the grass just south of Wilshire Boulevard. There were at least another twenty-five horses and riders standing fast and waiting for the demonstrators to come toward them. The demonstrators saw the crunch they were about to run into and decided to sit on the grass and submit to being captured rather than chance being hurt or killed by the converging forces.

I spoke later with Mike, my sergeant, about what I was doing with the car. He was certainly concerned about the action I was about to deploy, but we laughed it off nervously because of the possible serious consequences.

There was no need to hit anyone, because it wasn't justified in any book. Mike relaxed somewhat. I must admit I spooked him rather easily. We had worked together for a lengthy period of time when assigned at the sheriff's academy to at least two classes, so we knew one another pretty well.

Our unit was trained to the max and well versed in the use of force and firearms, combat tactics, and maneuvering. This complex knowledge was learned and reemphasized at this unit over a long time. It established our confidence and command presence and assured all other stations, details, bureaus, and personnel that we were well trained in all tactical matters and were a special culture and breed of men. We policed ourselves and critically hashed over flaws that could very well affect our bureau's pride and ability. It was very important that we maintain a good working ability with all units and assist all personnel in any and all tasks.

CHAPTER 85

A TEARFUL ADVERSARY

About my second week, we were at the bureau and about to go into the field at East Los Angeles Station. At that point we received a SWAT callout in the area of Lakewood Station. It was approximately a thirty-minute roll to the city of Cerritos.

We arrived and were given the details of a barricaded individual that was in a house at the end of a cul-de-sac. He apparently was in his own house, most likely alone.

The problem started the evening before when the man took a pair of his leather formal shoes and placed them into the middle of the cul-de-sac. Several neighbors were watching him, perplexed about what he was doing.

The man then went into his garage and brought out a small gas can and doused the shoes with the gas. He then took out a cigarette lighter and set the gasoline and shoes on fire. The shoes were ablaze for several minutes and smoldered for about twenty minutes.

The man then went back into his home and didn't come out again that night. The neighbors knew the man as a military veteran with several physical injuries and psychological problems.

The next day when the immediate neighbors on both sides came out of their homes to leave, when they came under fire. Bullets flew only when they tried to get into their cars. Fortunately, no one was injured or killed and the neighborhood was evacuated safely.

Ambulances and fire equipment were standing by several blocks away, ready for any eventuality. Our team was all geared up and ready to go, and the plan was going to be formulated as soon as Doug D. and I completed our scouting mission.

We started to advance on the objective, making notes of all cover and concealment modes of protection. We turned onto the street, crawling in our military green uniforms and darkened faces and hands. It seemed very quiet and well lit with no human activity at all. My partner was jotting down all sorts of info in his notebook as we crept past the first house on the east side of the street. Doug's only weapon was his sidearm, because he had to use both of his hands for writing and seeking available ways to position other team members.

Everything seemed okay as I followed Doug, armed with my sidearm and the AR-15 with a fifteen-round magazine. We were now poised near a small two-foot cinderblock wall that separated the adjoining home. That small wall tapered down close to the front sidewalk.

I was behind several medium-size bushes and leaned my face toward a small opening to get a better look when two blasts from what appeared to be a shotgun zinged off the cement about four inches past my face.

Doug and I rolled toward each other and paused briefly. There was no doubt what had just happened; fortunately the suspect missed us. Doug radioed the assault to our command post and requested a counter sniper and spotter to be moved up and positioned, so we could continue on without dancing around this suspect's bullets.

We continued on into the next property, hidden by a car and a motor home that were parked in the driveway. As we stood near the rear of the car, several more shotgun rounds slammed into the side of the car and other rounds whizzed by the sidewalk behind and under the car.

By this time our sniper and spotter were in position right behind us on the other side of the small cinderblock wall. Now we could count on them to watch out for what was coming from the targeted home and respond accordingly.

Doug and I were now getting our bearings, hiding behind the large motor home. Doug sprang out from the front of the motor home, crunched over, and began running to a pickup truck in an adjoining driveway. I moved to the front of the motor home and covered Doug's movements as he scurried across a small strip of open ground.

As Doug crept near the left rear wheel of the pickup, five or six rapidly fired rounds slammed into the opposite side of the truck and caused it to rock significantly from side to side. I saw Doug curled up like a sow-bug with his hands on top of his head, wadded up tightly like a wad of chewing gum around the wheel as the rounds were slamming into the truck.

Then several rounds hit the motor home where I was standing about a foot away from me, ricocheted past me, and hit the garage door. At that point, I fired two volleys of four rounds each into the open front door toward what I thought was the flash of the suspect's weapon.

We determined the numerous rounds of discharged shotgun rounds indicated the suspect knew exactly where we were, and any further scouting would be unnecessary and unsafe. Doug made it back to my position by a tall six-foot cinder-block wall, just in front of the truck in the driveway where he was last assaulted, and two doors away from the suspect's home.

The suspect's front door remained open, but no noise or movement was noted for two or three hours. The suspect's home, by the way, faced directly into the cul-de-sac and had an unobstructed view of the whole street.

Several attempts to call the suspect on his home phone went unanswered and quiet loomed, as if he was either waiting for further opportunities to shoot at someone or had been injured or killed. Finally he answered the phone and stated he would be coming out to surrender without any firearms. Our command post also indicated he would be walking out in the next three minutes.

Our sergeant, Dick P., and Doug were the ones that were designated to take the suspect into custody, and they both handed me their AR-15 rifles, as they were going to make the contact.

The suspect appeared suddenly, walking out the front door and onto the sidewalk and into the street. He appeared a bit bizarre, but surrendered nonetheless.

He was clad in a satin blue-and-black bathrobe, black slippers, and a black custom-fitted blindfold, and he carried a handsome black gold-edged Bible. He said nothing as he walked slowly into the lights and the middle of the cul-de-sac.

I followed Doug and the sergeant, Dick P., near the suspect and watched them both struggled with him like two saber-toothed tigers on a mammoth. They wrestled around his body as if examining him for lice.

They could not bring him down with their muscular gyrations or verbal commands. It was a little nerve racking they both couldn't drop him, possibly due to his ridgid stature and superior strength. He said nothing and just kept walking erect,taking minute steps because of the weight of both Doug and the sergeant.

I asked Doug and the sergeant to take the weapons from me and said I'd drop him quickly. Everyone on the team was watching. When they got off the suspect, I handed the weapons to the sergeant and brought the suspect to the ground immediately by sweeping his legs out from under him. I cuffed him quickly, and he still said nothing. This was odd because usually when someone is arrested and handcuffed, they scream as if all testosterone has left their body.

The call-out was over, and the SWAT lieutenant came over to me and chewed my ass out for destroying the shooting statistics of the bureau since its inception. In the past six years they had prided themselves as expending five rounds, on five different situations, and had five kills. My argument was I had to do something quick because the suspect was shooting at my partner, who was in a very vulnerable position. I had to shoot, and during my shooting, our sniper fired one round as well. (This reaction is commonly called "contagious fire.")

We examined the trajectories of our rounds and found out they hit the water heater, bedroom furniture, plastic casings of the shower stall, and hanging clothes in the bedrooms.

None of our rounds struck the suspect, and all were contained within the home except the .308 round fired by our sniper.

That .308 round went into the farthest bearing wall, through the one-inch-thick outer stucco wall, and into the backyard of the home.

Several of our guys had been moving into place at the rear without our knowledge. When the round came through the wall they heard the round whizzing past somewhere near them. This was determined to be an error by whoever gave the order to move extra personnel toward our position, without first conveying the information to the active SWAT personnel.

Several guys from the team and other teams came up to me and congratulated me for doing what I had to do and remarked that they had been at the bureau for five years and had never fired their weapons. Yet I had been there for only two weeks and shot off eight rounds justifiably. I thanked them for their opinions, but the final outcome had to come from the captain. He would make the final determination if my shooting was necessary and justified.

I was confronted the following day by another lieutenant, who informed me that the captain, Bob A., agreed with my perceptions and realized that the returned fire was the only way out of a deadly and dangerous predicament.

About a month later I was summoned to a preliminary trial for the suspect who had shot at us. He was in court seated in front next to his attorney. He was in shackles, chains, and cuffed to his waist.

I came to the witness stand and sat in the chair and described the events that had happened. As I talked about his assault on the whole team, he sat in his chair and agreed with my account and the descriptions of what had occurred. He was nodding his head and agreeing with me and smiled as if we were friends.

I soon found out the trial was a prelude for his sanity hearing. The information I obtained was that this guy was a Vietnam veteran and suffered grenade shrapnel wound that caused him to have a large metal plate in his head.

Just before his mind slipped into oblivion, he was pleading for the Veterans Administration to help him with the severe pain to his head apparently caused by the metal plate. The Veterans Administration refused to do anything and their response more than likely set him off.

When I found out why this guy was so incensed I felt like an idiot. This poor guy just wanted the pain to go away, and no one was helping him. I am so glad that I didn't hurt this guy and realized his reactions were to be expected.

God bless all military veterans, and I hope to God I'm never confronted again with anything close to that situation.

CHAPTER 86

BEAT IT!

We were working out of West Hollywood Station around five in the evening, and it was hot. There were lots of people, and traffic was jammed to a crawl eastbound on Santa Monica Boulevard nearing Kings Road.

My partner was driving, and I was looking for anything that might pop out of the woodwork. This place has many strange things that happen and those things would suddenly fall right into your lap.

There are no surprises in this area. Many men dress like women, including lipstick spread directly over their moustaches, and many women dress like men and sport moustaches. The term "be ready for anything" must have been crafted here.

We had just stopped a man a few blocks back who was standing alone by the curb and staring wildly into oblivion. He was gyrating his head as if he was spinning from within. As we slowly passed by him, he wouldn't look at us. He seemed rather peculiar, with his eyebrows raised and spaced out like the actor Bella Lugosi. I was thinking he was drunk on drugs or alcohol and I wanted to check on his well-being, because he was so near the street. We got out of our car and approached the man. He stood his ground and didn't move as we drew closer.

I stood directly in front of him, and he looked at me as if he couldn't focus on my face. I then noticed he had a three-inch silver-colored wood screw in each ear, with the sharpened tips pointed outward. He wouldn't talk with us, but another man who was nearby stated that the man was his friend and he was taking care of him. The unidentified man said his friend was undergoing some psychological problems and was okay as long as he was with him. The spaced-out male still maintained complete silence, so we asked his friend why the screws were in his ears.

His friend responded, "They're there to keep the gas off his dick!"

We paused for a moment and looked at the friend with empathy and despair, realizing that he was a tad off-kilter as well. We decided they were birds of a feather and to let well enough alone without any further strife. We returned to our car to slide back into the snarled traffic. We were still near the curb and attempting to ease ourselves into the traffic, when I noticed the older Ford station wagon in front of us with about six young children in the rear. They were pointing out the right side window at something that was making them excited.

We turned to our right and saw a thirty-year-old black man standing atop of a bus bench, buck naked, masturbating and looking directly at us. The bus bench was on Kings Road right in front of a large grocery store.

There had to be quite a few people watching us as we directed the car toward the bus bench. I jumped out and walked up near the bench.

He focused on me as he was playing with himself and screamed at me, "What the fuck are you looking at?" Knowing full well he was primed for conflict, I crossed my arms and turned away, but still carefully watching him. I said, "Go ahead and finish. I'll wait until you're done!"

I heard him groaning, huffing, and puffing as he was busily relieving himself. I heard quite a few clicks of cameras from the small crowd that started to gather. I was still carefully watching the suspect's movements.

I knew this could be a great photo op for the media depicting the wonderful contrast of the nude man on a bus bench, "whacking his willy," while a uniformed and helmeted deputy sheriff was nearby with his arms folded.

In about two minutes he finished his sexual bliss and carefully came down from the bus bench.

I pulled my handcuffs from my belt and tossed them underhanded to the suspect, who caught them rather handily. I told him to cuff himself. Without hesitation, he complied.

He remained calm, passive, and reserved as we drove him to the station and booked him for indecent exposure.

Surprisingly those unique photos never showed up, however time may prove me wrong.

CHAPTER 87

CHOKED BY A WOMAN

Doug D. and I were in the Lennox Station area over by LAX, passing in and out of the City of Hawthorne. This area is rife with crime and relatively close to Hollywood Park, not too far from Firestone Park.

We were southbound on Hawthorne Boulevard around eight in the evening. It was already dark for about an hour, and we were passing several older bungalows near 112th street. We spotted a male who turned away from us, just as we were lazily passing the main driveway. We decided to draw a little closer because of his evasive movements.

When we came upon him he was turning his head away from us as we drew closer. We both got out of the car quickly and called to him just as a woman was coming out of one of the small bungalows. She had something cupped in her left hand. She nearly walked right on top of us, standing in front of the small front porch.

You couldn't miss our car. The standard black-and-white four door took up nearly the whole driveway, yet she nearly walked into the car because it was so close to the bungalow door. The male adult was carrying a small brown satchel, and we asked him to place his hands on our car's fender.

He complied, by placing the satchel onto our patrol car hood and his hands on the fender. My partner asked the woman to place her hands on the fender as well. She started to comply, and Doug noticed her cupped left hand.

He called her attention to her cupped hand and told her to open it. That's when she took what appeared to be a twenty-five-dollar blue balloon of heroin and tossed it into her mouth.

Doug immediately recognized the familiar contraband and grabbed her neck. They both went backward over the two-stepped porch and into the bungalow's diminutive front room.

I saw them rolling around as Doug fought like a cowboy to hang on, both of his hands clasped around her throat. Suddenly the guy on the front fender grabbed the brown satchel and took off running full bore out the driveway and northbound on Hawthorne Boulevard.

I was reluctant to leave while my partner was scuffling with the female wrestler, but I figured he could certainly overcome her attempts to swallow the dope and cuff her. So I took off after the nitwit who was running like crazy and caught up with him after about fifty yards. I tapped him in the back of his head slightly with my left hand, which made him dive to the concrete like a runner coming to home plate. I grabbed him by his hair and told him we must hurry back, because if my partner was hurt I was going to break his legs. He complied and ran with me. I cuffed his right wrist and arm to our patrol car. I peered into the house and this time saw Doug being choked by the woman instead of him choking her.

I said, "Holy shit, Doug, is she whupping your ass?" He hollered back, "You could help, couldn't you?"

Instead of asking the male suspect not to try to escape, and knowing full well handcuffs can be slipped quite easily if not tightened firmly to both hands, I swept his two legs from underneath him. Surprised, he spun a full circle around the handle and slammed to the ground like a ham falling off a kitchen table.

I came in the room, carefully grabbed the female wrestler's hair, and pulled her head back, arching her back into submission. She spat out the balloon onto the wooden floor. Doug grabbed it, came over, and cuffed the wench from hell.

We all went outside and around the rear of the car. We placed the female into the backseat and closed the door. Doug and I came around to the rear, where the satchel was resting.

We were opening the satchel to see what was so valuable that the male suspect had taken off so fast but were interrupted by the male mumbling something undistinguishable. We came around to see what he was mumbling. He said, "I think my wrist is broken!"

We looked at his wrist and noted it was shaped like a rickety stove pipe, stretching downward from the handle. That injury must have happened when I swept his legs from under him, and no doubt the wrist was broken in transit. We ordered an ambulance to our location and completed searching the satchel. Inside the satchel was a baggie containing ten twenty-five-dollar balloons of heroin.

We ordered another one of our units to follow the ambulance to the hospital, get treatment for the injured suspect and then book him downtown in the jail medical ward. We went to Lennox Station to book the female and complete the reports. Both suspects were charged with possession of heroin for sales and court proceedings several months later held both of them over for trial.

Approximately a year later I received a subpoena for someone charged with possession of heroin for sales. I didn't recognize the name and called the district attorney's office to find out if it was some kind of a mistake. The deputy DA he informed me the name was correct, but the case number was from our arrest from Lennox Station a year earlier. He said that the two defendants were held over for trial in the municipal court matter, but as the court clerk went to reseal the evidence, she, the court clerk, skimmed and absconded with six of the eleven twenty-five-dollar balloons. Knowing full well the evidence would be accounted for in the near future, she apparently brushed aside prudence and integrity and took what she needed.

The court clerks' office was completely unaware that she had a severe drug problem and was in a position to take as much as she liked. Until she was caught.

Hopefully the county has put in place a series of checks and balances that precludes court clerks or anyone else from tampering with the chain of evidence admitted into the court system.

CHAPTER 88

THE GAY-SHOO

My partner was a sergeant, Art F., who was an admired fellow officer from Firestone Park, the academy, and the Special Enforcement Bureau. He and I were about the same height, and he was maybe thirty pounds heavier. He was well liked and had a great personality. We were summoned to the West Hollywood Station area. Our mission was to run the lingering transient homosexuals away from the established homosexuals' homes. Apparently the transient gays were actively engaged in sex with each other on the front yards of several gay community's homes. The transient boys who were doing "boom-boom" were apparently howling at the moon and making strange guttural humping noises in their acts of intense sexual ecstasy.

As requested from the gay community and the city administrators, our job was to frighten the gay prowlers and howlers. Our instructions were very clear: do not make any arrests, just scare the horny exhibitionists away. We were to dress in casual street attire. We knew the mode of dress was tight Levi's, T-shirts, black boots, and of course brown leather jackets.

The bonus for us to be working together was that we were both tall and clean-looking, with chiseled facial features and smiles that would make any man draw toward us at the snap of a finger. This specialized crew was none other than Sergeant Art F. and me.

We knew there must be something sensationalized, at some point, to make us literally "stick-out" from other similar studs in the group. So I took my inch and a half leather sap, which had powered lead at the broad end, and taped it onto my leg just above my right inside knee cap. This caused my "Levis" to outline the sap and it looked like I was super well-endowed.

Two other guys were staged out of view and acted as backup in case we stumbled onto a regular street thug.

So we set up just off of Robertson Avenue around three o'clock. We put our arms around each other and grasped each other's fannies and sashayed down the street. (I don't want any of you to get the wrong idea about this particular assignment; we had to really fight off laughing our asses off.) Many men and he/shes passed by us, and I believe we scared them away because of our sexual boldness. My profile worked perfectly, because every time we conversed with prospective clients they marveled at my well-outlined protrusion as an object of heavenly bliss.

I conversed sociably in "gayese" until I was about to laugh aloud, but I quickly whipped out my badge and ID. I reprimanded them for the offerings of explicit sexual conduct, which caused them to tighten their buttocks, and dash away. Then, and only then, I could laugh, but not too loudly, because that would be deemed offensive to the sensitive residents of the community.

We lingered around corners and driveways to gain maximum attention. We were coming into the evening hours, and expensive cars like Mercedeses, BMWs, and Cadillacs came cruising slowly down the street, zigzagging slightly for some unknown reason. The shiny new expensive cars would stop in the middle of the street, and the drivers would stare at us as if needing directions.

I approach a driver's door in my finest ankle-tied gait and saw the driver with his penis in hand, masturbating openly. Oddly enough, there was a large center-fold picture of a naked man, with all of his sexual equipment exposed, lying across the center console.

I made him giggle by asking if what was in his hand was a pet hamster. He showed me his pet snake and how handsome it was.

Of course symphony music was playing and amplified to lure me closer, but I didn't fall for it. I knew what this guy was up to and spoke to him about his handsome sexual appendage. When he responded flirtatiously, I became dizzy with all of the excitement and quickly flashed my badge and ID to make him stop and go away.

Most of them damn near crapped in their pants and lost the moment of surge and gave me their ID. Surprisingly, quite a few of them were chefs from the more elaborate hotels and eateries. We hit pay dirt and of course no arrests, but plenty got the bejesus scared out of them, and we completed a successful mission.

We concluded by driving around in an unmarked car to see if we could snag other types of exhibitionists. We drove into a commercial district off Santa Monica Boulevard near San Vicente. We came into a dark alley and noticed movement by a large Dumpster. One male was braced against the raunchy, foul smelling trash container, partially naked with his pants and underwear around his ankles. (Of course, there were no flies because it was nighttime and most of them are in bed.)

Another male, was also partially naked with his pants and underwear around his ankles as well, was firmly holding onto the bare, hairy rump of the man braced against the Dumpster. *Oh, let's skip all of the ambience and opulence of kings,* I thought. It was obvious they were in the throes of deep lovemaking until I shone my flashlight on them. Then they pulled up their pants and scurried away from us toward Santa Monica Boulevard.

Next we went over to a lesbian bar by Crescent Heights and Santa Monica and walked in just to get a drink. It was loaded with lesbians who gave us the raunchiest looks that would drive a starving lion away from a fresh gazelle.. I think the only thing that stopped most of the raw, robust made-up girls was our physical size.

If you ever want to test the waters of bias, just walk into one of these bars and attempt to snuggle up to the very few good-looking ones. You'd better think twice. They hate competition, especially from the masculine gender.

We finished our drinks and moseyed out to the parking lot and came upon two fine young ladies squatting between two parked cars and peeing. We stood there staring, and they became angered by our attention. We then identified ourselves and told them to use the restroom facilities instead of the open parking lot, where there is no expectation of privacy. We also informed them that urinating in public was a criminal offense and a violation of the penal code as well as the health and safety codes that list the offense as unhealthy.

We finished the night with sore stomachs from laughing so much. We didn't make a single arrest and actually released many for minor offenses and misdemeanors. I might add we sent many away laughing as well, and the mission turned out to be very productive and not too offensive.

CHAPTER 89

THE SETUP

Lennox Station is another prime spot where the stench of crime is all too familiar. This area is nothing but a generation behind Firestone Station's crime problems.

Lennox is between the fine cities of Inglewood and Hawthorne, close by LAX. Arrests are plentiful, and a variety of crimes seems to plague specific areas.

On a night that was not too much different than other nights, a two-man unit was summoned to a cul-de-sac where there was a call of a suspicious man acting strange. Unbeknown to the responding crew, a martial artist who had been to jail numerous times called in to Lennox Station to report himself as the suspicious suspect acting a little strange. The suspect's background of hatred toward law enforcement was extensive, and he'd had many contacts with them in the past. He had taught himself how to disarm law enforcement when they stopped him and taught many others the same attack scenario.

When the deputies arrived, they saw the man in the middle of the cul-de-sac. He stood there, erect, with his hands clasped comfortably below his belt. As the deputies drew near, the suspect watched them approach with his peripheral vision. In this mode, he did not send any alarm as to what he was about to do.

When the deputies were within three feet of the suspect, he refused to answer any questions they were asking, and he seemed to be in some sort of trance. That behavior drew the deputies even closer, so they were easily within reach of the suspect.

That's when the suspect exploded into action and slapped both officers on their respective right sides with both of his hands, almost like a martial artist's diversionary slap to turn them away from pending primary blows that generally follow such a movement. Both of the suspect's hands slipped down the deputies sides as if he was trying to grab their batons just at the junction of the deputies' utility belts. The problem this suspect was having, although he had practiced many times, was to be in close quarters, grab the officers' guns, and disarm them easily, if they weren't cautious.In this case, though, both of the deputies, training officer and trainee, were left-handed. This meant that both of the deputies had their holsters and guns positioned on their left sides.

The deputy said that he and his trainee were involved in a fight for their lives, and the suspect was not giving up. They grew extremely tired of hitting the suspect with their flashlights, but they didn't stop until he surrendered. Good fortune embraced them for being left-handed, and thank God both of them had the survival attitude burned into their training mantra not to give up.

This thug was found guilty of the assaults and was sentenced to prison for several years for the assaults on both deputies and was released in the late eighties. Right around the early nineties the same suspect was in a small bar on Olympic Boulevard in the East Los Angeles area.He became rather belligerent to several Hispanic patrons in the bar and went outside to leave. He was involved in another fight, but this time he was fatally stabbed in the eye with an ice pick. The suspect(s) who stabbed him were never apprehended.

The adage "What goes around comes around," couldn't be more eloquently portrayed.

CHAPTER 90

ROCK STARS

One thing we did at the Special Enforcement Bureau was to train, train, and then train some more. The more we practiced the better we got. My karate instructor and friend George B. worked us every day in numerous contorted defensive and offensive tactics if they had a slight possibility of arising in any SWAT callout.

George and I were selected to go to West Hollywood Station to do recruitment photo ops with a photographer. This was the first time we were selected to be rock stars for the department's publicity department. We had always made fun of the sheriff's administration for their action photos of passive-looking deputies in recruitment portfolios and handouts. So their answer was to take photos of us on car stops, in staged interaction with individuals inquiring about the sheriff's relationship with the public.

We had a good time and we ended up on several recruitment pamphlets and posters. We were elated. We were now at the top of our careers as rock stars and had nowhere else to go.

Several weeks later, we were ordered to accompany an actor from New York to go to Hyde Park in Los Angeles. This was going to be a Chevrolet Nova commercial. I was instructed to demonstrate to the actor of how to handle steering wheel maneuvers, sharp turns, fishtailing around corners, and hopping over large humps that made the car airborne. I thought, *Good God, they are going to pay me to act nuts!*

It was very important for the actor to understand the hazards behind the wheel and how to control the car. I was informed that actually there was going to be a camera mounted outside the driver's door and window, filming my hands with black gloves and my face with mirrored sunglasses and wearing my helmet. When outside the car, the actor would be talking to the camera, but when the car was doing the racing around, it would be George and me with our helmets, gloves, and mirrored sunglasses on.

It sounded like it would be fun, so away we went with the New York actor seated in the backseat watching us. I got out of the car before the cameras began shooting and let about fifteen pounds of pressure out of the tires to increase the squealing of tires and burning rubber for the visual effects as well.

We were approved to make the minor adjustments and were ready to take off. On the given signal, we took off, and away we went.

The whole episode was great and looked terrific with only one minor error.

The little actor in the backseat was curled up on the floor, scared to death. He was pleased that we didn't crash and kill him. Jesus, what a man.

Several more months went by, and I was called to do photo ops for recruitment posters with the Sheriff's Information Bureau photographer. I repeated numerous action stops as if in a combat mode in the twilight and evening shadows and modeled the uniform to display their well-groomed, trimmed uniform standards.

A couple of weeks later I received the photos that were taken and was told I didn't make the cut. I asked why. The photographer informed me that I was too mean-looking and looked as if I was in a hot combat mode all the time.

Since I was informed about my mean appearance, I've been working on my feminine side and a softer look, but this quest unfortunately was not successful.

Both George and I enjoyed our short rock star tenure and returned to our status quo lives, mingling with the rest of the guys and feeling ugly.

CHAPTER 91

THE THREE-STEP BIKER SHUFFLE

We were working in East Los Angeles, over on Olympic Boulevard near Ditman Avenue. One of our SEB units spotted a whole slew of outlaw bikers who had their hogs parked neatly aligned along Olympic Boulevard. These were all hard-core bikers occupying an outpost bar on the eastern edge of East Los Angeles Station's area.

Several individuals came out of the bar complaining that the bikers had taken over the whole bar and forced everyone else out. Fortunately we had about six two-man SEB units and all were still unattached with any other duties, so we decided to make a bar check.

My partner and I walked in first, while the other units were arriving and parking their cars. As I walked into the bar, I heard all kinds of noises and thuds. My best guess was that most bikers in the bar were packing heat and had dumped their guns and kicked them away from where they were sitting.

There were about thirty or forty the bikers and their sweethearts clustered inside the entire wraparound vinyl booths and maybe about six to eight other smaller tables scattered near the booths. We heard grumbling, which became increasingly loud as we came farther into the bar.

A couple of the larger men stood up. They started to growl about our presence and were starting to speak their contemptuous slander louder. I was in the farthest and noticed a large man slithering slowly toward the back door. With his left hand he was reaching for something in his left rear pocket. For some reason he was having great difficulty pulling whatever it was, and he kept his eyes on me as I drew closer to his position.

He was about six five and maybe 280 pounds, with shoulder-length hair, dirty in appearance. He sneered as I focused on his movements. About eight deputies were now in the bar with a fine command presence in neat, trim uniforms, shiny boots, and polished brown-and-green helmets. They spread themselves throughout the bar and watched the bikers' smug and brash movements.

The big thug by the rear door quickly scooted outside to the left of the doorway and disappeared momentarily. I came outside and spotted him still digging into his left rear pocket where he had a bulging biker-type wallet with a dog chain dangling from the wallet and connected to his belt loop.

I ordered him to pull his left hand out slowly and place his hands on the wall. I assisted placing his left arm and wrist against the wall. He said, "Hey, I'm not doing anything. Why are you fucking with me?"

While he was questioning me, I began to search him around the waist and then the pocket areas. When I came to the left rear pocket, I placed two of my fingers down along side of his bulky wallet with the chain clasp. I hit something hard, possibly a gun, and he pushed away from the wall and turned around. We were now face-to-face. He was absolutely foul smelling and grungy. I latched onto his wrists as he was trying to get his hand into his pocket.

He was "motherfucking" me to no end, as we wrestled backward and through the rear door and inside the bar. I stuck with him as if we were dancing partners. We slammed into several pinball machines and spun them askew like two bulls bumping into everything. I was about to smash him in the nose with my highly polished helmet as he was desperately trying to get into that left rear pocket, and gyrating from side to side and back and forth. The other bikers started yelling at us as we negotiated around the obstacles.

A couple of guns and large hunting knives were found at this time by other SEB deputies who had their backs to me. They were watching the other bikers and kept them from getting involved. The guns and knives were on the floor in front of several of the booths.

Several other units were called to assist in the bar fracas, and soon we had ten units at the scene. I was still waltzing around the bar and ended up near two green-felted pool tables. These pool tables were well lit with a long lamp hanging about four feet from the center of the table. I grabbed my dancing thug's long hair and yanked it backward, all the while holding tightly to his left wrist. I was able to bend him backward enough to create enough pain that he finally gave up.

I handcuffed him quickly and started to move out of the bar, when another one of the bikers jumped on top of one of the pool tables and began to sing a biker chant that raised the tempers of the other bikers to overpower us. The chant actually sounded pretty good as nearly everyone joined in the rhythmic biker mantra. I took the big boy outside and searched him thoroughly. From his left rear pocket I withdrew a two-shot .38 caliber derringer, fully loaded. I placed him in our patrol car, and another deputy watched him as I returned to the bar.

As I came in, the black-haired biker was still on the pool table, chanting louder than ever. By now the whole biker clan was involved in a unison incantation of magical biker words. Some were pounding on various tables to the beat of the song while other waved their arms and hands as if to draw the deputies' attention away from the fight, so they could dump more guns and knives, and numerous bags of dope.

That's when I reached upward and grabbed the biker cantor by his long locks, pulled him off the table, dropped him to the floor, and cuffed him. He was wiggling around like a fish out of water. He was arrested for "rout," which is an attempt to riot. Five others were arrested by other deputies and later on handed over to me to add their charges to our report.

A total of eight guns and two hunting knives were taken into custody, and a whole variety of narcotics. Most of the contraband was the same material that was tossed when we first came into the bar before the fight started.

To me this was a moment of pride when fellow deputies allowed me to carry on with my biker buddy performing the three-step biker shuffle.

The deputies put their backs to me and kept a constant vigil on the disruptive volley of chanting bikers and their discarded guns and dope. This was an excellent way to control this rowdy mob, and I was even more excited because every deputy knew what to do and performed extremely well.

No one was injured, and the whole ordeal was noted as a good reaction to a highly volatile situation.

CHAPTER 92

THE ROBBERY

We were going to lunch at a nice restaurant called Googie's in the Atlantic Plaza, on Atlantic Boulevard near Floral Avenue, in Monterey Park. It was only a short distance from the Special Enforcement Bureau, and they had pretty good food.

No one else wanted to go, so I went with my sergeant, Mike A. He was a very nice and polite sergeant and always had a smile on his face. I was driving our marked patrol car. As we pulled in to park, we noted the lot was pretty full. There was only one parking space, right next to the restaurant windows.

I pulled into the marked space and shut off the patrol car. I reached over near the sergeant's legs and pushed the lock inward to secure the shotgun.

Just before we stepped out, we spotted two cholos who were dressed the part (the duck theory), wearing buttoned-up plaid Pendletons, baggy khaki pants, and shined leather shoes. Their hair was long, dark, and slicked down and they were wearing wraparound shades.

They were coming out the front door of a Kids Mart store. They looked directly at us and then quickly turned their heads and covered the sides of their left cheeks and eyes with their open left hands. I believe they were attempting to conceal their profiles.

I spoke to Mike and said look at these two, what the hell are they up to? Mike stated, "Oh yeah, something's up!"

They walked to our left, two cars away and walked between them and around toward the rear of our car fifteen or so feet away.

As I turned in my seat, I looked at the cholo who was farther away and spotted the butt of an automatic pistol sticking out of his right rear pocket.

I yelled to Mike, "Gun," sprang out of the driver's seat, drew down on the two cholos, and ordered them to freeze!

One of them took off running around the front of the restaurant as Mike went after him. The one with the gun turned and faced me about twenty feet away. I ordered him to lie on the ground with his hands stretched outward.

He started to comply but then started to lower his hands as if he was going to try to grab his gun. I couldn't believe he was going to make the move. "Go ahead," I said and placed my pistol back into my holster. I stood ready for him to continue with his fatal move. He looked at me as if sizing me up and then decided not to make a dumb mistake. He stretched out his arms and lay down flat on the ground,with his nose touching the asphalt.

I heard two distinct shots off to my right as I straddled the brash, armed, skinny cholo with the wraparound shades. I thought it must be Mike shooting at the other nitwit.

I yelled, "Are you okay, Mike?" He responded quickly, "Yeah, that other guy pointed a gun at me!" I was infuriated at the brazen attitude of these two thugs. I saw the butt of an automatic pistol sticking out of my thug's right rear pocket.

I placed my left Cochran boot right onto the suspect's neck and leaned on him enough to control his entire body. I grabbed the pistol from his pocket and stuck it into my belt, and I told him not to move, or I would break his neck. He remained motionless as I cuffed him. I watched for my partner to reappear.

I grabbed the skinny guy by the butt of his baggy pants and grasped his shirt collar, and picked him up like I was offering him as a sacrifice to God. His back arched, as I had him in my outstretched arms so he wouldn't tumble free.

I walked over to our parked police unit as my partner approached. While standing about two feet from the trunk of our patrol car, I dropped the guy onto the trunk like a heavy side of lamb slamming onto a butcher's block.

I pulled his pistol from my waist and examined it. It was a pellet gun, not a real gun. It surprised me that the idiot was thinking to pull this gun to scare me; I didn't realize I looked that easy. I held his head on the trunk with my left hand on his throat. Surprised, I noticed about twenty to thirty patrons inside Googie's restaurant with their faces pressed to the picture windows. Apparently they had watched the entire event and enjoyed every minute of our capturing and arresting techniques. I think!

Mike told me that the other suspect dropped to one knee near the bank and pointed something shiny toward him from about fifty feet away. He added he must have missed, because the thug kept running away along the eastern wall of the same bank and was hidden somewhere between the parked cars.

Mike stood by the "trunked suspect" as I walked into the Kids Mart shop to talk with the employees. As I came in, I saw a young woman lying on the ground, crying. I told her who I was, and she readily stood up. I gave her a hug and told her we caught one of suspects and shot at the other one. I said she should not fear anything more.

She regained her composure and told me the two men came into the shop while she was there all alone. They demanded the money from the cash register, and she complied with their demands. She was then ordered to lie face down and not get up. They told her if she tried to get up, they would shoot her. She was scared they would shoot her, so she remained on the floor until I walked in.

I went back outside and searched the pockets of the captured bad guy. In his right front shirt pocket, I located a wad of money and six to eight checks made out to the Kids Mart. These items alone indicated we had the right guy.

A Monterey Park Police motor officer arrived and stood by me. The suspect was still lying atop the hood of my patrol car with my left hand grasping his throat. The officer was writing the information I was giving him when suddenly the suspect kicked his foot into the air and slapped the notebook from the motor officer's hands. The notebook landed on the asphalt over by the right front door of our patrol car.

I tempered the cholo's aggressive behavior by slapping his fanny with my right hand, and I gained his cooperation immediately. This event as well, was captured by the Googie's onlookers who were all smiling and apparently laughing at this imp's brash attitude.

A canine unit arrived and surprisingly the canine found the other suspect lying beneath a load of rubbish in a Dumpster near the rear of the bank. No weapon was found in the trash bin other than an eight-inch screwdriver. Even a screwdriver can be held like a gun, and consequences are inevitable.

CHAPTER 93

TWO CROOKS AFOOT

I was driving and my partner, Tony W., the team sergeant, was bookman in the right front seat. We were slowly traveling along Prairie Boulevard and shaking down as many gangbanging thugs as possible. Our goal was to wreak havoc on gang members because of the recent shootings and murders in and around the Hollywood Park Racetrack and of course the Lennox Station area, which was loaded with the criminal element.

Lennox Station was having a surge of gang-related shootings and requested the Special Enforcement Bureau to assist in trying to regain control of the neighborhoods. Our entire team, at least five two-man units, were in the area. The whole purpose for us being there was to quell the gang violence and settle the nervous feeling of the community. Most folks in the community were not aware that we were from an outside specialized unit, SEB, thoroughly trained to pop into action with typical street gangs and adept at controlling their antics.

Tony, my team sergeant, and I were very comfortable together. We tried very hard to beat the other guys to the first pinch, and hoping to get a gun or sizable amount of dope. That was the competitive nature and sprit of our unit. The regular Lennox units were deluged with calls, details, or other activities, and weren't constricted. We were allowed to roam about and aggressively and search for thugs and gang activity. What a job, getting paid to hunt!

We had already shaken down about ten individuals. On the curbside lane we noticed two gangbangers walking along the sidewalk in front of us and going in the same direction. This was a little strange, because it was still dusk, and usually these hoods don't come out until later in the evening hours to do their devious deeds. We were very fortunate to have seen their suspicious movement when we did, because we had only a fleeting moment to capture that move. Also the two were big enough to give us a run for our money and might go for their "stuff" before we could get out of the car. One of them looked at us over his left shoulder. When the one nearer the curb realized we were right behind them, he turned forward. They both did something with their right hands at their waistband areas.

Tony and I said, "See what they're doing?" We agreed they appeared to be either reaching for weapons or adjusting weapons in their waistbands so they were undetectable.

Instead of pulling right up to them—because they could turn at any moment—we stopped about ten feet behind them and got out of the car quietly as possible. We already had our guns out and alongside our legs at the ready. This is the time when a shooting is most likely to happen, and focus is paramount.

The two didn't turn around at all. We drew closer and made a loud announcement. "Put your hands out to each side, and don't turn around!" They stopped walking, and we repeated our command again. There was a pause for maybe two or three seconds and all four arms went up.

I went off to one side, about five feet, and told them not to turn around or they might get shot. Tony came alongside one of them and grabbed one of their wrists, and twisted it to draw him around in case the other one wanted to make a reach for his weapon. As Tony held the gangster against him closely, he holstered his weapon as I held a good bead on both of them; he ran his other hand around the front of him searching for a possible weapon.

Suddenly, Tony reinforced his tight grip, forcibly drew the suspect tighter against him, pulled out a black automatic pistol, and showed it to me. Tony placed the gun in his waistband and cuffed the suspect.

When he was finished, I ordered the other suspect to lie flat on the ground with his arms extended. The unsearched suspect said nothing; he was fully aware I was aiming my gun right at him.

Tony took the first suspect to the ground and backed away until the other suspect completed the instructions I gave him. He then approached the second suspect and grabbed his wrist, twisted it behind his back, and then he drew the other behind his back and cuffed it as well. Then Tony searched the second suspect and found a revolver in his waistband as well. He passed the gun to me and I placed it in my waistband. Tony helped the first suspect stand up. He escorted him to the patrol car, searched him thoroughly, and placed him into the backseat of our unit.

He returned to the second suspect and assisted him to stand. We all walked to the patrol car, where Tony searched him thoroughly as well. Nothing else was found other than the two guns, both of which were fully loaded and ready to go.

This find was pure luck, and it turned out pretty well, because no one was hurt. Had it been the local Lennox unit or anyone else, it might have had a different outcome. We were very pleased with our find and bragged about our catch over the radio in general radio terms as "10-15 with two!"

I worked with Tony many times, and we laughed a lot. He was no-nonsense cop, excellent as a partner, and ideal as our team sergeant.

CHAPTER 94

CLEARING LEATHER

Jimmy H. and I were working in the city of Carson because George B., his regular and longtime partner was ill. So we decided to pair up and dredge for low-feeding scum suckers in the south end. Working in Carson was a twist from other areas, with major industrial companies mixed in with the residential community.

Carson was the place where they had the infamous chlorine gas leak that came into a county fire station while the firemen were asleep. Several of those firemen were retired early from that catastrophe. The Los Angeles community called Wilmington was the southern border of Carson.

We often switched when either regular partner didn't come in. Time and experience was on our side, and we worked well together. Both of us were from Firestone Park Station and were able to communicate with each other rather easily. We knew what each other was thinking, and with coordinated hand signals, it made our attempts to flush out crooks rather easy.

We had already hooked and booked two male adults for guns and dope and finished our reports relatively quickly. We went back into the field and headed south of the station toward a small area called Scottsdale Estates. The area along Avalon Boulevard just north of Sepulveda Boulevard was rife with thugs. We stopped for a short bit and grabbed a couple of cups of coffee.

As we were driving around and shaking several possibilities, we were kidding each other about certain people we would run into. Jimmy was always in good humor and a lot of fun to be with. We were passing a large parking lot to a major market that was apparently closed. It was around nine in the evening, and no one was in the lot.

Then we spotted two cars parked farther back in the dimly lit distance along a dirt lot and closer to the store front, rather than the street side. We decided to check and see what the two cars were doing. As we came upon the two cars we noticed they were parked face-to-face, so two the drivers could communicate easily and touch each other's hands or exchange items without leaning or stretching. There were two adult Hispanic females in the first car facing outward from the dirt lot. The other car was facing the dirt lot, and a lone adult male, Hispanic, was seated in the driver's seat, apparently talking with the two females.

Suddenly what looked like a beer can was thrown in a high arching toss from between the cars. The can was leaking its contents as it traveled into the dirt lot, which was surrounded by a six-foot chain-link fence. As we drove by slowly Jimmy and I called out to them, "Hey, you guys dropped something!"

At this same time we noticed another male adult Hispanic seated inside a large shopping cart, backward, with both of his legs poking out the rear, movable portion. He was positioned between the drivers and smiled toward us when he heard our comment about dropping something.

The guy in the cart said, "No, we didn't drop anything!" Now, normally we would have left this alone, figuring these four were in the midst of a romantic rendezvous. But when they denied tossing the beer, we turned around in the lot and came upon them facing their cars.

We stepped from our car and stood near our respective doors and ordered all four to approach us. They complied and we searched all four. Nothing incriminating was found, and no one had contraband.

We asked all four to sit on the dry asphalt and relax. Jimmy said he was checking the cars. I stood behind all four individuals about ten feet to their rear.

Jimmy went through the cars for about two minutes. Without warning, he came out of the male driver's car. I distinctly heard his holster, which makes a distinct, unique sound of two pieces of hardened leather coming together. That meant one thing: he pulled his gun out. Something was very serious.

Jimmy ordered everyone to lie on the ground face down and not move at all. I drew my weapon and stood aside from Jimmy.

Jimmy told me to go check out the car facing away from us—there was a dead guy in the backseat. I thought, *What the hell?*

I left Jimmy with the four occupants lying on the ground and went directly to the car where the body was. I opened the two-door car and saw the body lying across the rear seat, face down. I crawled into the front seat, reached over the backrest, and placed two of my fingers on the man's neck near the carotid artery to see if there was a pulse.

I detected no pulse, so I elevated the man's head, opened one of his eyes, and poked my index finger into his eyeball. There was no reaction, and his body was cold to the touch. He was definitely dead with no obvious signs for his cause of death.

I came out of the car and told Jimmy of my findings. We hooked up all four. We called for paramedics to come and verify our dead body. Two other units were called to assist us with the four who needed to be isolated and transported immediately to the station. The station was advised to contact the homicide detectives and have them roll out as well.

The two women were separated, and they each explained they were going to the store when they ran into the two males who were in their car. Their conversation distracted them from their tasks. They said they had been talking for approximately a half hour and had absolutely no idea the men had a dead body in their backseat.

The women were very concerned, because they'd left their husbands at one of their homes waiting for the wives to come back with some beer and goodies. We assured them this would take at least five to ten hours if their stories were accurate. It was going to be up to the women to come up with a believable story for their husbands.

As for the men, they knew their friend was dead in the backseat from an overdose of heroin. When we stopped them, they'd had the dead body in the backseat for at least four hours. They were en route to Dominguez Hills, just east of Victoria Street, to dump their friend in one of the vast empty lots that ran along that area, to avoid embarrassing questions.

CHAPTER 95

CAMPING OUT!

The Angeles National Forest is a welcome sight to many campers. It has quite a few choice camping sites for people to relax and enjoy the outdoors. The campsites are generally full of anxious camping families, roughing it slightly and still enjoying nature, the aromas of the pine trees, and smoking campfires.

What they didn't expect was a large load of deadbeat biker gangsters to come into their campground, take the entire place over, pillage the campsites, and block off any escape for help. Then they began to rough up a dad who was attempting to fend off their amorous advances toward his teenaged daughter. One biker toyed with the young lady, who was repulsed by the urine-soaked, smelly biker. They didn't actually hit the dad, they just separated him from his daughter and intimidated him so he didn't know what was happening.

The bikers were also roughing up anyone who stood their ground and attempted to protect their belongings or leave to get help. Nothing could be done as long as they remained. Several hours passed until these marauders had their fill of rowdy behavior and finally left on their motorcycles, on their own accord, into the darkness.

This was the second time these thugs had pulled this stunt, and the forest rangers were afraid they would return soon, because no one had hindered their plunder and ruthless behavior. The forest rangers were easily outnumbered.

That's when the State Forestry Division requested help from the Los Angeles County Sheriff's Department. Our department assigned personnel from the Special Enforcement Bureau to resolve the problem quickly and efficiently.

Three of our teams were assigned the task. We came in the early afternoon and parked our cars and equipment approximately two miles from the designated campsite. No one knew we were coming, so we could benefit from the element of surprise.

We planned to assign teams to scout out the terrain and find positions of advantage to allow maximum cover and concealment. We were very quiet and had already darkened up, using a basic military camouflage stick on our faces and hands. We removed all of our shiny, reflective items, taped up our metal, and removed any gizmos that would make noise. We prepped our knives and guns and various other sundries needed for this special operation.

Our mood was formed based on the information we received about these thugs and what they had done, and we had to pray to the gods to keep our capturing advances reasonable and professional. When we were about a half mile away, our scouts went out with their backups, plus one extra deputy to bring up the rear.

The campsite was peaceful enough, filled with normal campers and their families. Everyone was enjoying their stay and had no idea we were in the area. It took about an hour to get set up. Everyone was in comfortable blinds that allowed the men to relax and wait. Our scouts were ready with their binoculars, and we all quietly waited for the rogue thugs to show up.

It started to get dark, and still they were a no show, but we knew very well that we were dealing with the risk of missing them altogether. We didn't know if they would show up or not, but we were set and anxiously awaiting their arrival.

All eyes were well focused, and we kept silent and very still. Our key was the surprise to all, including the campers.

Then, just at dusk, they rolled in, about thirty of them, on their noisy hogs and drove to the back part of the camp. They parked their bikes, assembled, and sat around some camping tables, laughing and greeting each other.

We were all aware of their presence and stood by watching their every move. There were about thirty-five of us. Noise and radio discipline was at it highest level, because any unnecessary chatter would certainly give our whole snagging system away, and these thugs escape capture and justice.

Several of the bikers began to saunter into campsites, disrupting their relaxation by asking, "Hey, you got any beer?" or "Are those hamburgers?"

Now, what would you think if several of these filthy, slovenly bikers came into your campsite asking for free beer or hamburgers?

We remained still until we knew we had most of them acting in concert with one another, intimidating people by scrounging around and taking things that no one could stop because of their size and psychological impact.

It was a no-brainer. We were watching for more offensive conduct and carefully looking for a crime that would initiate our bold response. Still no one was aware of our presence, and we were braced for an inevitable resolution.

It was dark now, and more of the bikers were wandering around and creating disruptions at several campsites, but not as outrageous as the prior information we had received. The bikers were getting louder and louder, roughhousing with one another and cussing as if they were in a biker camp.

We felt the campers were harassed and intimated enough, so we decided to overlook the smaller disruptions and not wait to find a much bigger cause to react. We figured that it wouldn't look good to hold off any more. So now we were going to start our antics and see what the bikers would do.

One biker slipped away from the group as if he was going to urinate and stepped away maybe thirty yards from the encampment. He walked to a small stream amid a cropping of rocks, across a large dome-faced rock that had a trickle of water and unzipped his pants. He fumbled briefly and began to urinate in a high arching stream as if just being silly. When he was buttoning up his pants, he looked up to see three darkened combat forms, armed to the hilt, surrounding him about ten feet away. He was startled and began to ask who they were, but all held a finger perpendicular against their lips, signaling him to keep quiet.

He understood and submitted without a stir. He was cuffed, and a small wrap of two-inch duct tape around his mouth insured his silent cooperation. He was taken away to a small designated holding spot by one of our guys.

Fifteen minutes went by, and three more bikers meandered to the same spot and began urinating. They too were surrounded quietly by our stealthy and darkened members who also demanded their silence. They all complied without further ado and were handcuffed and duct taped as well.

We were now facing approximately twenty-five more bikers who were left in the camp, and who started to call out for their missing comrades. We had already sent two of our smallest guys to go back, pick up one of our radio cars, and to clean up their camouflage paint. They were also instructed to come close to the camp on our signal, drive into the campgrounds, and convince the remaining bikers to step over to the radio car.

The point was to see if the majority of these raunchy bikers would cooperate with the diminutive deputies and not to try to overwhelm and intimidate them as well.

The signal was given around ten o'clock, and the radio car came into the campgrounds, driving slowly, taking in the eyes of the camping folks, and drifting toward the bikers who were amassed, wondering what the deputies wanted.

The radio car stopped near the biker group, and both deputies came out of the car and asked all of the bikers to step over to their car. Several of them were snickering and grumbling about the deputies who were about to question them.

As they drew closer to the car they obviously saw the difference in their sizes and were looking around as if they were going to try something dumb.

We were all poised and en masse came out of the foliage dressed in our fatigues, and camouflaged faces and hands, carrying a whole load of armament and flashlights. We surrounded the bikers who were startled to see us drop onto them so quickly.

Our green fatigues, of course, were easily identified by the black-and-green sewn-on badges and patches, and large "Sheriff" patch on the back of each member. The bikers' attitudes changed immediately. They listened very closely to what we were going to tell them.

First, we brought the four we had already detained into our meeting, released them, and demanded that they all pay very close attention. We advised them of our intentions, given the reported mistreatment and abuse of campers the prior week. We had planned to arrest the whole group. However, as we sat above them and watched their antics for several hours, their actions turned out to not be as blatant as expected. And of course their reaction to the smaller deputies when they came in, was of course paramount in our decision-making process.

It was our opinion that they were not ruthless outlaw types. They demonstrated a certain amount of intimidation, but not enough for criminal prosecutions.

Our orders for them were to let them know they all were going to be identified and listed for a field interview report and pictures to easily identify them. So if by chance they should appear again and intimidate or threaten any other campers, they would be sought out and arrested. We also informed them we had watched them for at least four hours when they first came into the campground. If any significant criminal activity had occurred, they would have been arrested immediately.

The bikers were gratified by our assessments and agreed not to create any further problems. This was a good lesson for them to know they were being watched carefully and could have been arrested easily.

Apparently our forest adventure proved successful. There was never another situation, and it all turned out perfectly. No one was arrested or hurt, and all involved were satisfied with the results.

CHAPTER 96

THE BARRICADED DA

Doug D. and I had been working the last couple of weeks mostly in the East Los Angeles Station area and had at least three to six arrests each night. We were pretty lucky, and we were determined to put a dent in crime and focus on the omnipresent criminal element.

Several weeks went by, and we heard the district attorney was making some snide remarks about the arrests by the Special Enforcement Bureau deputies that were in conflict with their principles. They said the procedures we were following in the field were illegal. This information irritated us to no end. We called the district attorney's office to arrange a meeting and get to the bottom of their accusations. Every time we tried to get ahold of the head district attorney, he wouldn't answer his phone, although the clerks stated he was in his office. We decided to go directly over to district attorney's office to see him personally.

We packed up our paperwork and headed over to see him. The clerks told us he was definitely in his private office, but he wouldn't answer the phone or come out of his locked room. We were informed that he'd gotten wind of our concern about his accusations and decided not to talk to us at all.

This had obviously gotten out of hand, and DA was in need of some administrative discipline real quick. We headed back to the bureau and made several contacts with his administrative superiors.

We were informed that five of our arrests were not filed, because they lacked necessary elements and we had illegally obtained the contraband. Those reports were rather lengthy and well written, covering all the indicated crimes. Everything was done by the book.

We called over to the district attorney's office and made an appointment to see a deputy district attorney. We informed him of our concerns, and he promised to review the five cases in light of what was going on with his immediate supervisor.

Everyone in our unit was highly upset because the accusations that were fabricated by the DA's office needed to be addressed and remedied immediately.

They would not prosecute any of our cases because of personal opinions, and some deputy DAs were anti-law enforcement. We learned this from several of the ELA detectives, who informed us that they were doing the same thing to their station arrests as well.

The station detectives' patience was strained, but they were restricted from any criticisms because of their politically correct captain. That captain wanted the detectives to work through the philosophical differences and ideals. This information was given to us in confidence, and it caused more aggravation than imagined.

The district attorney's office is supposed to work *with* law enforcement and prosecute individuals who have violated the law. They are not to undermine law enforcement's work product but are supposed to assist in the prosecution. We decided to make this an issue and take it right to the top if the fundamental structure was broken, flawed, or maligned.

We created a file folder, just like working a filing and prosecution case, and placed our five cases inside the folder. We went over them all, highlighting the elements and noted the case decisions that supported our arrests and searches. We were ready for our meeting and loaded for bear. On the outside of the folder, I constructed and contrived a black, silhouetted profile of two men engaged in spooning within a four-inch red circle, that had a four-inch slash across its face. This was to be our emblem.

Our meeting was at ten in the morning. My partner Doug and I walked into the DA's office ready to listen to him give a logical explanation for his contemptuous behavior and lack of a duty to prosecute. We met in the hallway, introduced ourselves, and shook hands. We were led into a small room where there was just enough room for the small desk and three Spartan-style chairs.

The deputy DA sat with his back to the wall and Doug and I sat in front of him. Doug talked first for a few minutes, laying out the information we received and the stories about the DA's office being anti-law enforcement.

As we continued, Doug started to lose his composure, excused himself, and stepped from the room. I remained seated and continued to talk about our cases and said that my partner had stepped out because he was so irritated.

I opened our folder and took out the first report, which was about six pages long. I placed the report in front of the deputy and explained the initial stop, the found evidence, and the reason why an arrest was made. While I was explaining the case, the deputy interrupted me and asked, "This is a trunk search, isn't it?" I said no, it wasn't a trunk search, and asked him if he read the report.

He replied it must have been a trunk search because the gun was found in the trunk. I said no, you must not have read the report. He was emphatic that he read the report carefully and determined it was a trunk search, and that's why it was rejected.

I heard Doug in the hallway starting to verbalize his indignation. It was becoming clear that just this report alone, was at an impasse.

I then displayed page-by-page notations of what had occurred and then sat back in my chair and waited for his reaction.

We stopped the car for speeding, and when we approached the car, we observed everyone had an open beer bottles in their possession. All were asked to step out, and the bottles were confiscated. Doug remained with the three, and I went into the car to get the remainder of the bottled beer.

I saw three unopened bottles in the backseat, so I opened the door to retrieve the evidence. The bottom of the rear seat was missing, but the back was still there. The six-pack with the three remaining bottles was firmly wedged between the back portion of the rear seat and the steel floor, just beneath where the bottom of the rear seat was normally positioned.

As I grabbed the cardboard handle of the six-pack container, the rear portion of the back seat flipped upward. I felt there was more beer behind the seat, so I lifted the rear portion and saw the butt end of a shotgun lying near where the six-pack carton was wedged. I pulled the stock of the shotgun upward and saw its barrel was sawed off and obviously illegal. I picked it up and examined it and found it was loaded with one round in the chamber.

My description of the events that occurred, and that there was absolutely no trunk search, left only two conclusions. Number one, that the report had not been read, or number two, there is an obvious lack of duty within the DA's office to perform their function and assist in the prosecution.

The deputy DA made some marks on the report and set it to the side, stating, "Okay, this one seems all right!"

The deputy was speechless, Doug was infuriated, and I was so inflamed I stood up and removed the second report from my folder. I laid it in front of the deputy to signify we were ready to go on to the second report.

Doug was now becoming so irate I could hear his disparaging words from the hallway and stepped out momentarily to quiet him down. I was only out in the hallway for a few seconds and I was probably overheard by the deputy DA. I came back into the room, and he was reading the narrative. I began to explain similar circumstances of the second arrest, but he began to argue about the merits of the case.

It was at this point I concluded that this whole incident was falling on deaf ears, and both these deputy DAs needed some heavy paper thrown on them to compel their removal or dismissal.

I made the comment to the deputy that it wasn't necessary to continue with the charade of proving that deception was prevalent in his office and yanked the second report from his hands. I informed him that his time in the district attorney's office was going to be over soon, and the same was going to happen to the head deputy district attorney, his boss, as well

Doug and I left and went to East Los Angeles Station and wrote a sixteen page complaint against both deputy DAs and sent them through our sheriff department channels. Within one week, both were transferred to the juvenile section of the district attorney's office.

What a shame, it was to deliberately discourage the filings of our excellent arrests because some errant deputy district attorneys felt compelled to stop our progress without any proof of misconduct, or they lacked proper judicial protocol.

Hopefully the two DAs will be used as a reminder that their office is a conduit for prosecution; it is not the jury. They are established to work along with law enforcement to prosecute violators of the law and let the courts decide who is in violation of the law and the consequences for those indiscretions. It is not the job of the DA's office to prejudge officers for any allegations of misconduct, or drop criminal filings because of their biased opinions.

CHAPTER 97

EVISCERATED

Phencyclidine, commonly called PCP, angel dust, or whack, was primarily used as an animal tranquilizer. Well, someone with the IQ of a rock found out how to get high from this drug. This drug was the main reason for the introduction of Tasers, which are a more desirable weapon than the lethal form, a firearm.

Law enforcement was inundated with individuals loaded on PCP who were highly aggressive and combative. Many PCP suspects were shot and killed because of their intensely bizarre behavior. There was one suspect who was shirtless (a symptom of PCP usage) in the East Los Angeles area. This area is plagued with gangs near Eastern Avenue and south of the 10 freeway.

Deputies received a call about some guy running around carrying a knife and bleeding heavily. When they arrived, they saw the shirtless suspect with a large kitchen knife and got out of their car to approach him with their guns drawn. The suspect, who was already covered with blood, took his knife and literally gutted himself while screaming obscenities, about twenty feet in front of them. The deputies stood their ground and aimed carefully in case he charged them.

Unexpectedly the suspect turned and ran from the deputies, up a hill on a small walkway that led to a hillside home. This area is covered with hillside homes that are quaint and charming. The deputies chased after their bloody, eviscerated suspect as he reached the front porch of a small home and entered the screen door. When the deputies approached, they stood back several feet awaiting some signal of the suspect's whereabouts inside.

Suddenly he came out of the front screen door full bore across the small porch attacking the deputies with the kitchen knife still in his hand, screaming.

The deputies opened fire and emptied their guns at the suspect, who dropped a couple of feet from their positions.

Although mortally wounded with numerous bullets and self-injury, the suspect lay on the ground growling and grinding his teeth with great contempt and despair. He continued his tirade for a couple of minutes and finally perished.

These types of self-induced anger and bizarre behaviors occurred all over the county, and the word was out to expect much more.

CHAPTER 98

WHO NEEDS SECURITY CAMERAS?

We had planned this entry for quite a few weeks. The home had a whole slew of security cameras and a vicious pit bull. He was a well-entrenched dope dealer and of course was paranoid about someone stealing his drugs.

We had done dozens of guys just like this one and he was not going to be any different. Nine cameras surrounded his expensive Ladera Heights home. The place was surrounded with tall fences and walls and we assumed the windows and doors were adequately barricaded as well.

The information we received was that the suspect cut and measured his cocaine in the front room, right in front of a large television set. A large wooden cabinet contained another TV screen that was segmented into nine frames for watching the security cameras. This security system was always on and easily scanned the approaches to the suspect's home.

The pit bull was to be neutralized by three of our guys as we approached the home. The security cameras were a problem, but not insurmountable.

We hit many other homes with security cameras and realized that most of the culprits had them on while under the influence and most likely didn't watch them. Only if this guy was different would he be able to see our approach and arm himself to defend his home and contraband.

Our concerns were proper timing, speed of approach, and entry. If we could visualize the terrain and the obstacles that we would encounter it would make the approach much easier, but there are always unseen obstacles and situations that they must be remedied on the run, as we're going in.

There was planning and many pictures of the layout. Drive-bys, walk-bys, aerial photos, and information from persons who had been in the house several times were included, and as much trivial intelligence as possible was all part of the preparation. The entire team was involved in the operation and all had input into the operation plan. This way none of the information was left out and all problems were jointly ironed out.

The morning came when we were all set and adequately prepped for any encounter. As we started to move in, the pit bull alerted to the men near the rear fence area. It started to bark and draw near the section of fence where the men were positioned. Within a second there was a zip, zip, zip, and the American 180, outfitted with a silencer, fired about eight or nine .22 caliber bullets into the body of the pit bull. The dog fell dead about five feet from the fence.

Without a missed step we continued on and hit the front door with a good-size steel ramming device that is motored by four men for heavy-impact deployment. When the door caved in on the first strike, taking about one second, we stormed in and rushed into the front room. The suspect was in the midst of cutting a large batch of cocaine. Fortunately, he was watching television and not monitoring the security cameras.

He was totally surprised. His automatic pistol was nearby on the same table, but it was not close enough to do battle with the team.

Our entry was was spectacular and very fast. He was down on the ground within seconds of our entry.

The cameras he had were perfectly angled on our paths coming into the yard, but our movements were only visible for seconds because of the speed of the entry team.

Thank God for practice and attention to detail. The unfortunate thing, of course, was that the vicious pit bull was put down quickly with no time to pamper the dog for fear we would be detected.

CHAPTER 99

THE EGG

We were working at Firestone Park Station, and it was pretty busy with patrol cars racing all over the place. Around nine in the evening we came upon a black male adult, totally naked, running and zigzagging across Firestone Boulevard.

His eyes were wild, and he ran full bore eastbound, carrying a large black bowling ball in both hands. He was actually clutching the bowling ball as if he was a running back carrying a football.

Initially we were going to set up a plan to capture this guy as he continued his zigzagging path, at first going eastbound and then westbound, running around cars that came to our request for help and dodging them as they drew closer. We assumed he was on whack, PCP, and were thinking about how to take him down. We followed behind him about twenty feet, and there were about three other cars behind us.

After several minutes of following him, it started to become quite obvious that we had to continue this trailing mode until he ran out of gas. This would whittle down the suspect's adrenaline and hopefully cause him to surrender without any confrontation.

While we were talking over the radio from car to car, one of the deputies remarked that the suspect appeared as if he was looking for a place to hide his egg. That comment alone was so hilarious, we decided if this guy got home without any injury to anyone, we would allow him a free pass and not arrest him. This went on for about fifteen minutes. He must have fallen ten times, dropping the bowling ball each time, skidding on the asphalt. The bowling ball would continue onward in a straight trajectory when it was released. The suspect had many small bleeding abrasions all over his naked sweaty body, screaming to high heaven for us to leave him alone.

As he continued eastbound on Firestone Boulevard, he finally turned onto southbound Fir Street. Around midblock, he ran through an open white picket gate, up the walkway, and into the house. Once he was inside, he slammed the door shut, pulled back the curtains on the door, and peered out the window to see what we were going to do.

It was our judgment call, and he acted as if on PCP, but he never hurt anyone. The only crime was his nudity, and that was a misdemeanor and not worth the trouble, considering his many minor injuries that would need medical attention.

We decided to leave him to his own care. No screams were coming from the home indicating that it must have been his home, so we decided to leave. We thanked the other assisting units for their help.

The bowling ball (egg) was recovered and used for several other tactical situations.

CHAPTER 100

A TERRIBLE ORDEAL

Deputies were summoned to a vehicle crash on the 405 freeway in Carson. Once they arrived they were contacted by the California Highway Patrol to assist with a full grown horse that was seriously injured with no hope for survival.

The deputy who responded was an excellent man who had been in the department many years. He was a good friend. He was a married man with children and a heart of gold, and he was deeply involved in his church.

Unlike many other officers, Randy J. hadn't developed the callous and apathetic mindset yet. He always had a positive outlook on life as a whole.

The CHP officer directed the deputy to the severely injured animal lying just outside of the overturned animal trailer. Several people were encouraging the deputy to dispatch the horse quickly, because of the intense pain it was suffering.

Without further ado, Randy drew his pistol and shot the horse in the head.

Unbeknown to Randy, that round he fired went through the horse's head, ricocheted off of the freeway asphalt, and traveled under a parked semitrailer. A California Highway Patrolman was passing by on the other side of the large trailer, not within view of anyone on the opposite side. The CHP officer was struck in the head by the bullet and died immediately.

As soon this calamity was brought to the attention of the deputy, it floored him and caused him great despair. He was was transported from the scene to the station for homicide to interview.

The entire event was a highly solemn situation that I could have ever imagined, and it had a major impact not only on Randy, who fired the shot, but on all of us in the law enforcement community.

Several years of counseling couldn't assuage the deputy's anguish, and he was nearing a nervous breakdown. Just before he left our department, he came up to me and said that the incident would not go away. He said that when he was firing on the range recently he couldn't keep his hands and arms from shaking, so his talent as an expert shot was eroded. He was in such terrible mental turmoil, he decided to leave, recuperate outside the department, and look elsewhere for relief.

He was a very good deputy and a tremendous loss to our department. This imprinted on us a simple factor that we all learned from his episode of grief— the ricochet factor. It must be considered in every shooting scenario as a factor that must be reckoned with and *never* overlooked.

CHAPTER 101

NORCO BANK ROBBERY

The city of Norco is nestled in Riverside County just off the 215 freeway between the 60 and 91 freeways. Around 3:40 p.m. on May 9, 1980, a robbery alarm went off at the Security Pacific Bank in Norco. A Riverside County deputy sheriff, "B," was almost right across the street from the bank when he received the call.

As the deputy came into the parking lot, four of the suspects came out of the bank and shot at the deputy's car. The suspects were armed with shotguns, assault rifle, pistols, and improvised explosive devices. The deputy's car was pummeled with a variety of bullets and his window was blown out. He exited in reverse to get the hell out of the way of the barrage of bullets.

Although under fire, the deputy was able to return fire and struck and killed the driver of the suspect van. The patrol car sustained over forty-seven hits out of the two hundred fired at him alone. The deputy suffered five hits, one in the face, one in the left shoulder, one in each forearm and one round in the left elbow.

These crooks fled their car and commandeered a plumber's truck, and the pursuit continued. This turned out to be a pursuit from hell. The suspects went northbound toward Lytle Creek in San Bernardino County. During that pursuit seven deputies were wounded and one San Bernardino Deputy, Evans, was killed. The suspects abandoned their commandeered truck and ran into the hills and mountainous terrain, eluding the officers.

It was pointed out the officers were totally outgunned, with only shotguns and .38 caliber revolvers at their disposal. The Los Angeles Sheriff's Department, Special Enforcement Bureau/Special Weapons and Tactics was called and caravanned to the location where the suspects were last seen. Everyone in our entire unit was called, activated, and put in service to find the bank robbers/murderers, except one—me. Apparently I was overlooked on the emergency mobilization roster, but all others joined in on a huge manhunt for the thugs.

Airdrops of supplies were dropped into the upper Lytle Creek mountainous area because of the intense cold in the evening hours. Early the next morning, several of the SWAT personnel from SEB shot and killed one suspect, and another was wounded.

Eventually the other two were captured as well. Two sets of these suspects were brothers, and they and another suspect were convicted of forty-six felonies and sentenced to life in prison without parole.

The injured Riverside deputy who shot it out with the suspects and was hit five times was awarded several awards for his gallantry in returning fire although wounded, and then he went on to become an officer in the US Air Force.

Since this bank robbery, this event has been used numerous times for officer training exercises.

———

Based on this information, why was the hell was LAPD outgunned in the Hollywood shootout on February 28, 1997? The LAPD administrators all knew about the Riverside bank robbery/pursuit seventeen years earlier.

Again political opinion stalled the necessary development and distribution of armament until after the Hollywood shootout, in which two thugs were armed with superior firepower. The LAPD officers were outgunned immediately. It was "divine intervention" that a nearby gun store readily loaned their guns to the officers to defeat the automatic-gun-toting thugs.

That gun store was able to privately outsource the officers' armament with the necessary powerful guns and ammo needed to suppress the onslaught.

Both suspects had full body armor and the officers' firepower initially was ineffective. Hopefully law enforcement will not try to outguess what is needed in the field, but knowing law enforcement administrators, I'll bet it will raise its ugly head again.

CHAPTER 102

THE COP STOP

We were coming in toward Carson Station on 215th Street with our unit's engine coughing and sputtering. The engine was missing terribly and was about to conk out. We were waiting at the eastbound red light at Avalon Boulevard, just west of and across the street from the Carson sheriff's station.

As we waited, we noticed a brand-new Honda two-door hatchback crossing the intersection directly in front of us southbound in the number two lane of Avalon Boulevard with the green light at 215th Street. Our attention was drawn to the Honda because it was racing its engine at about five thousand rpm and smoking as if it was in fifth gear from the takeoff. On top of that, it was whining at an unbelievable pitch, yet the car was passing in front of us at about 5 mph. Something was screwy, so we decided to investigate why the driver was ruining the engine in front of us. Was it a signal for help?

Our car spat and sputtered as we caught up to it. We positioned ourselves in the number-one southbound lane, next to the Honda. We flashed our spot lamp and a flashlight toward the driver's side window. Doug D. and I saw a young white woman driving and a black man was the passenger.

Neither of them looked at our flashing lights, and both were staring directly in front of the car, as if focused on going through a maze. The driver had a white-knuckle hold on the steering wheel and was nervously shaking her head as if she was going to crash.

They pulled over near the west curbline when we activated our red lights, but it took at least a whole block for them to pull over, traveling at approximately 5 mph. We stopped just south of Carson Street, and both occupants sat motionless in the car. Something was very strange about this one, and we were cautiously watching their every move.

The driver didn't even look in the rearview mirror, as most do. She still stared straight ahead. I cautiously approached the driver's side door, and Doug stood just behind the right side of their car, out of their view.

I began talking to the driver, although her window was up, but spoke in a loud voice, and motioned with my hand to roll down the window. She remained motionless, still white knuckling the steering wheel as if she was driving, staring off into oblivion.

I attempted several times to get her attention, but to no avail, so I reached for the handle and opened the door. As the door opened, she fell toward me sideways, nearly striking the asphalt. I grabbed her head and body with both of my hands. A strong odor of PCP emanated from her car, as I yelled a warning to my partner, "There's whack!"

As I was helping her up from falling onto the street, Doug was assisting the passenger from the seat; he was bombed out of his gourd as well. We met over by the right front fender of our patrol car with both of them in tow; and carefully sat them on the curbside next to our car.

We stood there for a few minutes and made sure they had no weapons, and Doug and I discussed our observations and what we were going to do next.

Since they were safe and unarmed, we decided I would return to the car to find the source of smell of the PCP. Doug stood back and away from the inebriated couple as I went to their car.

I opened the door and the pungent odor of PCP wafted all over the entire interior as if there was a large amount or a freshly sprayed, saturated cigarette close-by. The smell was overwhelming, and I had to step outside the car several times to avoid becoming intoxicated myself. I looked over the interior very carefully and didn't find anything. It was a hatchback, so the rear was accessible from the front if you could twist your way through the small car.

I grabbed the car keys from the ignition, and backed out of the driver's door, and walked to the rear to open the hatchback door.

As I reappeared, Doug was holding some small items and talking with the driver by the right front fender, about fifteen feet away from my position. Doug said, "Hey, Larry, she's a deputy!" He showed me an ALADS card. ALADS is the Association of Los Angeles Deputy Sheriffs.

We were both puzzled and thought possibly she was working our department's narco or vice unit and may have gotten in over her head or lost her team.

Doug told me she said that her 'shit' was in the rear, which meant to me her identification was hidden in the rear of the hatchback. I knew I had to examine the rear to determine the source of the PCP, but now I was more concerned whether this woman was being kidnapped.

I unlocked and popped the hatchback door. When that happened, the pungent odor of PCP slammed me in my face. I came upon a small cardboard box that had a LA County Sheriff's Department helmet atop some uniforms. I lifted the helmet and saw a class A jacket and a couple of class A long-sleeved shirts for the LA County Sheriff's Department.

Then I noticed the source of the smell, a small brown glass bottle, labeled "lemon extract," and I picked it up. There was no mistake—even without opening it, I knew it was full of liquid PCP. I saw a three-by-three-inch box of Little Actor cigarettes, used commonly as PCP-laced cigarettes, more than enough to use and enough liquid to saturate and sell. This meant to me that the driver was fully engaged in the possession and sales of PCP and the contraband was hidden with LA County Sheriff's Department uniforms. I personally was livid at the immense disrespect and taint of the work ethic I was so proud of.

We notified our sergeant over the radio and he came quickly to our location and informed of our findings. I made no effort to hide my personal feelings and said that I would like to tie her to the rear bumper of our car and drag her through the streets like Hector in *Troy*.

Of course that would be illegal, so we went to Carson Station to book both the driver and the passenger. I began the booking process, and Doug ran the arrests by the desk sergeant and watch commander. Presumably the station and staff already knew we had arrested a deputy and charged her with possession of a controlled substance and for sales of a sizable amount of PCP. I was advised by our SEB sergeant that the watch commander wanted to see me and my partner immediately.

I knew the watch commander and had worked with him at Firestone Park Station for several years. He was well liked by most hardworking deputies and we were on a first-name basis. When I arrived in his office he asked me if I knew who the deputy was that I just arrested. I said no, and it didn't matter if I knew her or not, she was scum and a disgrace to our department.

The watch commander then informed me that she was a recent graduate from the academy and her mother was a well-liked "services assistant" at Carson Station. The station had had a large party to celebrate her graduation from the academy. Her mother was very proud of her achievements and boasted of her daughter's unique qualities.

The lieutenant knew that I was irritated because of her affiliation with our department and the surrounding circumstances; he just wanted to let me know that he cared for the mother, and he knew this incident would create a lot of anguish and despair. We went over the stop and all of the elements surrounding both arrests and answered all of the questions to his satisfaction.

I went back to complete the booking and was standing at the booking cage when I heard her mom come into the station. It had to be her, because I heard crying coming from the watch commander's office, although his door was closed. We were then directed to transport the suspect to Sybil Brand Institute for Women, a female county jail facility in the East Los Angeles area.

We were to inform SBI over the radio when we were ten minutes out that we were coming in with a "special handling" inmate. That gave them ample opportunity to lock the whole facility down, because we were coming in with a deputy inmate.

This transfer took only thirty minutes, because they had been fully informed by the watch commander at Carson Station beforehand.

In the next several weeks, an internal investigation revealed that seven other deputies and a lieutenant were connected somehow with this case, and with an embezzlement case from the women's jail that involved patio furniture being made at the jail.

Of course it didn't stop there. The seven deputies were apparently lesbians, and they were acting in concert with inmate homosexuals to turn newly graduated cadets, to their sexual preference.

Now I must have been very sheltered not to be aware there was a problem with lesbians at the sheriff's facility. I'll admit, I was miffed and disappointed when the revelation was not scorned and cut off at the head, but it wasn't.

In today's politically correct environment and culturally diverse society, it probably is a mandatory indoctrination, championed by the new generation of lowered standards. These ideas are to produce a more generous, nonviolent deputy sheriff. To me and many others it is repulsive, but we are dinosaurs and just plain mean deputies with high standards and an excellent work ethic, without ever lowering the bar.

About a month had passed when we were subpoenaed to the preliminary trial at Compton Court. The courtroom was cleared of any audience. It was going to be isolated because of the sensitive information that was going to be discussed. Doug was up first and was questioned for two hours, and then it was my turn.

The attorneys hammered me for all the miniscule details of the stop, arrest, and what was said. I gave them the exact truth. The female driver/deputy sat at the defense table and seldom looked at me as I testified.

It took them three hours, and they were finally finished. When we were through, the judge deemed the search illegal, because it was a trunk search.

The district attorney went ballistic and assured us he was going to the appellate court to reverse this travesty of justice. We had already established that there were exigent circumstances, and all procedures were followed precisely.

We couldn't imagine why the judge ruled the way he did. We thought that he must have been a liberal judge or a former ACLU attorney. Several months went by, and then we learned that the appellate courts reviewed the case and reversed the judge's decision because of a conflict of interest.

What the hell—how can that be?

As it turned out the female suspect/deputy's father was the chief of the superior court clerk's office, and undue influence was placed upon the judge. Now what do you think of that?

Fortunately, the deputy pled out to a lesser crime, as a deal was cut to minimize court costs. We never followed up on the case, and I hope she was fired from our department or given an opportunity to resign in lieu of termination.

With this revelation it was only obvious that our (LASD) work ethic and integrity were in a perilous downward spin with its hiring practices, and that pointed to many other levels of government were in a downward spiral as well. Oh, but wait a minute—maybe it's progress, reaching out to more compassionate people!

CHAPTER 103

BEHIND THE EIGHT BALL

These are the same murders that the movie *Wonderland* depicted. Several of our SWAT teams were assigned the task of an operation in the Hollywood Hills area.

The operation was to arrest two individuals for the bludgeoning deaths of four young adults in the infamous Laurel Canyon murders.

We had ample time to locate the residence,—which happened to be unique because of its circular shape—and calculate the size and deployment characteristics needed for the arrest of both suspects in the murders.

When we hit the place, we had two full teams and had gone through the formalities before entering. Those formalities were of course our announcement in a loud voice of who we were and what we were doing. Our entry was fast after we determined there was ample time to answer our knock and notice.

I was in the lead and went directly to the large bedroom where we assumed the main thug slept. I was expecting to meet the large bodyguard first because it was his job to protect him. The bodyguard was the other suspect indicated on the warrant.

We came in unopposed and went into the bedroom. I focused on the large bed. There was a beautiful, naked, dark-haired female with handsome curves whom I grabbed first by her ponytail.

I pulled her up from the bed by her hair and held her about a foot and a half from my face. Her feet were dangling and wiggling all over as I quickly surveyed her unblemished torso from top to bottom, but only for a second or two. She was spectacular. Then I threw her by her hair to my partner, who was close behind me.

I grabbed the next naked female by her blond ponytail as well. Her body was just as beautiful as the first one's. I dangled her and admired her graceful curves and beautiful face for a few seconds and threw her to my partner as well.

Each time a body was passed, another deputy would come in, manacle them with flex ties, and escort them out.

I then came upon the main suspect, an chubby man with curly hair described by former friends as very mean and ruthless. He was also a major dope dealer and had a robust black bodyguard who was always nearby. I grabbed his hair, and his chubby naked body wiggled nervously. He whined like a puppy and was whisked from the satin sheets, like a fly being snatched off a tablecloth.

He too was flattened, cuffed, and towed out to the investigative bodies who were waiting just outside. Now we were on the prowl for the bodyguard, who obviously knew full well who we were because of all the noise. I knew we were going to run into him real quick, so we needed to be ready to take him down. My concern was that he might be armed—a gun, a knife, any conceivable weapon might be a tad troublesome.

We worked our way toward the rear area, and he approached us and surrendered himself to me. I cuffed him quickly and was about to come out with him in tow when someone said that the bodyguard capped one round through a frosted window at one of our guys.

We were unaware that any shots had been fired, probably because of all the noise we made when we entered.

We stopped for several minutes. The bodyguard was uncuffed, and he decided to take off all of his clothes and lie naked, belly down, on top of a brilliant green billiard table. He then placed each foot in a corner pocket, toes down, and both hands into two opposite corner pockets with an eight ball in his mouth.

He lay there for at least fifteen minutes as a gesture of good faith and repudiated knowing it was a deputy he had fired at. He explained he thought it was someone attempting to steal their dope.

This was his way of letting us know that he was sorry for shooting at one of our guys. He promised he would never do it again. The bullet had narrowly missed our guy, and it ended up no one was hurt.

The studly bad guy was allowed to dress. He was cuffed again and taken outside for all to see that he was okay and pleased to go to jail.

Both suspects were charged for and convicted of the four murders. Who knows when they'll get out—hopefully never.

Oh, by the way, what happened to the two main suspects when we arrested them was not covered nor discussed in the movie *Wonderland*. Hmm.

CHAPTER 104
EX-CHP SUSPECT

We were going after an ex-California Highway Patrol officer who went wayward and was running a large vice operation in the Lennox Station area. The suspect was well known in Hawthorne as well as the Lennox area and around the Hollywood Park Racetrack and Forum. Because of his knowledge of police procedures and the reliable information that he always carried a gun everywhere he goes, he was a prime candidate for the SWAT operation.

The local FBI office was also interested in this suspect for federal law violations and merely observed our takeover as the operation went down. Several other outside agencies had vested interests in this operation and assisted in some of the administrative issues.

The place we were going to hit was on the second story of a building that supported a large gambling operation that was owned and operated by the former officer. Our job was to get into the complex. where there were armed thugs acting as lookouts in the front and rear of the building. We had to remove the lookouts, plan the timing, approach, and attack plan with as little use of force as possible, and arrest the entire gambling operation, where as many as one hundred persons were involved.

Several of our department's undercover officers were in the mix of the hundred persons. They were to be treated the same as everyone else so their identities would remain confidential, even during this raid.

We planned this event for several weeks in advance and even had a couple of trial runs on some of the equipment we were going to use. We borrowed an older, slightly blemished, mobile extension, cherry-picker from the county's tree trimming unit and practiced coming down different streets. This was a unique way of approaching our destination with the picker almost fully extended.

This would allow us to immediately come upon the multiple-story structure without any delay, and as it turned out, pretty damn fast. The disadvantage was that we had to duck under power lines and a variety of utility wires to accomplish this task. We also had to pray that no other vehicular traffic was using the same road as we were for our two-minute jaunt.

As we came upon the target, the cherry picker allowed us rapid access to the roof door, and we only needed to break one door on the way into the second story structure.

About eight of us were on the cherry picker for quick entrance and arrest of entire operation while about twenty others waited outside to follow up with the investigation.

At least three SWAT personnel were assigned the tasks of neutralizing the two armed lookouts standing by just outside the building on the first or ground floor. Another ten personnel were to get in when two of our team unlocked the doors the minute we were in position on the upper level.

The two lookouts were bagged instantly. They had no prior warning, and our guys snuck up on them from three feet away when the signal was given.

When we got inside, one of our guys who was supposed to be an expert on booting doors found out the hard way that the door he was kicking was a sliding door, commonly called a pocket door. Later, we razzed him to no end, because we were stuck for about twenty seconds before we realized it was a sliding door, and it was unlocked.

We made our two-door grand entrance and hollered out that all were under arrest. There was little confrontation because of the surprise entry and the number of officers that flooded the entire room. The main suspect was arrested and immediately separated for processing.

The only injuries were the lookouts' egos. It was one of the fastest and cleanest operations most agencies had ever seen, and FBI agents lauded the operation as unparalleled and well done.

That same ex-CHP suspect was murdered in the early nineties in the city of Brea, allegedly by a competitor who was involved in devious shenanigans as well.

CHAPTER 105

SOMETHING STINKS

New bureau members were highly treasured, as was apparent from the selection system that was in place. When new personnel arrived, they were warmly greeted and given their team assignments. They needed extensive training in handling the special weapons, tear gas, and flash bangs, and the deployment operations. The whole idea was to keep everyone on their toes and ready for anything. The new men were able to pass the physical agility tests and were tested all the time. In all tactics, the impossible was always stretched and embraced by all to be expected from anyone.

One lieutenant, Joe C., came to our unit. I had worked with him before at the sheriff's academy. He was well liked, tactically proficient, and soundly qualified in officer survival. He had taught officer survival classes for several years at the academy, and he knew the errors in most shootings where deputies' lives were lost.

His first day was going to be an event that started off with a formal inspection where several division chiefs and commanders were honored. Everyone was getting ready for the formal inspection. The bathroom and locker room were packed. People were brushing their teeth, shaving, showering, and using the toilet. They were cleaning their uniforms, shoes, and leather gear, polishing their helmets, and prepping their firearms. All of this was to check that everyone knew what was expected, and being there on time was very important. Most came in an hour or two early to make sure everything was prepared.

The lieutenant went into the packed bathroom and into the second stall to do his personal business. There was a lot of commotion—laughter, loud talking, cussing—the usual bathroom antics. There were two people at every sink as well as in all the showers. Two guys in a shower? There was a line to take the first available shower or vacant toilet stall.

Everyone was comfortable with one another and reasonably peaceful. One large deputy, buck-ass naked, was quietly crawling across the top edges of the toilet stalls. When he got to the second stall, he carefully lowered himself along the bathroom wall. He balanced on the plumbing that protruded from the wall.

The lieutenant had no idea that the naked deputy was behind him as he did his business, and calmly gyrated, as if slightly uncomfortable from the hardened seat. The naked deputy then signaled to the onlookers that everything was okay, and the final lowering movement would occur shortly.

Then grasping the railings, he lowered himself the final foot and a half to the tiled floor and stood erect along the wall, not three inches from the lieutenant's rump. The deputy described the smell as odoriferous and beyond any colorful description by pinching his nose with his right hand, imploring slight laughter from twenty witnesses who knew what was about to happen.

Heads filled the bathroom door, and some of the laughter was observed by the new lieutenant eyeballing through the seams in the steel door where the hinges were mounted. He looked from side to side and shook his head slightly as if the laughter was meant for someone else.

He apparently was finished with his business and took several folded sheets from the toilet paper dispenser, wiped his buttocks, and then brought it to the his face as if he was checking for fecal worms. This was disgusting, so I slapped him gently with the rear of my left hand and commented, "What the hell do you have, worms?"

I stepped over the lieutenant's back crossways as he threw himself onto the tiled floor and screamed as if he was being consumed by demons. I unlocked the stall door and walked out as he continued to scream, spinning on the floor. The locker room and bathroom erupted into laughter so loud it should have shattered the windows. After the shock and hilarity ended, everyone scurried to get ready for the inspection, and nothing was said about the incident.

The inspection was held outside so we would have a large enough area to move around in and an area for the staff and command to assemble. It was the lieutenant's first formal inspection, and as he drew near my position, I could faintly hear some snickering about the incident and his dissatisfaction with the morning surprise. There were about sixty personnel, and I was in the third row and could sense the lieutenant's approach.

When he appeared in front of me, his teeth were grinding, and he appeared to be unshaven. I thought perhaps he was in a state of shock and was contemplating exacting some type of revenge. He whispered to me quietly and gave the order for me to march the guys when the inspection was through.

Apparently he surmised that the marching would put me in a very uncomfortable position with a strong likelihood of screwing up. He didn't realize that I was a former drill instructor and absolutely enjoyed marching. I replied, "Oh, please don't do that to me lieutenant, I'm sorry for what I did to you!"

The lieutenant wouldn't have any of that sorry stuff and scoffed at the assignment he gave me. He then went on to complete the inspection and when he was through, he rallied with the command staff.

The lieutenant then called my name out, and I scurried to his position. He commanded me to take the bureau and march them in a variety of marching drill movements to which I was especially accustomed. The command staff totaled fifteen persons. When I was given the task, all of the command staff was watching, so I was determined to do a very fine job of marching and needed the boys to pay close attention as we went through the drills and cadence.

The entire drill and marching went exceptionally well. As I drew close to the end of the marching I performed several column movements that would excite any drill instructor. I had noticed the rear gate was unlocked, and I directed the movement of the entire group to leave the facility and march off the property. The lieutenant was yelling at me, but the cadence count and "Jody-calls" drowned his voice out. The command staff realized what I had done and began to laugh. It all was done in jest, but kindly spirited by all.

The bathroom incident that occurred with the lieutenant was in fact one of many—done at least thirty or forty times to nearly all personnel. It became a novelty, and I performed it flawlessly and was never was noticed. Many said that it was impossible for anyone to do such a feat, but their confidence level was smashed.

Most of the SWAT personnel while I was there went through the same incident, and they all screamed to high heaven. The prank reminded them that no matter what you do in law enforcement,and especially in SWAT, you must look up and behind as often as possible. Also, it was an excuse for me to do stupid boyish pranks whenever I wanted. In today's litigious atmosphere, bureaus, units, and stations are sanitized to a point where bland is good and cultivated as if every word is microscopically examined for legality.

If this was not sufficiently explained, then look up the legal definition of "sexual harassment" and make your own assessment. If you're liberal and are disgusted at these childish frivolities, that is the very reason I'm writing these issues—to irritate you and the rest of your kind.

CHAPTER 106

BIG BOYS DON'T CRY: GEORGE AND JIMMY

I had been a cop by now for a little over twelve years and quite confident that I could handle just about anything that came my way. I worked the toughest parts of South Los Angeles in and around the Watts, Willowbrook, Compton, and Lynwood areas.

These areas are well known to all who live in the Los Angeles area as predominantly black and Hispanic and the toughest part of the entire area. These were the same parts where all the riots kicked off, a volatile crime nest waiting for something to set off another uprising. The population was 95 percent black in these area, and crimes were committed mostly by blacks.

Could it be a cultural hatred, drilled in by the maternal order of a fatherless family? Most likely, and no end in sight! My feelings were well known to all of my fellow officers. I believe I knew everything and how to handle anything that came along. I was arrogant, hard-nosed, and obdurate, and I loved my job so much I was absorbed in thinking about work, morning, noon, and night. I couldn't believe I was getting paid for this job; it was great! The thrill, the constant challenges testing my ability to notice criminal activity and then to respond to those threats of loss of life, injury, and physical confrontation.

I was part of a select group that was assigned to work these same areas without the interference and disruption of the monotonous routine calls or details. My experience was robust with volumes of arrests and confrontations. I came from a background of strict adherence to rules and regulations and believed that I was much more advanced than the average cop on the beat. After all, I didn't spend three and a half years as a cadet drill instructor at the sheriff's academy just to help young officers through all their difficulties. I pressured them hard and expected the best performance from men and women alike.

This special unit I belonged to was called the Special Enforcement Bureau and was also designated as the special weapons and tactics team (SWAT) We enjoyed the luxury of working out daily and training nearly every day so we could confront and handle any eventuality that may arise.

The guys I was working with were classified as the best in the department. They were the most enthusiastic, professional, and hardest-working guys that I've ever known—especially two of them I had worked with at the busiest station in the entire department—Firestone Park.

These two guys were unique, because they had worked together for about ten years. They had been in several shootings together and came out unscathed. They were well known for their work and held in high regard by all of the hardworking officers. In fact, they both were in the armed forces around the same time, during the Vietnam conflict. "Jimmy" was in the Marine Corps and George was in the distinguished Special Forces.

George always wore a brass bracelet given to him by the Montanyards, the tribesmen in the hills of Vietnam who gave these bracelets to the Special Forces who trained and aided them during the Vietnam conflict. George and Jimmy's tales of combat, endurance, and camaraderie were endless.

I worked with both of them in the late sixties at Firestone Park Station. I had a great time, running into them as we went through our day and evening routines, stirring up mind games and frivolous challenges that were really juvenile antics to brag about our endeavors, like hunting for the biggest and ugliest crook out there.

Whether it was a dope dealer, a burglar, a robber, or even a murderer, there were plenty of them. The calls were endless. In addition, you better have a strong stomach and able to endure long tedious hours, because there were plenty of shootings, stabbings, and fights. You had to laugh at a lot of this stuff, because it kept you sane and focused on life in this area and the way it was being lived.

One night when I was wasn't working, some moron came to Firestone Park Station, lobbed a hand grenade over the wall, and blew up several patrol cars and burned two others. How about that? It was a station to beat all! This grenade attack caused our station now to have two permanent outposts on our parking lot. Moreover, and unbelievably, we even made arrests from these outposts (10P1 and 10P2) and proudly proclaimed our captures over the radio. The word was out now that if you didn't work Firestone Park Station, you weren't a cop. Boy, we had it all!

George and Jimmy were quite the pair. Jimmy drove, and George booked; that's the way it was. This meant that Jimmy always drove the patrol car, and George always wrote the reports. Let me tell you, there were a lot of them. The brass loved them because of their arrests were always spectacular and followed up with noteworthy reports. The prosecution of their cases was sensational because of George and Jimmy's theatrical testimony, episodes of "The George and Jimmy Show."

One night our group was assigned to work out of Firestone Park and in south LA Willowbrook area. We were all racing around to see who would get the first hook.

I always prided myself as good competition to my fellow peers because of my immense ego. I could always do better than anyone else. I was very self-assured and demanded stern adherence to all the rules of our group, which in essence meant to work hard in order to obtain great results.

My gift to the department was to be unmoved by anything, be professional at all costs, command respect while in uniform, and of course lead the way by example. I knew the routine and challenged everybody and everything.

On this particular evening I was working with a deputy named Harry S.. We enjoyed each other's company, laughing at just about anything. This laughter helped pass the time.

We went to South LA to work in the Willowbrook/Watts areas at the request of the station to help hamper the onslaught of their everyday overabundance of crime. Our presence helped curtail the drug vending business and allowed the local cops to relax a bit because they knew we were around.

Harry and I had already made the first arrest for the night and were on our way out again. We met up with a fellow SEB unit and chatted for a short time, bragging about our recent arrest.

As we were talking with one another at an abandoned gas station on Imperial Highway just west of Wilmington Avenue. We were all seated in our cars facing in the opposite directions.

We saw Jimmy and George pass by us going westbound on Imperial Highway and thought nothing much of it. We knew that they were under pressure now to make a hook better than ours, and they were probably en route to the government housing projects located a little farther west on Imperial Highway near Central Avenue.

These areas had abundant crooks and crime action galore. This was the same scenario that covered the entire area. Cops weren't liked at all by most of the local thugs, but the community had to go along with their antics or face the consequences. We needed to watch ourselves in these areas, because occasionally we would get shot at or bushwhacked by some aspiring young thug or recent prison parolee. Shots rang out nightly and conveniently no one saw anything.

Whatever excitement or action prevailed, we had to be extra-attentive and alert, because we were easy targets, in uniform and black-and-white patrol cars.

We were chuckling at some stupid thing that happened that evening and about ready to go back to work when we heard somebody frantically calling over the radio saying he was under fire, wounded, and he needed help now. This call sent a rapid chill up our backs, because we knew this type of call was extremely serious. We didn't know who it was initially, just that it was a man's chilling voice, screaming for help, and we were nearby.

The voice said he was at Imperial Highway and Success Avenue. I thought, *Why, hell, that's just up the street from us, about a half mile away!* We took off at that cry for help, and I drove like blazes to get there.

During that short burst of speed in our car, Harry and I recognized the voice on the radio as Jimmy's. As we drew closer the call came in more clearly, and we noted Jimmy's somber tone. Unfortunately, it turned out to be the wrong location. The area had no activity whatsoever. We announced over our radio that it was the wrong location, as we sped into a leftward loop at around 60 mph and smoked up the intersection. We thought he must be in the projects just north of us and sped quickly northbound up Success Avenue.

Unintelligible sounds were coming over the radio, possibly because a lot of cops were asking what was happening as everyone raced to the location. They were all pumped up and stepping on each other's transmission, maybe even covering up further calls for help. It was imperative for all of us to stay off the air and only let the officer who needed help and the radio room clarify the emergency. We raced up the street a couple of blocks and then saw George and Jimmy's black-and-white radio car, just on the west side of 115th street.

We parked across the narrow street from their unit and rushed to see where they were. These dimly lit streets in the projects were very narrow and quite cluttered with parked cars and trash bins.

We saw two bodies on the ground near a tree in front of one of the project homes. We rushed to them; both apparently had been shot. George was face down. Jimmy was partially upright with his gun in his hand, stating, "My partner's shot; get him out of here. He's hurt bad—he's not talking!"

By now, another pair of officers arrived right behind us. (The same pair we were talking to before the shooting.) We realized that we had to get both Jimmy and George out of this area quick in order to save their lives.

We didn't know where George was hit; he was quiet and motionless. Jimmy had blood all over his face. We knew that Jimmy's call for help, was probably overheard by all, and the world was coming. If we didn't leave now there wasn't going to be any room to get George and Jimmy out or for rescue to come in. Harry and one of the other officers, Mike J., grabbed George, and I ran to our unit and got in the driver's seat to get ready to roll. The right rear door opened and Harry and Mike pushed George across the backseat feet first.

George's feet were partially stuck on the seat. I realized the gummed soles of his shoes were preventing him from sliding across, so I reached over the backseat, grabbed both of George's pants legs, and lifted George's legs enough for Harry and Mike to shove his body into the backseat and finally close the door.

Harry hopped in the passenger seat, and I turned around to begin driving. I noticed that in my haste I had knocked off the entire horn assembly, which also activates the siren, so I had to make some quick adjustments.

I then noticed my gun had somehow pried out of my holster and was seated barrel up and cocked, as if some unknown force was working against me in this critical time of emergency. I quickly uncocked my gun and holstered it. I reversed the car and drove like the wind out of the projects toward Saint Francis Hospital, which was approximately two and a half miles away.

Harry operated the radio as I drove. Firestone and Lynwood units blocked the major intersections as we approached and made it much easier and safer to transport as we closed our distance to the hospital.

I knew we were traveling pretty fast when we suddenly became airborne on Imperial Highway at Alameda Boulevard and landed about thirty feet past the intersection.

I looked back over my right shoulder at George several times and yelled to him to hang on, that we were getting him some help. He didn't say anything, but his chin nodded up and down and slightly from side from side on his chest because of the bumpy ride.

A large glob of coagulated blood oozed eerily from his mouth, down his chin, and throat and onto his T-shirt and tan uniform shirt. His eyes were closed, and for a brief moment I thought perhaps that maybe he was just faking, and this was part of a big joke. However, it clicked in that this wasn't a joke at all, and I was really getting angry and upset. I yelled several times at George to hang on in a feeble attempt to put positive thoughts into his mind so he wouldn't give up.

I began noticing a lot of other units going the opposite direction. Jesus, there were a lot of them, all red lights and sirens. It seemed the whole street was solid red lights going the opposite way. I knew that those units knew we had a wounded officer in our car and wanted to know what had just happened.

As we drew near the hospital I started to apply the brakes, but they were spongy and fading and skipping a little bit. I nearly passed the hospital up by traveling so fast. Finally, I negotiated a fast right turn and looped into the driveway. I sped toward a nearby stall close to the emergency dock and stopped. A nurse was almost at our car with a gurney as we got out, and we quickly pulled George out of the car and carefully placed him on the gurney. We quickly turned the gurney toward the hospital and guided it up the ramp. We started passing through several double doors on our way to one of the emergency operating rooms. It seemed as if we were in a slow-motion slide presentation as we passed everyone in the busy, crowded corridor and nursing station.

A nurse motioned us into one of the rooms, and an attending doctor came in asked us if we knew where George had been shot. We didn't know. We began assisting the doctors and nurses to remove George's uniform shirt and pants. There were approximately eight people in the room rushing ever so carefully and diligently searching for the wound.

In doing so, I realized one thing as we were taking off his Sam Brown belt with all the gear. George had a large wet spot in front of his pants zipper. He apparently had pissed on himself, and I thought about how I was going to make fun about this when George had pulled through this mess and was better. We couldn't find anything wrong until we took off his bulletproof vest and noticed a small hole in the upper right elastic Velcro fastener. This was it, a small-caliber shot that apparently had gone right into George's armpit and traversed his chest toward the other armpit. (It should be noted that George was the only one at our unit, SEB, who wore a bulletproof vest. He was an outspoken advocate of wearing a vest all of the time.) Talk about fate!

This wound looked bad, very bad, and George was unconscious, not responding at all to any of their lifesaving techniques.

I left the room to allow the emergency room staff to do their business and stood just across the hall. While standing there, I realized Jimmy was in the adjacent room. I overheard him asking about his partner's condition several times, as other doctors were analyzing the extent of his facial wounds. I thought, *Those damn marines; they're always thinking of their partners when the shit hits the fan.* Moreover, Jimmy was really raising a stink by screaming and hollering at everyone.

Before this day, I thought that any policeman who cried in uniform was a punk and a full-blown sissy. I was tough and wouldn't allow anyone in my profession to display such an emotion. I would chastise anyone who broke that unwritten rule. We were cops and worked in a tough neighborhood in tough times. We had an image to project to the common citizens and our job wouldn't allow such sentimental breakdowns to occur.

The hallway started to fill up with department brass and other officers looking to see what they could do to help and find out how the injured deputies were doing.

I was leaning against the wall when one of the doctors came out and told me they couldn't help George. They had just pronounced him dead.

I thought, *Shit, George, you motherfucker. You finally did it! You died on me, right when we had so much going!* This really hurt, and on top of it all he was my karate instructor, who constantly drilled us not to give up. Well, look at what he'd just done. He gave up, and this made me really mad. I liked him a lot, and now some fat shit-bird was out there who had just killed him. I really had to do something. I didn't know what right then, but I had to do it fast to ease the pain I was feeling.

Just about that same time, I realized that Jimmy was being pushed out of his room and was coming toward me on a gurney. He leaned slightly over and asked me, "Larry, how's George? Is he okay?" I said, "Yeah, he's doing okay right now. Just you hurry up and get yourself better."

I looked down the hallway and saw a whole bunch of guys now standing nearby, looking at me, and I felt like shit. *Holy fuck, I'm losing it, and I can't hold it back! I'm starting to tear up and I've got everyone watching me.*

I quickly started to walk away from everyone and down the long empty hallway, trying not to be seen. I guess several of the guys realized my dilemma and began to approach me. I increased my pace to get away from them. One of them was calling out to me again and again. "Larry, Larry, what's the matter?" Feeling the intense pressure to hide, I yelled at him to leave me alone. I needed time by myself. How embarrassing for anyone to see me cry. What a puss! I just kept walking and finally got a grip about ten minutes later.

I returned to the wall just outside the small room where I'd been when George was declared dead.

Twenty minutes later, George's wife, Mary, was escorted into the emergency area. I didn't see her, but I was aware she was there. She went into the room where George's body was resting. I heard her scream real loud and begin wailing. Again, I didn't see her, but I could envision her grabbing George and shaking him frantically.

I knew Mary pretty well because they lived near my home. Now I began crying openly—in my uniform, in front of the guys—and this time I didn't care if they saw me or not. It was the time to let it out and my emotions just wouldn't hold back anymore. It hurt too much.

Several hours later, detectives arrested one of the suspects, the one in the doorway, as they were scouring the surrounding neighborhoods. He was a heavyset gangbanger. The other two were rounded up after a brief interrogation of the first suspect. So much for gang loyalty.

We returned to our units of assignment about an hour later, and we were allowed to go home. Some of the guys stuck around and went together to have a few beers. They asked me to go with them, but I felt I needed the long drive home and the solitude to think about what happened that evening.

My feelings at that point were numb and ambivalent. I ran George and Jimmy's sequence of events over and over in my head and tried to figure out what exactly had occurred.

George, my friend, I am sorry for your loss so early in life, and I hope you won't look down on me because I cried for you and Mary. You were a lot of fun and a great partner, yet you caused me a lot of grief, as the incident made a permanent mark in my memory of your lively past.

You also made me eat those harsh words I believed until the time of your death. Big boys do cry.

CHAPTER 107

A TIME TO PONDER

Quite a few of the guys stayed after the night's work was completed to have a few beers and reflect on how they all admired George. Several asked me to stay, but I just wanted to go home and think about the situation in solitude. The rehashing of a dear friend was a psychological strain, and I just wanted to be alone.

I stopped across the street from East Los Angeles Station at a small liquor store to buy some liquid refreshments for the long drive home. I parked my car in a lined stall and prepared to exit my car. A flowered-up, pinkish cholo car pulled in right next to me, very close to my driver's car door. I had to squeeze myself out of my door so I wouldn't hit the pretty little cholo wagon. There were five Hispanic occupants in the car; two in the backseat and three in the front. The three in the front were the male driver and woman carrying a small infant, wrapped in several blankets.

The two in the backseat were male and female adults, and the male in the backseat had a black patch over one of his eyes. They all seemed a little intoxicated. As I opened my door, the door's edge touched their chrome bumper slightly. They were all looking at me coming from my car. A few comments were made, but I didn't pay attention. I just wanted to go home without any drama.

I walked into the liquor store and purchased two items for personal consumption. While at the cashier's counter, I heard a car door slam and some laughter coming from the outside.

I didn't think too much about the noise until I got to the door. I saw the driver stand up from the left rear tire of my car with a large knife in his right hand. Everyone in the cholo wagon was laughing as the driver rounded his car and returned to the driver's seat with the knife still in his hand. As he got in the car and closed his door, I came out and could distinctly hear the laughter coming from within the flowered-up cholo wagon.

The male in the backseat was machoing up, nodding and bobbing his head, smiling as the cholo wagon backed up slowly. My left rear tire was hissing and deflating rapidly, sporting a three-inch gash on the lower half. Seeing what this cockroach had just done, I walked toward his driver's door and told him to shut off his engine.

The driver starter to reach down to retrieve his knife, but I opened the side of my jacket, without drawing any weapon, and informed him if he pulled up a knife, I was going to blow his head clean off. He sized me up and decided not to make a foolish move. He shut the engine off.

Meanwhile everyone in the car called me every conceivable foul name in Spanish and English. I placed the two items I purchased on top of his car. He began to open the door. When he stood up I could plainly see the eight-inch knife, which he had slit my tire with, and a revolver lying on the floorboard right beneath the driver's seat. These weapons were easily within reach of the driver when he was seated.

As he came out, I kept my hand back by my right rear to indicate that if he did anything stupid I would quickly pull my weapon and drop him like a rock. He complied with my directions and placed his hands on the roof line. I shook him down briefly and while patting down his left leg, I grabbed the gun and the knife from the floorboard. The three adults challenged my every move with loud cussing, and threatening me the whole time that they were going to kick my ass and take care of me real quick.

In response to their ranting and threatening gestures and words, I unleashed my own diatribe of mean and nasty words.

I pulled the driver to the right, closed his door, and stood there waiting for a passing patrol car to help me. Ten minutes went by and I did not see one ELA unit. Inside the car, the others were getting out of control, wiggling around and gesturing as if arming themselves and getting ready to come out of the car.

Finally a female store clerk came outside with a corn broom and began sweeping the small area in front of the liquor store.

I called to her and she looked toward me with concern. I asked her to please call the East Los Angeles sheriff's station because I needed help. She quickly withdrew without any comment and went into the liquor store.

My biggest problem was that I was relying on the driver's .357 Ruger revolver, fully loaded with six rounds, and his eight-inch knife. I was hoping the gun was operable, and the knife, well, I'm a retired meatcutter and I'll leave it at that. You see my .38 caliber revolver was in my car, under my seat, so it might as well have been in China, because I couldn't get to it. When I pulled my jacket back and reached back as if I had a gun, I was bluffing, but the suspect bought it and gave up.

It took about three minutes for six patrol cars to come to my assistance. They surrounded the cholo car and all of us. Most of the deputies knew who I was, and I relayed my observations to the handling unit and the patrol sergeant. I handed the gun and knife that I had taken from the driver to the handling crew. After examination and review, they arrested the driver and towed his car. The man with the eye patch changed my tire for me, and all three adults, including the woman who was carrying the infant, were sent home on foot.

I was bushed from the incident and left for the hour-long homeward drive. I had to write a detailed memo to my captain the following day, informing him of the details and force used. Most deputies were amused at the drama I was involved in, and of course I had to relate the story quite a few times.

Weeks later, I received the subpoena from the East Los Angeles Municipal Court for the jury trial that was occurring within two weeks. Time came for me to go to trial on the driver, who was now being charged with possession of a loaded firearm, carrying a concealed firearm, and malicious mischief to my tire.

When I came into the courtroom, I was invited to sit with the prosecutor and assist in the processing for a possible lengthy trial. First, it was a jury trial, and selecting the jury took at least a full day. Then the actual trial started, with testimony from witnesses. I gave my version to the judge and jury and left no doubt about why I did what I did to arrest and detain the driver. It was direct and to the point.

The defense then asked about the incident and expressed his view of my state of mind. He stated that when I pulled up to the liquor store, I was already drunk. That was because of what had happened to my friend two nights before, and I was focused on that violent occasion.

He added that I was actively looking for a fight because of my friend's death. That's why I slammed my door into the cholo wagon, challenging them to see what they would do, and eagerly waited for them to react.

I did admit that the shooting was on my mind because of my close association with my murdered friend. I also admitted that that if someone challenged me physically, I would not retreat one bit but defend my life and possessions. I also admitted that I'd just wanted to go home and not have any drama thrown into my face, especially by a car full of pooh-butt gangsters.

Then the defense had its witness, the better-looking one who was with the driver and one-eyed hoodlum in the backseat. When she gave her version of what happened, she stated an obvious twist to the whole ordeal and wavered when trying to remember my exact words and actions.

She was asked specifically, "And what exactly did Deputy Rupp say to Mr. C. as he was getting out of the car?" She stated, "Deputy Rupp said..." She stopped talking and started to bawl and snivel dramatically. Of course the judge called for a short recess in order for her to regain her composure. About fifteen minutes passed, everyone came back into the courtroom, and the female resumed testifying about the exact words that I had used. This time she said, clearly and confidently, "Deputy Rupp told Mr. C. that he was going to change his tire, and he had better get it done in ten minutes or he, Deputy Rupp, was going to rip his nuts off and ram them down his throat!"

When the jury heard these words, they all turned their heads and peered at me at the prosecution table. I could feel them dissecting my every word and deed.

She went on to say that they were deprived of their only source of travel and were put further in jeopardy because the infant became cold on their long walk home.

I was recalled to the stand and asked if I made the statement the woman had testified to. I said I didn't recall her exact words, and the judge had the court stenographer read them back. She repeated what I allegedly told Mr. C. and then stopped.

The defense attorney again asked if those were the same words I used. I said, "Yes, I did!"

The prosecutor then jumped up and asked, "Why, then Deputy Rupp did you use those words?" I responded that I was scared that this event was going to get me hurt or killed. I was using the same level of foul language they were using, and I didn't have my gun. It was in my car. But when I cussed, they paid attention to me. I was using it as a defensive tool, and it was working.

The jury leaned back in their chairs and nodded. I couldn't figure out why they reacted that way and was a little perplexed.

The judge asked the jury to take a short recess while I was still on the stand. Once they all left, the judge looked at me and then the counsel table and stated, "Deputy Rupp I would like to commend you and your honesty, restraint, and determination in this situation." He further stated that he wished more officers would react in a similar manner—we would have a much better world. I thanked the judge for his compliments and that this event happened when I was in a state of depression and wouldn't tolerate any defiant acts of meanness.

The judge took a short break and came back in to continue the trial. When the trial was in its fourth day, the jury was led from the municipal court to the liquor store, which was about a hundred yards from the courthouse.

The jury was able to see how close the marked spaces were and how the event went down. Nothing could be said to the jury because the excursion was only for them to physically view the crime scene and not be persuaded by either the defense or the prosecution.

Finally, on Friday, the jury deliberated for approximately one hour and came out into the jury box. The findings were guilty on all accounts. The driver was also ordered to reimburse me seventy-five dollars for the slashed tire.

CHAPTER 108

MOM AND DAD TO THE RESCUE

We were in an operation in the Baldwin Park area. The target was a small home where a suspected gang member and shooter for a local gang lived with his mom and dad. He supposedly slept on a couch in the front room. He had a gun lying on the floor next to the couch, so he can shoot or return fire to anyone who threatened his home safety. How heroic—what a stud!

He was wanted for several murders, and he was supposedly nasty and mean to all. His toughness put him in a special category, the type who would love to die in a shootout with law enforcement. "Bravado mucho; no tiene sesos!"

We timed it early, around six in the morning, so there would be a lot of light and no argument about who we were. In fact, we had two sergeants coming in with us with automatic weapons to cut down any adversaries who might attempt to outshoot us.

One of the sergeants was very small and a bit questionable about defending himself, let alone a SWAT situation. He wanted us to simulate climbing over window ledges using tipped-over coffee tables in our assembly room. It seemed quite silly, but we practiced it for about an hour, because he kept stumbling over the tables. The sergeant was very apprehensive, so we assured him we would complete the mission safely, as long as he stayed close to us so we could help him over every obstacle.

I was first up with my bayonet out to unlock a flimsy aluminum screen door. Then I would toss the bayonet aside, because I was going kick the front door and go through quickly. The suspect was purportedly very close, just inches from the front door.

My focus was the gun and the suspect's ability to arm himself quickly. I rushed in, and there he was, grabbing the gun. There were around six SWAT men behind me, counting on me to neutralize the cockroach immediately. He screamed and I grabbed his hair and slammed him to the floor quite hard. The gun was under him. He kept trying to grab the gun from under his body, but I punched him as hard as I could every time his hand moved to his back area.

I had punched him five to six times when I was attacked by an elderly couple pounding on my back with their fists. I turned to see why the two were at my back and saw both sergeants standing back and trying to control the older male adult with one hand and the other controlling their automatic weapons.

The woman, around sixty-five years of age, was pounding on my back rapidly, and between hitting the suspect and slapping her, my patience was strained. I turned my body slightly as I pounded on the suspect's stomach.

I was able to raise my right leg high enough to kick the woman in the right clavicle area, hard enough to make her fly through the air and into the already dangling screen door and onto the front porch. Unfortunately she fell right on top of my bayonet, but she was not hurt by the knife. She was dragged farther out by several other officers who heard the commotion inside the home. That woman turned out to be the suspect's mother and the male who was striking me was the father. He was finally controlled and handcuffed without injury to himself.

Shortly thereafter I pulled the suspect from on top of his gun and cuffed him without further incident. While inside I voiced my displeasure and was very upset that the sergeants were overwhelmed so easily by the suspect's parents.

I described my lack of confidence in their inability to stop the parents from pounding on me without any significant resistance.

This debriefing was done inside the suspect's home, because if the lieutenants found out what had occurred, the sergeants would be held responsible and suffer consequences that would jeopardize their positions. We kept the situation to ourselves and discussed strengths and weaknesses of our sergeants coming inside with the team. All of the deputies were superb in tactical confrontations, but a sergeant's ability was limited by his ranking structure.

The SWAT lieutenants insisted that the sergeants go inside with the entry team to supervise combat situations, but they did not get involved with combat tactics and confrontations. I'm sure it remains the same today, but it must be realized that just because you are promoted doesn't mean you're able to defend yourself or the team.

I guess the sergeants or lieutenants, less agile and physically limited by stature, could come inside with the SWAT team with pointers or riding crops and direct combat tactics as the fight ensues. *Don't laugh. It happens and won't change.*

After the operation was completed, Baldwin Park Police Department acquired a bulldozer and dug a huge trench around the home looking for buried weapons from gang-style murders that were supposedly in the suspect's yard.

The final search left the small home with a "small house on a bluff" appearance. The entire yard's soil was removed down to eight feet. I sure hope it didn't rain, or they would have had a large moat surrounding their home.

CHAPTER 109

THE UNIVERSITY PROFESSOR

So you're in school, college, or a university, and you would expect the instructors are professional and socially accepted. Professors and teachers are elevated to a level where their words, decisions, and actions are held in high esteem, and they are viewed as unblemished characters seeking out truth and justice and good for all social ills.

Teachers and professors are presumed to be trusted without any review of their criminal backgrounds or illicit drug habits. (Columbia University in today's current events, knowingly employs former terrorists and murderers. How noble; such selection should be held in high regard.)

Teachers and professors allegedly receive exceptional training in first aid, so if an emergency should happen, they could simply jump right in and perform CPR, and you would expect nothing but excellent care.

Well, let's get into a situation that we ran into in the East Los Angeles Station area when were working for the Special Enforcement Bureau. We were on assignment to help curb the high crime rate that is always prevalent but not published.

We were traveling southbound in an alley east of and parallel to Atlantic Avenue near Fifth Street. It was around six in the evening, and just starting to get a little dark. We came upon an adult Hispanic male, nicely dressed in a business suit and tie, in his early forties. He was loading some small cameras and video equipment into his station wagon, which seemed a little peculiar because of the timing on a weekday evening.

The rear of these two-story buildings are actually on Atlantic Avenue and contain business offices. Normally all of these buildings are closed early, and the alley is pretty much free of cars and foot traffic. We stopped for just a quick check to see if the man had identification and business in the area.

A lot of times the businessmen are armed with guns because of all the numerous robberies that occur. Although possession of loaded firearms is illegal, many times the crime is overlooked by law enforcement if the person is a local business owner and has proper identification, and the gun he has in his possession is registered to him.

We approached the man, and he provided his driver's license indicating he was a local resident. The station wagon was ordinary, but it was loaded with teaching gear and electronics, including several overhead projectors and slide projectors. He said he was collecting some material for a class he teaches in the Malibu area and was in a rush because he had a long way to travel.

His story seemed plausible. He was neat and clean, and all of the equipment could very well be used for teaching. So we asked him for his university ID, and he presented it as well. It seemed it was official credentials with his picture sealed inside a university ID card that is typically worn around the neck.

I stayed by the patrol car and the professor, and my partner, Doug D., went up the switchback stairway to check out the rear door and the back of the business. Doug returned shortly and conferred with the professor. Doug asked for the key to the back door and the professor explained he had lost his key and unfortunately had had to pry the door open, because he needed the equipment desperately for his class. Doug asked the professor what the name of the business was he was taking the material from. The professor was hemming and hawing some name not even close to the actual name.

Something was amiss. The place he had removed the equipment from fortunately had a phone number to contact.

My partner talked to the owners, and they didn't know the professor, nor had they given him permission to break into their business or take any of their equipment.

When Doug learned of the illegal act, technically the professor was under arrest at that point for burglary of a business. We were discussing the burglary with the professor. He was slow in his speech and lethargic, nodding off while we were talking. Although he was leaning against our car, he nearly fell, but he caught himself when his head and body jerked.

It seemed as if he was under the influence of something, and because he knew he was already under arrest, we asked him to remove his jacket and roll up his white shirtsleeves. He complied, and lo and behold he had numerous injection marks and scabs over his right inside ditch and forearm.

When we spotted the injection sites, the professor admitted he was using a twenty-five-dollar balloon of heroin a day and needed the stolen material for resale to support his narcotics habit.

Now, I'm sure it's an uncontrollable urge and these kinds of people are suffering from a terrible habit, but this revelation shows that not all professionals are what they seem, and all may have questionable backgrounds.

I wonder many times what would happen if we were to require all elected officials to submit to mandatory urine tests four times a year. I believe it would benefit society.

If law enforcement is required to submit to random tests yearly, does that make them morally superior to those who don't? Well, in my mind, that's a no-brainer.

CHAPTER 110

THE GLOVE COMPARTMENT

The evening was coming on quickly. I was working at East Los Angeles Station. Everyone was busy, rushing all over the place, and chasing the radio. A few stabbings along the boulevard were classified as nonlife-threatening; weapon commonly used was the screwdriver. The variety that most gangsters used was eight to fourteen inches long, because they were legal to carry, innocuous and totally acceptable to the judicial system.

A Hispanic carrying a screwdriver would be equal to a miner carrying a pick. These kinds of weapons are like being stuck with a fencing foil or an ice pick, a choice weapon that can easily wound or kill.

Dusk was upon us, and there were about six Special Enforcement Bureau units working the area. Our job was to confront gangsters and let them know we were out in force to arrest as many as we could.

If you stopped some of the typical gangsters, and they were carrying screwdrivers, you couldn't even take the screwdriver from them, because it could legally be carried to fix common things.

One of our units spotted a brown Cadillac erratically driving southbound on Atlantic Avenue going toward Telegraph Road. The unit was Bob H. and Gerry T., who worked together several times. They were accustomed to each other's peculiarities and enjoyed each other's company. There was a certain uniqueness to these two; Bob was the president of the ALADS group that represented the majority of deputies in the department. Gerry, on the other hand, was multilingual in Spanish and Russian. He was also the national karate champion in 1971, and ran five well-known karate studios in the Los Angeles area. A quick punch from Gerry could injure you seriously or kill you.

These two cops were a good solid pair and had practiced many times for hypothetical situations that might undermine officer safety in combat operations.

Bob was driving and Gerry was the bookman. Bob pulled the Cadillac over right by the Winchell's Coffee and Donut shop parking lot; just north of Telegraph Road, on the west side of Atlantic Avenue.

The occupants of the Cadillac, three black adults, were asked to exit the car and step to the rear. The three guys came over to the radio car as directed by Gerry's verbal directions, and followed by Bob coming behind them.

Gerry shook the three down for weapons and found nothing. Once shaken down, Bob got the all clear for Gerry to return to the Cadillac of course with the driver's permission, and he began to search the car for contraband.

Meanwhile Gerry had the men resting against the radio car, as he was standing about fifteen feet away from them, favoring Bob's position in the Cadillac. This was a standard when a car was being searched.

At that same time a pursuit began over near the 710 freeway and Whittier Boulevard. A sheriff's unit was chasing a black Ford Bronco driving at a high rate of speed going eastbound on Whittier Boulevard, in and out of various small connecter streets, but always coming back to eastbound on Whittier Boulevard.

It was nearly dark when the pursuit was coming down Atlantic Avenue, blocks from where Bob and Gerry were on the car stop. Bob, meanwhile, was about to open small the glove compartment door in the Cadillac, unaware of the ongoing pursuit.

Gerry was watching the three adults who were resting with their rear ends on the right fender of the patrol car, as he was listening to the ongoing pursuit over the radio and looking sporadically for the Ford Bronco. He was occupied with the situation at hand, but the directions on the radio were most alarming.

At this point the pursuit was now coming directly toward Gerry and the three adults. The loud noise of the sirens and screeching wheels drew their attention to the Bronco. The Bronco was doing about 100 mph and was now about one hundred feet from the rear of the offset radio car and Cadillac—just seconds away.

Bob was starting to open the glove compartment door, when the three black guys started running southbound on Atlantic. Gerry scurried toward the parking lot of the donut shop, all fleeing because of the impending collision.

The Bronco crashed into the back of their parked patrol car with an enormous impact, causing it to lunge forward, ricochet off the Cadillac, and flip onto its side, Coming to rest on the sidewalk.

Bob was knocked into the backseat by the impact, and the Cadillac landed partly on the sidewalk. He was dazed and crawled out of the right rear passenger door. He couldn't focus very well because the radio car was now resting on its right side on the sidewalk. He was shaking his head to visualize what had just happened.

Gerry saw the Bronco flip on impact, where the radio car had been when stopped behind the Cadillac. He saw a Hispanic man crawl out of the rear smashed window of the Bronco, screaming wildly and flailing his arms and hands. When the man stood up, he looked at Gerry and rushed toward him, still screaming obscenities and yelling as if attacking the front line of a football lineup.

The man charged toward him, and Gerry readied himself for a combination of fast karate punches that would drop any man out of commission.

The crazy man was upon Gerry quickly, and boom, boom, boom, Gerry's fist was planted well into the man's chest. This lunatic's reaction was nil, so Gerry quickly pulled his pistol and pointed it at the man, who was now two feet away. The crazy man grabbed Gerry's gun. Gerry warned him twice to let go, but the man was still trying to pull the gun out of Gerry's hands.

Bob was out of the Cadillac and bleeding from a small head wound just above his right eye. He was coming up on Gerry's back side and able to see the madman's confrontation with Gerry, but not his hands.

Bob heard gunshots and saw blood splatter hitting the side of Gerry's face. He thought his partner was being shot right in front of him.

The blood splatter struck Bob's face as well. He quickly decided it was a deadly encounter as he instinctively pulled his gun out of his holster and aimed it at the screaming man.

Bob fired five rounds into the man and watched him fall right in front of Gerry, landing on his back. Bob then saw Gerry's gun out and realized Gerry had shot the suspect as well.

The man screamed several more times, sitting up and lying down at least three times. Finally the man fell backward, motionless and dead, with a tremendous loss of blood that quickly pooled around the body.

The madman was determined to be under the influence of phencyclidine, PCP, which gave him his superhuman strength. This drug was especially prevalent in the seventies and eighties, when many bizarre encounters happened. During this confrontation, another sheriff's department motor reserve deputy, JPH, who happened to work out of the Special Enforcement Bureau as well, arrived on the scene when the shooting was occurring. Reserve Deputy JPH fired several rounds as well and was caught up in the shooting. His rounds apparently missed their mark; however, he was hit by one of either Bob's or Gerry's rounds that struck the suspect, traveled all the way through his body, and hit Deputy JPH's leg. Fortunately he recovered from that shot quite well.

The Taser gun was introduced to law enforcement as possibly a less-than-lethal means to handle PCP users. Many suspects died while in transit to the hospital or jail because of preexisting conditions, like heart and lung ailments, that seemed to be exacerbated by the drug.

The thought when I first got into law enforcement was to legalize all victimless crimes, for instance public drunkenness, narcotics, prostitution, and gambling. Over the years the reins to control victimless crimes have been loosened substantially. The dope-smoking public wants to legalize marijuana for medicinal purposes; in a short time it may turn out to be required. I firmly believe it will happen.

I wonder what will happen when someone crashes his car because he's under the influence of marijuana—which will be totally acceptable—because of some vaguely painful ailment. Please pass this on. I feel sorry for the victims, who will severely suffer thanks to the dope-smoking community.

Now, let law enforcement get down to fighting crime, without the hue and cry from all of the screaming, freeloading liberals. We will hear from them later that their loved ones are mixed up because of the new freedom they will embrace that is the root cause to most crime.

But then I could be wrong. Watch and see what occurs over the next twenty to thirty years. I think you already know what the outcome will be.

CHAPTER 111
LETTER OF THE LAW!

We were all assembled in the briefing room at the Special Enforcement Bureau. An invited guest from the office of the Los Angeles County district attorney rose from his seat and presented himself behind the lectern. He introduced himself as a deputy DA from the Malibu Beach area and said he was about to inform us of a situation that occurred approximately a week earlier.

He started by telling us that a rape had occurred on Westward Beach over the weekend. As the suspect was raping and beating the female victim, approximately thirty onlookers cheered the suspect. Once finished, he fled and left his victim in tears on the beach. No one went to help her.

Westward Beach is adjacent to the infamous steep cliffs of Point Dume, where the final shot of the movie *Planet of the Apes*, starring Charlton Heston, was filmed.

This area is annexed to Zuma Beach, which is immediately north of Westward Beach. Zuma is the hangout for a huge crowd from the San Fernando Valley. The population of the entire area—Zuma Beach, Westward Beach, and Point Dume—is approximately three hundred thousand in the summer months.

Most of the beachgoers are relatively docile, but they had recently become more rowdy and irritable. The DA was upset about the rape and the behavior of the onlookers. He went on to say that the entire affluent community was incensed and demanding strict enforcement of all laws to restore civility. The DA pleaded with us to enforce all laws and ordinances to the letter and take as many as necessary until law and order prevailed. He then went through the county ordinances applicable to beachgoers and pointed out the necessary elements for rapid prosecution. The starting date was in two days and he said everyone would be happy for this turmoil to go away quickly.

This pumping up was never necessary to kindle or spark our arrest behavior, because it was well known already that we arrested more individuals than most stations do collectively. That was our job— we went out to jack up and arrest gangsters in all areas, soften them up, and specifically enforce weapons and narcotics laws which are tipically the root cause of most local crimes.

We surveyed all the necessary maps, operations plans, and mobile booking procedures. Initially we would start off with fifty deputies, dressed in our class Bs, sheriff's department white T-shirts, lightweight green pants, and high-top boots. A green baseball cap topped the uniform off with our black Sam Brown belt that held our gun, handcuffs, speedy-loaders, and other small items.

We hit the beach, focusing mostly on lifeguard tower number one. We headed for the extension cords that were connected to the bathroom electrical outlets. We yanked the cords from the wall outlets, started gathering up the cords, and came upon their attachments. They were all hooked up to large boom-box radios playing loudly on the beach. We asked who owned the radios, and they answered quickly as if nothing was wrong. When they approached, we ordered them to place their hands behind their backs. They were flex-cuffed and arrested for petty theft of electricity. That move sent at least twenty individuals to jail.

They were carted off to our mobile booking area and then processed for transport in one of the vans. Oh, there was a commotion, but we made sure our backup from the Malibu sheriff's station, the local California Highway Patrol, were easily seen.

The ample law enforcement presence stifled the large crowd with command presence, and a sure pass to injury or jail was enough to stave off any rescue attempts. This was anticipated and was a successful deterrent.

All parking and moving violations were strictly enforced. Local towing companies were lined up to haul illegally parked cars and many that had several unpaid parking violations. That really got their attention.

We were in two-man foot patrols, just like at other large festivals within LA County. As we traversed the beach, we stopped at each blanket that had visible alcoholic beverages. The people were asked for ID. The beverages were dumped into the sand, and citations were given to each violator. There was a multitude of violations, but we had to independently investigate each one, which slowed our processing, so we left an avenue for some to flee from the beach.

Each citation had to have a short report that accompanied it and the listed evidence. Many people were buck-ass naked. They were ordered to stand up and were flex-cuffed immediately. We marched them out to the mobile booking site and processed and placed them the jail van, naked. men and women were processed expeditiously.

Some of the soul mates, who were also inebriated, expressed their dissatisfaction at their mate's arrest. They were promptly warned once, and if we met resistance, then they were arrested as well.

Initially, our jail van was filling up every ten or fifteen minutes, carting our arrestees off to the Malibu sheriff's station. At the station there was a bus standing by for immediate transport to the central jail facility or Sybil Brand Institute for Women, near downtown Los Angeles. This process worked well for dispersing the crowd because of their immediate concern was how to get the hell out of the immediate zone of enforcement.

We shifted our attention to a bottleneck in the road along Westward Beach Road, which allowed traffic into the parking lots closer to Point Dume. Here we stood on both sides of the road, and that gave us a very good view into each car.

Case upon case of beer and alcoholic beverages were confiscated. We would first take pictures of the contraband and then pop all of the tabs and flip the case of beer upside down onto the cul-de-sac and began to build a pyramid-shaped stack of empty beer cases. Beer covered the cul-de-sac and the stench of beer evaporating on asphalt permeated the jail van and booking area.

Many men who were nude were appalled at our enforcement of nudity laws and were noisily outspoken even as they were flex-cuffed and led across the beach in their birthday suits. One gorgeous woman, basking naked as a jaybird, was asked to stand up and present valid ID. As she stood up, she said, "What is the problem, Officer?"

I stated that if she had valid ID, she would be given a citation for nudity on the beach. She said, "Well, I don't have any ID. Don't you like what you see?" I said, "That's not the point, ma'am, it's a county ordinance violation and indecent exposure!" She was flex-cuffed and taken across the beach to the jail van and transferred to the booking team.

We then ventured across the Point Dume cliffs and onto an area called pirate's cove. Here there were scads of gay men frolicking naked in the shallow tepid waters.

One guy had the cutest little plastic wings glued to his ankles and an English pith helmet, and he was splashing along the little ripples like the Mercury Man, an older generational symbol of a rapid deliveryman carrying hand messages or flowers. In fact that's what he said his moniker was inside the cove. He said he could display his wears provocatively as he scurried across the beach head.

Most of these nude bathers were cited, because they had proper identification, but we didn't want to attempt to cross over the jagged large rocks with a gaggle of naked men.

It would have been profound visual shock to all law abiders on the Westward Beach side of Point Dume.

The enforcement went on for the entire week. The following Monday you could have fired a cannon down the center of the beach and not hit a soul. The local residents were extremely pleased with the outcome and our patrol activities went on for three months.

After the first year, the patrol was kept up, but not as nearly aggressively as the first year, and it continued for another five years. All issues were subject to a reanalysis of the crime potential and the neighborhood's valued opinion when gauging or curtailing rude and rowdy behavior.

CHAPTER 112

PANDEMIC OR EPIDEMIC: FOOD FOR THOUGHT

We were working in the East Los Angeles Station area near Whittier Boulevard and Ford Avenue, right by the 710 freeway. We had stumbled on an abandoned building where several adult Hispanics were mingling and acting as if they were disturbed by our presence. We got out of our car and approached and discovered a whole slew of "hypes" (heroin users) who all appeared to have "gotten down" recently, because they all had constricted pupils.

We sat them all along the curbside and were talking to them about their identities and the necessity to take as many to jail as possible, because we viewed them as chronic thieves. I don't expect anyone would argue with that theory except an attorney.

There were nineteen of them, and they all admitted their usage. They were from all over Los Angeles County; five of them lived in Orange County. About half of them were married, and most said their wives didn't know they were hooked on heroin. We were in a learning moment and decided not to arrest any of them, but took their names and addresses, confirming their information with their driver's licenses and California identification cards.

They all admitted they had injected from the same needle, which seemed rather alarming, considering five of them stated they had active AIDS, acquired immunodeficiency syndrome, which meant that all involved were exposed directly to the AIDS virus. This wasn't such a big thing to them. They all said they didn't care; they were getting the high, and that's what counted.

Considering that all of those hypes went home to their sweethearts or wives and exchanged bodily fluids, what do you think of their outcomes? I'm sure if you're an AIDS scientist you could rationalize my findings that although appear limited in scope, may not establish anything other than nineteen addicts using the same needle.. On the other hand, those nineteen could carelessly or intentionally infect another nineteen, who would infect another nineteen, and so on and so forth is not a stretch. East Los Angeles is a haven of herion users and with AIDS in the mix an independent study would be alarming to all because most involved will not admit to their errant ways and deter true findings.

This is just one example, and we ran into it rather often. How about the real grungy areas, where the population of hypes is staggering? The unskewed statistics would shock the surgeon general.

CHAPTER 113

A TICKET, A COP, A LETTER

My wife came home late one night and told me she'd just received a moving violation from a California Highway Patrolman. This was for speeding—69 mph in a 65 mph zone on the I-5, passing through Irvine.

She told the CHP officer that her husband was going to be very upset because he was in law enforcement as well and with the Los Angeles County Sheriff's Department. He was stoic while filling out the citation and displayed no sense of compassion, brotherly sprit, or camaraderie.

When my wife said that the citation was for going four miles over on the freeway at around ten o'clock, my brotherly spirit diminished. I was angry, because I had stopped many officers—and many CHP officers and their wives—for a variety of violations and never cited one of them. (Now I know most of you who aren't cops think that that is terrible and firmly believe that cops are not above the law. But that's too bad. That's what we do, and most of us are very proud of the fact that it's the one minor pass we get aside from many free cups of coffee.)

I took it upon myself to write this officer a scathing letter of gratitude for stopping my wife and giving her a citation even though she'd told him I was a cop as well. The gist of the letter was to convey my sentiments about his display of courage for stopping the worst car an officer could ever pull over on a busy freeway late at night.

The vehicle was a Dodge van with large side windows covered with full curtains, which would prevent anyone or anything from being seen from the outside.

Sheer bravery pushed this fine professional officer to approach the driver's side and engage in a conversation with my wife, knowing full well that anyone with the slightest bit of provocation could have easily blown his balls off.

Despite being told of my connection with law enforcement, he took the liberty of issuing her a ticket (which could have been media fodder) for racing through the fine bedroom community of Irvine on the I-5 freeway, a little after ten in the evening.

I noted that the citation would be paid from my paycheck for arresting assholes, drug addicts, dope smokers, and thieves. Just because my wife was out late at night, probably whoring around and injecting vast amounts of heroin, it didn't mean she could deliberately violate the maximum speed law by boosting her speed well over 3 mph. I commended the officer for seeing through the cloud of deceit and insult of my wife. She was supposed to lead an exemplary lifestyle and possess an unblemished character, far from her performance that night.

Issuing that ticket would probably give him a spike in his productivity and keen awareness of criminal activity. I also assumed he'd receive a promotional stipend for exemplary performance in the face of danger. I assured him I was very lucky to pass through his area late at night, usually around two. I offered him ample weapon support and backup, if necessary.

I was allowed to take home a radio car because of my on-call status with the department and any opportunity to assist would be afforded to him and any other officer in need of help.

I finished the letter by stating that if he was to spot my wife coming through his neck of the woods again, up to her old antics of speeding 3–4 mph over the posted speed, he should cite her as much as possible to make her obey all laws. In order to let me know that she was continuing to speed through the area, he should stick his number-two pencil into her neck up to the eraser and shoot her in the right foot with his pistol to compel her to cooperate. I begged him not to use his shotgun, because it would blow her foot off, and she wouldn't be of much use to me with one foot. I thanked him for all of his due diligence and leniency for not arresting my wife.

Several of my coworkers and supervisors warned me not to send the letter because it would irritate our superiors, but I had to let this guy know my reaction to his zealous behavior, so I sent it to the California Highway Patrol via the Santa Ana office.

A week or two went by. One day a certain lieutenant from the night before left his locker unlocked and open. Someone took the lieutenant's pistol and disassembled it completely. That person placed all of the parts and frame into a clear plastic bag, took it to the top of our radio antenna, and tied it to the antenna. In order to retrieve the bag, you had to prove your courage by scaling the antenna—although the antenna drooped dramatically near the top, about five feet—grab the bag, and untie it.

If you had a fear of heights, this action would immediately put you in a death-gripping hold on the antenna, and you'd wish you hadn't pursued this feat.

Around nine o'clock in the morning the captain of the bureau approached several of us and ordered us to get the bag off the antenna and give the gun to him. He expressed his opinion that this would not be tolerated and was disrespectful to the lieutenant. We agreed that we would retrieve the gun at all costs and have it in the captain's hands within the hour. We assembled everyone working at the bureau in the briefing room and decided that we would retrieve the weapon together in order to conceal the true culprit.

We all went to the rooftop and made a line of approximately fifteen personnel. We climbed the antenna, untied the bag, and handed it to everyone, so all of our prints would be on the bag, thus frustrating any attempts to track a single guilty party. We then selected the newest bureau member and sent him into the captain's office to turn the bag over to him and to confess that no one else was involved.

Several minutes passed. I was paged over the public address system to report to the captain's office immediately. I dropped everything I was doing and stood just outside the office until I was motioned in by the captain and asked to close the door. I stood in front of the captain's desk, and he asked me to have a seat right in front of him. I complied. He came around the edge of his desk and threw a three-page typed letter onto his desk right in front of me. He exclaimed, "Did you write this?"

I picked the letter up and recognized it as the personal letter I wrote to the Santa Ana CHP officer.

I looked at the letter and read it very carefully, turning each page with conviction and focused attention. On the final page, which happened to be only a quarter of a page long, my typed name and signature were at the bottom. I pointed to the signature and stated to the captain, "Yes sir, that's my signature!"

The captain exclaimed, "Do you know what the media would do with the contents of this letter?" I responded, "For what reason? This is a personal letter from me to the officer. And by the way, how did you get it?" He responded, "Never mind how I got it, it's loaded with veiled threats!"

I said, "There are no threats whatsoever in the entire letter, and if the media got ahold of it, it would not reflect anything about our department at all, it was never mentioned!"

He seemed very frustrated and told me that it was going to cause a verbal reprimand to be issued to me.

I pointed out that there was no such thing as a verbal reprimand, because it has to be written down somewhere. Therefore, it would be a written reprimand.

He stood by his decision and said I would be getting the reprimand placed in my jacket. I argued that if it showed up in my jacket, I would protest.

The captain then went on about the situation with the lieutenant's gun. He stated that he was fully aware that I was one of the culprits responsible for the gun and its strategic placement. I quickly contradicted his claims and said the guilty party had already admitted to him that he was the only person responsible.

The captain stated that he knew very well that the person who gave him the disassembled gun and admitted to the hazing was not believable. He felt strongly that I had something to do with it, but he had no evidence. With that final accusation he allowed me to leave and continue with my day assignments.

For a month I carefully checked my personnel folder every day to see if the captain slipped in the written reprimand surreptitiously. The captain was transferred to Lynwood Station suddenly, and it seemed rather strange a SEB captain would be transferred to a patrol station, rather than to another specialized unit. It seemed he messed up somewhere and was leaving our unit. I felt he was going to slip the reprimand into my personnel folder on his way out the door. The day he was transferred, I happened to be working and checked my folder just as he left the bureau, and there it was, inside my folder.

I quickly sat down in a small room and started to write a grievance in response to the reprimand.

One of the other lieutenants came by and asked what I was doing. I told him what the captain had done. He asked if he could have the grievance form and said that he was going to run it by our new captain. Several minutes passed, and the lieutenant returned and said the new captain wanted to talk with me about the grievance. The new captain, Ray M., was very nice and asked me to sit down next to him. He asked, "You wrote this letter?" I responded, "Yes sir, I did, Captain!" He remarked, "I'm shocked at your poor judgment. Would you ever do this again?" I responded, "No sir, not again. I'm sorry!"

He replied with a wide smile, "Well, then, let's consider this over!" He took the letter and complaint, tore them up and tossed them into the trash can. We shook hands, and I welcomed him to the station.

Boy, did he hit a home run with me. I felt this guy was very charitable, a team player. He didn't want minor problems generated from his unit. I said, "Captain, sir, I could just kiss you on the lips!" He leaned back and warned me not to do that.

Since that moment with the new captain, I was impressed with him and his outright exuberance and quality way of handling nearly everything associated with the bureau. He was absolutely great and an honor to serve under. His support and ambitious behavior was tantamount to great leadership.

He made quite an impression on me and I felt responsible to keep him protected, as he did me. From that point on we remained in good contact and very comfortable with each other's company.

He was the first black captain ever assigned to our unit, and he was an excellent choice for the position. He blended in most favorably and was a delight to have on all assignments and missions of SWAT.

CHAPTER 114
GHETTO BARBECUE

We were in the north end of Firestone Park, dredging the streets for more quality arrests. We had just completed several and were on our way for more. My partner was a young whippersnapper named Billy M.

I call him that because he was one of my enlisted swine cadets, way back when I was a drill instructor. All kidding aside, I was very proud of him, but I would never admit to it. He already had an ego almost as large as mine. He was very good, and we partnered up as much as possible.

It was around ten in the evening, and we were southbound on Hoover Avenue coming to the Y at Central Avenue. There was a car slightly ahead of us, and no other cars were in sight. As we came to the red signal, we were able to see that the license tabs had expired on the Chevy four-door sedan.

The two occupants didn't even turn to see who was beside them. Our windows were down, and so were theirs. Most folks look toward us and nod, but some don't. They might have what is commonly known as "black-and-white fever," or they might have something to hide.

We felt that we should stop this car and see why they didn't have the required tabs. Billy,was driving, and we were watching closely, crime is rampant in the area, with gang activity, shootings, and many assaults. In fact quite a few officers had been shot nearby, and if we weren't watching, it could happen to us.

My partner walked up to the driver's side of the car and began conversing with the driver about the expired tabs. Meanwhile I came up on the right side and was able to see both occupants looking toward my partner.

The right front seat occupant had something between his legs, and I couldn't quite make it out. From my position it appeared to be a wine bottle with something protruding up out of the top of the bottle. The passenger was still watching my partner, with his hands steadying the bottle surreptitiously.

I shone my bright flashlight onto the object. I had my pistol at my leg, ready for any surprises. With the aid of my light, I saw what appeared to be a Molotov cocktail. The bottle was full of liquid, more than likely gasoline.

I told my partner that they had a Molotov cocktail, and he backed up as we ordered them from the car at gunpoint.

They complied and came over to the grassy area on the side of the road and lay face down as we handcuffed them. Upon closer examination we determined that they did have a Molotov cocktail, ready to go as if they were about use it nearby. My partner searched the entire car looking for more gas bombs, took the keys, and received permission to search the trunk. The trunk was huge, and my partner was actually inside the trunk searching for more contraband.

As he was searching, I was off to the side watching the cuffed suspects lying face down on the grass.

A radio car came upon us and it turned out to be an LAPD sergeant with a local TV newsman and his cameraman. They stopped slightly ahead of us, and the sergeant approached me, and after I had informed him of what we had, asked if it was okay for them to video us.

I agreed. The newsman and cameraman came over and started to film the suspects. They then went up to the trunk while my partner was searching the interior. He had no idea that they were there and turned around right when the bright lights illuminated the scene. My partner said, "What the fu—?"

I said the media was present and just needed some footage for the evening news. He was a little irritated, but he got over it because his picture was going to be on the news.

The newsman asked me what was going on and I told him that these individuals had been caught with a Molotov cocktail and were either going to a barbecue or were going to barbecue someone. I didn't smile at all and made the statement with sincerity and conviction.

When we came into Firestone Park Station I informed the watch commander of the news media contact, which is required. I repeated my statement which caused his eyes to light up, as if I gave them too much information for them to decipher.

All in all, the stop was a good stop, with excellent consequences. No one was injured or killed, and two thugs went to jail.

CHAPTER 115

PUNK ROCKER RIOTS

We were already assigned and working the East Los Angeles area when the dispatcher directed our SEB units to Huntington Park. The request was for immediate assistance for several Huntington Park policemen who were injured and overwhelmed by rioting punk rockers.

Nothing else needs to be said when peace officers need assistance, other than being directed to the location as quickly as possible, without delay. The response is an authorized code-three run for many, so our team met up and drove en convoy. My partner was Billy M. As we were coming up Florence Avenue traveling westbound, we noticed many other units traveling code three as well. A code-three response is using red lights and siren. We were watching very carefully, as other units were converging in the same small space, a narrow two-lane highway. Many traffic signals slowed our response. As we continued westbound, we came up on several other units, their red brake lights glowing brightly in the dark. We were anticipating an immediate sighting of a calamity or traffic accident directly in front of us, and it seemed was very real that something was amok. Our sight was obscured even more by the billowing puffs of smoke coming from the front of the forward merging radio cars. We were among a large batch of radio cars as the smoke was clearing, partially revealing a lone Sheriff's unit on a raised island, its four wheels perpendicular to the car.

Two uniformed deputies were outside the car checking the destroyed wheels and rims. The smoke was dissipating from under the damaged radio car, as we passed the beleaguered deputies. It was obvious the unit hadn't seen the center island, tried to pass another vehicle on its left, and had run right into the island at full speed.

We arrived at a large dance hall that rioters had trashed the place and run from law enforcement. Several of the Huntington Park officers were attacked and injured, and the remainder of the small force already there was being showered with bottles and anything else the rioters could throw. We went into the building and observed the punk rockers fleeing into the streets and the surrounding residential neighborhoods or mingling with the peaceful Hispanic population. The local police were overwhelmed by the vast numbers of rioters.

The bizarre way the punk rockers dressed and decorated their faces and hair was a perfect way to identify them on the fly, so we were able to separate them from the crowd. The locals stood their ground and actually froze in their tracks as the pursuing officers were running down the rioters. Several of the local stores' bay windows were broken and items on display were stolen.

We knew our job was to chase and smack down as many of the offenders as possible in order to restore civil law and order, so the local police could once again control the area. We would drive up to a batch of the running punkers, jump out of our cars, run them down, strike them once or twice. and move on. This event was treated just like a riot formation skirmish line, where driving the rioters out physically was the intended purpose and not to arrest.

Arresting rioters just complicates the situation and bogs the control method down by eliminating one or two officers each time they arrest someone. Resources become depleted with mass arrests and an inability to control becomes more likely. Riots are to be broken up as fast as possible, and law enforcement must regain physical control, or lives would be in danger and property would be destroyed. Most of them knew we were chasing them out of town, but most didn't count on how many officers would respond and actually trap them in areas they didn't know. Therefore most of the rioters ran in groups. As we came upon them, my partner many times jumped out of the patrol car while it was moving slowly, and scream at them to run. They ran like the wind and a few made snide remarks.

We came upon about twenty of the punkers in a residential backyard. Billy jumped out of the car and drew back his side-handled baton as the group ran by him. One in the group was a woman who saw what Billy was about to do and yelled, "You wouldn't hit a lady, would you?"

Of course Billy responded, "No, I wouldn't," and smacked her in the shoulder as she ran by. She screamed and fled as quickly as possible, supported by several of her friends.

This Huntington Park punker riot lasted for approximately three hours until the police regained control.

CHAPTER 116
MORE GRENADES

This time we were set to serve a search and arrest warrant for a group of family members who belonged to a major black gang dealing in dope and grenades. This was a rather unique warrant service, because we hadn't practiced grenade usage.

The warrant was going to be on Watts Avenue at 111th street. We had to really get close and get in quick. We had about two weeks to plan the assault and acquire any specialty gear needed to complete the mission.

We prearranged a unit to stop a pickup truck with a camper shell and a cholo driving the truck. The cholo was jacked up to the max just like a regular car stop, with two officers harassing the argumentative driver, Bobby A. aka canvasback. The issue was that inside the rear of the camper shell was our whole team. They were jotting important information about the characteristics of the home that we were to hit in approximately a week and a half. We were all busy jotting the whole scene, and assigning parts to the smallest detail, just as we had done many times before.

The stop turned out very good and lasted about fifteen minutes. The deputies who stopped the driver actually were pretty rough on him, as we suggested, and it turned out to be a beautiful opportunity to see firsthand any anomalies that might hinder the operation.

A lot of information was obtained and we discussed the info for several days, laying out the devised plan in every detail. Our philosophy is nothing great, but remarkable because the team has collectively the advantage over any one or two outspoken tacticians. The operation's critical areas were all addressed, and the plan of operation is a whole team's effort. Its application is all subject to the review of all team sergeants and bureau lieutenants. No one holds back, and everyone must have input.

We finished the operational plans and we were ready for deployment.

Some of the suspects were rather robust and plump, but we were sure we could reach everyone, including the mother, on the initial hit.

A significant diversion was necessary so the suspects wouldn't have time to arm themselves. A flash-bang was the tool we were going to use. It was a three-second timed cylinder of tightly packed gunpowder that made a horrendous noise, much like a military grenade.

Team members were assigned quadrants of the home to clear and nab all occupants, regardless of their involvement. During the commotion, one of our guys got into a fight in one of the bathrooms and both fell head first into a Jacuzzi. One suspect was believed to be hidden in the attic, so I climbed up after him and found him hidden beneath the insulation, just above the front room. As I grabbed him, we both fell through the ceiling joists about eight feet down to the front room floor, narrowly missing a mirrored glass coffee table and a baby grand piano. I'll admit the landing didn't feel good, and the sudden stop nearly knocked all of the snot out of my suspect and me. The entire operation went well, no one was seriously hurt, and all suspects were arrested without any significant harm.

When we finish an operation such as this one, we routinely turned the location, suspects, and final operation over to the detectives who were assigned the case from the initial investigation.

This means that the SWAT team is responsible for neutralizing the threat of any living suspects or animals and nothing more that could compromise the integrity of the entire investigation.

CHAPTER 117

NEAR DEATH'S SHADOW

I had been on the SWAT team for approximately seven years. Most of the time, I went in first as a backup or scout. We had been receiving callouts weekly, and each assignment was unique.

Camaraderie was an essential key to our success, and team compatibility and cooperation never went unnoticed. Trust was pushed to a high level of confidence; in times of darkness inside a building, you could reach around yourself and the person you touch would be a team member. In fact, several times, some of the more robust deputies needed to be separated from each other, administratively, because as a pair they complemented each other too much. The crews developed a bond that was too formidable and caused occasional confusion and frustration among supervisors.

Our teams competed with one another in all events, and training was essential for the successful completion of each mission and the after-action debriefing, which minutely criticized each event. The training was continuous and exhaustive, and the results were superb. We depended on one another, and some of us were involved in other outside activities that sharpened our skills even more.

I was taking my flight exam for a Cessna 172 at John Wayne Airport, studying like crazy in hopes of passing the check ride in several days. I started to learn to fly during the time I was instructing rappelling from the Sikorsky Choctaw and actively practicing departure techniques from the landing skids of the Bell helicopter. Several operations involved descending onto the complex high-rise rooftops in the downtown Los Angeles area. The helicopter operation was ferrying sticks of crews departing from a low-elevation hover. Three men on each skid would peel off and land on the rooftops.

Oh yeah, I nearly forgot—for proper ambience, the public address system played "Flight of the Valkyries" by the legendary German composer Richard Wagner as a prelude to each stick arriving on the roof. Talk about an orchestrated maneuver, this was spectacular from each member's viewpoint.

There were times I was hanging upside down from the skids while the helicopter was in flight, just to check my nerves and dexterity skills, while swooping in and out of combative positions.

Flight to me was uplifting and rewarded me with more and more ability in seemingly frightful antics for just plain excitement. Even when instructing rappelling and hovering a mere 150 feet from the deck, I would take up eight loops of the rappelling rope and face the new guys, holding the eights loops in my left hand, and warn them not to look down. If you did, everyone looked like ants, and it might very well scare the shit out of you.

So you should stand near the opening, make double sure you're hooked up to the rappelling line, and just jump. As you jumped, you released the eight loops and sailed down in a free fall, for approximately twenty feet. Oh, by the way, don't you dare let your off-hand get tangled up in the loose rope, or you'll wish you hadn't.

When the rope comes to the spot where it joins the "carabiner," you must simulate ramming your working thumb into the cheeks of your butt and the decent will stop.

The rapid stop and weight of the rappel would pull the heavy Choctaw downward, and it would drop slightly as well. That event alone is thrilling enough, followed up by a fast rappel down and into cover and concealment amid the dense brush and tall weeds.

My involvement made me practice and practice so much that the excitement pushed me into more adventure into the flying world and I was applying to federal agencies for combat positions.

My marriage was nearly trashed and on the brink of divorce, because of my total commitment and involvement in all training, callouts, and instruction. All brought about probably due to my lack of parenting skills and attention to being a committed father to my two sons.

Flying occupied a lot of my time, between studying and practicing the various flight maneuvers. I had aspirations of getting my own helicopter license after a hundred hours of fixed-wing aircraft, and then followed up with another fifty hours of rotorcraft training.

Those same aspirations sparked my ambitions of maybe quitting the department and becoming a private contractor/trainer in Central America. I know that idea sounded dumb, but that's where I was headed, once I achieved my helicopter license.

Several other fellow team members were also planning to follow my actions. They also were about to lose their marriages, so we were very much in tune with one another.

We had already set up a static parachute jump out in Perris, in Riverside County. Initially twenty-one of us signed up to take the jump, but as it turned out seven of us actually went. Of course I set the planning for the practice jumps, classes, and the main jump as well.

Only one lieutenant, John K., went with us. He was my mentor and a dynamic, bold leader who is discussed in other chapters of this book.

The helicopter training and licensing would allow us to quickly leave under any serious combat conditions and escape capture by insurgents. Or so the story goes. The landowners in Central America were often overwhelmed with guerrilla opposition and flight from the area was not only to evade capture, but to survive as well.

At this time as well, I was enrolled at Cal State Los Angeles taking political science as a major and Spanish language as a minor. Time was my worst enemy because there wasn't much to play with.

My aircraft training came from an instructor who was from Brazil and was very sharp and funny. He also taught me the essentials to pass my final flight exam for my private pilot's license. His name was Mike I., and he constantly messed with the flight instruments as I was flying and of course during take-offs and landings. I knew he was doing it to sharpen my skills, but he said he did it because he couldn't stand cops. Hmm, how different! He also told me he was taking his entire pay and sending it to his wife and family in Brazil.

We got along very well, and I had already switched upward from a Cessna 150 to a Cessna 152. Now I was getting serious and about to get into a much larger plane that seated four adults. The Cessna 172 was magnificent and really had much more oomph than the other planes I had flown. A total of five hours was necessary for the larger class of aircraft, so Mike was putting more and more pressure on me to pass my check flight.

I had spent quite a few hours with Mike, going over all of the peculiarities of the plane and the proper protocol for its operation. Mike was very diligent in his instruction and pushed me hard. He suggested that I come every day for three days, sit on the picnic bench and go over each and every flight maneuver, then go and prep the aircraft, taxi out to the tarmac, and take off.

I flew to my practice area and performed one maneuver. Then I returned to the airfield, landed, taxied back to the parking spot, shut the plane down, set the chocks in place, slipped in the gusset lock, locked the doors, and went directly back to the picnic bench and studied the next maneuver. I repeated the pattern for the whole day. For three days I did this repeatedly and felt very confident of what was necessary and required by the Federal Aviation Administration.

Then came the check flight; first I flew with Mike for about forty minutes, and then I returned to the flight business office to pick up the check pilot, who would put me through the rigors and requirements.

It was great. Mike trained me so well, I had no difficulty and aced the flight without any problems. When I returned, I came into the flight office and shook Mike's hand and gave him a "cop hug." I was so proud of my accomplishments I even threatened to kiss Mike on the lips. Of course he refused, but he smiled and congratulated me as well. When I achieved this rating, I believe I was so high in pride I needed someone to hold me down. My ego blossomed to the hilt.

I went home and informed my wife and neighbors of my accomplishments and was emotionally high the rest of the day. Now I would build up the necessary hours to go to the next step of helicopter instruction.

The following day, a fireman neighbor came over to my house, which was only two doors away, and asked if I'd heard about the Cessna 210 that collided with a King Air coming out of John Wayne Airport. My neighbor said he'd just heard about it on the news, so he called the Huntington Beach Fire Department. He spoke with the fire captain who handled the scene just minutes after the crash.

He said a Cessna 210 coming from Fullerton collided with a large King Air aircraft over Mile Square Park, in Fountain Valley. The multiengine King Air was climbing out of John Wayne Airport, and sheared the right wing completely off the Cessna 210. That Cessna 210 was coming into the flight pattern area for John Wayne Airport from Mile Square Park, a VFR (visual flight rules) checkpoint.

The multimillion-dollar King Air was able to make it back to John Wayne Airport, but the Cessna 210 with two aboard, did a flat pancake spin from three thousand feet to the street and sidewalk. The actual crash occurred on the border of Huntington Beach and Fountain Valley.

The occupants of the Cessna 210 were a chiropractor and his flight instructor. The investigation revealed that neither aircraft saw the other. Most likely the occupants were alive when the 210 rapidly descended and crashed.

The captain described the remnants of the two-man crew as a clumped-up mess of what appeared to be about three or four hundred pounds of hamburger.

I remembered the Compton helicopter crash from years before. I learned that when an aircraft crashes, everything between the impact point and the occupants will pass through the tissue of the occupants. Even the bones are sent flying away from the connective tissues. So when you see tissue, it will most likely not look human at all.

I immediately went home and called the flight business office at John Wayne Airport. I found out that Mike was the instructor who was killed. That floored me; he was instrumental in all of my flight achievements and a whole lot of fun to be with. All of the excitement and laughter of the previous day was stolen by the Grim Reaper. What a tragedy, and what a loss. He will be surely missed by me and all of his students, not to mention his wife and family in Brazil.

Mike was very safety conscious and always harped on me to keep my eyes front and to look for other aircraft constantly. He emphasized all airport settings, most important in the southern California area, because there were so many aircraft.

I returned to work and within two months, my marriage was strained so much I decided to leave my home and begin divorce proceedings. That heaped additional pain and misery on the recent trauma of my flight instructor's death. I moved to an apartment over by South Coast Plaza in Orange County, with a roommate and SWAT partner, Rich F., who was going through a divorce as well. It was a little rough for a month or so, but we managed. We were able to lick each other's wounds from our divorce traumas and split the living costs right down the middle. The best thing about this partnership was that it also served as a good listening board, as we discussed our marital relationships and downfalls.

Unfortunately, another source of trauma jumped right in both of our laps. We went to a callout in mid-April and our team sergeant was shot right in front of us. A gun battle ensued, and the suspect died as well. It seemed strange to me that people who were near to me were dying. Other team members were picking up on those vibes. Several of them started to imply that gloom and doom shadowed my presence. I didn't want to focus too much on what had happened in the last six months, but something or someone was watching over me. Fate had taken two names from the Special Enforcement Bureau roster. I was with both of them at their demise. No one else with my experience was involved in such tragedy, and it seemed imperative that I recover quickly from the psychological traumas, and tell their stories.

I was so busy the next several months caring for my seven-year-old boy every weekend, I didn't have time to dwell on the past too much. I remained intact and focused on assignments at the bureau, and where I should go next.

This kept me focused once a week on my son Chris. He came with me when I was cleaning swimming pools to help supplement my income. It forced me to pay attention to being a father at least once a week, if that was any consolation.

CHAPTER 118

THERE'S TROUBLE: LARRELL'S WREATH

Briefing was at four thirty that morning, and Larrell was running late. The briefing room was packed with forty or fifty guys dressed in battle gear and ready to go. This was a multiple SWAT function, and there were two full teams inside and awaiting updated information on both locations. The individuals we were after were Mexican crime partners. We had charted, mapped, and closely watched both places for the past two weeks.

I was particularly focused because of all the mishaps that occurred attempting to gain as much info as possible by intelligence from other team members. Some of the basic info was not panning out as easily as in the past, but we pressed on and finally answered the lingering questions. My position on the team was the scout, and I had to be fully aware of all the info and ready to parrot it to my team leader, Larrell, as soon as he came in.

Larrell was going through turmoil with the lieutenants, who didn't really consider him a strong team leader. They had recently informed him that he was going to get a low appraisal of promotability (AP), because he was too close to his men on the team. Larrell agreed that at times he acted more like a deputy than a sergeant. That meant most likely he was going to be passed up for the coming promotion, and he would be quite irritated. He spoke of the evaluation often and crudely announced his displeasure about their misgivings. He was an energetic, sharp, and talented SWAT sergeant and left most of the details up to me. I briefed him of every episode we were about to encounter, and he would give the report very well because he was briefed thoroughly. His communication skills were good and witty, capable of keeping the early SWAT crowd awake and optimistic.

Briefing lasted for approximately thirty minutes. We loaded up everyone and all the necessary equipment and drove out "in convoy" with roughly twenty-five cars, vans, and paramedic trucks toward the two designated locations. The convoy split up on the freeway, because the two locations were approximately four miles apart.

We assembled at the small service station with all of the crews three or four blocks away from the target home and quickly recapped personnel, plans, and strategies. Two of our bureau lieutenants came along with us on this warrant and were to stand by at the service station to assure all planning and strategies were going as anticipated. The two lieutenants were both exemplary in their positions. I knew them from my past tenure at Firestone and the academy.

We were all in the van, coming down the quiet residential street in a four-car convoy and ready to do business. We slowly crept up on the targeted house.

The heavy four-wheel paramedic truck was in front of us. After all, they were going to rip the burglar bars off with their hooks and they needed plenty of room. (To pull the burglar bars off a home, one end of the rope was secured to the heavy-duty paramedic truck's bumper and the other end of the rope had large hooks collared around the burglar bars. They would tighten up as the utility truck took up the slack by moving. We made sure no one was near the rope or the bars that were about to be ripped from the target's home's front face.) At times these bars would also include the anchoring bolts that were pulled from the framing and small chunks of stucco and chicken wire. The bars would rip from the window frame and travel across the lawn, often gouging out large tufts of grass and dirt and the surrounding fences, dragging those items along with the bars.

A lot of times the large rope would guide itself under the tires of parked cars and flip the cars on their sides as the bars and rope picked up speed. If anyone got in the way, they would be seriously injured, or more likely killed.

It was early, just after six o'clock in the morning, as the warrant demanded. We were all quiet as usual, eight of us huddled around, and armed to the hilt with our entry weapons, tear gas, and tools needed for this mission. We had planned this event for the past two to three weeks and knew our exact positions, responsibilities, limitations, and emergency procedures.

All questions about this operation had been asked and answered many times before and reviewed earlier at the four o'clock briefing. We were at our peak, strong and alert for any situation that may arise. After all we were the A team from the bureau. We were the best, we boasted and didn't hold back at all.

We knew the other team was about four miles away and ready to do the same thing. Both of these targets were bad actors from Mexico and had shot it out with the "federales" about a month earlier.

All van doors were held ajar, lessening the possibility of any noise. Just prior to our arrival, Larrell had joked, "That goddamn Art. Why doesn't he hit these places at noon?" Larrell was referring to the time of our entry, because the sun had been up for at least half an hour, and the tension of the situation was upon us.

We quietly came out of the van and went to our assigned positions. We cautiously followed each other up the driveway and onto the narrow walkway and stood by the corner of the front of the walkway and the garage. We remained there several seconds as the rest of the crew got into position and the hook-up team carefully placed the hooks on the burglar bars.

They were easily within our view to the left of us, maybe fifteen or twenty feet away. The entry team consisted of me, the scout, with, my backup and roommate, Rich, the team sergeant, Larrell, and "spot," Billy, our official Spanish announcer and fourth man in. Little Guy (Mike) and Half Foot (Gil) were at the rear, east wall, Nick was at the south wall near the dining room, and Canvasback (Bobby) and Gibber (Steve) covered the front.

We practiced many times going through the entry mode and what would, or might, occur. Spot announced the knock and notice in Spanish and in English in a loud tone as we drew closer to the door and banged on it loudly. We heard running inside and feared the occupants were up, aware of our presence, and possibly arming themselves or destroying the dope.

The signal to pull was by wave of hand and a nod. The all clear was announced to warn of the impending danger of the bars being pulled. The bars tore easily from the window and traveled across the front lawn. The noise at this point was ear shattering.

Doug and CB were the paramedics at the wheel and assigned to our operation and team. Doug was my partner for at least five years before and CB had been a paramedic for years and worked with me at Firestone Park Station. Both of these paramedics were well trained, seasoned, and above reproach.

Gibber had the long portion of a bumper jack and slammed it into the window, smashing the glass and raking the inside frame, clearing away the shards of glass that could complicate our entry. The bomb blanket went over the base ledge of the window, obviously to protect the entry team from cutting themselves on the small and medium remaining chards of window glass.

I could see into the living room and didn't see anyone moving around. I noticed a three-foot-tall television just inside the room, in front of the window. I had to stretch my right leg to climb over the wide window base frame to get into the living room.

Once inside, I took several small steps and saw a tall male figure, clad only in his white briefs, coming out of a doorway just inside the hallway. I was into my second announcement: "Sheriff's department, narcotics search warrant!"

The man looked directly at me and scoffed at my presence. He passed air through his teeth with no alarm or apprehension, although my handgun was pointing right at him. He turned away from me and went back through the same door without any emotion or missed step. I was focused on the doorway, thinking he was retrieving his gun or dumping his dope. I could hear the other guys behind me. (Our training was to keep visual control of the cones of responsibility and cover areas where other team member weren't looking; this function is developed stringently through constant training. It is based on a system that develops incrementally as each team member is introduced into the mix.)

A second or two later, I heard a muffled boom. My head was still focused on the doorway, but in my right peripheral vision I noted a drab green glob drop to the floor near the front window on the other side of the large TV.

I sensed it was a team member falling because of the muffled report of the gun—hopefully a miss. I saw the same man on his toes, crouched over. He was coming from the kitchen area, passing by the large sliding glass door. This time he was carrying a handgun and looking toward the front door, just to my right, about eight feet away. He passed the small garage door entrance and hunkered down in the dining room corner, just below the room divider and the door leading into the garage. These movements all occurred within one or two seconds after the muffled shot.

At that moment I thought it was my roommate who might have just got shot. This angered me so all I could do was to think that he was behind that little wall. I felt my feelings going numb and focused on the target behind the wall. (During our firearms training, we fired and shot into block walls, cement-filled block walls, brick, wood, stucco, lath and plaster, drywall, and a wide variety of doors, wooden and metal, solid and hollow core. We also carefully examined the structural characteristics of the walls and doors, each having an effect on our ammunition, .38 caliber, 9 mm, .45s, .223s, .308s, and tear gas projectiles, their travel and penetration capabilities through these building materials was of utmost importance to all team members both inside and outside.)

I noted the electrical outlet facing the living room on the room divider. (Training indicated that that outlet was approximately nine and one half inches from the ground and probably supported by a two-by-four stud, separated at least sixteen inches from each other by structural studs.)

I was armed with a Smith & Wesson model 66 revolver and directed my firing into the wall. (This was my choice of weapon because if I had to pistol whip anyone. it would remain together, whereas an automatic pistol had several times in the past fallen apart on impact and become inoperable.) I focused on the impact of my rounds near the top corner of the outlet's faceplate.

As the rounds struck the wall, I could easily see their pattern diagonally rising slightly toward the corner and within two and one half feet from the floor.

Realizing the wall was small and just large enough to conceal the suspect's body, I surmised my rounds were most probably striking him.

My six rounds were fired in rapid succession, and I was about to reload when I realized my roommate, Tripod, was to my left, a few feet from me. He was firing at the same target with his H&K MP5. (Later, Tripod informed me he was squatting and firing face-to-face with the suspect approximately eight feet away.)

At that point as I was about to reload I noticed another H&K MP5 at my feet without a sling. It must have come from whoever was shot at and now it was easily within my grasp. I quickly holstered my pistol and picked up the H&K and started to fire into the wall more randomly, but close to my pistol rounds.

I still couldn't see the suspect as I continued to fire through the wall as the suspect started to reveal his legs. He started to slither away from the corner and into my view. My rounds were directed away from the wall and into the suspect's chest and abdomen. I was yelling and cussing at the suspect as I was firing and stopped firing when I ran out of ammo. The suspect had stopped moving.

During this time shotgun blasts from the window entry by Gibber and Spot. Tripod had fired quite a few toward the suspect and didn't know if any of his rounds had struck him, but he had walked behind me as I was firing. Tripod went over to the window where CB and Doug were trying to lift Larrell's body from the floor just beneath the window.

Realizing I was again empty, and who was hit, I noticed they were picking Larrell's body up and away from the window, out of the firefight. (Later it was revealed that it was absolutely near impossible to get Larrell out of the home because of his own weight and the angle the paramedics had to operate. CB was exceedingly strong and no one else could have had his lifting capacity.)

I moved quickly toward Larrell's body as it was being lifted out the window and managed to grab two extra H&K 9 mm, magazines from his entry vest as he was being hoisted carefully out of the window.

I realized Tripod was okay and yelled to him to get out as I tossed two small handheld tear-gas grenades down the hallway, to counter and obscure our quick withdrawal. As I went out the window, I crossed the north side of the lawn and hopped over the small wall bordering the suspect's home.

I radioed our condition, and remained in a static hold on the home until the other team arrived.

Once outside, I noticed the paramedic utility truck was stalled because the stokes litter carrying Larrell was partially sticking out of the rear, unable to fit inside the truck properly.

Both paramedics were attempting to remedy the transportation problem. That took up several valuable seconds, and then they quickly drove off. The hospital was relatively close, and a map specifically directing the paramedic truck to the hospital was taped on the bench seat easily within view of the driver.

Several of the guys advised me that I was now the team leader. To be honest, I felt numb and searched my mind for what else had to be done while we held our position and waited for the other team to assist us. I was on the other side of the wall when Spot came up to me and repeated to me that Larrell was hit and was in bad shape. I was infuriated; my sensitivity was abandoned. I was focused on reloading and telling team members to remain in position. I yelled at Spot to shut up. There was no time to grieve a fallen team member. We had to hold and protect our positions. He complied.

Several minutes passed and I saw both the lieutenants pull up and get out of their car and stand by one house away. I crawled up toward them and told them what had happened. I said I was going to deploy tear gas. They acknowledged with a stunned look on their faces. I think they were in shock. They didn't say a word. I ran to the corner of the house near the entry window and began to toss a whole bag of tear-gas grenades one at a time into the window to drive anyone else in the home out and into the hands of awaiting team members.

I finished lobbing the tear gas into the window and returned to a position on the other side of the bordering north wall.

The gas was effective and within several minutes three kids (ages fourteen, twelve, and ten years old) came running out of the home and into the rear of awaiting team members. Quite a few neighbors began to come out of their homes, but were ordered to return to their homes because of the strong possibility that another gun battle would ensue.

Minutes passed and the second team, Art's team, pulled just south of our location, several homes away. Oddly enough when I saw them, they were in perfect alignment according to height, and very somber. They were a blessing to my mind; however, I was in haste to inform the sergeant. I recapped the series of events, who was in what position, and the obvious weaknesses of the perimeter security and concerns. The second team responded quickly to my demands.

Art listened to everything I said and then asked a few questions. This I remember distinctly, as we were conversing near the garage door, on the walkway. Art suggested putting in more gas, and his team was very concerned about how to get it inside. I suggested that they go the point of our entry, where I threw all of our gas. No one jumped at my suggestion.

Aware that I knew the suspect's position in the home firsthand, I offered to get to the corner of the house where we made entry. His team could lob the gas grenades to me underhand and I would pull the pins and toss each one inside. Art considered the suggestion and gave me the okay. I rushed over to the already smashed entry window; hidden from view to anyone on the interior, yet standing at the near corner.

I motioned I was ready, and the first grenade was tossed to me from the team member standing near the corner of the garage door and the front walkway. I pulled the pin holding the spoon and tossed it into the window with my right hand, and then leaned back, concealing my position. The grenade popped and released its gas and smoke into the living room and dining room. I motioned for another by extending my hands and arms, just as the next one was tossed. I caught it, and we repeated the sequence about ten times.

At that point, Art motioned for me to return to his position, and we started to discuss entry tactics. Art asked, "Larry, where exactly was the suspect the last time you saw him?"

I responded that he was lying face up in the living room, with his head right next to the garage door. I added, "I shot the shit out of that motherfucker until he stopped moving!"

Art seemed a little confused and wanted to picture where the suspect was lying. Apparently whatever I was saying, wasn't being conveyed, and I started to repeat myself. While I was talking to Art, I stepped a few feet away and reached for the handle in the middle of the garage door, grabbed it, and yanked it loose. The garage door rose and revealed two cars. A heavy haze of smoke and tear gas surrounded the upper portion of the cars. Smoke alarms could be heard distinctly and water was spraying from a pipe near the slightly elevated water heater.

I spoke loudly to Art. "That motherfucker is right next to that door!" while pointing at the garage door that went into the dining room.

Art spoke to several of the team members and was lining up the entry team to go inside. I reminded Art that the door he was going into was where the suspect was lying. Art said he understood and added, "Larry, you're not going in!"

I responded, "What the hell is wrong with me going in?"

Art stated, "Larry, you're not in any shape to go in right now."

It crushed my ego and I asked, "Am I that fucked up?" He nodded quietly and expected me to follow his directions. Knowing Art very well, and trusting his judgment wholeheartedly, I felt that apparently I was in a killing mood, mad, and expressing my intentions without actually realizing it.

I moved back a few feet and allowed Art and his crew to conclude their entry plans. I remained behind as they started to line up and go inside the garage.

The smoke alarms were still sounding off, but the gas and smoke had dissipated. I could now see bullet holes in both of the cars inside the garage. Water was still spraying nearby the water heater, and water was flowing from the garage and down the driveway apron.

It seemed like ten minutes passed without hearing a word from the team. We held our positions until the all clear was given. Art finally came out and said that the suspect was right where I said he was, and he was dead.

I went over to the lieutenants, who advised me that homicide was en route and wanted to talk with the team as soon as possible. So for the next hour or so we stood by in the street waiting for their arrival. The time went by slowly and very little talk was exchanged. The stillness was mind raking. I constantly went through my thoughts to examine if I had done anything in error.

I remembered seeing the suspect the first time. I was sure there was nothing in his hands, or I would have noticed. After all, that's the only place where suspects carry and shoot from. I kept going back to the suspect's first defiant glance as I was yelling at him. No, there was no gun, I was positive. So he must have picked up the gun in the short time he moved out of my view and then appeared in the kitchen.

Larrell was third man in, so he had to have seen the suspect before I did, because his angle of view of the kitchen and dining room was much better than mine.

When the homicide detectives arrived at the house, it was so densely permeated with tear gas and smoke the detectives couldn't get past the front door. They decided they couldn't see anything for now and must wait until the gas diminished and dissipated a great deal more. (It turned out later that it took three days before homicide detectives could enter.)

We were told to return to our unit and await homicide there until each was interviewed individually.

The homicide lieutenant just so happened to be my ex-academy staff sergeant, Lt. Don B. As I described what had happened, I felt comfortable with him, because he was always a fair man. He asked direct questions on the shots being fired. When he asked me how many shots I fired, I paused and started to think. I answered that I fired six bullets from my pistol, went to reload, and saw the H&K MP5 lying right in front of me and saw it was in the semimode. So I holstered my weapon and picked up the H&K MP5. I fired on the small wall on the semimode, and the suspect started to slither feet first across the floor. I continued to fire as the suspect kept moving, so I continued firing until he stopped moving, and when he stopped moving, I stopped shooting.

With that in consideration, my first six came from my revolver and possibly another thirty, if the magazine was full, from the H&K MP5. In total thirty-eight from me, possibly.

I was asked later on if there was anything that I regretted that I did during the shooting. I stated that when I ran out of ammo twice during the shooting, I realize that running out of ammo was not very smart to do, because it left me vulnerable both times. Should there have been another aggressive suspect, my position and other team members' lives would have been compromised. I was asked if there was anything else that should have occurred. I exclaimed I wished I'd had a five hundred-round magazine and a bayonet. That punk killed my friend and sergeant, and I wasn't through with him. Additionally, I was very pleased the young kids didn't come out during my shooting rage, because I probably would have shot them as well and would never have lived that situation down.

When we were back at the bureau awaiting homicide, I was walking around outside in the parking lot area constantly going through what had happened. I was out there for about a half hour and a fellow deputy, Rich D., came up to me from the rear, stuck five bucks in my hand, said, "That's for a few beers later, Larry!"

He was hinting to me, perhaps, that I was steaming with second guessing and about ready to blow apart. I barked at him that I felt he was watching me too much, and he should mind his own damn business. Later, I learned he was ordered to watch me closely and get me whatever I wanted— which is actually a department policy when there is an officer-involved shooting. Boy, did I feel stupid for being so mean, and to top it off, he was also one of my past cadets and now a team member. (Sorry, Rich, and thanks for keeping an eye on me.)

One of the two assistant sheriffs, Jerry H., drove by where I was walking. He stopped close by and paused, apparently wanting to talk. I approached him while he was seated in his car and placed both of my hands on the open window of the driver's door.

He asked, "You doing all right, Larry?" I responded, "I guess so, I'm just wondering what I could have done differently!"

He looked at me and said sincerely, "You did a good job out there, Larry. I'm proud of you!" That message felt good coming from him, because he was one of the most honored and treasured superiors I've ever work with. He also was one of my Firestone Station lieutenants over twelve years earlier and was well liked by many within the department. I certainly appreciated his remarks. They took a huge load off of my mind, thinking maybe I erred or was viewed as excessively violent. I didn't want either and was actually second guessing myself continually.

———

The funeral was huge. All of the LAPD/SWAT personnel came in uniform, and there had to be a couple of thousand friends, family, and onlookers present.

We had practiced for several hours folding the American flag and controlling our emotions. We stood proudly over the flag-draped casket of our sergeant and close companion. He was the second SWAT officer in the United States to be killed in the line of duty. Many times we discussed some very sensitive issues that would surface as we folded the American flag. It was very important to hold back our emotions until the flag was folded.

Well, unfortunately that didn't happen; Steve was the first to break down, and then it carried over to all of us. It was impossible to stop, but we finished our flag folding and passed it on to the sergeant, who in turn gave it to Larrell's wife.

This somber occasion lasted for about an hour, and during that time, our thoughts were on our team sprit and loyalty. The times we worked together will always be on our minds and probably for the rest of our lives.

Analysis: The bullet that struck Larrell actually was a ricocheting round from a Super .38 automatic pistol. That round initially struck diagonally across the top two-inch strap of a bulletproof Velcro attachment on his right shoulder. After the ricochet, the bullet struck and penetrated the lower right base of his skull. The bullet then traversed diagonally through his head and struck Larrell's upper left supraorbital ridge above his left eye and literally fell into his goggles.

If Larrell's body was in the window, he must have had his left foot stuck in the window, based on the trajectory of the fired round that caught him with his head turned away from the suspect. He was probably focused on his foot, in an arching motion. That would account for the killing round to have traveled in such an odd path.

On the other hand, Larrell may have seen the suspect pointing a weapon at him, and he turned away to his left to avoid being struck, which is unlikely. We've all been intensely trained to face the gunfire and never turn away.

Both paramedic deputies, of substantial strength, were having a rough time trying to pick up dead weight from the window area. Anyone of smaller stature or weakened strength would have never been able to lift a two-hundred-pound dead body weight from that angle, especially over a two-and-a-half-foot window ledge.

Those two ESD paramedics, who were in superb condition, braved the intense firing that was going on and were still strong enough to pick up the body and carry him from the window.

To empty my weapons twice was not very smart. Both times I was actually stuck with an empty gun, and just by chance I retrieved Larrell's gun and emptied it as well. I needed to go to the window as Larrell was being pulled out and was able to grab two additional thirty-round magazines from his vest.

Cross-training with all team firearms is a must. In this case I was fully aware of the weapon's function and was able to shoot it immediately.

When the bullets started to fly, the men in front of the garage door, Bobby A., and near the sliding glass doors, Nick and Gil were in the middle of a large volley of fired bullets and were ducking and dodging all projectiles that came outside the home. That in itself could have had inflamed the already tragic consequences and several team members might have been struck in the interior fire fight. Fortunately, they were behind a six-foot block wall that stopped all of the small arms fire from the .38 cal, 9 mm, and shotgun rounds. So it is very important to have rounds designed to stay close and not travel too far.

When Rich fired fourteen rounds from the inside wall near the kitchen/dining room access, quite a few of his rounds went into the wall behind the suspect next to the kitchen access to the garage, passed through the wall, and hit the cars and the water heater in the garage.

Many ricocheted into the garage door where they passed through easily narrowly missing Bobby A. outside on the driveway apron, causing him to dance around.

Knowledge of construction is a must. I knew full well my rounds were passing through dry wall easily and strike anything on the opposite side. It didn't really matter to me where I was hitting the suspect. Striking him anywhere was my focus.

CHAPTER 119

A FRIEND

I've stopped drunk drivers in nearly all areas of Los Angeles County. I've arrested many and have released many as well, taking them home and locking their keys in the trunk of their cars.

I've also had some chuck their car keys, or throw them, into dense tall foliage, where it would take a sober person to find them.

Many questioned my decision to release them because of the pressure from MADD, or the department policies and procedures that were changed in the midseventies because of one drunk driver who returned to his car shortly after being taken home by two deputies. That driver was involved in a crash that killed an innocent party in another car. The deputies in that case had found the driver asleep in his car and decided to drive him home, rather than arrest him. So much for spirit of the law, which I'm sure the deputies were pondering when deciding not to take the driver to jail. They suffered departmental discipline for their compassionate feelings, and maybe they were terminated as well.

I was working at Special Enforcement Bureau during the day when one of our guys came in and stated that a deputy was at the infamous Jap Shack, in East Los Angeles Station's area, and was very drunk. He mentioned his name, Tommy E., a former Firestone Park Station deputy who I worked with for several years. I was aware he had a drinking problem and was afraid he was going to try to go home in his car. I jumped into my own private car, drove the short distance to the bar, and met up with the deputy. I played several rounds of pool with him to size him up and determined he was way too inebriated to drive. I convinced him to come with me to SEB to continue with our pool games and that our pool tables, at SEB, were in much better condition.

He finally agreed to come with me because I promised him I would return him to the bar as soon as we were through. When we got to the bureau and got out of my car, he asked where the pool table was. I told him that there was no pool table and that he was way too drunk to drive. I said I would take him home, rather than to see him try to drive.

He cussed at me and told me to go to hell and walked toward the back gate to SEB. I followed him and watched him try to open the gate which was padlocked. He was very bitter toward me and was trying to scale the seven-foot block wall when I pulled him down and told him he wasn't going anywhere.

He began to fight me, but I put him in an arm lock and took him into the bureau hallway. He was yelling at me as I dragged him into the woman's restroom and handcuffed him to a leather lounge so he couldn't leave. I asked the desk to release him in four to five hours, but no sooner, because he was way too drunk. The desk followed my orders and released him about four hours later. They said he yelled and screamed for several minutes, but ultimately fell asleep.

I never heard from him again until a few months ago—actually twenty-five years later—and found out he left the department soon after our engagement and realized he had an alcohol problem.

Tommy approached me and told me what had happened, and it caught me by surprise. Our recent meeting was at an event where the life of a fellow Firestone Park Station deputy, SLD, was being celebrated at his passing.

It was good to see many of my fellow deputies from long ago, as we rehashed our experiences and friends.

I guess the old adage is true, that friends don't let friends drive drunk. Tommy passed away in 2011, and I hope he forgave me for my independent thoughts and deeds.

CHAPTER 120

I SMELL A CROOK

I arrived at my home in the Mission Viejo area, at around two thirty in the morning. It was at least an hour of driving from the Special Enforcement Bureau, where I just completed ten hours of saturation patrol in the East Los Angeles Station's area.

I was tired and ready to hit the sack, when a radio transmission indicated a call-out in the Rancho Palos Verdes Estates area at the top of the hill. The on-call team was activated and had to roll immediately. That distance was at least a fifty-minute hard drive. I didn't even get out of the patrol car and just cranked up the car, drove away from the front of my home, and drove like hell to get to the command post.

The command post was several blocks away from the targeted home, at the top of the posh residential area of Rancho Palos Verde Estates, just west of the city of Los Angeles and south of Torrance and Lomita. The area encompasses the cliffside area of Portuguese Bend and the coastline west of Cabrillo Beach, where I used to surf in my high-school days.

I got there in about an hour and quickly suited up in my SWAT gear, loaded up my weapons, and was ready in about ten minutes. Our team assembled behind one of the units. We were given the specifics of what had happened and directions to the home where the suspects were holed up.

There had been an armed robbery down the hill at a liquor store. The two men who pulled the robbery jumped into their car right in front of several sheriff's deputies just as they were arriving on the scene. The suspects and deputies saw one another as they converged. Needless to say, the chase was on. The suspects sped away with smoking tires, up the posh hill and into the elegant neighborhood that seldom comforted the obvious lowlife crooks on its upper-class streets. Security in this neighborhood was tight. Nearly every home had uniformed security guards. Bodyguards, usually off-duty policemen, are deployed to the rich and famous, depending on their security needs.

As they came into a tight turn, the suspect's car lost control, jumped the curb, and struck a boulder that was placed into the lawn by some landscaping artist, simulating the allure of a natural forest.

The suspects' left front tire flew off, rolled and hopped several times, and hit the front doors of a well-manicured Japanese-style home. Hearing the tremendous noise, the entire family of six fled the home and ran to the safety of their neighbors.

The two lowlife armed robbers were now stranded. They sought asylum in the pristine abode and were quickly surrounded by the sheriff's deputies, who ordered them out of the home. The suspects didn't respond to the warnings. Considering they were both armed during the robbery, the deputies established a guarded perimeter and a command post and requested SWAT.

By the time we arrived, were briefed, scouted the place out, and completed diagrams of the floor space, three hours had passed. The suspects were advised every ten minutes, from the public address system of the unit closest to the home, to come out and surrender because the SWAT team and several canine units were responding. That meant the crooks were warned at least six times per hour for three hours. Still no response!

The warnings continued, even as we were being deployed, and those warnings were recorded and noted. As far as the audibility was concerned, the command post was able to hear the announcements several blocks down the street.

The home was actually three stories, with the lower floor submerged in a small hill. This home was absolutely beautiful on the outside. We scouted the surroundings and took note of its niceties. The front doors were already torn from their hinges, creating easy access to the interior of the home.

We were ready, primed, and good to go about thirty minutes from the after-scout briefing, and moved into our respective positions. We made some small noises as we came into the home and again marveled at its surgical cleanliness; large floral ceramic urns that decorated the hallways seemed to be potential victims as well, if damaged by us or the soon-to-be-captured thugs.

One errant bullet would cause a large amount of damage in this home because of its uniqueness and the well-kept furniture, appliances, and artifacts.

I personally felt like a bull in a china shop, taking careful steps to ferret out these two cockroaches, hopefully without any severe damage to the home.

Everywhere we went in the home it was impeccably clean. We could see smudge marks across the floors, making it quite easy to track these fools, who were obviously hiding.

The five of us who were inside crept quietly and moved for a few seconds and then paused to listen for thirty seconds. This way, noise would give them away. We were using hand signals, the radios were very low, and talking and radio chatter were all in check. We used tape and cloth to keep the metal gear from clattering. Light discipline was a must and lights were sparingly used. We kept moving, followed the scuff marks, and watched each other's backs as we ventured up the two-level stairs, and then deciding which way to go at the top.

One disturbing factor was that something was about to "pop off" soon, because we were running out of unsearched space. We neared a child's bedroom at the end of a hallway. My partner stood near the right side of the doorway, and I peered into the room. I detected strong musky body odor and sweat close by. I edged myself in the door. The odor was stronger, emanating from the bed eight feet away. The bed was low profile; the box spring was four inches from the floor. The blankets and top white sheet were thrown back as if someone had jumped out of bed. I scanned the room and couldn't detect any movement or outward signs of a human form, but my eyes kept returning to the center of the bed, which seemed to be moving slightly upward, as if someone was under the bed.

Usually, if we were quiet, we could hear the heavy panting of a suspect as we drew closer. The suspect would be breathing heavier in anticipation of our contact and in reaction to their concealment. If this one was armed only with a pistol, he could not swing his arms and hands while the bed was on top of him. I signaled to my partner that the suspect was under the bed.

He gave me a thumbs-up signal, and I handed him my sawed-off shotgun to sling and prepare to cover me as I approached the bed.

I crept silently near the bed, put my arm up, and delivered the one, two, three countdown with three extended fingers. I jumped onto the center of the bed and bounced as if on a trampoline. I could hear moaning and groaning coming from under the mattresses and finished with the trampling after five to six times.

I jumped quickly from the bed and grabbed the edge of the box spring and flung it backward, exposing the male suspect unfolding his contorted body. If he had a gun, it didn't matter. I was all pumped up. I grabbed one wrist and the back of his pants and swung him swiftly across the room into a wall, hoping to knock him out.

Unfortunately the walls were constructed of drywall material on both sides. The suspect's head went entirely through both sides of the wall. His hair was visible just above the tile in the small bathroom. He was screaming as I manhandled him until I was satisfied that he was unarmed and presented no immediate threat to the other team members. I threw him to the floor and pounced on him, as if he was a small pony that was prepped, readied and saddled-up for a short ride. I flex-cuffed him and handed him off to another team member, who swiftly directed him outside the home.

During this brief ordeal he was screaming to high heaven. I guess after hearing his buddy scream so much, it caused the other suspect to come out of hiding, farther down the opposite side of the floor.

With his hands in the air, he surrendered himself without any prompting just as we were about to come his way. He, too, was bound, guided out quickly, and handed off to the uniformed handling deputies.

The only injuries the first suspect sustained were minor abrasions and bumps, probably from his head going through the wall. He was treated by the paramedics at the scene and taken to the hospital for examination and approval for booking.

CHAPTER 121

BEHIND THE CURTAIN

We were summoned to the Norwalk Station area to a home that was owned by a fireman, who told us he had several guns inside, available to anyone who might be in the house. In a bedroom closet there were a couple of handguns, shotguns, and rifles, and several boxes of ammo for each weapon on the shelf inside the closet as well. The problem was that at least one or two suspects were hunkered down in his home, unable to escape because of the rapid response and containment by the Norwalk deputies.

The crooks had been in the burglarized home for nearly two hours prior to our arrival. Announcements warned the suspects that canine units and SWAT were en route. There wasn't any response to the warnings; however, the warnings were repeated every ten to fifteen minutes.

There were no indicators of how many suspects were actually in the home other than the initial sightings of two Hispanic men. One was very thin, and the other was chubby.

We completed our scouting, briefing, and placement of team personnel and closed our approach near the front window. Several tear-gas canisters were lobbed inside, and we waited outside for a reaction for at least fifteen minutes. This was time to let the gas permeate the home. There was still no response, so entry was about to happen quickly, and we would confront the suspects one way or another.

We were ready to go, gas masks on. We made our way in, searching methodically in each room and working carefully not to overlook any nook or cranny where a thug could conceal himself. We moved slowly and tried to keep our positions quiet as possible, careful not to give away our interior movements.

We were moving down the narrow hallway, after clearing the front room and a bedroom. We came upon a medium-size bathroom; I looked behind the door, noting it was clear.

The only thing we were unable to easily see was what was behind the opaque, flowered shower curtain draped outside the white porcelain tub, just about six inches from the floor. I knew full well as I was moving that my M-17 tear-gas mask makes substantial breathing noises, especially when in confined empty rooms like a bathroom. The noise is just like Darth Vader in *Star Wars*. I was breathing steadily making the flutter valves open and close distinctly, making a sound like "shhcka- kaacc," as I shuffled across the room, passing the toilet to my right and coming upon the curtain. The noise from the gas mask was irritating, because it was too loud.

356

My partner was right behind me by the doorway, covering the curtain as I moved closer. I was armed with a sawed-off shotgun with a sling and poised to see if something moved behind the curtain.

The shower curtain was furled and folded vertically as they were designed to do, and it provided an excellent concealment if someone was standing right behind it, motionless, in the tub.

I was now about two feet from the shower curtain and could see the corner of a short-sleeved shirt just barely peeking beyond the edge of the curtain. I couldn't see much of anything else, but the vague shadow of a human being on the other side of the curtain. I turned to my backup and signaled that I saw someone inside the tub, by pointing two fingers just under my eyes.

He indicated he understood, as I readied my shotgun and grabbed both the stock and barrel for a butt stroke. I slammed the side of the sawed-off stock into the curtain, at around the suspect's jaw level.

There was a horrendous yell as the suspect fell backward and into the ceramic tub. The shower curtain was pulled with him into the tub, popping off the plastic hooks that were holding the curtain to a supporting rod above the tub. Those hooks popped and bounced all over the room and in the tub as well.

I jumped right on top of him as he was wiggling around, still concealed under the shower curtain. I jumped on him five to six times on top of the curtain and listened to him scream. I still didn't know if he was armed or not, and I pulled the shower curtain back to expose him. He was bleeding steadily from his head. Fresh blood and hot water were funneling down the drain.

Apparently, when the suspect fell backward, the side of his neck hit the hot water handle, turned it on, and knocked the spindle off the stem. This caused the hot water to turn on and pour down his neck. As I grabbed him by his hair and pulled him upward blood was pouring down his neck and all over his clothes.

We quickly cuffed him and wrapped a towel around his head to stop the bleeding. Then we completed the search of the home. As it turned out, the suspect we captured was the only one inside the house.

He received emergency treatment by our paramedics just outside the home. Later it was revealed that two other suspects had been in the home as well, but they got away prior to the initial perimeter containment.

CHAPTER 122

MEDIA APATHY: A DECISION FROM THE HEART

We were on our way back from Compton court in the northbound lanes of the Long Beach freeway and noticed cars braking and slowing down. Ahead we could see the black smoke billowing above gray smoke, as if there was a possible vehicle fire a short distance ahead.

We were in a marked patrol car, and we went over to the center lane, to go ahead of the pack of stopped cars to see if we could aid in the emergency. As we came upon the accident, my partner, Billy M., and I walked over to a sight that could only mean serious injuries or death.

A heavy-duty tractor trailer was precariously positioned atop a large passenger car. Both vehicles were steaming, with white smoke billowing above the blackened wreckage, emanating from the just-doused flames. The fire department was standing by a short distance away, because there was a lone passenger trapped inside the burned and crushed car.

The fire captain said there was nothing they could do for the passenger. The woman's body was in the rear seat, and her neck was pinned under the collapsed ceiling of the car which was crushed just inches above the front headrest. Fluids from the leaking tractor and car ignited and sparked a fire. The fire consumed the entire car and tractor, except the attached trailer.

The fire was quite intense and roared for about ten minutes until the fire department arrived to extinguish the flames. Several passengers and the driver escaped from the car, leaving the forty-year-old woman pinned inside.

The truck driver as well was able to escape, and all ran to the side of the freeway to avoid the raging fire and a possible explosion.

We stood there for a few seconds to see if we could help, but we couldn't discern where the body was positioned in all of the charred clumps of material inside the car. Suddenly I saw a slight movement on the middle portion of the headrest. I drew closer, and the clump of charred remnants opened its eyes and moved them as if trying to focus. The whites of her eyes contrasted with the surrounding charred interior and left the shape of the rest of her head to the imagination. She was blinking slowly. No words or tones were heard; only slight head movement and the delayed blinking of the eyes suggested the semblance of a life form. I felt extreme sorrow for her plight and could only wish the emergency equipment would arrive quickly.

All of a sudden a media photographer came to the front of the car and began to take pictures of the gruesome sight. I heard the rapid clicking of the camera, and the sound triggered a personal switch in my mind. He was inches away from the hood of the car, focused on the charred victim. This photographer had no empathy for the woman's misfortune and was capitalizing on the opportunity of a photo-op.

Without thinking too clearly, I grabbed the photographer by the shirt collar and the seat of his pants, ran him to the side of the freeway, and chewed his ass out for his lack of respect for the dignity of the dying woman. I felt that if I were the person inside the burned-out car, I would be incensed at anyone taking my picture as I was dying in such a grotesque way.

After admonishing the photographer for his lack of empathy, I warned him that if he returned to the front of the car, he would be taken to jail, although I knew I would be chastised by my department. I actually surprised myself, because I acted out of common decency, though rage provoked my reaction, just like in a shooting.

My partner, Billy M., was a little concerned. He agreed with me about the impropriety, but he didn't approve of the way I behaved. He nodded and smirked, as he always did, at my decision-making process.

When the rescue equipment arrived, and the California Highway Patrol took our position, we left without further ado. We never learned what happened to the poor soul in the car, but I believe she must have died from the entire body trauma.

When we returned to SEB, I immediately informed my sergeant and lieutenant and gave the circumstances to the ordeal. I'm sure they were comfortable with my reactions, but our department enjoys a special relationship with the media. In the end, I'm sure a call was made to the sheriff's information bureau, who located the photographer and the news outlet he worked with to remedy any wrongdoings.

CHAPTER 123
FATAL PROGNOSIS

To be selected to work the Special Enforcement Bureau can be viewed as an achievement for a hardworking patrol deputy with unique characteristics. He must be a hard-charging enthusiastic workaholic with an endless thirst for challenge and tasks no one else would even contemplate. When given an order, he must obey immediately, or there might be deadly consequences. Most who apply to the bureau have a desire for training for combat and tactical situations. The normal station officer couldn't even comprehend the amount of special training necessary to perfect the skills to reach successful outcomes.

At times there was a program that the Bureau offered for all patrol stations to send their best for an extra two weeks of special training in tactics, weapons training, and command-post operations. The deputies who came to those specialized classes were ecstatic about the training and the opportunity to meet and mingle with SWAT team members. This program also served to unify the bureau personnel and patrol deputies and show them that we were reasonable and approachable. Often station personnel thought of SEB as a batch of arrogant, pompous deputies who looked pretty in uniforms but followed too strict a disciplinary code that didn't match their method of operations.

The key is to be ready for anything. If someone is barricaded inside a house, garage, building, desert shack, industrial complex, bus, car, boat, or train, it may have dire and deadly consequences.

SWAT must work with hostage negotiators. While the negotiating experts negotiate, the team is working hard to prepare for the reasonable chance the bad guy will run out suddenly and attempt to escape at a moment's notice. Each team trains in numerous scenarios with possible different outcomes each time.

Team members train to the point where they perceive danger as a mere consequence that they hopefully have trained enough to overcome. Team members are so well adapted to stressful situations that their egos are cultivated sharpened to a fine point. Their attitude is they can handle anything and welcome adversity. SWAT will undoubtedly face complex situations from martial arts experts to combat veterans who have slipped into the morass of homelessness and are looking for what is known as a "suicide by cop."

Their class A uniform appearance as well as their grooming habits are above normal. They have performed internal security for the Academy Awards in formal civilian dress. It is not viewed as a difficult task and has been the assignment many times for several teams at once.

The mind-set at the bureau is competitive. If you're promoted coming from the Special Enforcement Bureau, more than likely you will be assured involvement in training elements wherever you are assigned. Most other units know full well how you were trained and will not question your tenacious ability and wisdom. We all competed with one another, and team competitiveness was encouraged to see who was the best and most tactically sound. Each team blended many different characters into a tight and efficient working unit, each member supporting the others, but too many of the best bulking up one team was discouraged.

One of our guys, B.W., was in his prime and well entrenched with his team. He was very pleased with his level of achievements and seemed very happy and content with life. He had a wife and two small children and lived in a nice house not too far from work.

While working out daily is required and top physical condition is a necessity, it is imperative that if something is giving you trouble physically, you must correct that ailment, quickly.

B.W. went to the doctor to find out why he was wearing out fast and tiring too quickly. He went to several doctors and was finally diagnosed with multiple sclerosis. He was alarmed and questioned the doctors. They reaffirmed their diagnosis of MS and also said that the prognosis was grim.

They informed him that within a year he would be an invalid and need at-home care to the point where he would be unable to care for his personal hygiene. He was absolutely shocked and discouraged by their prognosis.

He took time off from work and was at home for a couple of weeks and decided that he didn't want to go through the torment of this catastrophic illness. Many of his fellow team members came by his home and called to check on his well-being, and to see if they could help in any way with his grief or homelife.

He knew that his wife, kids, and friends were going to be run into the ground by his illness, and he couldn't bear their drawn-out grief.

Unfortunately, he decided to finish the disease early by ending his life and any further suffering by all.

May God console his talented young soul. He'll be missed by all and not forgotten.

I certainly hope the doctors who cared for him diagnosed his condition correctly, because if you are at the peak of life and then slammed head first into the ground, reason may not guide your judgment.

CHAPTER 124

THE TEACHER

I was asked by two of the most dedicated instructors in "officer survival" instruction, Sam M. and Carroll H., if I would like to accompany them to teach up north in Eureka, California. This was a week-long assignment at the College of the Redwoods, Humboldt County. The class was going to be approximately thirty officers from a wide variety of agencies from all over the country. The pay was $1,500 for the week, and airfare and accommodations would be paid fully.

I was honored to be asked by these two, because Carroll H. was now a lieutenant who was promoted and transferred from the Special Enforcement Bureau after serving as an honorable and great sergeant at the bureau. Carroll wrote a monthly article called "Keys to Survival" in a department paper. It provided persuasive information about survival on the streets for an ordinary street officer.

Sam M. was a gifted sergeant from the Special Enforcement Bureau as well. His talent was firearms, and if you took one of his classes you would definitely change your habits. He was now retired because of back injuries sustained on the job and now was running a variety of weapons classes on the go, throughout the entire state.

Both of these men had unmatched teaching skills and were embraced by all whom they instructed. I was deeply honored to be asked by them to teach with them, and I had plenty of available time to take off.

I was to catch a plane from Ontario to San Francisco and then transfer to a small puddle jumper to take me to Arcata, California. This was a airport just north of Eureka. From Arcata, the hotel shuttle would take me to the hotel, where I met up with Sam and Carroll. Several times I was accompanied by Carroll because he lived near me in the Baldwin Park area. At the hotel we would go over the agenda and what I would be doing. My part was going to be "weapon retention" and "weapon takeaway," which I felt very comfortable with, because I had taught several weapon retention/takeaway classes. The other classes were counter-sniper techniques and building searches. Our tasks of timing and class curriculum were very important and had to abide by the police officer standards of training (POST) requirements.

The class of police officers was great. They all appreciated the time away from their respective departments and thoroughly enjoyed the information we were giving them. Rain or shine—and it did rain heavily at times—the class continued without any glitches.

We usually started off our classes by stating the old adage, "Those who can, do, and those who can't, teach."

This described our attitude and the type of instruction they were about to receive. It usually broke any barriers the officers came in with by generating laughter.

The quality and level of instruction was the in-your-face type, meaning we were literally in each person's face and body to clearly demonstrate the class objectives. This was highly effective and very little instruction was given from the lectern. This was key. We would demonstrate on each other until it was performed correctly.

The area was surrounded by Victorian-style homes and had history at every turn. The city just south of Eureka is Ferndale, which might have had maybe fifty homes and a lighthouse.

Each home is distinctly early nineteen hundreds, their bushes are magnificent topiary examples, and their yards are beautiful.

We met the police chief of Ferndale, who was a retired chief petty officer from the navy. He had a five officers on his force, and three reserves. Although the pay was low, the surroundings would increase the lifespan ten years.

We even spent time passing through the graveyards to look at the dates of the deceased going back to the early eighteen hundreds. It was serene and peaceful and the foliage, trees, winding roads, dark green grasses on steeply sloped hills were beautiful. Deer romped about in dramatic splendor.

Another gorgeous area, a little farther south, is called the "Avenue of the Giants." Nothing could describe this area but the word amazing. A visit to this exceptionally tall redwood forest is breathtaking and a must-see by all.

Our off times were well spent at the famous Samoan Cookhouse, which was a large wharf house that fed lumberjacks near the port of Eureka, California. The food was abundant, as you could imagine, and great, so we ate there several times. Many bungalows housing the large lumberjack population, dot the surrounding hills. This cookhouse, which could probably serve several hundred at once, was neat and clean.

One afternoon we were all eating lunch. Carroll was seated immediately to my left. We were consuming our first course, split pea soup, while seated on one of the bench seats at the huge picnic tables. I was on about my third or fourth spoonful when I heard a distinct crack, liken to a small caliber weapon, coming from Carroll's position. Something ricocheted off the edge of my soup bowl and whatever it was settled in my soup. The next thing I heard was Carroll complain that part of his tooth blew out of his mouth as he was sipping the hot soup. The contrasting temperatures inside his mouth caused quarter-inch piece of his front tooth to dislodge and sail into my soup.

Carroll was a little miffed but wasn't in any pain. He was a bit humble about ruining my soup and that his body was prematurely falling apart. I didn't complain one bit because Carroll was such a nice and pleasant person. I did laugh a little, because it was the first time someone shot at me while I was eating.

In his years in the department, Carroll escaped death several times. Once near his home he was run over by a trash truck when he was driving his sports car. Another time, while assigned at the Special Enforcement Bureau, he had a major heart attack and was saved by another deputy, Ruly A., who gave him mouth to mouth resuscitation. After that episode it was necessary for Carroll to retire, because all of the attention he generated with his writing and instructional skills wore him out. Sam, on the other hand, had so many injuries he had difficulty moving around, and I figured out exactly why they picked me.

These two guys wanted me to pick up the slack and jump right in where they left off. That type of instruction required one or two of us to watch each other closely and blend in during the course.

We had excellent times teaching and being with one another, and we laughed as much as possible. We didn't care how poorly each officer thought of himself, it was our job to teach them skills to survive. There was nothing they could do wrong; we gave hand-to-hand instruction along the way. They all loved the instruction and our methods. Egos were checked at the door.

One afternoon, Sam was talking to the class and Carroll was team-teaching with Sam about bullet trajectories, specific objects that would stop a bullet, what type of round was being fired, and from what type of weapon.

The class started at noon, and it took about two hours to prep the class before coming to the range, where I was located. I had most of the displays set up and decided to walk up the embankment into the gorgeous surrounding forest. The trees were splendid. As I reached the top of the embankment I could see a dark hollow that seemed beautiful. It was well shaded by the tall trees. Right in the middle of the hollow there was one fallen tree with several branches jutting out from the four-foot trunk. The tree was bumpy with thick craggy bark, and a green waxy substance covered large sections of it.

This place was just over the hill from our range, with all of the concrete firing lines and well-defined bullet sand trap. It was relatively new and could easily accommodate a hundred shooters. It was extremely peaceful. There was a strong smell of pine needles. Cones were lying about by the hundreds. I thought that in about one hour, there was going to be a horrendous number of shots being fired from all of our automatic machine guns, including the AK-47s, which were really loud, like the shotguns. What a contrast to this serene forest atmosphere where I was seated on the fallen log. A slight breeze was coming through the tall pines and smaller redwood trees. The smell was very pleasing, and I was enjoying the calmness and tranquility.

I heard several small branches break and looked upward toward the edge of the shadowed hollow and saw five deer and a fawn coming my way. They were about fifty feet away and coming right toward me. The wind obviously was coming toward me as well, so the deer couldn't smell me. They couldn't see me unless I moved. I remained motionless and just watched them come closer and closer. I could hardly understand why they didn't realize my presence or miniscule movements. Maybe they just didn't expect a human in that area, because it was very rural. They came maybe ten feet from my seated position and were feeding on various items on the forest floor. The lead deer, of course the biggest, kept moving its head, attempting to capture a smell but couldn't quite figure it out. As the deer came closer, the others followed, curious. I think they could now sense I was close and were looking for some kind of movement, but I remained still. I was checking into an atmosphere of immense tranquility that not many people enjoy. I was ecstatic and I wanted to share it with friends and family. I knew if I moved, though, it would all be gone in a snap. These deer were clumped right in front of me, a splendid display of nature that no camera could ever capture.

This lasted maybe two minutes, at most, and then suddenly the lead deer alerted to a slight movement and probably detected my odor as well, and jumped away from my position. All of the other deer followed suit and dashed away from me, alarmed. The moment was indeed lost, but I remember it to this day. It will always be in my mind as one of the most beautiful moments I have ever seen, because it gave me a sense of clarity and introspection.

Unfortunately, the time was approaching for the demonstration, and soon the area would be anything but tranquil. I tried to share my observations with the class and my partners, but most of them thought I was nuts or had been drinking.

I argued that there wasn't any reason to scare the animals, so we should yell out "bang, bang" in lieu of firing all of the noisy machine guns. Of course that didn't go over well, and we immediately went back to the instruction at hand.

Six of the group was the Special Weapons Team from Sacramento. They were very receptive and quite enjoyable to be around. We spent several of our off hours at local bars, laughing and admiring each other's experiences. Their sergeant was a lot of fun and easy to get along with. The week was excellent.

Unfortunately, a couple of months later that same sergeant from the Sacramento SWAT team was shot in the head and killed as he leaned over a roof to get a better look at a suspect. This tragedy is often mentioned during trainings. It is always disturbing when someone whom we've known during training is torn from the long list of officer survival students and teammates.

I was involved in this type of instruction for nearly five years in Humboldt County, McClellan Air Force Base in Sacramento County, and Los Angeles

County at a variety of schools. It was a noble course of instruction and well accepted by all. I thoroughly enjoyed working with all and will remember the good instructional moments as well as the camaraderie. I certainly hope what they learned helped them in their daily endeavors.

(Point of information: A very interesting reading and history about Eureka is found in Wikipedia. Eureka was founded in 1856. Its history and treatment of the local American Indians is quite remarkable and should be published in its entirety. I'm sure today most Americans would cringe at the way our forefathers treated these people. Hopefully someone will make proper and suitable reparations.)

CHAPTER 125

E = MC2

The north end of Carson is a rather remote area where a lot of sneaky little buggers crawl around late at night stealing anything that isn't nailed down. There have been incidents where burglars entered a chrome plating building, where they have large areas with opened acid pits. You could only imagine what would be left if some nitwit burglar crawled into a building like this, late at night. I'm sure it has happened many times; but unfortunately there would be very little evidence left behind, other than random splashes of acid on the concrete walkway surrounding the pits. However that same risk goes for the cops who search the area as well. There would be nothing but a splash and a quick "yikes," and that would be the end of whoever fell in.

I'm of the opinion that being a thief is easy, to lie is easy, and to do something obviously wrong is easy. Yet there are individuals who claim it's because they were brought up wrong, grew up in a poor neighborhood, hung around the wrong people, were molested or beaten by their mom or dad, or were not breastfed. (Actually it's their lawyer who will quickly offer out some sort of bias or sad event that caused the idiot to murder his entire family.)

Whatever the excuse, it's just plain old stupidity. You know who I'm talking about—the ones who get stuck in precarious positions where they are apprehended quite easily because of "dumb luck." It's like the ones who get stuck in a chimney and have to wait for the fire department to rescue and bail them out so the police can take their lazy ass to jail.

I wish I could remember all of those times the stupid crooks were caught and the various assortments of snags that actually caught them. I can remember a few who really should have won the "idiot of the year" award. Some call me mean, but I say it is just the funniest thing in the world to see some of the suspects caught in these situations.

All along Wilmington Avenue, truckers parked their rigs along the soft shoulders of the road, with their freights in locked cargo containers or trailers or simply hooked directly to the trailers.

Most people see that these trucks are waiting for their delivery locations to open early the next day so they can off-load their material and get back to their home base to pick up another load. Truckers are a hardworking bunch and really don't need some idiot to come by and disrupt their workday by extending it for hours because of an investigation of a stolen or burglarized container.

There was one flatbed truck and trailer parked on the shoulder of Wilmington Avenue. It was loaded with three six-foot rolls of steel sheeting. It had the proper chain tie-downs, wooden wedges, and binder chains securely attached to prevent the rolls from moving or breaking loose from the flat-bed trailer. The binder chains are tightened by hand cranking the attached bar to the chains and trailer bed, making them very taut so there is no play whatsoever.

Well, it was around three in the morning, and there was very little vehicular or foot traffic. The rig had caught the eye of a brilliant thief. He lined up his half-ton, older-model pickup next to the full flatbed trailer. He parked it very close, hoping to transfer the valuable steel sheeting onto his truck and run off to enjoy the fruits of his plunder. I don't know the particulars of this theft or the actual IQ of the thief, but I'll leave that up to you, the reader.

It is unclear whether he released the binder chains, or gravity played a part, but somehow the roll of steel was set free to fall onto his pickup truck bed.

So what do you think happened? That small roll of steel weighs about ten to twelve thousand pounds, and when it rolled off of the trailer and onto the half-ton pickup, his scientific aim was accurate and the heavy roll landed on the center of the bed of his pickup beautifully. However a bigger problem revealed itself. The weight of the roll was so heavy it crushed the entire center of the pickup truck bed and part of the cab right down to the soft ground.

This error in calculation sent the now-truckless suspect running home to call the Carson sheriff's station to report his pickup truck stolen by some unknown persons. This is a typical response when suspects lose their vehicles during their crimes—they scurry home quickly to report the theft to the police.

Can you imagine what this thief told his buddies in jail when he was caught? I'll bet he'll tell everyone that he was wrongfully accused and was picked on because of his _____. I'll let you fill in the excuse.

CHAPTER 126

OH! OH!

The SWAT team was summoned to the Lennox Station area to capture two possible armed burglars trapped inside a house they were burglarizing. They were prevented from escaping by the rapidly responding station units.

It took about an hour for the team to respond and set up for deployment. The briefing was given. The station deputies were adamant that the burglars were trapped inside the home, unable to escape. Finally after a scouting detail returned, the entry plans were formulated and ready to go.

The burglars had been trapped for three hours, and they had ample time to prepare themselves for the impending onslaught of the SWAT team.

The team started off with the mandatory announcements deployment of tear gas. Then the team tossed two tear-gas grenades into the home. As training indicated, the team waited about ten minutes so the tear-gas elements would penetrate to optimum effect. They finally made entry and searched the entire home for over an hour. The team returned to the command post and stated the home was clear of any possible suspects. The house was about two thousand square feet of living space and a substantial area of attic space, all of which was methodically searched by the entry team.

When the team returned to the command post, they met up with the handling deputies from Lennox Station. The handling deputies were clear that the two suspects were inside—the SWAT team must have overlooked them.

An argument ensued, and SWAT returned and searched again, with more determination to find the burglars.

Again they finished and found no one. The team felt satisfied there was no one in the home and packed up their gear and returned to the bureau. They were a bit upset that the Lennox field deputies didn't believe them. Overlooking someone would be an embarrassment to the entire bureau.

Once the SWAT team left the location, the original handling Lennox Station deputies secured their supervisor's permission, masked up with their own tear gas masks, and went into the home a third time. It took them about twenty minutes to find them. They returned to the command post proudly, with the two crooks in tow. The watch commander of Lennox Station couldn't hold back his pride and called the SWAT team commander. He pompously reported their find and rightfully so.

When I found out the team had missed the suspects, and they were eventually found by the handling unit, I was flabbergasted. At a briefing later on that same evening, one of the team members admitted we all needed to practice searching attics more carefully. My response was that it was a very basic mistake to overlook someone if you and your team are not focused. I grabbed an empty cardboard box, threw it onto the ground, and declared, "You must treat a house like this box. It either has a human being inside or not. Careful searching is a must, and nothing can be overlooked."

Several critical problems could have occurred. One, if both handling deputies were so sure two burglars were inside, careful and more critical searching should have been done by perhaps another SWAT team. The other team might look in different places, which most likely would have revealed the burglars. Two, if the home was not carefully searched by either SWAT team or the returning handling deputies, it would have created an unsafe environment for whoever went in after the all-clear signal was erroneously announced.

It is no different to search a home today than in the years past. If handling deputies are adamant the suspects are in the home, then the team should believe them. To miss the suspects was a critical mistake, and no team should ever vacate the premises without the approval by all team members.

When an officer searches a vehicle, evidence may be overlooked. I've seen it many times. But if an assisting officer or partner searches the same vehicle a second time, then more than likely the evidence is found. This applies to searching everything, so don't take it personally when someone asks to search a second time. It's just good fundamental practice.

CHAPTER 127

"O CAPTAIN! MY CAPTAIN!"

Our captain wasn't too well liked, nor was he the sharpest knife in the drawer, but he was still the captain. He was very religious, and that helped inspire various mean pranks to discourage his efforts to find out who was involved and throw them out of the unit. I'm not admitting my involvement in any of the pranks, but let's say I knew very well those things that were going on. Several other guys were committing the pranks as a form of hazing.

I performed a few and forgot half of the ones I did, but now I feel that it was wrong. I am sorry, but I still encourage hazing of individuals. It's a sign of recognition and admiration, definitely not understood by nerds. Oh yes, there are some meanspirited people who have a another agenda and create hateful hazing, but that kind of frolic is not the same type, and it tarnishes all hazing. I preferred to haze individuals who were liked, to welcome them to a tight-knit unit of team members. I believe our captain was a nice man, a full-blown nice guy, very friendly, but just basically a nerd, in my view.

So he walked into his office on a Monday morning around eight o'clock. As he unlocked his office and opened the door, the three ducks that had been locked inside the office began quacking their heads off. The room was covered with duck crap. On his desk, floor, and file cabinets, the mire of malodorous aviary feces permeated the room and dirtied the Spartan administrative décor.

Because the Special Enforcement Bureau was located in an area that was about 150 feet from a large duck pond, sometimes errant ducks, mostly mallards, would find their way into the hallways and rooms of the Bureau, bunch up, and hide.

Most of the other surrounding buildings experienced the same problem as East Los Angeles Station, which was directly connected with SEB east of the pond, and the East Los Angeles County courthouse on the west side of the pond.

At first glance most deceptive minds would immediately think the ducks that were locked inside the room were placed there on purpose. But the intuitive mind would consider the possibility that the ducks might have cornered themselves without any human interaction. Yeah, really!

A month or two went by. The captain came in, unlocked his office door, and started his daily routine. He sat at his wooden desk, placed his paperwork on top of the desk, and went through his handwritten messages. He unlocked his desk drawers and settled down to the business affairs, adjusting small message notes in priority of importance, and handling several waiting telephone calls.

He then opened the right top desk drawer and let out a scream like a banshee. An emergency services sergeant heard the screams and rushed into the captain's office. He observed the captain wriggling in his large leather chair, his little feet barely touching the ground.

He pointed his shaking finger to the upper right top drawer with his eyes wide open, yelling for the sergeant to see what was in his drawer.

As the sergeant came around the desk and looked into the drawer, his eyes focused on a large colored photo of two nuns having oral sex with a naked man. The sergeant had to hold a serious, stoic face of disgust and painstakingly side with the captain's outrage of disgust and dismay.

I'll bet that picture was carefully scrutinized and examined for any evidence of fingerprints or DNA to reveal a suspect or suspects. I don't know if the captain had to go to therapy because of the intense shock he was subjected to, but I do know the room was sealed off until the forensic scientists had a crack at the evidence.

No one was identified as the culprit, and so the captain was very careful of his everyday habits and became much more circumspect. Hmm, some people just can't take a joke.

Time finally came when the captain of the Special Enforcement Bureau was transferred to Lynwood station. His loss was our gain. His replacement was a heavyset black captain with a smile that seemed a little deceptive and carried a certain amount of suspicion as what he was going to do. His first edict was related to me. We met to discuss a disciplinary action I happened to be contesting. That story will be discussed in another chapter.

Several of the boys did celebrate the new captain's arrival by going into his personal bathroom and gluing cotton balls all over the walls surrounding the toilet. On the floor, directly in front of the toilet was a current copy of *Jet*, a magazine geared for black people. This was obviously to point out his background and achievement of becoming the first black captain at the bureau.

The idea was to keep him entertained while he sat on the bowl. He could could pick cotton when he liked or read *Jet*. Oh yeah, that was racially motivated and just mean. How did he respond to the mischief, you ask? He laughed and shook his head and took it rather coolly. Nothing else was said and the removal of the cotton and book was done in the evening hours that same night.

These things that occurred to the new captain resonated a glorious welcome that he was good tough stuff and focused on our mission of readiness and intense training and immediate response.

To top it off this guy was about as nice a guy as you could imagine. He was married to a Caucasian wife. I don't know if that was a good sign, but he was taking Maalox by the quart. This is the heavy stuff when the acid in your system is wearing out your stomach lining.

He laughed a lot and fit like a glove. Bureau problems just plain disappeared, and this captain was involved in everything. He knew exactly what to do. He had a great spirit and knowledge of direction and purpose.

One day, I was working day shift for some reason, cleaning weapons in the assembly room, and I decided to play with the new captain. I knew he was in his office down the long hallway doing tedious paperwork.

I took the "egg," a black bowling ball, and set it on the linoleum floor just outside the assembly room. It had been tested before on the low gradient of the entire floor. It was at a pitch of about a quarter inch per ten feet. When the ball was placed on the floor at the opposite end of the hallway, it would roll very slowly all the way down to the other end of the hallway and stop right next to the captain's office door.

The distance was about 150 feet, so it took quite some time to roll the whole hallway. Any person who worked at the unit could discern the noise, as it lazily traveled its course. By the time it was at the end, the heavy ball would clunk against the metal doors, and its noise would echo in the empty hallway.

Apparently the captain was fully aware of what was coming, because he spoke out loudly right after the clunking noise, "Rupp, knock it off!" I swear he didn't see me at all, but drew the assumption that I had something to do with it. Maybe he was clairvoyant.

Yet another time, when we were about to serve a no-knock warrant, we needed a black deputy to drive a van loaded with team personnel up to the Nickerson housing projects.

We were fresh out of possible drivers and needed someone who wouldn't choke at the first sight of danger. Guess who volunteered and actually got the job. You're right—our fearless leader, the captain, who was itching to get involved in something with our teams.

When it came time to drive, he sported a porkpie hat and other casual clothes. The outfit made him look the part, so we could get up nice and close. He enjoyed it as much as we did his company. I'll always remember how much he fit into our plans, because it made him smile a whole lot.

When I got out of the van, I tried to shoot out the streetlight bordering the projects with a sawed-off shotgun. I hit the damn light three times, but it wouldn't break. On the fourth round it smashed the light, and I damn near stuck my thumb in my eye.

The captain and other team members were razzing me as if I was missing the light, but I wasn't. I believe the pellets were glancing off the heavy glass shroud, because sparks were flying everywhere every time I fired.

As I was trying to shoot out the street light, believe it or not, the entry announcement was being given over the air horn. Suddenly the person we were trying to apprehend came running out of the complex screaming, "Don't shoot me; please don't shoot me!" The suspect thought we were shooting at him and promptly surrendered.

The time this captain was at the bureau was good for our department and a great standard for all others who were going to try to fill this man's shoes.

CHAPTER 128

AW, NUTS—EXIT STAGE LEFT: ADIOS AMIGOS

It had been eight and a half years since I came to the Special Enforcement Bureau and was dealt a hand of great comrades in arms. The extensive training and a wealth of experiences are permanently branded in my memory.

I was offered a position at the sheriff's academy for a spot in the advance officer training unit. The job there was going to be all about officer survival and training and preparing the entire department for the 1984 Olympics for crowd and riot formations, command post operations, hazardous materials instruction, weapon retention and weapon takeaway.

This offer was very enticing and would give me an opportunity to adequately prepare for the upcoming sergeant exam, and I would be in an ideal spot for promotion. My last days were coming up and there was some training going on at the infamous Pitchess Honor Rancho, and an after-action barbecue. This was probably my last training day and an opportunity to be with all of the guys and the new captain.

The training was very active and mostly at the range with a whole lot of shooting on the range and at the tire house. These days were very physical, with timed volleys of fire in a complex series of obstacle courses.

In the afternoon, a couple of the lieutenants approached me and informed me that a large group of my comrades were going to jump me and haze me to the max. I thanked them for their info and mentally prepared myself for the onslaught. It was now nearing the latter part of the day, and the training wound up. We prepared ourselves for the barbecue. We were in a hidden area away from view and earshot of everyone. Everyone was drinking beer and relaxing, so I got two rubber baseball grenades. I pulled both of the pins and kept the spoons from springing away by holding the grenades in each hand.

If anyone offered me a beer, I took the beer and held it between the two live baseball grenades and drank my beer slowly.

This tactic prevented anyone from jumping me and attempting to do anything to me. If they did, they would suffer the consequences of tear-gas exposure.

I stayed among the lieutenants, who repeatedly warned me that the guys were going to jump me and do something really crass. My comments were curt, filled with expletives degrading my attackers and their lack of courage and strength to even get near me because of what I was capable of doing.

I saw quite a few of them conniving and mingling like a pack of female wolves, but lacking the initiative, stamina, and courage of real men. Of course this was increasing their anxiety to jump my rear end and do bad things. I said,

"There aren't enough of them to do anything," and continued to drink my beer slowly.

It took about an hour and a half for the boys to get inebriated enough to jump me. I was standing and talking with two lieutenants when the whole pack jumped me and took me down.

Of course the two baseball grenades fell and gassed everyone nearby. About five threw up everything they had just consumed.

Everyone else was gassed as they tried to run; I believe there were about thirty I caught with copious amounts of tear gas. They began to run including the bunch that grabbed me, although some fell trying to get away and others ran into each other. I know I got them good and expected swift retaliation.

They dragged me along a dirt road about fifty yards out, stretched my arms out across the road and tied each wrist with a knot using half-inch rope. They unbuckled my trousers and pulled them to my ankles and held them down. They took yellow foam and stuffed it into my mouth and duct-taped my mouth over the foam. They also placed duct tape over my eyes, so I was blinded to whatever was next. Someone yelled out they were going to piss on me, but fortunately my former partner and ex-cadet, Billy M., blurted out, "Nobody pisses on my partner or they'll deal with me!" Boy, what a nice guy!

After several seconds, I started to hear laughter from everyone and suddenly I felt someone squatting over me and dragging something over my taped mouth, nose and brow. I could only imagine what it could be, but just kept still, because I was stretched out and fully exposed.

One after another, at least thirty or forty of them dragged their hairy testicles across my nose, eyebrows, and forehead. Now I know why they stuffed and taped my mouth shut. It took about forty minutes, and they were finished. I was untied and left to pull up my pants and remove the tape from my eyes and mouth. I felt cheap and violated and probably needed to go to a psychiatrist to help alleviate guilt feelings for what had just happened. I had no room to complain, because I had done the same thing to most of them in the past eight and a half years. I was proud they'd taken the gassing like men and conjured up the nerve to jump me. They could have done much worse, but they were lenient in a gay way. I knew this was the end of a great time and a truly professional group of men. I was very thankful that they'd made me look good, most of the time, by letting me win all of the contests.

The common practice was to leave a small trophy or plaque dedicated to SEB, but I just couldn't do it. It was a unique unit of assignment in which I exposed my heart and soul. I lost a part of me with the deaths of my friends and companions. Those incidents were felt throughout the unit and we suffered from the same tragic losses. In my time at the bureau I enjoyed the company of like-minded individuals who gave all they could and in an exemplary manner.

May God bless all who work at the bureau in the future years. Let's not forget George B. and Larrell S. I hope both George and Larrell can look down upon me as an ambassador of good faith and exemplary skills to motivate others to emulate their excellent work skills and mind-set.

Hopefully at future bureau dinners and reunions a table will be always set up with two empty chairs. Several drinks could be placed upon that table in remembrance of both George and Larrell with a lit candle, as a reminder of their demise in the line of duty.

In my opinion there was no better place than the Special Enforcement Bureau to work, yet I felt compelled to leave to advance in rank after my next unit of assignment at the sheriff's academy, Advanced Officer Training Unit.

CHAPTER 129

ADVANCED OFFICER TRAINING:
HONEY, I'LL PUT THE KID DOWN!

We were a group of deputies who got together for a sergeant's exam study group. For the actual sergeant's exam, there were about eight of us coming together once a week at the new sheriff's academy in the city of Whittier. Some were from cadet training, advanced officer training, driver's training and a few were from the administration staff.

We were all serious about becoming sergeants, and the study group was the best way to drive home the important issues and focus us on test taking and choosing the proper answer. We all had reading assignments and specific research on topics that were going to be addressed on the exam. The weekly meetings were compulsory. The entire group counted on each other's assigned briefs, as a part of a designated reading chapter assignment. If you missed twice you might be kicked out because of lack of participation.

One of the guys in our group was a calm and quiet deputy from the driver's training center at the Pomona training facility, where he taught deputies how to drive. He was not the loud or obnoxious type, like several of us, and was rather gentlemanly and soft-spoken. He, like several others, were part of the group and trying to steal all of our vast sea of knowledge and taught a whole array of mandatory law enforcement classes, in the academy.

When he came in to our study group he had to drive through quite a bit of traffic to get to the group, which met weekly around five in the afternoon. It was much easier for our immediate group to gather because the meeting place was right next door on the academy grounds. Others, who were outside the academy proper, had to take an extra amount of time and effort to arrive at our meeting place.

We all knew that as academy staff we would enjoy a boost of confidence and accolades because we were usually on top of current events and legal instruction, and we had a good working knowledge of the department's policies and procedures.

One evening the deputy from driver's training and his wife went out to dinner with their small son. They had spent three to four hours out, and then came home around eight. When they arrived home, his wife was in the kitchen, and the deputy went into their son's bedroom to put the sleeping child to bed.

A loud gunshot came from the son's bedroom. His wife came running into the bedroom and found her husband shot in the head. Their little boy was okay, but the culprit was able to flee out the bedroom window. The wife screamed and called for help from the police and an ambulance. Unfortunately, the deputy died. He was twenty-nine years old.

The homicide detectives determined that the victim had been killed with his own service pistol. When he left for dinner, he neglected to take his weapon with him.

The burglar broke into his home and began to search for valuables. The family returned home and surprised and trapped the burglar. The burglar obviously had found the deputy's firearm and used it on the dad when he was carrying his sleepy son to his bedroom.

The burglar tossed the gun as he fled the home, and the weapon was confirmed as the murder weapon.

The burglar/murderer was never found, and the deputy died needlessly. But there's a moral to this story, and *all* should pay strict attention. Anyone who owns a gun *must* secure that weapon prior to leaving.

The California law of "strict liability" points out that responsibility lies with the owner of guns. If a child finds it and accidentally shoots him- or herself or anyone else, the gun owner will be held responsible. If a burglar breaks into your home without a gun, finds your gun, and uses it against you or someone else, you run the risk that the intruder will not be found guilty of your murder because it is not possible to prove intent to enter with a weapon to hurt anyone.

The possibility of a burglar coming into your home is very real. That gun that you own and didn't put away securely might be used on you or your family, as it was in this matter.

In my experience and opinion it is a good law. It holds that anyone with a gun must keep that weapon away from children at all times, and the law helps to curtail accidental discharges by children.

———

Quite a few years ago in another state, I was visiting some of my in-laws. My eldest son, Brian, was around five years old and was left at my brother-in-law's home with several adult women and several other young cousins. My ex-wife and I were directly across the street visiting a neighbor's home.

We had been at the home for maybe a half hour when suddenly one of the older cousins rushed over. She informed us that our son, Brian, and his cousin, Barney, of similar age, had gotten a hold of a gun and fired it. We ran to the house and found both Brian and Barney bawling inside a small bedroom. Apparently the door to the room was closed, and when the gun discharged, both kids were in a frantic state, desperately trying to get out of the room.

They were trying to open the door, but in their panic, they were trying to open it the wrong way. We examined both kids for any obvious signs of injury and were relieved there were only powder burns lightly tattooed along Brian's inner forearms.

Once they quieted down, we noted the damage and how these kids happened to get a hold of the gun, a .357 magnum revolver. First off, the gun was inside a leather cowboy belt and holster. draped over the headboard of the bed, as seen in old cowboy movies. It was obvious that the one who had the grip of the gun was Barney; evidenced by the absence of black powder tattooing. Both were in a tugging match over possession of the gun and one of them discharged the gun during the struggle. You can imagine how dangerous that was.

When the gun discharged, the bullet skipped across the top of a vacant bed and bored six holes in the bedspread. There were three holes each about a foot apart, and three other holes an inch apart, indicating there were folds in the bedspread before the gunshot.

The speeding bullet then hit a large jewelry box on the other side of the room, tore it to shreds, and scattered the contents on the floor.

My ex-brother-in-law started to yell at five-year-old Barney. He scolded Barney as if he were twelve—that he knew better than to touch the gun.

When I heard the reprimand I followed up with the question, "Do you mean, Clyde, you not only keep a real gun hanging over your bedpost, but a fully loaded one as well?" His response was, "Well, hell yeah, those kids know I keep that loaded gun there for our family."

I nodded my head in dismay and looked at my ex-wife as if that answer had to be the dumbest excuse I had ever heard. My ex-wife knew I was furious and wanted to leave as soon as possible.

I removed myself and made little attempt to communicate with Clyde again. There was no sense in discussing what had happened, but to stay would have put all of us in the position as contributors to the next shooting. We were now aware of the ignorance of gun safety in that home, and if we did not remove our son or the other kids from that gun, the possibility that there were other guns we didn't know about could be enough for us to be charged with a crime as well.

If you own a gun and disagree with me, please talk to a practicing criminal law attorney and see if I'm wrong. These two stories illustrate two complete failures of gun security and the consequences. If you decide to be a gun owner in the future, reread this chapter, the stories will never grow old.

CHAPTER 130

THE WILL TO SURVIVE: A POSTHUMOUS TRIBUTE TO A FIRESTONE PARK DEPUTY

It was Christmas season, and two deputies were assigned the wild car and were working the north end of the Florence and Firestone communities. They were driving around in the hopes of crossing paths with lowlifes on the prowl. Being in a slick car, or plain wrap, allowed the deputies a few seconds jump on closing the normal reaction time of a crook, as opposed to a marked patrol unit.

Working this area was tough stuff, and several deputies had been shot or killed. Everyone assigned to Firestone Park knew very well that danger always lurked nearby, and you had better keep your head on a swivel to stay alert for any eventuality that might show up. That was the heart and soul of working this station, and all other stations knew about Firestone Park's dangerous history.

Both of the deputies were in their civilian attire, and it just so happened to be a cold winter night. George decided to wear one of those sissy cowhide jackets with lamb's wool around the collar and lapels and peeking out of the sleeves. It was a little tight and uncomfortable.

Meanwhile Mike was anxious to get into the field and do some hooking and booking. Generally the streets abounded with crooks, dope, and guns. They were everywhere, so the unmarked unit would be most likely to run smack dab into trouble that was waiting for them.

They were patrolling around Florence Boulevard and looking for any suspicious activity that might need their attention. Nothing else was going on, so both decided to pass by an active gang party that was going on to see who was in attendance. Not much activity was going on at the party, so they decided to go over toward Central Avenue. As they were passing a Bank of America parking lot, they noticed three men walking toward them. Mike and George focused on the threesome and watched their reaction. When the three spotted the undercover car, they immediately made a one-eighty turn and began to walk away from them. This was a strong indication to the deputies that the three wanted to avoid contact with them but weren't being very discreet.

The unmarked unit turned into the parking lot and stopped just behind the men. George got out of the passenger door and told all three to stop. Mike got out of the driver's seat and watched their reaction to George's command. The three paid no attention, although his words were audible, clear, and direct.

George stepped slightly away from the passenger door and started to move toward the three when all three turned and bum-rushed George and Mike.

Although their guns were drawn, the three suspects were on them quickly and began to beat them. Suddenly a shot was fired, and it struck Mike right between the eyes. He fell just outside the driver's door and lay still. George had two of the large adults beating him with their pistols.

George felt as if he was passing out and was attempting to gather enough strength to repel the one adult who was on top of him. Meanwhile, although Mike was shot right between the eyes and had his glasses knocked off, he miraculously regained his strength and the will to survive. He turned toward his assailant, who was smashing his head in with a pistol, and shot him in the head.

Mike got up, crawled to the trunk area of the unmarked car, and leaned over the trunk. He took careful aim and shot the man beating his partner in the head. That shot slammed into the suspect's head but only knocked him off his partner. George was now able to stand up as well.

The third suspect apparently realized he was about to meet his maker and fled quickly into the nearby alley.

Mike and George caught up to the second suspect, who was still holding his pistol, and shot him repeatedly. Two of the three assailants were now dead and the other, although struck in the head, was able to run away.

Mike was able to get to the only radio inside the unmarked car and transmitted his chilling announcement. That call came over the airway and sent chills up most of the deputies' spines, and all raced to help them. One of the responding units, Sergeant Al K., was coming quickly and inadvertently ran broadside into a responding fire truck going to the same location. That sergeant was now near death himself, having sustained very serious injuries.

Another unit, Deputy Jim H., stopped by the collision and with the help of yet another deputy, and transported the injured sergeant to Saint Francis Hospital in Lynwood. Fortunately, that sergeant recovered, but ultimately had to retire from the department because of those injuries. Mike and George were themselves were transported to Saint Francis Hospital and recovered from their injuries.

About three hours after the incident on Florence Avenue, broadcasts were being delivered to all units in the area to be on the lookout for the third suspect and a brief, vague description was repeated. A Special Enforcement Bureau unit, spotted a suspicious car driving erratically a couple of miles from the shooting. That unit announced that they were in pursuit and many of the already emotionally pumped-up officers joined in the chase. That lead unit and others went on for several minutes and ended up in one of the streets in the city of Los Angeles. One of the assisting units right behind the primary pursuit car, took over when the evading car stopped and ran aground with a badly spent engine.

The lone suspect fled on foot, running up a residential driveway with a deputy on his heels. The suspect jumped a six-foot wooden fence and vaulted into the backyard. The pursuing SEB deputy, Doug D., followed him. As he reached the top of the fence, the suspect turned and fired one shot. That shot hit the top of the wooden fence, passed through the board, and went into and through Doug's ring finger, causing him to fall backward.

Doug retreated to the front of the home and met up with his partner, an SEB sergeant. Quite a few units, LAPD and LA sheriff units, were converging on the scene. Doug came out to where they were assembling, displayed his bloody hand to them, and announced that he was just shot by the suspect. That alone was enough to infuriate all of the officers, who became involved in the hunt. The suspect who was indeed close by. Several minutes passed when a whole line of officers, both LAPD and LA Sheriff's deputies rounded a corner of a tall wall and came upon the suspect cornered in a long side portion of an apartment complex.

Two tall walls boxed him in. He still had a pistol in his hand. The officers were gazing at him. Nothing much was said when as many as eight officers opened fire and dropped him like a rock to the asphalt. Several officers went up to the suspect to make sure he didn't have his pistol and carefully turned him over. Small wisps of steam rose from his perforated body.

Initially it was thought that the now-deceased man was the suspect who ran from the shooting on Florence Avenue. But further investigation revealed that this suspect was just another gunman looking for a victim when he was first observed.

I had just transferred to the academy from the Special Enforcement Bureau and was now assigned to the Advanced Officer Training Unit to teach officer survival, weapon retention, and weapon takeaway. The Olympics were coming and the entire department needed to be trained and refreshed in crowd and riot formations.

My partner, Deputy Jim H. and me were involved in videotaping officer survival training tapes, and we were blessed to be interviewing George A. about his and his partner Mike's near-death experiences after being shot, and George surviving a crushed skull from nearly seven years before.

This training film took about two months to direct, record all of the training points, and produce. George was humble and explicit about what he might have done wrong and readily discussed it for the training film. Everyone was pleased with the outcome of the training film, and we thanked George for his time, effort, candor, and polite demeanor.

Three months later, George A. was a new sergeant at the Men's Central Jail on Bauchet Street, downtown Los Angeles. He had recently been promoted and was working the night shift at MCJ. He got into his own private van to go home. He was on the 10 freeway eastbound when something happened. His van crossed the freeway, ran onto the soft shoulder, and crashed,just north of Aliso Village, Los Angeles.

CHP came onto the scene and discovered George A. was dead on the scene, apparently from the trauma of the impact. However, examination at the local hospital revealed he had been shot in the back of the head. That shot must have come from inside George's van, but there were no clues other than someone else's blood. There were no witnesses or evidence to point to anyone else and the crime stymied everyone. The blood was kept and held as evidence. At that time, DNA testing was not possible.

We were all dumbstruck. Suspicion pointed to his previous assignment at Operation Safe Streets. At OSS, George had a long list of gangbangers who may have wished him harm, but that thought wasn't enough for an investigation.

He was a well-liked deputy. Many came to his funeral, at which he was honored for his on-duty death.

Years went by, approximately fifteen, when a homicide detective was talking about George's death with George's ex-wife. She was asked if she had any idea who the killer might be. She admitted that she'd had one jealous suitor who might have been a prime candidate—Ted K. Ted was a deputy who had strong feelings for George's ex-wife. He coincidentally was assigned to patrol at East Los Angeles Station. George and his wife had separated just about the time when we were interviewing George for the training tape. Deputy Ted K. had been assigned to East Los Angeles Station patrol for many years and was actually a very good and hardworking deputy. The homicide detective informed the assigned investigating officer who acted on the new information. He called the former deputy, who had since retired and was now living in the Seattle area.

The former deputy, Ted K., was asked if he would mind if they came up to his home in Seattle and ask a few questions about George's death. Ted gave his approval and advised them he would answer any questions they had. So both homicide detectives flew up to Seattle, Washington, and went to Ted's home. Although he cooperated with the detectives, answering a lot of their questions, when asked if they could have a sample of his DNA, Ted refused and told them to get a warrant. To the detectives, this seemed highly suspicious, and in itself, it meant Ted may have had something to hide about the homicide.

The homicide detectives returned with the warrant and met Ted's new wife, who told them he was somewhere in the backyard. In the backyard they came upon Ted's body with a self-inflicted gunshot wound to his head. On top of that, the gun Ted used to commit suicide was the same gun used in the shooting death of George, fifteen years earlier.

———

This entire epic is chilling. The wrongdoing of criminals, who are often seen as bloodthirsty bottom-feeders who prey on the weak and defenseless, cause one's heart to skip a beat. George's tragedies could make a heart skip three beats; he died from the selfish desires of fellow officers.

I knew George, and I was fully aware of his work ethic and bravery from his experiences at Firestone Park Station. His will to survive was viewed as courageous, and he made it through quite a few years of excellent work. But because of some obscure romance, George A. paid a much higher price, owing to a forlorn attachment of a fellow deputy, who sought George's ex-wife's attention.

I know very well that God has already blessed George. God will use him as an example of a good hardworking deputy, and help the Lord reveal all who deceived, encouraged, and provoked his murder and early departure.

CHAPTER 131

NO TIME FOR VERTIGO

It was a relatively quiet night and routine evening calls were getting pumped out at a normal, manageable pace. Deputy Richard B., a Norwalk station deputy, was following up on several calls based on their procedural importance. At the top of that list are the priority calls such as assaults, murders (which, incidentally, are not put out over the air because of the excessive media draw), gang violence, rapes, missing juveniles, hazardous-material spills, and explosions. Any of these gets to the field sergeant in an audible call so he/she doesn't overlook the importance of the call.

Of course, the decision of priority rests with the field sergeant so he/she can choose which call to respond to. On this night everything was copacetic until a robbery alarm call went out. It was not too faraway, in the Norwalk area, in an open mall with plenty of shops. It was right around seven thirty, and the deputies were coordinating their response and converging on the area.

Deputy Richard B. was coming upon the store with his head lamps out and unsnapping his seatbelt. He was traveling about 10 mph and carefully transmitted his arrival over the car radio. He opened the door to hold it ajar as the car drew closer to the location.

A Hispanic man appeared in front of him not thirty yards away. He was armed with a handgun, pointing it directly at Richard, who was surprised at the sudden encounter. He was about to take evasive actions when he was struck in the face by multiple gunshots. One round slammed into Richard's cheek, causing immediate pain and apprehension of a deadly follow-up attack.

Richard reacted instinctively and fell to the floorboard of his patrol car. He put the car into reverse and hit the accelerator with his hand. He knew that he had to get quickly out of the kill zone, summon help, and caution other units.

His memory was impaired by the painful wound to his face, but he recalled that not knowing where he was traveling—at a high speed in reverse—was like falling into an empty abyss. He knew the longer he pressed on the accelerator and blindly steered the heavy patrol car the more likely there would be an impact that could hit innocent people wandering around the open mall. He added he had backed about fifty yards before he released the accelerator and came to a stop.

He grabbed the mike as he looked about to see if he could spot the assailant while broadcasting the attack and his injuries. Help was there moments later, and Richard was transported to the local hospital. He survived his wounds and returned to work several months later. A diligent search for the suspect proved fruitless, and unfortunately no one was arrested for the assault.

Richard's reaction was commendable and above reproach. Driving blindly in reverse was just as remarkable as surviving the wound. Richard's common sense and officer survival skills helped him to overcome adversity at which most folks would cringe. A factor in Richard's survival skills was that he was trained at Firestone Park Station by none other than Paul F. Paul F. was to be a very sharp deputy and was mentioned in another story while he was assigned to Firestone Park Station. Fortunately, Paul's fundamental skills may have been passed on to Richard B. without any further acknowledgments, but Paul may hold his head high in this case as well.

CHAPTER 132

LYNWOOD STATION: THE FIRST DAY

I parked my car and gathered some of my gear and uniforms and started in the back door of the Lynwood sheriff's station. It was early, and I was excited to start my assignment as a brand-spanking-new sergeant. Fresh from the Sheriff's Academy Advanced Officer Training Unit, and forewarned many times about a whole cluster of problems that had been recently plaguing that station, I disregarded those warnings and still chose to go. Although keenly aware of the internal strife, I chose to go to Lynwood because I knew the area and the mentality of deputies. I felt I possessed a strong desire to do a good job and could improve the morale and spirit of the station. I was in good spirits, anxious to see my new assignment, and get on with the routine I had done many times before.

As I was passing by the first set of stairs at the rear of the station, a lieutenant came walking out and stood by as I passed. I knew this lieutenant and had worked with him many times before at a deputy level. In fact I had worked at Firestone Station with him in the early seventies, and he had worked at the Special Enforcement Bureau for several years prior to my arrival.

I expected a friendly greeting or the standard remark, like "Oh no, not you! Boy, we're in trouble now!" It would have been welcome and would make the new assignment more pleasant. As I smiled, Lieutenant Spite blurted, "I just got off the phone with Mike and reassured him I'd take care of you when you get here."

He was referring to another lieutenant at the academy. They happened to be good friends. The heads-up call was to pay me back for getting him into administrative trouble. That contact set the tone for next three and a half years. I simply shrugged my head and nodded, implying that if "skirts" wanted to torment me and create an unpleasant atmosphere, then go right ahead and give it your best shot. To respond to such a gesture would be less than manly and simply give him all the rope he needed to "get me."

Wow, what a welcome! I needed to prepare to face this music everyday, or until the "girlie" threat was recompensed. A sort of prelude to this welcome mat was akin to the commonly known "three Ss," shit, shower, and shave, to start off a day when you first roll out of bed. However, this was a slight variation, Lynwood's three Ss.

I did find out later on that Lynwood Station was where the department put their mediocre lieutenants, so I was blessed with a small band of hard-ass, mediocre lieutenants, known mostly as the three Ss. These lieutenants will be identified as Spite, Snake, and last but not least, Scurry. The names were changed to make the three lieutenants seem briefly important to themselves, as is a sheet of toilet paper is prior to being used.

However, it appeared that putting these three at a very active station was a liability at best. Individually approached, you could understand why they were assigned to Lynwood Station. However, collectively they had a common bond, a thread of misdirection, and self-serving personal agendas.

Complacency and their obviously hidden agendas were not known by the department executives. They would certainly fuel the already-present patrol problems and would ignite the already-stoked kindling.

Prior to my promotion, I was asked by many if I was aware of the Viking problem at Lynwood. (That problem was that certain group of deputies were uniting together and forming a group called the "Vikings". Those deputies were collaborating with one another in several Lynwood station affairs and began to obtain tattoos of a Viking on their bodies to show that they were part of a selected group within the Lynwood station. They agreed to stick together on specific issues of camaraderie and build up alligence amoungst one another to do things a certain way. That form of association is not condoned at all by the sheriff's department and viewed as a illegal association that seems as if cops were acting against the department and its policies and procedures. The general public views these officers as formations of gangs that do illegal things and strain the departments integrity.) I knew about what was occurring and the accusations, but my feeling was that 99 percent of all deputies were good, hardworking deputies and that most of the problems were generated by lack of leadership and personal skills of the supervisors. With this in mind, I knew Lynwood was under the scrutiny of the department, and I also knew the executives knew me very well.

When coming from the sheriff's academy as a newly promotable item, you had a choice to go where you would like to go, rather than the routine of going to the jail facility, for the first couple of years. My choice, of course, with the aforementioned in mind, was Lynwood Station. That community was between Compton and my former station, Firestone Park. I knew the area very well, the makeup of the communities involved, and that Lynwood had the unfortunate distinction of the most deputies killed in the line of duty in the department's history.

Of course, I had the upper hand in all barricaded situations and riot behavior because of my background of eight and a half years with SWAT, the training of the entire department for the 1984 Olympics, and other independent police agencies on command post operations, crowd and riot control, and the physical instruction of weapon retention and officer survival. This way, when I walked in, I was an immediate asset loaded with the know-how and experience to make things run smoothly.

I wanted and loved the excitement of a busy station, and it was apparent from my work ethic and places I had chosen on a career path of a hands-on approach. I did not flinch from adversity and had a good sense of direction and knew the policies and procedures very well. I had been confronted by hundreds of angry citizens many times before and taught thousands of deputies and law enforcement officers how to survive and take care of themselves.

Most knew I was a good representative of law enforcement, honest, loyal, and not easily provoked into a confrontation. Most officers I've been around knew that I would assimilate very well, but in the cases where someone wanted to urinate down my back and tell me it was raining, I would react quickly, legally, and with great fervor.

The executives of the department knew me well enough, because we had worked together at Firestone Park Station, and they counted on me to continue with my work ethic unabated and relentlessly.

With that in mind, I felt that I had a calling to go to Lynwood and straighten those weak points out and redeem the robust quality of good deputy work ethics. A lot was a stake. My intentions were good, and I was stimulated to do a good job.

CHAPTER 133

BLACK MAMBA: LYNWOOD'S POISONOUS SNAKE

One lieutenant in particular was a philanderer and just plain lazy. He hated to respond to anything relating to the rigorous routine of law enforcement operations. He had women in his office a lot of times and was just having a great time entertaining them throughout most of the shift. He would spend countless hours on the office phone, obviously talking to women, discussing his sexual prowess and other matters that were not related to work. It didn't matter to me that he was lackadaisical and had stated many times to me he would rather step aside in a conflict than handle the problem straight on.

As the daily routine became a reality, all courses of activities seemed to raise their ugly head. I bathed myself in the morass of strife along with the rest of the sergeants. They too seemed very concerned about the lieutenants as time moved on. He was the very lieutenant I had previously discussed: Lt. Snake. What a classic numbskull. He was small in stature, balding, with a mediocre work ethic at best. And he was very, very black. In fact, he touted his race more than I've heard from many whites who barked out the same trashy racial hatred.

Time moved rather rapidly at Lynwood Station, because of all of the activity that went on day and night. Shootings here, robberies there, murders, rapes, assaults, blatant gang activities to the max, and just about everyone in the city was a victim several times over. When entrenched in all the activities—in the watch sergeant's office and out in the field—time flew throughout the shift with endless reports to read and process.

Several weeks passed, and I began to notice the booking cage lights were out. I was a little concerned, so I asked the jailer what was going on with the lights. He responded that when a certain lieutenant was on deck, nobody came to jail, so therefore the lights are out and the booking cage door was wide open.

I began to monitor the deputies' activities and inquiring why they weren't bringing anyone to jail. They agreed that when Lt. Snake was on, he would constantly badger them not to make any arrests. Keep in mind the crime in Lynwood was almost as bad as in the city of Compton. He was very open about his view, and everyone understood that if you wanted to get on the lieutenant's bad side; just arrest someone and see what happened.

Deputies who arrested anyone had to run the gauntlet of disparaging remarks and criticisms by Lieutenant Snake, who acted more like Captain Ahab in his quest for the white whale. Only in this instance, his focus was looking for an unholy war in his ultimate quest to find the black messiah. The thing Lt. Snake hated most was someone picking on his people, the "brothas and sistas." But the preponderance of Lynwood's population was black, so most of the crooks were black. Is there a problem? Should we all go around with pumped-up arms and tapered short-sleeved shirts in pimped-up police cars and chase women?

I'll leave that up to a much higher authority who knows the whole truth, and hopefully Lt. Snake will pay dearly later on. (He rose three more levels based on his mediocrity.)

The men and women who came to Lynwood were generally highly motivated and want to take as many crooks to jail as possible, but this lieutenant obviously was there to stop arrests. He wanted to minimize the appearance of crime, and especially the obvious guilt.

There was a barricaded suspect on Gibson Avenue just south of Rosecrans Avenue. The suspect was a black man who was holding his son at gunpoint.

This was a bitter custody dispute and the wife and mother of the six-year-old boy came to pick her child up after his stay with his father. Dad had different ideas and didn't want to let the child go, so he threatened the mom that he would kill the boy if she didn't leave him alone.

I was the field sergeant. I went to the home and began to set up a command post. Everything was going well and notifications were about to be sent out. Then Lt. Snake showed up. Oddly enough, he never came out of his office, although that's what was supposed to happen, according to department policy.

I was standing by my car with a pen and pad, ready to do business, when he came up to me and asked, "What do you have?

I relayed what the circumstances were and that the suspect was down the street barricaded in his home. Lt. Snake asked again, "What do you have?" As if he didn't hear my first explanation. Feeling something was strange here, I asked Lt. Snake, "What exactly do you want to happen, Lieutenant?" He said, "No one is hurt, right?" I said, "You're correct. No one is hurt *yet.*" He asked, "What if you and the guys just pack up and leave?" I said, "You've got to be kidding. Do you know what might happen?"

Lt. Snake said, "Nothing will happen if we just leave!" I said, "If that's what you want, Lieutenant, then so be it. We're out of here." Lt. Snake slithered away from the temporary command post and returned to the station posthaste. I gathered the deputies involved and gave them the order to abandon the suspect and hostage per the watch commander.

Quite a few deputies came over to me and inquired what had happened. I informed them of Lt. Snake's decision; it was his call. They grumbled, making accusations about Lieutenant Snake's mediocre field performance and abandoning his responsibilities. They said the whole event would disappear as long as no one was hurt or the situation publicized.

Most personnel were amazed at Lieutenant Snake's disregard of field procedures and departmental policies. They couldn't understand how he could stay out of trouble, although he ran from everything. They thought it surely would show up somehow or somewhere, and the administrators of the department would have a field day with the investigative results.

I was giving a briefing one afternoon, with fifteen or twenty deputies. Several deputies were talking about fight tactics, and I gave my opinion of how to handle the matters and how to safely engage suspects without losing your gun. My experience and training many deputies in the past was well known and these deputies expressed their gratitude for the hands-on explanations I often demonstrated.

I returned to my office after briefing to check on reports that might need correcting and processing, and I was called to the lieutenant's office. I stopped what I was doing and went to his office. He was concerned about why I was teaching the deputies how to protect themselves and retain their weapons during a fight.

I was surprised that he asked such a question because training is encouraged throughout the department, especially by sergeants at the station level. Confused about what the lieutenant was getting at, I asked, "What do you mean?" He then blurted out that I was a classified warmonger, persuading deputies to get into physical conflict with the citizens. I answered "I'm just teaching them the basic officer survival stuff and nothing more! Of course I emphasize never to give up when involved in a fight!"

He went off on me and started yelling that I was teaching the deputies how to injure and kill people for no reason, and then he called me a "Nazi"!

That set me off. I slammed his office door. Then I turned around and stood at the front of his desk. I pointed my finger at him as if I was going to shove it right through his chest and began barking out a long list of racial epithets and summed it up within two minutes—he was lazy, in the wrong business, and should be working for the social services department.

I pointed out that he disliked deputies, especially the white ones, and was afraid to go into the field. In the seven months I worked with him, he never went into the field, and I knew that the lieutenants were required by the department to get into the field as often as possible. I summed up my tirade by declaring that I would be in my office if he needed to respond to any of my accusations.

I returned to my office fully expecting him to react quickly, but he never showed up, and nothing became of the matter. From then on, Lieutenant Snake stayed clear of me. He knew I was not going to let him fly through his negligent command anymore and would report him at the drop of a hat if necessary. I decided that I was going to chart his faults and misdeeds and let the department know exactly what this jerk was up to.

Many times in briefings the sergeants had to read a specific warning to the deputies not to use the station phone system for personal phone calls. The administration was preparing to punish whoever violated that direct order, because of exorbitant phone costs. Over and over again the warnings went out. Several had been caught and had to pay the phone bill they created.

Lieutenant Snake was always on the phone, talking to someone about his personal problems, but nothing was said. Then one day he was hit with the phone bill for his long phone conversations that turned out to be personal as well, it was around three or four hundred dollars.

From that day on, he hung out in the station lobby where there was a pay phone, leaning against the wall, jawing with his long list of honeys. If anyone wanted to talk with him, they had to go to the lobby to listen to the deputies' presentation on how an arrest was made. He was about as discourteous as possible to the presenting deputy and mimicked or demeaned him while pulling on his crotch, as if bothered by someone interrupting him with business.

The deputies would come into my office right after talking with the lieutenant and discuss his demeaning comments and how he wouldn't accept their explanations for the arrest review forms. Although irritated as hell, there was nothing I could do except monitor his rude and unprofessional antics.

I knew that one day this man would be found out, and he'd fall somehow, like the rest of the other unproductive officers—right on his very own sword if left to his own deceptive devices.

CHAPTER 134

PETTY ILL WILL: SELECTIVE VENGEANCE

Now on the other hand, Lieutenant Spite, who threatened me on my first day, was a weasel who had to be watched all of the time. He was attending law school and made a total transformation into a major jerk. The problem is that he knew it. Because he was at the top of the heap, he wanted things his way, but he didn't want any trouble that would make him look unappealing.

One day Lieutenant Spite called me into his office. Two other sergeants were seated in front of his desk. He told me to follow up on an inquiry about two of Lynwood's better deputies who had beaten a suspect excessively and without justifiable reason. He wanted me to question the witnesses who allegedly saw the deputies beat the suspect.

Now, that request normally is taken at face value, but coming from this lieutenant, it was a bit comical, because I knew the lieutenant's past very well. I smirked and said I would look into the matter quickly and give the deputies a fair review.

The lieutenant was a little miffed about why I was smiling. I said that this investigation would be rather simple compared to the ones he was charged with when he was a deputy. He was angered by my comment and showed it to the new sergeants seated in front of him. He asked, "Just what do you mean?"

I said, "Well, for a person who cracked a man's head open with a flashlight and gave the recipient at least twenty stitches just to show a bunch of fellow officers how tough you were, this just doesn't seem too sincere." He knew exactly what I meant, because there were a lot of guys at the station who didn't like his brutality; he was nearly found out, but someone saved his ass.

Lieutenant Spite looked at me and tried to send fireballs from his eyes to slam into my head, but it didn't work. I obliged him and let the issue about him drop as I left the room.

Oh, rest assured, he watched me very closely and was all primed and ready to rip me apart with some violation to honor his friend and to follow through on his initial welcoming threat on my first day.

CHAPTER 135

DROWNED IN POLITICS

One day three of our units were involved in a dead body call over by Long Beach Boulevard on Euclid Street. This poor seventeen-year-old girl had been found drowned in a filthy, algae-ridden three-fourths-full pool. Everyone was in tears. The fire department had tried its best and took off to another call. We escorted the young woman, resting on a mobile gurney, to the waiting ambulance.

We had already planned the opening through the small crowd of people cluttering the driveway. I directed a couple of deputies to make sure the ambulance had an easy way out of the narrow street. As I was standing near the back door of the ambulance, now holding the deceased girl on a gurney, a deputy yelled to me about a problem he had with an adult woman in a car. She had just pulled up in her car as the deputy was attempting to clear the street so the ambulance could get through.

When asked to please move the car for a moment so the ambulance could get out, she said no—that she had every right to park where she intended to park. She was indignant and rude to the deputy. She was warned three times that the car would be towed and that she'd go to jail for hindering a peace officer in the performance of his duties. Her response was a curt, "Fuck you, I don't have to!"

I was guiding the ambulance as it was backing up through the tight space. The deputy called to me again, only this time he was about fifteen feet away and on an extremely narrow bend of the street.

The deputy said, "Hey, Sarge, she just told me to fuck off!" I looked puzzled at the deputy and noted the snide facial gesture of the driver as she was about to exit her car. I responded, "Then tow it and hook her up!"

The deputy took hold of the woman as she defiantly exited her car, put her in handcuffs and forcibly guided her over to his patrol car. She was screaming to high heaven as she was put in the backseat. She continued to scream as the deputy moved her car as we were coming past with the ambulance close behind.

We finally got the ambulance on the way. The girl had already been pronounced dead by the fire department. It was merely a compassionate gesture to expedite her removal.

A couple of deputies helped with the paperwork to tow the car. The deputy who made the arrest and I returned to the station to discuss it. As I came in, I was confronted immediately by Lieutenant Spite who scornfully questioned why I had ordered the arrest of the woman who had just come in. This was quite odd because he really never got involved in any arrest and never confronted me like he had now. This apparently had some very sour political overtones, and I was at a loss how it affected him.

Before I could answer he quickly snapped, "Do you know who she is?" All the while he was bobbing his head up and down like some gang member taking me on, with a touch of "whatever you say won't be considered anyway" attitude.

I said, "I don't give a shit who the hell she is. Do you know what she did?" Lieutenant Spite said, "And that's your problem, Larry. You don't care. She's a prominent attorney's secretary." I said, "You've got to be shitting me. What the hell does that have to do with the elements of her arrest?" He knew he was wrong to bring up an issue up about political influences and awareness while we were doing our work. He scurried to his office.

I heard her screaming in the back like a banshee. She was going wild and she was about to be transported to Los Angeles General Hospital for a seventy-two-hour evaluation by the psychiatric staff.

I knew full well Lieutenant Spite wasn't through with this and waited for the next step. Was it possibly a friend of his who employed this nut? What do you think occurred? Would the attorney, apparently well known to Lieutenant Spite, call and excoriate my judgment? Was it possible?

About a month passed, and the station was now under a new captain. I knew the new captain fairly well. When he was a sergeant, he had graciously helped all deputies under him at Firestone Park Station. He needed to know about these three jerks, but I didn't want to divulge my misgivings too soon.

We had already exchanged greetings and welcome-aboard salutations. He seemed high-spirited and much more enthusiastic than our previous captain.

Two weeks later I was summoned to the captain's office. He was seated in his chair behind his desk. "Larry, I frankly don't know what went on here." He was holding several pieces of paper in his hand. He showed me a typed reprimand condemning me for ordering a car to be towed in lieu of other remedies.

This was it; Lieutenant Spite wanted to have the last word. I nodded my head. "Captain, this guy"—I pointed to his name—"is an asshole and a jerk. If this is all that this prick could come up with, I'll take this and wear it as a badge of honor." I said I didn't appreciate Lieutenants Spite's mockery and feeble attempt to undermine our department's policy and ethical behavior and added, "That the jerk lieutenant needs to be watched, among several others, for incompetence."

The captain, a bit perplexed, was very kind and didn't understand the actions that were stated. I said I wouldn't beef or complain about this trivial crap, as long as he would carefully watch the lieutenants assigned under his command. I quickly signed the reprimand and promptly informed the other sergeants of what had happened.

Those interested sergeants were very concerned, because they were in the middle of their careers and just followed these three Ss and steered away from controversy.

CHAPTER 136

EARLY MORNING SHIFT

The early morning shift is a pleasant relief from all of the hectic action on the evening shift. On this shift you can shake a lot of thugs who sneak around and attempt to conceal themselves a variety of ways. I was into my shift for about the first three hours and was looking for a place to conceal myself from view in a used auto parking lot on Long Beach Boulevard, just above Imperial Highway.

The traffic was minimal. I pulled into the dark parking lot, parked my radio car among the unsold cars, and blended in nicely. I had just purchased a nice cup of hot coffee and was outside my car leaning back on the front fender.

There were all sorts of those goofy, triangular, small plastic, multicolored eye catching pennants lightly fluttering in the breeze. It was quiet, and the radio chatter was slowing down as well.

I was just resting and thinking about what the crews were up to and listening to the radio for any significant calls or requests for help. I would usually find a spot where I could be midstream and have a quick response. I didn't see anyone on the sidewalk, and vehicular traffic passed by without paying any attention to me, nestled in the middle of the used car lot.

I was sipping my coffee when I spotted a car being pulled over right in front of me by a single deputy. I noticed a lone woman driving the car directly in front of the radio car and pulling over to the northbound curb.

She appeared to keep her hands on the steering wheel. In her side-view mirror she watched the deputy get out of his patrol car. The deputy lit the car up with his spot lamp, and he had just switched on his amber, rear cautionary lamp.

I thought how odd it was that he'd pulled her over right smack dab in front of me and had no idea I was there. So I watched, all the while sipping my hot coffee. He came upon the car, slightly away from the side driver's window and was conversing with the woman. I noticed his radio car starting to move ever so slowly in reverse. No one else was in the car. The radio car was now drifting about fifteen feet from the stopped car and still moving backward, but unnoticed by the deputy who was focused on the driver of the stopped car.

The deputy apparently was informed by the driver that his car was moving. She obviously noticed the car's movement through the side-view mirror. By now the radio car was at least fifty feet away. The deputy went into a dead run after the car. Once the car was retrieved, the deputy drove back to the initial spot and went back to talking with the driver. They spoke for approximately five minutes and the woman drove away.

The deputy was going back to his car when he spotted me and waved to me. I waved back as he returned to his unit. He drove toward me and parked his car. He got out and approached me—I was still sipping my coffee—and asked me if I was following him.

I smiled and said no, not at all, but that trick you pulled on your last stop was really quite different. Embarrassed, he claimed that the gear had apparently slipped. I smiled and calmly complimented him for at least stopping cars and doing self-generated work at three in the morning.

He was pleased that I was just relaxing and not necessarily watching him, and he returned to his car and drove away.

Now I'm sure he will certainly tell quite a few other deputies that I'm always sneaking around and watching their actions. That would be okay with me; it would keep everyone on their toes.

CHAPTER 137

IDLE MINDS

Another time I was traveling on a very narrow street called Josephine Street just off of Santa Fe Avenue. It was around one in the afternoon. I was traveling westbound and passed by a residential driveway. I thought I saw a radio car way in the back of the driveway, almost out of sight. I stopped, backed up slightly, and noticed two individuals romping around on a light-colored patchwork quilt. They were lying upon a small front lawn on an elevated level, about three feet above street level.

It appeared to be a male clad in only pants, without any shirt or T-shirt, and a woman. They were romantically entwined, kissing as if it were a picnic outing to express their love. I continued backing a little bit more and spotted the car. Lo and behold, it was a radio car, and more important, one of ours.

The man sat up, and I recognized him as one of our day-shift deputies who was supposedly working. When he noticed it was me, he quickly got up, came over to my car, and said, "Hey, Sarge, how's it going?"

I didn't even get out of the car. I nodded my head in dismay and replied, "You've got to be shitting me." He said, "Hey, Sarge, I just stopped by to say hi to my girlfriend because it's her birthday."

I continued to nod. I ignored his reply, which was asinine. He apparently caught my askance look and quickly went to his unit. He put his clothes and shoes on, started his car, and began to back out of the driveway.

Now, most of the deputies knew that if they were identified as a slug, or if I caught them doing stupid stuff, I wouldn't write them up and have my allegations stripped of any quality noteworthy discipline. Instead I took care of the problems in the field. There were plenty of demeaning things for them to do in a patrol assignment, and I would use the most ridiculous tasks on the worst offenders. Many deputies knew very well I would torment them unmercifully until they left the shift, or transferred from the station, or had me killed.

The oddity of this observation was that this deputy's field performance was already marginally acceptable. (The county's evaluation system is hobbled with all sorts of rules that impede accurate assessments of an employee's true work ethic. Words are eliminated (by union intervention) that directly inform the reader of poor work by the employee. That's why poor employees can't be disciplined properly or terminated.

This deputy had been bragging to all that he had gone three years without paying taxes and laughed it all off. He insinuated that he had some sort of legal way to avoid paying taxes.

Well, that idea flopped after his three years were audited. He was now stuck with garnished wages that left him just enough money to live on. To top it off, it turned out he had a terrible gambling problem and was near suicidal.

Unfortunately, it all caught up with his three-packs-a-day smoking habit, when he had a severe heart attack and was forced out of the department.

CHAPTER 138

WHEN YOU NEED A COP...!

In the sheriff's department, and especially at the busy stations, there is a policy of no more than two units at one stop like a restaurant, taco stand, or any eatery. This is to avoid multiple units from congregating, which encourages an unfavorable opinion that law enforcement is wasting tax dollars. The policy is a good one and there is really no justification to see more than two units taking a lunch, dinner, or breakfast break at one place.

It was around one thirty in the morning, and I was traveling northbound on Long Beach Boulevard just north of Imperial Highway. I was coming upon Lucy's, a taco stand on the west side of the street. I looked at the parking lot and couldn't believe my eyes.

There in the parking lot, were about fifty (50) police cars from all sorts of agencies, including our department. Everyone was having a grand time until they saw me stop in the middle of the street, get out of my car, spread both arms outward as if I were the second coming of Christ—palms up, back arched, chin up—and screamed as loud as I could, "Holy shit! Are you all nuts?"

With that comment, they all ran like children to their respective radio cars and scooted out of Lucy's like wildfire. One of the deputies came near my car and had the gumption to exclaim, "Hey Sarge I was just grabbing a—" I cut him off by saying, "Get the hell out of here. or I'm going to get real mad." He too scooted and disappeared as well.

Now I knew very well that they would get away with this without trouble, because no lieutenant or administrator would believe it. But it happened once, so it could happen again unless supervisors were in the field and checking on their charges.

I knew the area very well, including where some of the station's deadbeats would go to sleep. I would monitor their calls and pay close attention to units that didn't receive calls at all. I would travel all around the different patrol areas in search of deputies on the in-service sheet, and I would make it a point to see each one at least four times each eight-hour shift.

That was a must, or the less-than-productive deputies became complacent and disappeared, hiding in some remote spot and possibly sleeping. I'm sorry, but that's what happens when it's early in the morning, radio activity is minimal and pedestrian and vehicular traffic is damn near nil.

I've climbed in to the backseat of many units where the deputies are sound asleep in the front seat and scared the bejesus out of them. I would also stand just outside of their cars and moan, as if in some sort of sexual bliss. Then I'd remind them that their survival skills were limited when they were asleep.

The key was to keep all on their toes and constantly check on their well-being. They knew I was going to find them one way or another, and some tried their best to avoid me.

One could only imagine conjuring up a plethora of ways to hurt or kill an officer, but sleeping leaves no avenue for help and provides easy access for anyone to vent their frustrations at the government to the fullest extent.

CHAPTER 139

"IS SHE GONE?"

It was around nine in the evening, and it had been raining for a short while. A female deputy pulled over a suspicious car going southbound. She asked the lone driver to step out of the car and over to the curbside. She asked him to place his hands on the fender of the car so she could search him for weapons, and he complied.

The deputy found no weapons and asked the man to sit on the curb as she awaited backup. The man was dressed in a three-piece suit and told the deputy that he wouldn't sit on the damp curb because it would ruin his brand-new suit. She became agitated at his response, and she repeatedly ordered him to sit on the curb with no regard for his suit. She pulled out her PR-24 baton and threatened that if he didn't comply, she would strike him.

He still refused, and she began to slam the PR-24 against his body. He asked her several times to stop, but she continued to strike him, so he grabbed the PR-24 away from her and tossed it away, which irritated her even more.

She then drew her pistol, and at gunpoint she ordered him to be seated on the curb, or she'd shoot. He again refused to comply and tried to grab her gun. She fired, and he immediately fell to the ground.

The deputy ran to the radio car and announced an officer-involved shooting just occurred, and one suspect was down. Of course when that type of call goes out, the entire station rolls, no questions asked.

Quite a few deputies arrived at once and ran up to the downed man, who was curled up sideways on the wet street, to check for his vital signs.

About twenty seconds passed. The downed suspect said something that was a bit muffled and indistinguishable. The deputy leaned closer and questioned the man, who asked in a low mellow voice, "Is that crazy bitch gone?"

To their surprise, the round she fired had missed him completely. The man was arrested and brought to the station, but he was quickly released when the whole story was revealed. The man waived his claim for any false arrest claims and promised not to hold the department responsible for any liability.

CHAPTER 140

A TEARFUL WOE

The evening had been relatively busy, but it started to slow down, and a two-man Lynwood crew was able to slip over and attempt to catch up on their paperwork. The importance of staying in the field and completing your paperwork cannot be overemphasized. Usually the units are encouraged to park near a busy intersection, so they can be seen by as many persons as possible, in cars and on foot. This positioning is a significant crime deterrent without going into details.

Once their reports were completed, the field sergeant would meet up with them and collect the paperwork. He would check the reports for errors and completion and sign them off. When the field sergeant came into the station he would then drop off the reports into the desk sergeant's tray. The station secretaries' would gather, sort, and confirm the accuracy of the file numbers, and then they would go into proper placement such as the detective, juvenile, and traffic bureaus.

This protocol would allow the deputies to remain in the field and patrol their respective districts. It was very effective, and all units would remain in the field unless coming in with a prisoner. This system worked, and the opportunity to keep as many units as possible in the field was appreciated by the citizens.

Just driving down the empty street, with or without your lights on, was a deterrent. Gangbangers—or the politically correct term, youth groups—were running all over the place up to their old tricks of stealing or killing someone because they missed their target or thought someone looked suspicious, or they were wearing the wrong colors. This was an ongoing major problem, because their parents were weak, and the youth groups were strong.

So this night was actually not really much different as the deputies drove slowly on Platt Street around four in the morning. They were chatting with each another, joking around quietly, but aware of what was going on around them, and what they might come upon.

The right front deputy noticed a person walking toward them on the south sidewalk. The streetlights were dim because of the abundant trees, with their broad leaf spread and branch configurations, reaching far over the individual lawns.

They focused their attention on the figure and realized it was a woman, clad only in her nightgown, walking slowly but staggering slightly and barefoot.

They pulled up to a vacant space near the curb, got out of their car, and approached the woman, who now appeared drunk and apparently lost. As they closed the distance, something appeared to be on top of her head, but they couldn't quite make out what it was. They also noted a moderate amount of blood oozing down both sides of her head and onto her shoulders.

When they reached her, the deputies' eyes widened. They couldn't believe what they saw on her head. It was a four-inch wooden handle of a common butcher knife. And based on the size of that handle, a blade of at least eight inches was probably buried deep inside her skull and possibly her throat as well.

She talked very slowly and deliberately. She said her boyfriend had put the knife in her head, and she needed help right now. Without hesitation an ambulance was summoned, and she was taken to Saint Francis Hospital. The poor victim managed to stay alive another three hours and gave explicit details of her attack.

The victim's boyfriend was arrested for her murder soon after.

One can only imagine the shock of seeing something like that. Such a horror will be in their minds for the rest of their lives.

CHAPTER 141

THE TEASE

He was an engineer in his midthirties and already at work around nine o'clock in the morning. He received a call from his soon-to-be-divorced wife's new boyfriend, who was rude and abrupt, demanding alimony and child support payments now. Apparently the engineer was a day or two late with his payments, but he was rather irritated at the boyfriend's testosterone-filled demands, especially when he said, "We want our money now!"

That statement reminded him of the loss of his lifestyle and the comfort and companionship of his six-year-old boy. He left work immediately after the phone call, went to his new residence, and loaded up his 12-gauge shotgun.

He went directly to his former home and came walking up the sidewalk, carrying the loaded shotgun. Apparently the boyfriend looked out the window and saw the husband carrying the shotgun. He quickly exited through the rear door.

The husband came into the home unannounced, and saw his six-year-old son watching cartoons on television. He told the boy to remain in the room and continue watching TV.

The engineer went to the bedroom where his ex-wife was sleeping and opened the door abruptly. As she sat up and attempted to hide, her ex-husband opened fire and shot her three times. One shot ripped off her right breast; another went through her left kidney, and the final shot blew off half of her buttocks. She was left on the floor, bleeding heavily. He fled the home in his car.

Neighbors heard the shots and called the station. We arrived within minutes of the shooting. The woman was treated by the paramedics and quickly transported to Saint Francis Hospital, and the son was taken into protective custody.

Just before the ambulance arrived, a call from another unit who overheard the emergency broadcast announced he had the suspect/husband on Bullis Road not too far from the Lynwood sheriff's station.

I immediately responded and came upon the deputy who had the suspect already in custody and seated in the backseat of his radio car. The deputy was standing just outside his patrol car. As I pulled up, he was looking down, scratching his head as if perplexed by something.

The deputy was looking at a pigeon that apparently was injured, flopping around on the sidewalk between the deputy and the patrol car.

The deputy he said, "Sarge, something's wrong with this pigeon. I can't figure it out!" I thought he was kidding and making light of his capture of the suspect, who had been en route to the station to turn himself in. The deputy wasn't kidding. He was still scratching his head, not watching the suspect at all, completely focused on the fluttering pigeon.

I asked if he was over on the street where the assault had occurred. He responded that he was one of the first units there, but he didn't have the handle on the call. I then asked if he'd seen the injured woman, who happened to be still alive but seriously injured.

He said that it looked like someone had taken fifty pounds of hamburger and thrown it into a high-speed fan. There was blood and flesh all over the room. When he was describing the scene, his eyes were constricted, and he was very emotional about what he'd seen.

Then he went right back to the injured pigeon and was staring at it as we talked. So I asked if he was okay, but I knew he was in shock. I raised my voice and told him to forget the damn pigeon and keep his attention on the suspect.

He quickly responded, "Yes, sir, I'm okay. I'll go book him right now." I asked him to hold up for a second, because I wanted to talk to the suspect briefly. I opened the opposite rear door and asked the suspect if he was okay.

The suspect replied, "Yeah I'm okay, and I'm sorry. Is she dead?"

I couldn't tell him anything because she was en route when I left the house and probably was at Saint Francis Hospital by then. I added that we would let him know her condition as time went on.

He was very thankful. He wanted to know where his six-year-old son was, and I told him he was coming to the station and would be handed over to children's services, and they would place him in a home.

The oddity of this provoked shooting is a lesson for all to be careful how rough you treat a human sometimes in a divorce proceeding. Sometimes the California court gives all to the wife bearing a child.

And in that judgment the court is sometimes too harsh and minimizes the effect it has on the man, a sort of tough-love situation giving way to gender bias.

In this situation the woman lived, but was minus half a buttock, one kidney and a breast. Do you think Mr. Boyfriend is still with her? I'll bet not, because he displayed his manliness when he ran out the back door and left the "defending" to the injured woman. I hope other brazen boyfriends who call up the soon to be ex-husband guard their mouths when you poke the tiger with a stick.

Also it is imperative that field supervisors watch their charges in the field very close and have a good understanding of Post Traumatic Shock Syndrome, and how it applies to law enforcement situations.

CHAPTER 142

BLINDSIDED

I had just finished my eight-hour night shift at Lynwood. I came in, changed my clothes, and went to my truck. It was a little foggy, so I drove over to the hose bib near the mechanic's bay. I was going to rinse my truck and shell off to get rid of the dew that had accumulated on the windows and mirrors.

The shift I just finished had several traffic accidents where the occupants of the crash were injured and lying in their cars, waiting anxiously for emergency responders to provide aid for their injuries and transport them to the hospital. While the injured were waiting, roving bands of thieves stole their money and jewelry, which they figured the injured parties wouldn't need anymore.

Not to be funny, but it's a bit like crossing the plains of the Serengeti and being injured just before nightfall. What do you think befalls the victims? Lions, hyenas, any meat-eating scavenger you could conjure up. Fortunately, these thieves haven't been consuming their prey yet, but they're just two clicks from being cannibals. They strip you of your property and money as you lie injured or dying. I'm sure if they saw a gold filling in your teeth, they would extract that as well. The lack of humanity and compassion would irritate even an attorney—maybe even a politician.

As I was rinsing my car I was thinking of those filthy cockroaches. I hoped to high heaven I would come across some as they were committing their atrocities, but that possibility seemed remote for someone prepared to take them on. I finished rinsing my car and neatly folded up the hose. I jumped into my warmed-up truck. I came out onto Bullis Road and then turned eastbound on Imperial Highway, heading home.

I couldn't help but notice that another deputy was right behind me, and he was heading away from the station as well. The traffic was light. It was still a little foggy and pretty well quiet. I was traveling at about 35 mph in the number one lane. I came to the red signal at Atlantic Boulevard. I was pretty relaxed. I looked at my watch and noted it was 12:05 a.m. Usually I put my driver's window down to catch the cool breeze, but this time I kept my windows rolled up to avoid the moisture from the rinsing.

The light turned green. No one else was holding at the intersection except me and the other deputy right behind me. My truck was going about 5 mph and beginning to increase speed. Out of nowhere, something slammed into my left side. My shoulder struck the driver's window, and my head followed as if I'd been struck by the base of a large tree.

My truck spun around to the right, and I nearly lost consciousness. When my truck stopped, the right door was opened as I was desperately gathering my wits. A bit dazed, I crawled out of the right door and almost into the lap of a large man who was saying, "Hey, man, you're all fucked up. Give me some money." He was about two feet away from me. I pulled my gun and told him to hit the road or I'd blow him away. He immediately backed off and disappeared. As I staggered through the wreckage, I looked at my truck and noticed it was now L shaped.

I began to realize I'd been struck by another car somehow. I rounded my truck and noticed the deputy who had been following me was stopped right behind me. His driver's door was open wide, and he was not close by.

I continued around my bent truck and saw a powder-blue Plymouth Duster across the street on the driveway apron of the 76 gas station on the southeast corner.

The driver's door was also open, the hood was up, and the whole engine was afire. Dark smoke was billowing just above the fire. No one was around, but I could hear a lot of sirens coming.

I didn't know if I was badly injured, so I stayed near my truck and watched as the Plymouth Duster was steadily consumed by the fire. I was also wondering whether the station had already switched their emergency shut-off control. (This switch is for any fire that is close enough to the gas pumps to spread.)

The deputy returned within minutes and asked how I was and if everything was okay. I said that my head and back hurt, but I was saved because my seatbelt had been fastened, and my windows were up.

I looked over my ruined truck and noticed the driver's door was bent at the top of the door. The impact caused my shoulder and head to bend the upper portion of the door out about four or five inches. I surmised at that point that if I had not kept that window up, I might have literally lost my head from the impact.

The deputy told me that I was struck by the Plymouth. The driver had blown the red signal and slammed right into me at approximately 60 mph. The Plymouth struck my left front wheel and fender. Had it struck my door, it would have killed me.

As we were talking, the fire department arrived. One of the firemen came to me and asked if I was okay. My response was the same except my head and center of my back was hurting quite a bit. The fireman examined my back and noticed a protrusion right in the center of my back and thought it might be a displaced vertebra. Everything else seemed okay. There was no bleeding, but I had quite a headache.

The deputy told me that when the Plymouth struck me, it careened across the intersection and stopped on the driveway apron of the 76 station.

The male driver jumped out of the car as the engine ignited into flames. The deputy stated he ran after the suspect but lost him about two blocks away. He decided to come back and check on my condition.

About ten other units showed up, and two helicopters searched the area for the hit-and-run suspect. Unfortunately, they didn't find him, but he left an open can of beer on the driver's seat right next to his wallet, which had all of his identification and license.

Another sergeant arrived and he assisted me into his car, because I wanted to go to Saint Francis Hospital and get a checkup.

I was extremely beholden to the deputy who was right behind me, and I offered personal sexual favors to him after I died, but he refused.

I was at the hospital for about an hour. The doctor examined me and noted the slight bulge between my shoulders. He asked me to take a deep breath and then let it all out. As I followed his instructions, he slapped the bulge with his open hand, and whatever it was popped back into place, and I felt great. I did have several small cuts inside my mouth, but not enough to need medical attention.

Two days later the suspect, who happened to live in Compton, turned himself in, because everyone was telling him a whole bunch of cops were looking for him because of a hit and run that involved his car.

Is there a moral to this story? The guy who appeared on the scene was nearly shot for approaching me at an inopportune time. We were both lucky that I persuaded him to go away.

The deputy behind me was the hero of the event. I owe him praise, and he deserves worthy thanks for backing me up.

CHAPTER 143

JUNKYARD DOGS: BRED TO BE MEAN

There is a special breed of canine that thrives in the areas of Watts, Willowbrook, Compton, and Lynwood. These areas have abundant packs of dogs that run about all over the territory, especially at night. Most officers, police and sheriff's deputies, who have worked these communities as patrolman for several years will attest to the large packs of dogs running amok and sometimes attacking humans, if they are out alone.

Who else would bring up this topic other than someone who is familiar with this unique setting? No one else seems the least bit concerned. Of course this is not apparent until expensive equipment, conveyances, and upscale money are mixed into an area (Willowbrook Mall, Metro Blue Line, and the new sheriff's station/jail facility at Century Station).

These cities and communities are all closely connected and notorious for their high rates of criminal behavior. There is a rare breed of junkyard dogs that have no borders and complete the picture of gangs and insouciant criminal behavior. To spot one of these junkyard dogs during the day is generally pretty hard, because most are plum tuckered out from the previous night's activities with roaming packs that meander all over these neighborhoods.

Some will attest that they will eat the leaf springs out of a '49 Studebaker and rest in a large pile of animal dung. They are tough and more easily spotted as the night ends and the morning dew begins to fall on parked cars. The only ones up at that time are the working officers desperately looking for criminals who move around surreptitiously stealing anything that isn't bolted down or feverishly guarded.

I wrote of another hectic situation that happened when I was assigned at Firestone Park Station in the chapter titled "Spooked." A freshly cut head of a large dog was placed into a chest of drawers and scared the dickens out of the woman living in the home. Some said this was a childhood prank or the work of prospective ghetto doctors. Go figure.

Most officers are aware of these packs of dogs. They know full well that if they are injured or killed on the streets, the dogs will consume the body before sunrise. We've had many cases of ghetto dogs biting and attacking individuals, and many gang members use them as weapons to attack rival gangs or keep law enforcement from accessing their homes. They have also pulled robberies on defenseless men and women for five or ten dollars. What studs! How manly!

So animal calls are not new and are very sensitive issues to many who live in the area, who condemn any attempts to curb the problems, because the dogs belong to them. Many— and I mean many—do not license their dogs because it costs too much, and the dogs do not have their required shots for rabies and other infectious animal diseases. They're not concerned with liability until a family member is bitten. It's the same as the gang shooting mentality: go ahead and shoot, and we will settle the problem without any police or government intervention. No one wants to give information because of fear of retaliation.

If you were assigned as an animal control officer in the Watts, Willowbrook, or Compton areas, you know full well that gangs are present that will kill you in an instant. Should you try to chase down dogs in their area? What would you do? Remember, you're alone most of the time, and most folks don't want you around. Oh, do you disagree?

It was a vicious animal call in the Willowbrook Community just north of 120th Street. I arrived just as two other one-man units did. The informant was over by a clearing of patchy grass and bare dirt bordered by a small wooden fence. There, nestled next to one of the poles was a large whitish-gray pit bull munching on the rear end of a live, ten-week-old puppy. The puppy was yelping like crazy as the hungry pit bull gnawed on its living morsel. The pit bull was not concerned with any of us including a huge crowd of onlookers who were yelling at us to shoot the dog and stop the poor puppy from suffering.

The dog wouldn't allow anyone near him, and he displayed his temper by jerking his head sharply from side to side, as the puppy's little body and head lingered behind. The handling unit stated that he would like to shoot the dog and stop the ruthless pit bull from its display of Serengeti carnivorous behavior.

I ordered the deputy to hold his fire, unless provoked, so I could check on the rear of the dog's position. There had to be a clear field of fire so no one would be harmed. (Remember the previous chapter describing ricochet factor?)

I carefully examined the field of fire and made damn sure the area was clear of children and adults. I told the deputy to use the shotgun, not the pistol, so the likelihood of missing would be minimized.

As the deputy charged the weapon, an Ithaca 12-gauge pump shotgun, I suggested to use only one round, which happened to be a number four buck, which has approximately twenty-seven pellets about the size of a .32 caliber round. I lightly questioned his accuracy, and he exclaimed, "Oh, Sarge, come on, give me a break."

I gave permission to fire. Unfortunately, his shot blew the puppy right out of the pit bull's mouth. The puppy lay dead a short distance away, although the pit bull was severely injured, with its jaw bleeding and partially dangling. I ordered the deputy to fire again, and his second round killed the pit bull.

I shook my head in dismay at the deputy's poor aim and advised him to await the arrival of LA County Animal Control to dispose of the dead animals.

We had to report and account for the rounds fired and provide proper follow-up information to justify the use of deadly force against a dangerous animal.

Several days later I had to follow up on yet another dog shooting in Lynwood. The lieutenant wanted me to investigate the deputies' reports of shooting another pit bull who had charged at them. There is generally no problem when great care is used with firearms, but in this case the pit bull was attacking them and was shot in the rump. Uh-oh! The investigation revealed that the deputies had been chasing the dog over a three-block area. Shooting at a running dog was not justified and absolutely unsafe. In this instance the deputies received days off for misconduct and poor decisions.

Thirty residents were contacted, and their views and opinions were recorded. Every one of them was concerned that the deputies chasing the dog were shooting at it on the run. That is probably one of the most unsafe shootings I've ever heard of, and many people were put in harm's way.

I might add that another situation occurred in the Willowbrook area right next to the central station of the Blue Line, the light rail system that was started in the late eighties. A woman who was despondent came to the light-rail platform to commit suicide. Fortunately the train was late, and she became irritated.

She rounded the fence bordering the light rail on Imperial Highway and crossed over to the Union Pacific Railroad heavy rail on the other side of the fence, closer to Wilmington Avenue. It just so happened there was a heavy-rail train coming southbound at approximately 10 mph, meandering through the snakelike curves approaching Imperial Highway.

The woman darted right in front of the oncoming train at the moment it was passing her. It mowed right over her, cutting both of her legs off just above her knees, and tossed her to the east a few feet, toward the Blue Line fence border.

Deputies ran to her aid as the train tried to stop, but there were at least a hundred heavily loaded attached cars.

As the deputies came upon her, she was trying to sit up and was pulling on one of her leg bones, which was fully exposed with a fair amount of blood oozing from the four-inch stumps. The woman was screaming, "Get this out of me, the devil is in me, take this out!" The deputy empathetically responded, "You're going to need that, ma'am. You had better leave it alone." Another deputy assisted in applying tourniquets to both legs to hold off the surge of blood. They anxiously awaiting the EMTs.

The deputies noted that the woman's bib overalls were knotted and wadded on her shoulders. It was unclear how they got that way in the first place.

One of her legs was located under the main locomotive about a quarter mile south of the initial impact. Unfortunately, her other leg was last seen being carried by a large junkyard dog heading southbound on the tracks and across Willowbrook Avenue, toward Mona Boulevard. That leg was never recovered, and we can guess what happened.

The woman was transported to the hospital quickly, and her life was saved.

The hysteria over the football player Michael Vick's involvement in dogfighting was understandable; it was a very mean thing to do. However, in the ghetto this type of activity occurs quite often.

Our department has a special unit that tries to chase down these people and it is called the vice bureau. Most of the organized dogfights are kept quiet and enjoyed by both blacks and Hispanics. In the Hispanic communities they have cockfights. And in Mexico it's a primary entertainment, just like bullfights. Do you think they have dogfights in Mexico or Canada? You know they do.

I wonder where Michael Vick was raised. I'll bet there was a lot of dogfighting going on, condoned by many affluent individuals as well as the poorer communities. I'll bet he didn't really think that what he was doing would be seen as contemptible and immoral. He wasn't killing humans, but he probably was around a lot of gangs and dope. What I'm saying is, if he was raised where there were dogfights, and he is nothing more than a product of his environment. I don't condone his behavior, but I certainly wouldn't treat him as a common criminal, or worse yet, a gangbanger.

Many of my friends were killed fighting the gangs and narcotics distribution. But none were killed attending dogfights or cockfights. Most people who attended those fights submitted to law enforcement and were easily arrested.

Michael Vick erred and paid a substantial price for it, including jail time. Enough is enough. Leave him alone and let him enjoy life as a normal man.

Now, as for the gangbanging athletes in football, baseball, and any other sport, don't let little children look up to them as idols. They should be thrown out without any further remedy and the team owners should be stiffly fined for lack of "due diligence." I don't mean the sponsors, I mean the individual who hires them. A million dollars is a good start, but it can be increased rather quickly.

I'll bet that'll change who's packing heat. (Four guns in a locker? Come on, is anyone watching? How much will it cost when several high-priced gangbangers are killed in their own locker room?)

Politicians and spokespersons will of course insist there are no packs of junkyard dogs running amok, and there are no dogfights or cockfights going on, but what do you think?

Take a stroll with the family down Willowbrook Avenue, just above El Segundo Boulevard going northbound around three in the morning, if the thugs miss you, the pack of junkyard dogs won't. And if you spot an animal control officer, you had better kick him real hard, because most likely he fell asleep or is dead. They don't work the early morning hours, do they?

Are there any snooping environmentalists lurking around ghettos in the late evening hours to spot animal cruelty? I'll bet not.

CHAPTER 144

GONE AWRY: MISSING LYNWOOD UNIT

I was headed south on Atlantic Avenue, just south of Rosecrans Avenue, looking for an East Compton unit with two deputies. The training officer and his trainee were close by, I hoped, moving around and being seen by the neighborhood and shaking down suspicious people.

The traffic was near nil, with occasional headlights popping in and out of my view, but with no alarming movements. It was a little after three in the morning, and the sheriff's radio was pretty quiet. I had been in the area for about twenty minutes and had seen neither hide nor hair of them.

I continued down Atlantic Avenue and then westbound on Alondra. Still nothing. I then decided I would go over by the Big Donut's darkened parking lot, at Atlantic and Alondra, and wait to see if they passed by, going to a call or making a pedestrian or car stop.

The radio was very quiet for another ten minutes, and then suddenly a call went out for the East Compton unit to respond to a disturbance call on Thorson Avenue just north of Greenleaf Boulevard. I readied myself to spot the unit, see where it was coming from, and then track the unit to the call without being seen. Still there was no vehicular traffic whatsoever, and then I spotted a lone unit coming from the city of Paramount. That unit came directly across from the Los Angeles Flood Control Bridge, which borders Compton and Paramount.

Instead of following the unit and revealing myself, I chose to take Greenleaf Avenue and come from the opposite direction toward the home on Thorson Avenue. As I rounded the corner on Thorson Avenue, I spotted the East Compton unit's headlights, pulled to the east side of the street, and waited patiently for ten minutes. I could easily see both deputies moving about near the front door of the home. They seemed unalarmed.

I felt the deputies were about to wind up the call, so I backed onto Greenleaf Avenue and returned to the Big Donut parking lot. Once there, if necessary, I would follow the unit.

Several minutes passed, and I heard the unit clear the call. I expected to see them shortly, and sure enough here they came, buzzing up and over the bridge and out of sight. I followed them about thirty seconds behind and came to the top of the bridge. I could see at least a mile to the east, but no cars at all were on the street. Now I looked around and figured they must have seen me and were hiding, but that was unlikely. I noticed a vacant construction site just to the north and veered toward the site. I looked around and couldn't spot anyone. I came back to the main street, thinking they must be close, but I just couldn't figure out where they were. So I returned to the top of the bridge with my lights out, stopped just short of the apex, and shut off my car engine.

I turned the radio very low and leaned partially out the window. Still nothing. I looked at the gated access to the LA Flood Control roadway and thought maybe they had the access key and went into the flood control. I pulled onto the driveway apron near the gate and saw a large chain draped around the framing poles of the gate. I got out of my car to see if there was a lock, and if it was secured. I carefully scanned the chain for the lock and discovered it was missing. I thought, *Ah, they could very well be in the flood control but doing what?* Nothing came into my mind, so I pulled the draped chain, which had a section welded to the cross member, so it could not be removed.

I drove onto the access road, closed the gate, and redraped the chain. I kept my head lamps off, so I wouldn't reveal myself too easily. I continued onto the isolated drive. The roadway is actually pretty well constructed. It sits high above the concrete flood-control channel. I drove slowly, so I could look to the east on the dirt overflow, which was loaded with shrubs that I used to hide in when playing with my friends and brother some thirty years before.

It was very dark as I crept along, the radio still very low and my head lamps off. About a mile down the path, I looked east and noticed a brake lamp flash momentarily, just under the next southern bridgeway, on the dirt overflow side.

Then the bright map light came on. I saw the driver quickly lean over and switch it off. The driver, most likely the training officer, must have seen me coming across his field of vision and tried to cover their whereabouts.

I continued southbound as if just wandering about slowly, without braking. I noticed the radio car in my rearview mirror, driving west toward the roadway, then onto the roadway and away from my position, returning to the gated access.

I couldn't imagine what the hell the unit was doing, but I was not in any position to order them to stop, because they could easily avoid me by accelerating. I needed to turn around or face backing up a significant distance to try to catch them as they drove forward.

I went a little way along the path, made laborious ten-point turn, and came back toward the gated access. When I reached the gate I saw it was closed and this time secured with a large heavy-duty padlock. They'd boxed me in for quite some time, and I would have to find another way out. That's what they thought, but I knew that the next egress was at Deforest Street in Long Beach, which I used when I lived with my parents on Dairy Avenue; I was familiar with the neighborhood.

So I drove to the exit and came back to east Compton. During that time I was thinking of how I was going to determine and prove who was in that unit, other than assuming it had to be the training officer and his trainee.

After an hour or two the sun started to come up, and there was a radio call of a burglar alarm going off at the Savon drugstore over on Atlantic Avenue and Compton Boulevard. I responded, as did the assigned unit, the east Compton unit with the training officer and his trainee. The trainee was a clean-cut Hispanic. He apparently was a black belt in karate and was doing pretty well, but his TO was questionable. He always seemed distant to me and a bit elusive. I couldn't quite sniff out what was going on, but after the flood control incident, I was a little perplexed.

The surrounding buildings appeared okay, and we talked a short bit about the likelihood of roof burglaries. I strongly urged them to check the roof. because roof burglars do frequent the area.

The TO of course told the trainee to climb up the ladder. He knew the sergeant's car always carried the ladder and urged all to use it.

But what the TO probably didn't know was that I always went up as well, to demonstrate initiative. We unfolded the ladder and extended it to its maximum length. I went up first. Once on the first roof landing, I motioned the trainee to come up, and he followed quickly.

I then pulled the ladder upward and positioned it again on the second main roof, which I scaled. The trainee and I checked the vents and all hatches for any signs of tampering. The roof appeared secure, and so we were about to descend. This time it was more relaxed, and we were somewhat at ease. I was casually discussing roof burglaries in the Compton area and how to spot them. I also said that if a roof burglar was found on top of the roof, he would most likely fight to get away, and we discussed the solutions with combat on the roof.

I suggested that the trainee go down first, and he started to climb onto the erect ladder. He appeared a little scared, so I asked, "Are you spooked of heights?" He said he was, so I replied, "Take your time and just move slowly."

I added, "Here, let me help you. It will make it a little easier." I grabbed his inside collar with my right hand and thumb and let him feel the strength of my grasp, and he slowly descended. When he was about two rungs down I ripped his collar back, causing his grip to loosen. He started to whimper.

I said loudly, "Now listen, you little shit, you locked that fuckin' gate, didn't you?" He quickly responded, "I didn't do it, sir, my training officer did!"

I yelled out to the training officer that his trainee had just snitched him off for locking the gate. He looked flabbergasted and had no reply. As I came down I looked at them and said I'd take care of them real soon. I retracted the ladder and returned it to my car.

Now I had both of them off guard. I needed to find something to set them straight so it would never happen again. Within several days something else did happen.

The training officer was removed from the station and was under investigation for an incident that occurred with his previous trainee. It turned out that the training officer and his previous trainees, both men, were sexually and romantically entangled with each other and under the influence of narcotics.

They were apparently allowed to resign from the department, in lieu of prosecution, which is often offered to wayward deputies.

The deputy I purposely jerked from the ladder turned out okay and finally made it off training. I never approached him again about the matter, but our eyes frequently locked. What do you think? Do you think I was too sneaky? Is there nothing wrong with two men entwined in lovemaking and under the influence of narcotics?

CHAPTER 145

ABANDONED: EMPTY HEADS

There was no indication this was going to be any different from any other evening shift. I came in early, as always, shined up my gear, and prepped my uniform. Then I geared up and went to the sergeant's office.

The station had recently removed the expensive bulletproof windows on the front desk area, because it appeared too offensive to the general public. That ought to give you an idea of the thinking at the time of these incidents. The first day they removed the windows, some idiot jumped the front desk and chased a secretary for a short bit until he was dropped like a rock and thrown into jail. Oh, how politics always weigh in and enter into the front lines. That's until another investigation reveals there is something very dumb about a line operation that is stripped of a fundamental necessity.

It was around six o'clock and getting pretty busy, but little did I know how busy it would become. This night was typical, with the intense calls for service and emergencies. And it would reveal another staff member not up to doing his or her job. The desk was busy as always, but calls still came in, and we were scurrying all over the place. Attention 250 Sam—that's me—a robbery just occurred here, an assault occurred there; they wanted me all over the damn place.

That's okay. I liked the action and the deputies did good jobs taking care of the injured, crime victims, suspects, and witnesses, doing this and doing that.

Then a more serious call came for a shooting over on Carlin Avenue, not too far from Atlantic Avenue. Several units arrived quickly, and then I pulled up several minutes later. I noticed the yellow tape barrier was set up around the scene. A black male teenager had been shot and killed, and important procedures had to be followed by the handling unit and assisting units.

The first units that arrived on the scene knew exactly what to do, and steadily worked to finish the emergency broadcast and tape off the area. They needed to locate all witnesses, separating them so they wouldn't talk with one another. They were waiting for me to arrive but still hustling to get things done.

When the teenager was shot, his girlfriend was struck in the leg as well, and she had already been transported to Saint Francis Hospital; accompanied by a deputy assigned to keep watch over her.

There were about fifty sightseers weaving near and about the scrimmage line and deputies were trying to establish a viable route for persons trying to get to their apartments. This crime line tape is intended to keep unnecessary people out of the crime scene and try to preserve evidence. In busy apartment complexes with well over a hundred occupants, it can be quite hectic when

422

everyone is law-abiding, and abides by rules established at the onset of the crime. However, in this case, the complex was inundated with gangs, who at any given moment, might disrupt the whole scene with all sorts of diversions.

Six units were there already, but the scene was getting out of hand. It was like a huge pot of stew brimming with ingredients and boiling over. Something else was about to occur—you could feel it. At these events you not only needed to watch and protect the crime scene, you needed to watch out for any eventuality that might occur, like another shooting, within an established crime scene.

There was yelling and screaming, but we held our own as I established a command post and instill stability so the deputies could get their work done. I was attempting to break loose some of our units that were needed elsewhere in the field for other important calls for service. That was an essential need in a crisis like this, to direct some units to stay and kick loose others, and of course inform the desk of our condition.

Three young black men pulled up in a dark car, jumped out, and came over to the crime tape. Together they ducked under the barricade tape and ran down the side access. They were met by a deputy, Byron W., who was in position to stop individuals trying to come onto the scene. Another deputy saw one of the gangsters dump a pistol in a large Dumpster as he whisked by, noticing the deputies were already chasing them down. It seemed like there was going to be another shooting within the taped-off murder scene. Our deputies were all trying to maintain security and control. I ran up to the deputy already involved in a donnybrook at the base of another large Dumpster. He had his hands full, attempting to maneuver and handcuff the gangster. There was no room for me to squeeze between the Dumpster and a small wall, so I watched Bryon to be sure he maintained control of his idiot and not get injured himself.

I heard noises coming from behind me and turned around. Lo and behold, there was another adult gangster, running toward me and about to clobber me, when I slapped him upside the head and swept his legs out from under him. He fell to the pavement like a tons of bricks. I stepped on his head like a basketball and held him in that position until Bryon got up with his thug in cuffs.

Then I brought my thug up by his hair and collar and cuffed him. He was yelling and crying that I had hurt him. (Compassion? You've got to be kidding!) The deputy told me that his idiot had thrown a brown paper bag into the Dumpster, and he was going in the Dumpster to retrieve it. When he reached in the Dumpster, he located the only brown paper bag sitting atop several large black plastic trash bags loaded with trash. Bryon opened the bag, and inside there were three biscuit-size rocks of cocaine worth several thousand dollars. The other man was apprehended by another crew not too far from us in the darkened side access. We released our hooked gangbangers to the custody of the two-man crew who took custody of all three and left for Lynwood Station to book them.

I tried again to establish another command post and was asking for more deputies, but none were available. I still continued to get everything ready and finally established a phone hookup with the desk at Lynwood Station. I was told that I was desperately needed at Saint Francis Hospital. The deputy there was having a rough time with the mother of the injured female juvenile and demanding that she be removed from custody as a material witness.

I explained that I was on the command post, and the policy of the department was to never abandon the command post under any conditions, because containment and control would be lost. The desk wouldn't relent and repeated the desperate need for me at the hospital. I was told to leave the command post operations to a deputy. They also advised me there were no other deputies available, and another robbery had just occurred on Atlantic Avenue just blocks away from my present position.

I was upset and irritated because I was the only sergeant in the field, and no one was available for any other emergent calls, but more so because of the stack of calls coming out for any available unit.

I picked Bryon to take over while I was gone. I came out of the driveway and saw a deputy walking around aimlessly. I ordered him to watch the Dumpster, which had a pistol inside. That pistol belonged to one of the assailants who ducked our tape line, so it was very important to maintain security of that Dumpster. The deputy acknowledged my concerns and stated he understood, so I walked away from him for a moment. I returned to the command post to tell Bryon about some other important matters to attend to.

When I was going back out toward the front of the complex to get into my car, I noticed the deputy whom I had assigned to watch the Dumpster was in fact out in the very front of the apartment complex. He was talking nonchalantly to another deputy, seated in a unit, not watching the Dumpster at all. I walked over to the deputy and yelled at him like a drunken cowboy digging in his spurs into the flesh of his horse. The deputy realized I was very mad at his slovenly attitude regarding preservation of evidence and that he was not obeying my orders. I'll admit I did demean him in front of his peers, but that was tough. Emergencies were occurring and this was no time for democracy or political correctness.

I quickly got into my car and sped to Saint Francis hospital. It took me approximately five minutes to arrive at the hospital. I parked on the side near the ambulance receiving dock and walked into the multidoor area and directly to the deputy standing by just outside one of the operating rooms. He began to tell me about his charge, who was argumentative and demanding release; however, she had been wounded in the thigh and was in protective custody.

She was about seventeen years of age and the girlfriend of the deceased gangster. She was cuffed to a gurney in the operating room, screaming, as the deputy was telling me about what was going on. She seemed to be a low priority for the emergency room staff until she stopped her antics. I could plainly hear her threats to the deputy as he was conversing with me.

He told me that the wounded female was the girlfriend of the decedent. He said that as the emergency staff was attempting to secure a signature from her mother for medical attention she, the mother, became caustic as well and wanted to take her daughter out of the hospital. The deputy informed the mother about the protocol and procedures when someone is in protective custody as a material witness to a murder. The mother was adamant that she wanted to take custody of her daughter and demanded her removal immediately. Well, that just wasn't going to happen; the daughter was remaining and would be treated with authorization from the Department of Children's Services, if necessary.

The mother, who cussed and threatened the deputy, left momentarily and was expected to return shortly. As the deputy was telling me the details of the rude mother's behavior, she overheard the deputy describing her poor attitude.

She chimed in abruptly and exclaimed, "That's right. I'm taking my motherfucking daughter, no matter what you say!" I blocked the doorway with my body. "Ma'am, you can't take her. She's in our custody."

With that comment she pushed me aside and attempted to pass by. I grabbed her arm and pulled her back.

She said, "Let me go, motherfucker, I want my daughter."

I informed her she was going to jail for obstructing and interfering with a peace officer in the performance of his duties. She rattled off obscenities as I was cuffing her wrists together in the doorway. She was twisting about and motherfucking this and motherfucking that. The hospital staff were watching the theatrics as I struggled to maintain control of her.

I told the deputy to remain with the daughter. I was taking this foul-mouthed banshee to the station. She kept dropping to the floor, trying to delay her extraction by fighting every step of the way. She twisted her body and jerked her arms trying to slip from my grasp. I then decided to put my arm under her cuffs, grab her blouse collar, and force her to stand up, which is a very effective way to make someone stand up straight. When I grabbed her collar I inadvertently grabbed her hair. Unfortunately her wig came off and into my hands, exposing her close-cropped hair, just as I hit the red button to open the two emergency doors to the ambulance docks. She refused to stand and collapsed her body to inhibit our progress.

As I dragged her along, we unfortunately passed the front lobby of the hospital. There, in the lobby were apparently twenty to thirty family members and friends of the mother, the woman I was taking to my car, cuffed up and still screaming her head off. They saw me with her in tow and charged toward me, yelling threats to take her from my custody. I ordered them to back away and not to interfere, all the while managing her weight and going down the stairs.

I overheard several threatening to jump me. They said they were going to kick my ass. They were way too close, and I had no time for needless verbiage. I got to my car and stumbled around stuffing the woman into the backseat. These friends and family members closed the gap even more and were within a couple of feet from me, when I pulled my gun. I ordered them back or someone was going to die.

They backed away momentarily, when I grabbed my radio and asked for assistance. The desk came back immediately and told me there was no one available, because all units were tied up at the murder scene, and three armed robberies that had just occurred along Atlantic Avenue.("Busy, you betcha!")

I was up to my ass in alligators. No help was around. I was holding twenty or more angry people at gunpoint, and I had to get away from this mob.

I fumbled around with my gun pointed at the lead males in the mob and started the engine quickly, with my gun shifted to my left hand and out the side window. Once the motor started, I put my gun back into my right hand, shifted with my left hand, and backed out as the crowd stood about ten feet away.

I then dropped the shift lever into drive and slammed the accelerator to the floor, and tore away from the hospital parking lot onto Imperial Highway eastbound to the station, just about two blocks away.

I was thinking how I was going to tell the lieutenant what had occurred in the last two hours, and that there were about fifty people from both places about to converge on the station to protest the excessive and unnecessary force used.

That's when I remembered it was Lieutenant Scurry on deck, He probably wouldn't be able to handle this mob when they came in. His command presence was not very good. He had a meek face and a slovenly appearance.

Well, it was too late to contemplate it any further. I drove into the parking lot and pulled up to the stairs near the watch commander's access. I got out of the car and leaned back on it and took a deep breath, knowing full well the lieutenant was going to be agitated and irritable because of all the work I was about to bestow upon him. I rested at that spot for about a minute and then stood up, still listening to the screaming woman in the backseat, yelling her head off.

I needed to get the lieutenant to meet me near the side door so I could tell him of the foreseeable problems. As I got to the top step, the side door opened. Lo and behold it was Lieutenant Scurry in his civilian clothes. I was anxious to inform him of the incidents that occurred first on Carlin Avenue and then at Saint Francis Hospital as they unfolded. I warned him that at least fifty mob types were coming to the station to complain about all incidents, which were somewhat connected. Lieutenant Scurry looked at me with an insouciant face and complete indifference. He laughed, raised his wristwatch in front of me, and stated, "Hey, I've got a plane to catch; you've got it!"

I looked at him with dismay and thought he was kidding. He wasn't; he walked down the stairs and went to his car.

I thought, *Holy shit, this is going to get much worse, and Lieutenant Scurry just abandoned me and left me in charge of the whole mess, and anything else that might pop up.* I thought more and decided that no one else could conjure up this kind of mess but me, a regular "shit magnet." I felt that I was more trained than most supervisors and could handle this, as well as any other failure of support, a hallmark of Lynwood Station's poor leadership.

I went inside to the jail, and dropped off the still-screaming female, and quickly went into the sergeant's office to prepare for the onslaught of complaints. I informed the desk and watch deputy of what was about to occur in the lobby, and they called in several units to back me up.

I was alone, but with a batch of good strong Lynwood deputies backing me up, and who could have asked for anything better? We all knew very well it might get dicey when the mob showed up in the lobby. There might be racial overtones, and threats because I didn't cower to their demands.

Ten minutes later, here they came, about fifty assembling along the walk, just before the door. They came in united and boisterous. I casually walked to the counter and noticed the lobby was already packed and streaming outside. Their loud and obnoxious demands were very disruptive. I told everyone, from the opposite side of the counter, to quiet down. I explained that Lynwood Station was a business office, and they were disturbing important service functions.

The group continued to loudly make all sorts of incoherent accusations about what had occurred on Carlin Avenue and Saint Francis Hospital, so I warned them again and added that if they didn't comply they would be arrested. I told them to go outside, away from the station's activities, and scream and yell all they wanted. That's when one male approached me and displayed his credentials as a member of the US Department of Justice and a private attorney.

He demanded to see his nephew who was jailed from the Carlin Avenue murder scene, and claimed he was beaten like a dog by some racist sergeant. I asked to see his federal credentials and attorney's ID, which he produced. I promptly took those pieces of identification and asked a deputy to copy them.

While we were waiting for the copies to return, I informed the man that there was a conflict with his request and he wouldn't be allowed to see his nephew. I explained that he couldn't use his federal ID for anything, because he was not acting within his capacity as an agent. He was there as a family member who was alarmed because one of his family was arrested and taken to jail.

I also told him that as an attorney he presented yet another conflict of interest, because he was acting as a family member without a valid court order. Because he was in the front of this group, he was placing himself in a position of inciting disruptive behavior. He pushed and used his credentials as instruments of authority and would be one of the first arrested if the need arose. I said that his nephew had not been beaten, on which he was vehemently insisting, and that I was the one who dropped him and stepped on his head like a bug because he attacked me. I added that that same suspect was in lockup, laughing, and only had a two-inch abrasion on the side of his head.

I lifted the counter portion that allows for foot traffic. I stepped into the lobby and among the loud protesters. I announced to the group that I was the sergeant in command at the Carlin Avenue murder scene, and of the investigation that was in progress, with several suspects involved, as well as the ones who ducked under the crime area with a gun and large amount of narcotics. I added that I was the sergeant in charge at Saint Francis Hospital and had arrested and handcuffed the mother. Furthermore, I was the one they had attacked at the ambulance docks, to whom I displayed my gun to prevent them from wresting her from my custody. I said I recognized many of them as active participants in that scene. I identified myself as the highest-ranking officer at Lynwood Station at that time, and the watch commander in charge of all operations.

The crowd quieted down, with some rumbling, but within reason. I passed out citizen complaint forms, tearing off individual sheets of paper, with fill-in lines for expediency sake, asserting wrongdoing by departmental employees. I informed all inside the foyer and in the vestibule of my full name, rank, and employee number.

I repeated my involvement at both the Carlin Avenue murder scene and at Saint Francis Hospital. I reemphasized I was the one in charge at both locations and the main one who used force on both parties. I also informed them that each and every complaint would be received and handed directly to the captain of Lynwood Station the following morning.

I remained standing in the foyer among most of them and illustrating how to fill out the complaints completely. When they finished I collected thirty-six complaints and combined them into a single stack. The protesters left the station without any further disruption. I wrote a short memo to the captain indicating that I would be in early the next day to discuss the complaints. My relief lieutenant came in around eleven o'clock, and I relayed the info to him as well.

When I left the station that night, I was miffed at Lieutenant Scurry for abandoning his position when I really needed help, but I knew down deep that I should've expected it. The old adage, "What goes around, comes around," is an expected reaction for the quality of leadership with any of the three Ss.(Lieutenants Snake, Spite and Scurry)

I came in an hour earlier the next day, and walked into the watch sergeant's office. The phone rang as I was looking through the scheduling board. It was a lieutenant summoning me as soon as I was available. I thought, *Well, this is it. The captain wants to speak to me now.*

The captain was fanning the thirty-six complaints in both of his hands. He asked, "Larry, what the hell happened last night?" I noted an empty aluminum chair surrounded by three lieutenants, one of whom was none other than Lieutenant Snake.

Boy, did this look like a one-stop snipe shot, so I had to make an opening announcement to set this record straight.

I stood directly in front of the empty chair and faced the captain, across his expansive desk. "Captain, number one, I'm not intimidated by rank." I took a moment and made eye contact with each seated lieutenant, letting them know I was not scared or intimated by them, individually or collectively. This was done primarily to set a tone that I would not be willing to stand by and let people pee down my back and tell me its raining.

I continued, "Number two, I have a wealth of experience and can handle anything in the field or at this station, except one thing. That one thing is, I don't know how to investigate myself, and I was perplexed, because I never heard of such a thing in my years on the department."

I went on, "Now I'll go into the whole matter and explain in detail who, what, when, where, how, and why these complaints were generated."

I'll admit I had the captain's whole attention, and thank God it was to him that I was explaining the sordid details up to and including my acceptance of the complaints in the lobby of the station.

When I finished the captain said, "What did Lieutenant Scurry say?" I repeated the lieutenant's words: "Hey, I've got a plane to catch, you've got it!" The captain leaned back in his chair and nodded. He told me this was going to Internal Affairs and would be a major investigation. I smiled and stated, "I hope they do a good job, because there's only one person who screwed up here, and I'll leave that decision up to them and to you."

I was excused. I went back to the sergeant's office, leaned against the file cabinet, and drew a deep breath of relief. Several sergeants came in and smiled, knowing full well what I just went through. I advised them I would let them know in a short while what had occurred and that the whole matter was going to Internal Affairs.

Now was the time to keep my loose mouth closed, because it might very well end up getting twisted during the investigation. I remained on the night shift for about another month, during which time I was asked to "body swap" with another sergeant who was assigned to East Los Angeles Station. Because of the unnecessary turmoil, dealing with the three Ss, I felt it was a no-brainer to swap with the other sergeant. Fortunately, it was approved, and I was transferred to East Los Angeles.

Several months passed. I was called at home by an Internal Affairs investigator who wanted to hear the exact words Lieutenant Scurry used when I gave him the details of that night's events. I repeated, "Hey, I've got a plane to catch, you've got it!" She replied, "You're sure?" "Yes, I am, positively." She said the investigation was almost complete and would be submitted to the chief.

I was excited about how the investigation was conducted; to be concluded in a matter of three months was quick. Two weeks later I was informed by departmental correspondence that I was completely exonerated.

I was further informed that Lieutenant Scurry was found in violation of many obligations set forth in the departmental manual of policies and procedures. Without going onto the detailed description of his "negligence and abandonment," the disciplinary action pretty much spells out his level of incompetence and defiance. The lieutenant was given thirty days off, the maximum in lieu of termination, and was transferred to Firestone Park Station. Lieutenant Scurry defiantly refused the discipline and the transfer and was allowed to retire from the department. Boy, what a move. So who really suffered from the fiasco? I'll let you figure that out. The false accusations hurt many people.

My rendition of this last experience with incompetent supervisors expresses exactly what was going on and how the three Ss were the essence of the problems in a high crime area, not the deputies. Lieutenant Spite was fixated on his own political ambitions and decided to discipline me on a whim of his arrogance. Lieutenant Scurry was after one thing, quite similar to Lieutenant Snake's avoidance of the decision-making process. They were determined to undermine the law enforcement work ethic.

The ones who succeeded were the deputies who backed me up many times and made me proud of their countless ways of operation. God bless those deputies and damn those morons who weakened their work ethic and pursuit of a law enforcement career.

CHAPTER 146

EAST LOS ANGELES STATION: A FAMILIAR RENDEZVOUS

It was my first night at East Los Angeles Station located just south of the 60 freeway, across from the infamous duck pond, just north of Third Street. It was almost like old home week for the Special Enforcement Bureau, because ELA's patrol car driveway leads directly to the SEB parking lot.

The Special Enforcement Bureau is situated on the northern portion of the same duck pond, where I spent an unforgettable eight and a half years.

Directly across from the front of ELA station's front doors is the municipal courthouse. The area is teeming with a Hispanic population and lots of small children play and have fun in the small grassy knolls that surround the pond. It was relatively safe, and the local families knew it. On the weekends there would be many colorful festivities, with mariachis playing their music while moving all about the park.

The reason it's so peaceful is because of the large presence of law enforcement in and out of the ELA sheriff's station, the Special Enforcement Bureau, and the municipal court building. Officers would be seen crossing the park and around the pond most of the day in uniform and many were seen in their running gear working out in the daytime and nighttime.

My first night in the field was with a fellow sergeant I knew well. He showed me the procedures and arrangements of the station's operating functions. It was very pleasing and a much nicer environment than my previous assignment, and the sergeant was excellent in his presentation. We went to the briefing and discussed assignments, and he introduced me to the deputy personnel.

Everyone was cordial, and I was feeling comfortable. No one had a confrontational attitude. The lieutenants were warm and friendly and had a genuine good work ethic. What a relief compared to the drudgery at Lynwood.

East Los Angeles was also the area where the sheriff's academy was located, where I started my law enforcement career with the Compton Police Department, first as a cadet and then as a staff member and drill instructor until mid-1975. Later I left the SEB and returned to the sheriff's academy as an advanced officer training staff member. During this first year the academy was moved to the former Monte Vista High School, which was being renovated into a new and much more multifaceted training facility. This new training facility was in an unincorporated area on Telegraph Road and Colima Road just north of the city of La Mirada.

My point is that this ELA patrol area was familiar to me for the past twenty years. In fact, I was about to marry again. My second wife, Gloria, was raised in the El Sereno area of Los Angeles, just north of East Los Angeles. Yep, she is Mexican, and in my mind quite the catch. Her whole family was very close to one another and always referred to me as the lovable gringo pendejo, which they told me meant that I was quite the catch for her as well, and a welcome addition to the Hispanic community and their family.

CHAPTER 147
SHITTY SITUATION

It was around seven in the evening when a call came out that there was a fight at one of the Hispanic bars over on Whittier Boulevard just east of Atlantic Avenue. I jumped into the sergeant's patrol car with the other sergeant, Fred O., who wanted to show me the area, which he knew well. He had already readied the patrol car with our personal gear.

Another sergeant, Joe P., who wanted to take the lead and display his driving skills, was just in front of us as both of our cars raced out of the parking lot. We were speeding down Third Street and coming up to Atlantic Avenue. The lead car, with Sergeant Joe P., apparently didn't see the median island that separated northbound and southbound traffic lanes. He sailed right across that center median and destroyed the front tires by collapsing both of them in the center of the concrete curbs.

We continued on, after determining Joe was okay, and sped to the bar fight. Three units were already there. We came into the bar and noticed about five involved in the melee move away and out the rear door. They ran to the rear outside portion of bar, where five passenger cars were parked and locked into the bar's inner perimeter.

When I went into the small hallway that led from the rear door, I came upon one of the men hiding near one of the parked cars and ordered him to stand up. He turned and tried to leap over the six-foot chain-link fence that surrounded the small area. I grabbed his collar and pulled him backward.

He began to swing wildly at me. I told him to cool down and talk to me. He swung again, this time much closer to my face, so I grabbed him around his neck and bent his arm behind his back as he struggled to break free. Then I almost lost my footing on something very slippery on the walkway. I looked down to see what the substance was. There were many piles of human excrement, stacked in little round, heaping piles between the parked cars.

It seemed as if the regular bar bathroom was occupied so much that most patrons just took a casual dump outside. There had to be at least twenty piles of that "crapola" between the cars, and I was right in the middle of a sea of waste.

The man I was attempting to control was swinging his free arm trying to strike me, but to no avail. I had a good lock on his head and left arm and was standing erect, very cautious not to fall.

Suddenly I noticed Fred O., the sergeant I came with, running across the hood of one of the parked cars, sounding like he was running with wet feet slapping on a damp floor.

As he drew closer to me, I noticed Fred had his 245 Gonzales sap in his right hand. In a downward motion from over his head, he slammed that puppy right onto my arms and continued to strike me as I was attempting to control the combative suspect. I wrestled with the man as he moved along the parked car with his body, and I was able to see the distinct feces footprints stepping across the hood as Fred continued to attempt to strike the suspect.

Although I was struck quite a few times by the sap, it didn't hurt that much, but I did yell to Fred to stop hitting me. My biggest concern was not to fall down or brush against the hood of the parked car that had the feces all over its entire hood.

The fight subsided after several minutes, and about six were arrested for fighting in public and public drunkenness. I also think my buddy/partner sergeant, Fred, ran out of gas from hitting me; his little arms tired so quickly.

No one was seriously hurt, but most had small abrasions and bruising. If those simple wounds made contact with the feces, the wounds would certainly have needed medical inspection and a thorough antiseptic cleansing.

A copy of the arrest report was directed to the LA County Health Department, the Sheriff's Licensing Detail and to the California Department of Alcohol and Beverage Control.

Hopefully the bar would be closed for noncompliance for operating a business with a deplorable open sewage and a biologically contaminated waste presence and brought up to code. I was a little perplexed as to why anyone would frequent the bar unless it was used for something other than drinking. Duh!

This was not one of the biggest fights or incidents I was involved in, but it was one of the worst for contact with waste.

Most other bar fights generally have much cleaner surroundings than this one presented, and I hoped this wouldn't happen again.

CHAPTER 148

EDISON MEDICINE: BACK SHOOTING

I was working the desk sergeant's position and monitoring the sheriff's radio communication regarding a large party. The party was getting out of hand, because some partygoers were smashing and breaking things up and extra help was arriving.

Apparently there was an established skirmish line set up, and the officers were about to clear the streets and cause the rowdy partygoers to leave. A lot of times in these situations, bottles and rocks are thrown by some idiots, which initiates a firm response from the officers. So the officers on the scene are damned because the partygoers are looped from all of the alcohol and moving in a slow defiant motion, not aware someone is tossing bottles and rocks at the police. When the officers start their forward movement, it is directly after the crowd has been warned of arrest if they linger. So what do you think happens? Those who linger and protest the force used by the officers are often battered by the slow-moving skirmish line or kicked to motivate them to leave or go to jail.

Even those who fall without any provocation and feign injury will be kicked to prove injury has taken place, or the feigning party will rise to the occasion as soon as the skirmish lines passes. Those individuals will then do harm to the skirmish line from the rear.

Of course the ones pelting the officers are generally not caught, but they are the ones who set the tone for use of force. The officers can receive pretty serious injury, especially to the head, when they are struck by stones or worse. These wounds could potentially be fatal, so the use of deadly force is not out of the question. Head wounds are very graphic and easily seen by assisting officers, who respond to those attacks. So guess what—if your partner or someone next to him or her is wounded, each person gets hit twice or kicked twice. Why just twice? Because the officers must conserve energy, and twice is enough. There are way too many to hit, and it's tiring to hit someone more than twice. The officers are instructed to hit bones—clavicle, shoulder, arm, wrist, finger, knee, shin, ankle, or the top of the foot are generally the best places to hit and cause the most pain. Head shots are discouraged, because the injury would be more severe. That way the rioters would likely not return the following day and would be sore for several days.

Apparently contact was made, and several were arrested and were on their way to the station. When they arrived, I met with several of the arrested suspects and shadowed the deputies as they brought them to the booking area. This shadowing was to be seen by all to discourage any independent action on each suspect. I knew the officers' tempers were on edge, and I was primarily there to watch and make sure the rules were strictly obeyed.

One of the individuals was extremely combative and had to be forcibly removed from the car and carried into the station. I stood slightly back as a trainee was attempting to get items ready for the booking process. While he was prepping the booking materials, the trainee turned his head and body away from the suspect, who was pinned against the booking cage counter by the trainee's weight and size. The suspect twisted free and was going to kick the trainee, so I stepped in and fired one Taser shot. The suspect dropped to the floor and began screaming. I held the trigger back for about eight seconds. The suspect urinated in his pants and continued to scream as I warned him not to fight or hit anyone.

After the Tasering, the suspect calmed down. The trainee was about to begin the booking process, when suddenly the suspect's head was gushing blood. I carefully looked at his scalp, and there was a two-inch gash. He was quickly bandaged and transported to the Los Angeles General Hospital medical jail ward for immediate medical attention and confinement. It wasn't understood how the suspect received such a wound; he certainly didn't hurt himself when Tased.

On the floor near the booking cage there wasn't anything that might have caused the suspect's injury, which strongly indicated that he had the injury prior to coming to the station. He needed twenty stitches to close the wound. It was also determined he might have been struck in the head when he was at the party, but no one would admit causing the wound. An internal investigation followed and the Internal Affairs Unit was unable to find the guilty party.

About year passed, and I was summoned to civil court and charged with being the one most likely to have hurt the suspect, but without any proof or criminal court trial. During that civil court testimony I was asked to describe the facts that led up to the suspect being Tased.

When I stated what I had done, one of the two attorneys bellowed, "Sergeant Rupp shot our client in the back and held the trigger for about eight seconds, making him shake violently and finally submit to his orders."

When asked why I shot him in the back, I explained that it was the easiest and nearest exposed surface to strike immediately and stop him from hurting the trainee.

The attorney made it seem that I was so inhumanely callous I defied the unwritten protocol of shooting suspects in the front of the body. When asked how many times I'd used the Taser, I acknowledged a plethora of occurrences. I informed the attorney that I taught the use of the Taser when I worked advanced officer training, while performing the actual procedures and policies of the sheriff's department. I said I must have instructed several hundred students. When I was assigned to Lynwood Station, I Tased at least three suspects a week who were using PCP. There were gallons of it confiscated in the Lynwood area, and many deputies were hurt and retired from the department early because of the seriousness of injuries inflicted by the drug users. I explained that many suspects were being shot multiple times because of their superhuman strength. Many of those suspects were killed, and the Taser was brought in to help curb those killings. I was at Lynwood for three and a half years. Forty-two months times twelve per month equals 504 times. Subtracting my training and vacation time of six weeks per year would reduce it to around 450 times. In East LA, I used the Taser maybe twice per month, again mostly for the PCP suspects and some violent cocaine users, that would be an additional forty-eight times.

During this trial I was already at another assignment for the sheriff's department called the Metro Blue Line, where I hadn't used the Taser at all and I had been there almost two years. So the total use was around five hundred times.

That testimony indicated I knew well the Taser and its effects. I added that the suspect did not strike anything that would have caused the two-inch gash on the top of his head.

The attorney then asked why I didn't just hit him with my hands, and I replied that I might have hurt him more than the Taser. Not only by the initial impact, but also by sharp-edged items that he might have come into contact with.

When finished with the testimony I was asked to gather my last three years of income tax returns and the names of the financial institutions where I bank. This was the punitive portion of the civil trial, and they were about to hit me with a punitive percentage of my financial worth. I discussed this dilemma with the attorney representing the county, and he said that because no one else had admitted to the use of force except me, the attorneys would seek a punitive action against me alone.

Well, isn't that a bunch of bull, I thought. So I made my own inquiries, and I found out that a former sergeant was the responsible party. He was afraid of what would happen to him, so he kept quiet. Of course this information was not usable in court because of the deceptive way I found out who it was. To top it all off, his father was one of my sergeants at Firestone Park Station and a recently retired division chief.

In the end, the civil trial was dismissed, and all parties were released from liability, because the suspect said the officer who hit him had a dark-colored jacket on with blue pants. That comment eliminated the sheriff's department and implicated several other agencies that were on the scene as well.

The moral of this story is that if you admit to using force, and you're the only one who admits it, and there is an unexplained injury sustained by the suspect, you could very well be charged as a guilty party. Their thinking is that you represent the department and whoever committed the injury was most likely a sheriff's department employee.

If I was going to be punitively charged, although I didn't cause the injury, I might have been hit with a 30 percent punitive fine of my net worth. Do you think the county would reimburse me for my loss?

Want to bet?

CHAPTER 149

GRAVE ROBBERS: NECROMANCY (WITCHCRAFT OR SORCERY) NEEDS

East Los Angeles is well known for its multitude of Hispanic gangs that are firmly entrenched and now politically referred as disrupted youth groups. Well, that rationale may sit well with individuals who skirt the issue of "titles to skew reporting," but I think we all know it is primarily done for political gain (obtaining votes) especially when the report is controlled by a political entity that publicizes it as authentic and accurate and fools the public into thinking the threat is no longer there, or has miraculously changed (i.e., bum/hobo to homeless). This is another version of the duck theory, which is recognized as racist and against the poorer class of people that can hardly survive. Oh, woe is me. Remember this the next time you come through ELA, and you inadvertently run into a group of those disrupted individuals.

This incident occurred several times and was brushed over as an anomaly because it occurred in a gang-infested area. It repulsed families from outside the area. The call came in from the Jewish cemetery caretaker that someone came into the cemetery and destroyed many tombstones. A unit was dispatched and discovered that the amount of damage was significant. The crew reported that several individuals had come into the cemetery and knocked over many tombstones and destroyed some of them. These gravestones had been in place undisturbed for twenty to thirty years. Many of the families who had visited the cemetery had stopped coming and assumed the plots were unmolested and peaceful.

Several local parties were going on in the surrounding gang-infested area. These parties were a slight deviation from normal, with a twist of gothic influence. You know the type, black makeup and clothing, freakish haircuts, silver studs in their noses, nipples, lips, eyebrows, and ears, all connected with a handsome small chain that signifies nerds with a touch of child abduction and cruelty.

Apparently the area folks, Hispanics mostly, are very much aware of the violent nature of the gangs and allow their carefully guarded kids to adopt the Gothic look, thinking that these antics are much better than shooting and stabbing each other, as the homegrown gangsters do so well.

These freaks entered the hallowed grounds of the deceased not only to toss their only remaining marker of life, but also their burial vaults. Several vaults were kicked in, causing the collapse of the cement chambers.

Then they unsealed the caskets and stole the left hands and heads of the interred. Now, I'm sure a psychologist could elaborate on the why this group needs such articles, but if it were my family member I would take it as personally as if they were alive. But then, that's my opinion, and I might be wrong.

Do you think this could happen in your area? Want to bet? Do you think the cemetery would notify you? How come there are so many graveyards without any noticeable security?

A similar shocking occurrence in the southern area of the city of Compton happened around the same time. The cemetery was over on Wilmington Avenue and Greenleaf Avenue, and numerous graves were dug up, and the human remains were burned. They were caught selling the same burial site many times and stacking the headstones behind a burial vault located in the rear of the cemetery. What happens to people who do these sorts of things?

An attorney would say, "Sue the bastards." But to sue, you would expect the manager, who was doing these sorts of things, to have money. In this case I wouldn't think so, considering the area and its surroundings. Do you think there would be any money whatsoever? Most likely not.

Remember the necrophiliac who lived in the Compton area, discussed in the chapter in my Compton years? Between the gravesites dug up and resold in Compton, the freaks who need the heads and hands of the interred, and the past history of cemetery management, not to mention centuries of stories about grave robbers, I would highly recommend cremation for all. Cremation would certainly eliminate grave molestation, and much cheaper than an expensive burial casket.

Another twist is the theft of flowers laid at the base of the tombstones. Frequently thieves steal the fresh flowers left by the mourners and sell them on freeway on-ramps. Is this the entrepreneurial spirit or just uncompassionate theft?

Many think of the thefts as a ghetto thing and think it is funny, but in my view it is just another lowlife theft that needs to be addressed by the masses who are the victims. How about reintroducing public caning?

Also keep this in mind, when you die you are no longer a live human, but merely a corpse or dead meat. The courts see it as only a disruption of human remains, and nothing else. Legislative action needs to be updated to change these crimes from misdemeanors to felonies.

CHAPTER 150

THE BIG PITCHER: ORGANIZED CRIME ANTICS

It was around ten thirty in the morning and a call came out that there was a shooting on Eastman Avenue just north of Whittier Boulevard. There a lone male Hispanic in his late thirties was walking, and someone drove by and fired several gunshots toward him. One of those rounds struck him in the thigh.

Now in East Los Angeles that's not unusual; it happens daily and this was at first glance no big deal, other than the normal youth group shooting at another youth group. As this shooting was being attended to by deputies, another situation was taking place not two blocks away.

Two tall men wearing wolf masks were walking across a playground, full of small children at an elementary school. Mysteriously, the usual playground adult monitor was not available to see these intruders as they drew closer to a small group of children. One of the men pushed his way brazenly through the group of kids and picked up an eight-year-old boy by his outer garments. He lifted him chest high, stuck a gun in the kid's face, and pulled the trigger. The child was attempting to wiggle free and screaming for help, and fortunately the gun didn't discharge.

The gunman pulled the trigger again, and once more the gun failed to discharge. One of the small boy's friends tried to make the man go away but was slapped to the ground. The gunman threw the small boy to the ground, and both masked gunmen fled the playground and out of view of any adult witnesses.

These events were connected. The man who was shot around the same time was the father of this child who'd just escaped serious harm. The message to the father was that his son was an example of what could happen if the father continued to help law enforcement in a previous gang shooting. That message was not from the local gangs, but from a much higher organized crime gang figure who is involved in all crime in the area.

Now, individually those crimes would have been missed if reported as one, but separately it was a much different picture.

Another example of the interaction of organized crime with the local gangs was that at the time, for anyone to join the gang, he must first donate $700 cash (1995 prices) and two guns in order to get in. That tidy sum goes directly to the organized crime figure as an initiation fee. He then can do anything in the organized crime figure's turf as long as it doesn't interfere with that person's operation. Also, it allows the local gangs to do contracted work at the organized crime figure's will.

442

Another time I was in a patrol car cruising by one of the local parks. I was alone and came upon about fifteen gang members who were all clustered around a cement park bench and seats. I was operating under the "duck" theory and recognized many of them, some of whom were the "heavies," main thugs of the gang. I got out of my car and asked for several units to back me up and had all of them surround my unit. Fifteen of them made a complete loop. They assumed the position with their hands on my car and their feet spread slightly.

As my backup arrived, I pulled each one of them from the group and learned from two of them that they were the local gang, meeting with two of the older homies. One by one I talked with them, shook each one of them down, and persuaded them to leave together when I was finished.

No guns or any weapons were found, but an interesting development was unveiled. The two older gangsters were parolees just out of prison. They were identified by two of the attendees as part of the organized gang, teaching the younger ones how and when to operate.

Now that revelation says a lot and underscores the seriousness of their open involvement and connection. So when your money goes to help the gangs in your area, does it apply to a joint meeting place where law enforcement can't view them? Want to bet? Every gang has former members instructing them how not get involved in gangs, right? That member who's talking to the younger guys is most likely a what? You've got to be kidding, right?

CHAPTER 151

PERFECT MATCH: WHO CRASHED OUR WEDDING?

We had a great wedding ceremony and reception. The boys behaved themselves throughout the festivities, and of course, I got "schnockered" on that double-sized champagne glass full of tequila.

The guys thought it was funny, thinking that I would balk, but I didn't. I guzzled that puppy down and surprised even myself. After that episode, I danced the night through with most of the men, women, and children alike.

It seems funny now that half of the reception, seated on the left, was loud-mouthed, boisterous SWAT cops and the other half was humble, Spanish-speaking-only Mexicans who looked so timid and decent.

It was near ending time, the mariachi band had already left and the DJ was working, so my new wife and I snuck out as soon as we could. We changed our clothes in the hotel room, next to the reception hall, and quickly jumped into the taxi and headed for LAX.

We were spending the night in one of the large nice hotels right next to the airport. Of course that macho move I made gulping that tequila defanged my performance. I fell asleep so fast I couldn't remember if we even got into bed together.

We woke up early so we wouldn't miss our flight and arrived at our air carrier's doorway without a hitch. We were on our way to Mexico. My new wife, of course a Mexican, and a very proud one at that, was all excited to show me what a beautiful place Mexico is. Its people are completely different from the common American folk and the cholos from Los Angeles.

She knew my philosophy about Hispanics was skewed because of all my experience with the sheriff's department. I had been on the department for about twenty years already and was a patrol sergeant at beautiful Lynwood Station, a small city just north of the glamorous, quaint city of Compton. I had already experienced enough sickness and depravity among all races of people.

I believed it was time to see something nice and pleasant to be around, so I trusted her judgment and prepared myself for culture shock.

She was so proud of her heritage and wanted me to see where her family came from and where many of whom still lived. She wanted to light up my life and expose me to the real Mexican culture—just plain, nice, and kind people. So I was ready and went for the whole package. It surely wouldn't hurt me to become more sophisticated and welcome diversity.

Our first stop was going to be Cancun. I thought it looked beautiful and very romantic, according to the brochures. Gloria seemed a little displeased that we were going to the Club Med route rather than some small quaint Mexican town a little more low-key. To Gloria, Club Med exemplified the flamboyant lifestyle of most gringos, very un-Mexican. However, she went along with my decision and away we went. We arrived at the airport and caught a small bus to the Club Med village.

Wow, this place looked great—white sandy beaches holding back the warm turquoise water, a backdrop of a pale-blue sky and white puffy clouds, and white hamlet-style buildings with thatched palm roofs. Expansive patios were cluttered with countless lounges, palm trees, and of course large open-air bars serving the scantly dressed, smiling customers. We were given the main tour as we went to to our assigned room.

The staff advised us to be careful of the crocodiles, and oh, by the way, "Please don't feed them!" There seemed to be hundreds of them. The countless crocodiles hardly went unnoticed, casually commanding their territory, with their ominous shapes and sizes, lazily moving about in a relatively slow, waddling fashion until disturbed. Then there followed a loud hissing from their bright pinkish gargantuan mouths, as they demonstrated their strength by strong sideward thrashing and rapid movements.

Occasionally, some would wander the hallways and all you had to do is call the front desk. They of course would send someone posthaste, to get rid of the always hungry, lurking predator. Boy, the danger seemed kind of sexually stimulating; an exotic honeymoon room where I can make love with my wife and know the presence of a hungry crocodile was just outside our door.

Another oddity that caught me unannounced, but was not as spectacular, was when we frequently crossed open areas on the Club Med grounds and saw frequent encounters of men in chef's attire. You know all of that typical white clothing and aprons they wear, with their stovepipe, extratall chef hats.

Please don't label me homophobic, but to see so many full-bearded men swapping spit with each other in dark little corners of the Village, it kind of made me think of the West Hollywood capers I mentioned earlier, where gay romance seemed very queer. Why just the chefs? Oh well.

We planned our week the first day, arranging our tours and events. We went to the club office to charter an airplane to the Mayan village of Chichen Itza. A chartered bus would take us to the airport, where we'd catch the plane to the Mayan village, a forty-five minute flight. We would stay for most of the day and then catch the return flight and bus back to the village.

As we were making preparations for the flight, we asked pertinent questions about the plane: How long has it been in service? How many passengers can it hold? Is it safe to fly?

The lady was pleasant and told us it was formally a US-made plane called a Convair 441, which seats approximately twenty-five people. It was built in the fifties and has been flying since.

I glanced over to a nearby wall and saw a picture of a plane and asked, "Is this it?" She looked at me as she conversed with my new wife and said, "That's it!"

The picture, alone on the wall in its wooden frame, appeared to be one of the original fifties posters from when it was new.

Suddenly, my eye caught a funny movement beyond a large window covered by a thin set of Venetian blinds. It looked like some little guy just outside the window, gazing with several other persons at a large group of ladies.

These ladies were outside, about thirty feet away, exercising in cadence with the boisterous physical fitness instructor, who was bellowing out commands.

The little guy seemed as if he was in a trance, shaking his hand awkwardly and a little offbeat to the exercising females' cadence. I drew closer to the window to see what he was doing. He had his penis in his right hand, masturbating.

His eyes were rolling back, and his eyelids were fluttering, as if staying in sync with the beat of the exercising women.

I brought his sexual exuberance to the attention of the scheduling chieftains who were talking to my wife and everyone turned toward the window and witnessed the sexual frolic the little guy was demonstrating.

The lady chieftain remarked, "Oh, that's nothing. He's one of the Mayan helpers, and they do things like that!"

That event served as a clue to what we were about to encounter. Furthermore, I spread the blinds right beside the little guy and tapped on the window to get his attention. To my amazement, he looked toward me and continued without missing a stroke.

Well, we were assured that the plane was safe and finally finished with our reservations. We went to our room and enjoyed the rest of the evening with lavish dining and dancing and romantic entanglements.

The following morning came quickly. I believe we awoke around six o'clock. As we were about to step out of our room, I carefully peeked out and around the door's edge, and scanned the hallway for any sign of the hotel's leathery, bumpy, uninvited guests that might be lurking about, looking for an quick bite to eat. It appeared all clear, so we quickly scurried out of our room and went to the restaurant area.

We ate an early breakfast and needed to board the bus around seven. We packed lightly and dressed in shorts and light shirts. It was going to be sultry.

We had been told that the bus ride itself was an adventure. Any person traveling the narrow unpaved paths would be jeopardy as the bus drew near. They had been known to speed right through persons on the road and rarely realized they had struck anyone, unless pointed out by one of the passengers.

We arrived rather quickly and unloaded our day gear and walked through the airport terminal. As we passed the exit to the tarmac, I couldn't help but notice a large banner draped on a ceiling supporting beam just ahead of us that depicted familiar icons of no guns or knives. You know the silhouette of a gun and a knife within a circle, and a diagonal slash across the silhouette.

Well this banner had another symbol that was a little out of sync with the others. This one depicted the icon of a "bomb." You know the black ball with a fuse sticking out of it. I thought to myself, *Gee, down here they carry bombs!* I made some smart-ass remark to my wife, indicating maybe this is going to be a little more exciting than expected, raising my eyebrow.

We walked onto the tarmac in somewhat of a single file and were led to an older airplane about fifty yards away. I overheard several passengers questioning their reasoning for this expedition. They seemed uncomfortable as we continued our walk, and their skepticism increased as we drew nearer the plane. Several of the passengers climbed the stairs to the older-looking plane and were also overheard remarking how unsafe the plane appeared. To me the plane looked all right—nothing fancy, but okay. As we boarded I had to duck a little more than usual; it seemed a little smaller than the jet models, but for a twin prop job, it still seemed all right.

I led my wife toward the rear portion, passing all our fellow passengers nervously sitting and watching anything and everything that moved. In this case there were a lot of bolts and screws moving, which didn't seem quite the norm. We sat in the rear because it's the safest spot on the plane, in an emergency.

Gloria wanted to sit near the window. We attempted to get comfortable in the older chairs. Still skepticism was at issue as we all sat back and awaited the plane to taxi. Our guide told us that Chichen Itza was forty-five minutes away.

Everything seemed pretty much okay as we began to take off, and everyone was relatively quiet. We got off the ground all right and started toward the ruins. We were cruising at approximately thirteen thousand feet. We could see below us the vast jungles, but not another city or village.

About forty minutes into our flight, one of the forward passengers spotted something unusual. It seemed a red fluid was coming from the left wing. He alerted the guide, who in turn pointed the problem out to one of the three uniformed crew. The crew conferred and determined we needed to turn around and shut down one of the engines. Now that decision frightened several of the passengers. They nervously began to criticize our planes' running capability and expected more things to occur.

Of course I was a private pilot, which gave some weight to my opinion about the crews' safe engine shutdown and turn around to Cancun. However, it did disturb me that the crew decided to go back to our departure point, rather than set the plane down at an alternate airport or landing spot.

This is basic flight procedure in the United States, and I'm pretty sure it's the same around the world. I was still able to converse with several other passengers and assured them everything seemed okay and there was no need for alarm. I hoped!

So we toiled in the air for approximately another thirty to forty minutes anxiously awaiting our return to Cancun. During this time I had leaned over my wife several times peering out the left window, in a feeble attempt to get our bearings, but to no avail.

I continued looking out the small window and realized we were flying very low, about five to six hundred feet, and it seemed we were about to land. This couldn't be; none of the crew had alerted us that we were about to land. It was a bit unnerving, because that also is a must in all normal landings, let alone in an engine out, return flight, I thought to myself, *Yikes!*

I was now leaning over my wife constantly looking out the window. We were now only about two hundred feet off the deck. I became alarmed and questioned my wife quietly, hoping she was awake and listening to me. "Babe, something's wrong! We're too high to land and too low to turn around, and where in the hell is this guy going? There's nothing but jungle ahead of us and we don't have any altitude!" She didn't seem overly alarmed, or probably I didn't make much sense in my cautionary statement. So I continued to peer out the window and carefully watched what the plane was doing.

About forty seconds later, and the aircraft was still losing altitude. We were now about fifty feet in the air when the plane started to turn into the dead engine.

This was absolutely the dumbest move I'd seen yet. I spoke in a loud voice as I grabbed my wife's seat belt and scrunched it on her lap as tight as possible. I stated loudly, "This dumb shit is going to crash!"

I saw the wing's edge clip the water and just miss the dense brush. I knew definitely we were going to crash, and most likely cartwheel, on top of that. I grabbed the back of my wife's head and pushed her body forward and onto her lap. Her head came to rest just above her knees, as she covered her face. I braced myself with my other hand, holding onto the back of the seat in front of me. I glanced outside and saw the left wing just edging into the water and creating a V-shaped ripple.

I thought, *Here goes, I bet this is going to hurt.* There was no more time to think of anything else but the impending crash, and the compounding injuries we would get with the intense momentum of the ass-over-teakettle cartwheeling.

Well, we hit, and all of those glass coke bottles in the back came forward at about 90 mph and hit everyone with their head up except me! Our plane started to cartwheel, but it must have been snagged by some of the large foliage, and we didn't.

However, the left wing grabbed onto something and caused the plane to rip open approximately seventeen feet from the nose. As a matter of fact, it ripped open right in front of where the little Mayan stewardess was seated. It tore open about eight feet to the left, and caused a small four-foot wave to come gushing in. *Yeah,* I thought to myself, *those crocodiles are coming in next, as soon as we settle down!* There were screams coming from men and women alike.

Finally everything stopped, and it was over. I stood up in the rear and announced to everyone that we needed to leave because there was going to be a fire. A lone woman in front of us shouted, "I can't find my purse!" My wife spoke up. "This thing is going to explode! Forget your purse; we've got to get out!" I just realized then that my wife's announcement actually relieved me, because it let me know that she was okay as well.

One woman opened the side door over the right wing and ran out onto the wing to get away. Everyone else was leaving carefully through the large tear, cautiously stepping into the murky water. Some of the passengers repeatedly expressed their concerned about the crocodiles as they slipped and sloshed into the shallow murky water covered with thick algae. It was raining pretty steadily and hotter than hell. This was getting worse as it went along. Blood was splattered around and leaching into the water, because several passengers had gashes in the back of their heads that were bleeding. We all figured that this would alarm, excite, and frustrate the presumably hungry crocodiles even more.

As we drew closer to the opening the woman on the wing came back inside the plane and decided to go out the same opening as everyone else.

I grabbed several of the seat bottoms in an attempt to use them as floatation devices, but the seats were sewn in; none of them would come out. As I stepped from the plane I was thinking that there had to be sharp pieces of metal along this tear. I surely didn't want to cut my leg at this point and warned Gloria.

We were the last ones to come out. We looked toward the plane and observed the three crewmen talking among themselves near the outside cockpit area, while standing hip-high in the murky water. I speculated they were hoping the plane would catch fire, so all of the required maintenance records would be destroyed.

In my opinion, their attention should have been on the passengers and their safety, not talking near the crashed plane. So I yelled to them in my broken Spanish, "Senores, Es muy peligreso, yo soy pelota, muy peligreso!" One of the crew yelled back, "Yo soy piloto, mi commandante!"

Apparently my Spanish was not totally up to par. Gloria said that I told the crew that I was a ball, and they probably didn't understand what I had said. In Spanish pilot is "piloto," and ball is pronounced "pelota"!

However this pilot knew exactly what I was saying. This was an obvious deviation from standard emergency procedures, unless he had a more important agenda, like getting rid of evidence that would prove an improperly maintained airplane. Also his tone was argumentative and confrontational.

Common sense would dictate looking after the injured passengers and making sure we were escorted out of the swamp. A crewman called to the stewardess by name. She appeared to understand what he said in Spanish. Gloria said that he wanted the stewardess to guide us out of the marsh, and not them.

The stewardess faced us. At first glance she was absolutely in a daze as if something had smacked her right in the face. Her eyes were rolling back as if she was going to pass out. She was desperately clutching a battered, gray steel box with a small Red Cross symbol in the center. It was obvious that she was in no shape to do anything, except stay awake and on her own two feet. Her injury was probably caused when the plane crashed, it tore open right near her feet and she most likely caught the onslaught of water, mud, and debris from the marsh right in her face, knocking her senseless.

Her first aid training apparently kicked in when she was clobbered by the water and debris, and she instinctively brought the first aid box. Gloria and I pried the steel box from her hands, and my wife spoke to her in Spanish. She resisted somewhat but then let the box go. Gloria took the box and carried it, and we assisted the stewardess wandering about in a daze. The water was about three feet deep with about two feet of mud. Bushes were on top and below the water; some were towering about eight to ten feet high. The mud was stirred and mixed up by our walking as we sloshed away from the crash.

About ten of the twenty-three passengers had cuts on the back of their heads that were bleeding steadily. Several of the male German passengers were very loud professing that they knew that there was going to be trouble when they first saw the plane at the airport.

One of the Germans had a pretty good gash on the back of his head, which he was holding with one of his hands. Of course his hand was covered with blood and it was dripping from his fingers into the water. Others were getting more frightened that crocodiles might appear at any time.

I jokingly commented, to ease the tension, that it was a known fact that crocodile mouths are very weak opening and that their mouths could be held shut with minimal human arm strength. I added that I'd got my two, how about them? Several laughed nervously, but we kept our eyes peeled for any signs of the formidable creatures. I believe we all knew that they were in the mix but didn't know exactly why they weren't being seen. All of the floating, clumpy green-and-brown algae and the clutter of debris added to the confusion.

A low-flying aircraft passed overhead a few times but disappeared just as quickly. Maybe it was just passing by to see where we were located. It was still raining and we were relatively close to one another. The crew was still busy near the aircraft, so one of the male passengers took the lead and began to walk toward where we thought the airport was located. We continued onward at a slow pace, snaking through the large brush and occasional sinkholes that would quickly allow the water to rise to chest height.

We all began to follow, but stopped briefly when one of the passengers began to video the situation and the crash site. I was the only one with a small camera suitable for underwater photos and began to snap colored photos.

As we began to move we thought it would a good idea to open the first aid box that the stewardess had grabbed. Gloria opened it and to our amazement there was only one dirty roll of yellow tape, nothing else! Boy, this was a script right out of a movie on how not to survive tactics.

After approximately a half an hour to forty-five minutes, we saw our rescuers on a hilltop about a hundred yards away, yelling to us in Spanish to come toward them. Of course they didn't want to come into the water most likely because of the crocodile infestation, and unnecessary risk.

We followed their directions and were about fifty yards from them when the male in the lead yelled, "Leeches"! He rose up as if he was walking on water and ran up the hill.

Just then I then felt something pinching the bottom of my left testicle. Of course I had a hold of Gloria's hand helping her struggling through the mud and water. This time the pain struck me again, but more intensely on the same testicle. Something small was biting me, and it was hurting. I figured it must be one of the leeches and pulled on the bottom of my testicle to scare the little bugger away but then felt a more severe bite in the same spot and knew it had to be them. I moved as fast as I could through the water, telling Gloria what was happening, and she began laughing. *Boy, what a wife,* I thought. We closed in on the leading male who at this time was standing near one of the rescue Volkswagen buses atop the hill. He had his pants down and was pulling one of the leeches from his pecker. That's right, pecker (aka penis). At this moment I reflected on a memory from a scene from the 1957 film *The Bridge on the River Kwai.*

When the soldiers found leeches on their legs, they had to first burn the back of their heads with cigarettes to make the leaches open their mouths, so their teeth would release the bite. Otherwise, their teeth would remain embedded and might cause a severe infection.

Here I was, on my honeymoon, supposedly having a great time. However, I would be in our honeymoon suite burning leeches from my testicles. This just didn't seem conducive to the honeymoon sex scenario. What else could a guy do, but try, right? I carefully and discreetly examined myself and noted that I only had a small amount of blood coming from a couple of spots on my testicle and brushed the matter off as a close call.

We loaded into the Volkswagen bus, about six or seven of us. They drove us back to the airport. There, we were told to go into an examining room where a doctor would examine and evaluate each of us.

We were guided into a large room with windows overlooking the airport and sat on several wooden benches. The medical crew was already examining several of our group across the room from us. We sat quietly and patiently in our wet and dirty summer attire discussing the crash and who was injured more severely.

I was more concerned who the doctors were, and if by chance I had a small pair of teeth imbedded in my scrotum or testicle. I could see a small blotch of blood on my white underwear and I was hoping that little bugger didn't have a chance to bite me directly and left his teeth in my shorts.

While we were talking, I looked suspiciously at one of the doctors in a white smock. He looked familiar, real familiar. I said to my wife, "Babe, doesn't that guy in the white smock look like someone we know? How about that stinking pilot that crashed our plane?"

Gloria said, "You've got to be kidding, he does!" Several of the other passengers agreed with me, and we determined this guy didn't know when to quit. He wanted to get a look at the women to get a free shot at them naked.

At this point, we decided that we'd had enough of this fiasco and said that we wanted to leave and not wait for the doctor. We loaded up again into the small Volkswagen bus and headed for the Club Med. Upon our arrival at the village we immediately went to the packed open-air bar. When everyone saw the condition we were in, they questioned why we were back so early and why we were so dirty. When they heard the story, they sat back in amazement, surprised we survived.

The bar was still closed, but the village chieftain announced the bar was open, realizing that after hearing the stories, people might cancel their upcoming excursions. The village chieftain yelled for the bartender to get us all a shot of tequila for our adventure. My wife remarked, "How about a bottle, hell!" The chieftain replied, "Okay, make it a bottle."

With that, Gloria and I and another couple went out of the bar with the bottle and a couple of glasses. We went into the beautiful, cool, and clean water and cleaned the filthy swamp water from our bodies. We polished that bottle off real quick and felt a lot better and refreshed. Then several others bought us a few more drinks and soon we were well onto thinking more positively about our honeymoon.

We went to our room to freshen up, and suddenly I became ill. I had a serious case of diarrhea. Someone from the village staff came to our room and suggested that we be examined by the village doctor assigned to Club Med. Because of my irritable bowel, coupled with the small bites on my testicle, we decided to take the advice. Besides that, both of us were now feeling pain in our lower backs, and we were afraid it might impair the entire vacation.

During the examination we stayed together and carefully watched the doctor. He was kind and methodical and said the cause of the diarrhea was probably from ingesting water from the crash. He informed us that the crash site was a marsh laden with infectious waste, as it was untreated sewage mire and that I probably had contracted a form of amebic dysentery. He gave me several small pills to help control the diarrhea. Then he looked at my testicles and determined they were okay; he couldn't detect any body parts of a leech.

He briefly examined our lower backs. He said that the crash caused quite a severe strain to both of our lower backs and we would probably experience more pain within the next couple of days. Several of the others weren't as fortunate: two had cracked vertebras, several had the same dysentery as I did, and about ten had lacerations on the backs of their heads and needed quite a few stitches.

I guess overall we came out pretty good, considering more severe consequences could have occurred.

On the following day, the Club Med village chieftain invited all of the passengers of the crash to a small meeting in a private room.

At that meeting we all sat around what appeared to be a small Polynesian luau-style party, with food, drinks and all the decorations. We were in company with the same tour guide who was with us during the crash and several other guides. The chieftain and tour guides were graciously apologizing for the mishap, trying to minimize the calamity as a forced landing and labeling it as another Club Med adventure. We voiced our objections to crew's blatant disregard for safety and demanded answers for the bizarre emergency procedures. We were not warned verbally of the impending crash, nor were we told to even buckle up and prepare for a nonroutine landing.

We demanded to speak to the crew; however, they were conveniently nowhere to be found. The party finally ended after several hours of passengers expressing their anger and quarrelling with the Club Med staff. They requested a list of all the passengers on that flight and the staff stated that that would be difficult because that information was confidential. Talk about a cover-up, this remark was absurd, and that didn't help matters at all.

We demanded answers and wanted to speak to someone from Club Med administration because the staffs' rationale was obviously misguided and self-serving. The chieftain stated that he would look into our requests and get back to us the following day.

Right after that meeting we all met near the pool lounge, where we discussed what was actually going on. It had all the appearance of a sham or cover-up. We determined that Club Med was not going to assist us in any way, because of the liability and possible lawsuit.

There was a vote to elect a spokesman for our group. Guess whom they voted as that spokesperson. Me. I think this was because they knew I was an off-duty peace officer, and I was the only other pilot aboard. During the meeting it was learned that I was a licensed pilot in the United States. I also learned from several telephone conversations that all emergency procedures for aircraft were in fact universal. I also informed all others that the operational safety procedures were totally in error from the beginning, when the red fluid first seen coming from the left wing.

Later on that evening we secretly made our own personal list, by hand and on one small piece of paper. We were very much afraid that Club Med or the Mexican government was going to keep us from making or having such a list and I assured everyone that I would do my best to get it through the border.

We all had also learned from that meeting, that American Express, a company based in New York City, owned Club Med. This situation was now becoming very suspicious. A little skullduggery seemed to be taking place, and we were right in the middle of it.

The next day we were summoned again to a private meeting in another area in the village. This meeting, again held by the chieftain, introduced two men who had recently arrived from New York City. They were all smiles and wearing shorts and sport shirts.

They informed us they represented an insurance company who wanted to resolve all rumors and innuendos arising from the crash. These guys projected themselves in a nonchalant manner; they appeared to be on a quest to minimize any and all claims involving the crash. They also seemed disingenuous and were highly motivated to persuade all of us that their company was not at fault. Several other Club Med tour guides joined in the conversation and summarized the crash as nothing but another adventurous outing.

Actually they expressed dissatisfaction with our direct questions and implications that somebody had screwed up. One of the lady passengers became really upset, got up from her chair, and stated, "I can't take this anymore!" She rushed from the room. I expressed my opinion feeling that the staff was rude to imply that this was just a little forced landing and no big thing. I assured the Club Med staff and the insurance agents that it was a big thing, and it would be settled when we returned to the United States.

I told them that I'd been involved in many dangerous situations. "If I was alone, without my wife present," I said, "and you threw a variety of danger-ous situations at me, I could handle them without any problems. But when you throw my wife into the mix, and scare the dickens out of her and get her injured, then you've got hell to pay. Someone here is going to face the music in a more legal setting. Here we are limited in resources. We are not going to let this drop because you said that Club Med had no fault. Well, we know better. And we'll take care of it, and exchange our own information without your help, or your impediments." The meeting quickly and quietly concluded.

When we returned home, and I discussed the incident with fellow officers, an East Los Angeles station deputy told me about his similar mishap at Cancun airport just three months before our crash. He said that they were on a similar aircraft about to take off. They were in midfield when the right engine caught fire.

The plane came to an abrupt stop. The crew pulled onto an adjoining taxi-way, stopped, and killed the engines. They started to repair the engine. The passengers were told that the crew was going to have the plane ready shortly, as soon as they repaired the damage. He said a woman jumped up from her seat and yelled, "Bullshit! I'm not flying on this piece of shit at all!"

She then exited the plane on the taxiway and walked back to the termi-nal across the tarmac. The rest of the passengers followed suit shortly and demanded that another, more serviceable plane be used. About thirty minutes later newer plane arrived, and they continued on to their original destination.

When we came back to the United States I was eager to convey my expe-riences to fellow officers and came by the Sheriff's Star Center, in the city of Whittier. Several friends of mine were assigned there as instructors, so I popped into an in-service class. As I came in, they were in the midst of their instruction of fifty or sixty officers, male and female.

My friend smiled as he saw me come into the rear of the room and started to heckle me obnoxiously in front of the class. He apparently had heard about the crash, and the pangs of the excursion, and was rubbing it in, so to speak, to ambush my honeymoon experience. The whole class turned around and laughed about me getting married, so I said loudly that I had a great time. I As I walked to the front of the class, I mentioned that I had videotaped the honeymoon. (This in-service training was for experienced detectives, most of whom I knew.)

When I loaded the video they all sat in awe that I would share my honeymoon with them, but I surreptitiously went past the wedding formalities and directly into the event in Cancun.

They were in awe that I survived an air crash and an adventurous campaign through the swamps and jungles of Mexico. I think I scared a lot of them, but my point was well taken about the precautions when traveling into another country. Not too many laughed and many came to me and asked questions. I'm sure it served as a good learning tool, and they probably warned others of my experiences.

The lesson learned in this adventure was that the Ninth Circuit Court of Appeals in San Francisco determined that we could not sue the airline because all airlines in Mexico belong to the country of Mexico. Therefore the suit was stopped in the interest of good relations with the country of Mexico, which was necessary to be maintained for a good economy. The entire suit was kicked out by a group of nerdy schmucks who judged our suit as invalid. No penalty could be imposed. Think of this ruling the next time you leave the country and something serious happens.

Do you want an attorney in a black robe to assist in the reevaluation of your concerns and side with the political influences of the very company that nearly killed or injured you, but contributed handsomely to the judges' appointment to an appeals court position? Not really, so you had better think twice before going on little excursions and running into trouble in a foreign country.

It apparently happens frequently, but no one hears about it. In our case, the Club Med defense was that claims on accidents involved on their property are grossly limited, like if you lose a foot you'll receive a grand total of $2,000 for each foot you lose. Don't laugh. I'll bet you thought your foot was worth a lot more. The next time, before you leave, look in the back of the booklet, and you'll see the contract. There is a specific scale they will pay, and you already agreed to it when you signed up for the event. That's what we were told. We never saw the rating injury scale, but they claimed they had proof they mailed it to us before we boarded the plane.

Just how, do you ask? The rule was simple: the mailbox rule. This is a legal ruling that establishes certain aspects of their insurance were met, even though you had already left the house and were en route to the airport to embark on your fabulous vacation. Yes, the insurance company or agent purposely delayed mailing the list until after you had already left. The mailbox rule states once the document is in the mail, it is an established contractual document and perfectly legitimate.

Second, Club Med claims that everything in the Club Med village and Club Med Inc., are separate contractors.

That means the food, the excursions by bus, airplane, or taxi, drinks at the bar, the bars themselves and all of the eateries are literally separate and not a part of "Club Med" or "Club Med Inc." Think about that. Is it possible in this day and age? You betcha! The next time anyone goes to a Club Med adventure and gets hurt parasailing, or stumbles on the slippery dance floor, or falls down the steps, or loses a leg to a hungry crocodile in the hallway, don't think for a moment you'll be cared for or compensated; you won't. Those established organizations will disallow this claim and claim you're lying and twisting the truth.

I would rather let you do the thinking and look into foreign adventures before you leave. Then seek extra insurance and see what they say. That alone will reveal the hazards of foreign travel. Yet here in the United States, all parties are held liable if minimum standards are not upheld.

CHAPTER 152

METRO BLUE LINE: A HOTBED OF ACTIVITY—THE LURE: 80,000 GANGSTERS

I was summoned by a lieutenant at the Metro Blue Line because it was going to be a hotbed of activity. The new light-rail line was cutting through gang-infested areas populated by approximately 80,000 thugs. I knew the lieutenant pretty well, and he said I would be at home in all of the neighborhoods because it was going through all of South Los Angeles, Watts, Willowbrook, Lynwood, Compton, and Long Beach.

To me it was actually tracking the old red car trolley line they tore up thirty years before, and this new line was going straight down Long Beach Boulevard. This is where I'd traveled five days a week to Saint Anthony's Boy's High School and Long Beach Polytechnic High.

This was quite the enticement—heavily inundated with thieves, thugs, murderers, robbers, rapists, and gun-toting idiots who hadn't been breastfed, or whatever the excuse was. Tons of dope and plenty of pushers and con artists abounded, pickpockets were going to be slithering about with their little fingers wrapped around other people's property and stealing like mad.

I went for it. It seemed like the most active place to go, and it was going to be a madhouse. So with only two years at East Los Angeles, the action appeared to most to be the Metro Blue Line. We had a whole week of schooling to learn all about the new high-voltage rail system. The electrical intensity that could cause immediate death, if you stepped on or near the tracks and many other electrical components, was alarming. We learned how to stay away from the dangerous electricity and got a brief rundown on how the electrical train operates.

Everyone was excited and expecting the worst, but for some strange reason this system had a lot of cover with security officers and sheriff's deputies working together. Each platform had many video cameras, and those cameras were being watched by specific personnel, who maintained strict vigilance at each bank of many centralized televised sets.

The planning seemed very good, and we just didn't know what amount of havoc would be stirred up as the trains started running.

Well, it started, and we had strong law enforcement presence. Every platform had deputies assigned. A patrol unit was assigned for every three platforms for backup support, prisoner pickup, and shuttling in paperwork. Our attention to the ridership was our primary focus, and being seen helped immensely. On top of the strength of our tan-and-green uniforms, we were virtually in Los Angeles, deep in their patrol areas. Our presence indeed caused many of the local thugs to think twice, because we would drag their skinny little butts off to the local stations, and they would be virtually lost in the jail system.

Most gangs and local crooks knew that our department didn't fool around with large or small gangs, and we were indifferent to their pinhead antics.

As it turned out, the Blue Line was a giant two-block swath that covered the entire rail system; from Seventh Street and Figueroa Avenue, Los Angeles, all the way down to one block from Ocean Boulevard, Long Beach, just blocks from the Queen Mary. Anyone who committed any crime within a half block from the rail, on either side, would be subject to arrest.

One assault occurred on the line in the Pico station area, where a small woman on the train politely asked a large man to remove his foot from the edge of her seat. He became enraged, stood up, grabbed the woman by the outer clothing, and punched her in the face; knocking her ass over teakettle, and into a steel barrier guarding the exit door.

The woman bravely stood up and produced her police badge to the tough guy, exclaiming she was a police officer. The tough thug then grabbed her badge and threw it toward other passengers. Several of the passengers complained to the train operator about what had happened, and he alerted the central station platform that they were pulling into the platform area within two minutes.

We went out to the platform, waited for the train to stop, boarded the train, and promptly took care of the off-duty LAPD, Newton Station female officer. She pointed out the suspect, who was seated directly in front of us with another woman, who happened to be his girlfriend.

He was immediately arrested for the assault, and everyone was happy that the whole ordeal was handled to conclusion with only a five minute delay. We, of course, gave the LAPD officer a ride home. I might add that the off-duty female officer was half the size of the big toughie who smashed her in the face, and she did pretty well without any major injuries and held her ground admirably.

Most of the ridership was faced with the honor system when paying their fares and subject to presenting their tickets when the deputies requested them. Quite a few got caught and were cited heavily to avoid a repeat offense. The fine was hefty, and there wasn't any question as to who was enforcing the laws. Other situations for ticketing were loud music, eating or chewing gum, or drinking. They were all ticketed as well, with no excuses. Well, not until some students from an organized black entitlement group sought out special compensation because they were black and loudly proclaimed to the deputies that they were racists.

This aggravated our Blue Line captain, and the whole militant group wanted to sit down and parley. I guess that's why I was only a sergeant, because

I possessed a limited mind. All that negotiating does is cultivate and give credence to the racist organizations and give them a special voice, rather than having to comply with all laws for all regular folks. (If you disagree with my opinion, then maybe you are an integral part of this screwed-up thought process.)

The day of the parley, I noticed our captain coming out of the office with a female black sergeant who was assigned to the Metro Blue Line and none other than the sheriff's department's secret Maoist, Lieutenant Snake, from Lynwood Station. I advised the captain that he should take me, because he might get jumped by the militant idiots and wouldn't have any backup.

The captain smiled and said, "No, Larry, I don't think I need you on this one." I said, "I'm sorry you think that way, Captain, I know exactly how this event will run its course."

Then Lieutenant Snake spoke up and shot his racist hot wind out, and I just nodded my head and said, "Special needs for special races, talk about taking a jerk to an event where only he could offer allegiance to the black race."

I believe that any racist views offered by any militant group with Marxist ideals and philosophy has no place in America, unless those idiots comply and obey the law as well as everyone else.

I'll leave what had happened in that meeting to you the reader, and let you contemplate the outcome.

CHAPTER 153

FOUR HUNDRED HELD UP

It was an early foggy morning around seven thirty, when I was dispatched to the 103rd Street platform of the Metro Blue line. It was pretty busy with a variety of calls to most of the foot patrols at various platform assignments. The call came to me over the radio as an "attention to a call" detail, about an animal on the tracks, holding up a Metro Blue Line train containing approximately four hundred passengers.

I arrived in about five minutes with several other units, just north of the stalled train, which was packed with passengers. The animal was a large black-and-white dog, literally cut in half, standing on its forelegs and rear stump, resting on the concrete railroad tie, and very much alive. The canine's entire rump, rear legs, and tail were missing. The dog was barking and snapping at anyone who came close to him.

Many of the passengers were standing and peering through the wet windows trying to see what we were doing. Many passengers were finding it difficult to see because of the position of the train. I surmised the Metro operator had announced the reason for the delay over the interior public address system, as well as our arrival.

The dog was right in the center of the rails, sitting upright and facing the motionless Metro Blue line. The Metro operator was seated inside the operator's cab at the front of the train. The train's operating lights were on and you could see a soft mist of foggy rain coming down.

The dog must have been cut in half by one of the fast-moving Metro line trains. The dog's upright position on the concrete railroad tie was surrounded by a bed of buffer, a term used by the railroad for the two-inch rock that surrounds the railroad ties and tracks.

Four of the deputies were closing in on the hyperalert and fatally struck dog as it began to snap at the deputies' approach.

I saw the train about a hundred feet south of us. I figured I would grab the large white sheet from the trunk of my patrol car that is usually used for covering dead bodies or treating injured citizens. The sheet would at least cover the injured dog and conceal its terrible injuries.

Using any sort of firearm—9 mm or buckshot—to dispose the seriously injured dog was out of the question. I was fully aware that any round fired might ricochet on any of the buffer, concrete ties, steel rails, or heavy metal spikes.

Because I was the field sergeant, the bewildered deputies looked to me, thinking this was a sensitive situation where animal cruelty and good judgment were about to be tested.

The light fog and rain made everything damp and slippery. The train had its exterior and interior lights on, and the passengers and motorman were watching our every move.

I asked the deputies to each grab a corner of the sheet and create a slight pocket in the sheet so they could easily scoop the fatally injured dog into its broad cupped center. They all understood what to do, and dragged the sheet slightly across the "buffer" and railroad tie just in front of the dog. The dog was barking intensely because of all the surrounding activity and the sheet closing in on his position.

The sheet captured the injured dog quite easily, and the deputies spun the dog as the ends of the sheet were brought together. I directed the deputies to carry the barking and howling dog, now encased in the sheet, to the east side of the large mound of buffer, and stand by as I directed the train to move onward, northbound with all of the passengers.

As they passed by us, a lot of the passengers were watching what we were doing.

I wanted them to pass because what I was about to do would be severely criticized if viewed by the general public.

Of course the dampness of the cloth caused the slowly expelling blood from the injured dog to literally bleed through the sheet and created a large, watered-down bloody mess. This created an oversensationalized image of the injured animal and accentuated the dog's blood loss.

The compassion of many passengers was obvious. When the train passed, I scanned the entire area to make sure no onlookers were around.

I surreptitiously pulled my "PR-24" side-handled baton and smacked the dog as hard as I could as the deputies held it entwined about two feet in the air by the closed ends. It took about six to eight hits, and the dog expired. Los Angeles City Animal Control was called to retrieve the remains.

Shortly afterward I was summoned to the Blue Line Central Command Center on Imperial Highway and Wilmington Avenue. I was immediately directed to the captain's office. The captain wanted to know why I had disposed of the dog in such a fashion. My answer was that I couldn't shoot the dog and indicated the ricochet factor. The dog was suffering great pain and a tremendous loss of blood, and the only humane way to quickly put the dog out of its misery was to strike it with a baton. I added that the baton was not heavy enough to cause its death from one or two blows, and that any future situations should be handled similarly with a baseball bat. I also assured him that the dispatching of the dog was done out of view of any spectators.

The captain frowned and was obviously annoyed at my decision and ordered me to assemble a meeting with all animal control concerns such as the county, city, and state animal control facilities and the local SPCA.

Several days later, approximately twenty individuals joined me and a lieutenant at the Central Control Facility. The situation with the dog that was halved was brought to their attention and my method of dispensing of the animal was thrown out for their evaluation and discussion.

My decision was determined to be a good, viable way to quickly dispose of the animal. All entities of the animal control business were in agreement. The outcome of that meeting was conveyed to the captain, who later smiled and agreed with the findings of that meeting.

Emphasis on the "ricochet factor" will be discussed in several other situations and must remain a constant variable in all shootings.

CHAPTER 154

QUEER MOVE

I believe most folks know that the Los Angeles Sheriff's Department has a larger number of gay deputies than any other department in the United States. It's not news. It's just plain common sense, since the gay community is huge in Southern California.

In fact, West Hollywood, a large gay community, is patrolled by deputies who understand their social needs and easily recognize the bashing that goes on by homophobes. I've worked around many gay deputies at a lot of assignments and really never gave a second thought to their personal views or lifestyle.

However, this time at the Blue Line was out of sync with the department's views and needed to be addressed to stop the homophobes from teaming up and doing stupid things that could get them fired.

There was an outspoken gay deputy assigned to our Metro Blue Line. Several deputies were aware his boyfriend was on the cover of some local gay newspaper. The deputies were laughing, but I didn't think much about their deportment as long as it didn't interfere with their assignments or duties.

The deputy in question was a very small guy, very quiet and polite, who performed his job well. He required little supervision and probably was intimidated by some of the more brash deputies with their sneaky innuendos demeaning his manhood. That same deputy asked for help one day when confronted with a belligerent passenger. I went to his assistance request and helped him settle the dispute, where he was issuing a citation. The disagreement was easily remedied, and I stayed awhile to see if other deputies would come to help him. They didn't. No one arrived, and I wanted to address that issue the very next day if I could do it before the gay deputy arrived at his usual time for late morning briefing.

That next morning another situation developed. I noticed many of the day-shift deputies in the hallway getting into their uniforms just outside the locker room in various stages of dress, some clad only in their underwear. I asked what was going on. One of them informed me that the gay deputy was in the locker room getting dressed, and these guys didn't want to be in the same room with him.

I nodded my head and told them to knock it off and not to be late for briefing. I couldn't believe these guys were afraid to be around this guy because of his personal sexual choices. I knew that I had to talk about this gay lynching as soon as possible, or someone was going to get hurt or fired.

It was time for briefing and everyone came into the briefing room, including the gay deputy. I asked the gay deputy to go out to the Dominguez platform and stay there until I arrived in about an hour. He complied with my request with no questions asked.

I then began to ream the whole group, without being specific, that yesterday's antics would not be tolerated. Every time I found out that someone did not respond to an assistance request from that deputy specifically, I would seek his dismissal from the unit immediately. "That is just downright chickenshit as hell and we, the department, will seek out the idiots who refuse to back him up for whatever bonehead reason."

Then I began addressing the incident in the locker room. My view was that many of the deputies assigned to this unit were misinformed and were downright afraid of the man because he wanted to get dressed in the locker room without being bashed or insulted. I expressed my beliefs and the policy of the department and suggested that if I saw anymore of these repulsive antics, I would deal with them individually or collectively and see how many I could get transferred out of the Blue Line in a single day.

My tone was tough, and the deputies knew very well I meant what I was saying. After all, I had the highest attrition rate in the department's history while at the sheriff's academy. They understood that I'd be watching and monitoring their calls, and if the gay deputy asked for help I would find out quickly who was available and who wasn't.

That warning seemed well understood until about a half hour later, when I was summoned to the captain's office. The captain was seated behind his desk with one of the lieutenants standing by his side. He said that a certain female sergeant had come to him and advised him that I was treading on very thin ice discussing the sensitive topic of homosexuality. She stated that one of the male deputies, thought to be gay, was left out of the conversation and the matter should not have been discussed. She added that it was sexual discrimination.

Although the captain was somber, I felt very comfortable talking about the topic. It was an advisory to all that sexual discrimination would not be tolerated.

I then described the two events and asked the captain why he was asking me. I thought that the accusing sergeant should be there as well. The captain stated that it was her concern that I was discussing a very sensitive topic and that I should handle any and all situations very carefully. I concurred,and added that I was faced dealing with it on the line level, but my assessment and delivery was being questioned by one of my peers who hadn't discussed it with me at all.

Again the captain stated that the female sergeant was worried that I was discussing something delicate and should leave it alone. I said that the sergeant who brought the issue up was hitting on me sexually a few times a day.

She used all of the female wiles, but I refused her advances because she was "butt ass ugly." I never gave it any further thought and left it like that. I carefully explained to the captain that this was a daily effort by the female sergeant, who thought I wouldn't have sex with her because she's black.

That was not the issue, but a possible excuse. I let each incident pass without any verbal reaction.

The captain then shifted in his seat. Personally, I don't think his feet were touching the floor because he was so small and needed to adjust himself in his seat because he was slipping. Once adjusted, the captain said that if that was going on, he would like me to wear a wire, a concealed microphone, to capture her sexual antics and talk. I laughed and said I wouldn't wear a wire for any reason. I explained that every man I knew would gladly accept any sexual request by a woman and wear that request as a medal of manly prowess in any language.

The captain disagreed with me on that issue, but I stood my ground that I would never complain about that sensitive content to anyone—only brag about it as often as possible. He told me to be very careful with the innuendos and to keep an eye out for any further acts of sexual discrimination relating to the male gay deputy. I assured him I would watch everyone closely and stop any other acts that might surface without hesitation.

I'll bet he called the female sergeant in and asked her about what I'd said, which seemed contrary to the initial complaint and just a ruse to gain favor with the administration.

This black female sergeant just so happened to be the one the captain selected, along with Lieutenant Snake from Lynwood Station, to meet with the militant black organization in a previous story.

CHAPTER 155
THE INTERVIEW

I had been at the Metro Blue Line since its inception. It was by far the most crime-free, boring assignment I had in law enforcement. Initially, when I was recruited to this new Metro blue line, the light-rail system, we, the staff, had thought it was going to be inundated with shootings, stabbings, robberies, assaults, rapes, and any other conceivable crime you could come up with.

Our thinking was influenced by the crime-roughened areas it was passing through. The whole area was seriously infested with gangs, roughly 80,000, serious crimes was prevalent and most likely to occur. In those two years, however, it turned out to be probably the safest place to be, because of all of the security. Cameras and someone assigned to watch those cameras full time, foot and radio car patrols, and of course the high degree of danger or death of electrocution from a variety of sources was the formula. This created an exemplary safe corridor of security through all of the gang-infested areas and remains secure and safe today.

Well, most gangsters didn't show up, and the Blue Line sheriff's department administration was in the crime-fighting doldrums, delving into nitpicking at things that were not relating to typical ghetto situations, and more prone to micromanaging its personnel. I have previously discussed several of the picayune, adverse situations that pretty much reflected the micromanagement, although if it was mentioned to those who were in charge, it was denied.

Those situations, coupled with low criminal activity were driving me to return to a busier station with much more activity. I had been there for almost two years and was ready to return to another patrol assignment. Several sergeants at East Los Angeles Station were attempting to persuade me to come back to ELA because of the activity, calls, and major ongoing gang issues. Not to mention the allure of working with like-minded staff, the lieutenants and the sergeants, and the reduced possibility of error. Without further ado on boring details, I set up an appointment with the administrative lieutenant at ELA for an interview with him. This interview was going to be about the likelihood of returning, and I felt very much welcomed and needed by the staff, who mostly knew me from my past assignments and experiences.

I vaguely knew the administrative lieutenant from when I had worked at the academy while training for the 1984 Olympics. He was part of a mass training exercise at that time, and was one of many lieutenants involved in the instructional exercise, while physically going through riot drills and formations.He knew me and my methods, because I was one of the main instructors for implementing several large platoon formations for crowd and riot control, command-post operations and tear-gas deployment. The lieutenant, like most of the patrol station personnel, was accustomed to my brash remarks and demands to perform that were, to say the least, provocative. Other than that training, we were aware of each other's presence, but never really crossed paths.

Now we were going to be face-to-face in this meeting, and hopefully unite, so I could return to ELA and get back to work with the staff in all of its hyperactivity and emergencies. I was excited, anticipating a shoe-in for the job, because they were shy one sergeant's position. I was fairly comfortable going to the interview. I prepared my dress tan-and-green uniform as if I was going to a formal inspection. I arrived around nine forty-five, fifteen minutes early, and met with the lieutenant, a small man, in a basement area near the assembly room.

He led me toward an empty table, where we sat and congenially exchanged greetings and shook hands. He was complimentary and smiled, making me more relaxed as we engaged in small talk about my assignment at the Metro blue line. We talked about how safe the light-rail system was initially and how it actually turned out. Instead of a calamity, it turned out to be a very safe mode of travel.

The small talk ended as the lieutenant was sipping coffee from one of those small machines and asked, "So, Larry, tell me about yourself. Exactly what kind of sergeant are you?" He then sipped the hot coffee slightly, and his eyebrows rose slightly.

I began to answer, "Well, I'm a hands-on, proactive kind of guy who keeps his eye on the ball at all times." During this opening statement the lieutenant was reaching down along side of the chair he was sitting in, and pulled up a beige manila envelope. He began opening the flap slowly leaning forward slightly and turning his head as if listening to me carefully.

I continued in a pretentious tone about my superior supervisory skills and leadership qualities. The lieutenant pulled a large paper from the envelope and placed it on the table in front of him. I continued elaborating about my personal traits, and the lieutenant placed his hand on top of the paper. That's when I realized it was an eight-by-ten glossy photo.

He slowly slid the photo toward me as I was talking. When it was right in front of me, he removed his hand and exposed a personal photo of me, in a captivating yet compromising position. That revelation stopped me from talking about myself. I carefully examined the photo.

I recognized it as a provocative picture that was taken several years ago when I was off duty, quite drunk, and in a private setting.

The photo was taken at a low angle, below my waistline, and in front of me, by someone who snapped the shot upward. The picture showed me holding a hot-dog bun, with catsup, mustard, and relish along each side of a weenie. The problem was that it wasn't a hot dog at all; it was my flaccid penis snuggled comfortably in the open-faced bun, as if it were being displayed for a commercial.

I was aware that this provocative photo was taken by a fellow officer at a party, absent anything that would've been an embarrassment to my department. It had been distributed to quite a few comrades-in-arms, and there was nothing I could do to control its distribution. The photo also clearly captured my face, so who was directly behind the loaded bun was clearly visible.

I asked the lieutenant where he got the photo, and I grimaced with despair. I wondered how the hell a photo like this came into this guy's hands, and ultimately in an oral interview setting.

The lieutenant just sat there and looked at me with disgust and a cold indifference. I boldly remarked to the lieutenant after his presentation of the photo, "Well, I guess that pretty much concludes this interview, huh?"

He didn't say a thing and continued to look at me with disgust, with his right eyebrow slightly elevated. I search my blameless mind for an excuse, but there wasn't any explanation for this type of photo, except stupidity and shame.

I nodded my head in a gesture of giving up, wondering why the hell this meeting ever took place. I thanked the lieutenant for the opportunity to express myself, and said I was sorry I had wasted his time. I walked away from the table, not shaking his hand or even looking back, but obviously contrite.

The lieutenant remained seated and didn't move; as I solemnly left the room, I listened for his gathering of papers and the photo or the sound of the heavy chair scooting backward on the linoleum floor. Not a sound was heard.

Everyone I knew at the station was noticeably absent from view as I came out of the interview, walked up the stairs, and passed by the front desk and dispatch center.

I left the station, hopped into my patrol car, and drove back to the Metro Blue Line central station, just south of Watts and on the border of Willowbrook Avenue and Imperial Highway. As I was driving back, I was reflecting on how the interview went and couldn't help but feel perplexed and stupid. I kept thinking, *Well, you numbskull, just whose fault was it?*

I continued asking myself, *Why in the hell did they let me come to the station, when they were aware of the ill-favored photo, and obviously had no intentions of allowing me to come back?*

I even thought maybe it was a situation where someone was very much aware of my past antics and wanted to drive home their disgust at my arrogant ways and lower the air pressure in my pride with a heaping dose of rejection. I felt humiliated and was actually looking forward to coming back to the Blue Line, where I would banish that recent image from my thoughts.

It took about twenty-five minutes to return, and I went to the locker room to freshen up, get ready to load up my gear, and go back out into the field.

I got my patrol gear, freshened up and stepped out into the hallway. I was paged that I had a phone call. I went to the operations desk and grabbed the nearest phone. The speaker on the other end stated he was the scheduling lieutenant at East Los Angeles Station. He asked me what shift I wanted to work at East Los Angeles, which caught me completely off guard. I advised him that I didn't do well at my interview, and that there must be a mix up.

He responded, "No, Larry, you're starting tomorrow, and we're all anxious to have you come back. It was the captain's decision, and he wants you here starting tomorrow. Do you understand?"

I acknowledged his advisory and was told that a transfer was in the making. All necessary parties had been advised.

With that information, I hung up the phone, took a deep breath and sat back in the chair, and realized it was a ploy thrown right into my face. Go figure, the prankster was set up! I felt relieved that this whole interview turned out to be an absolute fiasco. Someone had tainted the usual order of things and set the whole interview up to slap my feelings to the ground and deflate my ego.

Well, it worked, and now I needed to regain my composure, not let on how depressing it was, and mask anything that would reveal my true emotions about what had really happened.

After this episode I was forced to revaluate the mischievous notions that I enjoyed. I would be thankful and remember that when you do stupid things, they could very well come back later on and bite you right on the ass. Also, knowing full well there are compromising photos available to the public, I realized I could never run for a political office, unless I could withstand the scrutiny of those pictures and give a viable explanation, which of course is highly doubtful.

CHAPTER 156

EAST LOS ANGELES SECOND RUN: TRUE EXPRESSIONS, A GRAPHIC PICTORIAL

I was working as the desk sergeant in the early evening hours. The office adjoined the dispatcher's desk window and a large jail window next to the booking counter. The reason for this position is that this is the hub of most activity—field units are conversing, incoming phone calls are collected and disseminated, and proper follow-up action is determined. The jail booking activity is monitored both visually and audibly. Frequent communications between the dispatcher, jailer, and sergeant are necessary so proper protocol is followed and not overlooked. The department's policies and procedures are strictly adhered to, because the fundamental duties of both the front desk and the jailer's positions are very crucial and highly critical.

This night was no different. The desk was busy with a variety of calls and details. Field observations from the units assigned to specific patrol areas, called reporting districts, were noted. The jail was busy, and there was a lot of activity around the booking counter. Overall, the station's activity was bustling with the typical evening watch energy—deputies and secretaries coming in, going out, and passing by the high counter that sits directly in front of the watch sergeant's desk, doing all sorts of things.

A call came in from a woman who was having a party at her home on Lanfranco Street, with several of her family members and friends attending. Her concern was that she was recently separated from her husband and going through a very emotional and difficult divorce. She stated that her husband had called earlier, and stated that he had heard that she and her new boyfriend were together and at the party.

The husband was very irate that his wife's new boyfriend was at the party and apparently having a good time with his wife. He was angry that they were enjoying themselves in front of their two daughters, ages seven and five.

The husband was so incensed that he threatened to come over to kill both her and the boyfriend. She stated that he was a very violent man, and she already had a court order called a TRO, temporary restraining order, to keep him away from her, but he obviously didn't care. She was afraid he would carry out his threats and shoot them and anyone else who got in the way.

A female deputy handled the call and informed the woman that she should call back when her husband showed up, and they would then dispatch a unit. This remark apparently upset the female caller, who thought that it would certainly be too late for anyone to do anything, because he would already be there and following up with his threats.

The deputy explained to the woman that it was next to impossible to send a unit to her home, because the unit would be sitting out in front of their home. That wouldn't help matters much, because that detailed unit would have to be there for an unlimited amount of time without assurance the irate husband would ever come over.

The woman was very upset at the explanation the deputy gave her and argued extensively about the department's position in these situations. The female deputy went on to explain that it would be much simpler for the woman and her children to relocate until the TRO hearing was adjudicated. That way her husband wouldn't know where they were and he'd be unable to do any harm. The deputy who listened to her brash language, and held the phone line open until the woman hung up.

This call was handled properly and followed the guidelines of the departmental procedures and protocol.

About an hour later, quite a few calls came in that shots were heard coming from a house over on a street called Lanfranco, the same street where the female caller had requested protection from her spurned husband who had threatened her an hour earlier.

Units were sent to the home code three. When they arrived and entered the home, they saw a horrific bloodbath.

Apparently the spurned husband did return, only he came to the home from over the rear fence. He began shooting as soon as he climbed over the fence, shooting two, killing one. Then he came into the home and fired at his wife, his wife's mother, her aunt, and a family friend, killing all four, leaving the bodies stacked up in the kitchen like a cord of wood.

It was one of the worst shootings in the East Los Angeles area—five killed and a sixth one wounded. As it turned out the wounded one was the boyfriend of the now-deceased wife. Quite a few units converged on the scene and the sight caused several to be sick from the shock of so much blood and death.

The husband was easily apprehended and arrested and brought to the station without incident. Shortly afterward a couple of deputies brought in the two daughters. They were handled very carefully and handed off to several station secretaries to watch them until the Department of Child Services, DCS, investigators arrived approximately an hour or two later. Generally kids are seated at one of the many vacant desks and given a large sheet of unrolled shelf paper and a whole tub of crayons. This allows them to draw whatever they want and occupy their time until DCS investigators arrive.

When the husband passed by I looked at him with disgust, but I had some empathy for what he had just done and what the future of his life would be. He came in, very somber, and passed by my desk with his head down. He was very quiet and probably had a million things going on in his head. He needed to be watched very closely, because the possibility of a suicide is very high in situations like these.

When the girls came in, they seemed indifferent and a little nervous. The deputies advised me that they were apparently next door when the shooting had occurred. With that in mind, it seemed okay to keep them busy in the station's secretariat, without any further disturbances, out of sight and hearing of anything connected to the Lanfranco Street address.

As I followed up and made sure the girls were taken care of, I came upon the female deputy who took the call from the now-deceased wife. She was weeping in the adjacent room and feeling somewhat responsible for the event that cost five lives.

I empathized with her sad feelings and attempted to comfort her by pointing out that there wasn't a thing anyone could do about the situation, because the husband had it already planned in his mind to kill. I assured her she had followed the departmental policies and procedures and acted professionally and properly. She continued to weep and needed to be consoled more, so I informed the station watch commander of her feelings of guilt and said I thought she needed to be carefully watched.

In situations like this, it may very well become necessary to notify the department's psychological services and have them respond to the station because of the possibility of grave consequences.

About forty minutes had passed when one of the secretaries came to my desk and politely interrupted me while I was busy with some activity. She announced to me, "Sergeant Rupp, that little seven-year-old girl drew a very sensitive picture." She handed me the rolled-up shelf paper and asked me to review what the girl had drawn.

The secretary was very somber in her delivery and concerned about what I was about to view. I carefully unfurled the white sheet of paper and looked at the drawing.

It was the depiction of a small hill on the right side of the drawing, with splotches of green grass and a tree with verdant leaves. The large sun was a bright yellow in the background on the right side. There was a typical stick drawing of a two-inch woman with a simple triangular dress, stick fingers and toes, and curlicue hair on both sides of the head. The face had three dots, indicating the eyes and nose, and an upside U depicting a sad-shaped mouth.

In the background near the sketched woman, were one-inch letters that spelled, "Mommy, I love you." Then the most graphic illustration stood out in red crayon. It was a distinct tapered funnel, the small end at the right side of the neck of the drawn woman, flaring out to an inch and a half. Of course, the drawing indicated to me that the little seven-year-old had seen her dead mother, as illustrated in the drawing, but it was unknown if she or her five-year-old sister witnessed the entire shooting.

This was an extremely sensitive subject, not to be discussed with the children except by a professional psychiatrist. Critical boundaries were now revealed, and the highest concern for their safety and well-being, fragile to say the least, was recognized. This was a calamity in itself, and the damage to these two kids would most likely never be repaired. These girls would face years of intense professional counseling.

The drawing was given to the DCS investigators and passed on to their caseworkers. That detailed drawing was a genuine raw form of feelings that could be used today in many books because of its simplicity. The dramatic and tragic consequences from this shooting arose from a domestic conflict. The adult behavior of hatred and murder unfolded without any consideration of the tragic repercussions for small innocent children.

May God have mercy on those girls and let them live a life of happiness in all of their endeavors.

All of the deputies who responded to the Lanfranco address and witnessed the graphic scene suffered psychological consequences as well. Dramatic exposure of this nature was foreseen, and fortunately, the sheriff's department had a unit in place able to handle these types of situations. This professional intervention most likely prevented many long-term problems.

Should another situation like this occur, any department would be limited to the initial response. To allow a unit to go to the location and stand guard while the family partied is unreasonable. If a person is threatened, to remain at home is unsound reasoning. To move away and remain obscure and difficult to locate is a more reasonable move.

CHAPTER 157

FAMILIAR PLACES: THE DAISY CHAIN

Every year the Rose Parade comes to town, and it's a major commitment by the LA County Sheriff's Department to assist the Pasadena PD with resources such as deputies, vehicles, mobile command posts, transportation, and mobile mass bookings. I believe the count is around a million, give or take, in attendance.

The Rose Parade offers over four hundred million viewers a front-row seat. I might be off a bit, but I'll bet I'm still underestimating the amount of the world-wide viewing public. It's a perfect situation and spot for any moronic terrorist to snatch his seventy-two virgins in an epic slaughter with a mass audience.

Fortunately, the combined and coordinated efforts of law enforcement forces and the military are able to snatch these potential killers from the midst of all the excitement. They are able to throw those bomb-making, baby-killing idiots into jail, where hopefully they will meet "Bubba."

For several years, the corner of Colorado Boulevard and Orange Grove Boulevard is the epicenter of all excitement and the hoopla of the beginning and ending of the parade. The media is firmly entrenched at this location and the location could be a desirable stage for any fanatic to carry out their drama and be thoroughly noticed by many people.

I was assigned to this exact spot for nearly ten years in a row. It was the most highly publicized event of the year, and many important dignitaries such as the governor, city mayors and councilmen, entertainers, and the LA County Sheriff and their families.

A huge briefing was given in Pasadena every time for all agencies and law enforcement to meet one another and discuss the event and various difficulties. It always centered on the corner of Colorado and Orange Grove Boulevards.

This spot has a very large assemblage of high rise bleachers, L shaped at the corner, on both sides of the street. These bleachers are very long and seat thousands of spectators. The media is in these bleachers as well on both sides of the streets.

The commander of the LA Sheriff's Department entourage was one of the directors of the large law enforcement contingency. The commander always pointed out that the most sensitive spot in the entire parade was at Colorado and Orange Grove. He expressed his concerns about what might happen, because this place is where disruptions might be expected to take place. The commander would also illustrate that television coverage would allow over 450 million viewers to watch the celebration and the glorious parade floats, massive bands, cheerleaders, and all types of ceremonial groups and animals.

The commander then would add jokingly to the entire audience, "And who do we put there to watch over this entire mess? Sergeant Larry Rupp!" This comedian would always get a generous laugh.

With that, everything settled down, and everyone would receive their instructions for the reporting times and the small nuances that were discussed and ironed out.

The major problem in the position I was so carefully involved in was that the politicians, celebrities, and the affluent societal bureaucrats were seated comfortably and in full view of the parade. If something devious or dangerous was planned, it was going to be most likely right there.

Intelligence from the various departments would be viewed as critical and carefully scrutinized by the department heads. Of course when it comes time for intelligence gathers to spew out what they know, it always surprised me that there was no information. Now, think about that. No intelligence, or is it so sensitive that to announce it would be likely to scare the bejesus out of everyone, and then no one would come to the parade? Well, probably, yes, and you'd never hear about it. That's the way it goes.

Several days went by, and preparation for the parade was in full throttle. My reporting time was 4:30 a.m., allowing ample time to load up all necessities and get to my position. We arrived early, with no one in the stands. Most of the media had their equipment platform stands ready and in place, and were and awaiting the media crews to straggle in as well.

Bomb-sniffing dogs and their handlers were unobtrusively going through the giant bleachers and the entire perimeter and periphery. Security had actually been in place for a couple of days already, and as the time for the parade came near, security incrementally increased. When the day of the parade arrived, a noticeable security force was present, as were a variety of specialists, all with unique duties, yet another barrier for the unexpected.

Now we were ready. The crowd was arriving with their warm blankets, thermoses of hot coffee, chocolate and whatever other concoctions they might have. Red cheeks radiated, laughter was abundant, and the chilly air was noticeable when exhaled.

My thinking was that someone here was going to try something to make an announcement or disrupt the flow of the parade. That person or persons were probably watching me to measure my ability to react. I knew they saw me, so it was real important to stay focused.

I also had a responsibility to supervise the deputies who were watching the crowd as well. I'd remind them that the parade was for the public, and their primary job was to remain fluid, not make arrests or get involved in situations that would take their eyes off the crowd. They were to watch out for any disruptions or situations that might need specialized teams to respond. The assembly of a nearby platoon of law enforcement officers was ready to help should the necessity arise. However, they were hidden from the public's eye.

Cameras stands would start to fill with their crews, and the bleachers were filling rapidly. The hustle and bustle of activities abound. People moved everywhere, and I'd try to key in on someone who didn't fit in or was acting a little out of sync. (A duck in sheep's clothing?)

That's how the disruption would surface. It would come quickly, and we had to be able to respond with a flexible amount of necessary force to overcome the resistance.

My mind would go a hundred miles an hour to try to anticipate what might occur, but that's near impossible. My head was on a swivel and I was watching everyone nearby.

The lieutenant and I constantly checked on each other's positions and got a feel for the operative assessment of things going on. Some behavior was peculiar, but normal for this neck of the woods. Things were looking okay for now, but when would the inevitable problems pop up? Impossible to tell. The parade was beginning to start, and a surprise could surface anytime. The first floats were on their way and the bands were starting up, so here we go.

It would be imperative not to get tangled up in routine criminal matters and remain free to focus and observe the crowd's tempo and behavior.

Everyone generally focused on the parade and was enjoying it. Our jobs were to keep an open eye for the makings of something that might happen, but we just didn't know what.

What might occur, an idiot running out into the crowd with a bomb, a gun, a volatile chemical or substance? Let your imagination run wild, it could be something innocuous initially, but turn out to be dangerous or deadly.

Everything was going pretty well, and no significant delays or obstructions were noticed. Occasional float breakdowns were inevitable for a short interruption, but everything else seemed all right.

Close to midway through the parade, a group of protesters chained together demand more research for an AIDS cure. They came onto the parade quickly, running across the street all chained up. Some started to sit in the roadway, but we were able to grab most just as they were starting to sit down.

The US Marine Corp Mounted Brigade, on their horses and in full-dress uniforms, saw the interruption, drew their sabers, and began to approach, but they were asked not to bother the protesters and quickly complied.

There were fourteen in the daisy chain, and the last one was not able to sit at all. He was being dragged along, rolling around freestyle, chained to the whole group as we ran with them to the sidelines.

The last man on the chain was screaming as he was being dragged and flipping around uncontrollably. Once on the sidelines, just beneath one of the retractable booms used by the media, I placed each face into the rear end of the one before, because of the chains were very short. The protesters were able to lie face down, in each other's rear ends, like a centipede. It was the only way to get them out of the way quickly, and it seemed rather comical, as they were positioned beneath one of the media's extended booms that was photographing the entire ruckus.

The way they were coupled together wouldn't allow any other remedy to quickly organize the chained group and rapidly arrest all fourteen of them. They were all handcuffed with flex cuffs, and we created a small area to hold them until additional help came to cut the chain with bolt cutters.

The photo would have been priceless; however, I never saw it published. I'm sure the editors probably felt it would only frustrate the already sensitive and fragile public's molded support for the AIDS problem and chose to set the photos aside.

In my own mind, the attempt to disrupt the parade was a united attack. They may have had been orchestrated within the parade group organizers to get them that close to the parade without detection by either law enforcement or parade employees.

What do you think? If AIDS sympathizer(s) conspired to disrupt the parade, it might very well have been an internal problem within the Rose Parade organizers and possibly law enforcement. The chained group must have had internal help because the likelihood of detection would have been very high.

That was the only disruption, and it never slowed the parade at all because of quick reactions. Every year still has a load of problems, and personnel of the parade are the key requirement for a good presentation. One thing for sure, there must be several pairs of heavy-duty bolt cutters nearby at future events.

Only the most alert law enforcement personnel, armed with command posture, presence, and exceptional patrol skills, who are sharp-witted and have the ability to stay focused on the job at hand should be assigned to this sensitive spot.

The normal departmental obsequious toadies who are politically driven need not apply, because unexpected and outlandish situations will occur, and the personnel assigned will be taxed heavily to perform.

CHAPTER 158

TRUE LIARS: PROFESSIONAL PREVARICATORS

An event in my life set the stage for the following story, which occurred and was finalized in a courtroom setting with a court reporter, my sister Mary, a family law attorney from Oakland, and two other attorneys in the Orange County area. (I was in fact working at E.L.A. station, in the city of Commerce when this all surfaced and litigation was pursued.) Who would have thought, that an officer of the court was in fact a pathological prevaricator, who twisted an agreement and verbal contract into a fabricated mess that should have been publicized as a breach of ethics and a failed duty to perform.

Regardless how people feel about my arresting ability, this story is just as important as any other arrests I have made. I view anyone who deliberately violates the law in any profession, should suffer the same consequences. My job as a cop was to pursue crooks afoot, grab them by their tails and stick them in a cage. This story was no different, only this time my sister, Mary, was my partner.

Initial Complaint

It all started while I was in a sordid divorce, and the time was coming when my portion of the settlement was nearing the final date. I prematurely paid a title search to be performed on my home in Mission Viejo. This home is where my ex-wife was still living, with her boyfriend and my youngest son.

The title search revealed that the equity vested in my Mission Viejo home was suspiciously stripped by three independent loans that some how went around my mechanic's lien, which had been filed in the superior court in Santa Ana in 1984. That lien was brought about by processing my divorce court edict in the county seat.

I was going to law school at this time and was referred to an attorney who had an office near John Wayne Airport, Orange County. I scheduled a meeting with the attorney and stated my purpose. We exchanged salutations and talked briefly about my current attendance at the Western State Law School in Fullerton. It just so happened to be the same school she had graduated from, which made our meeting more comfortable.

She reviewed my title search and informed me that the fraud could cause my ex-wife to go to jail for the theft and asked me if I had any reservations about her going to jail. I remarked that if I had done the same thing, she would have certainly sent me to jail at the drop of a hat. Therefore, in simple terms I stated that I had no problem at all with the idea.

She informed me that I was a little premature because the money due to me was not going to be due for another six to eight months. Fine, I said, as long as we were ahead of the game. She advised me that we had ample time to secure any money due to me in the proper time allotted by the divorce court.

The attorney required $1700 as a fee for the processing and follow-up procedures. I wrote her a check for $800 in November and the remainder on another separate check toward the end of December 1993. I was pleased with her legal exuberance and felt sure I would be getting my final pay from the divorce settlement, and not be stiffed, like to holding a cookie jar with no cookies.

A month went by with no indication of my lawyer's research, so I began to call her office. More time passed, and I continued to call her office to find out what the plan was, and were we ready for legal pursuit. Every time I called my attorney, she was away or busy with another client. I was not able to contact my lawyer, but her secretary took many messages.

I assumed things were being done, and I was way ahead of the game, so I left her alone, other than calling to verify progress was in the works.

More time passed, and one day when I was talking it over with my sister Mary, a family law attorney in Oakland, she gave me some stern instructions. Mary stated that I should demand to speak with my attorney personally and find out exactly where we were at with the case. My sister was emphatic that time was of the essence, and I must review what the attorney had done to prepare my case.

No Contract!

I called and left another message for my attorney to call me, because the statute of limitations was near its end. Finally, my attorney returned my call. I asked where we were with the case, and she informed me, "Well, Larry, we never had a contract, so I haven't done anything at all!"

This floored me, and I responded, "We had a verbal contract, and I paid you the full price we agreed on. What do you mean we didn't have a contract?" She repeated her assertion and added, "If you hurry, you still may have some time before the statute of limitations runs out."

"What do you mean hurry? Hurry what and where? You are my paid attorney, and I expected performance. Where else can I go?" I informed her at that point that, based on her nonperformance and lack of "duty to perform," I had left no other alternative but to take her to court for a whole variety of "duty" responsibilities and the possible loss of my $60,000, settlement from the divorce decree.

As soon as I got off the phone, I called my sister and asked if she would represent me in court against my attorney, and she agreed. "What a sister!" I had never in my entire career, been left in the lurch by someone on whom I counted so much. It was as if I was being shoved into an abysmal legal morass.

Timeline

Time was at a premium, so I had to rush. Things had to be done to establish that a contract was made, and I had to show that my attorney and I were in communication with each other. I also must show that my reliance on her legal defenses was established, based on my beliefs and exchange of information.

I started to audit both of the phones I was using at home, and at the satellite station in the City of Commerce. This audit was over a two-and-a-half-year period when I was calling my attorney on a regular basis. I gathered the batch of phone bills from home and the satellite station, researched them intently, and faxes for calls to my attorney's office.

The audit revealed that I had called her twenty-seven times, and those calls matched with my notes of each communication and each time. The fax machine receipts verified three faxes of important messages, needed to be addressed. I called and informed my sister of the results, and she agreed that should be sufficient to prove we were communicating with each other and I was relying on her acting on my input.

My sister Mary asked me about when, where, who, how, and why way too many times, so I developed a timeline to indicate dates, times, and substance of all of the communications, and what matters were in play at the time that had a direct effect on me or what I was doing. When this timeline was completed, it stretched from floor to ceiling, printed in various colors of indelible ink.

This list of events was the icing on the cake, and coupled with the phone and fax lists of communication, it was compelling.

It appeared the statute of limitations had run its course, and now I was a victim of poor representation and an attorney who lacked protocol and legal knowledge and vacated her duty to perform.

Then my sister called me and told me that she just unloaded on my previous attorney about her poor ethical standards, and asked her to send my entire case folder to her. The attorney, Delilah, told my sister that there was nothing in my jacket because we did not have a contract.

That infuriated my sister, because although Delilah was in denial about the contract, she did know exactly when the statute was going to expire.

Bankruptcy Court

I was at a loss, because this whole thing was now in a denial stage, but somehow my sister found out that Delilah was in bankruptcy court. I needed to rush to the bankruptcy court and represent myself in a hearing where Delilah was finalizing her creditors list with the court and excluding me.

I quickly jumped into my suit and tie and drove like hell to the federal court in Santa Ana, and entered the courtroom of Judge Lynn Riddles. When

I arrived, the rear of the court was packed with attorneys. I was the only layperson to be heard by the court.

I was a little nervous, but I had to say something, and my sister was held up in other legal matters in Oakland, California.

Judge Lynn Riddles was talking with an attorney hired by my previous attorney, Delilah, both seated to my left, and were concluding their creditors' meeting that had taken place two weeks previously.

The new attorney was standing in front of a lectern, explaining the concluding matters of creditors. Judge Riddles interrupted and asked who I was, probably because I was standing directly behind the attorney representing Delilah.

I stood up to the lectern and stated that I was a creditor and that Delilah owed me $60,000. I had been purposely excluded from the list of creditors for no apparent reason.

Delilah's attorney spoke up and stated that I was in fact one of the creditors, but that I did not attend the meeting when summoned. So by default I was excluded. Judge Riddles explained to the co counsel that she needed to see the "proof of service" form to make a ruling. Co counsel leafed through a thick file as if looking for a "proof of service" form, when he knew there was none to be found. I was livid, knowing this person was lying before a federal court that I was served a summons. I wanted to slap the pee out of this person for insinuating something legal had transpired and that I failed to respond.

I think that in this case God stopped me. Judge Riddles focused on my reaction, this so called "officer of the court" was no better than a common heroin addict displaying his forearm to a cop, swearing he wasn't an addict, although recent puncture scabs lined up perfectly along his veins.

Judge Riddles said, "Council you know my ruling. If there is no proof of service, then there is no service at all!" He said he knew all about the edict, all the while still paging through the inch and a half of paper in the folder.

I believe I was seen as highly agitated by Judge Riddles, so she asked who was going to represent me when and if the hearing was delayed. I informed her that my sister Mary Catherine Rupp, who practiced law in Oakland, would be here within the next two weeks and would represent me in all legal matters.

A scheduled court hearing was set within the next two weeks, and my time before the court ended. I thanked the judge for her understanding of the matter, pleased with her ruling and continuance.

Superior Court

We went to court several times, my sister was successful by staying the bankruptcy hearing, and she reset a superior court hearing on the charges of lawyer misconduct and various breaches of a lawyer's fiduciary duties and obligations.

Each time my sister had to come to court, I had to pick her up at John Wayne Airport and drive her directly to the City of Santa Ana where she performed in an excellent manner.

In fact, the federal bankruptcy court judge, Lynn Riddles, commended Mary for her research and excellent preparation for trial and issues before the court.

I was so proud of my sister for doing this entire episode and all of its complexities, for which she never charged me a penny. Therefore, I owed her major. As soon as Mary was through, I would rush her back to the airport, where she caught the next flight out of Orange County and returned to her home base in Oakland.

The Deposition

We arrived at the law offices of Delilah and her co counsel. This was the deposition where Delilah would confront me in an odd jurisdictional moment. I was charging her with malpractice, abandoning a client, and seven other counts of misconduct. I did not feel comfortable at all because of my personal pride and thin skin for this sort of comical legal ethics and jurisprudence.

As we came into the small office, the introductions went okay. We all sat and acknowledged there was a court reporter present, and the legal proceeding went forward. The very person against whom I was charging misconduct asked a whole slew of mundane questions of me. Her attitude was arrogant, and she began to make facial gestures as I was testifying. This court officer was acting like a court jester, and I was compelled to respond without a sensible reaction.

Questioning went on, and Delilah began to introduce evidence. She passed a small stack of older wrinkled-up billing forms across the table to me and asked me if I would look at them. I took the small stack and reviewed them individually.

I realized that these billing forms were recently fabricated invoices that were downright fraudulent. I was infuriated.

Delilah leaned back with a smirk on her face. She rocked shoulders back and forth, firing off grimacing, facial gyrations at me. She knew that this would set me off, and she was in fact luring me into her planned web of outrage.

I could actually sense my blood pressure rising. I responded by moving forward in my seat, near the front edge of the chair, and leaning partially over the wooden table that was between us.

To add fuel to the fire, she stated, "You recognize those billing forms, don't you? They're copies of the billing I sent to you." She raised her eyebrow and lowered her jaw in the opposite direction, in a defiant gesture.

I pointed my right index finger toward her. "This is why this has to end. These were all made up recently, and you are mocking this entire proceeding."

My sister realized my outrage and grabbed my right elbow. "I think this is a good time to take a break." Co counsel responded in kind, "I think he's out of control." Mary said, "No, he's okay, his gun is out in his car. He's all right!" Mary and I discussed the situation outside, and she told me not to blow the case by losing my temper. I told her I could not take the taunting insolence. Something must be done to stop this lying "officer of the court" from creating an illusion of a legal proceeding and making it a laughingstock of ongoing fraud.

Mary was insistent that I hold back my emotions, or it would jeopardize the entire matter. I realized I had to contain myself in order to proceed with the deposition. I paid close attention to my sister's warnings and legal concerns, and we returned and concluded the deposition within thirty minutes. I behaved as expected and then took Mary to John Wayne Airport for her return home.

This volley went back and forth for nearly a year and a half, and my sister performed a lot of work while she was in Oakland. The finality was that we won our entire case, and Delilah owed me the monies that I lost due to her misconduct and misfeasance and poor lawyering practices.

Disbarred

Unfortunately, Delilah was also being sued by nine others and mine was in fact the case "in chief" when she lost everything. The attorney was brought before the California State Bar and suspended for four years.

During this time, she continually contrived wrongdoings and the outcome resulted in her being permanently disbarred, so she was no longer able to practice law again in the state of California.

As a tribute to my sister for all of the legal and personal work she performed, I felt it was fitting to create an ode for her diligence and professional behavior. The following is that ode, which outlines the legal track we went through, and the pride I have in her to this day.

ODE TO MARY: I AM MY BROTHER'S KEEPER?

Hurt, scorned, and bitterly mad,
I sat at home questioning life, "Why so sad?"
How could someone create such strife?
When I'd been so full of life.

Sick with despair, and with anger imbued
I knew deep inside, someone needed to be sued.
But wait, I knew someone close to me
Who is well versed in the legal sea.
I called upon 'er, a sister, sorely in need.
An attorney not paid, only for greed.
Never before had I sought 'er edge.
So keen to the world was 'er legal pledge.

Mom and Dad had babied this one.
Schooled 'er well, so it all would be fun.
She viewed the matter as a personal event,
Knowing full well 'er brother wouldn't relent.
'Er ambition and instructions were ever so clear;
No one should attack 'er brother so dear.

To the top of the fed, we focused our skills,
Going to battle against evil wills.
We scurried about with pride and ambitions,
Cautiously noting we may lose munitions.
Getting our stay was quite a venture.
Don't stop here, there's more adventure.

She's learned to lie and cheat very well.
This one will learn quickly; we've been trained n'r hell.
We loaded our quiver, with all of our points.
Flushing Mary's wisdom, to crush Delilah's joints.
Delilah scoffed aloud and snubbed our pains;
Though Judge Riddles rejected her claims.
To the top of the courts, we went to battle,
Protecting our points, duly embattled.

Though long and bitter, and never brief,
Mary coming through was no disbelief.

Like the time in the "depo," where I leaned real near;
Mary foresaw an impending fear.
'Er brother so mad, ready to punch,
She pulled him back and requested lunch.
Co council spouted, "He's out of control!"
Mary responded, "There's gun control!"

My brother's not dumb, he's just mad.
Thank god I'm here, or it'll be bad.
She told me to cool it. Go with the flow.
Nervously thinking, where she would go?
We went on to battle, and never gave up,
For we're the family whose proud name is Rupp.
Well, finally Delilah lost her license four years.
This brought both of us, nearly to tears.

In the end, Mary's performance was ever so great.
I'm proud as peaches for Delilah's fate.
Above the call for duty 'e wanted,
'is sister came and only jaunted.
Though money recovered was only a pittance,
'Er performance was patient; no need for remittance.

Mom and Dad knew I had to pay 'er something;
In order to prevent any family grumbling.
So for now, we will pay 'er a small tidy sum;
Only to keep 'er from being a bum.

The rest of the family should take heed,
Our little sister is not in need.
She has stature, talent, spirit, and tact
She's quite an attorney, and that's a fact!

For Mom and Dad to breed such stock,
Spiritually near the lifelong clock.
They'd boast of ventures their kids had stayed

Vince, Hank, and Mary would be their legal aid.
Of course Diana flew, and Larry hunted,
Both came to the plate and carefully bunted.

Our parents didn't talk a whole hell of a lot
Though encouraged our paths, like it or not.
I know full well they would follow this story;
In this "Ode to Mary" they would reap 'er glory!
To end this saga, I should personally thank,
Mary's on my side, take that to the bank.

Hugs and Kisses to Mary

Your loving brother Larry (April 8, 2005)

CHAPTER 159
CONSUMED

There are many pet owners in the East Los Angeles area, because for security's sake, a dog is probably the best alarm for the folks at home if something or someone is nearby. Having a dog around the home is very beneficial for the hard working community that goes in and out of the house all hours of the day and night. Everyone benefits from the canine's attention, although many complain of the incessant barking. But that's what dogs do and do well. They have protected many homes from burglaries just by their barking and alerting neighbors that someone is lurking about. Many of the neighborhood families treat their dog as if it was a cherished part of the family and care for their pets pretty well.

Many who choose to run the streets for exercise take their dogs along for the extra protection and as an obvious deterrent. In these neighborhoods, the folks don't linger too long in front of many homes because of the incessant barking.

I believe most care for their dogs fairly well and provide all the required health shots and necessary food and water to ensure the dogs' good health.

One day a call came to one of the patrol cars to check on the health and well-being of an older woman who hadn't been seen for several days. The relatives were the ones who called, concerned that something might have happened to the her, the sole occupant of the home.

When the deputy arrived, he went to the front door and knocked several times to no avail. He then went around to the rear door and knocked loudly as well. Still no response, so the deputy went around to the various windows to see if he could peer into the home and possibly see someone. Still nothing, so he went to the surrounding neighbors to see if they had seen the elderly woman.

All neighbors hadn't seen the woman either, so the deputy requested the phone number of the informant, who was a close relative but lived quite a distance away. The deputy informed the family member and sought permission to forcibly enter house. Once allowed to enter, he insisted that the family member come to secure the home.

The deputy went in and came across the elderly woman face down just inside the living room. Unfortunately, she was dead, and her buttocks were half eaten by her dog that had taken care of her all the while she was alive. Autopsy reports indicated that she had died a couple of weeks earlier.

Her faithful dog though, became increasingly hungry as days went by without any food and was drinking water from the small bathroom toilet.

Unfortunately the dog's hunger was exacerbated by the smell of its owner's flesh decaying. It obviously supplied some food for the dog, which is understandable, considering its starving condition.

This was the first time I had seen the photographs of a situation like this, but I'd heard of it several times before.

If you have a family member who lives alone with a dog, expect the same consequences. It is a natural reaction for animals to consume deceased individuals whom they cared for if they're left attended, and there's no other sustenance available.

CHAPTER 160

DOUBLE TASED

I had been at East Los Angeles Station for several months now, and I was persuaded to be Commerce dedicated sergeant. That meant that I was responsible for twenty-nine deputies assigned to patrol the contract city and make sure they provided good-quality service.

I knew the area pretty well. We were working on the new court injunction the city had obtained against the only known street gang. It was working great, and any former gang members who bragged about being in the gang had their statements used against them by the injunction. That court order specifically named each member and their affiliates to stay a certain distance from one another. They could not be together while in the city.

The cost for that injunction was high, but well worth it, because suddenly Commerce no longer had a gang problem and was now enjoying the ordinary bubble of crime. The crime in the area was not bad at all, as long as the deputies were seen patrolling around, checking on any suspicious activity, and communicating with individuals afoot.

Commerce is rather unique in that there is a population of about twelve thousand residents during the evening, but in the daytime it jumps to ninety thousand. That's because it is mostly a commercial city with an influx of many outside workers.

It was around eight in the evening one Saturday, and a call came that there was a large party going on in a home over by the Commerce city hall. Three units were dispatched, and I responded as well. When we arrived, there were approximately thirty to forty people in attendance. Most were cooperating pretty well, but then we came across several male Hispanics bordering on public drunkenness and feeling their oats.

We warned the party organizers that it was necessary for some of the other men to help these near drunks home before more trouble developed.

Of course, the ladies at the party inserted themselves into the mix and adamantly refused to leave just because their boyfriends were being ejected and sent home. Several other males began to horn in and offered to provide rides home for the ladies.

When the near-drunk young men heard about the other guys there at the party ready and willing to take their girlfriends home, it created more bad behavior. Several fistfights broke out right in and among eight of us deputies, and we were immediately overwhelmed by the sheer number of combative young men. We tried to separate several of the fighting men, but it was a no-win situation, and we needed more deputies to assist us.

There were about three fistfights near the rear door of one of the duplex homes. One was just outside about eight feet away, and another was going on inside the kitchen about six feet away. I ordered the fighters to stop what they were doing, but I had no deputies with me, because they were around the corner, trying to stop another fight. The fighting continued as if I wasn't there.

I advised both groups that I was going to use my Taser on the ones fighting, and this was going to be the last warning. They continued, apparently thinking I was alone, and there was nothing I could do until I got help, which didn't appear to be too soon.

I shot at the ones fighting just outside, who were now about six feet from my position. I struck one of the male adults. He began to scream and yell, as did the other, who was in contact with him, but they were able to jump away and the 50,000-volt charge was immediately focused on the man stuck with the barbs.

I immediately turned the Taser onto the group fighting in the kitchen. I fired the other chamber and hit another man about five feet away.

I kept the 50,000 volts on him until he stopped fighting. He was flopping up and down on the floor in agony. Once they both complied and stopped their fighting, I stopped pulling the trigger and had both of them arrested.

Several deputies came over to my location and assisted me in the double Tasering. Oddly enough, the marks were L shaped, with both of the fighters still attached to the barbs in case one of them wanted to continue to fight.

Fortunately no one was hurt except the two who were Tasered. They were arrested for fighting and taken to the hospital for Taser barb removal and then booked at the station.

CHAPTER 161
A QUIET NIGHT

It was about a quarter to four in the early morning. The radio was quiet, and traffic was very light. Once in a while my eyes would catch the movement of a distant car's headlights maybe three or four blocks away. I hadn't seen any pedestrians for a while and was getting pretty tired. I needed a break.

I drove over to Atlantic Avenue and Sixth Street to get a cup of coffee and maybe a fresh pastry. Those pastries were usually being made fresh about this time, and they were extremely tasty.

I hadn't seen a deputy's patrol car for quite a while so hopefully they were busy cruising around and being seen.

I pulled into the small L-shaped shopping center on the corner and parked my patrol car right near the front door. I got out and looked around and saw no one, so I decided to leave the engine running while I went inside.

As I waited at the counter, I continued to intermittently glance behind me to make sure no one would get near my car.

Although the streets appeared vacant, it was not at all unbelievable that a running car might be stolen, so I kept a watchful eye for thieves. As I was paying for my coffee and pastry, I heard the engine rev, and my patrol car was speeding in reverse away from me.

I left my coffee and pastry on the counter and ran after my radio car as fast as I could. The radio car was backing out onto Sixth Street and continued backing westbound past the first building and then into the north/south alley.

As I was closing in on my car, I saw a skinny male deputy, in uniform, running from the alley. He jumped into a waiting patrol car across the street and sped away.

I rounded the corner and fortunately my radio car was sitting on the very edge of the alley and SixthStreet, with the engine running and the keys still inside.

The deputy who took my car was someone I knew very well. I confronted him later with my observations and accusations. He adamantly denied the event, but I knew very well it was none other than Deputy Gregg G.

I promised him I would even the score at another time and kissed the whole thing off as a lesson that keeping a car running in the East Los Angeles area is not really a bright idea.

CHAPTER 162

IN A PINCH

Freddy was an older deputy assigned to the East Los Angeles patrol station for several years. He was an average worker and mostly rated competent in his yearly evaluations.

He drove to work on a motorcycle and dressed and groomed himself for the part as rough and tough. He was heavily mustachioed, average size, and relatively thin. His character was somewhat quiet and reserved and tainted slightly with a pessimistic attitude.

Freddy worked the day shift. He answered his calls in a timely manner. He seldom received complaints about his conduct and work ethic and remained in his area of assignment without equivocation. Other deputies worked with him when working on assignments, calls, and details.

Nothing seemed out of order in any way, other than the day-in–day-out routine of assigned calls for the multitude of crimes and gang activities that plague most ghetto stations.

Unbeknown to Freddy, the following week was going to be quite a surprise. Three days earlier the deputy had gone home after work and had dinner. Then he and his wife got into the family car and went to a local bar in the Industry Hills area. There, he and his wife were drinking and got into a quarrel with two other patrons. The quarrel became more heated as they continued drinking, so Freddy and his wife decided to leave. Once outside the back door the deputy turned in anger and fired several times through the rear door with his department-issued Berretta automatic pistol. They both jumped into the family car and drove home.

Unfortunately, Freddy failed to notify anyone of the discharge of his weapon into the public bar and pretty much brushed the entire incident off.

The LA Sheriff's Department requires all personnel to inform their station of assignment whenever any law enforcement action is taken. This incident at the bar was a no-brainer and reeked of misuse of a firearm, not to mention firing into an inhabited dwelling, which is of course a felony in California.

Little did the Freddy know that one of his rounds struck a patron seated at the bar on a high stool. The round penetrated the man's scrotum and leg. But what else would you expect? The patron was rushed to the hospital and treated. He was released several days later.

Now, I'm sure what went through the Freddy's head when he fired through the door in his fit of drunken anger was that he was a deputy sheriff and didn't need to inform anyone of his judgment, let alone that he'd shot blindly through a door leading into a crowded bar. Also, Freddy frequented this local bar with his wife, and both apparently had significant drinking problems, which they pretty much kept to themselves. His fellow deputies who knew him pretty well at the station weren't the wiser about his drinking problem.

The weekend went by, and the deputy reported to work for a couple of days and fulfilled his work assignments without any problems. Still he had not mention the shooting at the bar to anyone close to him. He apparently thought it was mysteriously forgotten, or at least he hadn't been identified.

On the third morning around ten thirty he received a detailed call to report to Men's Central Jail, near downtown LA, to pick up a prisoner and bring him to the detective bureau at East Los Angeles Station.

He promptly directed his patrol car to the jail and went into the building to report his presence, explain his business, and prepare the necessary paperwork and endorsements. Inside, Freddy stood outside the sally-port to secure and lock up his sidearm and baton. Once his weapons were secured, the large gate was electronically buzzed to allow him entry. That's just about the time the Sheriff's Department Internal Affairs Unit came into the sally-port as well and arrested the deputy for the shooting at the bar in the City of Industry.

Needless to say, when it was reported to his station right after his arrest, everyone was in shock. He was tried and convicted of assault with a deadly weapon and went away to prison.

Several years later, I was driving near the Commerce Casino and spotted that same deputy driving a bobtailed truck. I yelled to him, and he pulled over, and we chatted for about twenty minutes.

Freddy advised me he spent approximately a little over a year in prison and had lost his entire pension for his legal defense. He added that the only one who stood by him the whole time was his wife, and that alone was enough to amplify their affection. Both have stopped drinking.

He informed me he was now making seven fifty an hour driving the truck and delivering automotive supplies, but it was enough to get by on, coupled with his wife's salary. It should be noted that he was making about $4000 a month when he was working as a deputy.

Too bad for this deputy's indiscretions, but he served as an excellent example of consequences, so other deputies would realize that their behavior is monitored very closely. The lesson learned is that, on or off duty, all officers must follow the law as well as enforce it.

———

Note: Freddy's name was changed in this story.

CHAPTER 163

A WOMAN IN RED

There had been a series of local bank robberies at a very popular bank located in the city of Commerce. The bank hired two off-duty LAPD officers to provide a visible deterrent to the thugs. Commerce begins at Atlantic Boulevard and nearly centered right at the I-5 freeway. The East Los Angeles area is located at the Commerce's northern city limit.

The hiring of off-duty cops occurs quite frequently but in spurts several times every year. It usually occurs when a series of crimes are prominent and localized a reasonable distance from one another.

The policy of the LA Sheriff's Department does not permit their personnel to participate in security assignments, because of a conflict of interest with their law enforcement duties. This is laid out in the manual of policy and ethics.

In this case, the bank hired the two off-duty LAPD officers, because their department does allow them to work those security assignments with their prior approval and review. In this situation, the two cops were supervisors, one lieutenant and one sergeant. Their instructions were to be seen. Although they were in suits and ties, their mannerisms indicated they were cops indeed. One was assigned to be outside, while the other was inside. In this scenario those designated positions were a general good tactic involving two security personnel.

It was around eleven, and the bank was in its daily routine with about ten customers conducting banking business. It was a little slow, and the security personnel, the lieutenant and the sergeant, were seated inside the bank on a lobby bench seat, talking about personal matters.

A lone black woman in a red dress came in the rear door of the bank and was approaching a teller. The two officers noticed her as she drew closer to their seated position, but they didn't notice anything peculiar and continued talking to one another.

The woman in red was about ten feet from the two seated officers, but they still hadn't noticed she was wearing a long black wig and a heavy coat of red lipstick just below her full moustache. She focused her attention on the seated officers and pointed a large caliber handgun at them. He told them to lie on the floor without making any moves toward their guns, or they would get shot.

They complied without hesitation, because they were caught completely off guard and in a compromising position. While on the ground, another man came in and warned everyone not to move, or they would be shot. This man was wearing a baseball cap, sunglasses, and earpiece with an extended microphone boom. This implied that he had a communication contact with other bank robbers, probably outside in a getaway car or maybe in the bank as well but surreptitiously embedded among other banking customers.

The man came over to the two officers on the floor and handcuffed them with their own handcuffs. Both officers expressed total compliance and offered no resistance at all.

As the audacious suspects were completing their rounds of routing the bank's cash, one of the female tellers expressed her personal thoughts aloud while lying on the floor. The male with the baseball cap booted her in the head with his shoe and told her to keep her mouth shut.

Both of the suspects left through the rear door with a sizable amount of money and disappeared quickly. When deputies arrived the officers were already uncuffed, and a report was completed. The female teller suffered minor injuries to her face and was attended to by paramedics.

The suspects were not apprehended and the entire ordeal was used as an example of how not to perform security assignments. The two LAPD supervisors, noticeably shaken up by the ordeal, decided not to perform security off duty assignments again. .

Another point of advice for anyone lying on a floor during a robbery is not to treat the crooks as if they were scolding their husbands. Those comments should be kept in a safe, controlled environment and not put others in peril.

CHAPTER 164

YOUNG MARINES: A GOOD DOSE TO ELIMINATE GANGS

I was working as the dedicated sergeant to the city of Commerce when I became involved with the cities' code enforcement officer, Sal N. He was a comfort to work with, and I considered him an excellent ally. Anytime he needed help with any of his enforcement needs, we would put our heads together and resolve all problems rather quickly and professionally. Sal and I were in contact nearly every day and had many conversations about troubling persons and potential problems within the city. He was extremely easy to get along with and admittedly had a strong personality, akin to my own, and there was reason. In his office he had all sorts of US Marine Corps regalia decorating the walls and his desk. Sal had been a sergeant major for twenty-five years or better.

His military background was superb and quite interesting. As we continued our business contacts throughout the day, we would discuss some of the local young men and women. Several of them were getting into some small incidents with their immediate families and neighbors that could easily develop into more serious problems, like gang behavior.

The city of Commerce had monthly meetings among many of the social services and probation departments of the city and county. Additionally, there would be a psychologist available once a week for his input and confidence in the wide array of selected individuals. Selected individuals assigned to the city had immediate access to our gang units and the captain of the ELA station was in attendance.

I was there, of course, as uniformed personnel, along with my three-man special projects team of casually dressed deputies who focused special attention on whomever or whatever I suggested was problematic.

Meetings drew Sal and me closer because of his current contact with the Marine Corps, as a director of what is called the Young Marine Program. This program is developed for all kids ages eight to eighteen years of age. There is another program, sometimes confused with the Young Marine Program, that most folks are familiar with called the Devil Pups. The Devil Pups program geared to kids fourteen years of age and is a two-week exposure of young men and women to the working environment of the regular US Marine Corps.

Sal was drawing my interest into the Young Marine Program more and more as I was gathering information on errant young men and women. I was providing a list of parents for Sal to meet in the city of Commerce, and a few others from the East Los Angeles Area.

This program was a no-brainer, if it could offer a way out of the norm for the kids confined at home, doing mundane chores around the house and behaving well in school and bringing home good grades. It could create a new perspective on doing a good job. That was the Young Marine Program.

Think of it, kids of eight to eighteen are troubling to most parents, and having someone else with the same ideals and tenacity as the parents get involved with their children would be outstanding. Of course the necessary trust and comfort that their kids would benefit from each weekend were clear in the Young Marine Program.

The kids would board a Commerce bus and be transported to the Tustin Marine Air Station, located in the Orange County area. There the kids would unload on the grounds with plenty of supervision from the staff of former marines and other military services and assist the Young Marine staff in the coordination of specific programs. They would camp out, military fashion, and march, and do all sorts of structured military-type things to keep them moving in a direction that would make every parent proud of their accomplishments.

That's right, they would help in the food preparation and distribution and all jump in on mess cleanup and routine chores. They would learn about their uniforms and how to care for them. They would learn how to talk when spoken to, and how to deliver a polite, sensible response.

In a matter of one month's exposure to this program, they all were captivated by the stimulating environment and wanted to stay in the program. The interest in the Young Marine Program was climbing steadily with more and more interest. That's when Sal hit me being the executive officer, aka XO, and I was honored to provide my free time on the weekends as well.

I was there in LA County Sheriff's Department uniform, of course, and provided assurance for the parents that the sheriff's department was on the scene as well. Several nieces and nephews from my wife's side of the family joined as well. They added to the ongoing training on weekends, which was going very well.

To me it was very interesting that all of the kids coming from East Los Angeles and the city of Commerce were the borderline at-risk kids, and they took to the Young Marine Program like a duck takes to water. I was very proud that all of the somewhat troublesome kids were now enjoying their weekends and progressively changing their lives, and that they closely relied on one another for a common cause. They were hungry for discipline and acknowledgment of their achievements with various awards and peer accolades. What I feared was that people would excuse their kids from this program because it was too militaristic.

In these cases, the parent needed only to come to our weekend meetings and see how the kids responded to US Marine Corps type discipline.

If requested, the Young Marine staff would arrange to stop by a candidate's home and do a room check. This allowed the staff to go into private homes, with parental approval, observation, and direction to make sure the Young Marine maintained a well-kept room. That room would be searched for any contraband or evidence of gang activity. This of course was focused on the applicant's room only and not any other rooms.

The program also incorporated the review of the Young Marine's school attendance and grading. If there were problems, those problems could be remedied by some of the Young Marine staff, who would help with studies and deteriorating grades. On the home front, my position as a law enforcement entity allowed me to interact with the Young Marine if there was trouble at home. I would come by and observe the problems and give advice on their poor conduct or interact with the parents.

Unfortunately, because of my injuries, I had to retire and relinquish my interests because of the various ailments incurred from on-the-job injuries.

As time went on, the individuals who signed onto the Young Marine Program had to leave the program at age eighteen. However, quite a few of those who started went onto become authentic US Marines. Several were even slim, good-looking, and very proud Marine Corps drill instructors at Camp Pendleton Marine Base, Oceanside, California.

As mentioned before some of these Young Marines included some of my wife's nieces and nephews.

I was a little concerned because the war in Iraq had broken out, and I had a feeling the parents would hold their upbringing in the Young Marine Program against me if their kids were injured or killed. Fortunately none of them were injured or killed in the war, and some remained as career Marines.

I was offered several times the opportunity to return, although I was retired from the sheriff's department, but reluctantly declined the opportunity for a number of reasons.

Although I separated from this program, I was extremely proud of those who entered into the program and later on became full-blown marines as well.

It was an honor to curb the wayward appetites of so many young kids and redirect their focus into a good, strong, productive environment like the US Marine Corp.

I would strongly urge all areas that have a juvenile problem bordering on gang activity to look into this program and reap its benefits.

CHAPTER 165

FROZEN IN TIME

Another quiet day in the city of Commerce started off by going to the north annex and seeing if anything had gone on the previous evening. I had talked with several of the deputies driving around in their area and completing various things involving reporting protocol and final touches.

A radio dispatch to one of the southern units indicated a "927 D" call, dead human body, at a steel manufacturing plant and warehouse on east Slauson Avenue, just west of Garfield Boulevard, close to the I-5 freeway.

The handling unit and I arrived at about the same time at the plant and were directed by one of the supervisors to the huge warehouse. That warehouse had a large railroad car inside the hanging doors; just off a looping spur from the main railroad track. We met up with another supervisor, who was in charge of the incoming batches of steel material still loaded onto large railroad cars.

The man told us that he was inspecting a full railcar load of four-inch steel "L" brackets, approximately forty feet long. As the supervisor climbed onto the open railcar he noticed something strange at one end, near the large door. He drew closer and realized there were several human forms clustered in the dark, three-foot space, just at the end of the large four and a half-foot pile of heavy steel L bars, at least a full quarter-inch thick.

The human forms looked like human wax figures on display. He drew closer and saw they all were obviously dead, which "scared the dickens" out of him as he yelled out to others and jumped from the top of the steel load. That's when he called the station about his discovery. He assured us that no one had been near the car since he called, and he was glad we were there so quickly.

I climbed aboard the welded heavy duty ladder affixed to the railcar, near the end where the supervisor said the bodies were and I peered over the top. I saw three human figures that appeared to be black, dressed in casual street attire and warm thicker jackets, all staring forward down the full length of the railcar, as if watching a television screen amid pile of steel bars.

This was indeed an eerie sight and almost as if I'd walked inside a pool hall and looked at the spectators watching a pool match.

One was standing nearly straight up, with his head and shoulders slightly leaning forward. The man next to him and just behind the first one was standing and leaning forward with both hands and fingers cupped over his knees, and his butt against the steel end wall of the railcar. The third one was squatting with one knee on the floor of the railcar and one of his hands was draped casually across his knee at the wrist level; the other hand was on the left side, as if he was balancing himself from falling over. This man was to the right and slightly foreword of the squatting man.

These three men were all close to one another; which may have contributed to causing them to stay together and appear very lifelike. They weren't moving at all, and posed as if real-life mannequins had been placed in the empty section of the car.

I climbed over the L-angle bars and noticed they were adult Hispanic males all looking directly toward me and were black in appearance as if they had been in the sun for a long period of time. All three had angled two-inch chunks of their faces and heads missing. There were some large maggots scurrying near the huge open wounds that displayed only dried blood, indicating all three had been dead for several days prior to their discovery.

The missing chunks of skull, flesh and hair appeared to mysteriously have similar cookie cutter pieces of the same size as each of the heavy, quarter-inch thick, forty-foot L brackets. The fatal wounds were along the scalp area of the man standing and the one next to him along his temple area and the one squatting was struck right through the middle of his forehead and center scalp.

It struck me that these guys must have hopped into this railcar, possibly to hide from someone, or maybe they were just sneaking across the Mexican border.

Then, when the car started to move, like most trainloads of long unfastened metal loads, the load shifted and several random "L" bars slid out of the neatly stacked four-and-a-half-foot-high heavy load and slammed forward stopping only on the heavy-gauge metal wall. As the load shifted when the car began moving forward, those random bars returned to their original position, as if neatly stacked without any significant movement. Hence the outward appearance of the "frozen in time" threesome seemed obvious; lacking the presence of any other evidence indicating wrongdoing.

I inquired when the load had arrived, and the supervisor informed me it was dropped off the day before by the train onto the spur track. They also advised me the load had been in the Coachella Valley for a period of six days and had originated from San Yisidro the previous day. So that meant the three were in the car possibly for seven whole days and nights.

With that information, it made sense that the three were probably illegal aliens who were sneaking across the border and found refuge and concealment within the railcar.

Those three persons had no idea that the load would shift and thought perhaps they had a wonderful place to hide from everyone in the spacious three foot void on one end of the railcar.

Our homicide bureau's detectives confirmed our suspicions. They determined the men had been dead for at least seven days and that the load had shifted and caused their demise.

That would account for the three men's blackened appearance, because they were subjected to the intense 120-degree heat in the arid Coachella Valley for at least six full hot days. That temperature, coupled with the heated-up steel, literally baked the three and preserved their lifelike appearance without much of an outward deterioration to their bodies.

CHAPTER 166

THE MEXICAN CONNECTION

I believe it was a Friday morning around ten when a call came in about an abandoned car over on the other side of the I-710 freeway just off Telegraph. It was in a small residential neighborhood locked in by all of the surrounding businesses and freeway abutments. This area was quite inconspicuous and free of any cholo gang members and the typical graffiti. This was a small pocket, quiet and serene amid the surrounding commercial area.

One of the Commerce community service specialists reported a suspicious car that seemed out of place in the community. These specialists are generally retired police officers who patrol the community and answer many minor city ordinance calls and miscellaneous misdemeanor reports. This is in lieu of the regular deputies, so the deputies could pay more attention to other significant law enforcement hazards and calls.

As I drove up and saw the car in question, I noted it was a light-colored, four-door Chevrolet sedan. The doors were all closed and the windows were rolled up.

Nothing much seemed out of place other than that the car was parked along the bland empty parkway, sitting all alone, away from eyesight of most of the surrounding homes. No one was in the car as I approached on foot. The CSS man was pointing inside the car at the right front floorboard area.

As I drew closer upon the car I looked in and saw a black cotton running suit, pants and top shirt with a hood, lying on the floor as if someone had evaporated from the garment. Both pants legs were lying gathered up on the floor, and the top garment was lying next to the pants as if held up by the hood and slowly placed on top of each of the folds. Right next to the pants was what appeared to be a 9 mm or .45 caliber nickel-plated automatic pistol.

In the back seat was another black running suit. Again, each piece was carefully lying in a stack, and the barrel of another nickel-plated firearm was protruding from under the clothes. There was another firearm, but we couldn't distinguish it from outside the window, only the long dark barrel stuck out, and it wasn't immediately distinguishable. It could be a rifle or shotgun, but who knew from this distance.

We entered the car very carefully, knowing full well this was going to be a whodunit scenario, so preservation of evidence was our primary focus.

The nearly identical running suits were collected and placed individually in a paper bag to preserve any valuable evidence. The two pistols were examined. Both were nickel-plated Smith & Wesson model 39 automatics. Both were fully loaded with rounds in the chambers.

The weapon on the back floorboard was a fully automatic, Kalashnikov AK 47, drum fed, with a large round drum attached to the bottom of the weapon, and it too was fully loaded with nearly eighty rounds. We handled these weapons very carefully, in order to preserve all possible trace evidence.

Once all of the weapons were retrieved, the auto and all of its contents were confiscated as well for detectives to comb the entire car for evidence and hopefully link the items to someone,

The car turned out to be registered to an auto sales lot in the border city of San Ysidro, California.

The recovered items were highly suspicious because of the excellent quality of the weapons and their tremendous amount of firepower.

No one could imagine where they might have come from, and for what purpose. About two days later, the results came back from the sheriff's crime lab.

That report indicated all three guns did have prints on them, but unfortunately revealed the prints belonged to one of the supervisory community service officers, who was also a retired LA County sheriff's sergeant. I was infuriated that an experienced, retired sergeant had previously insisted that no one had touched the weapons at all.

Well, that fell right by the wayside, and he was censured by the social services director for his untimely and nonprofessional exuberance that might have compromised the follow-up investigation.

The information obtained from the investigation was that the weapons and the car came back as possibly items used in the assassination of a Roman Catholic cardinal. He was gunned down in an airport just outside Guadalajara, Mexico. That shooting occurred just several days earlier on May 24, 1993. The shooting also killed the driver, chauffeur of the cardinal, and five bystanders.

Supposedly the shooting was a result of rival drug gangs, but another more plausible story was that the cardinal was very outspoken about the Colombian/Mexican drug cartels, and his outspoken beliefs were not appreciated, so his words might very well have led to his demise.

So do you think crime from other countries is deplorable, compared to our vast sea of higher-class crooks in the United States? Think again. Those lowlife crooks from other countries are here and moving around quite freely among our own.

CHAPTER 167

FIVE LAUNCHED INTO RAIL YARD PRECIPITATED A LAW

It was around one thirty and the traffic was relatively light, and they were coming home from a night out tagging. They were all in the small pickup truck, two in the small front seat and five others lying down on the rear empty bed, exposed to the elements.

They were out having their thrills, spraying the town with their graffiti and unaware that anything out of the ordinary was about to occur. The pickup was traveling at approximately 65 mph, northbound on the 710 freeway coming up to the large bridge covering the expansive Union Pacific Railroad yards near the Bandini off ramp, in the city of Commerce.

Somehow a car in an adjoining lane began to lose control as both the truck and the car were crossing the bridge. Possibly the driver fell asleep at the wheel.

Both vehicles were traveling at about the same speed when they brushed against each other. This contact was near the apex of the bridge; which was spanning a good fifty feet above an array of railroad tracks.

The pickup lost control because of the impact and careened into the bridge guardrails head on and the five in the bed of the truck, were launched helplessly into the air.

Three of the victims slammed into two heavy-duty steel lighting towers slightly lower than the bridge's height. Those three died on impact. The other two victims continued down to the actual rail yards and died as well, only seconds later than the initial three.

The two remaining in the truck were inside the front cab and seat belted securely. All five of the deceased were under the age of eighteen years of age. The remaining two suffered moderate injuries and were pulled from their truck, which fortunately was dangling from the bridge by its rear wheels. Their seat belts were the prime reason they survived the collision.

The driver of the car that hit their truck sustained minor injuries only. An investigation of the incident revealed that the female driver was under the influence of alcohol. She was promptly arrested. A record check of the female showed she had five prior drunk driving charges. In fact, she was on probation at the time of this accident that took five juvenile lives.

This accident sparked community anger and persuaded the California legislature to enact strict seat belt laws for all occupants inside pickup trucks. Each passenger must have secured seats with belts in the beds of pickups.

Also, this case drew attention to the California Judiciary to follow strict punishments for repeat offenders of all DUI laws.

Nothing can describe the anguish suffered by the families at the deaths of the juveniles. However, a law was enacted for the good of all, and its value and importance to the community at large cannot be overemphasized.

CHAPTER 168

A FOUL GNOME: THE JERK IN UNIFORM

It was a Friday night, and I was at home washing some dishes when Gloria, my wife, walked in from work around nine. She was a desk operations assistant, DOA, working the desk operations at East Los Angeles sheriff's station.

Gloria had been working that assignment for approximately ten years, answering phone calls coming into the station, including 911 emergent calls, and occasionally acting as a dispatcher. She was born and raised in the area just above ELA called El Sereno. She was Mexican, bilingual, and she was often used by the detectives for Spanish interpretation.

She started to inform me of a situation that had occurred on the desk. She was really disturbed by the outcome. I listened attentively as she went through the situation.

Gloria and three other women were working at their desk assignments when a Sergeant Rich M. walked in, leaned against Gloria's desk, and began talking with the three other women on a topic that was vulgar and sexually explicit. The conversation was loud and very graphic. My wife thought maybe he was on drugs. He was a supervisor and could get into trouble very easily, since he was supposed to monitor such conversations and overt acts of sexual misconduct.

Now, I have told my wife several times that when any idiot deputy comes into the desk area—or any other work area in the entire station—and starts to talk trash or display pornographic material, books, pictures, etc., she should stand up and walk out immediately without any comment. When the person figures out what you just did, he will immediately disappear from the desk, because he knows you'll be asked why you aren't at your work station by some authority figure.

Sergeant M. continued with his sexually explicit vernacular and had the audience of the three women, two deputies, and another younger DOA. As he continued with his sexual banter, Gloria was seated in her work station pretending to converse on the phone, feigning not listening to the sergeant. It was pretty hard to not hear the sergeant's raunchy talk because he was resting his rear end against Gloria's desk with his back toward Gloria.

She felt she had heard enough of the offensive talk. She stood up and walked toward the dispatch door. As she began to open the door, the sergeant blurted out, "Well, look who can't take it," implying to everyone in the dispatch area that because she was married to me, she should certainly be able withstand his foul mouth.

She went to the ladies' bathroom and remained for approximately fifteen minutes. She then returned to her work area, now that the foulmouthed sergeant had left. Nothing else was discussed that evening. Gloria left at her normal time and came home.

As she described the ordeal to me, I became very irritated at the sergeant's foul demeanor and explained to Gloria that I would handle the matter come Monday. In fact, that poor behavior she passed on to me irritated me more and more as the weekend went on.

When Monday came, I was all primed to go to the station early and seek out the foulmouthed stud. I was ready to confront him about his poor deportment within my wife's hearing and then calling her on it when she attempted to leave.

Actually, I was set to confront Sergeant M. physically and challenge his manhood to a point where he should swing at me. Furthermore, if he didn't, I was willing to deck the little turd for his idiotic topic, confrontation, and blatant rudeness to my wife.

I came into the station and was seeking Sergeant M. He was nowhere to be found. I checked with the desk and found out he took the day off. I was furious and was confronted by the day watch commander as to why I was so upset. I explained the matter to him. The administrative lieutenant came out as well and listened to my concerns. I explained my wife's story and said that I was going to kick the sergeant's butt.

The administrative lieutenant asked me to come into the captain's office and explain. The captain was visibly upset about the sergeant's foul mouth but was more concerned that I was going to kick his ass. He let me know in no uncertain terms that if I hit or hurt Sergeant M. in any way that I would receive thirty days off. When the captain said that, I paused briefly and thought, *Hmm, thirty days, huh?* He could see I was contemplating taking the thirty days willingly in order to settle the point.

The captain was very understanding and ordered an immediate internal investigation into the matter. He also ordered Sergeant M.'s immediate transfer to another station. That actually cooled me down somewhat, but I still had a seething internal conflict about whether to pummel the little nitwit on his ass. Well, I was given the day off and went home to let off some steam. The following day I came to work and found out the sergeant was transferred to Temple Station.

To most that would seem an okay move—to assign him to a different station while he was under investigation. I was a little more concerned because Temple Station is the station area where my home is located. However, I figured that if they weren't concerned, then I had better leave well enough alone unless something else happened.

About a month went by and I was at home, outside by the parkway watering my lawn, when I spotted a sheriff's unit coming by slowly.

I thought, *What if it's Sergeant M.? What should I do?*

The car cruised by slowly, and lo and behold, who do you think it was? Yep, that's right. It was Sergeant M., slumped in the driver's seat much like a gang-banger slumps, "mad dogging" me with a defiant, pompous glare that had the fear factor of a garden gnome. No words were exchanged, just the defiant look. He didn't stop, and I was shaking my head from side to side as if he was about to do something stupid.

I shined it on, as if maybe the little squirt was lost and just came by my home by mere coincidence, but I knew he was up to something. (Duck Theory?) I came to work and informed my captain of the sighting and that I thought it was more than coincidence. I hoped he would phone the Temple Station captain to warn him of what the sergeant was up to. Well, as time went on, that same sergeant came by the house at least six times with the same gangbanger look, "mad dogging" me each time.

So I called Temple Station and spoke with the administrative lieutenant. I informed her that if he stopped for anything, I was going to pull him out of the sheriff's unit, pull his pants down, and spank him. Then I would take his PR24, ram it where the sun doesn't shine, and ask for help over the sheriff's radio.

When the deputies came to arrest me they could book me at Temple Station, but I'd bet I wouldn't be in jail an hour before I was released. Since that call, and informing my captain as well, Sergeant M. stopped coming my home.

Oh, in the investigation, all three women on the desk that day said they didn't hear anything sexually explicit from the supervisor. They didn't back up my wife at all.

Also, I was coming down the hall one day and saw Sergeant M. leaning against the wall, talking with six other deputies in uniform. I was carrying my patrol gear and was about to pass right by him. All of the deputies saw me coming and backed away quickly, leaving the sergeant leaning against the wall.

As I started to pass by, I stopped right in front of him with my left side exposed carrying my valise. I turned my head slowly and looked at him, and he lowered his head downward in shame and didn't say a word. He knew full well I was ready to drop him real quick, but I kept thinking his forehead was at my shoulder height. I thought for a moment that it would seem like child abuse if I hit him and walked on without a word.

A couple of days later, several deputies who were friends of his approached me and asked why I snitched him off. That type of question infuriated me. I responded that it had nothing to do with law enforcement; it was personal. I also informed them that if they thought I was wrong and didn't like what I was doing, they knew very well where I parked my car in the back, in the dark, and they could jump me, pound the hell out of me, or shut up about his character.

At the end of the investigation, the sergeant was given a whopping three days off for his rude and threatening antics. In retrospect I should have dropped him in the hallway and taken the thirty days off, which would have been more equal in justice and longer lasting.

CHAPTER 169

TOUGH GANGSTER? HOW TO USE A BABY AS A HOSTAGE

It was a slow day, and an extra sergeant wanted to ride around with me in the city of Commerce. He was well known to me from the years past and had worked with me at Firestone Park Station and at the Special Enforcement Bureau. His name was Steve V. We were traveling around meeting with various deputies and monitoring their calls.

It was nice to have someone else in the patrol car, and we enjoyed each other's company. We stopped for a bite to eat and gabbed for the better part of the day, all the while monitoring the radio and watching vehicular traffic pass by.

We decided to go south on Eastern Avenue near Gage Avenue right next to the Bell Gardens boundary line. We happened by a Bell Gardens police unit with two officers, one on the small front porch and another standing close by. As we were passing the officer closest to the curb, Steve stuck out his hand and signaled four fingers, asking if everything was okay. We expected a return four fingers, indicating everything was all right, but instead he flashed an alerting signal, a halt sign, indicating that they needed help.

We stopped and listened to the conversation of the officer on the porch and his partner standing by watching very carefully. As we drew closer, we noticed a Hispanic man, approximately nineteen years old, standing right in front of the officer on the porch. This young man had a small baby in his arms and was halfway inside the home, standing about a foot away from the officer.

We didn't say anything, but we stood closer to the officer near the door. We could now hear the officer talking with the man. There was obviously some problem going on, and we heard the officer trying to get the man to give the baby to his mother, who was standing inside, right by the door.

My partner, Steve, asked the officer standing by and learned that the two officers had an arrest warrant for the man for a felony, but the suspect was refusing to give the child up safely so he could be arrested. It was now apparent the Hispanic man was a gangbanger—duck theory—using his own eighteen-month-old baby as a hostage, because he didn't want to go to jail. Wow, what a stud. Only real men use their own child to stave off the cops when they come to nab you.

We could hear the family inside arguing with the officers about the legality of the warrant. It was a sensitive situation. I wondered if the family planned this event, and the baby was to be a part of the operation. Do you think this was the first time the police had been to this home?

Both Steve and I were above six foot tall and moving close enough so the officer at the door could see us. He now knew he had ample backup to proceed with his advisory about the arrest. He told the man to surrender the child to the mother inside the door.

Then we heard, "I'm not going!" and he began to move away from the officer on the porch. The officer grabbed him by the arm and stopped him from going inside the home. Both Steve and I stepped up and grabbed ahold of the suspect as well. We knew very well we needed to avoid injury to the baby at all costs. We had to quickly pry the child from this he-man.

Several people inside the home came spilling outside and across the porch, screaming. The Bell Gardens officer was squeezed out of the melee because we were bigger than Bell Gardens officer.

We were attempting to control the suspect's arms and keep him upright. I placed a good choke hold on him, and kept his other hand off to the side while his free hand was holding the baby. Then suddenly Steve got a can of capsicum pepper spray and began to spray the suspect in the face.

Well, Steve inadvertently sprayed me in the face as well because I was right behind the suspect's head, locking his jaw off to the side. Fortunately I had my sunglasses on and received only a minor amount of overspray. We both fell backward on top of me, on the sidewalk and front lawn area. This fall cushioned the suspect's impact and certainly protected the baby, now held outward away from the suspect.

Everyone was screaming, the parents, the baby, who had caught a small amount of pepper overspray, and now some neighbors.

As I was rolling around grasping the suspect rather tightly, I heard and saw about six cholos running toward me, as if to join in and get in a few kicks. I overheard one of the gangbangers say, "Let's fuck this one up." I believed that was me they were talking about beating to set their friend and the baby free.

I released the suspect's right hand, pulled my gun out and said to the six cholos, "Stop, or I'd blow you into next week!"

Apparently this warning worked. They all stood back, afraid I would shoot someone. Then a whole bunch of police units and sheriff's units arrived, and the situation was controlled. The suspect finally surrendered the baby, and he was taken to jail.

I was still trying to rinse the pepper spray out of my face when I was informed by Steve that an immediate investigation of excessive and unnecessary force had been lodged against both Steve and me.

I didn't even have time to brush myself off when I ordered to respond to the Office of Internal Affairs Investigation Unit that just so happened to be close by in the city of Commerce. I believe the city of Bell Gardens had complained about the incident to my captain, who was especially sensitive about the eighteen-month-old baby who was inadvertently sprayed with the pepper spray, and the complaint of injury by the studly gangbanger I was choking. I might add the suspect only had a slight reddening of the eyes and a few scuff marks.

Both Steve and I arrived quickly, met with the two internal affairs sergeants, and delivered our rendition. The meeting was very cordial, and the investigators were very professional.

Within one week the entire incident was over. It was determined that our judgment was correct. A minimal amount of force was necessary, and the injuries suffered were justifiable.

Both Steve and I were completely exonerated.

CHAPTER 170
AN OBVIOUS PREDICTION

So now, if any officer is involved in any altercation, it seems apparent that an investigation on top of another investigation may be expected—which means double the work and double the personnel because some idiot gangbanger and family seeks retribution, although they initiated the fight and accosted the police.

I guess it's time to leave law enforcement, because the internal affairs unit staff will be bigger than the count of officers in the field. Maybe we all were wrong now and police are no longer needed because of these overreaction antics.

This must be the indicator that unarmed police armed only with compassion and kindness are needed. The new cop on the beat, wearing a pink blazer and tie and smelling good will quietly respond on his or her Segway and handle calls.

Going to all calls will be delayed as much as possible to avoid conflict. Officers will simply take reports. Suspects will not be arrested unless a warrant is prepared indicating reasonable cause.

Want to bet? Do you think I'm wrong? Watch—the response time from now on will be shockingly delayed, and services will be curtailed. Wait and see over the coming years. Observe the notable absence of law enforcement on the streets. All confrontation will diminish.

Ask all agencies how many of their police personnel and their ranks are assigned to internal investigations? Compare that number to the personnel assigned to any station.

At the time of this writing, a patrol car is rarely seen. At neighborhood meetings, persons are asked to contact their legislators, because there aren't enough patrol personnel to cover our streets. For twenty years there were always visible patrol cars with two deputies, now there are none. Gee, where did they go?

My personal opinion is that the jail system should be staffed by civilians, and all the deputies should work in the field. Jail is no place for a highly paid deputy; civilian guards makes more sense. Think of the difference from an economics point of view.

CHAPTER 171

SECOND SIGHTING

It was around nine in the evening when I opened my garage door to go to my truck and drive to the grocery store.

I was walking onto my driveway and saw the same two cockroaches I'd seen in Perry and Lally's driveway two weeks earlier, now squatting between the doors of my two parked cars on the driveway.

I was on them in a flash, and they began to run immediately as one of them, the smaller one, turned around holding up a three-foot galvanized pipe saying, "I'll fuck you up," indicating he was going to hit me with the pipe.

Unbeknown to the armed thieves, I had my Beretta 9 mm automatic pistol in my waistband and I was ready for a confrontation.

I responded to the armed thief that I was going to take the pipe he was threatening me with and "shove it where the sun doesn't shine." I was coming toward him at full bore, and ready to catch or dodge the three-foot pipe.

The thief turned quickly and followed his thieving partner, already thirty feet northbound, running full bore away from me. I ran after both of them and slowly closing the distance between us. They quickly turned running westbound on another connecting street and into the darkness, but still within my sight.

About two blocks from my home I was almost upon them when they ducked behind a parked pickup truck with a camper shell. I stopped short of the pickup truck and called out to them to come out of hiding and give it up, or they were going to get hurt or shot.

I gave them several seconds to respond and finally one of them came into the street with his hands in the air and followed my directions to lie down and place his face on the ground.

He followed my directions as I approached him and put my foot on the side of his head and leaned on him slightly and ordered him not to move.

As I waited for the other suspect, I could distinctly hear his movements on the other side of the pickup. He was moving across dried leaves on the grassy surface, and the noise made it easy to determine his exact position.

So I yelled out in a clear voice that if he came at me with the pipe I would shoot him right between the eyes. I could still hear him moving about, until several of the neighbors came out with shovels and rakes and asked me if I needed help. I asked someone to call the police or sheriff's department and let them know I needed their help now.

Five or six male neighbors came to my aid and stood by as I told them that the suspect with the pipe was nearby and about to come out and attack me, after I had already warned him I had a gun.

All the while, I was still standing on the other suspect's head, slightly leaning on that foot and twisting my shod foot onto his face and into the asphalt surface.

One of the neighborhood men asked me if he should get his own gun to help me, but I declined, saying that I had control with one in custody; the other was deciding whether to do something soon before the police arrived. We were talking loudly; I knew full well the other suspect was listening to our conversation.

Then the distinct sounds of sirens were in the distance. The arrival of more neighbors coming to my aid may have caused the other suspect to leave the area. I couldn't hear any further movements from the stalking, slithering suspect. I stood my ground and asked the many onlookers to keep an eye on me, should the other suspect decide to attack me. I knew full well that if I had to shoot someone I would need as many witnesses as possible.

Within two minutes, the first unit arrived from Arcadia Police Department, then two more, and then two units from Monrovia Police Department. They assisted me in helping the one suspect up, while the others looked for the remaining suspect. They concluded that the other suspect had fled the area. An Arcadia patrol sergeant drove up and approached the one suspect in their custody.

I was exchanging information with the Arcadia Police Department when the sergeant came up to me and stated that I was overzealous in the capture of the suspect, because he had abrasions on the side of his head where I was stepping and twisting his head into the asphalt. I defended my use of force, telling the sergeant that the suspect was evasive and reluctant to give up; I was alone and knew full well that the other suspect was about to pummel me from behind with a three-foot piece of galvanized pipe. I defended my lone position and the restraint I had to maintain in order not to use deadly force. He didn't seem pleased, but I wasn't concerned, because I was the victim in this case and in my view, the suspect was able to walk to the patrol car unimpaired.

As it turned out the suspect I had was already on probation. His two brothers were presently in prison for multiple burglaries. This suspect lived only three blocks, away near the 210 freeway. I was sure if the Arcadia Police talked to this suspect,they would learn his thieving associate's name.

Every time an off-duty deputy sheriff is involved in a law enforcement action, it is mandatory to notify your supervisor at your present assignment as soon as possible. I made those notifications and completed a lengthy memo the following day. No further action was necessary, and no court summons was initiated.

CHAPTER 172

NOW DON'T BE A RACIST!

Several months went by, and again I was at home doing my nighttime watering routine, right after I came home around one o'clock in the morning. As I was gingerly sprinkling my lawn, I looked down two streets from the corner of my home. The streets were empty of any vehicle or pedestrian traffic, and the quiet of the night was deep.

I casually looked to the south of one of the streets and noticed an adult male, about six foot tall and maybe 180 pounds, dressed in a Levi's leisure suit with an open collar, walking toward my position. As he drew near, our eyes met, and I said, "Howdy."

He said hi, and followed up with a casual nod. He seemed a little unusual, because he was walking by himself in a residential area, the leisure suit was rather outdated and his medium Afro hairstyle was a tad outdated as well.

I was listening very cautiously as he passed behind me by approximately five feet, and I slowly turned around after about ten seconds passed. I didn't want to seem too focused on his movements and was really trying to pretend that everything was all right.

As I turned around and faced westbound I couldn't see him anywhere. Now that was puzzling, because of the late hour, and a lone pedestrian not from my residential area had been visible not thirty seconds earlier.

I focused on the two driveways closest to my house, because that would be the area where the man should have been when I turned around. I moved closer to my western property line and looked carefully, and then I spotted two moving feet pointing toward the street under my neighbor's car. Those feet were easy to spot because of the contrast between the dark shoes and the whitish cement driveway.

He appeared slumped over as he scurried into the street from that driveway. Then he stood erect and walked by me again as I stood there watching his every move. I was thinking should I squirt him with the hose, but decided not to because he might have been visiting friends that I was unaware of.

As he passed me once again, he knew full well I was watching his every move and yet kept quiet. He continued onward southbound on the adjacent street and out of sight. I decided to let the whole matter go by until the following day.

The following morning, around ten, I stopped by my neighbor's home and asked about the late night visit. The man of the house was thinking of what had occurred and responded that his gasoline cap was unscrewed and hanging outside the small hatch compartment when he went out to his car an hour earlier.

He said he thought it was strange that the cap was dangling because he remembered he had secured the cap two days prior. We decided that's what the man was doing—preparing for a gas theft later on, after he readied the victim's car for a fast siphoning.

From the resting point of a car on an elevated driveway, all he would have to do is to stick a garden hose into the car in the driveway and lead the other end to a waiting car.

The neighbor also stated that about a month ago they were driving their pickup truck for about an hour when they ran out of gas. The problem was that they had filled their tank with gasoline the night before and couldn't figure out how they lost the gasoline. But now, with my observation, it seemed apparent that the late night marauder had returned to the scene of his former victim to help himself with about sixty dollars worth of gas.

So the message to me was again, "If it looks, walks, talks and acts like a duck…"

CHAPTER 173
WEST SIDE STORY

My dogs were barking, and I went to the large front window of my home to see what was going on. It was around one thirty in the morning and quite peaceful until the dogs began barking. I split the wooden shades and peered through the blinds. I saw at least twenty males, ranging from sixteen to twenty years of age, covering the whole breadth of the street, coming toward the corner of my home. It looked just like the theme cutout of the movie *West Side Story*.

They appeared to be joyfully entertaining themselves and were a bit rowdy. Because of the hour and their youth, I figured something was about to happen. I knew they were passing by my front door, so I lowered the slit of blind I was watching from. I was walking by the front door of my house when I heard two distinct pops hitting my front door. I thought they might have been small-caliber shots and quickly opened the front door to see the entire mob running north. I was clad only in my sweat pants and T-shirt. I was barefoot but I immediately chased after the mob. I yelled to my wife, who was seated in the front room, to call the cops.

I ran full bore one block north and then one block west and was coming upon the biggest of them, who was sporting a ponytail. My intention was to hit him hard and display his pain in front of the others to make them stop.

I grabbed him by his ponytail and throat with my hands and yelled to the whole group, "Okay, you butt licks, pull out your guns and knives and let's play. I'll let you guess what I've got."

My appearance and announcement caught all of them by surprise. Half turned around and ran full blast away from me, and the other half stopped.

I had about nine who were paying very close attention to me, because I had their friend by his throat and was pulling on his ponytail. He was arching back in pain.

I ordered them all to line up together and march back to my home. They complied and emphatically claimed they had no weapons of any kind. I released my grasp on the biggest male and demanded they keep their mouths shut and quickly move out.

As we came back to my home, the sirens could be heard in the distance. I had all nine take a seat on the curb and await the police. My wife came to the door and asked if she could help. I told her to keep the shotgun on them until the police arrived, causing them to think she actually had a shotgun.

I noticed that two of the nine had already pissed in their pants; they were all noticeably shaken up by my actions.

The Temple sheriff's deputies arrived at my home and drove their cars close up to the marauders. I began to inform several of the deputies what had occurred.

When I was describing my observations I walked up toward the front door of my home to see the damage from what ever the marauders had fired or thrown.

I noticed several pieces of egg shells with a smattering of yokes and whites splattered across my front door, threshold, and wall. I was certainly dismayed at the revelation, because I could have hurt several of them just for egging my home.

I thought, *What a stupid prank. Where did they come from?*

To me this was a lesson in restraint that kept me from going any further. I also thought, *What if I'd had my gun or nightstick?* I could only imagine. Certainly someone would have been hurt.

Then several of them stated they were having an overnight Bible study group at another home some two blocks north of my home, and their minister fell asleep, so they all decided to leave and go out and egg several homes.

Just at that time their minister showed up and identified himself. I chewed his ass out for falling asleep and letting his flock get into mischief. I told him that I was a deputy sheriff and worked at very rough stations, where I had dealt with many gangsters, and I had thought perhaps his flock could have been a whole slew of gangsters out pillaging the neighborhood.

Egging the homes of several of the older single women in the neighborhood might have caused them to nearly have heart attacks by scaring the wits out of them.

He was very apologetic and pleaded forgiveness for what his charges had done, and of course, I forgave him and let all matters drop. There was no way in hell I was going to have them arrested for such a trivial matter.

The following day around ten o'clock, about five of that group rang my doorbell and offered to clean the mess up. I told them it was not necessary. I was going to clean it up shortly. I also told them I was sorry for being so mean to them, and I was grateful that I didn't hurt any of them and only scared most of them, and I thanked the group for their offer.

An Overview of Law Enforcement

Many of my injuries were sustained from car crashes, and many repeated injuries that occurred in the vast array of skirmishes and conflicts caused me to retire at the age of fifty-three from the East Angeles sheriff's station. It came upon me rather quickly when my doctor said that if I did not retire, I might not retire at all. He added that if I did not retire most likely I could very well injure or cause serious injury to another officer on an emergency. My back injury and legs were at a point I could not get out of a car unless I backed up physically. The constant seating in the deep seat of a patrol car made my back injury more aggravated and I was in pain most of the time. The captain at E.L.A. station asked me if I could handle the idea of retirement, realizing I was somewhat depressed. I assured him I was fully capable of the transition, but was slightly surprised.

For the next year and a half, I went to many doctors who reevaluated my physical capabilities. All assessments revealed a limited physical condition that obviously impaired my ability classified as *arduous*. That was the sheriff's department standard that classifies a deputy's physical agility and anything outside that ability was not satisfactory.

At a retirement meeting by the county, a bow tie wearing county attorney sarcastically questioned me, suggesting my injuries were possibly conjured up for an early retirement. I was insulted at the accusation and removed the small clasped microphone, attached to my collar, and announced that I needed a break in order to cool down. I guess that attorney felt obligated to harass me as if I were a charlatan seeking an early out from a job that I disliked. After a five-minute break I returned and informed the attorney that he was rude and was attempting to goad me into stating something he was pursuing to disprove my valid injuries, and relinquish my early path to retirement. Fortunately, my retirement was completed, with proper council and representation, and my departure date was on July 14, 1998.

As this book goes to print, the Federal Bureau of Investigation arrested as many as twenty deputies, one lieutenant and a sergeant, last December 2013. Two other investigators from the internal affairs unit were arrested as well for acting as an organized gang, and threatened a female F.B.I. investigator and accused of hiding a federal witness. This along with the undersheriff who resigned, and his position was actually eradicated, followed up by the sheriff himself, resigned a month later and awaiting possible charges. This alone speaks volumes of where the department has been going. Now watch what will happen to all of those suspected under the organized crime law covered by the "RICO" statute. Most of those arrested will spill the beans of what was going on and all of the king's men, and women, will fall. (Meaning more will be filed upon and they will divulge all other conspirators) I guess we all can wait to see what will happen, and a full disclosure will not occur for at least two years from now.

When I started with the department, the sheriff, Peter Pitchess himself, was a former F.B.I. agent that came in the early fifties, to correct the corruption on the department and now history is repeating itself. For all of those who are cops on the street and doing a fine job and staying away from all of this wrong doing I hope they will survive the onslaught of unnecessary criticism and hopefully prevail. I hope they will keep working on keeping the peace and put thugs in jail where they belong and stay away from any organized affiliations that may appear unethical.

When I worked at Lynwood Station for three and one half years, the same group of "Vikings" was congregating and our job, as sergeants, was to discourage that group from becoming larger and have them disband. Everyone knew where I stood on the "Vikings" issue and I made no bones about it. Now look what happened, something failed and the same group became bigger, but this time with impunity from the upper level echelon. They allegedly did things that were outside the department policy and procedures and felt empowered by someone of much higher authority.

I could be wrong, but remember my thirty-one years in uniform, caused me to develop an opinion of *where law enforcement should be and where it is now.*

I would now venture to say between both the L.A.P.D. and L.A.S.D. time has come to seriously consider combining these two forces and create a new command staff and of course a citizens review committee. This would be a metropolitan police department but with a twist of an elected official as the head. Elected officials are much more responsive and have an ear for the community. Also if elected and not fulfilling their job, voters can simply throw them out on the next election. Please, no commissioners, leave the politics out of this formation. Talk about a savings of money, effort and resources, do the math. There have been too many mistakes by both command staff of each department. *It is time to vet everyone.* Corruption seems excessively close to all and raises its ugly head too frequently.

I have three sons. Two of them have expressed interest in law enforcement. I have discouraged them from becoming a police officer because of the present law enforcements opposite view of the way things should be handled. I felt they would be unnecessarily viewed as dinosaurs when offering an opinion and run into too much opposition carrying my last name. I only have one nephew on the department now and I hope he is successful in his career, he has been duly warned.

CHAPTER 174

PRIVATE INVESTIGATOR: FLIGHT TRAINING— SEPTEMBER 12, 2001

I was taking flying lessons out of a small flight office at Brackett Airport, Pomona.

I had accumulated approximately 180 hours of training toward my commercial and instrument certificate. The owner of this flight business office was an Israeli named Aries.

The flight instruction was all part of a vocational rehabilitation education package, teaching me skills for another field of work.

This was occurring just after my disability retirement in July of 1998. I had aspirations of becoming a skilled subcontract pilot for hire on local flights in and out of southern California.

My instructor, Darius, was a former Iranian soldier and a very qualified instructor, and he helped me immensely with my training and through a recent lull in advancing. I just couldn't get the timing and points aligned properly in making the approach passing through Paradise VOR, just outside of Chino Airport. I must have tried this maneuver five or six times each lesson and was at a plateau in my training by not initiating the proper procedures en route to Chino approach. I tried hard to nail down my altitude and speed requirements.

My instructor had informed me he was going to take a month-long hiatus in August 2001 so he could go to Florida and take jet flight training.

He was anxious to acquire this flight training so he could advance in the expansion of his flight credentials.

It was nice to have the time off and gain some simulator flight training hours of repetitive takeoffs and tracking signals going to "Paradise VOR" and coordinating the different altitudes and speeds. This was as good as it got without my instructor.

The flight office had been very busy, and seeing the other students in and out of the office was a common sight. The check flight instructors would check out my skills when the time came up.

The chief pilot, Mark W., was a former Australian fighter pilot and very helpful with direction and support. His enthusiasm was refreshing and he was nice to talk with. This particular flight business office was loaded with many Arab student pilots, and they were as friendly as my instructor. We chatted and studied together.

Darius had a friend he met nearly every time we taxied out onto the tarmac. He was a former Russian fighter pilot. As we crossed the tarmac to the fuel area, they would meet by the fueling depot and exchange their friendly greetings and speak to each other as I was fueling our plane.

They both had pretty heavy accents but were still easy to understand. They treated me very well, and I enjoyed their company and the tales of their experiences.

Darius had already been gone for about a month and it was about time to resume my training in September. Then it happened. It was all over the news and on every channel. It was very discernable as an attack on the United States by Arab terrorists. Stories went all over the place about the terrorists being able only to fly the planes, but not land or take off.

I watched and listened intently as the twin towers fell. My curiosity was a bit tormented, because I was drawing a comparison with the group of Arab students at our flight business office. I was really fighting off the infamous "duck theory" and trying to make sense out of the whole affair, but it felt like it had some connection with my instruction somehow, and it really disturbed me.

I decided the following day to go to the flight business office early and discuss the matter with the chief pilot, Mark W. I arrived around nine o'clock.

The place looked abandoned and spooky as I exited my car and entered the office. There was only one person, who was standing at the counter in a business suit, watching Mark, who was apparently busily stacking some paperwork in his hands and walking from room to room.

Mark saw me and stated, "I'll be right with you, Larry, but this gentleman was before you." I jokingly responded to the man in the suit, "Well, who the hell are you?" He turned around to face me and stated, "I'm an agent with the FBI." I brashly stuck out my right hand and declared, "I'm Larry Rupp, a retired sergeant from the LA Sheriff's Department. How the hell are you doing?"

He was a little shocked and said, "I'm okay, how are you?"

I responded likewise and asked," What's going on? Is this about what happened yesterday?" He said, "Yes, I'm here to pick up all the applications for the Arab student pilots in training here."

I asked, "Well just how many were being trained here?" He responded, "About sixty." I said, "Holy shit, that many?" He politely stated, "Yep, and we're collecting all of them for an assessment." I wished him good luck. We shook hands again as he went out the door.

Mark called me into his office and I sat down with him and had quite an exchange about what was presently occurring. Mark was closing the flight business office for the next couple of days.

Mark informed me that my instructor, Darius, was no longer working out of their office and may have been returned to Iran. He also informed me that my training was in a period of transition. I would have to forego it for a time until the the office was investigated thoroughly and resolved.

I was alarmed, but what do you say when it involved national security on a grand scale?

I thanked Mark for his inspiration and help and stated that I would come back or call back in a month or two, when this would, I hoped, be over. We shook hands, and I left the business office and sat in my car in the parking area and listened to all of the breaking news.

The news programs were saying that many Arab individuals were involved in training in the United States and that the federal government was looking into the complexity of a possible terrorist conspiracy within our borders.

It went through my mind that this office might very well close, and the remainder of my training would be dissolved. This was a very serious situation. We unknowingly might have been exposed to some of the deception of the grand-scale conspiracy.

I was expecting some kind of contact, but I was never contacted by the federal government. I guess the information I might have had was not necessary or relevant, and I passed the whole thing off as another daunting experience.

I waited several months before returning to the office; in fact almost a year had passed. When I arrived the business sign was gone and only a few abandoned aircraft were on the parking area. I went inside and talked with a new owner who was running a helicopter training business.

I inquired what had happened to the fixed base office. He advised me that they had folded up and closed the training facility. I informed him that the business owed me $5000 worth of training.

He informed me to go to the airport manager located at the airport business office, midfield. I went there to the office and spoke with the manager, who thought the office had closed permanently and might have gone bankrupt.

He did inform me that the owner might have gone to Chino Airport and opened up in another name. To me this was becoming more and more convoluted and any further follow-up would prove fruitless.

I was concerned about my lost training money, but it would probably become more complex and obviously into ongoing federal investigations, so I dropped my interest in the training and changed my focus to private investigation.

CHAPTER 175

THE BODYGUARD

This job started in 2003, when I was hired with two other men to be body-guards for a female country-singing trio. It was going to be a learning experience for an "on the road" trip for four months. This trip covered sixty-five shows in the United States and eight shows in Canada. We were selected to be with this group called "The Dixie Chicks" which was quite remarkable in all accounts because of their outspoken opinions about racism, President Bush and most important about "A guy named Earl", who happened to be one of their songs about how they handled a guy that beat his wife. Their songs were great and quite a hit among their huge fan base. Each show had nearly eighteen to twenty-thousand in attendance.

My partners were both about twenty years younger than I, very opinionated, and were and a lot of fun to be with. Richard D. was an ex L.A.P.D. officer for over ten years and pretty serious about all matters. Richard was raised in the Watts area of South Central Los Angeles, and a sensei in the martial arts of taekwondo. The other partner was Lorenzo W., had no police experience at all, and spent most of his younger years in the back seat of a police car, so he says. In fact, Lorenzo thinks I may have nearly run him over several times in a sheriff's patrol car when he was a kid living on Carlin Avenue, Lynwood.

These two partners and I were very close and personal. We slept, ate and lived with one another on our security bus and thoroughly enjoyed each other's company. We kept a sharp eye out for one another and several times needed to stay close together for our own work integrity and keep each other well informed of all rumors that may surface and scare the "Chicks". We communicated very well with each other and at times had to stand up for one another from other security forces. Those forces seemed very curt and outspoken about certain dislikes of Richard and Lorenzo and their lack of experience. I was personally insulted when these objections surfaced about my two partners and spoke out about the opposition's assessment. It was flawed and I placed my reputation against theirs in a final spat and the "Chicks" dismissed the other security force because they had created quite a stir with other show staff as well.

Our job was to make sure the "Chicks" were not interrupted, nor molested by anyone. Several threats, mostly from the internet, were alarming and specific. Those threats may have been caused by the ladies outspoken view about President Bush. My charge was "Marty" the violinist. She was extremely talented and in my view, especially when playing the violin. Richard's charge was "Natalie" the main singer, and Lorenzo's charge was "Emily." Both Marty and

Emily are sisters. The entire show was country western music and singing, and all of us liked county music very well.

The routine was I would come out first in an all black suit and walk around the figure eight shaped twenty-three million dollar stage called the "river walk." As I rounded the stage I glared at all the close-by seated audience and let them know without saying a word that I was the one to be reckoned with, when anyone came near the stage that stood approximately three and a half to four foot high. The top floor was illuminated quite nicely and that illumination helped see the "Chicks" as they musically strolled by. If someone drew close, they would reach out for one of the "Chicks" and extended their hand and one of the "Chicks" would grasp the fans' hands and greet them while they were singing. As the fan reached each time, I would position myself immediately next to them as they were shaking the hand and advised them to politely release the "Chick's" hand and not tug on them in any way. Everyone complied nicely once the hand was released, as others drew closer and repeated the gesture. The splendor and roar of the fans was loud and everyone was having a nice time. There was actually no threat seen through each show, yet we kept a sharp eye out for any possibilities.

I think we were in Chicago and standing outside the "Chicks" dressing room door when the infamous writer Stephen King came walking towards the door to meet the "Chicks." One of the "Chicks" handlers introduced Stephen King and family as they approached. Stephen King extended his hand to me as they were being ushered into the dressing room. That is when I arched my back and leaned back fluttering my eyes and vibrated my right hand rapidly and said, "Aahhhh" as if being electrocuted. At that moment, Stephen King realized I was kidding him about the type of stories he has written which were mostly scary and horrific. He laughed at me as I smiled which meant I conveyed my awareness of his writings in a comical way simply by a hand gesture.

To me that contact along with another notable character I guarded later on, was that if I can make these guys laugh, I might be good at entertaining and possibly try my hand at writing. I thought about writing a few times and figured if I have the unique talent to convey the many stories I have experienced, then why not?

When the "Chicks" were going to open a show in Vancouver, Canada, our security bus went ahead of us from Salt Lake City. Our entourage boarded a jet, flew to Vancouver, and was to meet up with the show in the nearby arena. Everything was uneventful until I walked from our hotel several blocks away from the arena and located our security bus that was parked near an overpass on the arena's large parking lot. When I came on board our security bus I noticed my clothing duffle bag was missing. I looked around and realized someone came into the bus and took my duffle bag and exited the automatic door.

Outside, I noticed several pieces of my clothing sporadically dropped on the ground and strewn about as if the thief was discarding items of clothing on his or her way leaving the bus. I followed the trail of the clothing just under the overpass and noticed it led me to a cardboard shanty, constructed obviously by one of the many homeless that were lingering about.

I thought for a moment if I pull the cardboard shanty down, I would see the homeless thief inside and most likely, a fight would ensue. I realized that although I had every right to pursue the person who stole my clothing, but considered the fact that I was in another country. I know that we were guests in Canada and if I did anything to its citizens, it would not look good at all, yet alone injuring that person and causing him or her court action. Those issues alone seemed risky and avoidable. I decided that by just walking away, suffer the loss without all of the aggravation, would be a much smarter move. I returned to my hotel, informed production of the loss, and had to make a fast run to the local clothing store and purchase new clothing that would last for several more weeks.

Overall this entire event was quite an experience, our job was simplified because of the staff, and "Chicks" were exceptional people. We had an enjoyable atmosphere the whole time. There were many comical moments and everyone's job melded into one another, which simplified the four-month venture. The "Chicks" songs never became tiring and were enjoyable to be in the direct mix of the show. The "Chicks" were very polite and accommodating to us and very easy to talk with about any subject.

I certainly hope the "Chicks" get back together because of their singing ability is outstanding, and their high fan base were exemplary in their behavior and attention to the "Chicks" as the show went on.

Bodyguard for a Movie Star- The Oscars

Right after the "Dixie Chicks", we were hired by one of the top five movie stars for the next four years. Because of a personal confidential agreement, I will refer to that movie star as "Jack." The importance of this man cannot be over emphasized, he was very talented, a pleasure to be with and talk to, as if he were part of our team. He was a family man that had two small children and a woman who was just as graceful as he was. "Jack" and his family lived in the Hollywood Hills area and lived in an estate anyone would be jealous of by its size and eye catching style of a home with many personal things to enjoy.

His fame allowed Richard D. and I to travel to England and France escorting the family to whatever he was involved in. We enjoyed the pleasant surroundings of the city of Bath, England and Paris, France. We were given the same opulence of all matters concerning "Jack" and his family, and interacted with them as certain occasions arose that caused a security concern and communications with the family's daily agendas.

I guess many folks would be jealous of what both Richard and I were involved in, however keep this in mind, both of us were married and by ourselves in beautiful surroundings without our wives, and far away for weeks at a time. The time spent with "Jack", and his family was very appealing. They treated us very well as if we were a part of their family. That made the job of bodyguarding rather unique and very comfortable.

Many times "Jack" would come out of his room or setting and converse with us as if he was a close friend. He made quite an impression on us that he liked to talk about all matters and certainly enjoyed laughter.

The mother of his children was very kind as well, both called us on many things associated with their daily routine to mind the children and help with some of the travels in the local community. There was no question as to who needed to be carefully watched, the children regardless if both mother and father were around. The children were first and primary to guard on any daily routine. The kids were well behaved and quickly responded to any suggestions of safety we may have brought up.

Several times both Richard and I enjoyed the red carpet at the Academy Awards ceremony, just as much as "Jack" and the whole family. The ride in the limousine to the drop off point "Jack" would always comment on how people were spooked at my focus of protection. I knew someone, along the route of the slow moving cars, may very well come up to "Jack's" door and attempt to open it. My job was to keep those things from happening, so I intentionally kept a stoical face on all that came close to the car. Once any of the bystanders looked towards me, they seemed to lean or move backwards.

On our arrival, I was first out and looking briefly at all to see if any eyes were focused too sharply on our charge, as if I were guarding a political dignitary.

Because of my own imagination and ego, I envisioned myself as the main character as all of the hundreds of cameras that were flickering to capture myself in a captivating pose. Of course, that was but a brief moment and my focus on the primary and his family regained their momentum. To say the least, it was exhilarating. This was his moment of fame and I am sure he felt the same accolades as he passed by in-review. The audience cheered him as he slowly made his way up the red carpet. He was pulled aside occasionally to deliver a short interview or two with some of local TV networks, but kept up with the cadence of the program.

Once inside the Kodak Theater both Richard and I went to a private waiting room for other bodyguards until the ending of the program. This wait could last several hours until we were summoned to return to "Jack's" home.

In fact, many times "Jack" would come out to our security shack and talk. This is when he brought up the suggestion to write a book on my many adventures as a cop. The way he conveyed this suggestion was the repeated visits he made several times just to laugh at many of the adventures I was involved in and the way I delivered the stories. He is quite a funny character and enjoys laughter as well as anyone else with a good sense of humor. Many times he asked me to sit with him at a table and enjoy a drink or two, but I hesitantly informed him that would compromise his safety. I knew my own limitations and if someone were to come close to threaten us, I would be at a disadvantage because of our closeness and most likely unable to react quickly to any threat being somewhat inebriated.

I think he just enjoyed our company that made him laugh a lot and he realized we had a job to do, to protect him and his family.

Time went on and we spent many hours patrolling his home and grounds assuring he was in well guarded care and safe. "Jack" was comfortable with us around, protecting all of his cherished possessions. As time would have it I had to move on after four years and was offered another job with another celebrity, but this one was much prettier.

Bodyguard of a Spanish Beauty

To say the least she was one to look at and I marveled at her beauty. Her friends were just as gorgeous, and well known. Unbelievably, I was actually paid to guard Penelope Cruz at her home in the Hollywood Hills area. This was a tough job, but someone had to do it. She was eloquent to talk with and to look at. She was very friendly and frequently came out to chat, because some of the other bodyguards had fallen asleep and she did not want to pay someone to sleep while on her payroll. In a sense, she was checking on our alertness.

Her brother "Edwardito", a celebrated singer in Mexico, occasionally visited her and she had me drive them and her other close friend Selma Hyek. Boy talk about gorgeous women, these two were very kind and friendly, spoke to me as if I was their long time friend and made me feel very proud to watch over them and keep pesky paparazzo at bay. They were very amiable and gave specific directions on where to go and how long we would stay. One night I drove Penelope's car and we were travelling down the Sunset Strip, Selma was in the right front seat, putting on makeup and conversing with Penelope who was behind me and Edwardito sat in the right rear seat. We were on our way to grab something to eat and they chatted as if I was part of the conversation. To describe them was easy, they were very close and personable, just like anyone else.

The job lasted for approximately a year and then Javier Bardem came into her life again and they both were smitten with one another. One time coming out of a restaurant on Robertson Avenue in the West Hollywood area, an ambitious paparazzi and at least eight others came very close to Penelope's face with his camera and scared her to a point when Javier charged him and others in a "bum rush" and knocked several of them down. Javier was ticked, and rightfully so, and took matters into his own hands. I advised him that I would handle the paparazzo because they knew who I was and they know that I would ask help from the West Hollywood Station if any breech of personal security would occur. I suggested to both to get into my car and I would persuade the paparazzo to cool it or suffer consequences from the responding sheriff deputies. They complied and we started to come home. When travelling in my car a relatively short distance, a whole barrage of alerted paparazzo appeared in their cars and motorcycles. The guys on the motorcycles in fact were seated back to back with the cameraman on the rear, seated backwards, taking as many pictures as possible. Talk about unsafe riding, "geese Louise", they were driving after me lickedy split going to Penelope's home.

I called the West Hollywood Station and asked for help when we were about to arrive at her home. That took approximately five minutes and when we arrived paparazzo were on her lawn and near her front door. I got out and went into the paparazzo leading as Javier and Penelope followed closely behind, just as the deputies arrived and the paparazzo dispersed. One time when we were travelling I mentioned to Javier that he reminded me very much of the actor Anthony Quinn. He responded how so? I said his facial structure and voice was very similar to that famous actor and after viewing him in the 2007 film, "No Country for Old Men." He smiled and thanked me for the comparison and felt honored to be similar to such a famous actor.

My bodyguard career continued with several other celebrities, but not too much to discuss in specific detail, several were embarrassing to me and short lived. Other celebrities were an exact opposite of my values, and at best kept silent.

CHAPTER 176

OH, DEER ME

I arrived at my usual time, just a little before nine in the evening. I parked inside the gated residence, in the same spot where the inside of my car couldn't be seen from the street. The neighborhood was quiet, and I could hear several dogs barking in the distance.

A few nearby departing guests of the neighboring homes could be overheard saying their good-byes as they were getting into their cars. Noises were easily heard that evening, because several afternoon rain showers had dampened everything and amplified the usual sounds.

I got out of my car and began to look over the property for anything that seemed out of order. I used my flashlight frequently, splashing the light generously over the home and the surrounding shrubbery. My intentions were rather basic—I looked for anything that might be out of the ordinary and visually checked the premises for any signs of intruders or unsafe conditions.

By waving my flashlight, I was sure that anyone inside the home would see the light and know that I was outside patrolling the property until dawn. All appeared safe and sound, which meant that it would probably lead to another uneventful night.

My biggest worry was to stay awake and make the night pass quickly.

Around midnight I made another pass around the home, but this time I was being very careful to remain as silent as possible. The family was asleep, and I didn't want to alarm them by my presence. I returned to my car and stood in the shadows in my dark clothing.

I could hear the sounds of the crowded freeway a couple of miles away, listening to thousands of tires on the asphalt pavement. I was in the posh Brentwood area, on a very quiet narrow street that serpentines gracefully through the hills of the affluent community. Time was passing very slowly. It was hard to focus on anything that didn't move or make noise.

I struggled staying awake and occupied myself by looking and listening for the deer that usually passed by on the dimly lit street, in a small group of approximately six to eight. The deer generally moved around this time, at about nine-thirty in the evening, in single file, en route to graze on the enriched lawns and shrubs. Then around three thirty to four o'clock, the deer would return to their habitats.

Oddly enough, on several occasions, I'd seen packs of coyotes following the same trail the deer had taken, rambunctiously sniffing the semifresh odors not an hour or two old. The coyotes were sniffing close to the ground in a semicircular fashion and tracking forward ambitiously, seeking their bounty.

Many times in the past, these deer would approach my position as I stood in the bushes, concealing myself from intruders or guests. It was obvious the deer smelled me as they passed within feet of my position.

The deer would bob their noses up and down gently and then whisk from left to right in order to get a bearing on what they were detecting. I remained quiet and motionless, hidden in the bushes, and amazed that I could nearly touch the animal with my hands.

That's what my client liked—being elusive to the local sightseer, yet by design, purposely seen occasionally, armed and ominous.

My client's concerns were to stay vigilant and keep anyone and anything from disrupting his family while he was away. This job seemed relatively easy, considering my lengthy tenure and experience with law enforcement.

Offenders in this neck of the woods were no match for my experience as a cop; yet I was the family's personal bodyguard and responsible for their safety.

At about three thirty one morning, I was waiting for the deer to pass by again, when I noticed a small red car coming toward me, zigzagging from side to side, as if delivering newspapers.

As it drew closer I could hear music coming from the car and recognized it as Mexican frontera music. A lone male occupant had a carload of throwaway newspaper advertisements and was tossing them onto each residential driveway. As he passed by me, he tossed one of them toward the main gate, right in front of where I happened to be standing. He was passing by my position and suddenly stopped. He quickly backed up onto the driveway apron, just short of the tall wrought-iron main gate.

He didn't see me at all, because I was well hidden in the bushes. The bushes were actually red bougainvilleas just inside the wrought iron fence, yet within inches of the roadway.

I was very close to him, and he had no clue I was there. I was so close that I could have easily reached through the wrought-iron fence and tapped the driver on the top of his head.

He kept looking toward my car, which was parked in front of the garage. I later came to realize that he must have been looking at the two canvas camping chairs. I set up those chairs all the time; with opened books lying on each seat, as if several persons were close by, yet suggesting suspicious activity was in question.

He seemed puzzled and was fixated on the empty chairs, as if wondering where these two guys were there in the first place. He paused several times, trying to realize what was going on, as the engine and radio kept running and playing. Finally, he turned around and faced forward. He appeared perplexed. He looked down onto the flowering bougainvillea draping from the iron fence onto the asphalt. He began to look slowly upward until he reached where my face was blended into and among the flowers and leaves.

Then it happened. His eyes squinted, and he leaned forward slightly and began to focus on my face, which was blended in with the flora, but apart from the plant. Suddenly he realized that he was looking at my face, and I was looking directly at him, not three feet away from his nose.

He screamed, hit the gas pedal, and sped off. I thought for sure that if he survived the first one hundred feet without crashing into anything, he would notify the local authorities as soon as he could. So I came out of the bushes and stood near the front gate, awaiting their response.

No one else came by that evening, and the rest of the night passed by rather quickly. I can only imagine what that man was thinking after he noticed me mixed in with the flowers, and what he told his friends.

CHAPTER 177

BUSHWHACKED

I had been working most of the day in the Riverside County area as a private investigator and was growing tired as evening approached. I called my wife and made arrangements to meet up with her at Mimi's Café in Monrovia. It is a nice, clean French-style restaurant near our home, and the food is great, especially the onion soup.

My wife had already finished her work as a Spanish teacher and was already at the restaurant, awaiting my arrival. It was approximately seven thirty and darkness had fallen. I was running several minutes late and anxious to meet up with my wife and enjoy a nice dinner.

As I drove up the driveway apron I noticed the parking lot was packed. The restaurant was in a conglomerate of large and small stores and other restaurants like Mervyn's, Applebee's, Black Angus, and other fast-food services.

I drove around Mimi's and couldn't find a parking space. I was feeling a tad impatient. I drove around a second time and realized the nearby parking was full. But on the other hand, the adjoining Mervyn's rear parking lot had several empty spaces, probably because the added distance was an uncomfortable walk for most other patrons.

I quickly drove into the space and noticed it was darkened by the yellowish streetlights along Mayflower Avenue. The lighting was blocked by the verdant tree limbs that bordered the street, sidewalk, and parking lot area. Anyway, I shut off the noisy diesel engine of my Ford Excursion and turned off the headlights.

I grabbed my gun, a Glock .45 that was neatly tucked between the driver's seat and the large center console, and placed it on my lap. I unstrapped the seatbelt and grabbed my tweed sports coat from the right front seat with my right hand. I then switched the coat to my left hand as I opened the door, as I normally do.

I picked up my gun with my right hand, slung the jacket over the gun, and started to push the door open slightly with my left hand. I usually do this to conceal the fact that I have a gun when I step out into view. I would then simply place the gun into my waistband and put my jacket on.

As I started to step outward from the driver's door, a tall, lean young Hispanic male, approximately sixteen to eighteen years old, stepped toward me as the door opened, with his right hand in his right front pants pocket.

He looked directly at me and ordered, "Give me your motherfucking money!" I looked more carefully, especially at the bulging pants pocket, where his hand was positioned. I determined that this guy was simulating a gun in his pocket. If there was a real gun in his pocket, it might blow his private parts away, and he knew that fact very well. On top of that, my gun was already in my hand, finger on the trigger, and my tweed sports coat was draped neatly over my arm and hand, concealing my armament.

This all went through my mind rather quickly, in nanoseconds, because I never balked or lost stride. My gun was pointing at the thief's chest less than a foot away.

I responded to the thief, "Go fuck yourself, punk!" I said in a convincing manner and added, "You little shit—go play on the freeway!" He really irritated me, and I talked to him like I was scolding a child holding a squirt gun. I didn't stop at any point in my forward momentum. He backed up quickly and nearly fell as he neared my rear bumper.

I kept a steady focus on the right hand in the suspect's pocket. If anything that looked like a gun began to come into view, I would shoot him, hopefully twice in the chest in quick succession.

I knew that I would be lucky if I was able to squeeze off two rounds, because a single .45 caliber bullet is well known to cartwheel a human target in an upper body shot.

I sensed this crook was bluffing, and I was in a position to correct the bluff at any moment. I also realized that if I shot the suspect, it would certainly poke at least four to six holes in my tweed jacket and maybe even cause it to catch fire.

I sensed my attitude angered the suspect, because he repeated his demand for my "motherfucking money." However, he was so startled at my displeasure, abusive language, and daunting physical stature, he kept backing up faster and faster.

He yelled to me something indistinguishable as we were parting, but I couldn't understand him and frankly didn't care, or more important, didn't seem to care.

He turned away from me when he was halfway into the street and ran across Mayflower Avenue and then directly into a driveway of a darkened apartment complex.

I rounded the rear bumper of my car and kept a peripheral open view for the suspect, who I felt might reappear. He didn't, so I continued to walk briskly two to three cars from my car and ducked between two other cars and raised my head up slightly.

This was to see if I could spot this lucky "road agent" poking his little pointed head out from the driveway and see what he was about to do. My thinking was that he was going to return to my car and "key" the painted finish in retaliation for the bungled robbery.

He reappeared, skulking at the edge of darkness and looked across the street toward my car, then looked north and south on Mayflower Avenue.

Then he looked northbound again and started to walk toward the McDonald's at Mayflower Avenue and Huntington Drive. He continually looked around, I believe in an attempt to locate me, but he was unable to see me crouched between two parked cars.

I finally lost sight of the suspect as I stood up and began walking toward Mimi's Café.

A uniformed security officer driving a small golf cart with a little bed in the rear of the cart, came driving toward me, and I flagged him down.

I told him of the incident and said that I was a retired sergeant from the Los Angeles Sheriff's Department, and I'd almost shot the robbery suspect. I decided not to, because of his youthful appearance and his clumsy and fumbling robbing antics, which were feeble.

I was on somewhat of a rant because of the incident and attributed it to the dense trees that block the street lamps and the lack of lighting by Mervyn's store that invited the criminal element to the area. I informed the security guard that had I shot the crook, the entire shopping complex would have been compromised, and police and detective units would have inundated the area.

I also informed the security officer that I was going into Mimi's Café to meet up with my wife for a nice and quiet dinner. If the police came, he should please let them know where I'd be. I would be glad to talk to them. He was very polite and understanding and expressed his concern about the lighting and the near calamity.

I walked for a short distance, trying to cool down, and entered the restaurant. Apparently it was obvious something had happened, because when I approached my wife, she asked, "What happened, babe?"

It took about five minutes to inform her of the incident. I was waiting for the local police to come into the restaurant, but they never did.

We finished our meal and walked to our respective cars and went home.

Several weeks went by. Lo and behold, all of the trees along the side of Mervyn's were thinned out and cut back.

This alone illuminated the parking lot immensely. About a week later the dark side of Mervyn's was illuminated with two bright floodlights that really cut into the criminals' environment.

Within two or three months, the aged apartment complex across the street from Mervyn's was demolished, and a whole new condominium complex replaced the lair that hid the bonehead would-be robber.

CHAPTER 178

DEATH OF A FRIEND

I hadn't seen Jimmy in quite a while and knew he was in trouble quite a few times with the department for making some poor decisions while on the job. Jimmy always had a tendency to make fun of other persons and their beliefs, and he was always amused at the fervor it sparked.

Several individuals told me he was one of the ones in the jail who were going through the gang block of the jail with small crossed sticks ablaze as if in some sort of mini Klansmen skit or episode. These antics threatened the peaceful surroundings of the incarcerated gang members.

Well, that wasn't a very smart idea, considering the gang was black. Jimmy was always one for a joke, but this situation was very serious and caused claims racial prejudice by all for doing such a dumb thing. He was of course looked upon as a role model until this event occurred, and he was quickly reprimanded and disciplined.

Still, he was a friend and former Firestone Park and SWAT member who was at my side many times. We laughed many times together with his long-time friend and companion, George B. and went through many shocking and exciting situations as partners in arms, including George's death in 1979.

We never really hung out together, but he knew I loved him like a brother and would go out of my way to help him in any endeavor. I still remember he used to cut out hundreds of women's colorful lips, in various contorted positions, and paste the cutouts onto the inside of his locker door.

He was a ladies' man, but he had a real hard time staying with one for a long time. I think his ego was very big, and he knew he was very good in all combat positions because of all of his experiences and training while at Firestone Park station, SWAT assignments, and of course his Vietnam experience and commitment with the US Marine Corps. Needless to say he dressed sharply and had a definite command presence.

If someone pulled a gun on him in the dark or in broad daylight, he would just smile and outshoot anyone who tried. His courage was never questioned. If we were partnered up in complete darkness and I were to reach to the side, I knew very well the person I touched would be Jimmy. He knew where to be at all times and was a natural tactician.

His downfall was George. George was everything to Jimmy until that fateful night in April 1979. Most of us knew full well Jimmy was having a real tough time. He started off with quite a few mistakes while still on the SWAT team. A lot of little things began to surface that pushed Jimmy into the limelight and caused quite a bit of consternation and trouble within the department and its supervisors. This was all brought on by the death of his close friend, partner, and confidant.

Prior to George's death, George was the one who many times had to negotiate with fellow workers to resolve personality conflicts created by Jimmy's brash comments. George was always Jimmy's mouthpiece and had the gift to make the argument go away. Now with the death of his spokesman and friend, trouble seemed to flourish.

Jimmy finally left SWAT and went to a jail assignment. He was lost within the abundance of young impressionable deputies who looked upon Jimmy as a role model, and anything he said was the gospel truth.

I had already retired and was a private investigator in the Riverside County area when I got word that Jimmy had had a severe heart attack and managed to drive himself to the hospital, where he died shortly thereafter.

When I heard he passed away, I had tears in my eyes because of our past friendship and of course my close friendship with George as well.

The services were at Forest Lawn in Covina, and there was an open casket for viewing. I went in a dress black suit and tried to prepare myself for his viewing. I tried desperately not to break down emotionally. I knew it was going to be tough, and that there were going to be quite a few people there as well.

I came in quietly and said hello to several guys I hadn't seen in years. Without further ado, I went directly to the open casket. I noticed three women standing about ten feet away from the casket in their dark, formal dresses. They were very quiet.

On the other side of the casket were approximately fifty to sixty young deputies, standing quietly aside and closely monitoring anyone who came near the casket of their role model, Jimmy H., who had guided them faithfully and definitely sharpened their skills.

I guess they were going to be puzzled by my appearance in a black suit and tie, sporting a long ponytail as if I were a high-end dope pusher from some Hollywood dope den. I made my approach slowly, alone, and drew closer to the large portrait of Jimmy, sitting just ahead of the casket, yet close enough for anyone to draw a comparison to the individual cradled in the casket.

It surely didn't look like him at all, I noticed everyone was watching me as I drew closer. I couldn't help but start to reflect on my friend and partner in arms, who was now right in front of me, silent, eyes closed, wearing a lot of makeup.

I know personally if Jimmy had been aware of that thick gaudy makeup, he would have wiped that crap off of his face before I approached, but unfortunately he couldn't, because now he was relying on good friends to make him look presentable. Oh well!

I paused briefly, laid my hand on top of his, and nodded my head at the sorrowful display. I then leaned over and kissed him on the forehead and bade my friend farewell. I started to tear up. Although I tried to hide my emotions, it was very hard to hold back the tears, and I needed to exit as soon as possible without any further delay. As I rose from the casket, I felt all eyes were upon me, and I did not want to make any eye contact with anyone else.

This event was very fast, with no explanations about who Jimmy was to me, and I felt no qualifying or quantifying statements were necessary.

I walked away briskly. I didn't want to turn back, because my anguish was hurting too much.

"Good-bye, Jimmy. Take care, and save a place for me wherever you go."

CHAPTER 179

"DON'T ANSWER THE DOOR"—MOM'S WARNING

I was lollygagging around the house in my underwear around nine thirty in the morning and went to the kitchen contemplating whether I should have another cup of coffee. It was our twenty-second wedding anniversary as well. However, I was alone, and Gloria was at the local hospital attending to her diabetic mom, who was going into surgery to have her left foot and calf amputated because of her long-term and ongoing diabetic complications.

I couldn't go to the hospital, because I was recovering from conjunctivitis, "pink eye," which is contagious for seven to ten days.

I was standing in front of the sink, peering out the kitchen window, and I noticed a gold-colored Altima car stopped just in front of my neighbor's driveway about three feet from the curb. My neighbors were at work, so there was no one at home, and their driveway was empty of their cars.

The driver of the gold Altima was a female Hispanic in her early twenties. She had shoulder-length black hair and was looking toward the passenger-side door, as a lone black man exited. He then walked toward the rear of the Altima. He appeared to be slightly stooped forward as he quickly rounded the rear of the car.

Still stooped over, he cut diagonally across the street. He then went toward my son's red Jeep Cherokee which was parked on the west side of the street.

I know pretty much everyone in the neighborhood, and this guy didn't look familiar at all. His quick exit from the car indicated to me that something suspicious was going on. I went to the bedroom, threw on my shorts, and walked quickly out the front door. The gold Altima now parked directly behind my son's car, and no one appeared to be inside. Now my suspicions were elevated even more because of the position of the car, and the fact that both of its young occupants were absent.

I walked to the car from the rear and carefully peered at the license plate, trying to focus on its numbers and letters so I would remember them, should anything suspicious occur.

I walked alongside the car, on the driver's side and noticed that the female Hispanic driver was lying nearly flat on the front seat. She was still seated behind the steering wheel with her head away from me, face down on the seat. This position seemed to be an odd position for comfort and very suspicious.

It seemed to me that she was hiding from my view by design, or she was trying not to be seen by anyone afoot or in passing cars. As I continued walking toward the front of the Altima, the woman raised her head, keeping her face turned to her right and away from my view. This movement alarmed me even more, so I backed another foot away from the car, sensing she might very well come up with a gun.

She sat upright in the driver's seat, still with her head twisted to her right and away from my view. This seemed an obvious furtive move to keep her from facing me, as if to conceal her identity.

Just then the male passenger appeared, coming from my neighbor's driveway apron and near an open chain-link double gate, just a few feet west from the street.

Uniquely, my neighbor works at the German Embassy, downtown Los Angeles, and I casually talk with him and his wife daily.

The black male was walking toward me and looking directly at me. In a somewhat contentious tone he asked, "You need something?" He was now about eight feet from me and stopped.

I noticed his clean red shirt, black shorts, and red high-top tennis shoes. This seemed a bit out of whack because the local gangsters, not too far from here, did not wear red at all. However, that was a Compton thing, and I might have been out of touch with current gang colors.

I said, "Yeah. What are you doing?" He responded again, "What's it to you?" I said, "I'm a neighborhood-watch kind of guy. I'm keeping an eye on what's going on in the neighborhood. What are you doing?"

He said he was just visiting a friend, so I asked, "What's your friend's name?" He retorted, "It's none of your fucking business." I said, "Well, it is my business, and I am noting suspicious activity and making mental notes of any and all events that may occur."

I glanced again at the driver, who still had her face turned away slightly. I was now really alarmed at their antics. It felt to me like these two might produce a gun to discourage me from snooping in their business.

The arrogant young man walked between my son's Jeep and the Altima and went to the front passenger's door. He reached down, grabbed his groin, and jestured as if he was lifting up his testicles, obviously insulting my inquisitiveness and persistence. Then he opened the passenger door and stepped inside. The car started up and began to back away from me as I gazed at the suspect's face and the front license plate.

I thought something was wrong, but I didn't know for sure. I focused on the driver and her tattoos, the man's face, and the license plate.

The driver kept her head turned away from me the whole time, making it difficult for me to see her face. I would be less likely to identify her other than by the large tattoos she had on her left rear bicep coming from her shoulder and down to her left elbow.

I began to walk toward my neighbor's home to see if I could quickly see if there were any outward signs of tampering with the doors or the windows.

The gold Altima passed me and made a quick right turn onto Altern Street. It sped up to approximately 25 mph. Its tires were screeching. Then it made another quick left turn onto southbound Rochelle Street, picking up more speed until out of sight.

These collective suspicious actions made me think the two were in fact scoping out my neighbor's home to burglarize, so I kept repeating the license number to myself as I walked home.

I went into my home, grabbed a pen and a pink sticky note, and jotted the license number down. I grabbed my fanny pack, which was holding my pistol and went back into the street. I returned to my neighbor's home while calling the Temple Sheriff's Station, which happened to be on speed dial on my cell phone.

I contacted the front desk and informed the officer of the circumstances of what had just occurred, a description of the gold Altima, and its license number.

While I was talking with the desk officer, I was carefully examining my neighbors' doors, windows, and screens to see if there had been any tampering or pry marks.

The desk person then informed me that the gold Altima had a felony stop on its announcement return for a burglary that had occurred the previous day by Glendora Police Department. This information irritated me, because both of the suspects were within reach and could've been arrested. I thought, *Oh well, maybe this will turn out a little better by observing and reporting and letting the detectives and patrol personnel follow up.*

I asked the person to please dispatch a unit to my location so I could make a verbal report about the incident.

The unit arrived approximately a half hour later. During the time while I was waiting for the unit, I closely examined my neighbor's windows, screens, and doors several more times and was unable to detect any obvious signs of depression marks, cut screens, or jimmied windows.

When the deputy arrived, I introduced myself to her and informed her of my findings. I gave her the pink sticky note with the license number on its face. While we were talking, a detective from the Glendora Police Department arrived and informed us that the gold Altima was wanted for five residential burglaries the previous day. The detective also informed us that both of the occupants of the Altima were the same suspects I had confronted.

The detective took the necessary information and informed me that another detective would arrive soon and ask me to attempt to select the suspects I confronted in a photo array.

Approximately fifteen minutes later, the other Glendora detective arrived and introduced himself to me. He came into my home, where he had me pick both of the suspects from a selection of other similar suspects without any prompting or persuasion. We finished the mug photos presentation and went outside, where I ran the whole incident again in detail. We went to my neighbor's home and again looked very carefully at the windows, screens, and doors.

He seemed very pleased with my observations and said he would call me if needed. A half hour later, I went again to the front door of my neighbor's home and noticed their thirteen-year-old daughter sitting on the porch.

I approached her and asked if she was at home when both the detectives and I were trying the doors and windows earlier.

She said that she was. I asked how come she didn't open the door, and she replied, "My mom told me not to answer the door."

I replied, "Well, that was very good of you to do that, because we were looking for evidence of a man who was possibly at your door."

She said that a black man had come to her front porch. He rang the doorbell three times and then leaned over the railing and looked into the house. She added that she was on the phone with her mother and informing her of what was going on. Her mother told her repeatedly not to answer the door at all.

I congratulated the young lady for her courage and obedience and told her I would contact her parents later on during the day.

My biggest concern was that the suspect was obviously ringing the front doorbell and peering into the home because he was about to go around to the blind side of the home and break into one of the windows on the west side of the home.

I can only speculate what he would have done to the girl, who would have been a witness. The outcome of the whole incident would have had much more serious consequences had the burglar and the girl met in the small home.

Several days later I learned that seven people were arrested for this incident and that most were gangbangers from the neighboring city (*Pasadena Star News*, 06/24/10, page A-5).

Another suspect from the same gang, equally involved in the local burglaries, was arrested by a special weapons and tactics team that went to his home and arrested him. He was wanted for an assault with a deadly weapon charge and had a combative criminal history.

Several of my neighbors congratulated me on my observations and thanked me for preserving the peace in the neighborhood.

My initial observations were lucky and were combined with divine intervention and, of course, " the duck theory".

———

An important matter in this scenario has raised concern for anyone who leaves strict instructions for our loved ones on how to behave in a crisis.

We expect our rules for safety and survival to be met with strict adherence. However, there must be an exit strategy when situations like this suggest strongly that "the devil is at your door." Should you leave your home if a culprit comes inside? This would have been in direct contradiction of the orders from her mom and dad. I've advised this family to discuss this with their daughter, who may elect to arm herself with a weapon to overcome the overwhelming force that she might face if alone in the home.

The following ideas are mere suggestions, based on my education and experience:

1. Keep pepper spray, gun, kitchen knife, baseball bat, etc. where you can reach them.
2. Use the cell phone while the authorities are en route to keep them informed of the gravity of the situation as it unfolds, and of course, stay on the line until police arrive.
3. Keep your eyes and ears on the perpetrator and know exactly how close he is.
4. Exiting the home while talking to a parent or the authorities may be a safer strategy than remaining inside the home.
5. Leave the home quickly and quietly. Then go into the street and scream for help.
6. Purchase a pepper spray that can be carried conveniently in the car and on your house keys. The spray is good for about one year, and it is effective.
7. Purchase a US Coast Guard-approved air horn. (They are carried at the Big Five stores and sell for about ten dollars). This is a great attention getter at all hours in nearly every neighborhood. It is so loud a perpetrator would most likely run away from the intense blast. It might cause him to change his mind about whatever illegal intentions he might have.
8. Have the son or daughter enroll in a jujitsu class or take self-defense classes to at least a brown-belt level.

9. Consider building a safe room or panic room with all of the aforementioned supplies at hand as well as food and water. Keep in mind that panic or safe rooms are usually good for a twenty-minute attack, while the authorities are responding. Now, with the delayed responses of law enforcement to all calls, maybe a panic room should be reinforced for at least a one-hour siege.

CHAPTER 180

RANCH SECURITY – A FINAL REVIEW FROM HEAVEN'S GATE

I have been working on a huge ranch in North San Diego County since the latter part of 2011. Its size is roughly thirty-seven square miles. This ranch is called Rancho Guejito, and is classified as the jewel of southern California. Its borders are from Highway 78 and north to nearly Highway 76 with five Indian reservations on our northern borders. The elevation is approximately 4300 feet at the top of the bordering mountains. It is crammed full of endangered Engelmann Oaks, Coast Live Oaks at all levels and Black Oaks mostly in the higher elevations.

Rancho Guejito is rife with mountains lions, deer, coyotes, eagles, hawks, turkeys, skunks, rabbits, rattlesnakes, and an occasional badger sighting that roam the streambeds. Birds of every size and color chirp throughout the land and grab any food morsel they can spot. Many rocks and boulders, some the size of a house, decorate the vast land throughout all of the property. Grasslands spread throughout various levels of the oak trees and rocky protuberances that create shapely figures of animals and human faces, marking many of the way-points easy to navigate the ranch at a moments notice.

Rodriguez mountain is a mountaintop that designates a northerly direction and easily seen from the many different plantations that sport avocado and citrus groves.

A herd of nearly 1200 cattle, 30 horses and 400 goats feed from the grass-lands and drink from the many small tributaries of the Guejito creek.

There are about fifteen vaqueros, Mexican cowboys, who handle the cattle, horses and goats. They also handle many ranch chores like fence building and repairs.

Our job is to be seen and resolve most security issues within the ranch. We are armed, write reports relating anything affecting the operations of the ranch. We report illegal aircraft operations that land on ranch property or buzz the livestock to spook them and are a constant problem. We also report all problems and unusual activities such as illegal hunters, environmental shenan-igans and illegal trespassers. Our job is unique that most who enjoy four wheel-ing and riding on quads would pay to do what we do on their off time. This is in sharp contrast to patrol operations with the L.A. Sheriffs Department in the cities of Compton, South L.A. or East Los Angeles.

I wear Levis, a western shirt and handkerchief, armed to the hilt with pis-tols, twelve-gage shotgun and a good hunting knife. My boots are high and laced up nice and tight and if riding the quad I will don my handsome leather chaps to keep the brush from poking through my leg. Most of the time I wear a western straw hat with a chin strap primarily to keep the harsh sun from my face.

I drive a large Ford pickup, four by four, diesel powered, and have many tools needed for mending the barbed wire fences and many other broken amenities that requires a quick repair. Since I started working on the ranch, I have seen three mountain lions. Two of them were two-hundred pounders and they wonder the dirt roads and primarily hunt down the many deer often seen all over the ranch.

One afternoon I was travelling along a dirt road at four p.m. I thought I noticed a coyote on the left hand side of the road, just in front of me. It seemed rather peculiar that the coyote did not run, which they normally do when they hear my loud diesel engine. This one was traveling at a slow pace and I thought that maybe it was sick or injured.

Therefore, I continued to come abreast with the animal and when I was right along side of it, I looked out my opened driver's window and looked down to the animal and realized it was a hundred pound mountain lion. "Yikes!" He looked at me as if contemptuous with my sudden appearance. The mountain lion then looked left and without skipping a step, it turned away from me into the brush along side of the road and disappeared. Had I opened my truck door when along side the mountain lion I could have easily struck it in the head. Now that was as close as one could be without any injuries? California mountain lions are an endangered species, protected from hunters, and are left alone unless they start to harm the ranch animals. Then and only then a large trap will be set with the Department of Fish and Game's approval and removed to another location.

Another time I was on a dirt road and coming through some oak trees and saw a large badger crawling out of a burrow, looked at me and then turned around and rushed right back into the same hole, lickedy split. This was the first time anyone had seen a badger on the property and so I took the time to place a trail camera on a steel stake to recapture and validate my sighting. The next day it turned out the badger was a "ham" and apparently sensed the infrared light and put his face right against the camera and the picture came out magnificently. I "Googled" the badger name to see its characteristics and found out if molested the badger may very well attack an intruder and cause serious wounds with its teeth and three-inch claws. From there on, I left it alone and just carefully watched for its reappearance.

There are hundreds of turkeys and seeing them in large numbers makes one feel like being in Jurassic Park. I believe I have the turkey mating call down now, and at times have been asked to make the call and have the turkeys appear for guests. Surprisingly the turkeys do appear and it makes me feel like I am now the ranches official turkey caller.

The ranch is quite the place for seeing the natural beauty of land, that is the last of the intact Mexican land grants with scenery that would soften ones soul by just catching the rare sights most folks have not seen. I can envision myself seated on any one of the granite rocks in the hilly area and take in the raw beauty of it all. It is just pleasant and makes one think of being in a time machine or just outside heaven's gate.

I suppose if I were to perish one day, I would like to have my ashes scattered about the ranch in a serene location away from most of the hustle and bustle of any city's usual busy activities. I think I might mention my ideas to the owner, and see if it could be arranged for keeping a dedicated, watchful eye on her property. That way when I am dust and dirt combined, I may reappear as an apparition and roam the land from the other side of heavens gate and rejoin my fallen friends and family, but this time I would be listening to their stories of adventure.

Made in the USA
Las Vegas, NV
24 November 2021